The title no longer ships with a companion disc. All references within the text to a CD/DVD should be considered to refer instead to this website. http://booksite.elsevier.com/9781558607491/

Materials on this website are provided in versions current as of the date of publication. They have not been updated for performance or compatibility with operating systems or other software released since the date of publication.

T0264253

The System Designer's Guide to VHDL-AMS

Analog, Mixed-Signal, and
Mixed-Technology Modeling

The Morgan Kaufmann Series in Systems on Silicon

Series Editors: Peter J. Ashenden, Ashenden Designs Pty. Ltd. and Adelaide University, and Wayne Wolf, Princeton University

The rapid growth of silicon technology and the demands of applications are increasingly forcing electronics designers to take a systems-oriented approach to design. This has led to new challenges in design methodology, design automation, manufacture and test. The main challenges are to enhance designer productivity and to achieve correctness on the first pass. The Morgan Kaufmann Series in Systems on Silicon presents high quality, peer-reviewed books authored by leading experts in the field who are uniquely qualified to address these issues.

The Designer's Guide to VHDL, Second Edition
Peter J. Ashenden

The System Designer's Guide to VHDL-AMS
Peter J. Ashenden, Gregory D. Peterson, and Darrell A. Teegarden

Readings in Hardware/Software Co-Design
Edited by Giovanni De Micheli, Rolf Ernst, and Wayne Wolf

Forthcoming Titles

Rosetta User's Guide: Model-Based Systems Design
Perry Alexander, Peter J. Ashenden, and David L. Barton

Rosetta Developer's Guide: Semantics for Systems Design
Perry Alexander, Peter J. Ashenden, and David L. Barton

The System Designer's Guide to VHDL-AMS

Analog, Mixed-Signal, and Mixed-Technology Modeling

Peter J. Ashenden

EDA CONSULTANT, ASHENDEN DESIGNS PTY. LTD.
VISITING RESEARCH FELLOW, ADELAIDE UNIVERSITY

Gregory D. Peterson

UNIVERSITY OF TENNESSEE

Darrell A. Teegarden

MENTOR GRAPHICS CORPORATION

MK®

MORGAN KAUFMANN PUBLISHERS

AN IMPRINT OF ELSEVIER SCIENCE

AMSTERDAM   BOSTON   LONDON   NEW YORK
OXFORD   PARIS   SAN DIEGO   SAN FRANCISCO
SINGAPORE   SYDNEY   TOKYO

Senior Editor   Denise E. M. Penrose
Publishing Services Manager   Edward Wade
Editorial Coordinator   Alyson Day
Series Art Direction, Cover Design, & Photography   Chen Design Associates, SF
Text Design   Rebecca Evans & Associates
Copyeditor   Ken DellaPenta
Proofreader   Ann Wood
Printer   The Maple-Vail Book Manufacturing Group

This book was author typeset using FrameMaker 7.0 and Illustrator 10.0 for Windows.

Figure 21-8 and Appendix B reprinted with permission from IEEE Std. 1076.1-1999, *IEEE Standard VHDL Analog and Mixed-Signal Extensions,* Copyright 1999 by IEEE. Section C.1 of Appendix C reprinted with permission from IEEE Std. 1164-1993, *IEEE Standard Multivalue Logic System for VHDL Model Interoperability (Std_logic_1164),* Copyright 1993 by IEEE. Section C.2 of Appendix C reprinted with permission from IEEE Std. 1076.2-1996, *IEEE Standard VHDL Mathematical Packages,* Copyright 1997 by IEEE. The IEEE disclaims any responsibility or liability resulting from the placement and use in the described manner.

Morgan Kaufmann Publishers
An imprint of Elsevier Science
340 Pine Street, Sixth Floor
San Francisco, California 94104-3205
www.mkp.com

Library of Congress Control Number: 2002110023

ISBN: 1-55860-749-8

This book is printed on acid-free paper.

To the memory of Al Dewey, VHDL pioneer

Contents

Preface   xix

1 **Fundamental Concepts**   **1**

1.1   Modeling Systems   2

1.2   Domains and Levels of Modeling   5
Digital Modeling Example   5
Analog Modeling Example   10
Mixed-Signal Modeling Example   12
Energy Domains and Conservation   12

1.3   Modeling Languages   13

1.4   VHDL-AMS Modeling Concepts   15
Elements of Behavior   16
Elements of Structure   18
Mixed Structural and Behavioral Models   21
Test Benches   21
Analysis, Elaboration and Execution   24

1.5   Learning a New Language: Lexical Elements and Syntax   26
Lexical Elements   27
Syntax Descriptions   32

Exercises   35

2 **Scalar Data Types, Natures and Operations**   **39**

2.1   Constants and Variables   40
Constant and Variable Declarations   40
Variable Assignment   42

2.2   Scalar Types   43
Type Declarations   43
Integer Types   44
Floating-Point Types   46
Physical Types   48
Enumeration Types   51

2.3   Type Classification   57
      Subtypes   57
      Type Qualification   60
      Type Conversion   60
2.4   Scalar Natures   61
      Nature Declarations   61
      Standard Natures   64
      Subnatures   65
2.5   Attributes of Scalar Types and Natures   66
2.6   Expressions and Operators   70
Exercises   72

Sequential Statements   **75**

3.1   If Statements   76
3.2   Case Statements   79
3.3   Null Statements   84
3.4   Loop Statements   86
      Exit Statements   87
      Next Statements   90
      While Loops   91
      For Loops   93
      Summary of Loop Statements   96
3.5   Assertion and Report Statements   96
Exercises   102

Composite Data Types and Operations   **105**

4.1   Arrays   106
      Multidimensional Arrays   111
      Array Aggregates   113
      Array Attributes   117
4.2   Unconstrained Arrays   118
      Strings   120
      Real Vectors   120
      Bit Vectors   121
      Standard-Logic Arrays   121
      String and Bit-String Literals   121
      Unconstrained Array Ports   122
4.3   Array Operations and Referencing   123
      Array Slices   125
      Array Type Conversions   126
4.4   Records   127
      Record Aggregates   131
Exercises   132

5   **Digital Modeling Constructs**   **135**

5.1   Entity Declarations   136

5.2   Architecture Bodies   138
Concurrent Statements   139
Signal Declarations   140

5.3   Digital Behavioral Descriptions   141
Signal Assignment   141
Signal Attributes   144
Wait Statements   146
Delta Delays   150
Transport and Inertial Delay Mechanisms   153
Process Statements   160
Concurrent Signal Assignment Statements   161
Concurrent Assertion Statements   167
Entities and Passive Processes   168

5.4   Digital Structural Descriptions   170
Component Instantiation and Port Maps   170

Exercises   179

6   **Analog Modeling Constructs**   **187**

6.1   Free Quantities   188
Quantity Ports   190

6.2   Terminals and Branch Quantities   192
Terminal Declarations   192
Branch Quantity Declarations   193
Terminal Ports   200

6.3   Attributes of Terminals and Quantities   201
Attributes of Terminals   202
Attributes of Quantities   202
Quantity Attributes of Signals   213

6.4   Simultaneous Statements   217
Simple Simultaneous Statement   218
Simultaneous If Statement   221
Simultaneous Case Statement   224
Simultaneous Null Statement   227

6.5   Analog Structural Descriptions   228

6.6   Discontinuities and Break Statements   232
Concurrent Break Statements   239

6.7   Step Limit Specifications   244

6.8   Mixed-Signal Descriptions   247
Analog-to-Digital Conversion   248
Digital-to-Analog Conversion   250

6.9   Mixed-Technology Descriptions   253

Exercises   256

7   Design Processing   **261**

7.1   Analysis   262
       Design Libraries, Library Clauses and Use Clauses   267
7.2   Elaboration   269
       Requirements for Solvability   275
7.3   Execution   277
Exercises   280

8   Case Study 1: Mixed-Signal Focus   **281**

8.1   System Overview   282
8.2   Command and Control System Design   282
       Control Sticks   283
       Digitize/Encode Block   283
       Decoder/Pulse-Width Block   290
       Pulse-Width/Analog Converter   290
8.3   Design Trade-Off Analysis   294
       Converter Accuracy   295
       System Analysis   296
Exercises   299

9   Subprograms   **303**

9.1   Procedures   304
       Return Statement in a Procedure   309
9.2   Procedure Parameters   310
       Signal Parameters   314
       Default Values   317
       Unconstrained Array Parameters   319
       Summary of Procedure Parameters   321
9.3   Concurrent Procedure Call Statements   322
9.4   Functions   325
       Functional Modeling   327
       Pure and Impure Functions   327
       Functions in Simultaneous Statements   329
       The Function Now   330
9.5   Simultaneous Procedural Statements   333
9.6   Overloading   338
       Overloading Operator Symbols   339
9.7   Visibility of Declarations   341
Exercises   345

10   Packages and Use Clauses   **349**

10.1   Package Declarations   350
       Subprograms in Package Declarations   355
       Constants in Package Declarations   356

10.2 Package Bodies   358

10.3 Use Clauses   360

10.4 The Predefined Package Standard   363

10.5 IEEE Standard Packages   364
Std_Logic_1164 Multivalue Logic System   364
Standard VHDL Synthesis Packages   366
Standard VHDL Mathematical Packages   366
Proposed Standard Analog Packages   371

Exercises   375

11 **Aliases**   **377**

11.1 Aliases for Data Objects   378

11.2 Aliases for Non-Data Items   383

Exercises   386

12 **Generic Constants**   **389**

12.1 Parameterizing Behavior   390

12.2 Parameterizing Structure   394

Exercises   398

13 **Frequency and Transfer Function Modeling**   **401**

13.1 Frequency-Based Modeling   402
Spectral Source Quantities   405

13.2 Noise Modeling   409

13.3 Laplace Transfer Functions   412

13.4 Discrete Transfer Functions and Sampling   423
Zero-Order Hold (ZOH)   423
Z Transfer Function (ZTF)   426
Summary of Transfer Function Attributes   428
Z-Domain Sampling   431

Exercises   433

14 **Case Study 2: Mixed-Technology Focus**   **437**

14.1 Rudder System Overview   438
Rudder System Specifications and Development   439

14.2 *S*-Domain Implementation   440
Servo Controller   441
Motor Model   444
Gearbox   446
Rudder Load   447
S-Domain System Performance   447

14.3 Mixed Mechanical/*S*-Domain Implementation   454
Servo/Amplifier   455
Motor Model   455

Gearbox   457
Control Horn Assembly   458
Rudder Model   460

14.4 Design Trade-Off Analysis   461
Deriving *Z*-Domain Coefficients   463
Implement Compensator as Difference Equations   464
Exercises   467

15 Resolved Signals   469

15.1 Basic Resolved Signals   470
Composite Resolved Subtypes   474
Summary of Resolved Subtypes   478

15.2 IEEE Std_Logic_1164 Resolved Subtypes   479

15.3 Resolved Signals and Ports   481
Resolved Ports   483
Driving Value Attribute   485

15.4 Resolved Signal Parameters   485
Exercises   487

16 Components and Configurations   493

16.1 Components   494
Component Declarations   494
Component Instantiation   495
Packaging Components   496

16.2 Configuring Component Instances   498
Basic Configuration Declarations   498
Configuring Multiple Levels of Hierarchy   501
Direct Instantiation of Configured Entities   504
Generic and Port Maps in Configurations   505
Deferred Component Binding   512

16.3 Configuration Specifications   514
Incremental Binding   515
Exercises   521

17 Generate Statements   529

17.1 Generating Iterative Structures   530

17.2 Conditionally Generating Structures   536
Recursive Structures   541

17.3 Configuration of Generate Statements   543
Exercises   549

18 Case Study 3: DC-DC Power Converter   557

18.1 Buck Converter Theory and Design   558
Selecting a Switching Regulator Topology   558

18.2 Modeling with VHDL-AMS   565
    Capacitor Model   565
    Ideal Switch Model   566

18.3 Voltage-Mode Control   568

18.4 Averaged Model   569

18.5 Closing the Loop   571
    Compensation Design   572
    Load Regulation   576
    Line Regulation   578

18.6 Design Trade-Off Study   578

Exercises   582

19   **Guards and Blocks**   **585**

19.1 Guarded Signals and Disconnection   586
    The Driving Attribute   591
    Guarded Ports   591
    Guarded Signal Parameters   593

19.2 Blocks and Guarded Signal Assignment   595
    Explicit Guard Signals   598
    Disconnection Specifications   600

19.3 Using Blocks for Structural Modularity   601
    Generics and Ports in Blocks   604
    Configuring Designs with Blocks   605

Exercises   608

20   **Access Types and Abstract Data Types**   **613**

20.1 Access Types   614
    Access Type Declarations and Allocators   614
    Assignment and Equality of Access Values   617
    Access Types for Records and Arrays   618

20.2 Linked Data Structures   620
    Deallocation and Storage Management   625

20.3 Abstract Data Types Using Packages   626
    Container ADTs   631

Exercises   640

21   **Files and Input/Output**   **643**

21.1 Files   644
    File Declarations   644
    Reading from Files   645
    Writing to Files   648
    Files Declared in Subprograms   651
    Explicit Open and Close Operations   653
    File Parameters in Subprograms   656

Portability of Files   657

21.2 The Package Textio   658
      Textio Read Operations   660
      Textio Write Operations   664
      Reading and Writing User-Defined Types   667
Exercises   667

22   Attributes and Groups   **671**

22.1 Predefined Attributes   672
      Attributes of Scalar Types   672
      Attributes of Scalar Natures   673
      Attributes of Array Types and Objects   673
      Attributes of Signals   674
      Attributes of Terminals   675
      Attributes of Quantities   675
      Attributes of Named Items   676

22.2 User-Defined Attributes   683
      Attribute Declarations   683
      Attribute Specifications   684
      The Attribute Foreign   694

22.3 Groups   696
Exercises   699

23   Case Study 4: Communication System   **703**

23.1 Communication System Overview   704
23.2 Frequency Shift Keying   705
23.3 FSK Detection   708
      Non-Coherent Detection   709
      Phase-Locked Loop Detection   711
23.4 Trade-Off Study   714
Exercises   716

24   Miscellaneous Topics   **719**

24.1 Buffer and Linkage Ports   720
24.2 Conversion Functions in Association Lists   722
24.3 Postponed Processes   727
24.4 Shared Variables   730
Exercises   731

25   Integrated System Modeling   **735**

25.1 Top-down Design   736
25.2 System Specification   738
25.3 Partitioning the System   739

25.4 Refining the Design 740

25.5 Model Calibration 742

25.6 System Verification 744

25.7 Synthesis and Reuse 745

25.8 Design Trade-Offs and Optimization 746
Architectural Trade-Offs 747
Parametric Analysis 747
Optimization 747
Response Surface Models 748

Exercises 749

26 **Case Study 5: RC Airplane System** 751

26.1 RC System Overview 752

26.2 Interfacing Command and Control to the Rudder System 752

26.3 System Power Supply Effects 754
Supply Level and Servo Error 755
Rudder Servo with Buck Converter 757

26.4 Propeller System 762
Propeller System Performance 768

26.5 Human Controller 770
Modeling the Human 770
System Accuracy 773

26.6 Summary 773

Exercises 774

A **Using SPICE Models in VHDL-AMS** 777

A.1 SystemVision/ADMS (Mentor Graphics Corporation) 777

A.2 VeriasHDL (Synopsys, Inc.) 780

A.3 Auriga (FTL Systems, Inc.) 782

B **The Predefined Package Standard** 785

C **IEEE Standard Packages** 789

C.1 Std_Logic_1164 Multivalue Logic System 789

C.2 Standard 1076.2 VHDL Mathematical Packages 792

D **Related Standards** 797

D.1 IEEE VHDL Standards 797

D.2 Other Design Automation Standards 801

E **VHDL-AMS Syntax** 807

E.1 Design File 809

E.2 Library Unit Declarations 809

E.3   Declarations and Specifications   811

E.4   Type Definitions   813

E.5   Concurrent Statements   814

E.6   Simultaneous Statements   816

E.7   Sequential Statements   817

E.8   Interfaces and Associations   819

E.9   Expressions   819

F   Answers to Exercises   **821**

G   CD-ROM Guide   **851**

References   **853**

Index   **857**

Preface

VHDL-AMS is a language for describing digital, analog and mixed-signal systems. It is an extension of the digital hardware description language VHDL, which arose out of the United States government's Very High Speed Integrated Circuits (VHSIC) program. In the course of this program, it became clear that there was a need for a standard language for describing the structure and function of integrated circuits (ICs). Hence the VHSIC Hardware Description Language (VHDL) was developed. It was subsequently developed further under the auspices of the Institute of Electrical and Electronic Engineers (IEEE) and adopted in the form of the IEEE Standard 1076, *Standard VHDL Language Reference Manual,* in 1987. This first standard version of the language is often referred to as VHDL-87.

Like all IEEE standards, the VHDL standard is subject to review every five years. Comments and suggestions from users of the 1987 standard were analyzed by the IEEE working group responsible for VHDL, and in 1992 a revised version of the standard was proposed. This was eventually adopted in 1993, giving us VHDL-93. A second round of revision of the standard was started in 1998. That process was completed in 2001, giving us the current version of the digital language, VHDL-2001.

In the early 1990s, the need for a hardware description language supporting analog and mixed-signal modeling became apparent, and an IEEE Working Group was established. The Working Group developed a set of design objectives for an extension to VHDL and completed a draft Language Reference Manual in 1997. The draft was refined and subsequently approved in 1999, becoming IEEE Standard 1076.1 *Definition of Analog and Mixed Signal Extensions to IEEE Standard VHDL.*

VHDL-AMS is designed to fill a number of needs in the design process. First, it allows description of the structure of a system, that is, how it is decomposed into subsystems and how those subsystems are interconnected. Second, it allows the specification of the function of a system using familiar programming language and equation forms. Third, as a result, it allows the design of a system to be simulated before being manufactured, so that designers can quickly compare alternatives and test for correctness without the delay and expense of hardware prototyping. Fourth, it allows the detailed structure of a design to be synthesized from a more abstract specification, allowing designers to concentrate on more strategic design decisions and reducing time to market.

This book presents a structured guide to the modeling facilities offered by the VHDL-AMS language, showing how they can be used for the design of digital, analog, mixed-signal and mixed-technology systems. The book does not purport to teach engineering design, since that topic is large enough by itself to warrant several textbooks covering its various aspects. Instead, the book assumes that the reader has at least a basic grasp of electronics design concepts, such as might be gained from a first course in electronics design in an engineering degree program. Some exposure to computer programming and to analog and radio-frequency system design will also be beneficial. An understanding of multidisciplinary engineering will be useful for those interested in using VHDL-AMS for "mechatronics" design. Unlike some other books on VHDL-AMS, this book does not assume the reader is already familiar with VHDL for digital system modeling. Instead, it presents the whole of VHDL-AMS as a unified language for digital, analog and mixed-signal modeling. This book is suitable for use in an intermediate or advanced-level course in analog and mixed-signal circuit design or "mechatronics" design. It will also serve practicing engineers who need to acquire VHDL-AMS fluency as part of their changing job requirements.

One pervasive theme running through the presentation in this book is that modeling a system using a hardware description language is essentially a software design exercise. This implies that good software engineering practice should be applied. Hence the treatment in this book draws directly from experience in software engineering. There are numerous hints and techniques from small-scale and large-scale software engineering presented throughout the book, with the sincere intention that they might be of use to readers.

We are particularly pleased to be able to include this book in the Morgan Kaufmann *Series in Systems on Silicon*. Modeling for simulation and synthesis is a vital part of a design methodology for large-scale systems. VHDL-AMS allows models to be expressed at a range of levels of abstraction, from device level up to algorithmic and architectural levels. It will play an important role in future design processes for analog, mixed-signal and mixed-technology systems, many of which must function correctly in environments that are neither digital nor electronic.

Structure of the Book

The Designer's Guide to VHDL-AMS is organized so that it can be read linearly from front to back. This path offers a graduated development, with each chapter building on ideas introduced in the preceding chapters. Each chapter introduces a number of related concepts or language facilities and illustrates each one with examples. Scattered throughout the book are five case studies, which bring together preceding material in the form of extended worked examples.

Chapter 1 introduces the idea of a hardware description language and outlines the reasons for its use and the benefits that ensue. It then proceeds to introduce the basic concepts underlying VHDL-AMS, so that they can serve as a basis for examples in subsequent chapters. The next three chapters cover the aspects of VHDL-AMS that are most like conventional programming languages. These may be used to describe the behavior of a system in algorithmic terms. Chapter 2 explains the basic type system of the language and introduces the scalar data types. Chapter 3 describes the sequential control structures, and Chapter 4 covers composite data structures used to represent collections of data elements.

In Chapter 5, the main facilities of VHDL-AMS used for modeling digital hardware are covered in detail. These include facilities for modeling the basic behavioral elements in a design, the signals that interconnect them and the hierarchical structure of the design. In Chapter 6, the facilities of VHDL-AMS used for modeling analog and mixed-signal hardware are covered. These include facilities for modeling the equations that represent analog behavior, the terminals and quantities that interconnect parts of a design and the facilities for expressing the interaction between the analog and digital portions of a design. Chapter 7 describes the way in which VHDL-AMS models are processed for simulation or other forms of analysis and discusses execution of models and solution of equations. The combination of facilities described in these early chapters is sufficient for many modeling tasks, so Chapter 8 brings them together in the first case study.

The next group of chapters extends this basic set of facilities with language features that make modeling of large systems more tractable. Chapter 9 introduces procedures and functions, which can be used to encapsulate behavioral aspects of a design. Chapter 10 introduces the package as a means of collecting together related parts of a design or of creating modules that can be reused in a number of designs. It also describes a number of packages standardized by the IEEE for use in VHDL-AMS designs. Chapter 11 then covers aliases as a way of managing the large number of names that arise in a large model. Chapter 12 describes generic constants as a means of parameterizing the behavior and structure of a design. Chapter 13 deals with Laplace and discrete transforms for frequency domain modeling and with small-signal noise modeling. The material in this group of chapters is brought together in the next case study in Chapter 14.

The third group of chapters covers advanced modeling features in VHDL-AMS. Chapter 15 deals with the important topic of resolved signals. While this language facility forms the basis of many real-world models, its treatment in this book is left to this late chapter. Experience has shown that the ideas can be difficult to understand without a solid foundation in the more basic language aspects. Chapter 16 deals with the topics of component instantiation and configuration. These features are also important in large real-world models, but they can be difficult to understand. Hence this book introduces structural modeling through the mechanism of direct instantiation in earlier chapters and leaves the more general case of component instantiation and configuration until this later chapter. In Chapter 17, generated regular structures are covered. Chapter 18 brings the material in this group of chapters together in the third case study.

The fourth group of chapters covers language facilities generally used for system-level modeling. Chapter 19 is a detailed treatment of the related topics of guarded signals and blocks. Chapter 20 introduces the notion of access types (or pointers) and uses them to develop linked data structures. This leads to a discussion of abstract data types as a means of managing the complexity associated with linked data structures. Chapter 21 covers the language facilities for input and output using files, including binary files and text files. Chapter 22 describes the attribute mechanism as a means of annotating a design with additional information. Chapter 23 then presents the fourth case study.

The last group of chapters draws the tour of VHDL-AMS to a close by covering the remaining language facilities and addressing system design issues. Chapter 24 is a miscellany of advanced topics not covered in the previous chapters. Chapter 25 discusses the use of VHDL-AMS features for modeling the integrated system of analog and digital subsystems and their interactions. Chapter 26 concludes with the final case study.

The Case Studies

The case studies explore the design of a radio-controlled (RC), electric-powered airplane system. They are intended for educational purposes and include analog, mixed-signal and mixed-technology models. They demonstrate VHDL-AMS language features and embody clear guidelines for system design and analysis.

The system from which all of the case studies are derived is shown in Figure P-1. The overall system works as follows. The ground-based operator gives analog throttle (propeller) and rudder commands using control joysticks as shown in the upper left-hand corner of the diagram. The command signals are digitized, encoded into a serial format and transmitted over an FM radio link. The signals are picked up by receiver electronics on the airplane, decoded and converted to pulse-width modulated signals that are proportional to the original analog control settings. These varying pulse-width signals are converted back to analog signals and sent to the amplifiers and servos controlling the propeller speed and rudder position. The system architecture provides an expandable design to which channels for control surfaces or other functions can easily be added.

FIGURE P-1

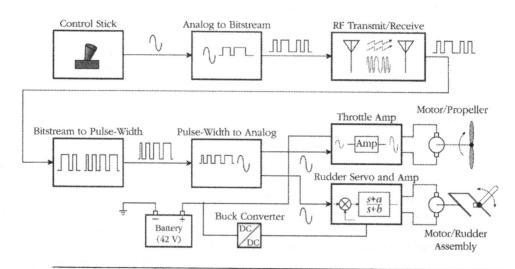

System diagram for the RC airplane system.

At first glance this may appear to be a rather simple system. However, under closer inspection, it contains a wide variety of modeling challenges: digital, analog, mixed-signal, mixed-technology, as well as behavioral and structural VHDL-AMS models, represented with multiple levels of hierarchy. Various aspects of the RC airplane system are explored in this book in five case studies. Each case study is designed to illustrate specific uses of VHDL-AMS.

Case Study 1: Mixed-Signal Focus

The first case study focuses on the encoding, transmission and decoding of the analog throttle and rudder command signals as they make their way through the system. Analog-to-digital and digital-to-analog conversions are highlighted to show mixed-signal modeling with VHDL-AMS.

Case Study 2: Mixed-Technology Focus

This case study focuses on the mixed-technology (mixed-domain) capabilities of VHDL-AMS. In particular, the *s*-domain servo control blocks and the electrical and mechanical system components are discussed.

Case Study 3: Power Systems Focus

This case study shows how power systems can be modeled with VHDL-AMS. A buck converter is modeled with two useful levels of abstraction, and the effects of power fluctuations on the system are simulated.

Case Study 4: Communications System Focus

This case study compares phase-locked loop and discrimination methods for signal recovery in the RF receiver.

Case Study 5: Full System Analysis

This case study looks at the RC airplane as an entire system. It also highlights how different modeling abstraction levels may be used to make large system simulations as efficient as possible. The value of early requirements exploration, frequent subsystem integration and validation, and bottom-up design verification are explored.

Notes to Instructors

Whereas a complete reading of this book provides a complete coverage of the language, there are several shorter paths through the material. Some suggested minimal paths for readers with different requirements are as follows:

- For an introductory course in modeling using VHDL-AMS: Chapters 1 to 7, 9, 10, 12 and 15, plus the case study in Chapter 8. Chapter 11 may be included if time permits.

- For a more advanced course: add Chapters 13, 16 and 17; the case studies in Chapters 14 and 18; and a selection of the remaining chapters as time permits. Chapter 25 will be helpful in formulating a modeling flow around VHDL-AMS.

- For readers who wish to focus primarily on analog modeling: Chapters 1, 2, 6, 7, 13 and 25 are the most relevant.

- For readers proficient in using conventional programming languages: treat Chapters 2 to 4 as review.

- For readers with some previous introductory-level background in VHDL-AMS: treat Chapters 1 to 4 as review.

Each chapter in the book is followed by a set of exercises designed to help the reader develop understanding of the material. Where an exercise relates to a particular topic described in the chapter, the section number is included in square brackets. An approximate "difficulty" rating is also provided, expressed using the following symbols:

- ❶ quiz-style exercise, testing basic understanding

- ❷ basic modeling exercise—10 minutes to half an hour effort

- ❸ advanced modeling exercise—one half to two hours effort

- ❹ modeling project—half a day or more effort

Answers for the first category of exercises are provided in Appendix F. The remaining categories involve developing VHDL-AMS models. Readers are encouraged to test correctness of their models by running them on a VHDL-AMS simulator. This is a much more effective learning exercise than comparing paper models with paper solutions.

CD-ROM

This book includes a CD-ROM containing source code of all of the case study and example models in the book, supplemental resources related to the text and examples and a library of models that are useful building blocks for building larger systems or for learning the power of VHDL-AMS "by example." The case studies and model library have been coordinated to work with the SystemVision simulation and modeling environment offered as a commercial product by Mentor Graphics Corporation. The SystemVision environment includes a schematic entry tool, a VHDL-AMS simulator and a waveform viewing facility. Full hierarchical SystemVision schematics are available for the case studies in this book. To learn more, you can visit the Web site *mentor.com/SystemVision*. A downloadable version of the environment, for educational purposes, is available from this Web site. The limited-capacity educational-version tools allow you to experiment with the example models and to verify designs suggested in the exercises. They can also be used with selected portions of the case studies.

Resources for Help and Information

While this book attempts to be comprehensive in its coverage of VHDL-AMS, there will no doubt be questions that it does not answer. For these, the reader will need to seek other resources. A valuable source of experience and advice, often overlooked, is one's colleagues, either at the workplace or in user groups. User groups generally hold regular meetings that either formally or informally include a time for questions and answers. Many also run e-mail lists and on-line discussion groups for problem solving.

Accellera, an EDA industry association, sponsors the EDA Industry Working Groups Web server (*www.eda.org*). The server has links to Web pages and repositories of several VHDL standards groups and user groups. Another Web site of interest is *www.vhdl-ams.com,* hosted by Avant! Systems. It provides tutorial material and example models provided by VHDL-AMS tool vendors.

Readers who have access to the Usenet electronic news network will find the news group *comp.lang.vhdl* a valuable resource. This discussion group is a source of announcements, sample models, questions and answers and useful software. Participants include VHDL and VHDL-AMS users and people actively involved in the language standard working group and in VHDL and VHDL-AMS tool development. The "frequently asked questions" (FAQ) file for this group is a mine of useful pointers to books, products and other information. It is archived at *www.eda.org.*

One resource that must be mentioned is IEEE Standard 1076.1, *Definition of Analog and Mixed Signal Extensions to IEEE Standard VHDL.* It extends the standard for digital VHDL, IEEE Standard 1076, *IEEE Standard VHDL Language Reference Manual.* Together, the two standards are the authoritative sources of information about VHDL and VHDL-AMS. However, since they are definitional documents, not a tutorial, they are written in a complex legalistic style. This makes them very difficult to use to answer the usual questions that arise when writing VHDL-AMS models. They should only be used once you are somewhat familiar with VHDL-AMS. They can be ordered from the IEEE at *standards.ieee.org.*

This book contains numerous examples of VHDL-AMS models that may also serve as a resource for resolving questions. The VHDL-AMS source code for these examples and the case studies, as well as other related information, is available for on-line access at

www.mkp.com/vhdl-ams

Although we have been careful to avoid errors in the example code, there are no doubt some that we have missed. We would be pleased to hear about them, so that we can correct them in the on-line code and in future printings of this book. Errata and general comments can be e-mailed to us at *vhdl-book@ashenden.com.au*

Acknowledgments

The development of this book has been very much a team effort, and the authors are extremely grateful to all who have contributed. Most important, we would like to acknowledge the generous support of Mentor Graphics Corporation, for contributing staff time and other resources to the development of the case studies. After we decided on the RC airplane as the system to be designed, Mike Donnelly developed the system specification and detailed architecture. He created the original "back of the napkin" sketch and worked out how to partition the system into the individual case studies. From this starting point, Scott Cooper and Tom Egel worked through the detailed design and drafted the case study chapters. Scott also took on the Herculean effort of testing the code examples, not only in the case study chapters, but in other chapters also. In addition, Rehan Shaukat from Portland State University assisted with preparation of the CD-ROM during his internship at Mentor. Without the efforts of these people and the support provided by Mentor, the case studies, which are central to the book, would not have been possible.

We are also grateful to Ken Bakalar, one of the developers of VHDL-AMS, for helping us to resolve questions of interpretation of the language definition and to formulate modeling guidelines. Gary Pratt also helped us with modeling guidelines and suggestions for examples to illustrate them. Thanks are due to Alan Mantooth of the University of Arkansas, who used a draft of this book in his course.

This book has also benefited greatly from the input of the reviewers: Gary Pratt and Maged Fikry of Mentor Graphics, Steve Drager of Air Force Research Labs, Peter Wilson of the University of Southampton, Peter Frey of Cadence, Paul Menchini, Jim Barby of the University of Waterloo and David Barton of AverStar. Also, Hal Carter of the University of Cincinnati helped to shape the structure of the book. Any remaining errors or omissions are our fault.

Finally, and by no means least, we would like to thank the staff at Morgan Kaufmann Publishers, led by Senior Editor Denise Penrose, for their support for this project. Denise has kept us focused, and her commitment to quality has been an inspiration to us.

chapter one

Fundamental Concepts

In this introductory chapter, we describe what we mean by digital, analog and mixed-signal system modeling and see why modeling and simulation are an important part of the design process. We see how the hardware description language VHDL-AMS can be used to model digital, analog and mixed-signal systems and introduce some of the basic concepts underlying the language. We complete this chapter with a description of the basic lexical and syntactic elements of the language, to form a basis for the detailed descriptions of language features that follow in later chapters.

1.1 Modeling Systems

If we are to discuss the topic of modeling digital, analog and mixed-signal systems, we first need to agree on what we mean by each of these terms. Different engineers would come up with different definitions, depending on their background and the field in which they were working. The primary difference between digital and analog systems is their representation of values and behavior with respect to time.

First, we focus on what we mean by a digital system. Some designers may consider a single VLSI circuit to be a self-contained digital system. Others might take a larger view and think of a complete computer, packaged in a cabinet with peripheral controllers and other interfaces, as a system. In both of these cases, it is not the size or complexity of the system that makes it digital; rather, it is how data values are represented. For the purposes of this book, we consider any digital circuit that processes or stores information quantized over time into discrete values to be a digital system. We thus consider both the system as a whole and the various parts from which it is constructed.

With this definition of digital systems in mind, we now turn to analog systems. In contrast to digital systems, information in analog systems has values that vary continuously with time. We often use continuous ordinary differential and algebraic equations to describe the varying values within analog systems. Like a digital system, we can consider an analog system as a whole or as an assembly of constituent components. An analog system may be a single device, such as a resistor or capacitor, or it may be a complete system including components such as mixers, oscillators, filters and amplifiers.

Given these definitions of digital and analog systems, we now consider how these systems interact. We call combined analog and digital systems *mixed-signal* systems. In such systems, the analog and digital portions interact via analog-to-digital and digital-to-analog converters. An example of a mixed-signal system is a chemical-process control system with analog sensors, filters and actuators combined with digital computers to determine flow rates for different fluids. The interactions between the digital and analog portions of the system are accomplished by analog-to-digital converters that sample sensor values for processing by the computer and by digital-to-analog converters that enable the computers to control actuators and thus fluid flow.

In addition to electronic systems, we can also consider mechanical, optical, fluidic, thermal and electromagnetic systems, since they also represent information in continuously varying form. Note that we may view a particular system from more than one of these perspectives. For example, a microelectromechanical accelerometer used to control deployment of an automobile's airbag may include digital and analog electrical, mechanical and thermal functionality. Similarly, the thermal effects on the operation of a transistor involve multiple domains in a single component. Thus our discussion covers a range of systems modeled in different energy domains and spanning levels of abstraction from the low-level devices that make up the components to the top-level functional units.

If we are to encompass this range of views of digital, analog and mixed-signal systems, we must recognize the complexity with which we are dealing. It is not humanly possible to comprehend such complex systems in their entirety. We need to find methods of dealing with the complexity, so that we can, with some degree of confidence, design components and systems that meet their requirements.

The most important way of meeting this challenge is to adopt a systematic methodology of design. If we start with a requirements document for the system, we can design an abstract structure that meets the requirements. We can then decompose this structure into a collection of components that interact to perform the same function. Each of these components can in turn be decomposed until we get to a level where we have some ready-made, primitive components that perform a required function. The result of this process is a hierarchically composed system, built from the primitive elements.

The advantage of this methodology is that each subsystem can be designed independently of others. When we use a subsystem, we can think of it as an abstraction rather than having to consider its detailed composition. So at any particular stage in the design process, we only need to pay attention to the small amount of information relevant to the current focus of design. We are saved from being overwhelmed by masses of detail.

We use the term *model* to mean our understanding of a system. The model represents that information which is relevant and abstracts away from irrelevant detail. The implication of this is that there may be several models of the same system, since different information is relevant in different contexts. One kind of model might concentrate on representing the function of the system, another kind might represent the way in which the system is composed of subsystems, and further kinds might focus on different energy domains. We will come back to this idea in more detail in the next section.

There are a number of important motivations for formalizing this idea of a model. First, when a system is needed, the requirements of the system must be specified. The job of the engineers is to design a system that meets these requirements. To do that, they must be given an understanding of the requirements, hopefully in a way that leaves them free to explore alternative implementations and to choose the best according to some criteria. One of the problems that often arises is that requirements are incompletely and ambiguously spelled out, and the customer and the design engineers disagree on what is meant by the requirements document. This problem can be avoided by using a formal model to communicate requirements.

A second reason for using formal models is to communicate understanding of the function of a system to a user. The designer cannot always predict every possible way in which a system may be used, and so is not able to enumerate all possible behaviors. If the designer provides a model, the user can check it against any given set of inputs and determine how the system behaves in that context. The ability to model interactions between multiple energy domains provides a particularly powerful tool for expressing system functionality in emerging technology areas, such as mixed-signal systems on a chip or mixed-technology nanotechnology devices. Thus a formal model is an invaluable tool for documenting a system.

A third motivation for modeling is to allow testing and verification of a design using simulation. If we start with a requirements model that defines the behavior of a system, we can simulate the behavior using test inputs and note the resultant outputs of the system. According to our design methodology, we can then design a circuit from subsystems, each with its own model of behavior. We can simulate this composite system with the same test inputs and compare the outputs with those of the previous simulation. If they are the same (within some tolerances), we know that the composite system meets the requirements for the cases tested. Otherwise we know that some revision of the design is needed. We can continue this process until we reach the bottom level in our design hierarchy, where the components are real devices whose behavior we know. Subsequently, when the design is manufactured, the test inputs and outputs from simulation can be used to verify that the physical circuit functions correctly. This approach to testing and verification of course assumes that the test inputs cover all of the circumstances in which the final circuit will be used. The issue of test coverage is a complex problem in itself and is an active area of research.

When we are modeling for testing or verification, it is instructive to remember that digital designs are abstractions or approximations of analog circuits. In reality, the high and low voltage levels used to encode digital binary signal values are analog and vary continuously. By using rigorous design methodologies, such as that embodied in synchronous digital design, we can normally ensure that the digital abstraction is consistent with the behavior of the fabricated circuit. However, as feature sizes shrink or the operating frequency increases, the digital model of a circuit may no longer be accurate. In such cases, we can resort to more detailed analog models to achieve the necessary modeling fidelity to test our design.

A fourth motivation for modeling is to allow formal verification of the correctness of a design. Formal verification requires a mathematical statement of the required function of a system. This statement may be expressed in the notation of a formal logic system, such as temporal logic. Formal verification also requires a mathematical definition of the meaning of the modeling language or notation used to describe a design. The process of verification involves application of the rules of inference of the logic system to prove that the design implies the required function. While formal verification is not yet in everyday use, it is an active area of research. There have already been significant demonstrations of formal verification techniques in real design projects, and the promise for the future is bright. In recent years, a number of commercial formal verification tools have become available for digital models. The most common type of tool provides equivalency checking between two digital models. This allows designers to ensure that detailed implementations have equivalent functionality as a more abstract model serves as a specification. The application of formal verification to analog designs is not as mature, but it is an active area of research. There have already been significant demonstrations of formal verification techniques in real analog design projects, particularly in the area of symbolic analysis.

One final, but equally important, motivation for modeling is to allow automatic synthesis of circuits. If we can formally specify the function required of a system, it is in theory possible to translate that specification into a circuit that performs the function. The advantage of this approach is that the human cost of design is reduced, and engineers are free to explore alternatives rather than being bogged down in design detail. Also, there is less scope for errors being introduced into a design and not being detected. If we automate the translation from specification to implementation, we can be more confident that the resulting circuit is correct.

The application of synthesis to digital design is now commonplace, with typical development projects using a synthesis-based design flow. The analog synthesis technology is not as mature, although there has been explosive growth in recent years. A number of research tools exist that successfully synthesize analog circuits, and there are several forthcoming commercial tools for analog synthesis. Mixed-signal synthesis is also an emerging technology based on work leveraging the more mature digital synthesis algorithms. As analog synthesis capabilities improve, mixed-signal synthesis capabilities will leverage these improvements as well. For mixed-technology systems, synthesis research promises the ability to automate the implementation of microelectromechanical or nanotechnology machines.

The unifying factor behind all of these arguments is that we want to achieve maximum reliability in the design process for minimum cost and design time. We need to ensure that requirements are clearly specified and understood, that subsystems are used correctly and that designs meet the requirements. A major contributor to excessive cost is having to revise a design after manufacture to correct errors. By avoiding errors, and by providing better tools for the design process, costs and delays can be contained.

1.2 Domains and Levels of Modeling

In the previous section, we mentioned that there may be different models of a system, each focusing on different aspects. We can classify these models into three domains: *function, structure* and *geometry*. The functional domain is concerned with the operations performed by the system. In a sense, this is the most abstract domain of description, since it does not indicate how the function is implemented. The structural domain deals with how the system is composed of interconnected subsystems. The geometric domain deals with how the system is laid out in physical space.

Each of these domains can also be divided into levels of abstraction. At the top level, we consider an overview of function, structure or geometry, and at lower levels we introduce successively finer detail. Figure 1-1 (devised by Gajski and Kuhn, see reference [18]) represents the domains on three independent axes and represents the levels of abstraction by the concentric circles crossing each of the axes. Figure 1-2, inspired by this work, shows a similar "Y-chart" representing domains for analog systems.

Let us look at these classifications in more detail, showing how at each level we can create models in each domain. We start with a digital example, a single-chip microcontroller system used as the controller for some measurement instrument, with data input connections and some form of display outputs. We then consider as an analog example circuitry used to condition the inputs from a sensor. Finally, we consider a mixed-signal example combining these digital and analog systems and including mixed-signal converter circuitry.

Digital Modeling Example

At the most abstract level, the function of a digital system may be described in terms of an algorithm, much like an algorithm for a computer program. This level of functional modeling is often called *behavioral modeling,* a term we shall adopt when

FIGURE 1-1

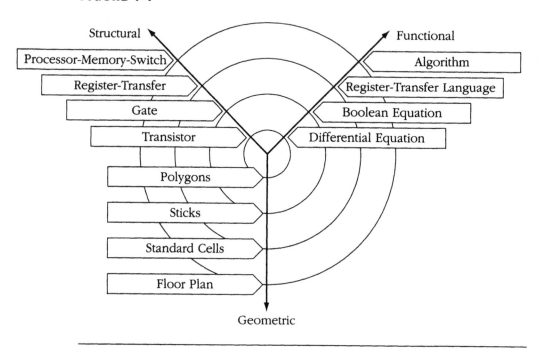

Domains and levels of abstraction. The radial axes show the three different domains of modeling. The concentric rings show the levels of abstraction, with the more abstract levels on the outside and more detailed levels toward the center.

presenting abstract descriptions of a system's function. A possible algorithm for our instrument controller is shown in Figure 1-3. This model describes how the controller repeatedly scans each data input and writes a scaled display of the input value.

At this top level of abstraction, the structure of a system may be described as an interconnection of such components as processors, memories and input/output devices. This level is sometimes called the Processor Memory Switch (PMS) level, named after the notation used by Bell and Newell (see reference [4]). Figure 1-4 shows a structural model of the instrument controller drawn using this notation. It consists of a processor connected via a switch to a memory component and to controllers for the data inputs and display outputs.

In the geometric domain at this top level of abstraction, a system to be implemented as a VLSI circuit may be modeled using a floor plan. This shows how the components described in the structural model are arranged on the silicon die. Figure 1-5 shows a possible floor plan for the instrument controller chip. There are analogous geometric descriptions for digital systems integrated in other media. For example, a personal computer system might be modeled at the top level in the geometric domain by an assembly diagram showing the positions of the motherboard and plug-in expansion boards in the desktop cabinet.

FIGURE 1-2

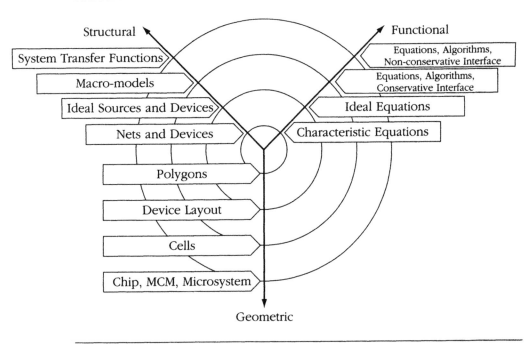

Analog domains and levels of abstraction.

FIGURE 1-3

```
loop
    for each data input loop
        read the value on this input;
        scale the value using the current scale factor for this input;
        convert the scaled value to a decimal string;
        write the string to the display output corresponding to this input;
    end loop;
    wait for 10 ms;
end loop;
```

An algorithm for a measurement instrument controller.

FIGURE 1-4

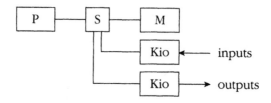

A PMS model of the controller structure. It is constructed from a processor (P), a memory (M), an interconnection switch (S) and two input/output controllers (Kio).

FIGURE 1-5

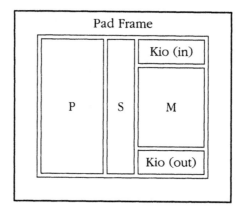

A floor plan model of the controller geometry.

The next level of abstraction in modeling, depicted by the second ring in Figure 1-1, describes the system in terms of units of data storage and transformation. In the digital structural domain, this is often called the *register-transfer* level, composed of a *data path* and a *control section*. The data path contains data storage registers, and data is transferred between them through transformation units. The control section sequences operation of the data path components. For example, a register-transfer-level structural model of the processor in our controller is shown in Figure 1-6.

In the functional domain, a *register-transfer language* (RTL) is often used to specify the operation of a system at this level. Storage of data is represented using register variables, and transformations are represented by arithmetic and logical operators. For example, an RTL model for the processor in our example controller might include the following description:

FIGURE 1-6

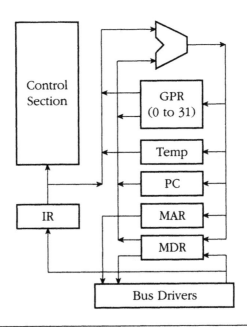

A register-transfer-level structural model of the controller processor. It consists of a general-purpose register (GPR) file; registers for the program counter (PC), memory address (MAR), memory data (MDR), temporary values (Temp) and fetched instructions (IR); an arithmetic unit; bus drivers and the control section.

```
MAR ← PC,  memory_read ← 1
PC ← PC + 1
wait until ready = 1
IR ← memory_data
memory_read ← 0
```

This section of the model describes the operations involved in fetching an instruction from memory. The contents of the PC register are transferred to the memory address register, and the **memory_read** signal is asserted. Then the value from the PC register is transformed (incremented in this case) and transferred back to the PC register. When the **ready** input from the memory is asserted, the value on the memory data input is transferred to the instruction register. Finally, the **memory_read** signal is negated.

In the geometric domain, the kind of model used depends on the physical medium. In our example, standard library cells might be used to implement the registers and data transformation units, and these must be placed in the areas allocated in the chip floor plan.

The third level of abstraction shown in Figure 1-1 is the conventional logic level. At this level, structure is modeled using interconnections of gates, and function is modeled by Boolean equations or truth tables. In the physical medium of a custom integrated circuit, geometry may be modeled using a virtual grid, or "sticks," notation.

At the most detailed level of abstraction, we can model structure using individual transistors, function using the differential equations that relate voltage and current in the circuit, and geometry using polygons for each mask layer of an integrated circuit. Most digital designers do not need to work at this detailed level, as design tools are available to automate translation from a higher level. However, should the need arise to model detailed effects at this level, we can use analog and mixed-signal modeling techniques.

Analog Modeling Example

We illustrate analog modeling by considering a sensor system that includes filtering and amplifier circuitry to condition the input signal. As with the digital system discussed above, the function of an analog system may be described in terms of an algorithm or a set of characteristic equations. This level of functional modeling of analog systems is also known as behavioral modeling.

VHDL-AMS supports modeling continuous time systems described with sets of simultaneous equations. These equations are differential and algebraic equations with sets of unknowns that are continuous, analytic functions of time. We can model the function of analog systems at different levels of abstraction in ways similar to those just discussed for digital systems. First we can form system-level models using transfer functions as with digital design. We can then decompose the system into subsystems and employ a set of macro-models for each. Finally, we can further decompose the macro-models into device-level models. The complexity of the models grows as more detailed models are developed and representations of the structural, functional and geometrical views are refined.

Structural aspects of a system are refined from abstract views that may consist of a set of connected functional blocks or system transfer functions, to a collection of macro-models and nets, then to ideal sources, devices and interconnects, and finally to primitive devices including wires and channels. Similarly, the functional aspects of a system are refined from abstract models using simple equations, to equations representing ideal components, then to more complex modeling equations that include device second-order effects. The physical aspects of a system may span from circuit boards or multichip modules, to floor-planned cells, then to device layout, and finally to polygons as we saw with digital designs.

At the highest level of abstraction, the function of an analog system may be described using transfer functions or some other mathematical description. Typically we express the function not with a single, complex transfer function, but rather by using a collection of steps or stages, with a transfer function associated with each. The corresponding structure of the system can be represented using an interconnection of such n-port devices or of functional blocks. A structural block diagram illustrating analog conditioning circuitry to filter and amplify sensor inputs is shown in Figure 1-7. In the case of a simple one-pole low-pass filter, a transfer function describing its function is shown in Figure 1-8.

FIGURE 1-7

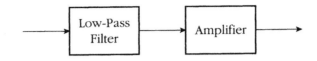

A block diagram for analog conditioning circuitry.

FIGURE 1-8

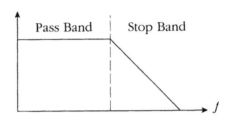

The transfer function for a low-pass filter.

Because the system will be implemented as a VLSI circuit or multichip module (MCM), the abstract geometric domain for this analog system may be represented using a floor plan like that used for a digital system. The arrangement of the functional blocks on one or more dice, MCMs or boards is illustrated in this manner.

The next levels of abstraction in modeling analog systems are macro-modeling and device-level modeling. The transfer-function description gives a functional model for the circuit, then models at lower levels of abstraction flesh out the details of the implementation. For example, a device-level model of the circuit for the simple one-pole low-pass filter is shown in Figure 1-9.

The low-pass filter circuit can be structurally modeled using the resistor and capacitor devices as shown. As with digital modeling, we can consider the function, structure and geometry for an analog system at different levels of abstraction.

FIGURE 1-9

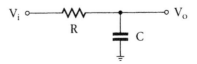

A circuit for a simple low-pass filter.

Mixed-Signal Modeling Example

Having considered both digital and analog systems, we now turn to modeling mixed-signal systems. Mixed-signal models include both analog and digital components, and often focus on the interface between analog and digital systems. For example, a sensor system could include an analog front end that conditions the signal as discussed above, analog-to-digital conversion circuitry and digital processing of the resulting data. Figure 1-10 illustrates such a mixed-signal sensor system with analog and digital subsystems as well as an analog-to-digital converter subsystem that is a mixed-signal system itself. The block diagram presents an abstract functional view of the system with some structure implied by the blocks and their interconnection.

As with the digital processor and analog conditioning circuitry examples above, the function, structure and geometry can be expressed in models. They may be refined from initial abstract representations to more detailed representations as implementation decisions are made during the design process. A simple behavioral model of an analog-to-digital converter is shown in Figure 1-11. We will revisit this analog-to-digital converter block in Section 1.4.

Energy Domains and Conservation

In Figures 1-1 and 1-2, we used Y-charts to illustrate the structural, functional and geometric domains for digital and analog electrical systems. We have also mentioned the

FIGURE 1-10

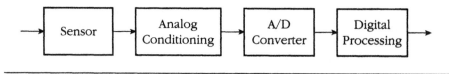

A block diagram for a mixed-signal sensor system.

FIGURE 1-11

```
wait until input voltage crosses threshold
    read input voltage with respect to ground
    if input voltage above threshold then
        output high value as result
    else
        output low value as result
    end if;
end wait until;
```

A behavioral model of an analog-to-digital converter.

need to model composite or coupled-energy systems from multiple energy domains, such as electromechanical, electro-optical and electro-fluidic systems. We use ordinary differential and algebraic equations as the modeling framework for these analog systems. We can classify sets of ordinary differential and algebraic equations as *conservative* or *non-conservative*. Conservative sets of equations represent systems in which energy is conserved, whereas non-conservative sets represent systems where energy is not conserved. Examples of conservative systems include the analog conditioning circuitry and the analog-to-digital converter circuitry described above that use Kirchoff's current and voltage laws to describe the system functionality. Conservative electrical systems are typical of lumped systems with no electrical field effects. Conservative mechanical systems arise from systems in dynamic equilibrium. Non-conservative sets of equations can be used to model systems at abstract levels, to model systems in which the physical phenomena governing behavior are not precisely understood or to improve modeling productivity or simulation speed when approximations do not significantly degrade model fidelity. In the case of conservative systems, energy conservation laws result in additional implicit equations that can be used by an analog solver to represent the system behavior. In contrast, there are no implicit equations for non-conservative systems.

A common application for non-conservative sets of equations is abstract signal-flow models of system behavior. For example, we can describe the transfer functions of blocks in a control system using non-conservative equations without addressing the implementation details of each block. Subsequently, as we progress through the design process, we implement each of the blocks as a digital processing element or as a circuit described by a conservative set of equations.

Another example is a non-conservative set of equations representing Newton's law of cooling. We use this law to model the time rate of heat dissipated from a body into a medium in which the body is immersed. The time rate of temperature change for the body can be represented using a simple ordinary differential equation as follows:

$$\frac{dT(t)}{dt} = k(A - T(t))$$

where A is the constant temperature of the medium, $T(t)$ is the temperature of the body over time and k is a positive constant coefficient for thermal conductivity.

1.3   Modeling Languages

In the previous section, we saw that different kinds of models can be devised to represent the various levels of function, structure and physical arrangement of a system. There are also different ways of expressing these models, depending on the use made of the model.

As an example, consider the ways in which a structural model may be expressed. One common form is a circuit schematic. Graphical symbols are used to represent subsystems or sub-circuits, and instances of these are connected using lines that represent wires. This graphical form is generally the one preferred by designers. However, the same structural information can be represented textually in the form of a net list. For example, analog circuit designs created using a schematic capture tool are often extracted into an equivalent SPICE netlist.

When we move into the functional domain, we usually see textual notations used for modeling. Some of these are intended for use as specification languages, to meet the need for describing the operation of a system without indicating how it might be implemented. For digital systems, these notations are usually based on formal mathematical methods, such as temporal logic or abstract state machines. For analog and mixed-signal systems, the notations may use equations or transfer functions. Other notations are intended for simulating the system for test and verification purposes and are typically based on conventional programming languages. Yet other notations are oriented toward hardware synthesis and usually have a more restricted set of modeling facilities, since some programming language constructs are difficult to translate into hardware.

The purpose of this book is to describe the modeling language VHDL-AMS. VHDL-AMS includes facilities for describing structure and function at a number of levels, from the most abstract down to the device level. It also provides an attribute mechanism that can be used to annotate a model with information in the geometric domain, a feature that can prove very useful for detailed device modeling. VHDL-AMS is intended, among other things, as a modeling language for specification and simulation. We can also use it for hardware synthesis if we restrict ourselves to a subset that can be automatically translated into hardware.

VHDL-AMS was developed to allow designers to represent both analog and digital functionality of a system in the same model. Existing hardware description languages, such as VHDL and Verilog, support digital systems modeling, while languages such as SPICE and its numerous variants support analog systems modeling. Integrating these two modeling domains is a significant new capability for designers.

As System-on-a-Chip (SoC) design becomes more prevalent, designers seek to integrate ever more functionality onto the same die. Analog and digital subsystems are being implemented together more often, requiring the mixed-signal modeling capabilities of VHDL-AMS to adequately describe such systems. As clock frequencies increase and feature sizes continue to shrink, the assumptions underlying digital design no longer hold, and analog models for digital components must be employed instead. In addition, the high-speed interconnects between the processor, memory and switches in a digital system such as the one described above may require more accurate analog transmission line models to adequately represent their function. VHDL-AMS can be used to express these analog models in SoC designs.

VHDL-AMS is an extension of VHDL, a modeling language for digital systems. Digital design with VHDL is mature and widespread in industry, which is why VHDL was used as the base language for the development of VHDL-AMS. Readers specifically interested in VHDL or the digital modeling portions of VHDL-AMS are encouraged to read *The Designer's Guide to VHDL* [1].

1.4 VHDL-AMS Modeling Concepts

In Section 1.2, we looked at the three domains of modeling: function, structure and geometry. In this section, we look at the basic modeling concepts in each of these domains and introduce the corresponding VHDL-AMS elements for describing them. This will provide a feel for VHDL-AMS and a basis from which to work in later chapters. As an example, we look at ways of describing a 1-bit sampling analog-to-digital converter (ADC) with gain, shown in Figure 1-12.

Using VHDL-AMS terminology, we call the module **adc** a design *entity,* and the inputs and outputs are *ports.* Figure 1-13 shows a VHDL-AMS description of the interface to this entity. This is an example of an *entity declaration.* The first two lines of the figure indicate that the entity involves aspects of analog electrical-energy systems. We will explain the precise meaning of these lines in due course, but for now we will treat them as VHDL-AMS "magic" to be included when we describe models in the electrical domain. The entity declaration introduces a name for the entity and lists the input and output ports. The port named **gain** is an analog *quantity port,* representing a voltage level that is a continuous function of time. The port named **a** is an analog *terminal port* of the **electrical** nature, representing a circuit node. The nature specifies that the terminal has voltage and current properties associated with it, and that rules governing conservation of energy apply at the terminal. The ports named

---

FIGURE 1-12

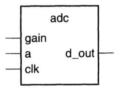

A 1-bit sampling analog-to-digital converter (ADC) module. It is named adc *and has two analog inputs* gain *and* a, *one digital input* clk *and one digital output* d_out.

FIGURE 1-13

```
library ieee_proposed; use ieee_proposed.electrical_systems.all;
entity adc is
    port ( quantity gain : in voltage;
           terminal a : electrical;
           signal clk : in bit;
           signal d_out : out bit );
end entity adc;
```

A VHDL-AMS entity description of an analog-to-digital converter.

clk and d are digital *signal ports* of type bit. They carry '0' and '1' values into and out of the entity. From this we see that an entity declaration describes the external view of the entity.

Elements of Behavior

In VHDL-AMS, a description of the internal implementation of an entity is called an *architecture body* of the entity. There may be a number of different architecture bodies of the one interface to an entity, corresponding to alternative implementations that perform the same function. We can write a *behavioral* architecture body of an entity, which describes the function in an abstract way. Such an architecture body includes only *process statements*, which are collections of actions to be executed in sequence, or *simultaneous statements*, which describe equations governing analog system behavior. Process statements are typically used to describe digital functionality, whereas simultaneous statements are used to describe analog functionality.

The actions of processes are called *sequential statements* and are much like the kinds of statements we see in a conventional programming language. The types of actions that can be performed include evaluating expressions, assigning values to variables, conditional execution, repeated execution and subprogram calls. In addition, there is a sequential statement that is unique to hardware modeling languages, the *signal assignment* statement. This is similar to variable assignment, except that it causes the value on a signal to be updated at some future time.

Similarly, simultaneous statements model analog behavior using mathematical equations involving the kinds of expressions we see in programming languages. The simultaneous statements express explicit differential and algebraic equations that describe the values of the analog quantities of a model. The continuously varying values represent the analog behavior of the system.

To illustrate these ideas, let us look at a behavioral architecture body for the ADC entity, shown in Figure 1-14. The architecture begins with the declaration of a constant, ref, representing the reference voltage used by the ADC. Following this is a declaration of an analog *branch quantity*, vin, representing the voltage level across the terminal **a**. The value of a branch quantity such as this is constrained by the values of the voltage and current properties of the associated terminal. Next is a declaration of a *free quantity*, v_amplified, representing the amplified input voltage. Unlike a branch quantity, a free quantity is not constrained by any terminal. Its value is determined solely by the equations in the model.

The first part of the architecture body after the first **begin** keyword is a simultaneous statement that relates the value of the quantity v_amplified to the values of the quantities v_in and gain. Since v_in and gain are inputs to the system, the value of v_amplified is constrained to be their product.

The next statement is a process statement, which describes how the analog-to-digital converter behaves. The process statement starts with the process name, adc_behavior, and finishes with the keywords **end process**. It includes sequential statements that define a sequence of actions that are to take place when the system is simulated. These actions control how the values on the entity's signal ports change

FIGURE 1-14

```
architecture ideal of adc is
    constant ref : real := 5.0;
    quantity v_in across a;
    quantity v_amplified : voltage;
begin
    v_amplified == v_in * gain;
    adc_behavior: process is
        variable stored_d : bit;
    begin
        if clk = '1' then
            if v_amplified > ref / 2.0 then
                stored_d := '1';
            else
                stored_d := '0';
            end if;
        end if;
        d_out <= stored_d after 5 ns;
        wait on clk;
    end process adc_behavior;
end architecture ideal;
```

A behavioral architecture body of the ADC entity.

over time; that is, they control the digital behavior of the entity. This process can modify the values of the entity's signal ports using signal assignment statements.

The way this process works is as follows. When the simulation is started, the output signal value is set to '0', and the process is activated. The process's variable (declared after the keyword **variable**) is initialized to '0', then the statements are executed in order. The first sequential statement is a condition that tests whether the value of the clk input is '1'. If it is, the inner condition is tested to determine whether the value of the v_amplified quantity exceeds the threshold of half the reference voltage. If it does, the value of the variable stored_d is updated to '1'; otherwise it is updated to '0'. After the conditional statements there is a signal assignment statement that causes the output signal d_out to be updated 5 ns later.

When all of these statements in the process have been executed, the process reaches the *wait statement* and *suspends;* that is, it becomes inactive. It stays suspended until the signal to which it is *sensitive* changes value. In this case, the process is sensitive to changes on the signal clk. When that signal changes, the process is resumed. The statements are executed again, starting from the keyword **begin**, and the cycle repeats. Notice that while the process is suspended, the values of the process's variable is not lost. This is how the process can represent the state of a system.

Elements of Structure

An alternative way of describing the implementation of an entity is to specify how it is composed of subsystems. We can give a structural description of the entity's implementation. An architecture body that is composed only of interconnected subsystems is called a *structural* architecture body. Figure 1-15 shows how the adc entity might be composed of resistors, a voltage-controlled amplifier, a comparator and a D-flipflop. If we are to describe this in VHDL-AMS, we will need entity declarations and architecture bodies for the subsystems, shown in Figure 1-16.

The entity statements used for the resistor, amplifier, comparator and D-flipflop components are similar to the adc entity we declared above. The resistor architecture body declares two branch quantities associated with the terminals. The quantity v is an across branch quantity, representing the difference in voltage between the terminals. The quantity i is a through branch quantity, representing the current flow in the resistor between the terminals. The simultaneous statement in the architecture body relates the branch quantities using Ohm's law. The amplifier architecture body declares branch quantities for the voltages across the input and output terminals and the current through the output terminal, and specifies the amplification behavior in the simultaneous statement. The architecture bodies for the comparator and D-flipflop use process statements to give behavioral descriptions of the components' operation. In the case of the comp_behavior process, the process is sensitive to a signal represented by diff'above(0.0). This signal changes from false to true when the value of the quantity diff rises above the specified threshold (0.0 in this case), and changes from true to false when the value falls below the threshold.

Figure 1-17 is a VHDL-AMS architecture body declaration that describes the structure shown in Figure 1-15. The declarative region before the keyword **begin** is where internal signals and terminals of the architecture are declared. In this case, the terminal a_amplified is an internal node declared to represent the amplified input voltage, ref represents the reference voltage source and half_ref represents the negative analog input to the comparator. The quantity v_ref is declared as the voltage across the ref terminal. The signal d is declared to connect the comparator output to the D-flipflop input. In general, VHDL-AMS quantities represent analog values, terminals represent nodes pertaining to various energy domains and signals can be declared to carry arbitrarily complex values. Within the architecture body the ports of the entity are also treated as signals, quantities or terminals.

In the second part of the architecture body, a number of *component instances* are created, representing the subsystems from which the adc entity is composed. Each component instance is a copy of the entity representing the subsystem, using the corresponding specified architecture body. (The name work refers to the current working library, in which all of the entity and architecture body descriptions are assumed to be held.)

The *port map* specifies the connection of the ports of each component instance to signals, quantities and terminals within the enclosing architecture body. For example, res1, an instance of the resistor entity, has its port p1 connected to the terminal ref and its port p2 connected to the terminal half_ref. Similarly, comp, an instance of the comparator entity, has its value port connected to the signal d.

FIGURE 1-15

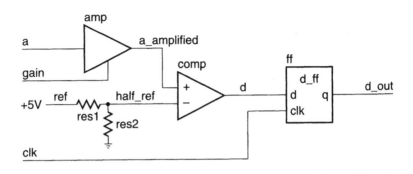

A structural composition of the adc *entity.*

FIGURE 1-16

```
library ieee_proposed;  use ieee_proposed.electrical_systems.all;
entity resistor is
     port ( terminal p1, p2 : electrical );
end entity resistor ;

architecture ideal of resistor is
     quantity v across i through p1 to p2;
     constant resistance : real := 10000.0;
begin
     v == i * resistance;
end architecture ideal;
```

```
library ieee_proposed;  use ieee_proposed.electrical_systems.all;
entity vc_amp is
     port ( quantity g : in voltage;
          terminal a, o : electrical );
end entity vc_amp;

architecture ideal of vc_amp is
     quantity v_in across a;
     quantity v_out across i_out through o;
begin
     v_out == v_in * g;
end architecture ideal;
```

(continued on page 20)

(continued from page 19)

```vhdl
library ieee_proposed;  use ieee_proposed.electrical_systems.all;
entity comparator is
    port ( terminal plus, minus: electrical,
        signal value : out bit );
end entity comparator;
architecture ideal of comparator is
    quantity diff across plus to minus;
begin
    comp_behavior: process is
    begin
        if diff > 0.0 then
            value <= '1' after 5 ns;
        else
            value <= '0' after 5 ns;
        end if;
        wait on diff'above(0.0);
    end process comp_behavior;
end architecture ideal;

_____

entity d_ff is
    port ( d, clk : in bit;  q : out bit );
end d_ff;
architecture basic of d_ff is
begin
    ff_behavior : process is
    begin
        if clk = '1' then
            q <= d after 2 ns;
        end if;
        wait on clk;
    end process ff_behavior;
end architecture basic;
```

Entity declarations and architecture bodies for resistor, comparator and D-flipflop.

FIGURE 1-17

```vhdl
architecture struct of adc is
    terminal a_amplified, ref, half_ref: electrical;
    quantity v_ref across i_ref through ref;
    signal d : bit;
```

```
begin
    res1 : entity work.resistor(ideal)
        port map ( ref, half_ref);
    res2 : entity work.resistor(ideal)
        port map ( half_ref, electrical_ref );
    amp : entity work.vc_amp(ideal)
        port map ( gain, a, a_amplified );
    comp : entity work.comparator(ideal)
        port map ( a_amplified, half_ref, d);
    ff : entity work.d_ff(basic)
        port map ( d, clk, d_out );
    v_ref == 5.0;
end architecture struct;
```

A VHDL-AMS structural architecture body of the adc *entity.*

Mixed Structural and Behavioral Models

Models need not be purely structural or purely behavioral. Often it is useful to specify a model with some parts composed of interconnected component instances, and other parts described using processes or simultaneous statements. We use signals, terminals and quantities as the means of joining component instances, processes and simultaneous statements. A signal can be associated with a port of a component instance and can also be assigned to or read in a process. A terminal can also be associated with a port of a component instance to represent a circuit node. A quantity can be associated with a port of a component instance and can be read in a process.

We can write such a hybrid model by including component instance, process and simultaneous statements in the body of an architecture. Component instance and process statements are called *concurrent statements*, since the corresponding processes all execute concurrently when the model is simulated. An outline of such a model is shown in Figure 1-18.

This model describes a propeller-based propulsion system consisting of a direct-current, voltage-controlled motor, rotational mechanical shafts with gears, inertial effects, a propeller and a control section. The motor, gears and propeller are described structurally using a number of component instances. The control section is described behaviorally using a process that assigns to the control signals for the motor and gears. Hence we see a mix of energy domains as well as structure and behavior within a model.

Test Benches

In our introductory discussion, we mentioned testing through simulation as an important motivation for modeling. We often test a VHDL-AMS model using an enclosing

FIGURE 1-18

```
library ieee_proposed;
use ieee_proposed.mechanical_systems.all;
use ieee_proposed.electrical_systems.all;
entity propulsion is
    port ( signal clk, reset : in bit;       -- control inputs
            signal rpm : in natural;         -- requested rpm
            signal forward : in bit );       -- requested direction
end entity propulsion;
architecture mixed of propulsion is
    terminal p1, p2 : electrical;
    terminal shaft1, shaft2, shaft3 : rotational_v;
    signal forward_gear : bit;
    ...
begin
    motor : entity work.dc_motor(ideal)
        port map ( p1, p2, shaft1 );
    gear : entity work.gear_av(ideal)
        port map ( forward_gear, shaft1, shaft2 );
    intertia : entity work.inertia_av(ideal)
        port map ( shaft2, shaft3 );
    prop : entity work.propeller(ideal)
        port map ( shaft3 );
    control_section : process is
        -- variable declarations for control_section to control voltage inputs
        -- and gear shifting
        ...
    begin
        ...
        wait on clk, reset;
    end process control_section;
    ...
end architecture mixed;
```

An outline of a mixed structural and behavioral model for a propeller-based propulsion system.

model called a *test bench*. The name comes from the analogy with a real hardware test bench, on which a device under test is stimulated with waveform generators and observed with probes. A VHDL-AMS test bench consists of an architecture body containing an instance of the component to be tested and processes that generate stimuli on signals, terminals or quantities connected to the component instance. The architecture body may also contain processes that test that the component instance produces the expected values on its outputs. Alternatively, we may use the monitoring facilities of a simulator to observe the outputs.

A test bench model for the behavioral implementation of the **propulsion** example is shown in Figure 1-19. The entity declaration has no port list, since the test bench is entirely self-contained. The architecture body contains signals that are connected to the input ports of the component instance **dut**, the device under test. The process labeled **stimulus** provides a sequence of test values on the inputs by performing signal assignment statements, interspersed with wait statements. Each wait statement specifies a pause during which the control process within the propulsion system sets voltage values for the motor, and the gear and propeller velocities are updated. We can use a simulator to observe the values on the output signals and terminals to verify that the propulsion system operates correctly. When all of the stimulus values have been applied, the stimulus process waits indefinitely, thus completing the simulation.

FIGURE 1-19

```
library ieee_proposed;
use ieee_proposed.mechanical_systems.all;
use ieee_proposed.electrical_systems.all;

entity test_bench is
end entity test_bench;

architecture example of test_bench is
    signal clk, reset: bit;
    signal rpm : natural;
    signal forward : bit;
begin
    dut : entity work.propulsion(mixed)
        port map ( clk, reset, rpm, forward );

    stimulus: process is
    begin
        clk <= '1'; reset <= '0'; rpm <= 0; forward <= '1'; wait for 10 sec;
        clk <= '0'; wait for 10 sec;
        clk <= '1'; rpm <= 50; wait for 20 sec;
        clk <= '0'; wait for 20 sec;
        clk <= '1'; rpm <= 0; wait for 20 sec;
        clk <= '0'; wait for 20 sec;
        clk <= '1'; rpm <= 50; forward <= '0'; wait for 20 sec;
        clk <= '0'; wait for 20 sec;
        ...
        wait;
    end process stimulus;
end architecture example;
```

A VHDL-AMS test bench for the propulsion model.

Analysis, Elaboration and Execution

One of the main reasons for writing a model of a system is to enable us to simulate it. This involves three stages: *analysis, elaboration* and *execution*. Analysis and elaboration are also required in preparation for other uses of the model, such as synthesis.

In the first stage, analysis, the VHDL-AMS description of a system is checked for various kinds of errors. Like most programming languages, VHDL-AMS has rigidly defined *syntax* and *semantics*. The syntax is the set of grammatical rules that govern how a model is written. The rules of semantics govern the meaning of a program. For example, it makes sense to perform an addition operation on two numbers but not on two processes.

During the analysis phase, the VHDL-AMS description is examined, and syntactic and static semantic errors are located. The whole model of a system need not be analyzed at once. Instead, it is possible to analyze *design units,* such as entity and architecture body declarations, separately. If the analyzer finds no errors in a design unit, it creates an intermediate representation of the unit and stores it in a library. The exact mechanism varies between VHDL-AMS tools.

The second stage in simulating a model, elaboration, is the act of working through the design hierarchy and creating all of the objects defined in declarations. The ultimate product of design elaboration is a collection of processes interconnected by nets and characteristic expressions, with each process possibly containing variables. The characteristic expressions describe analog behavior and interactions between processes, and the nets describe digital interactions between processes. A model must be reducible to a collection of processes, signals and characteristic expressions in order to simulate it.

We can see how elaboration achieves this reduction by starting at the top level of a model, namely, an entity, and choosing an architecture of the entity to simulate. The architecture comprises signals, terminals, quantities, processes, simultaneous statements and component instances. Each component instance is a copy of an entity and an architecture. Instances of the signals, terminals, quantities, processes and simultaneous statements of the architecture corresponding to the component instance are created, and then the elaboration operation is repeated for the subcomponent instances. Ultimately, a component instance is reached that is a copy of an entity with a purely behavioral architecture, containing only processes and simultaneous statements. This corresponds to a primitive component for the level of design being simulated. Figure 1-20 shows how elaboration proceeds for the structural architecture body of the **adc** entity. As each instance of a process is created, its variables are created and given initial values. We can think of each process instance as corresponding to one instance of a component. The elaboration of terminal declarations involves the creation of implicit equations that describe the interaction of the terminal with other objects according to energy conservation laws.

The third stage of simulation is the execution of the model. For the digital portion of the simulation, the passage of time is simulated in discrete steps, depending on when events occur. At some simulation time, a process may be stimulated by changing the value on a signal to which it is sensitive. The process is resumed and may schedule new values to be given to signals at some later simulated time. This is called *scheduling a transaction* on that signal. If the new value is different from the previous

FIGURE 1-20

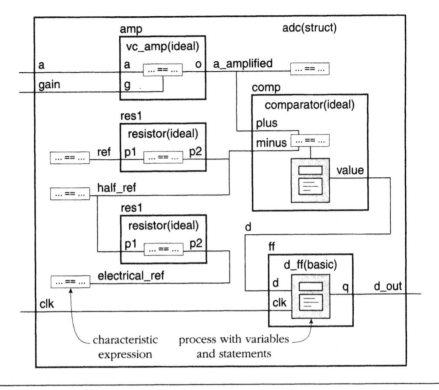

The elaboration of the adc *entity using the structural architecture body. Each instance of the* vc_amp, resistor, comparator *and* d_ff *entities is replaced by the contents of the corresponding architecture. These consist of characteristic equations and processes with their variables and sequential statements. There are also characteristic equations corresponding to the declared terminals and simultaneous statements in the structural architecture body of the* adc *entity.*

value on the signal, an *event* occurs, and other processes sensitive to the signal may be resumed.

Analog portions of the simulated system are evaluated by an *analog solver* at *analog solution points* in continuous time. The solver uses three sets of equations. The *structural set* comprises those equations that are implied by the declaration and interconnection of quantities and terminals. The *explicit set* of equations corresponds to the simultaneous statements that appear in architecture bodies. The *augmentation set* of equations depends on the kind of simulation being performed, including quiescent state, time domain, frequency domain or noise simulation. We discuss structural sets, explicit sets and augmentation sets in more detail in Chapters 7 and 13.

The simulation starts with an *initialization phase,* followed by repetitive execution of a *simulation cycle.* During the initialization phase, each signal and analog quantity is given an initial value, depending on its type. The simulation time is set to zero, then each process instance is activated and its sequential statements executed. Usually, a process will include a signal assignment statement to schedule a transaction on a signal at some later simulation time. Execution of a process continues until it reaches a wait statement, which causes the process to be suspended.

During the simulation cycle, the analog solver is first executed. Second, the simulation time is advanced to the next time at which a transaction on a signal has been scheduled. Third, all the transactions scheduled for that time are performed. This may cause some events to occur on some signals. Fourth, all processes that are sensitive to those events are resumed and are allowed to continue until they reach a wait statement and suspend. Again, the processes usually execute signal assignments to schedule further transactions on signals. When all the processes have suspended again, the simulation cycle is repeated. When the simulation gets to the stage where there are no further transactions scheduled, it stops, since the simulation is then complete.

1.5   Learning a New Language: Lexical Elements and Syntax

When we learn a new natural language, such as Greek, Chinese or English, we start by learning the alphabet of symbols used in the language, then form these symbols into words. Next, we learn the way to put the words together to form sentences and learn the meaning of these combinations of words. We reach fluency in a language when we can easily express what we need to say using correctly formed sentences.

The same ideas apply when we need to learn a new special-purpose language, such as VHDL-AMS for describing digital, analog and mixed-signal systems. We can borrow a few terms from language theory to describe what we need to learn. First, we need to learn the alphabet with which the language is written. The VHDL-AMS alphabet consists of all of the characters in the ISO 8859 Latin-1 8-bit character set. This includes uppercase and lowercase letters (including letters with diacritical marks, such as 'à', 'ä' and so forth), digits 0 to 9, punctuation and other special characters. Second, we need to learn the *lexical elements* of the language. In VHDL-AMS, these are the identifiers, reserved words, special symbols and literals. Third, we need to learn the *syntax* of the language. This is the grammar that determines what combinations of lexical elements make up legal VHDL-AMS descriptions. Fourth, we need to learn the *semantics,* or meaning, of VHDL-AMS descriptions. It is the semantics that allow a collection of symbols to describe a design. Fifth, we need to learn how to develop our own VHDL-AMS descriptions to describe a design we are working with. This is the creative part of modeling, and fluency in this part will greatly enhance our design skills.

In the remainder of this chapter, we describe the lexical elements used in VHDL-AMS and introduce the notation we use to describe the syntax rules. Then in subsequent chapters, we introduce the different facilities available in the language. For each of these, we show the syntax rules, describe the corresponding semantics and give examples of how they are used to model particular parts of a system. We also include some exercises at the end of each chapter to provide practice in the fifth stage of learning described above.

Lexical Elements

In the following section, we discuss the lexical elements of VHDL-AMS: *comments, identifiers, reserved words, special symbols, numbers, characters, strings* and *bit strings.*

Comments

When we are writing a hardware model in VHDL-AMS, it is important to annotate the code with comments. The reason for doing this is to help readers understand the structure and logic behind the model. It is important to realize that although we only write a model once, it may subsequently be read and modified many times, both by its author and by other engineers. Any assistance we can give to understanding the model is worth the effort.

A VHDL-AMS model consists of a number of lines of text. A comment can be added to a line by writing two dashes together, followed by the comment text. For example:

... a line of VHDL-AMS description ...   *-- a descriptive comment*

The comment extends from the two dashes to the end of the line and may include any text we wish, since it is not formally part of the VHDL-AMS model. The code of a model can include blank lines and lines that only contain comments, starting with two dashes. We can write long comments on successive lines, each starting with two dashes, for example:

-- The following code models
-- the flicker noise of the circuit
... some VHDL-AMS code ...

Identifiers

Identifiers are used to name items in a VHDL-AMS model. It is good practice to use names that indicate the purpose of the item, so VHDL-AMS allows names to be arbitrarily long. However, there are some rules about how identifiers may be formed. A basic identifier

- may only contain alphabetic letters ('A' to 'Z' and 'a' to 'z'), decimal digits ('0' to '9') and the underline character ('_');

- must start with an alphabetic letter;

- may not end with an underline character; and

- may not include two successive underline characters.

Some examples of valid basic identifiers are

A X0 Vdd Next_Value leakage_current

Some examples of invalid basic identifiers are

```
last@value      -- contains an illegal character for an identifier
5bit_counter    -- starts with a nonalphabetic character
_Vcb            -- starts with an underline
Vbc_            -- ends with an underline
clock__pulse    -- two successive underlines
```

Note that the case of letters is not considered significant, so the identifiers **cat** and **Cat** are the same. Underline characters in identifiers are significant, so **This_Name** and **ThisName** are different identifiers.

In addition to the basic identifiers, VHDL-AMS allows *extended identifiers,* which can contain any sequence of characters. Extended identifiers are included to allow communication between computer-aided engineering tools for processing VHDL-AMS descriptions and other tools that use different rules for identifiers. An extended identifier is written by enclosing the characters of the identifier between '\' characters. For example:

```
\differential amplifier\  \global.clock\  \923\  \d#1\  \start__\
```

If we need to include a '\' character in an extended identifier, we do so by doubling the character, for example:

```
\A:\\name\      -- contains a '\' between the ':' and the 'n'
```

Note that the case of letters is significant in extended identifiers and that all extended identifiers are distinct from all basic identifiers. So the following are all distinct identifiers:

```
name  \name\  \Name\  \NAME\
```

Reserved Words

Some identifiers, called reserved words or keywords, are reserved for special use in VHDL-AMS. They are used to denote specific constructs that form a model, so we cannot use them as identifiers for items we define. The full list of reserved words is shown in Figure 1-21. Often, when a VHDL-AMS program is typeset, reserved words are printed in boldface. This convention is followed in this book.

Special Symbols

VHDL-AMS uses a number of special symbols to denote operators, to delimit parts of language constructs and as punctuation. Some of these special symbols consist of just one character. They are

```
"  #  &  '  (  )  *  +  -  ,  .  /  :  ;  <  =  >  [  ]  |
```

FIGURE 1-21

abs	disconnect	label	package	sla
access	downto	library	port	sll
across		limit	postponed	spectrum
after	else	linkage	procedural	sra
alias	elsif	literal	procedure	srl
all	end	loop	process	subnature
and	entity		pure	subtype
architecture	exit	map		
array	file	mod	quantity	terminal
assert	for			then
attribute	function	nand	range	through
		nature	record	to
begin	generate	new	reference	tolerance
block	generic	next	register	transport
body	group	noise	reject	type
break	guarded	nor	rem	
buffer		not	report	unaffected
bus	if	null	return	units
	impure		rol	until
case	in	of	ror	use
component	inertial	on		
configuration	inout	open	select	variable
constant	is	or	severity	
		others	shared	wait
		out	signal	when
				while
				with
				xnor
				xor

VHDL-AMS reserved words.

Other special symbols consist of pairs of characters. The two characters must be typed next to each other, with no intervening space. These symbols are

    =>   **   :=   /=   >=   <=   <>   ==

Numbers

There are two forms of numbers that can be written in VHDL-AMS code: *integer literals* and *real literals*. An integer literal simply represents a whole number and consists of digits without a decimal point. Real literals, on the other hand, can represent fractional numbers. They always include a decimal point, which is preceded by at least one digit and followed by at least one digit. Real literals represent an approximation to real numbers.

Some examples of decimal integer literals are

    23   0   146

Note that −10, for example, is not an integer literal. It is actually a combination of a negation operator and the integer literal 10.

    Some examples of real literals are

    23.1   0.0   3.14159

    Both integer and real literals can also use exponential notation, in which the number is followed by the letter 'E' or 'e', and an exponent value. This indicates a power of 10 by which the number is multiplied. For integer literals, the exponent must not be negative, whereas for real literals, it may be either positive or negative. Some examples of integer literals using exponential notation are

    46E5   1E+12   19e00

Some examples of real literals using exponential notation are

    1.234E09   98.6E+21   34.0e−08

    Integer and real literals may also be expressed in a base other than base 10. In fact, the base can be any integer between 2 and 16. To do this, we write the number surrounded by sharp characters ('#'), preceded by the base. For bases greater than 10, the letters 'A' through 'F' (or 'a' through 'f') are used to represent the digits 10 through 15. For example, several ways of writing the value 253 are as follows:

    2#11111101#   16#FD#   16#0fd#   8#0375#

Similarly, the value 0.5 can be represented as

    2#0.100#   8#0.4#   12#0.6#

Note that in all these cases, the base itself is expressed in *decimal*.

    Based literals can also use exponential notation. In this case, the exponent, expressed in decimal, is appended to the based number after the closing sharp character. The exponent represents the power of the base by which the number is multiplied. For example, the number 1024 could be represented by the integer literals:

    2#1#E10   16#4#E2   10#1024#E+00

    Finally, as an aid to readability of long numbers, we can include underline characters as separators between digits. The rules for including underline characters are similar to those for identifiers; that is, they may not appear at the beginning or end of a number, nor may two appear in succession. Some examples are

    123_456   3.141_592_6   2#1111_1100_0000_0000#

Characters

A character literal can be written in VHDL-AMS code by enclosing it in single quotation marks. Any of the printable characters in the standard character set (including a space character) can be written in this way. Some examples are

```
'A'      -- uppercase letter
'z'      -- lowercase letter
','      -- the punctuation character comma
'''      -- the punctuation character single quote
' '      -- the separator character space
```

Strings

A string literal represents a sequence of characters and is written by enclosing the characters in double quotation marks. The string may include any number of characters (including zero), but it must fit entirely on one line. Some examples are

```
"A string"
"We can include any printing characters (e.g., &%@^*) in a string!!"
"00001111ZZZZ"
""       -- empty string
```

If we need to include a double quotation mark character in a string, we write two double quotation mark characters together. The pair is interpreted as just one character in the string. For example:

```
"A string in a string: ""A string"". "
```

If we need to write a string that is longer than will fit on one line, we can use the concatenation operator ("&") to join two substrings together. (This operator is discussed in Chapter 4.) For example:

```
"If a string will not fit on one line, "
& "then we can break it into parts on separate lines."
```

Bit Strings

VHDL-AMS includes values that represent bits (binary digits), which can be either '0' or '1'. A bit-string literal represents a sequence of these bit values. It is represented by a string of digits, enclosed by double quotation marks and preceded by a character that specifies the base of the digits. The base specifier can be one of the following:

- B for binary,

- O for octal (base 8) and

- X for hexadecimal (base 16).

For example, some bitstring literals specified in binary are

B"0100011"   B"10"   b"1111_0010_0001"   B""

Notice that we can include underline characters in bit-string literals to separate adjacent digits. The underline characters do not affect the meaning of the literal; they simply make the literal more readable. The base specifier can be in uppercase or lowercase. The last of the examples above denotes an empty bit string.

If the base specifier is octal, the digits '0' through '7' can be used. Each digit represents exactly three bits in the sequence. Some examples are

O"372"   -- equivalent to B"011_111_010"
o"00"   -- equivalent to B"000_000"

If the base specifier is hexadecimal, the digits '0' through '9' and 'A' through 'F' or 'a' through 'f' (representing 10 through 15) can be used. In hexadecimal, each digit represents exactly four bits. Some examples are

X"FA"   -- equivalent to B"1111_1010"
x"0d"   -- equivalent to B"0000_1101"

Notice that O"372" is not the same as X"FA", since the former is a sequence of nine bits, whereas the latter is a sequence of eight bits.

Syntax Descriptions

In the remainder of this book, we describe rules of syntax using a notation based on the Extended Backus-Naur Form (EBNF). These rules govern how we may combine lexical elements to form valid VHDL-AMS descriptions. It is useful to have a good working knowledge of the syntax rules, since VHDL-AMS analyzers expect valid VHDL-AMS descriptions as input. The error messages they otherwise produce may in some cases appear cryptic if we are unaware of the syntax rules.

The idea behind EBNF is to divide the language into *syntactic categories*. For each syntactic category we write a rule that describes how to build a VHDL-AMS clause of that category by combining lexical elements and clauses of other categories. These rules are analogous to the rules of English grammar. For example, there are rules that describe a sentence in terms of a subject and a predicate, and that describe a predicate in terms of a verb and an object phrase. In the rules for English grammar, "sentence", "subject", "predicate", and so on, are the syntactic categories.

In EBNF, we write a rule with the syntactic category we are defining on the left of a "⇐" sign (read as "is defined to be"), and a pattern on the right. The simplest kind of pattern is a collection of items in sequence, for example:

variable_assignment ⇐ target := expression ;

This rule indicates that a VHDL-AMS clause in the category "variable_assignment" is defined to be a clause in the category "target", followed by the symbol ":=", followed by a clause in the category "expression", followed by the symbol ";". To find out whether the VHDL-AMS clause

    d0 := 25 + 6;

is syntactically valid, we would have to check the rules for "target" and "expression". As it happens, "d0" and "25+6" are valid subclauses, so the whole clause conforms to the pattern in the rule and is thus a valid variable assignment. On the other hand, the clause

    25 fred := x if := .

cannot possibly be a valid variable assignment, since it doesn't match the pattern on the right side of the rule.

The next kind of rule to consider is one that allows for an optional component in a clause. We indicate the optional part by enclosing it between the symbols "⟦" and "⟧". For example:

    function_call ⇐ name ⟦ (association_list) ⟧

This indicates that a function call consists of a name that may be followed by an association list in parentheses. Note the use of the outline symbols for writing the pattern in the rule, as opposed to the normal solid symbols that are lexical elements of VHDL-AMS.

In many rules, we need to specify that a clause is optional, but if present, it may be repeated as many times as needed. For example, in this simplified rule for a process statement:

    process_statement ⇐
        process is
            { process_declarative_item }
        begin
            { sequential_statement }
        end process ;

the curly braces specify that a process may include zero or more process declarative items and zero or more sequential statements. A case that arises frequently in the rules of VHDL-AMS is a pattern consisting of some category followed by zero or more repetitions of that category. In this case, we use dots within the braces to represent the repeated category, rather than writing it out again in full. For example, the rule

    case_statement ⇐
        case expression **is**
            case_statement_alternative

{ ... }
end case ;

indicates that a case statement must contain at least one case statement alternative, but may contain an arbitrary number of additional case statement alternatives as required. If there is a sequence of categories and symbols preceding the braces, the dots represent only the last element of the sequence. Thus, in the example above, the dots represent only the case statement alternative, not the sequence "**case** expression **is** case_statement_alternative".

We also use the dots notation where a list of one or more repetitions of a clause is required, but some delimiter symbol is needed between repetitions. For example, the rule

identifier_list ⇐ identifier { , ... }

specifies that an identifier list consists of one or more identifiers, and that if there is more than one, they are separated by comma symbols. Note that the dots always represent a repetition of the category immediately preceding the left brace symbol. Thus, in the above rule, it is the identifier that is repeated, not the comma.

Many syntax rules allow a category to be composed of one of a number of alternatives. One way to represent this is to have a number of separate rules for the category, one for each alternative. However, it is often more convenient to combine alternatives using the "|" symbol. For example, the rule

mode ⇐ **in** | **out** | **inout**

specifies that the category "mode" can be formed from a clause consisting of one of the reserved words chosen from the alternatives listed.

The final notation we use in our syntax rules is parenthetic grouping, using the symbols "(" and ")". These simply serve to group part of a pattern, so that we can avoid any ambiguity that might otherwise arise. For example, the inclusion of parentheses in the rule

term ⇐ factor { (* | / | **mod** | **rem**) factor }

makes it clear that a factor may be followed by one of the operator symbols, and then another factor. Without the parentheses, the rule would be

term ⇐ factor { * | / | **mod** | **rem** factor }

indicating that a factor may be followed by one of the operators "*", "/" or **mod** alone, or by the operator **rem** and then another factor. This is certainly not what is intended. The reason for this incorrect interpretation is that there is a *precedence,* or order of priority, in the EBNF notation we are using. In the absence of parentheses, a sequence of pattern components following one after the other is considered as a group with higher precedence than components separated by "|" symbols.

This EBNF notation is sufficient to describe the complete grammar of VHDL-AMS. However, there are often further constraints on a VHDL-AMS description that relate to the meaning of the lexical elements used. For example, a description specifying connection of a signal to a named object that identifies a component instead of a port is incorrect, even though it may conform to the syntax rules. To avoid such problems, many rules include additional information relating to the meaning of a language feature. For example, the rule shown above describing how a function call is formed is augmented thus:

function_call ⇐ *function*_name ⟦ (*parameter*_association_list) ⟧

The italicized prefix on a syntactic category in the pattern simply provides semantic information. This rule indicates that the name cannot be just any name, but must be the name of a function. Similarly, the association list must describe the parameters supplied to the function. (We will describe the meaning of functions and parameters in a later chapter.) The semantic information is for our benefit as designers reading the rule, to help us understand the intended semantics. So far as the syntax is concerned, the rule is equivalent to the original rule without the italicized parts.

In the following chapters, we will introduce each new feature of VHDL-AMS by describing its syntax using EBNF rules, and then we will describe the meaning and use of the feature through examples. In many cases, we will start with a simplified version of the syntax to make the description easier to learn and come back to the full details in a later chapter. For reference, Appendix E contains a complete listing of VHDL-AMS syntax in EBNF notation.

Exercises

1. [❶ 1.4] Briefly outline the purposes of the following VHDL-AMS modeling constructs: entity declaration, behavioral architecture body, structural architecture body, process statement, signal assignment statement, simultaneous statement and port map.

2. [❶ 1.5] Comment symbols are often used to make lines of a model temporarily ineffective. The symbol is added at the front of the line, turning the line into a comment. The comment symbol can be simply removed to reactivate the statement. The following process statement includes a line to assign a value to a test signal, to help debug the model. Modify the process to make the assignment ineffective.

```
apply_transform : process is
begin
    d_out <= transform(d_in) after 200 ps;
    debug_test <= transform(d_in);
    wait on enable, d_in;
end process apply_transform;
```

3. [❶ 1.5] Which of the following are valid VHDL-AMS basic identifiers? Which are reserved words? Of the invalid identifiers, why are they invalid?

    last_item   prev item   value–1   limit

    element#5   _opamp   93_999   gain_

4. [❶ 1.5] Rewrite the following decimal literals as hexadecimal literals.

    1   34   256.0   0.5

5. [❶ 1.5] What decimal numbers are represented by the following literals?

    8#14#   2#1000_0100#   16#2C#

    2.5E5   2#1#E15   2#0.101#

6. [❶ 1.5] What is the difference between the literals **16#23DF#** and **X"23DF"**?

7. [❶ 1.5] Express the following octal and hexadecimal bit strings as binary bit-string literals.

    O"747"   O"377"   O"1_345"

    X"F2"   X"0014"   X"0000_0001"

8. [❷ 1.4] Write an entity declaration and a behavioral architecture body for a two-input multiplexer, with input ports **a**, **b** and **sel** and an output port **z**. If the **sel** input is '0', the value of **a** should be copied to **z**, otherwise the value of **b** should be copied to **z**. Write a test bench for the multiplexer model, and test it using a VHDL-AMS simulator.

9. [❷ 1.4] Write an entity declaration and a structural architecture body for a 4-bit-wide multiplexer, using instances of the 2-bit multiplexer from Exercise 8. The input ports are **a0**, **a1**, **a2**, **a3**, **b0**, **b1**, **b2**, **b3** and **sel**, and the output ports are **z0**, **z1**, **z2** and **z3**. When sel is '0', the inputs **a0** to **a3** are copied to the outputs, otherwise the inputs **b0** to **b3** are copied to the outputs. Write a test bench for the multiplexer model, and test it using a VHDL-AMS simulator.

10. [❷ 1.4] Write an entity declaration and structural architecture body for a 2-bit analog-to-digital converter as shown in Figure 1-22. Use the resistor and comparator entities defined in Figure 1-16 and the multiplexer from Exercise 8.

11. [❷ 1.4] Write an entity declaration and a behavioral architecture body for an opamp with an open-loop gain of 1000. The opamp has two input terminals, **plus_in** and **minus_in**, and an output terminal, **output**. The voltage at the output is the difference between the input-terminal voltages multiplied by the open-loop gain.

12. [❷ 1.4] Write an entity declaration and structural architecture body for the amplifier circuit shown in Figure 1-23, using the opamp entity from Exercise 11 and the resistor entity from Figure 1-16.

FIGURE 1-22

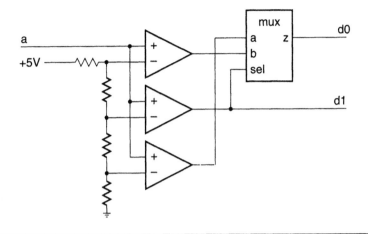

A 2-bit analog-to-digital converter.

FIGURE 1-23

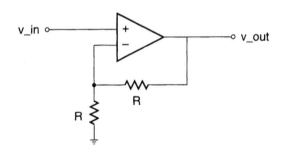

An amplifier circuit.

chapter two

Scalar Data Types, Natures and Operations

The concepts of type and nature are very important when describing data in a VHDL-AMS model. The type or nature of a data object defines the set of values that the object can assume, as well as the set of operations that can be performed on those values. A scalar type consists of single, indivisible values. A scalar nature defines values that are associated with a single terminal. In this chapter we look at the basic scalar types and natures provided by VHDL-AMS and see how they can be used to define data objects that model the internal state of a module.

2.1 Constants and Variables

An object is a named item in a VHDL-AMS model that has a value of a specified type or, in the case of a terminal, has a specified nature. There are six classes of objects: constants, variables, signals, terminals, quantities and files. In this chapter, we look at constants and variables; signals are described fully in Chapter 5, terminals and quantities in Chapter 6, and files in Chapter 21. Constants and variables are objects in which data can be stored for use in a model. The difference between them is that the value of a constant cannot be changed after it is created, whereas a variable's value can be changed as many times as necessary using variable assignment statements.

Constant and Variable Declarations

Both constants and variables need to be declared before they can be used in a model. A *declaration* simply introduces the name of the object, defines its type and may give it an initial value. The syntax rule for a constant declaration is

> constant_declaration ⇐
>   **constant** identifier ⟨ , ₀₀₀ ⟩ : subtype_indication ⟦ := expression ⟧ ;

The identifiers listed are the names of the constants being defined (one per name), and the subtype indication specifies the type of all of the constants. We look at ways of specifying the type in detail in subsequent sections of this chapter. The optional part shown in the syntax rule is an expression that specifies the value that each constant assumes. This part can only be omitted in certain cases that we discuss in Chapter 10. Until then, we always include it in examples. Here are some examples of constant declarations:

> **constant** number_of_bytes : integer := 4;
> **constant** number_of_bits : integer := 8 * number_of_bytes;
> **constant** e : real := 2.718281828;
> **constant** prop_delay : time := 3 ns;
> **constant** q : real := 1.60218E–19;
> **constant** resistivity : real := 2.5E5;

The reason for using a constant is to have a name and an explicitly defined type for a value, rather than just writing the value as a literal. This makes the model more intelligible to the reader, since the name and type convey much more information about the intended use of the object than the literal value alone. Furthermore, if we need to change the value as the model evolves, we only need to update the declaration. This is much easier and more reliable than trying to find and update all instances of a literal value throughout a model. It is good practice to use constants rather than writing literal values within a model.

The form of a variable declaration is similar to a constant declaration. The syntax rule is

variable_declaration ⇐
    variable identifier ⟦ , ... ⟧ : subtype_indication ⟦ := expression ⟧ ;

Here also the initialization expression is optional. If we omit it, the default initial value assumed by the variable when it is created depends on the type. For scalar types, the default initial value is the leftmost value of the type. For example, for integers it is the smallest representable integer. Some examples of variable declarations are

variable index : integer := 0;
variable temperature : real;
variable start, finish : time := 0 ns;

If we include more than one identifier in a variable declaration, it is the same as having separate declarations for each identifier. For example, the last declaration above is the same as the two declarations

variable start : time := 0 ns;
variable finish : time := 0 ns;

This is not normally significant unless the initialization expression is such that it potentially produces different values on two successive evaluations. The only time this may occur is if the initialization expression contains a call to a function with side effects (see Chapter 9).

Constant and variable declarations can appear in a number of places in a VHDL-AMS model, including in the declaration parts of processes. In this case, the declared object can be used only within the process. One restriction on where a variable declaration may occur is that it may not be placed so that the variable would be accessible to more than one process. This is to prevent the strange effects that might otherwise occur if the processes were to modify the variable in indeterminate order. The exception to this rule is if a variable is declared specially as a *shared* variable. We will leave discussion of shared variables until Chapter 24.

Example   Figure 2-1 outlines an architecture body that shows how constant and variable declarations may be included in a VHDL-AMS model.

_____

FIGURE 2-1

architecture sample **of** ent **is**
    constant pi : real := 3.14159;
begin
    process is
        variable counter : integer;

(continued on page 42)

(continued from page 41)

```
    begin
        ...       -- statements using pi and counter
    end process;
end architecture sample;
```

An architecture body showing declarations of a constant pi *and a variable* counter.

Variable Assignment

Once a variable has been declared, its value can be modified by an assignment statement. The syntax of a variable assignment statement is given by the rule

variable_assignment_statement ⇐ [[label :]] name := expression ;

The optional label provides a means of identifying the assignment statement. We will discuss reasons for labeling statements in Chapter 22. Until then, we will simply omit the label in our examples. The name in a variable assignment statement identifies the variable to be changed, and the expression is evaluated to produce the new value. The type of this value must match the type of the variable. The full details of how an expression is formed are covered in the rest of this chapter. For now, just think of expressions as the usual combinations of identifiers and literals with operators. Here are some examples of assignment statements:

```
program_counter := 0;
index := index + 1;
resonance_frequency := L * C;
```

The first assignment sets the value of the variable **program_counter** to zero, overwriting any previous value. The second example increments the value of **index** by one. The third assignment computes the resonance frequency of a circuit and updates the value of the variable **resonance_frequency**.

It is important to note the difference between a variable assignment statement, shown here, and signal assignment and simultaneous statements, introduced in Chapter 1. A variable assignment immediately overwrites the variable with a new value. A signal assignment schedules a new value to be applied to a signal at some later time. A simultaneous statement creates one or more characteristic equations that are used by the analog solver to model continuously valued behavior. We will return to signal assignments in Chapter 5 and to simultaneous statements in Chapter 6. Because of the significant difference between these kinds of assignment, VHDL-AMS uses distinct symbols: ":=" for variable assignment, "<=" for signal assignment and "=="
for simultaneous statements.

2.2 Scalar Types

The notion of *type* is very important in VHDL-AMS. We say that VHDL-AMS is a *strongly typed* language, meaning that every object may only assume values of its nominated type. Furthermore, the definition of each operation includes the types of values to which the operation may be applied. The aim of strong typing is to allow detection of errors at an early stage of the design process, namely, when a model is analyzed.

In this section, we show how a new type is declared. We then show how to define different *scalar* types. A scalar type is one whose values are indivisible. In Chapter 4 we will show how to declare types whose values are composed of collections of element values. VHDL-AMS also includes *natures*, which are extensions to types used to express analog quantities from various energy domains. We discuss scalar natures in Section 2.4.

Type Declarations

We introduce new types into a VHDL-AMS model by using type declarations. The declaration names a type and specifies which values may be stored in objects of the type. The syntax rule for a type declaration is

type_declaration ⇐ **type** identifier **is** type_definition ;

One important point to note is that if two types are declared separately with identical type definitions, they are nevertheless distinct and incompatible types. For example, if we have two type declarations:

type apples **is range** 0 **to** 100;
type oranges **is range** 0 **to** 100;

we may not assign a value of type **apples** to a variable of type **oranges**, since they are of different types.

An important use of types is to specify the allowed values for ports of an entity. In the examples in Chapter 1, we saw the type name **bit** used to specify that ports may take only the values '0' and '1'. If we define our own types for ports, the type names must be declared in a *package,* so that they are visible in the entity declaration. We will describe packages in more detail in Chapter 10; we introduce them here to enable us to write entity declarations using types of our own devising. For example, suppose we wish to define an adder entity that adds small integers in the range 0 to 255. We write a package containing the type declaration, as follows:

package int_types **is**
    type small_int **is range** 0 **to** 255;
end package int_types;

This defines a package named int_types, which provides the type named small_int. The package is a separate design unit and is analyzed before any entity declaration that needs to use the type it provides. We can use the type by preceding an entity declaration with a *use clause,* for example:

```
use work.int_types.all;

entity small_adder is
    port ( a, b : in small_int;  s : out small_int );
end entity small_adder;
```

When we discuss packages in Chapter 10, we will explain the precise meaning of use clauses such as this. For now, we treat it as "magic" needed to declare types for use in entity declarations.

Integer Types

In VHDL-AMS, integer types have values that are whole numbers. An example of an integer type is the predefined type integer, which includes all the whole numbers representable on a particular host computer. The language standard requires that the type integer include at least the numbers $-2,147,483,647$ to $+2,147,483,647$ ($-2^{31} + 1$ to $+2^{31} - 1$), but VHDL-AMS implementations may extend the range.

We can define a new integer type using a range-constraint type definition. The simplified syntax rule for an integer type definition is

integer_type_definition ⇐
    range simple_expression (**to** ▯ **downto**) simple_expression

which defines the set of integers between (and including) the values given by the two expressions. The expressions must evaluate to integer values. If we use the keyword **to**, we are defining an *ascending range,* in which values are ordered from the smallest on the left to the largest on the right. On the other hand, using the keyword **downto** defines a *descending range,* in which values are ordered left to right from largest to smallest. The reasons for distinguishing between ascending and descending ranges will become clear later.

Example   Here are two integer type declarations:

```
type day_of_month is range 0 to 31;
type year is range 0 to 2100;
```

These two types are quite distinct, even though they include some values in common. Thus if we declare variables of these types:

```
variable today : day_of_month := 9;
variable start_year : year := 1987;
```

it would be illegal to make the assignment

    start_year := today;

Even though the number 9 is a member of the type **year**, in context it is treated as being of type **day_of_month**, which is incompatible with type **year**. This type rule helps us to avoid inadvertently mixing numbers that represent different kinds of things.

If we wish to use an arithmetic expression to specify the bounds of the range, the values used in the expression must be *locally static;* that is, they must be known when the model is analyzed. For example, we can use constant values in an expression as part of a range definition:

    constant number_of_bits : integer := 32;
    type bit_index **is range** 0 **to** number_of_bits − 1;

The operations that can be performed on values of integer types include the familiar arithmetic operations:

+   addition, or identity

−   subtraction, or negation

*   multiplication

/   division

mod   modulo

rem   remainder

abs   absolute value

**   exponentiation

The result of an operation is an integer of the same type as the operand or operands. For the binary operators (those that take two operands), the operands must be of the same type. The right operand of the exponentiation operator must be a non-negative integer.

The identity and negation operators are unary, meaning that they only take a single, right operand. The result of the identity operator is its operand unchanged, while the negation operator produces zero minus the operand. So, for example, the following all produce the same result:

    A + (−B),   A − (+B),   A − B

The division operator produces an integer that is the result of dividing, with any fractional part truncated toward zero. The remainder operator is defined such that the relation

$$A = (A / B) * B + (A \text{ rem } B)$$

is satisfied. The result of **A rem B** is the remainder left over from division of **A** by **B**. It has the same sign as **A** and has absolute value less than the absolute value of **B**. For example:

5 **rem** 3 = 2, (–5) **rem** 3 = –2, 5 **rem** (–3) = 2, (–5) **rem** (–3) = –2

Note that in these expressions, the parentheses are required by the grammar of VHDL-AMS. The two operators, **rem** and negation, may not be written side by side. The modulo operator conforms to the mathematical definition satisfying the relation

$$A = B * N + (A \text{ mod } B) \qquad \text{-- for some integer N}$$

The result of **A mod B** has the same sign as **B** and has absolute value less than the absolute value of **B**. For example:

5 **mod** 3 = 2, (–5) **mod** 3 = 1, 5 **mod** (–3) = –1, (–5) **mod** (–3) = –2

When a variable is declared to be of an integer type, the default initial value is the leftmost value in the range of the type. For ascending ranges, this will be the least value, and for descending ranges, it will be the greatest value. If we have these declarations:

```
type set_index_range is range 21 downto 11;
type mode_pos_range is range 5 to 7;
variable set_index : set_index_range;
variable mode_pos : mode_pos_range;
```

the initial value of **set_index** is 21, and that of **mode_pos** is 5. The initial value of a variable of type **integer** is –2,147,483,647 or less, since this type is predefined as an ascending range that must include –2,147,483,647.

Floating-Point Types

Floating-point types in VHDL-AMS are used to represent real numbers. Mathematically speaking, there is an infinite number of real numbers within any interval, so it is not possible to represent real numbers exactly on a computer. Hence floating-point types are only an approximation to real numbers. The term "floating point" refers to the fact that they are represented using a mantissa part and an exponent part. This is similar to the way in which we represent numbers in scientific notation.

There is a predefined floating-point type called **real**, which includes at least the range −1.0E+38 to +1.0E+38, with at least six decimal digits of precision. This corresponds to the IEEE standard 32-bit representation commonly used for floating-point numbers. Some implementations of VHDL-AMS may extend this range and may provide higher precision.

In the 2001 update to VHDL, the definition of floating-point types is revised to conform to the IEEE Standard 754 or 854 for floating-point computation. Floating-point numbers are represented using at least 64 bits, giving approximately 15 decimal digits of precision and a range of approximately −1.8E+308 to +1.8E+308. An implementation may choose to use a larger representation, providing correspondingly greater precision or range. For most implementations, the predefined floating-point type **real** will support the range of the IEEE 64-bit double-precision representation. Since VHDL-AMS is based on the 1993 edition of VHDL, the IEEE 754 or 854 floating-point precision is, strictly speaking, not required. VHDL-AMS language revision efforts under way will require the adoption of IEEE 754 or 854 floating point, and most tool vendors are already supporting IEEE 754 or 854. So we may safely assume the higher-precision floating point is available.

We define a new floating-point type using a range-constraint type definition. The simplified syntax rule for a floating-point type definition is

floating_type_definition ⇐
    range simple_expression ⟦ **to** ⟧ **downto** ⟧ simple_expression

This is similar to the way in which an integer type is declared, except that the bounds must evaluate to floating-point numbers. Some examples of floating-point type declarations are

    type input_level **is range** −10.0 **to** +10.0;
    type probability **is range** 0.0 **to** 1.0;

The operations that can be performed on floating-point values include the arithmetic operations addition and identity ("+"), subtraction and negation ("−"), multiplication ("*"), division ("/"), absolute value (**abs**) and exponentiation ("**"). The result of an operation is of the same floating-point type as the operand or operands. For the binary operators (those that take two operands), the operands must be of the same type. The exception is that the right operand of the exponentiation operator must be an integer. The identity and negation operators are unary (meaning that they only take a single, right operand).

Variables that are declared to be of a floating-point type have a default initial value that is the leftmost value in the range of the type. So if we declare a variable to be of the type **input_level** shown above:

    variable input_A : input_level;

its initial value is −10.0.

Physical Types

The remaining numeric types in VHDL-AMS are physical types. They are used to represent real-world physical properties, such as length, mass and time. The definition of a physical type includes the *primary unit* of measure and may also include some *secondary units,* which are integral multiples of the primary unit. The simplified syntax rule for a physical type definition is

physical_type_definition ⇐
    range simple_expression ⟦ **to** ⟧ **downto** ⟧ simple_expression
        units
            identifier ;
            ⟦ identifier = physical_literal ; ⟧
        end units ⟦ identifier ⟧

physical_literal ⇐ ⟦ decimal_literal ⟧ based_literal ⟧ *unit*_name

A physical type definition is like an integer type definition, but with the units definition part added. The primary unit (the first identifier after the **units** keyword) is the smallest unit that is represented. We may then define a number of secondary units, as we shall see in a moment. The range specifies the multiples of the primary unit that are included in the type. If the identifier is included at the end of the units definition part, it must repeat the name of the type being defined.

Example   Here is a declaration of a physical type representing electrical resistance:

```
type resistance is range 0 to 1E9
    units
        ohm;
    end units resistance;
```

Literal values of this type are written as a numeric literal followed by the unit name, for example:

5 ohm   22 ohm   471_000 ohm

Notice that we must include a space before the unit name. Also, if the number is the literal 1, it can be omitted, leaving just the unit name. So the following two literals represent the same value:

ohm   1 ohm

Note that values such as –5 ohm and 1E16 ohm are not included in the type resistance, since the values –5 and 1E16 lie outside of the range of the type.

Now that we have seen how to write physical literals, we can look at how to specify secondary units in a physical type declaration. We do this by indicating how many primary units comprise a secondary unit. Our declaration for the resistance type can now be extended:

```
type resistance is range 0 to 1E9
    units
        ohm;
        kohm = 1000 ohm;
        Mohm = 1000 kohm;
    end units resistance;
```

Notice that once one secondary unit is defined, it can be used to specify further secondary units. Of course, the secondary units do not have to be powers of 10 times the primary unit; however, the multiplier must be an integer. For example, a physical type for length might be declared as

```
type length is range 0 to 1E9
    units
        um;             -- primary unit: micron
        mm = 1000 um;   -- metric units
        m = 1000 mm;
        inch = 25400 um;  -- English units
        foot = 12 inch;
    end units length;
```

We can write physical literals of this type using the secondary units, for example:

```
23 mm    2 foot    9 inch
```

When we write physical literals, we can write non-integral multiples of primary or secondary units. If the value we write is not an exact multiple of the primary unit, it is rounded down to the nearest multiple. For example, we might write the following literals of type **length**, each of which represents the same value:

```
0.1 inch    2.54 mm    2.540528 mm
```

The last of these is rounded down to 2540 um, since the primary unit for **length** is **um**. If we write the physical literal **6.8 um**, it is rounded down to the value **6 um**.

Many of the arithmetic operators can be applied to physical types, but with some restrictions. The addition, subtraction, identity and negation operators can be applied to values of physical types, in which case they yield results that are of the same type as the operand or operands. A value of a physical type can be multiplied by a number of type **integer** or **real** to yield a value of the same physical type, for example:

```
5 mm * 6  =  30 mm
```

A value of a physical type can be divided by a number of type **integer** or **real** to yield a value of the same physical type. Furthermore, two values of the same physical type can be divided to yield an integer, for example:

18 kohm / 2.0 = 9 kohm,   33 kohm / 22 ohm = 1500

Finally, the **abs** operator may be applied to a value of a physical type to yield a value of the same type, for example:

abs 2 foot = 2 foot,   **abs** (–2 foot) = 2 foot

The restrictions make sense when we consider that physical types represent actual physical properties, and arithmetic should be done so as to produce results of the correct dimensions. It doesn't make sense to multiply two lengths together to yield a length; the result should logically be an area. So VHDL-AMS does not allow direct multiplication of two physical types. Instead, we must convert the values to abstract integers to do the calculation, then convert the result back to the final physical type. (See the discussion of the 'pos and 'val attributes in Section 2.5.)

A variable that is declared to be of a physical type has a default initial value that is the leftmost value in the range of the type. For example, the default initial values for the types declared above are 0 ohm for **resistance** and 0 um for **length**.

Time

The predefined physical type **time** is very important in VHDL-AMS, as it is used extensively to specify delays. Its definition is

```
type time is range implementation defined
    units
        fs;
        ps = 1000 fs;
        ns = 1000 ps;
        us = 1000 ns;
        ms = 1000 us;
        sec = 1000 ms;
        min = 60 sec;
        hr = 60 min;
    end units;
```

By default, the primary unit **fs** is the *resolution limit* used when a model is simulated. Time values smaller than the resolution limit are rounded down to zero units. A simulator may allow us to select a secondary unit of **time** as the resolution limit. In this case, the unit of all physical literals of type **time** in the model must not be less than the resolution limit. When the model is executed, the resolution limit is used to determine the precision with which time values are represented. The reason for allowing reduced precision in this way is to allow a greater range of time values to be represented. This may allow a model to be simulated for a longer period of simulation time.

In addition to the physical type time, a VHDL-AMS simulator also makes use of a floating-point representation of time. Digital simulation time is defined in terms of the physical type, whereas the analog solver uses the floating-point representation. We discuss the way in which these two representations interact in Chapter 6. In particular, note that the resolution limit referred to above is different from the step limit used by the analog solver to determine the time step for computation of analog solution points. We discuss step limits in Section 6.7.

Enumeration Types

Often when writing models of hardware at an abstract level, it is useful to use a set of names for the encoded values of some signals, rather than committing to an encoding straightaway. VHDL-AMS *enumeration types* allow us to do this. For example, suppose we are modeling a transistor, and we want to define names for its operating region. A suitable type declaration is

type transistor_region **is** (linear, saturation);

Such a type is called an *enumeration*, because the literal values used are enumerated in a list. The syntax rule for enumeration type definitions in general is

enumeration_type_definition ⇐ (⟨ identifier ▯ character_literal ⟩ ⟨ , ∘∘∘ ⟩)

There must be at least one value in the type, and each value may be either an identifier, as in the above example, or a character literal. An example of this latter case is

type octal_digit **is** ('0', '1', '2', '3', '4', '5', '6', '7');

Given the above two type declarations, we could declare variables:

variable transistor_state : transistor_region;
variable last_digit : octal_digit := '0';

and make assignments to them:

transistor_state := linear;
last_digit := '7';

Different enumeration types may include the same identifier as a literal (called *overloading*), so the context of use must make it clear which type is meant. To illustrate this, consider the following declarations:

```
type logic_level is (unknown, low, undriven, high);
variable control : logic_level;
type water_level is (dangerously_low, low, ok);
variable water_sensor : water_level;
```

Here, the literal **low** is overloaded, since it is a member of both types. However, the assignments

```
control := low;
water_sensor := low;
```

are both acceptable, since the types of the variables are sufficient to determine which low is being referred to.

When a variable of an enumeration type is declared, the default initial value is the leftmost element in the enumeration list. So **unknown** is the default initial value for type **logic_level**, and **dangerously_low** is that for type **water_level**.

There are four predefined enumeration types defined as

```
type severity_level is (note, warning, error, failure);
type file_open_status is (open_ok, status_error, name_error, mode_error);
type file_open_kind is (read_mode, write_mode, append_mode);
type domain_type is (quiescent_domain, time_domain, frequency_domain);
```

The type **severity_level** is used in assertion statements, which we will discuss in Chapter 3, and the types **file_open_status** and **file_open_kind** are used for file operations, which we will discuss in Chapter 21. The type **domain_type** is used to indicate whether the simulation is in the quiescent domain to find the DC operating point, the time domain for time-based simulation or the frequency domain for spectral and noise analysis. This type is used with an implicit signal, **domain**, to allow us to write behavior for these different simulation domains. We return to this topic in Chapter 13. For the remainder of this section, we look at the other predefined enumeration types and the operations applicable to them.

Characters

In Chapter 1 we saw how to write literal character values. These values are members of the predefined enumeration type **character**, which includes all of the characters in the ISO 8859 Latin-1 8-bit character set. The type definition is shown in Figure 2-2. Note that this type is an example of an enumeration type containing a mixture of identifiers and character literals as elements.

The first 128 characters in this enumeration are the ASCII characters, which form a subset of the Latin-1 character set. The identifiers from **nul** to **usp** and **del** are the non-printable ASCII control characters. Characters **c128** to **c159** do not have any standard names, so VHDL-AMS just gives them nondescript names based on their position in the character set. The character at position 160 is a non-breaking space character, distinct from the ordinary space character, and the character at position 173 is a soft hyphen.

FIGURE 2-2

```
type character is (
    nul,      soh,      stx,      etx,      eot,      enq,      ack,      bel,
    bs,       ht,       lf,       vt,       ff,       cr,       so,       si,
    dle,      dc1,      dc2,      dc3,      dc4,      nak,      syn,      etb,
    can,      em,       sub,      esc,      fsp,      gsp,      rsp,      usp,
    ' ',      '!',      '"',      '#',      '$',      '%',      '&',      ''',
    '(',      ')',      '*',      '+',      ',',      '-',      '.',      '/',
    '0',      '1',      '2',      '3',      '4',      '5',      '6',      '7',
    '8',      '9',      ':',      ';',      '<',      '=',      '>',      '?',
    '@',      'A',      'B',      'C',      'D',      'E',      'F',      'G',
    'H',      'I',      'J',      'K',      'L',      'M',      'N',      'O',
    'P',      'Q',      'R',      'S',      'T',      'U',      'V',      'W',
    'X',      'Y',      'Z',      '[',      '\',      ']',      '^',      '_',
    '`',      'a',      'b',      'c',      'd',      'e',      'f',      'g',
    'h',      'i',      'j',      'k',      'l',      'm',      'n',      'o',
    'p',      'q',      'r',      's',      't',      'u',      'v',      'w',
    'x',      'y',      'z',      '{',      '|',      '}',      '~',      del,
    c128,     c129,     c130,     c131,     c132,     c133,     c134,     c135,
    c136,     c137,     c138,     c139,     c140,     c141,     c142,     c143,
    c144,     c145,     c146,     c147,     c148,     c149,     c150,     c151,
    c152,     c153,     c154,     c155,     c156,     c157,     c158,     c159,
    ' ',      '¡',      '¢',      '£',      '¤',      '¥',      '¦',      '§',
    '¨',      '©',      'ª',      '«',      '¬',      '',      '®',      '¯',
    '°',      '±',      '²',      '³',      '´',      'µ',      '¶',      '·',
    '¸',      '¹',      'º',      '»',      '¼',      '½',      '¾',      '¿',
    'À',      'Á',      'Â',      'Ã',      'Ä',      'Å',      'Æ',      'Ç',
    'È',      'É',      'Ê',      'Ë',      'Ì',      'Í',      'Î',      'Ï',
    'Ð',      'Ñ',      'Ò',      'Ó',      'Ô',      'Õ',      'Ö',      '×',
    'Ø',      'Ù',      'Ú',      'Û',      'Ü',      'Ý',      'Þ',      'ß',
    'à',      'á',      'â',      'ã',      'ä',      'å',      'æ',      'ç',
    'è',      'é',      'ê',      'ë',      'ì',      'í',      'î',      'ï',
    'ð',      'ñ',      'ò',      'ó',      'ô',      'õ',      'ö',      '÷',
    'ø',      'ù',      'ú',      'û',      'ü',      'ý',      'þ',      'ÿ');
```

The definition of the predefined enumeration type character.

To illustrate the use of the **character** type, we declare variables as follows:

variable cmd_char, terminator : character;

and then make the assignments

```
cmd_char := 'P';
terminator := cr;
```

Booleans

One of the most important predefined enumeration types in VHDL-AMS is the type boolean, defined as

type boolean **is** (false, true);

This type is used to represent condition values, which can control execution of a behavioral model. There are a number of operators that we can apply to values of different types to yield Boolean values, namely, the relational and logical operators. The relational operators equality ("=") and inequality ("/=") can be applied to operands of any type (except files), including the composite types that we will see later in this chapter. The operands must both be of the same type, and the result is a Boolean value. For example, the expressions

123 = 123,   'A' = 'A',   7 ns = 7 ns

all yield the value **true**, and the expressions

123 = 456,   'A' = 'z',   7 ns = 2 us

yield the value **false**.

The relational operators that test ordering are the less-than ("<"), less-than-or-equal-to ("<="), greater-than (">") and greater-than-or-equal-to (">=") operators. These can only be applied to values of types that are ordered, including all of the scalar types described in this chapter. As with the equality and inequality operators, the operands must be of the same type, and the result is a Boolean value. For example, the expressions

123 < 456,   789 ps <= 789 ps,   '1' > '0'

all result in **true**, and the expressions

96 >= 102,   2 us < 4 ns,   'X' < 'X'

all result in **false**.

The logical operators **and, or, nand, nor, xor, xnor** and **not** take operands that must be Boolean values, and they produce Boolean results. Figure 2-3 shows the results produced by the binary logical operators. The result of the **not** operator is **true** if the operand is **false**, and **false** if the operand is **true**.

The operators **and, or, nand** and **nor** are called "short-circuit" operators, as they only evaluate the right operand if the left operand does not determine the result. For example, if the left operand of the **and** operator is **false**, we know that the result is **false**, so we do not need to consider the other operand. This is useful where the left operand is a test that guards against the right operand causing an error. Consider the expression

FIGURE 2-3

A	B	A and B	A nand B	A or B	A nor B	A xor B	A xnor B
false	false	false	true	false	true	false	true
false	true	false	true	true	false	true	false
true	false	false	true	true	false	true	false
true	true	true	false	true	false	false	true

The truth table for binary logical operators.

(b /= 0) **and** (a/b > 1)

If **b** were zero and we evaluated the right-hand operand, we would cause an error due to dividing by zero. However, because **and** is a short-circuit operator, if **b** were zero, the left-hand operand would evaluate to **false**, so the right-hand operand would not be evaluated. For the **nand** operator, the right-hand operand is similarly not evaluated if the left-hand is **false**. For **or** and **nor**, the right-hand operand is not evaluated if the left-hand is **true**.

Bits

Since at times VHDL-AMS is used to model digital systems and subsystems, it is useful to have a data type to represent bit values. The predefined enumeration type **bit** serves this purpose. It is defined as

type bit **is** ('0', '1');

Notice that the characters '0' and '1' are overloaded, since they are members of both **bit** and **character**. Where '0' or '1' occurs in a model, the context is used to determine which type is being used.

The logical operators that we mentioned for Boolean values can also be applied to values of type **bit**, and they produce results of type **bit**. The value '0' corresponds to false, and '1' corresponds to true. So, for example:

'0' **and** '1' = '0',   '1' **xor** '1' = '0'

The operands must still be of the same type as each other. Thus it is not legal to write

'0' **and** true

The difference between the types **boolean** and **bit** is that **boolean** values are used to model abstract conditions, whereas **bit** values are used to model digital hardware logic levels. Thus, '0' represents a low logic level and '1' represents a high logic level. The logical operators, when applied to **bit** values, are defined in terms of positive logic, with '0' representing the negated state and '1' representing the asserted state. If we need to deal with negative logic, we need to take care when writing logical expressions to get the correct logic sense. For example, if write_enable_n, select_reg_n and write_reg_n are negative logic bit variables, we perform the assignment

write_reg_n := **not** (**not** write_enable_n **and not** select_reg_n);

The variable write_reg_n is asserted ('0') only if write_enable_n is asserted and select_reg_n is asserted. Otherwise it is negated ('1').

Standard Logic

VHDL was designed for modeling digital hardware, so modelers found it necessary to include types to represent digitally encoded values. The predefined type **bit** shown above can be used for this in more abstract models, where we are not concerned about the details of digital electrical signals. However, as we refine our models to include more detail, we need to take account of the electrical properties when representing signals. With VHDL-AMS, we can directly model the differential and algebraic equations to represent detailed electrical behavior. Alternatively, we can use standard data representations for digital simulation at an intermediate level of detail. There are many ways we can define data types to do this, but the IEEE has standardized one way in a package called std_logic_1164. The full details of the package are included in Appendix C. One of the types defined in this package is an enumeration type called std_ulogic, defined as

```
type std_ulogic is ( 'U',    -- Uninitialized
                     'X',    -- Forcing Unknown
                     '0',    -- Forcing zero
                     '1',    -- Forcing one
                     'Z',    -- High Impedance
                     'W',    -- Weak Unknown
                     'L',    -- Weak zero
                     'H',    -- Weak one
                     '–' );  -- Don't care
```

This type can be used to represent signals driven by active drivers (forcing strength), resistive drivers such as pull-ups and pull-downs (weak strength) or three-state drivers including a high-impedance state. Each kind of driver may drive a "zero", "one" or "unknown" value. An "unknown" value is driven by a model when it is unable to determine whether the signal should be "zero" or "one". For example, the output of an and gate is unknown when its inputs are driven by high-impedance drivers. In addition to these values, the leftmost value in the type represents an "uninitialized" value. If we declare signals of std_ulogic type, by default they take on 'U' as their initial value. If a model tries to operate on this value instead of a real logic value, we have detected a design error in that the system being modeled does not start up properly. The final value in std_ulogic is a "don't care" value. This is sometimes used by logic synthesis tools and may also be used when defining test vectors, to denote that the value of a signal to be compared with a test vector is not important.

Even though the type **std_ulogic** and the other types defined in the **std_logic_1164** package are not actually built into the VHDL or VHDL-AMS languages, we can write models as though they were, with a little bit of preparation. For now, we describe some "magic" to include at the beginning of a model that uses the package; we explain the details in Chapter 10. If we include the line

library ieee; **use** ieee.std_logic_1164.**all**;

preceding each entity or architecture body that uses the package, we can write models as though the types were built into the language.

With this preparation in hand, we can now create constants, variables and signals of type **std_ulogic**. As well as assigning values of the type, we can also use the logical operators **and**, **or**, **not** and so on. Each of these operates on **std_ulogic** values and returns a **std_ulogic** result of 'U', 'X', '0' or '1'. The operators are "optimistic," in that if they can determine a '0' or '1' result despite inputs being unknown, they do so. Otherwise they return 'X' or 'U'. For example '0' **and** 'Z' returns '0', since one input to an and gate being '0' always causes the output to be '0', regardless of the other input.

The standard-logic package is very commonly used for modeling digital systems with VHDL. We can enjoy similar benefits from using the standard-logic package with VHDL-AMS for digital portions of mixed-signal designs. However, VHDL-AMS allows more detailed modeling of electrical behavior than the standard-logic package. This is particularly useful for designing deep submicron integrated circuits. We may use standard-logic values for most of the physical wires in the circuit and more detailed analog models of critical nets.

2.3   Type Classification

In the preceding sections we have looked at the scalar types provided in VHDL-AMS. Figure 2-4 illustrates the relationships between these types, the predefined scalar types and the types we look at in later chapters. We discuss scalar natures in the next section.

The scalar types are all those composed of individual values that are ordered. Integer and floating-point types are ordered on the number line. Physical types are ordered by the number of base units in each value. Enumeration types are ordered by their declaration. The discrete types are those that represent discrete sets of values and comprise the integer types and enumeration types. Floating-point and physical types are not discrete, as they approximate a continuum of values.

Subtypes

In Section 2.2 we saw how to declare a type, which defines a set of values. Often a model contains objects that should only take on a restricted range of the complete set of values. We can represent such objects by declaring a *subtype,* which defines a restricted set of values from a *base type.* The condition that determines which values

FIGURE 2-4

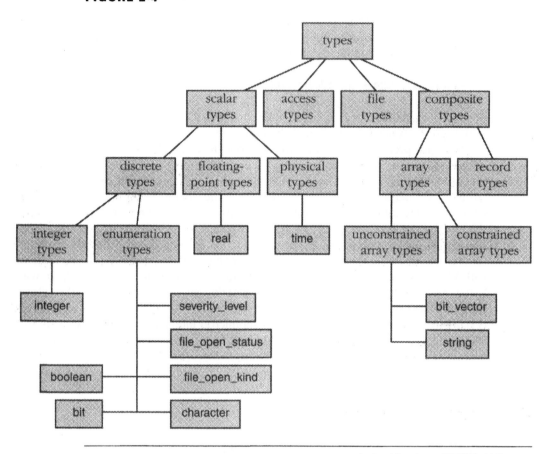

A classification of VHDL-AMS types.

are in the subtype is called a *constraint*. Using a subtype declaration makes clear our intention about which values are valid and makes it possible to check that invalid values are not used. The simplified syntax rules for a subtype declaration are

subtype_declaration ⇐ **subtype** identifier **is** subtype_indication ;

subtype_indication ⇐
    type_mark ⟦ **range** simple_expression (**to** ▯ **downto**) simple_expression ⟧
    ⟦ **tolerance** *string*_expression ⟧

We will look at more advanced forms of subtype indications in later chapters. The subtype declaration defines the identifier as a subtype of the base type specified by the type mark, with the range constraint restricting the values for the subtype. The constraint is optional, which means that it is possible to have a subtype that includes all of the values of the base type.

The optional tolerance clause may be used for floating-point types. If a subtype indication includes a tolerance clause, the string expression defines a *tolerance group*. The tolerance group of a subtype is used by a simulator to determine how accurately to compute values of analog quantities of the subtype. The format of the tolerance group string is implementation defined. Tolerances can only be used for floating-point types.

Example   Here is a declaration that defines a subtype of integer:

     subtype small_int **is** integer **range** –128 **to** 127;

Values of small_int are constrained to be within the range –128 to 127. If we declare some variables:

     variable deviation : small_int;
     variable adjustment : integer;

we can use them in calculations:

     deviation := deviation + adjustment;

Note that in this case, we can mix the subtype and base type values in the addition to produce a value of type integer, but the result must be within the range –128 to 127 for the assignment to succeed. If it is not, an error will be signaled when the variable is assigned. All of the operations that are applicable to the base type can also be used on values of a subtype. The operations produce values of the base type rather than the subtype. However, the assignment operation will not assign a value to a variable of a subtype if the value does not meet the constraint.

Another point to note is that if a base type is a range of one direction (ascending or descending), and a subtype is specified with a range constraint of the opposite direction, it is the subtype specification that counts. For example, the predefined type integer is an ascending range. If we declare a subtype as

     subtype bit_index **is** integer **range** 31 **downto** 0;

this subtype is a descending range.

Example   The following subtype with a tolerance clause may be used for modeling pressure quantities in fluidic systems. All quantities declared to be of this subtype have the same tolerance group, so a simulator will compute their values to the same accuracy.

     subtype pressure **is** real **tolerance** "default_pressure";

The VHDL-AMS standard includes two predefined integer subtypes, defined as

subtype natural **is** integer **range** 0 **to** *highest_integer*;
subtype positive **is** integer **range** 1 **to** *highest_integer*;

Where the logic of a design indicates that a number should not be negative, it is good style to use one of these subtypes rather than the base type **integer**. In this way, we can detect any design errors that incorrectly cause negative numbers to be produced. There is also a predefined subtype of the physical type **time**, defined as

subtype delay_length **is** time **range** 0 fs **to** *highest_time*;

This subtype should be used wherever a non-negative time delay is required.

Type Qualification

Sometimes it is not clear from the context what the type of a particular value is. In the case of overloaded enumeration literals, it may be necessary to specify explicitly which type is meant. We can do this using *type qualification,* which consists of writing the type name followed by a single quote character, then an expression enclosed in parentheses. For example, given the enumeration types

type logic_level **is** (unknown, low, undriven, high);
type transistor_state **is** (unknown, unsaturated, saturated);

we can distinguish between the common literal values by writing

logic_level'(unknown),   transistor _state'(unknown)

Type qualification can also be used to narrow a value down to a particular subtype of a base type. For example, if we define a subtype of **logic_level**

subtype valid_level **is** logic_level **range** low **to** high;

we can explicitly specify a value of either the type or the subtype

logic_level'(high),   valid_level'(high)

Of course, it is an error if the expression being qualified is not of the type or subtype specified.

Type Conversion

When we introduced the arithmetic operators in previous sections, we stated that the operands must be of the same type. This precludes mixing integer and floating-point values in arithmetic expressions. Where we need to do mixed arithmetic, we can use *type conversions* to convert between integer and floating-point values. The form of a type conversion is the name of the type we want to convert to, followed by a value in parentheses. For example, to convert between the types integer and real, we could write

    real(123),   integer(3.6)

Converting an integer to a floating-point value is simply a change in representation, although some loss of precision may occur. Converting from a floating-point value to an integer involves rounding to the nearest integer. Numeric type conversions are not the only conversion allowed. In general, we can convert between any closely related types. Other examples of closely related types are certain array types, discussed in Chapter 4.

One thing to watch out for is the distinction between type qualification and type conversion. The former simply states the type of a value, whereas the latter changes the value, possibly to a different type. One way to remember this distinction is to think of "*qu*ote for *qu*alification."

2.4 Scalar Natures

As we discussed in Chapter 1, VHDL-AMS enables us to model continuously valued behaviors of systems from different energy domains. When we model the properties of a system, we typically do so in terms of circuit nodes. In VHDL-AMS, nodes are represented by *terminals*. A terminal is of a specified *nature*, which defines the continuous values associated with the terminal. The nature represents the energy domain for the terminal. We have seen examples of electrical and rotational-velocity natures in Chapter 1. Natures are similar to types in that they define data templates or structures for objects. In addition, a nature defines a reference terminal, such as a ground terminal for an electrical nature. In this section, we discuss concepts relating to *scalar* natures. As with scalar types, scalar natures are indivisible. We defer discussion of composite natures to Chapter 4.

Nature Declarations

We introduce a new nature into a VHDL-AMS model by using a nature declaration. The declaration names a nature and specifies which values may be taken on by objects of that nature. The syntax rule for a scalar nature declaration is

    nature_declaration ⇐ **nature** identifier **is** scalar_nature_definition ;

    scalar_nature_definition ⇐
        type_mark **across**
        type_mark **through**
        identifier **reference**

The two types referred to in the nature declaration are called the *across type* and the *through type,* respectively. The across type models the effort or force associated with the energy domain represented by the nature, and the through type models the flow or velocity. Each of these types must be a floating-point type or subtype and may include a tolerance group as described in the previous section.

The identifier immediately before the keyword **reference** names a *reference terminal* defined by the nature declaration. The across quantities of terminals are taken to be relative to the reference terminal of their nature. For example, in models of electrical systems, the reference terminal is typically ground, whereas in rotational-velocity mechanical systems, the reference terminal is typically the stationary frame of reference.

Example   The electrical nature that we used in the examples in Chapter 1 is defined as follows:

```
subtype voltage is real tolerance "default_voltage";
subtype current is real tolerance "default_current";

nature electrical is
    voltage across
    current through
    electrical_ref reference;
```

Here, the across type is voltage, the through type is current and the reference terminal is called electrical_ref. We can use the electrical nature to declare terminals:

```
terminal in_plus, in_minus, preamp_out : electrical;
```

In order to write equations relating voltage and current at the terminals, we need to declare branch quantities, for example:

```
quantity signal_level across in_plus to in_minus;
quantity output_level across output_current through preamp_out;
```

The quantity signal_level, being declared as an across branch quantity, is of type voltage, since that is the across type of the electrical nature. The quantity is constrained to be the difference between the voltage of the in_plus terminal and the in_minus terminal. The quantity output_level is likewise an across branch quantity, but because only one terminal is mentioned in the quantity declaration, the voltage is measured with respect to the reference terminal of the electrical nature. The quantity output_current is declared as a through branch quantity, and so takes on values of type current. Its value is constrained to be the current flowing between the preamp_out terminal and the electrical_ref terminal.

Just as operations with incompatible types are erroneous, VHDL-AMS does not allow branch quantities between two terminals of different natures. As with types, if two natures are declared separately with identical nature definitions, they are nevertheless distinct and incompatible natures. For example, if we have the following nature declarations for thermal and cryogenic domains:

```
subtype temperature is real tolerance "default_temperature";
subtype heat_flow is real tolerance "default_heat_flow";
subtype cryo_temp is real tolerance "default_temperature";
subtype cryo_flow is real tolerance "default_heat_flow";

nature thermal is
    temperature across
    heat_flow through
    thermal_ref reference;

nature cryogenic is
    cryo_temp across
    cryo_flow through
    cryo_ref reference;
```

we cannot declare a branch quantity relating a terminal of nature thermal and another nature cryogenic. If we really need to model interaction between natures, we must create an explicit entity with terminals of each nature and an architecture body that contains equations to model the interaction.

As we have mentioned, natures are used in VHDL-AMS to define a physical energy domain. The nature defines the fundamental effort and flow concepts of the domain. Figure 2-5 illustrates the effort and flow for a number of common domains and shows how the across and through types of a VHDL-AMS nature can be combined with other generalized variables to model the domains.

Example One example of an energy domain we may wish to include for systems modeling is optical radiance. In the radiant energy domain, the illuminance and optic flux represent the across and through quantities corresponding to the effort and flow of radiant energy. A nature declaration to express this is

```
subtype illuminance is real tolerance "default_illuminance";
subtype optic_flux is real tolerance "default_optic_flux";

nature radiant is
    illuminance across
    optic_flux through
    radiant_ref reference;
```

The illuminance subtype uses the default_illuminance tolerance group, and the optic_flux subtype uses the default_optic_flux tolerance group. The radiant_ref reference is used for the illuminance calculations at each terminal of nature radiant.

FIGURE 2-5

Generalized Variable	Electrical	Mechanical Translation	Mechanical Rotation	Fluidic
Effort (e) (across branch type)	voltage (V)	velocity (V)	angular velocity (ω)	pressure (P)
Flow (f) (through branch type)	current (I)	force (F)	torque (τ)	volumetric flow rate (Φ)
Momentum (p)	flux linkage (λ)	momentum (p)	angular momentum (p_θ)	pressure momentum (p_v)
State (q)	charge (q)	translation (x)	angle (θ)	volume (V)
Energy (W)	$\int_q V dq, \int_\lambda I d\lambda$	$\int_x F dx, \int_p V dp$	$\int_\theta \tau d\theta, \int_{p_\theta} \omega dp_\theta$	$\int_V P dV, \int_{p_v} \Phi dp_v$
Power (P)	$V(t) \times I(t)$	$F(t) \times V(t)$	$\tau(t) \times \omega(t)$	$P(t) \times \Phi(t)$

Energy domains.

Standard Natures

A variety of energy domains are of interest to modelers using VHDL-AMS. As Figure 2-5 illustrates, the mathematics underlying the physical processes we wish to model are quite similar. By declaring natures for each of these physical energy domains, we can model a very broad range of system behaviors. Just as the standard multivalued-logic package described in Section 2.2 makes digital modeling and simulation easier, standard nature definitions make analog modeling easier and improve model portability. Therefore, the VHDL-AMS community has developed a set of packages containing nature declarations for conservative energy domains. The natures defined are

electrical	electrical domain
magnetic	electromagnetic domain
translational	translational domain (linear displacement)
translational_v	translational velocity domain
rotational	rotational domain (angular displacement)
rotational_v	rotational velocity domain
fluidic	fluidic domain
thermal	thermal domain

radiant   radiant domain

Note that domains for mechanical systems allow for descriptions in terms of displacement or velocity. The packages are under consideration for IEEE standardization, and so are placed in a library called **ieee_proposed**. Recall from our discussion in Section 2.2 that we can make use of a library package by including a library and use clause preceding an entity or architecture declaration. Thus, to use the electrical nature package, we would include the line

library ieee_proposed; **use** ieee_proposed.electrical_systems.**all**;

We will explain the details behind this VHDL-AMS "magic" in Chapter 10. The packages are described in more detail in Section 10.5.

Subnatures

Subnatures are related to natures in the same way that subtypes are related to types. A subnature declaration can be used to associate different tolerance groups with different terminals of the same base nature. The simplified syntax rule for a subnature declaration is

subnature_declaration ⇐ **subnature** identifier **is** subnature_indication ;

subtype_indication ⇐
    nature_mark
      ⟦ **tolerance** *string*_expression **across** *string*_expression **through** ⟧

We will discuss more advanced forms of subnature indications in later chapters. If a subnature indication includes a tolerance specification, the tolerance group of the across type of the subnature is the value of the string expression preceding the keyword **across**. Similarly, the tolerance group of the through type of the subnature is the value of the string expression preceding the keyword **through**. Note that terminals of subnatures of the same base nature may be interconnected.

Example   Suppose we know that the power supply terminals of an electrical system are well conditioned and so their values need not be calculated by a simulator to a high degree of accuracy. We can declare a subnature with a separate tolerance group for the power supply terminals:

    subnature coarse_electrical **is** electrical
      tolerance "coarse_voltage" **across** "coarse_current" **through**;

We can then declare terminals of both the base electrical nature, which has a default tolerance group, and the subnature with the coarse tolerance group:

> **terminal** supply_plus, supply_minus : coarse_electrical;
> **terminal** bias : electrical;

Since the terminals are of the same base nature, we can declare branch quantities that interconnect them, for example:

> **quantity** bias_pullup_v **across** supply_plus **to** bias;
> **quantity** bias_pulldown_v **across** bias **to** supply_minus;

2.5   **Attributes of Scalar Types and Natures**

A type defines a set of values and a set of applicable operations, and a nature defines a set of values associated with a terminal. There is also a predefined set of *attributes* that are used to give information about the values included in the type or nature. Attributes are written by following the type name with a quote mark (') and the attribute name. The value of an attribute can be used in calculations in a model. We now look at some of the attributes defined for the types and natures we have discussed in this chapter.

First, there are a number of attributes that are applicable to all scalar types and provide information about the range of values in the type. If we let T stand for any scalar type or subtype, x stand for a value of that type and s stand for a string value, the attributes are

T'left	first (leftmost) value in T
T'right	last (rightmost) value in T
T'low	least value in T
T'high	greatest value in T
T'ascending	true if T is an ascending range, **false** otherwise
T'image(x)	a string representing the value of x
T'value(s)	the value in T that is represented by s

The string produced by the 'image attribute is a correctly formed literal according to the rules shown in Chapter 1. The strings allowed in the 'value attribute must follow those rules and may include leading or trailing spaces. These two attributes are useful for input and output in a model, as we will see when we come to that topic.

Example   To illustrate the attributes listed above, we include some declarations from previous examples:

```
type resistance is range 0 to 1E9
    units
        ohm;
        kohm = 1000 ohm;
        Mohm = 1000 kohm;
    end units resistance;
type set_index_range is range 21 downto 11;
type logic_level is (unknown, low, undriven, high);
```

For these types:

```
resistance'left = 0 ohm
resistance'right = 1E9 ohm
resistance'low = 0 ohm
resistance'high = 1E9 ohm
resistance'ascending = true
resistance'image(2 kohm) = "2000 ohm"
resistance'value("5 Mohm") = 5_000_000 ohm

set_index_range'left = 21
set_index_range'right = 11
set_index_range'low = 11
set_index_range'high = 21
set_index_range'ascending = false
set_index_range'image(14) = "14"
set_index_range'value("20") = 20

logic_level'left = unknown
logic_level'right = high
logic_level'low = unknown
logic_level'high = high
logic_level'ascending = true
logic_level'image(undriven) = "undriven"
logic_level'value("Low") = low
```

Next, there are attributes that are applicable to just discrete and physical types. For any such type T, a value x of that type and an integer n, the attributes are

T'pos(x)	position number of x in T
T'val(n)	value in T at position n
T'succ(x)	value in T at position one greater than that of x
T'pred(x)	value in T at position one less than that of x
T'leftof(x)	value in T at position one to the left of x
T'rightof(x)	value in T at position one to the right of x

For enumeration types, the position numbers start at zero for the first element listed and increase by one for each element to the right. So, for the type logic_level shown above, some attribute values are

```
logic_level'pos(unknown) = 0
logic_level'val(3) = high
logic_level'succ(unknown) = low
logic_level'pred(undriven) = low
```

For integer types, the position number is the same as the integer value, but the type of the position number is a special anonymous type called *universal integer*. This is the same type as that of integer literals and, where necessary, is implicitly converted to any other declared integer type. For physical types, the position number is the integer number of base units in the physical value. For example:

```
time'pos(4 ns) = 4_000_000
```

since the base unit is fs.

Example We can use the 'pos and 'val attributes in combination to perform mixed-dimensional arithmetic with physical types, producing a result of the correct dimensionality. Suppose we define physical types to represent length and area, as follows:

```
type length is range integer'low to integer'high
    units
        mm;
    end units length;
type area is range integer'low to integer'high
    units
        square_mm;
    end units area;
```

and variables of these types:

```
variable L1, L2 : length;
variable A : area;
```

The restrictions on multiplying values of physical types prevents us from writing something like

```
A := L1 * L2;    -- this is incorrect
```

To achieve the correct result, we can convert the length values to abstract integers using the 'pos attribute, then convert the result of the multiplication to an area value using 'val, as follows:

A := area'val(length'pos(L1) * length'pos(L2));

Note that in this example, we do not need to include a scale factor in the multiplication, since the base unit of **area** is the square of the base unit of **length**.

For ascending ranges, T'succ(x) and T'rightof(x) produce the same value, and T'pred(x) and T'leftof(x) produce the same value. For descending ranges, T'pred(x) and T'rightof(x) produce the same value, and T'succ(x) and T'leftof(x) produce the same value. For all ranges, T'succ(T'high), T'pred(T'low), T'rightof(T'right) and T'leftof(T'left) cause an error to occur.

There is a single attribute, 'tolerance, that is applicable to floating-point subtypes. It provides a string whose value is the tolerance group for that subtype. For example, given the declarations

subtype voltage **is** real **tolerance** "default_voltage";
subtype high_current **is** real **tolerance** "coarse_current";

the values of the 'tolerance attribute for these subtypes are

voltage'tolerance = "default_voltage"
high_current'tolerance = "coarse_current"

The last attribute we introduce here is T'base. For any subtype T, this attribute produces the base type of T. The only context in which this attribute may be used is as the prefix of another attribute. For example, if we have the declarations

type gear **is** (unknown, park, reverse, neutral, first, second, third, fourth, fifth);
subtype forward **is** gear **range** first **to** fifth;

then

forward'base'left = unknown
forward'base'succ(reverse) = neutral

The only predefined attributes for natures in VHDL-AMS are 'across and 'through. Each of these produces a type that can be used in declarations or with the attributes shown above, as with the 'base attribute. The 'across attribute produces the across type of the nature prefix, and the 'through attribute produces the through type of the nature prefix.

Example   If we define a translational-mechanical nature with the following declarations,

subtype displacement **is** real **tolerance** "default_displacement";
subtype force **is** real **tolerance** "default_force";
nature translational **is**

        displacement **across**
        force **through**
        translational_ref **reference**;

    then the attributes

        translational'across
        translational'through

    yield displacement and force, which can be used as follows:

        quantity qdisp : translational'across;   *-- declares quantity of type displacement*
        quantity qforce : translational'through;   *-- declares quantity of type force*

    to declare quantities with the appropriate tolerance groups.

2.6 Expressions and Operators

In Section 2.1 we showed how the value resulting from evaluation of an expression can be assigned to a variable. We have also seen examples of expressions used in equations in analog models. In this section, we summarize the rules governing expressions. We can think of an expression as being a formula that specifies how to compute a value. As such, it consists of primary values combined with operators. The precise syntax rules for writing expressions are shown in Appendix E. The primary values that can be used in expressions include

- literal values,
- identifiers representing data objects (constants, variables, quantities and so on, but not including terminals),
- attributes that yield values,
- qualified expressions,
- type-converted expressions and
- expressions in parentheses.

We have seen examples of these in this chapter and in Chapter 1. For reference, all of the operators and the types they can be applied to are summarized in Figure 2-6. We will discuss array operators in Chapter 4.

The operators in this table are grouped by precedence, with "******", **abs** and **not** having highest precedence and the logical operators lowest. This means that if an expression contains a combination of operators, those with highest precedence are applied first. Parentheses can be used to alter the order of evaluation, or for clarity.

FIGURE 2-6

Operator	Operation	Left operand type	Right operand type	Result type
**	exponentiation	integer or floating-point	integer	same as left operand
abs	absolute value		numeric	same as operand
not	negation		bit, boolean or 1-D array of bit or boolean	same as operand
*	multiplication	integer or floating-point	same as left operand	same as operands
		physical	integer or real	same as left operand
		integer or real	physical	same as right operand
/	division	integer or floating-point	same as left operand	same as operands
		physical	integer or real	same as left operand
		physical	same as left operand	universal integer
mod	modulo	integer	same as left operand	same as operands
rem	remainder	integer	same as left operand	same as operands
+	identity		numeric	same as operand
−	negation		numeric	same as operand
+	addition	numeric	same as left operand	same as operands
−	subtraction	numeric	same as left operand	same as operands
&	concatenation	1-D array	same as left operand	same as operands
		1-D array	element type of left operand	same as left operand
		element type of right operand	1-D array	same as right operand
		element type of result	element type of result	1-D array

(continued on page 72)

(continued from page 71)

Operator	Operation	Left operand type	Right operand type	Result type
sll	shift-left logical	1-D array of bit or	integer	same as left operand
srl	shift-right logical	boolean		
sla	shift-left arithmetic			
sra	shift-right arithmetic			
rol	rotate left			
ror	rotate right			
=	equality	any except file or	same as left operand	boolean
/=	inequality	protected type		
<	less than	scalar or 1-D array of	same as left operand	boolean
<=	less than or equal	any discrete type		
>	greater than			
>=	greater than or equal			
and	logical and	bit, boolean or 1-D	same as left operand	same as operands
or	logical or	array of bit or boolean		
nand	negated logical and			
nor	negated logical or			
xor	exclusive or			
xnor	negated exclusive or			

VHDL-AMS *operators in order of precedence, from most binding to least binding.*

Exercises

1. [❶ 2.1] Write constant declarations for the number of bits in a 32-bit word and for the number π (3.14159).

2. [❶ 2.1] Write variable declarations for a counter, initialized to 0; a status flag used to indicate whether a module is busy; and a standard-logic value used to store a temporary result.

3. [❶ 2.1] Given the declarations in Exercise 2, write variable assignment statements to increment the counter, to set the status flag to indicate the module is busy and to indicate a weak unknown temporary result.

4. [❶ 2.2] Write a package declaration containing type declarations for small non-negative integers representable in eight bits; fractional numbers between –1.0 and +1.0; electrical currents, with units of nA, µA, mA and A; and traffic light colors.

5. [❶ 2.4] Write a package declaration containing subtype and nature declarations for modeling pneumatic systems. The effort aspect of such systems is pressure, and the flow aspect is volumetric flow rate. The across type should have the tolerance group "default_pressure", and the through type should have the tolerance group "default_flow".

6. [❶ 2.4] Write a subnature declaration that uses the pneumatic nature of Exercise 5 as the base nature and specifies the tolerance groups "detailed_pressure" for the across type and "detailed_flow" for the through type.

7. [❶ 2.5] Given the subtype declarations

    subtype pulse_range **is** time **range** 1 ms **to** 100 ms;
    subtype word_index **is** integer **range** 31 **downto** 0;

    what are the values of 'left, 'right, 'low, 'high and 'ascending attributes of each of these subtypes?

8. [❶ 2.5] Given the type declaration

    type state **is** (off, standby, active1, active2);

    what are the values of

    state'pos(standby)   state'val(2)
    state'succ(active2)   state'pred(active1)
    state'leftof(off)   state'rightof(off)

9. [❶ 2.6] For each of the following expressions, indicate whether they are syntactically correct, and if so, determine the resulting value.

    2 * 3 + 6 / 4   3 + –4
    "cat" & character'('0')   true **and** x **and not** y **or** z
    B"101110" **sll** 3   (B"100010" **sra** 2) & X"2C"

10. [❷ 2.1] Write a counter model with a clock input **clk** of type **bit**, and an output **q** of type **integer**. The behavioral architecture body should contain a process that declares a count variable initialized to zero. The process should wait for changes on **clk**. When **clk** changes to '1', the process should increment the count and assign its value to the output port.

11. [❷ 2.2] Write a model that represents a simple ALU with integer inputs and output, and a function select input of type **bit**. If the function select is '0', the ALU output should be the sum of the inputs; otherwise the output should be the difference of the inputs.

12. [❷ 2.2] Write a model for a digital integrator that has a clock input of type **bit** and data input and output each of type **real**. The integrator maintains the sum of successive data input values. When the clock input changes from '0' to '1', the inte-

grator should add the current data input to the sum and provide the new sum on the output.

13. [❷ 2.2] Following is a process that generates a regular clock signal.

```
clock_gen : process is
begin
    clk <= '1';  wait for 10 ns;
    clk <= '0';  wait for 10 ns;
end process clock_gen;
```

Use this as the basis for experiments to determine how your simulator behaves with different settings for the resolution limit. Try setting the resolution limit to 1 ns (the default for many simulators), 1 ps and 1 μs.

14. [❷ 2.2] Write a model for a tristate buffer using the standard-logic type for its data and enable inputs and its data output. If the enable input is '0' or 'L', the output should be 'Z'. If the enable input is '1' or 'H' and the data input is '0' or 'L', the output should be '0'. If the enable input is '1' or 'H' and the data input is '1' or 'H', the output should be '1'. In all other cases, the output should be 'X'.

chapter three

Sequential Statements

In the previous chapter we saw how to represent the internal state of models using VHDL-AMS data types and natures. In this chapter we look at how that data may be manipulated within processes and procedurals. This is done using sequential statements, *so called because they are executed in sequence. We have already seen one of the basic sequential statements, the variable assignment statement, when we were looking at data types and objects. The statements we look at in this chapter deal with controlling actions within a model; hence they are often called* control structures. *They allow selection between alternative courses of action as well as repetition of actions.*

3.1 If Statements

In many models, the behavior depends on a set of conditions that may or may not hold true during the course of simulation. We can use an *if statement* to express this behavior. The syntax rule for an if statement is

```
if_statement ⇐
    ⟦ if_label : ⟧
    if boolean_expression then
        { sequential_statement }
    { elsif boolean_expression then
        { sequential_statement } }
    ⟦ else
        { sequential_statement } ⟧
    end if ⟦ if_label ⟧ ;
```

At first sight, this may appear somewhat complicated, so we start with some simple examples and work up to examples showing the general case. The label may be used to identify the if statement. We will discuss labeled statements in Chapter 22. A simple example of an if statement is

```
if en = '1' then
    stored_value := data_in;
end if;
```

The Boolean expression after the keyword **if** is the condition that is used to control whether or not the statement after the keyword **then** is executed. If the condition evaluates to true, the statement is executed. In this example, if the value of the object en is '1', the assignment is made; otherwise it is skipped. We can also specify actions to be performed if the condition is false. For example:

```
if sel = 0 then
    result <= input_0;     -- executed if sel = 0
else
    result <= input_1;     -- executed if sel /= 0
end if;
```

Here, as the comments indicate, the first signal assignment statement is executed if the condition is true, and the second signal assignment statement is executed if the condition is false.

In many models, we may need to check a number of different conditions and execute a different sequence of statements for each case. We can construct a more elaborate form of if statement to do this, for example:

```
if mode = immediate then
    operand := immed_operand;
elsif opcode = load or opcode = add or opcode = subtract then
```

```
        operand := memory_operand;
else
        operand := address_operand;
end if;
```

In this example, the first condition is evaluated, and if true, the statement after the first **then** keyword is executed. If the first condition is false, the second condition is evaluated, and if it evaluates to true, the statement after the second **then** keyword is executed. If the second condition is false, the statement after the **else** keyword is executed.

In general, we can construct an if statement with any number of **elsif** clauses (including none), and we may include or omit the **else** clause. Execution of the if statement starts by evaluating the first condition. If it is false, successive conditions are evaluated, in order, until one is found to be true, in which case the corresponding statements are executed. If none of the conditions is true, and we have included an **else** clause, the statements after the **else** keyword are executed.

We are not restricted to just one statement in each part of the if statement. This is illustrated by the following if statement:

```
if gear = neutral then
        max_acceleration := 0.0;
        reverse_indicator := false;
        gear_engaged <= false;
end if;
```

If the condition is true, all three statements are executed, one after another. On the other hand, if the condition is false, none of the statements are executed. Furthermore, each statement contained in an if statement can be any sequential statement. This means we can nest if statements, for example:

```
if phase = wash then
        if cycle_select = delicate_cycle then
                agitator_speed <= slow;
        else
                agitator_speed <= fast;
        end if;
        agitator_on <= true;
end if;
```

In this example, the condition **phase = wash** is first evaluated, and if true, the nested if statement and the following signal assignment statement are executed. Thus the assignment **agitator_speed <= slow** is executed only if both conditions evaluate to true, and the assignment **agitator_speed <= fast** is executed only if the first condition is true and the second condition is false.

Example Let us develop a behavioral model for a simple heater thermostat. The device can be modeled as an entity with an integer input that specifies the desired temperature, an analog quantity input that is connected to a thermometer, and one Boolean output that turns a heater on and off. The thermostat turns the heater on if the measured temperature falls below two degrees less than the desired temperature, and turns the heater off if the measured temperature rises above two degrees greater than the desired temperature. Figure 3-1 shows the entity and architecture bodies for the thermostat. The entity declaration defines the input and output ports.

Since it is a behavioral model, the architecture body contains only a process statement that implements the required behavior. The process statement includes a *sensitivity list* after the keyword **process**. This is a list of signals to which the process is sensitive. When any of these signals changes value, the process resumes and executes the sequential statements. After it has executed the last statement, the process suspends again. In this example, the process is sensitive to changes in three signals. The first is the **desired_temp** input port. The second and third are Boolean signals denoted by the 'above attribute of the **sensor_temp** input quantity. Each of these Boolean signals is true when the value of the quantity is greater than the specified threshold, and false otherwise. (We discuss the 'above

FIGURE 3-1

```
library ieee_proposed;  use ieee_proposed.thermal_systems.all;
entity thermostat is
    port ( quantity sensor_temp : in temperature;
           signal desired_temp : in real;
           signal heater_on : out boolean );
end entity thermostat;
```

```
architecture example of thermostat is
begin
    controller : process ( desired_temp,
                           sensor_temp'above(desired_temp + 2.0),
                           sensor_temp'above(desired_temp – 2.0) ) is
    begin
        if sensor_temp < desired_temp – 2.0 then
            heater_on <= true;
        elsif sensor_temp > desired_temp + 2.0 then
            heater_on <= false;
        end if;
    end process controller;
end architecture example;
```

An entity and architecture body for a heater thermostat.

attribute in more detail in Chapter 6.) Thus, if we adjust the desired temperature, or if the measured temperature from the sensor crosses one of the thresholds at two degrees above or below the desired temperature, the process is resumed. The body of the process contains an if statement that compares the actual temperature with the desired temperature. If the actual temperature is too low, the process executes the first signal assignment to turn the heater on. If the actual temperature is too high, the process executes the second signal assignment to turn the heater off. If the actual temperature is within the range, the state of the heater is not changed, since there is no **else** clause in the if statement.

3.2 Case Statements

If we have a model in which the behavior is to depend on the value of a single expression, we can use a *case statement*. The syntax rules are as follows:

case_statement ⇐
    ⟦ *case*_label : ⟧
    case expression **is**
        ⦇ **when** choices => ⦃ sequential_statement ⦄ ⦈
        ⦃ ₀₀₀ ⦄
    end case ⟦ *case*_label ⟧ ;

choices ⇐ ⦇ simple_expression ⫾ discrete_range ⫾ **others** ⦈ ⦃ ⫾ ₀₀₀ ⦄

The label may be used to identify the case statement. We will discuss labeled statements in Chapter 22. We start with some simple examples of case statements and build up from them. First, suppose we are modeling an arithmetic/logic unit, with a control input, **func**, declared to be of the enumeration type:

type alu_func **is** (pass1, pass2, add, subtract);

We could describe the behavior using a case statement:

```
case func is
    when pass1 =>
        result := operand1;
    when pass2 =>
        result := operand2;
    when add =>
        result := operand1 + operand2;
    when subtract =>
        result := operand1 – operand2;
end case;
```

At the head of this case statement is the *selector expression,* between the keywords **case** and **is**. In this example it is a simple expression consisting of just a primary value. The value of this expression is used to select which statements to execute. The body of the case statement consists of a series of *alternatives.* Each alternative starts with the keyword **when** and is followed by one or more *choices* and a sequence of statements. The choices are values that are compared with the value of the selector expression. There must be exactly one choice for each possible value. The case statement finds the alternative whose choice value is equal to the value of the selector expression and executes the statements in that alternative. In this example, the choices are all simple expressions of type alu_func. If the value of func is **pass1**, the statement result := operand1 is executed; if the value is **pass2**, the statement result := operand2 is executed; and so on.

A case statement bears some similarity to an if statement in that they both select among alternative groups of sequential statements. The difference lies in how the statements to be executed are chosen. We saw in the previous section that an if statement evaluates successive Boolean expressions in turn until one is found to be true. The group of statements corresponding to that condition is then executed. A case statement, on the other hand, evaluates a single selector expression to derive a selector value. This value is then compared with the choice values in the case statement alternatives to determine which statement to execute. An if statement provides a more general mechanism for selecting between alternatives, since the conditions can be arbitrarily complex Boolean expressions. However, case statements are an important and useful modeling mechanism, as the examples in this section show.

The selector expression of a case statement must result in a value of a discrete type, or a one-dimensional array of character elements, such as a character string or bit string (see Chapter 4). Thus, we can have a case statement that selects an alternative based on an integer value. If we assume index_mode and instruction_register are declared as

```
subtype index_mode is integer range 0 to 3;
variable instruction_register : integer range 0 to 2**16 – 1;
```

then we can write a case statement that uses a value of this type:

```
case index_mode'((instruction_register / 2**12) rem 2**2) is
    when 0 =>
        index_value := 0;
    when 1 =>
        index_value := accumulator_A;
    when 2 =>
        index_value := accumulator_B;
    when 3 =>
        index_value := index_register;
end case;
```

Notice that in this example, we use a qualified expression in the selector expression. If we had omitted this, the result of the expression would have been **integer**, and we would have had to include alternatives to cover all possible integer values. The type qualification avoids this need by limiting the possible values of the expression.

Another rule to remember is that the type of each choice must be the same as the type resulting from the selector expression. Thus in the above example, it is illegal to include an alternative such as

when 'a' => ...   *-- illegal!*

since the choice listed cannot be an integer. Such a choice does not make sense, since it can never match a value of type **integer**.

We can include more than one choice in each alternative by writing the choices separated by the "|" symbol. For example, if the type **opcodes** is declared as

type opcodes **is**
    (nop, add, subtract, load, store, jump, jumpsub, branch, halt);

we could write an alternative including three of these values as choices:

when load | add | subtract =>
    operand := memory_operand;

If we have a number of alternatives in a case statement and we want to include an alternative to handle all possible values of the selector expression not mentioned in previous alternatives, we can use the special choice **others**. For example, if the variable **opcode** is a variable of type **opcodes**, declared above, we can write

case opcode **is**
    when load | add | subtract =>
        operand := memory_operand;
    when store | jump | jumpsub | branch =>
        operand := address_operand;
    when others =>
        operand := 0;
end case;

In this example, if the value of **opcode** is anything other than the choices listed in the first and second alternatives, the last alternative is selected. There may only be one alternative that uses the **others** choice, and if it is included, it must be the last alternative in the case statement. An alternative that includes the **others** choice may not include any other choices. Note that, if all of the possible values of the selector expression are covered by previous choices, we may still include the **others** choice, but it can never be matched.

The remaining form of choice that we have not yet mentioned is a *discrete range,* specified by these simplified syntax rules:

discrete_range ⇐
   *discrete*_subtype_indication
    ⫿ simple_expression ⦅ **to** ⫿ **downto** ⦆ simple_expression

subtype_indication ⇐
   type_mark
     ⟦ **range** simple_expression ⦅ **to** ⫿ **downto** ⦆ simple_expression ⟧

These forms allow us to specify a range of values in a case statement alternative. If the value of the selector expression matches any of the values in the range, the statements in the alternative are executed. The simplest way to specify a discrete range is just to write the left and right bounds of the range, separated by a direction keyword. For example, the case statement above could be rewritten as

```
case opcode is
    when add to load =>
        operand := memory_operand;
    when branch downto store =>
        operand := address_operand;
    when others =>
        operand := 0;
end case;
```

Another way of specifying a discrete range is to use the name of a discrete type, and possibly a range constraint to narrow down the values to a subset of the type. For example, if we declare a subtype of **opcodes** as

```
subtype control_transfer_opcodes is opcodes range jump to branch;
```

we can rewrite the second alternative as

```
when control_transfer_opcodes | store =>
    operand := address_operand;
```

Note that we may only use a discrete range as a choice if the selector expression is of a discrete type. We may not use a discrete range if the selector expression is of an array type, such as a bit-vector type. If we specify a range by writing the bounds and a direction, the direction has no significance except to identify the contents of the range.

An important point to note about the choices in a case statement is that they must all be written using *locally static* values. This means that the values of the choices must be determined during the analysis phase of design processing. All of the above examples satisfy this requirement. To give an example of a case statement that fails this requirement, suppose we have an integer variable **N**, declared as

```
variable N : integer := 1;
```

If we wrote the case statement

```
case expression is       -- example of an illegal case statement
    when N | N+1 => ...
    when N+2 to N+5 => ...
    when others => ...
end case;
```

the values of the choices depend on the value of the variable **N**. Since this might change during the course of execution, these choices are not locally static. Hence the case statement as written is illegal. On the other hand, if we had declared **C** to be a constant integer, for example with the declaration

```
constant C : integer := 1;
```

then we could legally write the case statement

```
case expression is
    when C | C+1 => ...
    when C+2 to C+5 => ...
    when others => ...
end case;
```

This is legal, since we can determine, by analyzing the model, that the first alternative includes choices 1 and 2, the second includes numbers between 3 and 6 and the third covers all other possible values of the expression.

The previous examples all show only one statement in each alternative. As with the if statement, we can write an arbitrary number of sequential statements of any kind in each alternative. This includes writing nested case statements, if statements or any other form of sequential statements in the alternatives.

Although the preceding rules governing case statements may seem complex, in practice there are just a few things to remember, namely:

- all possible values of the selector expression must be covered by one and only one choice,

- the values in the choices must be locally static and

- if the **others** choice is used it must be in the last alternative and must be the only choice in that alternative.

Example   We can write a behavioral model of a multiplexer with a select input **sel**; four data inputs **d0**, **d1**, **d2** and **d3**; and a data output **z**. The data inputs and outputs are of the IEEE standard-logic type, and the select input is of type **sel_range**, which we assume to be declared elsewhere as

```
type sel_range is range 0 to 3;
```

We show in Chapter 10, when we discuss packages, how we define a type for use in an entity declaration. The entity declaration defining the ports and a behavioral architecture body are shown in Figure 3-2. The architecture body contains just a process declaration. Since the output of the multiplexer must change if any of the data or select inputs change, the process must be sensitive to all of the inputs. It makes use of a case statement to select which of the data inputs is to be assigned to the data output.

FIGURE 3-2

```
library ieee;  use ieee.std_logic_1164.all;
entity mux4 is
    port ( sel : in sel_range;
           d0, d1, d2, d3 : in std_ulogic;
           z : out std_ulogic );
end entity mux4;
```

```
architecture demo of mux4 is
begin
    out_select : process (sel, d0, d1, d2, d3) is
    begin
        case sel is
            when 0 =>
                z <= d0;
            when 1 =>
                z <= d1;
            when 2 =>
                z <= d2;
            when 3 =>
                z <= d3;
        end case;
    end process out_select;
end architecture demo;
```

An entity and architecture body for a four-input multiplexer.

3.3 Null Statements

Sometimes when writing models we need to state that when some condition arises, no action is to be performed. This need often arises when we use case statements, since we must include an alternative for every possible value of the selector expression. Rather than just leaving the statement part of an alternative blank, we can use a *null statement* to state explicitly that nothing is to be done. The syntax rule for the null statement is simply

null_statement ⇐ ⟦ label : ⟧ **null** ;

The optional label serves to identify the statement. We discuss labeled statements in Chapter 22. A simple, unlabeled null statement is

null;

Example Suppose we are modeling a control stick with a throttle position declared to be of the enumeration type

```
type stick_position is (down, center, up);
```

If the control stick is in the center position, the engine speed should remain unchanged. We can use a null statement within a case statement to model this:

```
case throttle is
    when down =>
        speed := speed – decrement;
    when up =>
        speed := speed + increment;
    when center =>
        null;      –– no change to speed
end case;
```

We can use a null statement in any place where a sequential statement is required, not just in a case statement alternative. A null statement may be used during the development phase of model writing. If we know, for example, that we will need an entity as part of a system, but we are not yet in a position to write a detailed model for it, we can write a behavioral model that does nothing. Such a model just includes a process with a null statement in its body:

```
control_section : process ( sensitivity-list ) is
begin
    null;
end process control_section;
```

Note that the process must include the sensitivity list, for reasons that are explained in Chapter 5.

3.4   **Loop Statements**

Often we need to write a sequence of statements that is to be repeatedly executed. We use a *loop statement* to express this behavior. There are several different forms of loop statements in VHDL-AMS; the simplest is a loop that repeats a sequence of statements indefinitely, often called an *infinite loop*. The syntax rule for this kind of loop is

> loop_statement ⇐
>   ⟦ *loop*_label : ⟧
>   **loop**
>   ⦃ sequential_statement ⦄
>   **end loop** ⟦ *loop*_label ⟧ ;

In most computer programming languages, an infinite loop is not desirable, since it means that the program never terminates. However, when we are modeling hardware systems, an infinite loop can be useful, since many hardware devices repeatedly perform the same function until we turn off the power. Typically a model for such a system includes a loop statement in a process body; the loop, in turn, contains a wait statement.

Example   Figure 3-3 is a model for a counter that starts from zero and increments on each clock transition from '0' to '1'. When the counter reaches 15, it wraps back to zero on the next clock transition. The architecture body for the counter contains a process that first initializes the **count** output to zero, then repeatedly waits for a clock transition before incrementing the count value.

    The wait statement in this example causes the process to suspend in the middle of the loop. When the **clk** signal changes from '0' to '1', the process resumes and updates the count value and the **count** output. The loop is then repeated starting with the wait statement, so the process suspends again.

FIGURE 3-3

```
entity counter is
    port ( clk : in bit;  count : out natural );
end entity counter;
```

```
architecture behavior of counter is
begin

    incrementer : process is
        variable count_value : natural := 0;
    begin
        count <= count_value;
        loop
```

```
            wait until clk = '1';
            count_value := (count_value + 1) mod 16;
            count <= count_value;
        end loop;
    end process incrementer;
end architecture behavior;
```

An entity and architecture body for a counter.

Another point to note in passing is that the process statement does not include a sensitivity list. This is because it includes a wait statement. A process may contain either a sensitivity list or wait statements, but not both. We will return to this in detail in Chapter 5.

Exit Statements

In the previous example, the loop repeatedly executes the enclosed statements, with no way of stopping. Usually we need to exit the loop when some condition arises. We can use an *exit statement* to exit a loop. The syntax rule is

```
exit_statement ⇐
    [ label : ] exit [ loop_label ] [ when boolean_expression ] ;
```

The optional label at the start of the exit statement serves to identify the statement. We discuss labeled statements in Chapter 22. The simplest form of exit statement is just

```
exit;
```

When this statement is executed, any remaining statements in the loop are skipped, and control is transferred to the statement after the **end loop** keywords. So in a loop we can write

```
if condition then
    exit;
end if;
```

where *condition* is a Boolean expression. Since this is perhaps the most common use of the exit statement, VHDL-AMS provides a shorthand way of writing it, using the **when** clause. We use an exit statement with the **when** clause in a loop of the form

```
loop
    ...
    exit when condition;
```

```
        ...
    end loop;
    ...        -- control transferred to here
               -- when condition becomes true within the loop
```

Example   We now revise the previous counter model to include a **reset** input that, when '1', causes the **count** output to be reset to zero. The output stays at zero as long as the **reset** input is '1' and resumes counting on the next clock transition after **reset** changes to '0'. The revised entity declaration, shown in Figure 3-4, includes the new input port.

The architecture body is revised by nesting the loop inside another loop statement and adding the **reset** signal to the original wait statement. The inner loop performs the same function as before, except that when **reset** changes to '1', the process is resumed, and the exit statement causes the inner loop to be terminated. Control is transferred to the statement just after the end of the inner loop. As the

---

FIGURE 3-4

```
entity counter is
    port ( clk, reset : in bit;  count : out natural );
end entity counter;
```

```
architecture behavior of counter is
begin
    incrementer : process is
        variable count_value : natural := 0;
    begin
        count <= count_value;
        loop
            loop
                wait until clk = '1' or reset = '1';
                exit when reset = '1';
                count_value := (count_value + 1) mod 16;
                count <= count_value;
            end loop;
            -- at this point, reset = '1'
            count_value := 0;
            count <= count_value;
            wait until reset = '0';
        end loop;
    end process incrementer;
end architecture behavior;
```

An entity and architecture body of the revised counter, including a reset *input.*

comment indicates, we know that this point can only be reached when **reset** is '1'. The count value and **count** outputs are reset, and the process then waits for **reset** to return to '0'. While it is suspended at this point, any changes on the clock input are ignored. When **reset** changes to '0', the process resumes, and the outer loop repeats.

This example also illustrates another important point. When we have nested loop statements, with an exit statement inside the inner loop, the exit statement causes control to be transferred out of the inner loop only, not the outer loop. By default, an exit statement transfers control out of the immediately enclosing loop.

In some cases, we may wish to transfer control out of an inner loop and also a containing loop. We can do this by labeling the outer loop and using the label in the exit statement. We can write

```
loop_name : loop
    ...
    exit loop_name;
    ...
end loop loop_name ;
```

This labels the loop with the name **loop_name**, so that we can indicate which loop to exit in the exit statement. The loop label can be any valid identifier. The exit statement referring to this label can be located within nested loop statements.

To illustrate how loops can be nested, labeled and exited, let us consider the following statements:

```
outer : loop
    ...
    inner : loop
        ...
        exit outer when condition-1;   -- exit 1
        ...
        exit when condition-2;         -- exit 2
        ...
    end loop inner;
    ...                                -- target A
    exit outer when condition-3;       -- exit 3
    ...
end loop outer;
    ...                                -- target B
```

This example contains two loop statements, one labeled **inner** nested inside another labeled **outer**. The first exit statement, tagged with the comment **exit 1**, transfers control to the statement tagged **target B** if its condition is true. The second exit statement, tagged **exit 2**, transfers control to **target A**. Since it does not refer to a label, it only exits the immediately enclosing loop statement, namely, loop **inner**. Finally, the exit statement tagged **exit 3** transfers control to **target B**.

Next Statements

Another kind of statement that we can use to control the execution of loops is the *next statement*. When this statement is executed, the current iteration of the loop is completed without executing any further statements, and the next iteration is begun. The syntax rule is

next_statement ⇐
    ⟦ label : ⟧ **next** ⟦ *loop*_label ⟧ ⟦ **when** *boolean*_expression ⟧ ;

The optional label at the start of the next statement serves to identify the statement. We discuss labeled statements in Chapter 22. A next statement is very similar in form to an exit statement, the difference being the keyword **next** instead of **exit**. The simplest form of next statement is

next;

which starts the next iteration of the immediately enclosing loop. We can also include a condition to test before completing the iteration:

next when *condition*;

and we can include a loop label to indicate for which loop to complete the iteration:

next *loop-label*;

or

next *loop-label* **when** *condition*;

A next statement that exits the immediately enclosing loop can be easily rewritten as an equivalent loop with an if statement replacing the next statement. For example, the following two loops are equivalent:

```
loop                             loop
    statement-1;                     statement-1;
    next when condition;             if not condition then
    statement-2;                         statement-2;
end loop;                            end if;
                                 end loop;
```

However, nested labeled loops that contain next statements referring to outer loops cannot be so easily rewritten. As a matter of style, if we find ourselves about to write such a collection of loops and next statements, it's probably time to think more carefully about what we are trying to express. If we check the logic of the model, we may be able to find a simpler formulation of loop statements. Complicated loop/next structures can be confusing, making the model hard to read and understand.

While Loops

We can augment the basic loop statement introduced previously to form a *while loop,* which tests a condition before each iteration. If the condition is true, iteration proceeds. If it is false, the loop is terminated. The syntax rule for a while loop is

loop_statement ⇐
    ⟦ *loop*_label : ⟧
    while *boolean*_expression **loop**
        ⦃ sequential_statement ⦄
    end loop ⟦ *loop*_label ⟧ ;

The only difference between this form and the basic loop statement is that we have added the keyword **while** and the condition before the **loop** keyword. All of the things we said about the basic loop statement also apply to a while loop. We can write any sequential statements in the body of the loop, including exit and next statements, and we can label the loop by writing the label before the **while** keyword.

There are three important points to note about while loops. The first point is that the condition is tested before each iteration of the loop, including the first iteration. This means that if the condition is false before we start the loop, it is terminated immediately, with no iterations being executed. For example, given the while loop

```
while index > 0 loop
    ...           -- statement A: do something with index
end loop;
    ...           -- statement B
```

if we can demonstrate that **index** is not greater than zero before the loop is started, then we know that the statements inside the loop will not be executed, and control will be transferred straight to **statement B**.

The second point is that in the absence of exit statements within a while loop, the loop terminates only when the condition becomes false. Thus, we know that the negation of the condition must hold when control reaches the statement after the loop. Similarly, in the absence of next statements within a while loop, the loop performs an iteration only when the condition is true. Thus, we know that the condition holds when we start the statements in the loop body. In the above example, we know that **index** must be greater then zero when we execute the statement tagged **statement A**, and also that **index** must be less than or equal to zero when we reach **statement B**. This knowledge can help us reason about the correctness of the model we are writing.

The third point is that when we write the statements inside the body of a while loop, we must make sure that the condition will eventually become false, or that an exit statement will eventually exit the loop. Otherwise the while loop will never terminate. Presumably, if we had intended to write an infinite loop, we would have used a simple loop statement.

Example We can develop a model for an entity **cos** that might be used as part of a specialized signal processing system. The entity has one input, **theta**, which is a real number representing an angle in radians, and one output, **result**, representing the cosine function of the value of **theta**. We can use the relation

$$\cos\theta \ = \ 1 - \frac{\theta^2}{2!} + \frac{\theta^4}{4!} - \frac{\theta^6}{6!} + \dots$$

by adding successive terms of the series until the terms become smaller than one millionth of the result. The entity and architecture body declarations are shown in Figure 3-5.

The architecture body consists of a process that is sensitive to changes in the input signal **theta**. Initially, the variables **sum** and **term** are set to 1.0, representing the first term in the series. The variable n starts at 0 for the first term. The cosine function is computed using a while loop that increments n by two and uses it to calculate the next term based on the previous term. Iteration proceeds as long as the last term computed is larger in magnitude than one millionth of the sum. When the last term falls below this threshold, the while loop is terminated. We can determine that the loop will terminate, since the values of successive terms in the series get progressively smaller. This is because the factorial function grows at a greater rate than the exponential function.

FIGURE 3-5

```
entity cos is
    port ( theta : in real;  result : out real );
end entity cos;
```

```
architecture series of cos is
begin
    summation : process (theta) is
        variable sum, term : real;
        variable n : natural;
    begin
        sum := 1.0;
        term := 1.0;
        n := 0;
```

```
            while abs term > abs (sum / 1.0E6) loop
                n := n + 2;
                term := (–term) * theta**2 / real(((n–1) * n));
                sum := sum + term;
            end loop;
            result <= sum;
        end process summation;

end architecture series;
```

An entity and architecture body for a cosine module.

For Loops

Another way we can augment the basic loop statement is the *for loop*. A for loop includes a specification of how many times the body of the loop is to be executed. The syntax rule for a for loop is

```
loop_statement ⇐
    〖 loop_label : 〗
    for identifier in discrete_range loop
        〖 sequential_statement 〗
    end loop 〖 loop_label 〗 ;
```

We saw on page 81 that a discrete range can be of the form

```
simple_expression 〖 to ▯ downto 〗 simple_expression
```

representing all the values between the left and right bounds, inclusive. The identifier is called the *loop parameter,* and for each iteration of the loop, it takes on successive values of the discrete range, starting from the left element. For example, in this for loop:

```
for count_value in 0 to 127 loop
    count_out <= count_value;
    wait for 5 ns;
end loop;
```

the identifier count_value takes on the values 0, 1, 2 and so on, and for each value, the assignment and wait statements are executed. Thus the signal count_out will be assigned values 0, 1, 2 and so on, up to 127, at 5 ns intervals.

We also saw that a discrete range can be specified using a discrete type or subtype name, possibly further constrained to a subset of values by a range constraint. For example, if we have the enumeration type

```
type controller_state is (initial, idle, active, error);
```

we can write a for loop that iterates over each of the values in the type:

```
for state in controller_state loop
    ...
end loop;
```

Within the sequence of statements in the for loop body, the loop parameter is a constant whose type is the base type of the discrete range. This means we can use its value by including it in an expression, but we cannot make assignments to it. Unlike other constants, we do not need to declare it. Instead, the loop parameter is implicitly declared over the for loop. It only exists when the loop is executing, and not before or after it. For example, the following process statement shows how not to use the loop parameter:

```
erroneous : process is
    variable i, j : integer;
begin
    i := loop_param;                    -- error!
    for loop_param in 1 to 10 loop
        loop_param := 5;                -- error!
    end loop;
    j := loop_param;                    -- error!
end process erroneous;
```

The assignments to i and j are illegal since the loop parameter is defined neither before nor after the loop. The assignment within the loop body is illegal because loop_param is a constant and thus may not be modified.

A consequence of the way the loop parameter is defined is that it *hides* any object of the same name defined outside the loop. For example, in this process:

```
hiding_example : process is
    variable a, b : integer;
begin
    a := 10;
    for a in 0 to 7 loop
        b := a;
    end loop;
    -- a = 10, and b = 7
    ...
end process hiding_example;
```

the variable a is initially assigned the value 10, and then the for loop is executed, creating a loop parameter also called a. Within the loop, the assignment to b uses the loop parameter, so the final value of b after the last iteration is 7. After the loop, the loop parameter no longer exists, so if we use the name **a**, we are referring to the variable object, whose value is still 10.

As we mentioned above, the for loop iterates with the loop parameter assuming successive values from the discrete range starting from the leftmost value. An important point to note is that if we specify a null range, the for loop body does not execute at all. A null range can arise if we specify an ascending range with the left bound greater than the right bound, or a descending range with the left bound less than the right bound. For example, the for loop

```
for i in 10 to 1 loop
    ...
end loop;
```

completes immediately, without executing the enclosed statements. If we really want the loop to iterate with i taking values 10, 9, 8 and so on, we should write

```
for i in 10 downto 1 loop
    ...
end loop;
```

One final thing to note about for loops is that, like basic loop statements, they can enclose arbitrary sequential statements, including next and exit statements, and we can label a for loop by writing the label before the **for** keyword.

Example   We now rewrite the cosine model in Figure 3-5 to calculate the result by summing the first 10 terms of the series. The entity declaration is unchanged. The revised architecture body, shown in Figure 3-6, consists of a process that uses a for loop instead of a while loop. As before, the variables **sum** and **term** are set to 1.0, representing the first term in the series. The variable n is replaced by the for loop parameter. The loop iterates nine times, calculating the remaining nine terms of the series.

FIGURE 3-6

```
architecture fixed_length_series of cos is
begin
    summation : process (theta) is
        variable sum, term : real;
    begin
        sum := 1.0;
        term := 1.0;
        for n in 1 to 9 loop
            term := (-term) * theta**2 / real(((2*n-1) * 2*n));
            sum := sum + term;
```

(continued on page 96)

(continued from page 95)

```
        end loop;
        result <= sum;
    end process summation;
end architecture fixed_length_series;
```

The revised architecture body for the cosine module.

Summary of Loop Statements

The preceding sections describe the various forms of loop statements in detail. It is worth summarizing this information in one place, to show the few basic points to remember. First, the syntax rule for all loop statements is

```
loop_statement ⇐
    ⟦ loop_label : ⟧
    ⟦ while boolean_expression ▯ for identifier in discrete_range ⟧ loop
        ⦃ sequential_statement ⦄
    end loop ⟦ loop_label ⟧ ;
```

Second, in the absence of exit and next statements, the while loop iterates as long as the condition is true, and the for loop iterates with the loop parameter assuming successive values from the discrete range. If the condition in a while loop is initially false, or if the discrete range in a for loop is a null range, then no iterations occur.

Third, the loop parameter in a for loop cannot be explicitly declared, and it is a constant within the loop body. It also shadows any other object of the same name declared outside the loop.

Finally, an exit statement can be used to terminate any loop, and a next statement can be used to complete the current iteration and commence the next iteration. These statements can refer to loop labels to terminate or complete iteration for an outer level of a nested set of loops.

3.5 Assertion and Report Statements

One of the reasons for writing models of mixed-technology systems is to verify that a design functions correctly. We can partially test a model by applying sample inputs and checking that the outputs meet our expectations. If they do not, we are then faced with the task of determining what went wrong inside the design. This task can be made easier using *assertion statements* that check that expected conditions are met within the model. An assertion statement is a sequential statement, so it can be included anywhere in a process body. The full syntax rule for an assertion statement is

assertion_statement ⇐
　　⟦ label : ⟧ **assert** *boolean*_expression
　　　　⟦ **report** expression ⟧ ⟦ **severity** expression ⟧ ;

The optional label allows us to identify the assertion statement. We will discuss labeled statements in Chapter 22. The simplest form of assertion statement just includes the keyword **assert** followed by a Boolean expression that we expect to be true when the assertion statement is executed. If the condition is not met, we say that an *assertion violation* has occurred. If an assertion violation arises during simulation of a model, the simulator reports the fact. During synthesis, the condition in an assertion statement may be interpreted as a condition that the synthesizer may assume to be true. During formal verification, the condition may be interpreted as a condition to be proven by the verifier. For example, if we write

　　assert initial_value <= max_value;

and initial_value is larger than max_value when the statement is executed during simulation, the simulator will let us know. During synthesis, the synthesizer may assume that initial_value <= max_value and optimize the circuit based on that information. During formal verification, the verifier may attempt to prove initial_value <= max_value for all possible input stimuli and execution paths leading to the assertion statement.

If we have a number of assertion statements throughout a model, it is useful to know which assertion is violated. We can get the simulator to provide extra information by including a **report** clause in an assertion statement, for example:

　　assert initial_value <= max_value
　　　　report "initial value too large";

The string that we provide is used to form part of the assertion violation message. We can write any expression in the report clause provided it yields a string value, for example:

　　assert current_character >= '0' **and** current_character <= '9'
　　　　report "Input number " & input_string & " contains a non–digit";

Here the message is derived by concatenating three string values together.

In Section 2.2, we mentioned a predefined enumeration type severity_level, defined as

　　type severity_level **is** (note, warning, error, failure);

We can include a value of this type in a **severity** clause of an assertion statement. This value indicates the degree to which the violation of the assertion affects operation of the model. The value note can be used to pass informative messages out from a simulation, for example:

```
assert free_memory >= low_water_limit
    report "low on memory, about to start garbage collect"
    severity note;
```

The severity level **warning** can be used if an unusual situation arises in which the model can continue to execute, but may produce unusual results, for example:

```
assert packet_length /= 0
    report "empty network packet received"
    severity warning;
```

We can use the severity level **error** to indicate that something has definitely gone wrong and that corrective action should be taken, for example:

```
assert clock_pulse_width >= min_clock_width
    severity error;
```

Finally, the value **failure** can be used if we detect an inconsistency that should never arise, for example:

```
assert (last_position – first_position + 1) = number_of_entries
    report "inconsistency in buffer model"
    severity failure;
```

We have seen that we can write an assertion statement with either a **report** clause or a **severity** clause, or both. If both are present, the syntax rule shows us that the report clause must come first. If we omit the **report** clause, the default string in the error message is "Assertion violation." If we omit the **severity** clause, the default value is **error**. The severity value is usually used by a simulator to determine whether or not to continue execution after an assertion violation. Most simulators allow the user to specify a severity threshold, beyond which execution is stopped.

Usually, failure of an assertion means either that the entity is being used incorrectly as part of a larger design or that the model for the entity has been incorrectly written. We illustrate both cases.

Example   A set/reset (SR) flipflop has two inputs, S and R, and an output Q. When S is '1', the output is set to '1', and when R is '1', the output is reset to '0'. However, S and R may not both be '1' at the same time. If they are, the output value is not specified. Figure 3-7 is a behavioral model for an SR flipflop that includes a check for this illegal condition.

The architecture body contains a process sensitive to the S and R inputs. Within the process body we write an assertion statement that requires that S and R not both be '1'. If both are '1', the assertion is violated, so the simulator writes an "Assertion violation" message with severity error. If execution continues after the violated assertion, the value '1' will first be assigned to Q, followed by the value '0'. The resulting value is '0'. This is allowed, since the state of Q was not

FIGURE 3-7

```
entity SR_flipflop is
    port ( S, R : in bit;  Q : out bit );
end entity SR_flipflop;

------------------------------------------------------------

architecture checking of SR_flipflop is
begin
    set_reset : process (S, R) is
    begin
        assert S = '1' nand R = '1';
        if S = '1' then
            Q <= '1';
        end if;
        if R = '1' then
            Q <= '0';
        end if;
    end process set_reset;
end architecture checking;
```

An entity and architecture body for a set/reset flipflop, including a check for correct usage.

specified for this illegal condition, so we are at liberty to choose any value. If the assertion is not violated, then at most one of the following if statements is executed, correctly modeling the behavior of the SR flipflop.

Example   To illustrate the use of an assertion statement as a "sanity check," let us look at a model, shown in Figure 3-8, for an entity that has three integer inputs, a, b and c, and produces an integer output z that is the largest of its inputs.

FIGURE 3-8

```
entity max3 is
    port ( a, b, c : in integer;  z : out integer );
end entity max3;

------------------------------------------------------------

architecture check_error of max3 is
begin
    maximizer : process (a, b, c)
        variable result : integer;
    begin
```

(continued on page 100)

(continued from page 99)

```
              if a > b then
                  if a > c then
                      result := a;
                  else
                      result := a;      -- Oops! Should be: result := c;
                  end if;
              elsif  b > c then
                  result := b;
              else
                  result := c;
              end if;
              assert result >= a and result >= b and result >= c
                  report "inconsistent result for maximum"
                  severity failure;
              z <= result;
          end process maximizer;
      end architecture check_error;
```

An entity and architecture body for a maximum selector module, including a check for a correctly generated result.

The architecture body is written using a process containing nested if statements. For this example we have introduced an "accidental" error into the model. If we simulate this model and put the values a = 7, b = 3 and c = 9 on the ports of this entity, we expect that the value of **result**, and hence the output port, is 9. The assertion states that the value of **result** must be greater than or equal to all of the inputs. However, our coding error causes the value 7 to be assigned to **result**, and so the assertion is violated. This violation causes us to examine our model more closely, and correct the error.

Another important use for assertion statements is in checking timing constraints that apply to a model. For example, most clocked devices require that the clock pulse be longer than some minimum duration. We can use the predefined primary **now** in an expression to calculate durations. We return to **now** in a later chapter. Suffice it to say that it yields the current simulation time when it is evaluated.

Example   An edge-triggered register has a data input and a data output of type **real** and a clock input of type **bit**. When the clock changes from '0' to '1', the data input is sampled, stored and transmitted through to the output. Let us suppose that the clock input must remain at '1' for at least 5 ns. Figure 3-9 is a model for this register, including a check for legal clock pulse width.

The architecture body contains a process that is sensitive to changes on the clock input. When the clock changes from '0' to '1', the input is stored, and the

FIGURE 3-9

```
entity edge_triggered_register is
    port ( clock : in bit;
              d_in : in real;  d_out : out real );
end entity edge_triggered_register;
```

```
architecture check_timing of edge_triggered_register is
begin
    store_and_check : process (clock) is
        variable stored_value : real;
        variable pulse_start : time;
    begin
        case clock is
            when '1' =>
                pulse_start := now;
                stored_value := d_in;
                d_out <= stored_value;
            when '0' =>
                assert now = 0 ns or (now – pulse_start) >= 5 ns
                    report "clock pulse too short";
        end case;
    end process store_and_check;
end architecture check_timing;
```

An entity and architecture body for an edge-triggered register, including a timing check for correct pulse width on the clock input.

current simulation time is recorded in the variable **pulse_start**. When the clock changes from '1' to '0', the difference between **pulse_start** and the current simulation time is checked by the assertion statement.

VHDL-AMS also provides us with a *report statement,* which is similar to an assertion statement. The syntax rule for the report statement shows this similarity:

report_statement ⟸
    〖 label : 〗 **report** expression 〖 **severity** expression 〗 ;

The differences are that there is no condition, and if the severity level is not specified, the default is **note**. Indeed, the report statement can be thought of as an assertion statement in which the condition is the value **false** and the severity is **note**, hence it always produces the message. One way in which the report statement is useful is as a means of including "trace writes" in a model as an aid to debugging.

Example   Suppose we are writing a complex model and we are not sure that we have got the logic quite right. We can use report statements to get the processes in the model to write out messages, so that we can see when they are activated and what they are doing. An example process is

```
transmit_element : process (transmit_data) is
    ...        -- variable declarations
begin
    report "transmit_element: data = "
            & data_type'image(transmit_data);

    ...

end process transmit_element;
```

Exercises

1. [◐ 3.1] Write an if statement that sets a variable **odd** to '1' if an integer **n** is odd, or to '0' if it is even.

2. [◐ 3.1] Write an if statement that, given the year of today's date in the variable **year**, sets the variable **days_in_February** to the number of days in February. A year is a leap year if it is divisible by four, except for years that are divisible by 100. However, years that are divisible by 400 are leap years. February has 29 days in a leap year and 28 days otherwise.

3. [◐ 3.2] Write a case statement that strips the strength information from a standard-logic variable **x**. If **x** is '0' or 'L', set it to '0'. If **x** is '1' or 'H', set it to '1'. If **x** is 'X', 'W', 'Z', 'U' or '–', set it to 'X'. (This is the conversion performed by the standard-logic function **to_X01**.)

4. [◐ 3.2] Write a case statement that sets an integer variable **character_class** to 1 if the character variable **ch** contains a letter, to 2 if it contains a digit, to 3 if it contains some other printable character or to 4 if it contains a non-printable character. Note that the VHDL-AMS character set contains accented letters, as shown in Figure 2-2.

5. [◐ 3.4] Write a loop statement that samples a bit input **d** when a clock input **clk** changes to '1'. So long as **d** is '0', the loop continues executing. When **d** is '1', the loop exits.

6. [◐ 3.4] Write a while loop that calculates the exponential function of **x** to an accuracy of one part in 10^4 by summing terms of the following series:

$$e^x = 1 + \frac{x}{1} + \frac{x^2}{2!} + \frac{x^3}{3!} + \frac{x^4}{4!} + \dots$$

7. [❶ 3.4] Write a for loop that calculates the exponential function of x by summing the first eight terms of the series in Exercise 6.

8. [❶ 3.5] Write an assertion statement that expresses the requirement that a flip-flop's two outputs, q and q_n, of type **std_ulogic**, are complementary.

9. [❶ 3.5] We can use report statements in VHDL-AMS to achieve the same effect as using "trace writes" in software programming languages, to report a message when part of the model is executed. Insert a report statement in the model of Figure 3-4 to cause a trace message when the counter is reset.

10. [❷ 3.1] Develop a behavioral model for a limiter with three integer inputs, **data_in**, **lower** and **upper**; an integer output, **data_out**; and a bit output, **out_of_limits**. The **data_out** output follows **data_in** so long as it is between **lower** and **upper**. If **data_in** is less than **lower**, **data_out** is limited to **lower**. If **data_in** is greater than **upper**, **data_out** is limited to **upper**. The **out_of_limit** output indicates when **data_out** is limited.

11. [❷ 3.2] Develop a model for a floating-point arithmetic unit with data inputs x and y, data output z and function code inputs f1 and f0 of type **bit**. Function codes f1 = '0' and f0 = '0' produce addition; f1 = '0' and f0 = '1' produce subtraction of y from x; f1 = '1' and f0 = '0' produce multiplication; and f1 = '1' and f0 = '1' produce division of x by y.

12. [❷ 3.4] Write a model for a counter with an output port of type **natural**, initially set to 15. When the **clk** input changes to '1', the counter decrements by one. After counting down to zero, the counter wraps back to 15 on the next clock edge.

13. [❷ 3.4] Modify the counter of Exercise 12 to include an asynchronous load input and a data input. When the load input is '1', the counter is preset to the data input value. When the load input changes back to '0', the counter continues counting down from the preset value.

14. [❷ 3.4] Develop a model of an averaging module that calculates the average of batches of 16 real numbers. The module has clock and data inputs and a data output. The module accepts the next input number when the clock changes to '1'. After 16 numbers have been accepted, the module places their average on the output port, then repeats the process for the next batch.

15. [❷ 3.5] Write a model that causes assertion violations with different severity levels. Experiment with your simulator to determine its behavior when an assertion violation occurs. See if you can specify a severity threshold above which it stops execution.

chapter four

Composite Data Types and Operations

Now that we have seen the basic data types, natures and sequential operations from which the processes of a VHDL-AMS model are formed, it is time to look at composite data types. We first mentioned them in the classification of data types and natures in Chapter 2. Composite data objects consist of related collections of data elements in the form of either an array *or a* record. *We can treat an object of a composite type or nature as a single object or manipulate its constituent elements individually. In this chapter, we see how to define composite types and natures and how to manipulate them using operators and sequential statements.*

4.1 **Arrays**

An *array* consists of a collection of values, all of which are of the same type or nature as each other. The position of each element in an array is given by a scalar value called its *index*. To create an array object in a model, we first define an array type in a type declaration. The syntax rule for an array type definition is

    array_type_definition ⇐
        array (discrete_range ⟦ , ... ⟧) **of** *element*_subtype_indication

This defines an array type by specifying one or more index ranges (the list of discrete ranges) and the element type or subtype.

Alternatively, to create an array terminal in a model, we first define an array nature in a nature declaration. The syntax rule is

    array_nature_definition ⇐
        array (discrete_range ⟦ , ... ⟧) **of** *element*_subnature_indication

As with array types, this defines an array nature by specifying one or more index ranges and the element nature or subnature.

Recall from previous chapters that a discrete range is a subset of values from a discrete type (an integer or enumeration type), and that it can be specified as shown by the simplified syntax rule

    discrete_range ⇐
        *discrete*_subtype_indication
        ⟦ simple_expression ⟨ **to** ⟨ **downto** ⟩ simple_expression

Recall also that a subtype indication can be just the name of a previously declared type (a type mark) and can include a range constraint to limit the set of values from that type. It can also include a tolerance clause to specify the required numeric accuracy for floating-point subtypes. These possibilities are shown by the simplified syntax rule

    subtype_indication ⇐
        type_mark ⟦ **range** simple_expression ⟨ **to** ⟨ **downto** ⟩ simple_expression ⟧
                  ⟦ **tolerance** *string*_expression ⟧

Similarly, a subnature indication can be just the name of a previously declared nature (a nature mark) and can include a tolerance clause to specify the required numeric accuracy, as shown by the simplified rule

    subnature_indication ⇐
        nature_mark ⟦ *index*_constraint ⟧
                    ⟦ **tolerance** *string*_expression **across** *string*_expression **through** ⟧

We illustrate these rules for defining arrays with a series of examples. We start with single-dimensional arrays, in which there is just one index range. Here is a simple example to start off with, showing the declaration of an array type to represent words of data:

type word **is array** (0 **to** 31) **of** bit;

Each element is a bit, and the elements are indexed from 0 up to 31. An alternative declaration of a word type, more appropriate for "little-endian" systems, is

type word **is array** (31 **downto** 0) **of** bit;

The difference here is that index values start at 31 for the leftmost element in values of this type and continue down to 0 for the rightmost.

We can declare an array nature in a similar manner. To create a bus of wires of an electrical nature, we simply use the following definition:

nature electrical_bus **is array** (0 **to** 31) **of** electrical;

This declares an array nature in which each element is of **electrical** nature. Terminals declared with this array nature have 32 elements indexed from 0 up to 31. Alternatively, we can order the elements with a descending index range:

nature electrical_bus **is array** (31 **downto** 0) **of** electrical;

The index values of an array do not have to be numeric. For example, given this declaration of an enumeration type:

type controller_state **is** (initial, idle, active, error);

we could then declare an array as follows:

type state_counts **is array** (idle **to** error) **of** natural;

This kind of array type declaration relies on the type of the index range being clear from the context. If there were more than one enumeration type with values idle and error, it would not be clear which one to use for the index type. To make it clear, we can use the alternative form for specifying the index range, in which we name the index type and include a range constraint. The previous example could be rewritten as

type state_counts **is**
    array (controller_state **range** idle **to** error) **of** natural;

Array natures can also be indexed with enumeration types, illustrated by the following enumerated type identifying nodes within an engine:

```
type engine_nodes is (intake, compressor, combustion, exhaust);
```

We could then declare an array nature to model the fluid dynamics inside an engine as follows:

```
nature engine_flows is array (intake to exhaust) of fluidic;
```

If we need an array element for every value in an index type, we need only name the index type in the array declaration without specifying the range. For example:

```
subtype coeff_ram_address is integer range 0 to 63;
type coeff_array is array (coeff_ram_address) of real;
```

The same applies to array natures, for example:

```
subtype bus_lines is integer range 0 to 31;
nature electrical_bus is array (bus_lines) of electrical;
```

This declares an array nature that can be used for terminals to model 32-wire buses.

Once we have declared an array type, we can define objects of that type, including constants, variables, signals and quantities of that type. For example, using the types declared above, we can declare variables as follows:

```
variable buffer_register, data_register : word;
variable counters : state_counts;
variable coeff : coeff_array;
```

Each of these objects consists of the collection of elements described by the corresponding type declaration. An individual element can be used in an expression or as the target of an assignment by referring to the array object and supplying an index value, for example:

```
coeff(0) := 0.0;
```

If **active** is a variable of type controller_state, we can write

```
counters(active) := counters(active) + 1;
```

An array object can also be used as a single composite object. For example, the assignment

```
data_register := buffer_register;
```

copies all of the elements of the array **buffer_register** into the corresponding elements of the array **data_register**.

In Chapter 2 we saw how we can declare a subtype with a tolerance clause. We can use such a subtype as the element type for an array. For example, if we declare two subtypes as follows:

```
subtype pressure is real tolerance "default_pressure";
subtype pipes is integer range 0 to 15;
```

we can define an array of pressures for a chemical process or hydraulic application using the following type declaration:

```
type gas_pressures is array (pipes) of pressure;
```

Example   Figure 4-1 is a model for a memory that stores 64 real-number coefficients, initialized to 0.0. We assume the type coeff_ram_address is previously declared as above. The architecture body contains a process with an array variable representing the coefficient storage. When the process starts, it initializes the array using a for loop. It then repetitively waits for any of the input ports to change. When rd is '1', the array is indexed using the address value to read a coefficient. When wr is '1', the address value is used to select which coefficient to change.

FIGURE 4-1

```
entity coeff_ram is
    port ( rd, wr : in bit;  addr : in coeff_ram_address;
            d_in : in real;  d_out : out real );
end entity coeff_ram;

------------------------------------------------------------

architecture abstract of coeff_ram is
begin
    memory : process is
        type coeff_array is array (coeff_ram_address) of real;
        variable coeff : coeff_array;
    begin
        for index in coeff_ram_address loop
            coeff(index) := 0.0;
        end loop;
        loop
            wait on rd, wr, addr, d_in;
            if rd = '1' then
                d_out <= coeff(addr);
            end if;
            if wr = '1' then
                coeff(addr) := d_in;
```

(continued on page 110)

(continued from page 109)

```
                    end if;
                  end loop;
                end process memory;
      end architecture abstract;
```

An entity and architecture body for a memory module that stores real-number coefficients. The memory storage is implemented using an array.

Array natures are useful for declaring collections of terminals. Given the declaration of an array nature in a model, we can define terminals of that nature. For example, using the natures declared above, we can declare terminals as follows:

```
terminal system_bus : electrical_bus;
terminal ferrari_engine, chevy_engine : engine_flows;
```

Recall that a terminal has across and through types defined by its nature. If the nature of a terminal is an array nature, the across and through types are arrays. So if we define branch quantities interconnecting terminals of an array nature, the branch quantities are themselves arrays. For example, the declaration

```
quantity bus_voltages across bus_currents through
      system_bus to electrical_ref;
```

defines two array branch quantities that we can use in equations to describe analog behavior. We will look at one further example of array terminals and quantities here, and discuss the topic in more detail in Chapter 6.

Example   Figure 4-2 is a model for a bus of transmission lines that also translates the values on bus wires into digital form. We assume the array nature **electrical_bus** and the type **word** are declared as above. The architecture body contains a process that sets each bit of the signal port depending on whether the corresponding bus wire is above or below a threshold level.

FIGURE 4-2

```
entity transmission_lines is
    port ( terminal data_bus : electrical_bus;
          signal clk : in bit;  signal data_out : out word );
end entity transmission_lines;
```

```
        architecture abstract of transmission_lines is
            constant threshold : voltage := 1.5;
            quantity bus_voltages across bus_currents through
                    data_bus to electrical_ref;
begin
        logic_value_maps : process (clk) is
        begin
            if clk = '1' then
                for index in bus_lines loop
                    if bus_voltages(index) > threshold then
                        data_out(index) <= '1';
                    else
                        data_out(index) <= '0';
                    end if;
                end loop;
            end if;
        end process logic_value_maps;

        -- additional VHDL-AMS code to describe reflections and attenuation
        ...

end architecture abstract;
```

An entity and architecture body for a transmission line model of a bus with its resulting waveform translated to digital form. The bus is implemented using an array of electrical terminals.

Multidimensional Arrays

VHDL-AMS also allows us to create multidimensional arrays, for example, to represent matrices or tables indexed by more than one value, or to represent collections of terminals arranged regularly in two or three dimensions. A multidimensional array type is declared by specifying a list of index ranges, as shown by the syntax rule on page 106. For example, we might include the following type declarations in a model for a finite-state machine:

```
type symbol is ('a', 't', 'd', 'h', digit, cr, error);
type state is range 0 to 6;
type transition_matrix is array (state, symbol) of state;
```

Similarly, we might include the following type and nature declarations in a model for an aircraft:

```
type engine_nodes is (intake, compressor, combustion, exhaust);
type engines is range 1 to 4;
nature aircraft_engine_flows is array (engine_nodes, engines) of fluidic;
```

Each index range can be specified as shown above for single-dimensional arrays. The index ranges for each dimension need not all be from the same type, nor have the same direction. An object of a multidimensional array type is indexed by writing a list of index values to select an element. For example, if we have a variable declared as

variable transition_table : transition_matrix;

we can index it as follows:

transition_table(5, 'd');

Note that a multidimensional array declares a collection of elements with multiple indices, but each element in the array is of the same type or nature.

Example   In three-dimensional graphics, a point in space may be represented using a three-element vector [x, y, z] of coordinates. Transformations, such as scaling, rotation and reflection, may be done by multiplying a vector by a 3 × 3 transformation matrix to get a new vector representing the transformed point. We can write VHDL-AMS type declarations for points and transformation matrices:

```
type point is array (1 to 3) of real;
type matrix is array (1 to 3, 1 to 3) of real;
```

We can use these types to declare point variables p and q and a matrix variable transform:

```
variable p, q : point;
variable transform : matrix;
```

The transformation can be applied to the point p to produce a result in q with the following statements:

```
for i in 1 to 3 loop
    q(i) := 0.0;
    for j in 1 to 3 loop
        q(i) := q(i) + transform(i, j) * p(j);
    end loop;
end loop;
```

Example   Suppose we model a seismic sensor as a device that measures linear displacement of the earth's surface. We can declare a two-dimensional array nature to represent values produced by a grid of sensors:

nature sensor_matrix **is array** (1 **to** 100, 1 **to** 100) **of** translational;

We can model the grid itself as a terminal of this array nature:

```
terminal sensor_grid : sensor_matrix;
```

To acquire data from the sensor grid, we declare an across branch quantity, since the displacement is the across type for the translational nature:

```
quantity sensor_data across sensor_grid to translational_ref;
```

This quantity is a 100 × 100 array of displacement values. We can thus find the average displacement over the entire grid at any time with the following statements in a process:

```
total_displacement := 0.0;
for x in 1 to 100 loop
    for y in 1 to 100 loop
        total_displacement := total_displacement + sensor_data(x, y);
    end loop;
end loop;
average_displacement := total_displacement / 10000.0;
```

Array Aggregates

We have seen how we can write literal values of scalar types. Often we also need to write literal array values, for example, to initialize a variable, quantity or constant of an array type. We can do this using a VHDL-AMS construct called an array *aggregate,* according to the syntax rule

aggregate ⇐ (⦇ ⟦ choices => ⟧ expression ⦈ ⦃ , ₒₒₒ ⦄)

Let us look first at the form of aggregate without the choices part. It simply consists of a list of the elements enclosed in parentheses, for example:

```
type point is array (1 to 3) of real;
constant origin : point := (0.0, 0.0, 0.0);
variable view_point : point := (10.0, 20.0, 0.0);

subtype resistance is real tolerance "default_resistance";
type resistance_array is array (1 to 4) of resistance;
quantity resistances : resistance_array := (10.0, 20.0, 50.0, 75.0);
```

This form of array aggregate uses *positional association* to determine which value in the list corresponds to which element of the array. The first value is the element with the leftmost index, the second is the next index to the right, and so on, up to the last value, which is the element with the rightmost index. There must be a one-to-one correspondence between values in the aggregate and elements in the array.

An alternative form of aggregate uses *named association,* in which the index value for each element is written explicitly using the choices part shown in the syntax rule. The choices may be specified in exactly the same way as those in alternatives of a case statement, discussed in Chapter 3. As a reminder, here is the syntax rule for choices:

choices ⇐ ⦇ simple_expression ⫿ discrete_range ⫿ **others** ⦈ ⦃ ⫿ ... ⦄

For example, the variable declaration and initialization could be rewritten as

variable view_point : point := (1 => 10.0, 2 => 20.0, 3 => 0.0);

and the free quantity declaration and initialization could be rewritten as

quantity resistances : resistance_array := (1 => 10.0, 2 => 20.0, 3 => 50.0, 4 => 75.0);

The main advantage of named association is that it gives us more flexibility in writing aggregates for larger arrays. To illustrate this, let us return to the coefficient memory described above. The type declaration was

type coeff_array **is array** (coeff_ram_address) **of** real;

Suppose we want to declare the coefficient variable, initialize the first few locations to some non-zero value and initialize the remainder to zero. Following are a number of ways of writing aggregates that all have the same effect:

variable coeff : coeff_array := (0 => 1.6, 1 => 2.3, 2 => 1.6, 3 **to** 63 => 0.0);

Here we are using a range specification to initialize the bulk of the array value to zero.

variable coeff : coeff_array := (0 => 1.6, 1 => 2.3, 2 => 1.6, **others** => 0.0);

The keyword **others** stands for any index value that has not been previously mentioned in the aggregate. If the keyword **others** is used, it must be the last choice in the aggregate.

variable coeff : coeff_array := (0 | 2 => 1.6, 1 => 2.3, **others** => 0.0);

The "|" symbol can be used to separate a list of index values, for which all elements have the same value.

Note that we may not mix positional and named association in an array aggregate, except for the use of an **others** choice in the final postion. Thus, the following aggregate is illegal:

variable coeff : coeff_array := (1.6, 2.3, 2 => 1.6, **others** => 0.0);   *-- illegal*

We can also use aggregates to write multidimensional array values. In this case, we treat the array as though it were an array of arrays, writing an array aggregate for each of the leftmost index values first.

Example   We can use a two-dimensional array to represent the transition matrix of a finite-state machine (FSM) that interprets simple modem commands. A command must consist of the string "atd" followed by a string of digits and a **cr** character, or the string "ath" followed by **cr**. The state transition diagram is shown in Figure 4-3. The symbol "other" represents a character other than 'a', 't', 'd', 'h', a digit or **cr**. An outline of a process that implements the FSM is shown in Figure 4-4.

The type declarations for **symbol** and **state** represent the command symbols and the states for the FSM. The transition matrix, **next_state**, is a two-dimensional array constant indexed by the state and symbol type. An element at position (*i*, *j*) in this matrix indicates the next state the FSM should move to when it is in state *i* and the next input symbol is *j*. The matrix is initialized according to the transition diagram. The process uses the **current_state** variable and successive input symbols as indices into the transition matrix to determine the next state. For each transition, it performs some action based on the new state. The actions are implemented within the case statement.

FIGURE 4-3

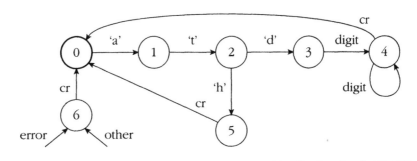

The state transition diagram for a modem command finite-state machine. State 0 is the initial state. The machine returns to this state after recognizing a correct command. State 6 is the error state, to which the machine goes if it detects an illegal or unexpected character.

FIGURE 4-4

```
modem_controller : process is
        type symbol is ('a', 't', 'd', 'h', digit, cr, other);
        type symbol_string is array (1 to 20) of symbol;
        type state is range 0 to 6;
        type transition_matrix is array (state, symbol) of state;
```

(continued on page 116)

(continued from page 115)

```
    constant next_state : transition_matrix :=
        ( 0 => ('a' => 1, others => 6),
          1 => ('t' => 2, others => 6),
          2 => ('d' => 3, 'h' => 5, others => 6),
          3 => (digit => 4, others => 6),
          4 => (digit => 4, cr => 0, others => 6),
          5 => (cr => 0, others => 6),
          6 => (cr => 0, others => 6) );
    variable command : symbol_string;
    variable current_state : state := 0;
begin
    ...
    for index in 1 to 20 loop
        current_state := next_state( current_state, command(index) );
        case current_state is
            ...
        end case;
    end loop;
    ...
end process modem_controller;
```

An outline of a process that implements the finite-state machine to accept a modem command.

Another place in which we may use an aggregate is the target of a variable assignment or a signal assignment. The full syntax rule for a variable assignment statement is

variable_assignment_statement ⇐
    〚 label : 〛 〘 name ⫾ aggregate 〙 := expression ;

If the target is an aggregate, it must contain a variable name at each element position. Furthermore, expression on the right-hand side of the assignment must produce a composite value of the same type as the target aggregate. Each element of the right-hand side is assigned to the corresponding variable in the target aggregate. The full syntax rule for a signal assignment also allows the target to be in the form of an aggregate, with each element being a signal name. We can use assignments of this form to split a composite value among a number of scalar signals. For example, if we have a variable flag_reg, which is a four-element bit vector, we can perform the following signal assignment to four signals of type **bit**:

```
    ( z_flag, n_flag, v_flag, c_flag ) <= flag_reg;
```

Since the right-hand side is a bit vector, the target is taken as a bit-vector aggregate. The leftmost element of flag_reg is assigned to z_flag, the second element of flag_reg is assigned to n_flag, and so on. This form of multiple assignment is much more compact to write than four separate assignment statements.

Array Attributes

In Chapter 2 we saw that attributes could be used to refer to information about scalar types and natures. There are also attributes applicable to array types and natures; they refer to information about the index ranges. Array attributes can also be applied to array objects, such as constants, variables, signals, quantities and terminals, to refer to information about the types or natures of the objects. Given some array type, nature or object A, and an integer N between 1 and the number of dimensions of A, VHDL-AMS defines the following attributes:

A'left(N)	Left bound of index range of dimension N of A
A'right(N)	Right bound of index range of dimension N of A
A'low(N)	Lower bound of index range of dimension N of A
A'high(N)	Upper bound of index range of dimension N of A
A'range(N)	Index range of dimension N of A
A'reverse_range(N)	Reverse of index range of dimension N of A
A'length(N)	Length of index range of dimension N of A
A'ascending(N)	true if index range of dimension N of A is an ascending range, false otherwise

For example, given the array declarations

    type A is array (1 to 4, 31 downto 0) of boolean;
    nature B is array (1 to 10, 19 downto 0) of thermal;

some attribute values are

A'low(1) = 1	B'left(1) = 1
A'high(2) = 31	B'right(2) = 0
A'reverse_range(2) is 0 to 31	B'range(1) is 1 to 10
A'length(2) = 32	B'length(1) = 10
A'ascending(2) = false	B'ascending(1) = true

For all of these attributes, to refer to the first dimension (or if there is only one dimension), we can omit the dimension number in parentheses, for example:

A'low = 1	A'length = 4
B'high = 10	B'length = 10

In the next section, we see how these array attributes may be used to deal with array ports. We will also see, in Chapter 9, how they may be used with subprogram parameters that are arrays. Another major use is in writing for loops to iterate over elements of an array. For example, given an array variable **free_map** that is an array of bits, we can write a for loop to count the number of '1' bits without knowing the actual size of the array:

```
count := 0;
for index in free_map'range loop
    if free_map(index) = '1' then
        count := count + 1;
    end if;
end loop;
```

The 'range and 'reverse_range attributes can be used in any place in a VHDL-AMS model where a range specification is required, as an alternative to specifying the left and right bounds and the range direction. Thus, we may use the attributes in type and subtype definitions, in nature and subnature definitions, in subtype constraints, in for loop parameter specifications, in case statement choices and so on. The advantage of taking this approach is that we can specify the size of the array in one place in the model and in all other places use array attributes. If we need to change the array size later for some reason, we need only change the model in one place.

4.2   Unconstrained Arrays

The array types and natures we have seen so far in this chapter are called *constrained* arrays, since the type or nature definition constrains index values to be within a specific range. VHDL-AMS also allows us to define *unconstrained* array types and natures, in which we just indicate the type of the index values, without specifying bounds. An unconstrained array type definition is described by the alternate syntax rule

```
array_type_definition ⇐
    array ( 〖 type_mark range <> 〗 〖 , ... 〗 )
        of element_subtype_indication
```

Similarly, an unconstrained nature definition is described by the alternate syntax rule

```
array_nature_definition ⇐
    array ( 〖 type_mark range <> 〗 〖 , ... 〗 )
        of element_subnature_indication
```

The symbol "<>", often called "box," can be thought of as a placeholder for the index range, to be filled in later when the type or nature is used. An example of an unconstrained array type declaration is

type sample **is array** (natural **range** <>) **of** integer;

An example of an unconstrained array nature is

nature electrical_vector **is array** (natural **range** <>) **of** electrical;

An important point to understand about unconstrained array types is that when we declare an object of such a type, we need to provide a constraint that specifies the index bounds. We can do this in several ways. One way is to provide the constraint when an object is created, for example:

variable short_sample_buf : sample(0 **to** 63);

This indicates that index values for the variable **short_sample_buf** are natural numbers in the ascending range 0 to 63. Another way to specify the constraint is to declare a subtype of the unconstrained array type. Objects can then be created using this subtype, for example:

subtype long_sample **is** sample(0 **to** 255);
variable new_sample_buf, old_sample_buf : long_sample;

These are both examples of a new form of subtype indication that we have not yet seen. The syntax rule is

subtype_indication ⇐ type_mark 〖 (discrete_range 〖 , ₀₀₀ 〗) 〗

The type mark is the name of the unconstrained array type, and the discrete range specifications constrain the index type to a subset of values used to index array elements. Each discrete range must be of the same type as the corresponding index type.

By analogy with types, when we declare a terminal using an unconstrained array nature, we need to provide a constraint for the index bounds of the terminal. We can provide the constraint when we declare the terminal, for example:

terminal local_bus : electrical_vector(15 **downto** 0);

Alternatively, we can declare a subnature of the unconstrained nature and create terminals of the subnature, for example:

subnature long_bus **is** electrical_vector(7 **downto** 0);
terminal remote_bus : long_bus;

When we declare a constant of an unconstrained array type, there is a third way in which we can provide a constraint. We can infer it from the expression used to initialize the constant. If the initialization expression is an array aggregate written using named association, the index values in the aggregate imply the index range of the constant. For example, in the constant declaration

> **constant** lookup_table : sample := (1 => 23, 3 => –16, 2 => 100, 4 => 11);

the index range is 1 to 4.

If the expression is an aggregate using positional association, the index value of the first element is assumed to be the leftmost value in the array subtype. For example, in the constant declaration

> **constant** beep_sample : sample := (127, 63, 0, –63, –127, –63, 0, 63);

the index range is 0 to 7, since the index subtype is **natural**. The index direction is ascending, since **natural** is defined to be an ascending range.

Strings

VHDL-AMS provides a predefined unconstrained array type called **string**, declared as

> **type** string **is array** (positive **range** <>) **of** character;

In principle the index range for a constrained string may be either an ascending or descending range, with any positive integers for the index bounds. However, most applications simply use an ascending range starting from 1. For example:

> **constant** LCD_display_len : positive := 20;
> **subtype** LCD_display_string **is** string(1 **to** LCD_display_len);
> **variable** LCD_display : LCD_display_string := (**others** => ' ');

Real Vectors

VHDL-AMS also provides a predefined unconstrained array type called **real_vector**, declared as

> **type** real_vector **is array** (natural **range** <>) **of** real;

This type can be used to represent collections of continuous data. For example, subtypes for representing a set of gains for a set of amplifiers might be declared as

> **subtype** gains **is** real_vector(15 **downto** 0);

Alternatively, we can supply the constraint for a real vector when an object is declared, for example:

> **quantity** max_temperatures : real_vector(1 **to** 10);

Bit Vectors

VHDL-AMS provides a further predefined unconstrained array type called bit_vector, declared as

    type bit_vector **is array** (natural **range** <>) **of** bit;

This type can be used to represent words of data at the architectural level of modeling. For example, subtypes for representing bytes of data in a little-endian processor might be declared as

    subtype byte **is** bit_vector(7 **downto** 0);

Alternatively, we can supply the constraint when an object is declared, for example:

    variable channel_busy_register : bit_vector(1 **to** 4);

Standard-Logic Arrays

The standard-logic package std_logic_1164 provides an unconstrained array type for vectors of standard-logic values. It is declared as

    type std_ulogic_vector **is array** (natural **range** <>) **of** std_ulogic;

This type can be used in a way similar to bit vectors, but provides more detail in representing the electrical levels used in a design. We can define subtypes of the standard-logic vector type, for example:

    subtype std_ulogic_word **is** std_ulogic_vector(0 **to** 31);

Or we can directly create an object of the standard-logic vector type:

    signal csr_offset : std_ulogic_vector(2 **downto** 1);

String and Bit-String Literals

In Chapter 1, we saw that a string literal may be used to write a value representing a sequence of characters. We can use a string literal in place of an array aggregate for a value of type **string**. For example, we can initialize a string constant as follows:

    constant ready_message : string := "Ready   ";

We can also use string literals for any other one-dimensional array type whose elements are of an enumeration type that includes characters. The IEEE standard-logic array type **std_ulogic_vector** is an example. Thus we could declare and initialize a variable as follows:

> **variable** current_test : std_ulogic_vector(0 **to** 13) := "ZZZZZZZZZZ----";

In Chapter 1 we also saw bit-string literals as a way of writing a sequence of bit values. Bit strings can be used in place of array aggregates to write values of bit-vector types. For example, the variable **channel_busy_register** defined above may be initialized with an assignment:

> channel_busy_register := b"0000";

We can also use bit-string literals for other one-dimensional array types whose elements are of an enumeration type that includes the characters '0' and '1'. Each character in the bit-string literal represents one, three or four successive elements of the array value, depending on whether the base specified in the literal is binary, octal or hexadecimal. Again, using **std_ulogic_vector** as an example type, we can write a constant declaration using a bit-string literal:

> **constant** all_ones : std_ulogic_vector(15 **downto** 0) := X"FFFF";

Unconstrained Array Ports

An important use of an unconstrained array type or nature is to specify the type of an array port. This use allows us to write an entity interface in a general way, so that it can connect to array signals, quantities or terminals of any size or with any range of index values. When we instantiate the entity, the index bounds of the array signal, quantity or terminal connected to the port are used as the bounds of the port.

Example   Suppose we wish to model a family of and gates, each with a different number of inputs. We declare the entity interface as shown in Figure 4-5. The input port is of the unconstrained type **bit_vector**. The architecture body includes a process that is sensitive to changes on the input port. When any element changes, the process performs a logical and operation across the input array. It uses the **'range** attribute to determine the index range of the array, since the index range is not known until the entity is instantiated.

FIGURE 4-5

```
entity and_multiple is
    port ( i : in bit_vector;  y : out bit );
end entity and_multiple;
```

```
architecture behavioral of and_multiple is
begin
    and_reducer : process ( i ) is
        variable result : bit;
    begin
        result := '1';
        for index in i'range loop
            result := result and i(index);
        end loop;
        y <= result;
    end process and_reducer;
end architecture behavioral;
```

An entity and architecture body for an and gate with an unconstrained array input port.

To illustrate the use of the multiple-input gate entity, suppose we have the following signals:

```
signal count_value : bit_vector(7 downto 0);
signal terminal_count : bit;
```

We instantiate the entity, connecting its input port to the bit-vector signal:

```
tc_gate : entity work.and_multiple(behavioral)
    port map ( i => count_value, y => terminal_count);
```

For this instance, the input port is constrained by the index range of the signal. The instance acts as an eight-input and gate.

4.3   Array Operations and Referencing

Although an array is a collection of values, much of the time we operate on arrays one element at a time, using the operators described in Chapter 2. However, if we are working with one-dimensional arrays of scalar values, we can use some of the operators to operate on whole arrays, combining elements in a pairwise fashion.

First, the logical operators (**and, or, nand, nor, xor** and **xnor**) can be applied to two one-dimensional arrays of bit or Boolean elements. The operands must be of the same length and type, and the result is computed by applying the operator to matching elements from each array to produce an array of the same length. Elements are matched starting from the leftmost position in each array. An element at a given position from the left in one array is matched with the element at the same position from the left in the other array. The operator **not** can also be applied to a single array of bit or Boolean elements, with the result being an array of the same length and type as the operand. The following declarations and statements illustrate this use of logical operators when applied to bit vectors:

```
subtype pixel_row is bit_vector (0 to 15);
variable current_row, mask : pixel_row;

current_row := current_row and not mask;
current_row := current_row xor X"FFFF";
```

Second, the shift operators introduced in Chapter 2 (**sll**, **srl**, **sla**, **sra**, **rol** and **ror**) can be used with a one-dimensional array of bit or Boolean values as the left operand and an integer value as the right operand. A shift-left logical operation shifts the elements in the array n places to the left (n being the right operand), filling in the vacated positions with '0' or **false** and discarding the leftmost n elements. If n is negative, the elements are instead shifted to the right. Some examples are

```
B"10001010" sll 3  =  B"01010000"      B"10001010" sll –2  =  B"00100010"
```

The shift-right logical operation similarly shifts elements n positions to the right for positive n, or to the left for negative n, for example:

```
B"10010111" srl 2  =  B"00100101"      B"10010111" srl –6  =  B"11000000"
```

The next two shift operations, shift-left arithmetic and shift-right arithmetic, operate similarly, but instead of filling vacated positions with '0' or **false**, they fill them with a copy of the element at the end being vacated, for example:

```
B"01001011" sra 3  =  B"00001001"      B"10010111" sra 3  =  B"11110010"
B"00001100" sla 2  =  B"00110000"      B"00010001" sla 2  =  B"01000111"
```

As with the logical shifts, if n is negative, the shifts work in the opposite direction, for example:

```
B"00010001" sra –2  =  B"01000111"    B"00110000" sla –2  =  B"00001100"
```

A rotate-left operation moves the elements of the array n places to the left, transferring the n elements from the left end of the array around to the vacated positions at the right end. A rotate-right operation does the same, but in the opposite direction. As with the shift operations, a negative right argument reverses the direction of rotation. Some examples are

```
B"10010011" rol 1  =  B"00100111"      B"10010011" ror 1  =  B"11001001"
```

Relational operators form the third group of operations that can be applied to one-dimensional arrays. The array elements can be of any discrete type. The two operands need not be of the same length, so long as they have the same element type. The way these operators work can be most easily seen when they are applied to strings of characters, in which case they are compared according to case-sensitive dictionary ordering.

To see how dictionary comparison can be generalized to one-dimensional arrays of other element types, let us consider the "<" operator applied to two arrays **a** and **b**. If both **a** and **b** have length 0, **a** < **b** is false. If **a** has length 0, and **b** has non-zero length, then **a** < **b**. Alternatively, if both **a** and **b** have non-zero length, then **a** < **b** if a(1) < b(1), or if a(1) = b(1) and the rest of **a** < the rest of **b**. In the remaining case, where **a** has non-zero length and **b** has length 0, **a** < **b** is false. Comparison using the other relational operators is performed analogously.

The one remaining operator that can be applied to one-dimensional arrays is the concatenation operator ("&"), which joins two array values end to end. For example, when applied to bit vectors, it produces a new bit vector with length equal to the sum of the lengths of the two operands. Thus, b"0000" & b"1111" produces b"0000_1111".

The concatenation operator can be applied to two operands, one of which is an array and the other of which is a single scalar element. It can also be applied to two scalar values to produce an array of length 2. Some examples are

```
"abc" & 'd'  =  "abcd"
'w' & "xyz"  =  "wxyz"
'a' & 'b'  =  "ab"
```

Array Slices

Often we want to refer to a contiguous subset of elements of an array, but not the whole array. We can do this using *slice* notation, in which we specify the left and right index values of part of an array object. For example, given arrays **a1**, **a2** and **a3** declared as follows:

```
type array1 is array (1 to 100) of integer;
type array2 is array (100 downto 1) of integer;
type array3 is array (10 downto 1) of real tolerance "default";

variable a1 : array1;
variable a2 : array2;
quantity a3 : array3;
```

we can refer to the array slice **a1(11 to 20)**, which is an array of 10 elements having the indices 11 to 20. Similarly, the slice **a2(50 downto 41)** is an array of 10 elements but with a descending index range. The slice **a3(5 downto 1)** is an array of 5 elements, also with a descending index range. Note that the slices **a1(10 to 1)**, **a2(1 downto 10)** and **a3(1 downto 10)** are *null* slices, since the index ranges specified are null. Furthermore, the ranges specified in the slice must have the same direction as the original array. Thus we may not legally write **a1(10 downto 1)**, **a2(1 to 10)** or **a3(1 to 10)**.

Example   Figure 4-6 is a behavioral model for a byte-swapper that has one input port and one output port, each of which is a bit vector of subtype **halfword**, declared as follows:

>   **subtype** halfword **is** bit_vector(0 **to** 15);

The process in the architecture body swaps the two bytes of input with each other. It shows how the slice notation can be used for signal array objects in signal assignment statements.

FIGURE 4-6

```
entity byte_swap is
    port (input : in halfword;  output : out halfword);
end entity byte_swap;
```

```
architecture behavior of byte_swap is
begin
    swap : process (input)
    begin
        output(8 to 15) <= input(0 to 7);
        output(0 to 7) <= input(8 to 15);
    end process swap;
end architecture behavior;
```

An entity and architecture body for a byte-swapper module.

Array Type Conversions

In Chapter 2 we introduced the idea of type conversion of a numeric value to another value of a closely related type. A value of an array type can also be converted to a value of another array type, provided both array types have the same element type, the same number of dimensions and index types that can be type converted. The type conversion simply produces a new array value of the specified type, with each index converted to the value in the corresponding position of the new type's index range.

To illustrate the idea of type-converting array values, suppose we have the following declarations in a model:

>   **subtype** name **is** string(1 **to** 20);
>   **type** display_string **is** array (integer **range** 0 **to** 19) **of** character;

```
variable item_name : name;
variable display : display_string;
```

We cannot directly assign the value of **item_name** to **display**, since the types are different. However, we can using a type conversion:

```
display := display_string(item_name);
```

This produces a new array, with the left element having index 0 and the right element having index 19, which is compatible with the assignment target.

A common case in which we do not need a type conversion is the assigment of an array value of one subtype to an array object of a different subtype of the same base type. This occurs where the index ranges of the target and the operand have different bounds or directions. VHDL-AMS automatically includes an implicit subtype conversion in the assignment. For example, given the subtypes and variables declared thus:

```
subtype big_endian_upper_halfword is bit_vector(0 to 15);
subtype little_endian_upper_halfword is bit_vector(31 downto 16);

variable big : big_endian_upper_halfword;
variable little : little_endian_upper_halfword;
```

we could make the following assignments without including explicit type conversions:

```
big := little;
little := big;
```

4.4   Records

In this section, we discuss the second class of composite types and natures, *records*. We start with record types, and return to record natures subsequently, since there are some significant differences between them. A value of a record type comprises elements that may be of different types from one another. Each element is identified by a name, which is unique within the record. This name is used to select the element from the record value. The syntax rule for a record type definition is

```
record_type_definition ⇐
    record
        ( identifier { , ... } : subtype_indication ; )
        { ... }
    end record [ identifier ]
```

Each of the names in the identifier lists declares an element of the indicated type or subtype. Recall that the curly brackets in the syntax rule indicate that the enclosed part may be repeated indefinitely. Thus, we can include several elements of different types within the record. The identifier at the end of the record type definition, if included, must repeat the name of the record type.

The following is an example record type declaration and variable declarations using the record type:

```
type time_stamp is record
        seconds : integer range 0 to 59;
        minutes : integer range 0 to 59;
        hours : integer range 0 to 23;
    end record time_stamp;
variable sample_time, current_time : time_stamp;
```

Whole record values can be assigned using assignment statements, for example:

```
sample_time := current_time;
```

We can also refer to an element in a record using a *selected name,* for example:

```
sample_hour := sample_time.hours;
```

In the expression on the right of the assignment symbol, the prefix before the dot names the record value, and the suffix after the dot selects the element from the record. A selected name can also be used on the left side of an assignment to identify a record element to be modified, for example:

```
current_time.seconds := clock mod 60;
```

Example   In the early stages of designing a new instruction set for a CPU, we don't want to commit to an encoding of opcodes and operands within an instruction word. Instead we use a record type to represent the components of an instruction. We illustrate this in Figure 4-7, an outline of a system-level behavioral model of a CPU and memory that uses record types to represent instructions and data.

FIGURE 4-7

```
architecture system_level of computer is
    type opcodes is (add, sub, addu, subu, jmp, breq, brne, ld, st, ...);
    type reg_number is range 0 to 31;
    constant r0 : reg_number := 0;  constant r1 : reg_number := 1;  ...

    type instruction is record
            opcode : opcodes;
            source_reg1, source_reg2, dest_reg : reg_number;
            displacement : integer;
        end record instruction;
```

```
        type word is record
                instr : instruction;
                data : bit_vector(31 downto 0);
            end record word;
    signal address : natural;
    signal read_word, write_word : word;
    signal mem_read, mem_write : bit := '0';
    signal mem_ready : bit := '0';
begin
    cpu : process is
        variable instr_reg : instruction;
        variable PC : natural;
            ...       -- other declarations for register file, etc.
    begin
        address <= PC;
        mem_read <= '1';
        wait until mem_ready = '1';
        instr_reg := read_word.instr;
        mem_read <= '0';
        PC := PC + 4;
        case instr_reg.opcode is      -- execute the instruction
                ...
        end case;
    end process cpu;
    memory : process is
        subtype address_range is natural range 0 to 2**14 - 1;
        type memory_array is array (address_range) of word;
        variable store : memory_array :=
            ( 0  => ( ( ld, r0, r0, r2, 40 ), X"00000000" ),
              1  => ( ( breq, r2, r0, r0, 5 ), X"00000000" ),
                ...
              40 => ( ( nop, r0, r0, r0, 0 ), X"FFFFFFFE"),
              others => ( ( nop, r0, r0, r0, 0 ), X"00000000") );
    begin
        ...
    end process memory;
end architecture system_level;
```

An outline of a behavioral architecture body for a computer system comprising a CPU and a memory, using record values to represent instructions and data values.

The record type **instruction** represents the information to be included in each instruction of a program and includes the opcode, source and destination register numbers and a displacement. The record type **word** represents a word stored in memory. Since a word might represent an instruction or data, elements are included in the record for both possibilities. Unlike many conventional programming languages, VHDL-AMS does not provide variant parts in record values. The record type **word** illustrates how composite data values can include elements that are themselves composite values, provided the included elements are of a constrained subtype. The signals in the model are used for the address, data and control connections between the CPU and the memory.

Within the CPU process the variable **instr_reg** represents the instruction register containing the current instruction to be executed. The process fetches a word from memory and copies the instruction element from the record into the instruction register. It then uses the opcode field of the value to determine how to execute the instruction.

The memory process contains a variable that is an array of word records representing the memory storage. The array is initialized with a program and data. Words representing instructions are initialized with a record aggregate containing an instruction record aggregate and a bit vector, which is ignored. Similarly, words representing data are initialized with an aggregate containing an instruction aggregate, which is ignored, and the bit vector of data.

We now return to record natures. The syntax rule for a record nature definition is

```
record_nature_definition ⇐
    record
        ⟨ identifier ⟨ , ... ⟩ : subnature_indication ; ⟩
        ⟨ ... ⟩
    end record ⟦ identifier ⟧
```

On the surface, this appears analogous to a record type definition. However, unlike elements of record types, the elements of a record nature cannot be of arbitrary different types. All of the scalar sub-elements of the record nature's elements must be of the same scalar nature. For example, we can declare a record nature as follows:

```
nature electrical_bus is record
        strobe : electrical;
        bus_lines : electrical_vector(0 to 15);
    end record electrical_bus;
```

since the element **strobe** and the scalar sub-elements of **bus_lines** are all of the scalar nature **electrical**. We could not, however, declare a record nature with elements of natures **electrical** and **thermal**.

Provided we work within this restriction on the element natures, we otherwise use record natures analogously with record types. For example, we can declare terminals of the **electrical_bus** nature as follows:

```
terminal address_bus, data_bus : electrical_bus;
```

Analogously with array natures, the through and across branch types of a record nature are themselves record types with elements corresponding to those of the record nature. So if we declare branch quantities:

quantity data_voltages **across** data_currents **through** data_bus;

the quantity **data_voltages** is a record containing a **strobe** element of type **voltage** and a **bus_lines** element that is an array of 16 **voltage** elements. Similarly, the quantity **data_currents** is a record containing a **strobe** element of type **current** and a **bus_lines** element that is an array of 16 **current** elements.

Record Aggregates

We can use a record aggregate to write a literal value of a record type—for example, to initialize a record variable or constant. Using a record aggregate is analogous to using an array aggregate for writing a literal value of an array type (see page 113). A record aggregate is formed by writing a list of the elements enclosed in parentheses. An aggregate using positional association lists the elements in the same order as they appear in the record type declaration. For example, given the record type **time_stamp** shown above, we can initialize a constant as follows:

constant midday : time_stamp := (0, 0, 12);

We can also use named association, in which we identify each element in the aggregate by its name. The order of elements identified using named association does not affect the aggregate value. The example above could be rewritten as

constant midday : time_stamp := (hours => 12, minutes => 0, seconds => 0);

Unlike array aggregates, we can mix positional and named association in record aggregates, provided all of the named elements follow any positional elements. We can also use the symbols "|" and **others** when writing choices. Here are some more examples, using the types **instruction** and **time_stamp** declared above:

```
constant nop_instr : instruction :=
        ( opcode => addu,
          source_reg1 | source_reg2 | dest_reg => 0,
          displacement => 0 );
variable latest_event : time_stamp := (others => 0);      -- initially midnight
```

Note that unlike array aggregates, we can't use a range of values to identify elements in a record aggregate, since the elements are identified by names, not indexed by a discrete range.

Exercises

1. [❶ 4.1] Write an array type declaration for an array of 30 integers, and a variable declaration for a variable of the type. Write a for loop to calculate the average of the array elements.

2. [❶ 4.1] Write an array type declaration for an array of bit values, indexed by standard-logic values. Then write a declaration for a constant, **std_ulogic_to_bit**, of this type that maps standard-logic values to the corresponding bit value. (Assume unknown values map to '0'.) Given a standard-logic vector **v1** and a bit-vector variable **v2**, both indexed from 0 to 15, write a for loop that uses the constant **std_ulogic_to_bit** to map the standard-logic vector to the bit vector.

3. [❶ 4.1] Write declarations for an array nature representing four electrical nodes. Write declarations for two composite terminals of the array nature and for branch quantities representing the voltage and current between the terminals.

4. [❶ 4.1] The example on page 112 shows declarations for types **point** and **matrix** and shows an algorithm for coordinate transformation. Write a constant declaration for a matrix to scale a point by a factor of 2. The matrix has the value 2.0 for each element on the diagonal and zero elsewhere. Write a free quantity declaration for two points **p** and **q** and simultaneous statements to apply the transform matrix to **p** to determine the value of **q**. Hint: write a separate simultaneous statement for each element of **q**.

5. [❶ 4.1] Suppose we wish to model the electrical connections in a plug that connects a trailer's lights to the electrical system of an automobile. There are connections for tail lights, brake lights, left and right turning indicators, reversing light, auxiliary light, negative return and chassis ground. Write an enumeration type for these connections and a declaration of an array nature indexed by the enumeration type.

6. [❶ 4.1] The data on a diskette is arranged in 18 sectors per track, 80 tracks per side and two sides per diskette. A computer system maintains a map of free sectors. Write a three-dimensional array type declaration to represent such a map, with a '1' element representing a free sector and a '0' element representing an occupied sector. Write a set of nested for loops to scan a variable of this type to find the location of the first free sector.

7. [❶ 4.2] Write a declaration for a subtype of **std_ulogic_vector**, representing a byte. Declare a constant of this subtype, with each element having the value 'Z'.

8. [❶ 4.2] Write a for loop to count the number of '1' elements in a bit-vector variable **v**.

9. [❶ 4.2] Write a declaration for a subtype of **real_vector** representing an (x, y, z) coordinate. Declare a free quantity of this subtype to represent the spacial position of a robot hand. Initialize the quantity to the origin (all coordinate elements being zero).

10. [❶ 4.3] An 8-bit vector **v1** representing a two's-complement binary integer can be sign-extended into a 32-bit vector **v2** by copying it to the leftmost eight positions of **v2**, then performing an arithmetic right shift to move the eight bits to the right-most eight positions. Write variable assignment statements that use slicing and shift operations to express this procedure.

11. [❶ 4.4] Write a record type declaration for a test stimulus record containing a stimulus bit vector of three bits, a delay value and an expected response bit vector of eight bits.

12. [❷ 4.1] Develop a model for a register file that stores 16 words of 32 bits each. The register file has data input and output ports, each of which is a 32-bit word; read-address and write-address ports, each of which is an integer in the range 0 to 15; and a write-enable port of type **bit**. The data output port reflects the content of the location whose address is given by the read-address port. When the write-enable port is '1', the input data is written to the register file at the location whose address is given by the write-address port.

13. [❷ 4.1] Develop a model for a priority encoder with a 16-element bit-vector input port, an output port of type **natural** that encodes the index of the leftmost '1' value in the input and an output of type **bit** that indicates whether any input elements are '1'.

14. [❷ 4.1] Use the nature declaration from Exercise 3 in a model of a quad-amplifier module. The amplifiers should all have a fixed voltage gain of 10.

15. [❷ 4.1] Develop a model of a hex-comparator module (a module comprising six comparators). The comparators have independent plus terminal inputs and standard-logic outputs, but have a common minus terminal. Use an array nature for the plus terminal inputs and a standard-logic vector for the digital outputs.

16. [❷ 4.2] Write a package that declares an unconstrained array type whose elements are integers. Use the type in an entity declaration for a module that finds the maximum of a set of numbers. The entity has an input port of the unconstrained array type and an integer output. Develop a behavioral architecture body for the entity. How should the module behave if the actual array associated with the input port is empty (i.e., of zero length)?

17. [❷ 4.2/4.3] Develop a model for a general and-or-invert gate, with two standard-logic vector input ports **a** and **b** and a standard-logic output port **y**. The output of the gate is

$$\overline{a_0 \cdot b_0 + a_1 \cdot b_1 + \ldots + a_{n-1} \cdot b_{n-1}}$$

18. [❷ 4.4] Develop a model of a 3-to-8 decoder and a test bench to exercise the decoder. In the test bench, declare the record type that you wrote for Exercise 11 and a constant array of test record values. Initialize the array to a set of test vectors for the decoder, and use the vectors to perform the test.

chapter five

Digital Modeling Constructs

The description of a module in a digital system can be divided into two facets: the external view and the internal view. The external view describes the interface to the module, including the number and types of inputs and outputs. The internal view describes how the module implements its function. In VHDL-AMS, we can separate the description of a module into an entity declaration, *which describes the external interface, and one or more* architecture bodies, *which describe alternative internal implementations. These were introduced in Chapter 1. In this chapter, we discuss the general aspects of entity declarations and architecture bodies that are common to both digital and analog modeling, and then focus on the features of VHDL-AMS that are specific to digital modeling.*

5.1   **Entity Declarations**

Let us first examine the syntax rules for an entity declaration and then show some examples. We start with a simplified description of entity declarations and move on to
a full description later in this chapter. The syntax rules for this simplified form of entity declaration are

> entity_declaration ⇐
>   **entity** identifier **is**
>   ⟦ **port** (*port*_interface_list) ; ⟧
>   ❴ entity_declarative_item ❵
>   **end** ⟦ **entity** ⟧ ⟦ identifier ⟧ ;
>
> interface_list ⇐
>   (⟦ **signal** ⟧ identifier ❴ , ₀₀₀ ❵ : ⟦ mode ⟧ subtype_indication
>   ⟦ := expression ⟧) ❴ ; ₀₀₀ ❵
>
> mode ⇐ **in** ⃒ **out** ⃒ **inout**

The identifier in an entity declaration names the module so that it can be referred
to later. If the identifier is included at the end of the declaration, it must repeat the
name of the entity. The port clause names each of the *ports,* which together form the
interface to the entity. We can think of ports as being analogous to the pins of a circuit; they are the means by which information is fed into and out of the circuit. In
general, a port can be a digital signal or an analog quantity or terminal. We confine
our attention to signal ports in this chapter, and return to quantity and terminal ports
in Chapter 6. In VHDL-AMS, each signal port of an entity has a *type,* which specifies
the kind of information that can be communicated, and a *mode,* which specifies
whether information flows into or out from the entity through the port. These aspects
of type and direction are in keeping with the strong typing philosophy of VHDL-AMS,
which helps us avoid erroneous circuit descriptions. A simple example of an entity
declaration is

> **entity** adder **is**
>   **port** (a : **in** word;
>   b : **in** word;
>   sum : **out** word);
> **end entity** adder;

This example describes an entity named **adder**, with two input ports and one output port, all of type **word**, which we assume is defined elsewhere. By default, ports
are signals, so we have omitted the keyword **signal** in this example. We can list the
ports in any order; we do not have to put inputs before outputs. Also, we can include
a list of ports of the same mode and type instead of writing them out individually.
Thus the above declaration could equally well be written as follows:

```
entity adder is
    port (    a, b : in word;
              sum : out word );
end entity adder;
```

In this example we have seen input and output ports. We can also have bidirectional ports, with mode **inout**. These can be used to model devices that alternately sense and drive data through a pin. Such models must deal with the possibility of more than one connected device driving a given signal at the same time. VHDL-AMS provides a mechanism for this, *signal resolution,* which we will return to in Chapter 15.

The similarity between the description of a port in an entity declaration and the declaration of a variable may be apparent. This similarity is not coincidental, and we can extend the analogy by specifying a default value on a port description, for example:

```
entity and_or_inv is
    port ( a1, a2, b1, b2 : in bit := '1';
           y : out bit );
end entity and_or_inv;
```

The default value, in this case the '1' on the input ports, indicates the value each port should assume if it is left unconnected in an enclosing model. We can think of it as describing the value that the port "floats to." On the other hand, if the port is used, the default value is ignored. We say more about use of default values when we look at the execution of a model.

Another point to note about entity declarations is that the port clause is optional. So we can write an entity declaration such as

```
entity top_level is
end entity top_level;
```

which describes a completely self-contained module. As the name in this example implies, this kind of module usually represents the top level of a design hierarchy.

Finally, if we return to the first syntax rule on page 136, we see that we can include declarations of items within an entity declaration. These include declarations of constants, types, signals and other kinds of items that we will see later in this chapter. The items can be used in all architecture bodies corresponding to the entity. Thus, it makes sense to include declarations that are relevant to the entity and all possible implementations. Anything that is part of only one particular implementation should instead be declared within the corresponding architecture body.

Example   Suppose we are designing an embedded controller using a microprocessor with a program stored in a read-only memory (ROM). The program to be stored in the ROM is fixed, but we still need to model the ROM at different levels of detail. We can include declarations that describe the program in the entity declaration for the

ROM, as shown in Figure 5-1. These declarations are not directly accessible to a user of the ROM entity, but serve to document the contents of the ROM. Each architecture body corresponding to the entity can use the constant **program** to initialize whatever structure it uses internally to implement the ROM.

FIGURE 5-1

```
entity program_ROM is
    port ( address : in std_ulogic_vector(14 downto 0);
           data : out std_ulogic_vector(7 downto 0);
           enable : in std_ulogic );

    subtype instruction_byte is bit_vector(7 downto 0);
    type program_array is array (0 to 2**14 – 1) of instruction_byte;
    constant program : program_array
        := ( X"32", X"3F", X"03",          -- LDA  $3F03
             X"71", X"23",                 -- BLT   $23
             ...
           );
end entity program_ROM;
```

An entity declaration for a ROM, including declarations that describe the program contained in it.

5.2 Architecture Bodies

The internal operation of a module is described by an architecture body. An architecture body for a digital system generally applies some operations to values on input ports, generating values to be assigned to output ports. The operations can be described either by processes, which contain sequential statements operating on values, or by a collection of components representing sub-circuits. Where the operation requires generation of intermediate values, these can be described using *signals,* analogous to the internal wires of a module. The syntax rule for architecture bodies shows the general outline:

```
architecture_body ⇐
    architecture identifier of entity_name is
        ⟦ block_declarative_item ⟧
    begin
        ⟦ concurrent_statement ⟧
    end ⟦ architecture ⟧ ⟦ identifier ⟧ ;
```

The identifier names this particular architecture body, and the entity name specifies which module has its operation described by this architecture body. If the identifier is included at the end of the architecture body, it must repeat the name of the architecture body. There may be several different architecture bodies corresponding to a single entity, each describing an alternative way of implementing the module's operation. The block declarative items in an architecture body are declarations needed to implement the operations. The items may include type and constant declarations, signal declarations and other kinds of declarations that we will look at in later chapters.

Concurrent Statements

The *concurrent statements* in an architecture body describe the module's operation. One form of concurrent statement, which we have already seen, is a process statement. Putting this together with the rule for writing architecture bodies, we can look at a simple example of an architecture body corresponding to the **adder** entity on page 136:

```
architecture abstract of adder is
begin
    add_a_b : process (a, b) is
    begin
        sum <= a + b;
    end process add_a_b;
end architecture abstract;
```

The architecture body is named **abstract**, and it contains a process **add_a_b**, which describes the operation of the entity. The process assumes that the operator **+** is defined for the type **word**, the type of **a** and **b**. We will see in Chapter 9 how such a definition may be written. We could also envisage additional architecture bodies describing the adder in different ways, provided they all conform to the external interface laid down by the entity declaration.

We have looked at processes first because they are the most fundamental form of concurrent statement for digital modeling. All other forms can ultimately be reduced to one or more processes. Concurrent statements are so called because conceptually they can be activated and perform their actions together, that is, concurrently. Contrast this with the sequential statements inside a process, which are executed one after another. Concurrency is useful for modeling the way real circuits behave. If we have two gates whose inputs change, each evaluates its new output independently of the other. There is no inherent sequencing governing the order in which they are evaluated. We look at process statements in more detail in Section 5.3. Then, in Section 5.4, we look at another form of concurrent statement, the component instantiation statement, used to describe how a module is composed of interconnected submodules.

Signal Declarations

When we need to provide internal signals in an architecture body, we must define them using *signal declarations*. The syntax for a signal declaration is very similar to that for a variable declaration:

signal_declaration ⇐
    signal identifier ⟦ , ... ⟧ : subtype_indication ⟦ := expression ⟧ ;

This declaration simply names each signal, specifies its type and optionally includes an initial value for all signals declared by the declaration.

Example   Figure 5-2 is an example of an architecture body for the entity **and_or_inv**, defined on page 137. The architecture body includes declarations of some signals that are internal to the architecture body. They can be used by processes within the architecture body but are not accessible outside, since a user of the module need not be concerned with the internal details of its implementation. Values are assigned to signals using signal assignment statements within processes. Signals can be sensed by processes to read their values.

FIGURE 5·2

```
architecture primitive of and_or_inv is
     signal and_a, and_b : bit;
     signal or_a_b : bit;
begin
     and_gate_a : process (a1, a2) is
     begin
          and_a <= a1 and a2;
     end process and_gate_a;
     and_gate_b : process (b1, b2) is
     begin
          and_b <= b1 and b2;
     end process and_gate_b;
     or_gate : process (and_a, and_b) is
     begin
          or_a_b <= and_a or and_b;
     end process or_gate;
     inv : process (or_a_b) is
     begin
          y <= not or_a_b;
     end process inv;
```

end architecture primitive;

An architecture body corresponding to the **and_or_inv** *entity shown on page 137.*

An important point illustrated by this example is that the ports of the entity are also visible to processes inside the architecture body and are used in the same way as signals. This corresponds to our view of ports as external pins of a circuit: from the internal point of view, a pin is just a wire with an external connection. So it makes sense for VHDL-AMS to treat signal ports like signals inside an architecture of the entity.

5.3   Digital Behavioral Descriptions

At the most fundamental level, the digital behavior of a module is described by signal assignment statements within processes. We can think of a process as the basic unit of digital behavioral description. A process is executed in response to changes of values of signals and uses the present values of signals it reads to determine new values for other signals. A signal assignment is a sequential statement and thus can only appear within a process. In this section, we look in detail at the interaction between signals and processes.

Signal Assignment

In all of the digital examples we have looked at so far, we have used a simple form of signal assignment statement. Each assignment just provides a new value for a signal. The value is determined by evaluating an expression, the result of which must match the type of the signal. What we have not yet addressed is the issue of timing: when does the signal take on the new value? This is fundamental to modeling hardware, in which events occur over time. First, let us look at the syntax for a basic signal assignment statement in a process:

signal_assignment_statement ⇐
　　⟦ label : ⟧ name <= ⟦ delay_mechanism ⟧ waveform ;

waveform ⇐ (*value*_expression ⟦ **after** *time*_expression ⟧) { , ₀₀₀ }

The optional label allows us to identify the statement. We will discuss labeled statements in Chapter 22. The syntax rules tell us that we can specify a delay mechanism, which we come to soon, and one or more waveform elements, each consisting of a new value and an optional delay time. It is these delay times in a signal assignment that allow us to specify when the new value should be applied. For example, consider the following assignment:

```
y <= not or_a_b after 5 ns;
```

This specifies that the signal **y** is to take on the new value at a time 5 ns later than that at which the statement executes. The delay can be read in one of two ways, depending on whether the model is being used purely for its descriptive value or for simulation. In the first case, the delay can be considered in an abstract sense as a specification of the module's propagation delay: whenever the input changes, the output is updated 5 ns later. In the second case, it can be considered in an operational sense, with reference to a host machine simulating operation of the module by executing the model. Thus if the above assignment is executed at time 250 ns, and **or_a_b** has the value '1' at that time, then the signal **y** will take on the value '0' at time 255 ns. Note that the statement itself executes in zero modeled time.

The time dimension referred to when the model is executed is *simulation time,* that is, the time in which the circuit being modeled is deemed to operate. This is distinct from real execution time on the host machine running a simulation. For digital systems or subsystems, we measure simulation time starting from zero at the start of execution and increasing in discrete steps as events occur in the model. Not surprisingly, this technique is called *discrete event simulation.* In contrast, we simulate analog systems or subsystems using continuous time. We discuss analog simulation and its relation to digital simulation within VHDL-AMS in Chapter 6. A discrete event simulator must have a simulation time clock, and when a signal assignment statement is executed, the delay specified is added to the current simulation time to determine when the new value is to be applied to the signal. We say that the signal assignment schedules a *transaction* for the signal, where the transaction consists of the new value and the simulation time at which it is to be applied. When simulation time advances to the time at which a transaction is scheduled, the signal is updated with the new value. We say that the signal is *active* during that simulation cycle. If the new value is not equal to the old value it replaces on a signal, we say an *event* occurs on the signal. The importance of this distinction is that processes respond to events on signals, not to transactions.

The syntax rules for signal assignments show that we can schedule a number of transactions for a signal, to be applied after different delays. For example, a clock driver process might execute the following assignment to generate the next two edges of a clock signal (assuming **T_pw** is a constant that represents the clock pulse width):

```
clk <= '1' after T_pw, '0' after 2*T_pw;
```

If this statement is executed at simulation time 50 ns and **T_pw** has the value 10 ns, one transaction is scheduled for time 60 ns to set **clk** to '1', and a second transaction is scheduled for time 70 ns to set **clk** to '0'. If we assume that **clk** has the value '0' when the assignment is executed, both transactions produce events on **clk**.

This signal assignment statement shows that when more than one transaction is included, the delays are all measured from the current time, not the time in the previous element. Furthermore, the transactions in the list must have strictly increasing delays, so that the list reads in the order that the values will be applied to the signal.

Example We can write a process declaration for a clock generator using the above signal assignment statement to generate a symmetrical clock signal with pulse width T_pw. The difficulty is to get the process to execute regularly every clock cycle. One way to do this is by making it resume whenever the clock changes and scheduling the next two transitions when it changes to '0'. This approach is shown in Figure 5-3.

FIGURE 5-3

```
clock_gen : process (clk) is
begin
    if clk = '0' then
        clk <= '1' after T_pw, '0' after 2*T_pw;
    end if;
end process clock_gen;
```

A process that generates a symmetric clock waveform.

Since a process is the basic unit of a digital behavioral description, it makes intuitive sense to be allowed to include more than one signal assignment statement for a given signal within a single process. We can think of this as describing the different ways in which a signal's value can be generated by the process at different times.

Example We can write a process that models a two-input multiplexer as shown in Figure 5-4. The value of the **sel** port is used to select which signal assignment to execute to determine the output value.

FIGURE 5-4

```
mux : process (a, b, sel) is
begin
    case sel is
        when '0' =>
            z <= a after prop_delay;
        when '1' =>
            z <= b after prop_delay;
    end case;
end process mux;
```

A process that models a two-input multiplexer.

We say that a process defines a *driver* for a signal if and only if it contains at least one signal assignment statement for the signal. So this example defines a driver for the signal **z**. If a process contains signal assignment statements for several signals, it defines drivers for each of those signals. A driver is a *source* for a signal in that it provides values to be applied to the signal. An important rule to remember is that for normal signals, there may only be one source. This means that we cannot write two different processes each containing signal assignment statements for the one signal. If we want to model such things as buses or wired-or signals, we must use a special kind of signal called a *resolved signal,* which we will discuss in Chapter 15.

Signal Attributes

In Chapter 2 we introduced the idea of attributes of types, which give information about allowed values for the types. Then, in Chapter 4, we saw how we could use attributes of array objects to get information about their index ranges. We can also refer to attributes of signals to find information about their history of transactions and events. Given a signal **S**, and a value **T** of type **time**, VHDL-AMS defines the following attributes:

S'delayed(T)	A signal that takes on the same values as **S** but is delayed by time **T**.
S'stable(T)	A Boolean signal that is true if there has been no event on **S** in the time interval **T** up to the current time, otherwise false.
S'quiet(T)	A Boolean signal that is true if there has been no transaction on **S** in the time interval **T** up to the current time, otherwise false.
S'transaction	A signal of type **bit** that changes value from '0' to '1' or vice versa each time there is a transaction on **S**.
S'event	True if there is an event on **S** in the current simulation cycle, false otherwise.
S'active	True if there is a transaction on **S** in the current simulation cycle, false otherwise.
S'last_event	The time interval since the last event on **S**.
S'last_active	The time interval since the last transaction on **S**.
S'last_value	The value of S just before the last event on **S**.
S'ramp(t_rise, t_fall)	A quantity that follows the value of **S** with specified rise and fall times.
S'slew(rising_slope, falling_slope)	A quantity that follows the value of **S** with specified rising and falling slopes.

The 'ramp and 'slew attributes are used in mixed-signal modeling. We return to them in Chapter 6 when we describe quantities in detail. The first three attributes, 'delayed, 'stable and 'quiet, take an optional time parameter. If we omit the parameter, the value 0 fs is assumed. These attributes are often used in checking the timing behavior within a model. For example, we can verify that a signal d meets a minimum setup time requirement of Tsu before a rising edge on a clock clk of type std_ulogic as follows:

```
if clk'event and (clk = '1' or clk = 'H')
        and (clk'last_value = '0' or clk'last_value = 'L') then
    assert d'last_event >= Tsu
        report "Timing error: d changed within setup time of clk";
end if;
```

Similarly, we might check that the pulse width of a clock signal input to a module doesn't exceed a maximum frequency by testing its pulse width:

```
assert (not clk'event) or clk'delayed'last_event >= Tpw_clk
    report "Clock frequency too high";
```

Note that we test the time since the last event on a delayed version of the clock signal. When there is currently an event on a signal, the 'last_event attribute returns the value 0 fs. In this case, we determine the time since the previous event by applying the 'last_event attribute to the signal delayed by 0 fs. We can think of this as being an infinitesimal delay. We will return to this idea later in this chapter, in our discussion of delta delays.

Example   We can use a similar test for the rising edge of a clock signal to model an edge-triggered module, such as a flipflop. The flipflop should load the value of its D input on a rising edge of clk, but asynchronously clear the outputs whenever clr is '1'. The entity declaration and a behavioral architecture body are shown in Figure 5-5.

FIGURE 5-5

```
entity edge_triggered_Dff is
    port ( D : in bit;  clk : in bit;  clr : in bit;
            Q : out bit );
end entity edge_triggered_Dff;
```

```
architecture behavioral of edge_triggered_Dff is
begin
    state_change : process (clk, clr) is
```

(continued on page 146)

(continued from page 145)

```
    begin
        if clr = '1' then
            Q <= '0' after 2 ns;
        elsif clk'event and clk = '1' then
            Q <= D after 2 ns;
        end if;
    end process state_change;
end architecture behavioral;
```

An entity and architecture body for an edge-triggered flipflop, using the 'event *attribute to check for changes on the* clk *signal.*

If the flipflop did not have the asynchronous clear input, the model could have used a simple wait statement such as

wait until clk = '1';

to trigger on a rising edge. However, with the clear input present, the process must be sensitive to changes on both clk and clr at any time. Hence it uses the 'event attribute to distinguish between clk changing to '1' and clr going back to '0' while clk is stable at '1'.

Wait Statements

Now that we have seen how to change the values of signals over time, the next step in behavioral modeling is to specify when processes respond to changes in signal values. This is done using *wait statements*. A wait statement is a sequential statement with the following syntax rule:

wait_statement ⇐
    〖 label : 〗 **wait** 〖 **on** *signal*_name 〖 , ... 〗 〗
                    〖 **until** *boolean*_expression 〗
                    〖 **for** *time_or_real*_expression 〗 ;

The optional label allows us to identify the statement. We will discuss labeled statements in Chapter 22. The purpose of the wait statement is to cause the process that executes the statement to suspend execution. The *sensitivity* clause, *condition* clause and *timeout* clause specify when the process is subsequently to resume execution. We can include any combination of these clauses, or we may omit all three. Let us go through each clause and describe what it specifies.

The sensitivity clause, starting with the word **on**, allows us to specify a list of signals to which the process responds. If we just include a sensitivity clause in a wait statement, the process will resume whenever any one of the listed signals changes value, that is, whenever an event occurs on any of the signals. This style of wait statement is useful in a process that models a block of combinatorial logic, since any change on the inputs may result in new output values; for example:

```
half_add : process is
begin
    sum <= a xor b after T_pd;
    carry <= a and b after T_pd;
    wait on a, b;
end process half_add;
```

The process starts execution by generating values for **sum** and **carry** based on the initial values of **a** and **b**, then suspends on the wait statement until either **a** or **b** (or both) change values. When that happens, the process resumes and starts execution from the top.

This form of process is so common in modeling digital systems that VHDL-AMS provides the shorthand notation that we have seen in many examples in preceding chapters. A process with a sensitivity list in its heading is exactly equivalent to a process with a wait statement at the end, containing a sensitivity clause naming the signals in the sensitivity list. So the **half_add** process above could be rewritten as

```
half_add : process (a, b) is
begin
    sum <= a xor b after T_pd;
    carry <= a and b after T_pd;
end process half_add;
```

Example   Let us return to the model of a two-input multiplexer shown in Figure 5-4. The process in that model is sensitive to all three input signals. This means that it will resume on changes on either data input, even though only one of them is selected at any time. If we are concerned about this slight lack of efficiency in simulation, we can write the process differently, using wait statements to be more selective about the signals to which the process is sensitive each time it suspends. The revised model is shown in Figure 5-6. In this model, when input **a** is selected, the process only waits for changes on the select input and on **a**. Any changes on **b** are ignored. Similarly, if **b** is selected, the process waits for changes on **sel** and on **b**, ignoring changes on **a**.

FIGURE 5-6

```
entity mux2 is
    port ( a, b, sel : in bit;
           z : out bit );
end entity mux2;
```

(continued on page 148)

(continued from page 147)

```
architecture behavioral of mux2 is
    constant prop_delay : time := 2 ns;
begin
    slick_mux : process is
    begin
        case sel is
            when '0' =>
                z <= a after prop_delay;
                wait on sel, a;
            when '1' =>
                z <= b after prop_delay;
                wait on sel, b;
        end case;
    end process slick_mux;
end architecture behavioral;
```

An entity and architecture body for a multiplexer that avoids being resumed in response to changes on the input signal that is not currently selected.

The condition clause in a wait statement, starting with the word **until**, allows us to specify a condition that must be true for the process to resume. For example, the wait statement

wait until clk = '1';

causes the executing process to suspend until the value of the signal **clk** changes to '1'. The condition expression is tested while the process is suspended to determine whether to resume the process. A consequence of this is that even if the condition is true when the wait statement is executed, the process will still suspend until the appropriate signals change and cause the condition to be true again. If the wait statement doesn't include a sensitivity clause, the condition is tested whenever an event occurs on any of the signals mentioned in the condition.

Example   The clock generator process from the example on page 143 can be rewritten using a wait statement with a condition clause, as shown in Figure 5-7. Each time the process executes the wait statement, **clk** has the value '0'. However, the process still suspends, and the condition is tested each time there is an event on **clk**. When **clk** changes to '1', nothing happens, but when it changes to '0' again, the process resumes and schedules transactions for the next cycle.

FIGURE 5-7

```
clock_gen : process is
begin
    clk <= '1' after T_pw, '0' after 2*T_pw;
    wait until clk = '0';
end process clock_gen;
```

The revised clock generator process.

If a wait statement includes a sensitivity clause as well as a condition clause, the condition is only tested when an event occurs on any of the signals in the sensitivity clause. For example, if a process suspends on the following wait statement:

wait on clk **until** reset = '0';

the condition is tested on each change in the value of **clk**, regardless of any changes on **reset**.

The timeout clause in a wait statement, starting with the word **for**, allows us to specify a maximum interval of simulation time for which the process should be suspended. We may specify the interval either as a value of **time** value or as a real-number value. If we also include a sensitivity or condition clause, these may cause the process to be resumed earlier. For example, the wait statement

wait until trigger = '1' **for** 1 ms;

causes the executing process to suspend until **trigger** changes to '1', or until 1 ms of simulation time has elapsed, whichever comes first. Similarly, the wait statement

wait until disp'above(min_high) **for** 2.0;

suspends execution until the **disp** quantity goes above the **min_high** threshold or until 2.0 seconds have elapsed. If we just include a timeout clause by itself in a wait statement, the process will suspend for the time given.

Example   We can rewrite the clock generator process from the example on page 143 yet again, this time using a wait statement with a timeout clause, as shown in Figure 5-8. In this case we specify the clock period as the timeout, after which the process is to be resumed.

FIGURE 5·8

```
clock_gen : process is
begin
    clk <= '1' after T_pw, '0' after 2*T_pw;
    wait for 2*T_pw;
end process clock_gen;
```

A third version of the clock generator process.

If we refer back to the syntax rule for a wait statement shown on page 146, we note that it is legal to write

wait;

This form causes the executing process to suspend for the remainder of the simulation. Although this may at first seem a strange thing to want to do, in practice it is quite useful. One place where it is used is in a process whose purpose is to generate stimuli for a simulation. Such a process should generate a sequence of transactions on signals connected to other parts of a model and then stop. For example, the process

```
test_gen : process is
begin
    test0 <= '0' after 10 ns, '1' after 20 ns, '0' after 30 ns, '1' after 40 ns;
    test1 <= '0' after 10 ns, '1' after 30 ns;
    wait;
end process test_gen;
```

generates all four possible combinations of values on the signals **test0** and **test1**. If the final wait statement were omitted, the process would cycle forever, repeating the signal assignment statements without suspending, and the simulation would make no progress.

Delta Delays

Let us now return to the topic of delays in signal assignments. In many of the example signal assignments in previous chapters, we omitted the delay part of waveform elements. This is equivalent to specifying a delay of 0 fs. The value is to be applied to the signal at the current simulation time. However, it is important to note that the signal value does not change as soon as the signal assignment statement is executed. Rather, the assignment schedules a transaction for the signal, which is applied after the process suspends. Thus the process does not see the effect of the assignment until the next time it resumes, even if this is at the same simulation time. For this reason, a delay of 0 fs in a signal assignment is called a *delta delay*.

To understand why delta delays work in this way, it is necessary to review the simulation cycle, introduced in Chapter 1 on page 25. Recall that the digital portion of the simulation cycle includes two phases: a signal update phase followed by a process execution phase. In the signal update phase, simulation time is advanced to the time of the earliest scheduled transaction, and the values in all transactions scheduled for this time are applied to their corresponding signals. This may cause events to occur on some signals. In the process execution phase, all processes that respond to these events are resumed and execute until they suspend again on wait statements. The simulator then repeats the simulation cycle.

Let us now consider what happens when a process executes a signal assignment statement with delta delay, for example:

```
data <= X"00";
```

Suppose this is executed at simulation time *t* during the process execution phase of the current simulation cycle. The effect of the assignment is to schedule a transaction to put the value X"00" on **data** at time *t*. The transaction is not applied immediately, since the simulator is in the process execution phase. Hence the process continues executing, with **data** unchanged. When all processes have suspended, the simulator starts the next simulation cycle and updates the simulation time. Since the earliest transaction is now at time *t*, simulation time remains unchanged. The simulator now applies the value X"00" in the scheduled transaction to **data**, then resumes any processes that respond to the new value.

Writing a model with delta delays is useful when we are working at a high level of abstraction and are not yet concerned with detailed timing. If all we are interested in is describing the order in which operations take place, delta delays provide a means of ignoring the complications of timing. We have seen this in many of the examples in previous chapters. However, we should note a common pitfall encountered by most beginner VHDL-AMS designers when using delta delays: they forget that the process does not see the effect of the assignment immediately. For example, we might write a process that includes the following statements:

```
s <= '1';
...
if s = '1' then ...
```

and expect the process to execute the if statement assuming **s** has the value '1'. We would then spend fruitless hours debugging our model until we remembered that **s** still has its old value until the next simulation cycle, after the process has suspended.

Example   Figure 5-9 is an outline of an abstract model of a computer system. The CPU and memory are connected with address and data signals. They synchronize their operation with the **mem_read** and **mem_write** control signals and the **mem_ready** status signal. No delays are specified in the signal assignment statements, so synchronization occurs over a number of delta delay cycles, as shown in Figure 5-10.

When the simulation starts, the CPU process begins executing its statements and the memory suspends. The CPU schedules transactions to assign the next instruction address to the **address** signal and the value '1' to the **mem_read** signal, then suspends. In the next simulation cycle, these signals are updated and the memory process resumes, since it is waiting for an event on **mem_read**. The memory process schedules the data on the **read_data** signal and the value '1' on **mem_ready**, then suspends. In the third cycle, these signals are updated and the CPU process resumes. It schedules the value '0' on **mem_read** and suspends. Then, in the fourth cycle, **mem_read** is updated and the memory process is resumed, scheduling the value '0' on **mem_ready** to complete the handshake. Finally, on the fifth cycle, **mem_ready** is updated and the CPU process resumes and executes the fetched instruction.

FIGURE 5·9

```
architecture abstract of computer_system is
    subtype word is bit_vector(31 downto 0);
    signal address : natural;
    signal read_data, write_data : word;
    signal mem_read, mem_write : bit := '0';
    signal mem_ready : bit := '0';
begin
    cpu : process is
        variable instr_reg : word;
        variable PC : natural;
        ...     -- other declarations
    begin
        loop
            address <= PC;
            mem_read <= '1';
            wait until mem_ready = '1';
            instr_reg := read_data;
            mem_read <= '0';
            wait until mem_ready = '0';
            PC := PC + 4;
            ...     -- execute the instruction
        end loop;
    end process cpu;

    memory : process is
        type memory_array is array (0 to 2**14 – 1) of word;
        variable store : memory_array := (
            ...
        );
```

```
    begin
        wait until mem_read = '1' or mem_write = '1';
        if mem_read = '1' then
            read_data <= store( address / 4 );
            mem_ready <= '1';
            wait until mem_read = '0';
            mem_ready <= '0';
        else
            ...        -- perform write access
        end if;
    end process memory;
end architecture abstract;
```

An outline of an abstract model for a computer system, consisting of a CPU and a memory. The processes use delta delays to synchronize communication, rather than modeling timing of bus transactions in detail.

FIGURE 5-10

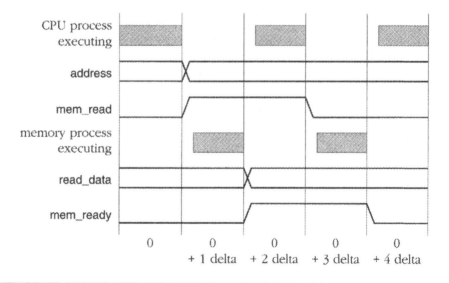

Synchronization over successive delta cycles in a simulation of a read operation between the CPU and memory shown in Figure 5-9.

Transport and Inertial Delay Mechanisms

So far in our discussion of signal assignments, we have implicitly assumed that there were no pending transactions scheduled for a signal when a signal assignment statement was executed. In many models, particularly at higher levels of abstraction, this will be the case. If, on the other hand, there are pending transactions, the new transactions are merged with them in a way that depends on the *delay mechanism* used in the signal assignment statement. This is an optional part of the signal assignment syntax shown on page 141. The syntax rule for the delay mechanism is

delay_mechanism ⇐ **transport** ⏐ ⟦ **reject** *time*_expression ⟧ **inertial**

A signal assignment with the delay mechanism part omitted is equivalent to specifying **inertial**. We look at the *transport* delay mechanism first, since it is simpler, and then return to the *inertial* delay mechanism.

We use the transport delay mechanism when we are modeling an ideal device with infinite frequency response, in which any input pulse, no matter how short, produces an output pulse. An example of such a device is an ideal transmission line, which transmits all input changes delayed by some amount. A process to model a transmission line with delay 500 ps is

```
transmission_line : process (line_in) is
begin
    line_out <= transport line_in after 500 ps;
end process transmission_line;
```

In this model the output follows any changes in the input, but delayed by 500 ps. If the input changes twice or more within a period shorter than 500 ps, the scheduled transactions are simply queued by the driver until the simulation time at which they are to be applied, as shown in Figure 5-11.

FIGURE 5-11

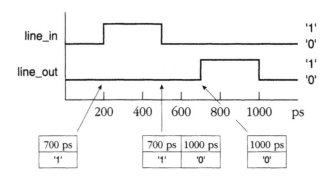

Transactions queued by a driver using transport delay. At time 200 ps the input changes, and a transaction is scheduled for 700 ps. At time 500 ps, the input changes again, and another transaction is scheduled for 1000 ps. This is queued by the driver behind the earlier transaction. When simulation time reaches 700 ps, the first transaction is applied, and the second transaction remains queued. Finally, simulation time reaches 1000 ps, and the final transaction is applied, leaving the driver queue empty.

In this example, each new transaction that is generated by a signal assignment statement is scheduled for a simulation time that is later than the pending transactions queued by the driver. The situation gets a little more complex when variable delays are used, since we can schedule a transaction for an earlier time than a pending transaction. The semantics of the transport delay mechanism specify that if there are pending transactions on a driver that are scheduled for a time later than or equal to a new transaction, those later transactions are deleted.

Example Figure 5-12 is a process that describes the behavior of an asymmetric delay element, with different delay times for rising and falling transitions. The delay for rising transitions is 800 ps and for falling transitions 500 ps. If we apply an input pulse of only 200 ps duration, we would expect the output not to change, since the delayed falling transition should "overtake" the delayed rising transition. If we were simply to add each transition to the driver queue when a signal assignment statement is executed, we would not get this behavior. However, the semantics of the transport delay mechanism produce the desired behavior, as Figure 5-13 shows.

FIGURE 5-12

```
asym_delay : process (a) is
    constant Tpd_01 : time := 800 ps;
    constant Tpd_10 : time := 500 ps;
begin
    if a = '1' then
        z <= transport a after Tpd_01;
    else  -- a = '0'
        z <= transport a after Tpd_10;
    end if;
end process asym_delay;
```

A process that describes a delay element with asymmetric delays for rising and falling transitions.

FIGURE 5-13

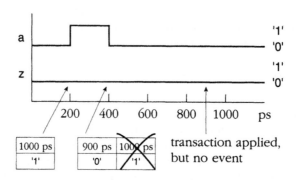

Transactions in a driver using asymmetric transport delay. At time 200 ps the input chang-
es, and a transaction is scheduled for 1000 ps. At time 400 ps, the input changes again,
and another transaction is scheduled for 900 ps. Since this is earlier than the pending
transaction at 1000 ps, the pending transaction is deleted. When simulation time reaches
900 ps, the remaining transaction is applied, but since the value is '0', no event occurs on
the signal.

Most real electronic circuits don't have infinite frequency response, so it is not appropriate to model them using transport delay. In real devices, changing the values
of internal nodes and outputs involves moving electronic charge around in the presence of capacitance, inductance and resistance. This gives the device some inertia; it
tends to stay in the same state unless we force it by applying inputs for a sufficiently
long duration. We can choose to model such systems with higher-fidelity analog
modeling constructs, which we discuss in Chapter 6, or we can use a more realistic
delay mechanism with our digital model. This is why VHDL-AMS includes the inertial
delay mechanism, to allow us to model devices that reject input pulses too short to
overcome their inertia. Inertial delay is the mechanism used by default in a signal
assignment, or we can specify it explicitly by including the word **inertial**.

To explain how inertial delay works, let us first consider a model in which all the
signal assignments for a given signal use the same delay value, say, 3 ns, as in the
following inverter model:

```
inv : process (a) is
begin
     y <= inertial not a after 3 ns;
end process inv;
```

So long as input events occur more than 3 ns apart, this model does not present
any problems. Each time a signal assignment is executed, there are no pending transactions, so a new transaction is scheduled, and the output changes value 3 ns later.
However, if an input changes less than 3 ns after the previous change, this represents
a pulse less than the propagation delay of the device, so it should be rejected. This

behavior is shown at the top of Figure 5-14. In a simple model such as this, we can interpret inertial delay as saying if a signal assignment would produce an output pulse shorter than the propagation delay, then the output pulse does not happen.

Next, let us extend this model by specifying a pulse rejection limit, after the word **reject** in the signal assignment:

```
inv : process (a) is
begin
        y <= reject 2 ns inertial not a after 3 ns;
end process inv;
```

We can interpret this as saying if a signal assignment would produce an output pulse shorter than (or equal to) the pulse rejection limit, the output pulse does not happen. In this simple model, so long as input changes occur more than 2 ns apart, they produce output changes 3 ns later, as shown at the bottom of Figure 5-14. Note that the pulse rejection limit specified must be between 0 fs and the delay specified in the signal assignment. Omitting a pulse rejection limit is the same as specifying a limit equal to the delay, and specifying a limit of 0 fs is the same as specifying transport delay.

Now let us look at the full story of inertial delay, allowing for varying the delay time and pulse rejection limit in different signal assignments applied to the same signal. As with transport delay, the situation becomes more complex, and it is best to describe it in terms of deleting transactions from the driver. Those who are unlikely

FIGURE 5-14

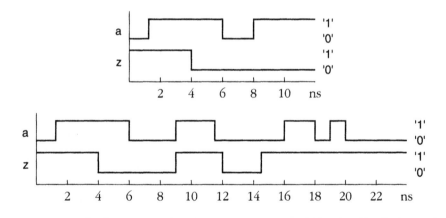

Results of signal assignments using the inertial delay mechanism. In the top waveform, an inertial delay of 3 ns is specified. The input change at time 1 ns is reflected in the output at time 4 ns. The pulse from 6 to 8 ns is less than the propagation delay, so it doesn't affect the output. In the bottom waveform, an inertial delay of 3 ns and a pulse rejection limit of 2 ns are specified. The input changes at 1, 6, 9 and 11.5 ns are all reflected in the output, since they occur greater than 2 ns apart. However, the subsequent input pulses are less than or equal to the pulse rejection limit in length, and so do not affect the output.

to be writing models that deal with timing at this level of detail may wish to move on to the next section.

An inertially delayed signal assignment involves examining the pending transactions on a driver when adding a new transaction. Suppose a signal assignment schedules a new transaction for time t_{new}, with a pulse rejection limit of t_r. First, any pending transactions scheduled for a time later than or equal to t_{new} are deleted, just as they are when transport delay is used. Then the new transaction is added to the driver. Second, any pending transactions scheduled in the interval $t_{new} - t_r$ to t_{new} are examined. If there is a run of consecutive transactions immediately preceding the new transaction with the same value as the new transaction, they are kept in the driver. All other transactions in the interval are deleted.

An example will make this clearer. Suppose a driver for signal **s** contains pending transactions as shown at the top of Figure 5-15, and the process containing the driver executes the following signal assignment statement at time 10 ns:

s <= **reject** 5 ns **inertial** '1' **after** 8 ns;

The pending transactions after this assignment are shown at the bottom of Figure 5-15.

One final point to note about specifying the delay mechanism in a signal assignment statement is that if a number of waveform elements are included, the specified mechanism only applies to the first element. All the subsequent elements schedule transactions using transport delay. Since the delays for multiple waveform elements must be in ascending order, this means that all of the transactions after the first are just added to the driver transaction queue in the order written.

FIGURE 5-15

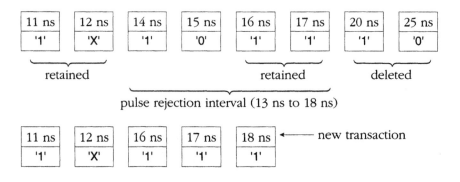

Transactions before (top) and after (bottom) an inertial delay signal assignment. The transactions at 20 and 25 ns are deleted because they are scheduled for later than the new transaction. Those at 11 and 12 ns are retained because they fall before the pulse rejection interval. The transactions at 16 and 17 ns fall within the rejection interval, but they form a run leading up to the new transaction, with the same value as the new transaction; hence they are also retained. The other transactions in the rejection interval are deleted.

Example A detailed model of a two-input and gate is shown in Figure 5-16. When a change on either of the input signals results in a change scheduled for the output, the **delay** process determines the propagation delay to be used. On a rising output transition, spikes of less than 400 ps are rejected, and on a falling or unknown transition, spikes of less than 300 ps are rejected. Note that the result of the **and** operator, when applied to standard-logic values, is always 'U', 'X', '0' or '1'. Hence the **delay** process need not compare result with 'H' or 'L' when testing for rising or falling transitions.

FIGURE 5-16

```
library ieee;  use ieee.std_logic_1164.all;

entity and2 is
    port ( a, b : in std_ulogic;  y : out std_ulogic );
end entity and2;
```

```
architecture detailed_delay of and2 is

    signal result : std_ulogic;

begin
    gate : process (a, b) is
    begin
        result <= a and b;
    end process gate;
    delay : process (result) is
    begin
        if result = '1' then
            y <= reject 400 ps inertial '1' after 1.5 ns;
        elsif result = '0' then
            y <= reject 300 ps inertial '0' after 1.2 ns;
        else
            y <= reject 300 ps inertial 'X' after 500 ps;
        end if;
    end process delay;
end architecture detailed_delay;
```

An entity and architecture body for a two-input and gate. The process **gate** *implements the logical function of the entity, and the process* **delay** *implements its detailed timing characteristics using inertially delayed signal assignments. A delay of 1.5 ns is used for rising transitions, 1.2 ns for falling transitions.*

Process Statements

We have been using processes quite extensively in examples in this and previous chapters, so we have seen most of the details of how they are written and used. To summarize, let us now look at the formal syntax for a process statement and review process operation. The syntax rule is

process_statement ⇐
    〖 *process*_label : 〗
    process 〖 (*signal*_name 〖 , ... 〗) 〗 〖 **is** 〗
        〖 process_declarative_item 〗
    begin
        〖 sequential_statement 〗
    end process 〖 *process*_label 〗 ;

Recall that a process statement is a concurrent statement that can be included in an architecture body to implement all or part of the behavior of a module. The process label identifies the process. While it is optional, it is a good idea to include a label on each process. A label makes it easier to debug a simulation of a system, since most simulators provide a way of identifying a process by its label. Most simulators also generate a default name for a process if we omit the label in the process statement. Having identified a process, we can examine the contents of its variables or set breakpoints at statements within the process.

The declarative items in a process statement may include constant, type and variable declarations, as well as other declarations that we will come to later. Note that ordinary variables may only be declared within process statements, not outside of them. The variables are used to represent the state of the process, as we have seen in the examples. The sequential statements that form the process body may include any of those that we introduced in Chapter 3, plus signal assignment and wait statements. When a process is activated during simulation, it starts executing from the first sequential statement and continues until it reaches the last. It then starts again from the first. This would be an infinite loop, with no progress being made in the simulation, if it were not for the inclusion of wait statements, which suspend process execution until some relevant event occurs. Wait statements are the only statements that take more than zero simulation time to execute. It is only through the execution of wait statements that simulation time advances.

A process may include a sensitivity list in parentheses after the keyword **process**. The sensitivity list identifies a set of signals that the process monitors for events. If the sensitivity list is omitted, the process should include one or more wait statements. On the other hand, if the sensitivity list is included, then the process body cannot include any wait statements. Instead, there is an implicit wait statement, just before the **end process** keywords, that includes the signals listed in the sensitivity list as signals in an **on** clause.

Concurrent Signal Assignment Statements

The form of process statement that we have been using is the basis for all digital behavioral modeling in VHDL-AMS, but for simple cases, it can be a little cumbersome and verbose. For this reason, VHDL-AMS provides us with some useful shorthand notations for *functional* modeling, that is, behavioral modeling in which the operation to be described is a simple combinatorial transformation of inputs to an output. We look at the basic form of two of these statements, *concurrent signal assignment* statements, which are concurrent statements that are essentially signal assignments. Unlike ordinary signal assignments, concurrent signal assignment statements can be included in the statement part of an architecture body. The syntax rule is

> concurrent_signal_assignment_statement ⇐
>   〖 label : 〗 conditional_signal_assignment
>   ▏ 〖 label : 〗 selected_signal_assignment

which tells us that the two forms are called a *conditional signal assignment* and a *selected signal assignment*. Each of them may include a label, which serves exactly the same purpose as a label on a process statement: it allows the statement to be identified by name during simulation or synthesis.

Conditional Signal Assignment Statements

The conditional signal assignment statement is a shorthand for a collection of ordinary signal assignments contained in an if statement, which is in turn contained in a process statement. The simplified syntax rule for a conditional signal assignment is

> conditional_signal_assignment ⇐
>   name <= 〖 delay_mechanism 〗
>   〖 waveform **when** *boolean*_expression **else** 〗
>   waveform 〖 **when** *boolean*_expression 〗 ;

The conditional signal assignment allows us to specify which of a number of waveforms should be assigned to a signal depending on the values of some conditions. Let us look at some examples and show how each conditional signal assignment can be transformed into an equivalent process statement. First, the top statement in Figure 5-17 is a functional description of a multiplexer, with four data inputs (**d0, d1, d2** and **d3**), two select inputs (**sel0** and **sel1**) and a data output (**z**). All of these signals are of type **bit**. This statement has exactly the same meaning as the process statement shown at the bottom of Figure 5-17.

The advantage of the conditional signal assignment form over the equivalent process is clearly evident from this example. The simple combinatorial transformation is obvious to the reader, uncluttered by the details of the process mechanism. This is not to say that processes are a bad thing, rather that in simple cases, we would rather hide that detail to make the model clearer. Looking at the equivalent process shows us something important about the conditional signal assignment statement, namely, that it is sensitive to all of the signals mentioned in the waveforms and the conditions.

FIGURE 5·17

```
zmux : z <= d0 when sel1 = '0' and sel0 = '0' else
             d1 when sel1 = '0' and sel0 = '1' else
             d2 when sel1 = '1' and sel0 = '0' else
             d3 when sel1 = '1' and sel0 = '1';
```

```
zmux : process is
begin
    if sel1 = '0' and sel0 = '0' then
        z <= d0;
    elsif sel1 = '0' and sel0 = '1' then
        z <= d1;
    elsif sel1 = '1' and sel0 = '0' then
        z <= d2;
    elsif sel1 = '1' and sel0 = '1' then
        z <= d3;
    end if;
    wait on d0, d1, d2, d3, sel0, sel1;
end process zmux;
```

Top: a functional model of a multiplexer, using a conditional signal assignment statement. Bottom: the equivalent process statement.

So whenever any of these change value, the conditional assignment is reevaluated and a new transaction scheduled on the driver for the target signal.

If we look more closely at the multiplexer model, we note that the last condition is redundant, since the signals sel0 and sel1 are of type bit. If none of the previous conditions are true, the signal should always be assigned the last waveform. So we can rewrite the example as shown in Figure 5-18.

A very common case in function modeling is to write a conditional signal assignment with no conditions, as in the following example:

```
PC_incr : next_PC <= PC + 4 after 5 ns;
```

At first sight this appears to be an ordinary sequential signal assignment statement, which by rights ought to be inside a process body. However, if we look at the syntax rule for a concurrent signal assignment, we note that this can in fact be recognized as such if all of the optional parts except the label are omitted. In this case, the equivalent process statement is

```
PC_incr : process is
begin
    next_PC <= PC + 4 after 5 ns;
    wait on PC;
end process PC_incr;
```

FIGURE 5-18

```
zmux : z <= d0 when sel1 = '0' and sel0 = '0' else
             d1 when sel1 = '0' and sel0 = '1' else
             d2 when sel1 = '1' and sel0 = '0' else
             d3;
```

```
zmux : process is
begin
    if sel1 = '0' and sel0 = '0' then
        z <= d0;
    elsif sel1 = '0' and sel0 = '1' then
        z <= d1;
    elsif sel1 = '1' and sel0 = '0' then
        z <= d2;
    else
        z <= d3;
    end if;
    wait on d0, d1, d2, d3, sel0, sel1;
end process zmux;
```

A revised functional model for the multiplexer, with its equivalent process statement.

Another case that sometimes arises when writing functional models is the need for a process that schedules an initial set of transactions and then does nothing more for the remainder of the simulation. An example is the generation of a reset signal. One way of doing this is as follows:

```
reset_gen : reset <= '1', '0' after 200 ns when extended_reset else
                     '1', '0' after 50 ns;
```

The thing to note here is that there are no signals named in any of the waveforms or the conditions (assuming that **extended_reset** is a constant). This means that the statement is executed once when simulation starts, schedules two transactions on **reset** and remains quiescent thereafter. The equivalent process is

```
reset_gen : process is
begin
    if extended_reset then
        reset <= '1', '0' after 200 ns;
    else
        reset <= '1', '0' after 50 ns;
    end if;
    wait;
end process reset_gen;
```

Since there are no signals involved, the wait statement has no sensitivity clause. Thus after the if statement has executed, the process suspends forever.

If we include a delay mechanism specification in a conditional signal assignment statement, it is used whichever waveform is chosen. So we might rewrite the model for the asymmetric delay element shown in Figure 5-12 as

```
asym_delay : z <= transport a after Tpd_01 when a = '1' else
                  a after Tpd_10;
```

One problem with conditional signal assignments, as we have described them so far, is that they always assign a new value to a signal. Sometimes we may not want to change the value of a signal, or more specifically, we may not want to schedule any new transactions on the signal. We can use the keyword **unaffected** instead of a normal waveform for these cases, as shown at the top of Figure 5-19.

FIGURE 5-19

```
scheduler :
    request <= first_priority_request after scheduling_delay
                    when priority_waiting and server_status = ready else
              first_normal_request after scheduling_delay
                    when not priority_waiting and server_status = ready else
              unaffected
                    when server_status = busy else
              reset_request after scheduling_delay;
```

```
scheduler : process is
begin
    if priority_waiting and server_status = ready then
        request <= first_priority_request after scheduling_delay;
    elsif not priority_waiting and server_status = ready then
        request <= first_normal_request after scheduling_delay;
    elsif server_status = busy then
        null;
    else
        request <= reset_request after scheduling_delay;
    end if;
    wait on first_priority_request, priority_waiting, server_status,
            first_normal_request, reset_request;
end process scheduler;
```

Top: a conditional signal assignment statement showing use of the **unaffected** *waveform. Bottom: the equivalent process statement.*

The effect of the **unaffected** waveform is to include a null statement in the equivalent process, causing it to bypass scheduling a transaction when the corresponding condition is true. (Recall that the effect of the null sequential statement is to do nothing.) So the example at the top of Figure 5-19 is equivalent to the process shown at the bottom. Note that we can only use **unaffected** in a concurrent signal assignment, not in a sequential signal assignment.

Selected Signal Assignment Statements

The selected signal assignment statement is similar in many ways to the conditional signal assignment statement. It, too, is a shorthand for a number of ordinary signal assignments embedded in a process. But for a selected signal assignment, the equivalent process contains a case statement instead of an if statement. The simplified syntax rule is

> selected_signal_assignment ⇐
>   **with** expression **select**
>   name <= 〚 delay_mechanism 〛
>   〖 waveform **when** choices , 〗
>   waveform **when** choices ;

This statement allows us to choose between a number of waveforms to be assigned to a signal depending on the value of an expression. As an example, let us consider the selected signal assignment shown at the top of Figure 5-20. This has the same meaning as the process statement containing a case statement shown at the bottom of Figure 5-20.

A selected signal assignment statement is sensitive to all of the signals in the selector expression and in the waveforms. This means that the selected signal assignment in Figure 5-20 is sensitive to **b** and will resume if **b** changes value, even if the value of alu_function is alu_pass_a.

An important point to note about a selected signal assignment statement is that the case statement in the equivalent process must be legal according to all of the rules that we described in Chapter 3. This means that every possible value for the selector expression must be accounted for in one of the choices, that no value is included in more than one choice and so on.

Apart from the difference in the equivalent process, the selected signal assignment is similar to the conditional assignment. Thus the special waveform **unaffected** can be used to specify that no assignment take place for some values of the selector expression. Also, if a delay mechanism is specified in the statement, that mechanism is used on each sequential signal assignment within the equivalent process.

FIGURE 5-20

```
alu : with alu_function select
        result <=  a + b after Tpd        when alu_add | alu_add_unsigned,
                   a – b after Tpd        when alu_sub | alu_sub_unsigned,
                   a and b after Tpd      when alu_and,
                   a or b after Tpd       when alu_or,
                   a after Tpd            when alu_pass_a;
```

```
alu : process is
begin
    case alu_function is
        when alu_add | alu_add_unsigned => result <= a + b after Tpd;
        when alu_sub | alu_sub_unsigned => result <= a – b after Tpd;
        when alu_and                    => result <= a and b after Tpd;
        when alu_or                     => result <= a or b after Tpd;
        when alu_pass_a                 => result <= a after Tpd;
    end case;
    wait on alu_function, a, b;
end process alu;
```

Top: a selected signal assignment statement. Bottom: its equivalent process statement.

Example   We can use a selected signal assignment to express a combinatorial logic function in truth-table form. Figure 5-21 shows an entity declaration and an architecture body for a full adder. The selected signal assignment statement has, as its selector expression, a bit vector formed by aggregating the input signals. The choices list all possible values of inputs, and for each, the values for the **c_out** and **s** outputs are given.

FIGURE 5-21

```
entity full_adder is
    port ( a, b, c_in : bit;  s, c_out : out bit );
end entity full_adder;
```

```
architecture truth_table of full_adder is
begin
    with bit_vector'(a, b, c_in) select
        (c_out, s) <= bit_vector'("00") when "000",
                      bit_vector'("01") when "001",
                      bit_vector'("01") when "010",
                      bit_vector'("10") when "011",
```

bit_vector'("01") **when** "100",
bit_vector'("10") **when** "101",
bit_vector'("10") **when** "110",
bit_vector'("11") **when** "111";

end architecture truth_table;

An entity declaration and functional architecture body for a full adder.

This example illustrates the most common use of aggregate targets in signal assignments. Note that the type qualification is required in the selector expression to specify the type of the aggregate. The type qualification is needed in the output values to distinguish the bit-vector string literals from character string literals.

Concurrent Assertion Statements

VHDL-AMS provides another shorthand process notation, the *concurrent assertion statement,* which can be used in behavioral modeling. As its name implies, a concurrent assertion statement represents a process whose body contains an ordinary sequential assertion statement. The syntax rule is

concurrent_assertion_statement ⇐
    〖 label : 〗
    assert *boolean*_expression
        〖 **report** expression 〗〖 **severity** expression 〗 ;

This syntax appears to be exactly the same as that for a sequential assertion statement, but the difference is that it may appear as a concurrent statement. The optional label on the statement serves the same purpose as that on a process statement: to provide a way of referring to the statement during simulation or synthesis. The process equivalent to a concurrent assertion contains a sequential assertion with the same condition, report clause and severity clause. The sequential assertion is then followed by a wait statement whose sensitivity list includes the signals mentioned in the condition expression. Thus the effect of the concurrent assertion statement is to check that the condition holds true each time any of the signals mentioned in the condition change value. Concurrent assertions provide a very compact and useful way of including timing and correctness checks in a model.

Example We can use concurrent assertion statements to check for correct use of a set/reset flipflop, with two inputs s and r and two outputs q and q_n, all of type **bit**. The requirement for use is that s and r are not both '1' at the same time. The entity and architecture body are shown in Figure 5-22.
    The first and second concurrent statements implement the functionality of the model. The third checks for correct use and is resumed when either s or r changes value, since these are the signals mentioned in the Boolean condition. If

FIGURE 5-22

```
entity S_R_flipflop is
    port ( s, r : in bit;  q, q_n : out bit );
end entity S_R_flipflop;

architecture functional of S_R_flipflop is
begin

    q <= '1' when s = '1' else
        '0' when r = '1';

    q_n <= '0' when s = '1' else
        '1' when r = '1';

    check : assert not (s = '1' and r = '1')
                report "Incorrect use of S_R_flip_flop: s and r both '1'";

end architecture functional;
```

An entity and architecture body for a set/reset flipflop, including a concurrent assertion statement to check for correct usage.

both of the signals are '1', an assertion violation is reported. The equivalent process for the concurrent assertion is

```
check : process is
begin
    assert not (s = '1' and r = '1')
        report "Incorrect use of S_R_flip_flop: s and r both '1'";
    wait on s, r;
end process check;
```

Entities and Passive Processes

We complete this section on behavioral modeling by returning to declarations of entities. We can include certain kinds of concurrent statements in an entity declaration, to monitor use and operation of the entity. The extended syntax rule for an entity declaration that shows this is

```
entity_declaration ⇐
    entity identifier is
        〖 port ( port_interface_list ) ; 〗
        〖 entity_declarative_item 〗
    〖 begin
        〖 concurrent_assertion_statement
        ⏐ passive_concurrent_procedure_call_statement
```

⟦ *passive*_process_statement ⟧ ⟧
end ⟦ **entity** ⟧ ⟦ identifier ⟧ ;

The concurrent statements included in an entity declaration must be *passive;* that is, they may not affect the operation of the entity in any way. A concurrent assertion statement meets this requirement, since it simply tests a condition whenever events occur on signals to which it is sensitive. A process statement is passive if it contains no signal assignment statements or calls to procedures containing signal assignment statements. Such a process can be used to trace events that occur on the entity's inputs. We will describe the remaining alternative, concurrent procedure call statements, when we discuss procedures in Chapter 9. A concurrent procedure call is passive if the procedure called contains no signal assignment statements or calls to procedures containing signal assignment statements.

Example   We can rewrite the entity declaration for the set/reset flipflop of Figure 5-22 as shown in Figure 5-23. If we do this, the check is included for every possible implementation of the flipflop and does not need to be included in the corresponding architecture bodies.

FIGURE 5-23

```
entity S_R_flipflop is
    port ( s, r : in bit;  q, q_n : out bit );
begin
    check : assert not (s = '1' and r = '1')
                report "Incorrect use of S_R_flip_flop: s and r both '1'";
end entity S_R_flipflop;
```

The revised entity declaration for the set/reset flipflop, including the concurrent assertion statement to check for correct usage.

Example   Figure 5-24 shows an entity declaration for a read-only memory (ROM). It includes a passive process, **trace_reads**, that is sensitive to changes on the **enable** port. When the value of the port changes to '1', the process reports a message tracing the time and address of the read operation. The process does not affect the course of the simulation in any way, since it does not include any signal assignments.

FIGURE 5-24

```
entity ROM is
    port ( address : in natural;
            data : out bit_vector(0 to 7);
            enable : in bit );
begin
    trace_reads : process (enable) is
    begin
        if enable = '1' then
            report "ROM read at time " & time'image(now)
                    & " from address " & natural'image(address);
        end if;
    end process trace_reads;
end entity ROM;
```

An entity declaration for a ROM, including a passive process for tracing read operations.

5.4 Digital Structural Descriptions

A structural description of a digital system is expressed in terms of subsystems interconnected by signals. Each subsystem may in turn be composed of an interconnection of sub-subsystems, and so on, until we finally reach a level consisting of primitive components, described purely in terms of their behavior. Thus the top-level system can be thought of as having a hierarchical structure. In this section, we look at how to write digital structural architecture bodies to express this hierarchical organization.

Component Instantiation and Port Maps

We have seen earlier in this chapter that the concurrent statements in an architecture body describe an implementation of an entity interface. In order to write a structural implementation, we must use a concurrent statement called a *component instantiation* statement, the simplest form of which is governed by the syntax rule

```
component_instantiation_statement ⇐
    instantiation_label :
        entity entity_name [ ( architecture_identifier ) ]
            [ port map ( port_association_list ) ] ;
```

This form of component instantiation statement performs *direct instantiation* of an entity. We can think of component instantiation as creating a copy of the named entity, with the corresponding architecture body substituted for the component instance. In general, the port map specifies which ports of the entity are connected to which signals, quantities and terminals in the enclosing architecture body. In this chapter, we focus on connection of signal ports to signals, and we return to analog connections in Chapter 6. The simplified syntax rule for a signal-port association list is

port_association_list ⇐
    ([[*port*_name =>] (*signal*_name ⫾ expression ⫾ **open**)) { , ⚬⚬⚬ }

Each element in the association list associates one port of the entity either with one signal of the enclosing architecture body or with the value of an expression, or leaves the port unassociated, as indicated by the keyword **open**.

Let us look at some examples to illustrate component instantiation statements and the association of ports with signals. Suppose we have an entity declared as

```
entity DRAM_controller is
    port ( rd, wr, mem : in bit;
              ras, cas, we, ready : out bit  );
end entity DRAM_controller;
```

and a corresponding architecture called fpld. We might create an instance of this entity as follows:

```
main_mem_controller : entity work.DRAM_controller(fpld)
    port map ( cpu_rd, cpu_wr, cpu_mem,
                    mem_ras, mem_cas, mem_we, cpu_rdy );
```

In this example, the name **work** refers to the current working library in which entities and architecture bodies are stored. We return to the topic of libraries in Chapter 7. The port map of this example lists the signals in the enclosing architecture body to which the ports of the copy of the entity are connected. *Positional association* is used: each signal listed in the port map is connected to the port at the same position in the entity declaration. So the signal **cpu_rd** is connected to the port **rd**, the signal **cpu_wr** is connected to the port **wr** and so on.

One of the problems with positional association is that it is not immediately clear which signals are being connected to which ports. Someone reading the description must refer to the entity declaration to check the order of the ports in the entity interface. A better way of writing a component instantiation statement is to use *named association,* as shown in the following example:

```
main_mem_controller : entity work.DRAM_controller(fpld)
    port map ( rd => cpu_rd, wr => cpu_wr,
                    mem => cpu_mem, ready => cpu_rdy,
                    ras => mem_ras, cas => mem_cas, we => mem_we );
```

Here, each port is explicitly named along with the signal to which it is connected. The order in which the connections are listed is immaterial. The advantage of this approach is that it is immediately obvious to the reader how the entity is connected into the structure of the enclosing architecture body.

In the preceding example we have explicitly named the architecture body to be used corresponding to the entity instantiated. However, the syntax rule for component instantiation statements shows this to be optional. If we wish, we can omit the specification of the architecture body, in which case the one to be used may be chosen when the overall model is processed for simulation, synthesis or some other purpose. At that time, if no other choice is specified, the most recently analyzed architecture body is selected. We return to the topic of analyzing models in Chapter 7.

Example In Figure 5-5 we looked at a behavioral model of an edge-triggered flipflop. We can use the flipflop as the basis of a 4-bit edge-triggered register. Figure 5-25 shows the entity declaration and a structural architecture body.

We can use the register entity, along with other entities, as part of a structural architecture for the two-digit decimal counter represented by the schematic of Figure 5-26. Suppose a digit is represented as a bit vector of length four, described by the subtype declaration

subtype digit **is** bit_vector(3 **downto** 0);

Figure 5-27 shows the entity declaration for the counter, along with an outline of the structural architecture body. This example illustrates a number of important points about component instances and port maps. First, the two component instances **val0_reg** and **val1_reg** are both instances of the same entity/architecture

FIGURE 5-25

```
entity reg4 is
    port ( clk, clr, d0, d1, d2, d3 : in bit;  q0, q1, q2, q3 : out bit );
end entity reg4;
```
```
architecture struct of reg4 is
begin
    bit0 : entity work.edge_triggered_Dff(behavioral)
        port map (d0, clk, clr, q0);
    bit1 : entity work.edge_triggered_Dff(behavioral)
        port map (d1, clk, clr, q1);
    bit2 : entity work.edge_triggered_Dff(behavioral)
        port map (d2, clk, clr, q2);
    bit3 : entity work.edge_triggered_Dff(behavioral)
        port map (d3, clk, clr, q3);
end architecture struct;
```

An entity and structural architecture body for a 4-bit edge-triggered register, with an asynchronous clear input.

FIGURE 5-26

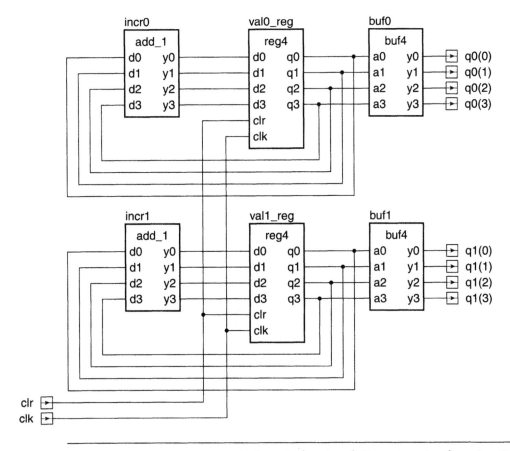

A schematic for a two-digit counter using the **reg4** *entity.*

pair. This means that two distinct copies of the architecture **struct** of **reg4** are created, one for each of the component instances. We return to this point when we discuss the topic of elaboration in Chapter 7. Second, in each of the port maps, ports of the entity being instantiated are associated with separate elements of array signals. This is allowed, since a signal that is of a composite type, such as an array, can be treated as a collection of signals, one per element. Third, some of the signals connected to the component instances are signals declared within the enclosing architecture body, **registered**, whereas the **clk** signal is a port of the entity **counter**. This again illustrates the point that within an architecture body, the ports of the corresponding entity are treated as signals.

FIGURE 5-27

```
entity counter is
    port ( clk, clr : in bit;
            q0, q1 : out digit );
end entity counter;
```

```
architecture registered of counter is
    signal current_val0, current_val1, next_val0, next_val1 : digit;
begin
    val0_reg : entity work.reg4(struct)
        port map ( d0 => next_val0(0), d1 => next_val0(1),
                   d2 => next_val0(2), d3 => next_val0(3),
                   q0 => current_val0(0), q1 => current_val0(1),
                   q2 => current_val0(2), q3 => current_val0(3),
                   clk => clk, clr => clr );

    val1_reg : entity work.reg4(struct)
        port map ( d0 => next_val1(0), d1 => next_val1(1),
                   d2 => next_val1(2), d3 => next_val1(3),
                   q0 => current_val1(0), q1 => current_val1(1),
                   q2 => current_val1(2), q3 => current_val1(3),
                   clk => clk, clr => clr );

    incr0 : entity work.add_1(boolean_eqn) ...;

    incr1 : entity work.add_1(boolean_eqn) ...;

    buf0 : entity work.buf4(basic) ...;

    buf1 : entity work.buf4(basic) ...;
end architecture registered;
```

An entity declaration of a two-digit decimal counter, with an outline of an architecture body using the reg4 entity.

We saw in the above example that we can associate separate ports of an instance with individual elements of an actual signal of a composite type, such as an array or record type. If an instance has a composite port, we can write associations the other way around; that is, we can associate separate actual signals with individual elements of the port. This is sometimes called *subelement association*. For example, if the instance DMA_buffer has a port status of type FIFO_status, declared as

```
type FIFO_status is record
        nearly_full, nearly_empty, full, empty : bit;
    end record FIFO_status;
```

we could associate a signal with each element of the port as follows:

```
DMA_buffer : entity work.FIFO
    port map ( ..., status.nearly_full => start_flush,
                    status.nearly_empty => end_flush,
                    status.full => DMA_buffer_full,
                    status.empty => DMA_buffer_empty, ... );
```

This illustrates two important points about subelement association. First, all elements of the composite port must be associated with an actual signal. We cannot associate some elements and leave the rest unassociated. Second, all of the associations for a particular port must be grouped together in the association list, without any associations for other ports among them.

We can use subelement association for ports of an array type by writing an indexed element name on the left side of an association. Furthermore, we can associate a slice of the port with an actual signal that is a one-dimensional array, as the following example shows.

Example   Suppose we have a register entity, declared as shown at the top of Figure 5-28. The ports **d** and **q** are arrays of bits. The architecture body for a microprocessor, outlined at the bottom of Figure 5-28, instantiates this entity as the program status register (PSR). Individual bits within the register represent condition and interrupt flags, and the field from bit 6 down to bit 4 represents the current interrupt priority level.

FIGURE 5-28

```
entity reg is
    port ( d : in bit_vector(7 downto 0);
           q : out bit_vector(7 downto 0);
           clk : in bit );
end entity reg;
```

```
architecture RTL of microprocessor is
    signal interrupt_req : bit;
    signal interrupt_level : bit_vector(2 downto 0);
    signal carry_flag, negative_flag, overflow_flag, zero_flag : bit;
    signal program_status : bit_vector(7 downto 0);
    signal clk_PSR : bit;
    ...
begin
    PSR : entity work.reg
        port map ( d(7) => interrupt_req,
                   d(6 downto 4) => interrupt_level,
                   d(3) => carry_flag,  d(2) => negative_flag,
```

(continued on page 176)

(continued from page 175)

```
                        d(1) => overflow_flag,  d(0) => zero_flag,
                        q => program_status,
                        clk => clk_PSR );
    ...

end architecture RTL;
```

An entity declaration for a register with array type ports, and an outline of an architecture body that instantiates the entity. The port map includes subelement associations with individual elements and a slice of the d port.

In the port map of the instance, subelement association is used for the input port d to connect individual elements of the port with separate actual signals of the architecture. A slice of the port is connected to the interrupt_level signal. The output port q, on the other hand, is associated in whole with the bit-vector signal program_status.

We may also use subelement association for a port that is of an unconstrained array type. The index bounds of the port are determined by the least and greatest index values used in the association list, and the index range direction is determined by the port type. For example, suppose we declare an and gate entity:

```
entity and_gate is
    port ( i : in bit_vector;  y : out bit );
end entity and_gate;
```

and a number of signals:

```
signal serial_select, write_en, bus_clk, serial_wr : bit;
```

We can instantiate the entity as a three-input and gate:

```
serial_write_gate : entity work.and_gate
    port map ( i(1) => serial_select,
               i(2) => write_en,
               i(3) => bus_clk,
               y => serial_wr );
```

Since the input port i is unconstrained, the index values in the subelement associations determine the index bounds for this instance. The least value is one and the greatest value is three. The port type is bit_vector, which has an ascending index range. Thus, the index range for the port in the instance is an ascending range from one to three.

The syntax rule for a port association list shows that a port of a component instance may be associated with an expression instead of a signal. In this case, the value of the expression is used as a constant value for the port throughout the simulation. If real hardware is synthesized from the model, the port of the component instance would be tied to a fixed value determined by the expression. Association with an expression is useful when we have an entity provided as part of a library, but we do not need to use all of the functionality provided by the entity. When associating a port with an expression, the value of the expression must be *globally static;* that is, we must be able to determine the value from constants defined when the model is elaborated. So, for example, the expression must not include references to any signals.

Example   Given a four-input multiplexer described by the entity declaration

```
entity mux4 is
    port ( i0, i1, i2, i3, sel0, sel1 : in bit;
            z : out bit );
end entity mux4;
```

we can use it as a two-input multiplexer by instantiating it as follows:

```
a_mux : entity work.mux4
    port map ( sel0 => select_line, i0 => line0, i1 => line1,
            z => result_line,
            sel1 => '0', i2 => '1', i3 => '1' );
```

For this component instance, the high-order select bit is fixed at '0', ensuring that only one of line0 or line1 is passed to the output. We have also followed the practice, recommended for many logic families, of tying unused inputs to a fixed value, in this case '1'.

Some entities may be designed to allow inputs to be left open by specifying a default value for a port. When the entity is instantiated, we can specify that a port is to be left open by using the keyword **open** in the port association list, as shown in the syntax rule on page 171.

Example   The and_or_inv entity declaration on page 137 includes a default value of '1' for each of its input ports, as again shown here:

```
entity and_or_inv is
    port ( a1, a2, b1, b2 : in bit := '1';
            y : out bit );
end entity and_or_inv;
```

We can write a component instantiation to perform the function **not ((A and B) or C)** using this entity as follows:

```
f_cell : entity work.and_or_inv
    port map ( a1 => A, a2 => B, b1 => C, b2 => open, y => F );
```

The port **b2** is left open, so it assumes the default value '1' specified in the entity declaration.

There is some similarity between specifying a default value for an input port and associating an input port with an expression. In both cases the expression must be globally static (that is, we must be able to determine its value when the model is elaborated). The difference is that a default value is only used if the port is left open when the entity is instantiated, whereas association with an expression specifies that the expression value is to be used to drive the port for the entire simulation or life of the component instance. If a port is declared with a default value and then associated with an expression, the expression value is used, overriding the default value.

Output and bidirectional ports may also be left unassociated using the **open** keyword, provided they are not of an unconstrained array type. If a port of mode **out** is left open, any value driven by the entity is ignored. If a port of mode **inout** is left open, the value used internally by the entity (the *effective value*) is the value that it drives on to the port.

A final point to make about unassociated ports is that we can simply omit a port from a port association list to specify that it remain open. So, given an entity declared as follows:

```
entity and3 is
    port ( a, b, c : in bit := '1';
            z, not_z : out bit);
end entity and3;
```

the component instantiation

```
g1 : entity work.and3 port map ( a => s1, b => s2, not_z => ctrl1 );
```

has the same meaning as

```
g1 : entity work.and3 port map ( a => s1, b => s2, not_z => ctrl1,
                                    c => open, z => open );
```

The difference is that the second version makes it clear that the unused ports are deliberately left open, rather than being accidentally overlooked in the design process. This is useful information for someone reading the model.

Exercises

1. [❶ 5.1] Write an entity declaration for a lookup table ROM modeled at an abstract level. The ROM has an address input of type lookup_index, which is an integer range from 0 to 31, and a data output of type real. Include declarations within the declarative part of the entity to define the ROM contents, initialized to numbers of your choice.

2. [❶ 5.3] Trace the transactions applied to the signal s in the following process. At what times is the signal active, and at what times does an event occur on it?

   ```
   process is
   begin
       s <= 'Z', '0' after 10 ns, '1' after 30 ns;
       wait for 50 ns;
       s <= '1' after 5 ns; 'H' after 15 ns;
       wait for 50 ns;
       s <= 'Z';
       wait;
   end process;
   ```

3. [❶ 5.3] Given the assignments to the signal s made by the process in Exercise 2, trace the values of the signals s'delayed(5 ns), s'stable(5 ns), s'quiet(5 ns) and s'transaction. What are the values of s'last_event, s'last_active and s'last_value at time 60 ns?

4. [❶ 5.3] Write a wait statement that suspends a process until a signal s changes from '1' to '0' while an enable signal en is '1'.

5. [❶ 5.3] Write a wait statement that suspends a process until a signal ready changes to '1' or until a maximum of 5 ms has elapsed.

6. [❶ 5.3] Suppose the signal s currently has the value '0'. What is the value of the Boolean variables v1 and v2 after execution of the following statements within a process?

   ```
   s <= '1';
   v1 := s = '1';
   wait on s;
   v2 := s = '1';
   ```

7. [❶ 5.3] Trace the transactions scheduled on the driver for z by the following statements, and show the values taken on by z during simulation.

   ```
   z <= transport '1' after 6 ns;
   wait for 3 ns;
   z <= transport '0' after 4 ns;
   wait for 5 ns;
   z <= transport '1' after 6 ns;
   wait for 1 ns;
   z <= transport '0' after 4 ns;
   ```

8. [❶ 5.3] Trace the transactions scheduled on the driver for **x** by the following statements, and show the values taken on by **x** during simulation. Assume **x** initially has the value zero.

    x <= **reject** 5 ns **inertial** 1 **after** 7 ns, 23 **after** 9 ns, 5 **after** 10 ns,
                    23 **after** 12 ns, −5 **after** 15 ns;
    wait for 6 ns;
    x <= **reject** 5 ns **inertial** 23 **after** 7 ns;

9. [❶ 5.3] Write the equivalent process for the conditional signal assignment statement

    mux_logic :
        z <= a **and not** b **after** 5 ns **when** enable = '1' **and** sel = '0' **else**
              x **or** y **after** 6 ns **when** enable = '1' **and** sel = '1' **else**
              '0' **after** 4 ns;

10. [❶ 5.3] Write the equivalent process for the selected signal assignment statement

    with bit_vector'(s, r) **select**
        q <= **unaffected when** "00",
              '0' **when** "01",
              '1' **when** "10" | "11";

11. [❶ 5.3] Write a concurrent assertion statement that verifies that the time between changes of a clock signal, **clk**, is at least **T_pw_clk**.

12. [❶ 5.4] Write component instantiation statements to model the structure shown by the schematic diagram in Figure 5-29. Assume that the entity **ttl_74x74** and the corresponding architecture **basic** have been analyzed into the library **work**.

FIGURE 5-29

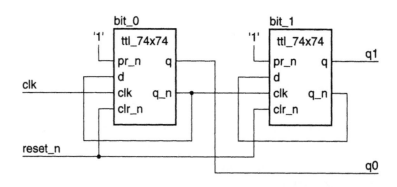

A schematic diagram of a 2-bit counter.

13. [❶ 5.4] Sketch a schematic diagram of the structure modeled by the following component instantiation statements.

> decode_1 : **entity** work.ttl_74x138(basic)
> **port map** (c => a(2), b => a(1), a => a(0),
>   g1 => a(3), g2a_n => sel_n, g2b_n => '0',
>   y7_n => en_n(15), y6_n => en_n(14),
>   y5_n => en_n(13), y4_n => en_n(12),
>   y3_n => en_n(11), y2_n => en_n(10),
>   y1_n => en_n(9), y0_n => en_n(8));
>
> decode_0 : **entity** work.ttl_74x138(basic)
> **port map** (c => a(2), b => a(1), a => a(0),
>   g1 => '1', g2a_n => sel_n, g2b_n => a(3),
>   y7_n => en_n(7), y6_n => en_n(6),
>   y5_n => en_n(5), y4_n => en_n(4),
>   y3_n => en_n(3), y2_n => en_n(2),
>   y1_n => en_n(1), y0_n => en_n(0));

14. [❷ 5.3] Develop a behavioral model for a four-input multiplexer, with ports of type bit and a propagation delay from data or select input to data output of 4.5 ns. You should declare a constant for the propagation delay, rather than writing it as a literal in signal assignments in the model.

15. [❷ 5.3] Develop a behavioral model for a negative-edge-triggered 4-bit counter with asynchronous parallel load inputs. The entity declaration is

> **entity** counter **is**
>   **port** (clk_n, load_en : **in** std_ulogic;
>   d : **in** std_ulogic_vector(3 **downto** 0);
>   q : **out** std_ulogic_vector(3 **downto** 0));
> **end entity** counter;

16. [❷ 5.3] Develop a behavioral model for a D-latch with a clock-to-output propagation delay of 3 ns and a data-to-output propagation delay of 4 ns.

17. [❷ 5.3] Develop a behavioral model for an edge-triggered flipflop that includes tests to verify the following timing constraints: data setup time of 3 ns, data hold time of 2 ns and minimum clock pulse width of 5 ns.

18. [❷ 5.3] Develop a model of an adder whose interface is specified by the following entity declaration:

> **entity** adder **is**
>   **port** (a, b : **in** integer; s : **out** integer);
> **end entity** adder;

For each pair of integers that arrive on the inputs, the adder produces their sum on the output. Note that successive integers on each input may have the same value, so the adder must respond to transactions rather than to events. While integers in a pair may arrive in the inputs at different times, you may assume that neither value of the following pair will arrive until both values of the first pair have arrived. The adder should produce the sum only when both input values of a pair have arrived.

19. [❷ 5.3] Develop a behavioral model for a two-input Muller-C element, with two input ports and one output, all of type bit. The inputs and outputs are initially '0'. When both inputs are '1', the output changes to '1'. It stays '1' until both inputs are '0', at which time it changes back to '0'. Your model should have a propagation delay for rising output transitions of 3.5 ns, and for falling output transitions of 2.5 ns.

20. [❷ 5.3] The following process statement models a producer of data:

```
producer : process is
    variable next_data : natural := 0;
begin
    data <= next_data;  next_data := next_data + 1;
    data_ready <= '1';
    wait until data_ack = '1';
    data ready <= '0';
    wait until data_ack = '0';
end process producer;
```

The process uses a four-phase handshaking protocol to synchronize data transfer with a consumer process. Develop a process statement to model the consumer. It, too, should use delta delays in the handshaking protocol. Include the process statements in a test-bench architecture body, and experiment with your simulator to see how it deals with models that use delta delays.

21. [❷ 5.3] Develop a behavioral model for a multitap delay line, with the following interface:

```
entity delay_line is
    port ( input : in std_ulogic;  output : out std_ulogic_vector );
end entity delay_line;
```

Each element of the output port is a delayed version of the input. The delay to the leftmost output element is 5 ns, to the next element is 10 ns and so on. The delay to the rightmost element is 5 ns times the length of the output port. Assume the delay line acts as an ideal transmission line.

22. [❷ 5.3] Develop a functional model using conditional signal assignment statements of an address decoder for a microcomputer system. The decoder has an address input port of type natural and a number of active-low select outputs, each activated when the address is within a given range. The outputs and their corresponding ranges are

ROM_sel_n	16#0000# to 16#3FFF#
RAM_sel_n	16#4000# to 16#5FFF#
PIO_sel_n	16#8000# to 16#8FFF#
SIO_sel_n	16#9000# to 16#9FFF#
INT_sel_n	16#F000# to 16#FFFF#

23. [❷ 5.3] Develop a functional model of a BCD-to-seven-segment decoder for a light-emitting diode (LED) display. The decoder has a 4-bit input that encodes a numeric digit between 0 and 9. There are seven outputs indexed from 'a' to 'g', corresponding to the seven segments of the LED display as shown in the margin. An output bit being '1' causes the corresponding segment to illuminate. For each input digit, the decoder activates the appropriate combination of segment outputs to form the displayed representation of the digit. For example, for the input "0010", which encodes the digit 2, the output is "1101101". Your model should use a selected signal assignment statement to describe the decoder function in truth-table form.

24. [❷ 5.3] Write an entity declaration for a 4-bit counter with an asynchronous reset input. Include a process in the entity declaration that measures the duration of each reset pulse and reports the duration at the end of each pulse.

25. [❷ 5.4] Develop a structural model of an 8-bit odd-parity checker using instances of an exclusive-or gate entity. The parity checker has eight inputs, i0 to i7, and an output, p, all of type **std_ulogic**. The logic equation describing the parity checker is

$$P = ((I_0 \oplus I_1) \oplus (I_2 \oplus I_3)) \oplus ((I_4 \oplus I_5) \oplus (I_6 \oplus I_7))$$

Note: in this equation, the symbol "$\oplus$" denotes the exclusive-or operation.

26. [❸ 5.4] Develop a structural model of a 14-bit counter with parallel load inputs, using instances of the 4-bit counter described in Exercise 15. Ensure that any unused inputs are properly connected to a constant driving value.

27. [❸ 5.3] Develop a behavioral model for a D-latch with tristate output. The entity declaration is

```
entity d_latch is
    port ( latch_en, out_en, d : in std_ulogic;  q : out std_ulogic );
end entity d_latch;
```

When latch_en is asserted, data from the d input enters the latch. When latch_en is negated, the latch maintains the stored value. When out_en is asserted, data passes through to the output. When out_en is negated, the output has the value 'Z' (high-impedance). The propagation delay from latch_en to q is 3 ns and from d to q is 4 ns. The delay from out_en asserted to q active is 2 ns and from out_en negated to q high-impedance is 5 ns.

28. [❸ 5.3] Develop a functional model of a 4-bit carry-look-ahead adder. The adder has two 4-bit data inputs, a(3 **downto** 0) and b(3 **downto** 0); a 4-bit data output, s(3 **downto** 0); a carry input, c_in; a carry output, c_out; a carry generate output, g; and a carry propagate output, p. The adder is described by the logic equations and associated propagation delays:

$$S_i = A_i \oplus B_i \oplus C_{i-1} \quad \text{(delay is 5 ns)}$$

$$G_i = A_i B_i \quad \text{(delay is 2 ns)}$$

$$P_i = A_i + B_i \quad \text{(delay is 3 ns)}$$

$$C_i = G_i + P_i C_{i-1}$$

$$\quad = G_i + P_i G_{i-1} + P_i P_{i-1} G_{i-2} + \dots + P_i P_{i-1} \dots P_0 C_{-1} \quad \text{(delay is 5 ns)}$$

$$G = G_3 + P_3 G_2 + P_3 P_2 G_1 + P_3 P_2 P_1 G_0 \quad \text{(delay is 5 ns)}$$

$$P = P_3 P_2 P_1 P_0 \quad \text{(delay is 3 ns)}$$

where the G_i are the intermediate carry generate signals, the P_i are the intermediate carry propagate signals and the C_i are the intermediate carry signals. C_{-1} is c_in and C_3 is c_out. (In the equation for S_i, the symbol "$\oplus$" denotes the exclusive-or operation.) Your model should use the expanded equation to calculate the intermediate carries, which are then used to calculate the sums.

29. [❸ 5.3] Develop a behavioral model for a four-input arbiter with the following entity interface:

    entity arbiter **is**
        port (request : **in** bit_vector(0 **to** 3);
                  acknowledge : **out** bit_vector(0 **to** 3));
    end entity arbiter;

    The arbiter should use a round-robin discipline for responding to requests. Include a concurrent assertion statement that verifies that no more than one acknowledgment is issued at once and that an acknowledgment is only issued to a requesting client.

30. [❸ 5.3] Write an entity declaration for a 7474 positive edge-triggered JK-flipflop with asynchronous active-low preset and clear inputs, and Q and $\overline{Q}$ outputs. Include concurrent assertion statements and passive processes as necessary in the entity declaration to verify that

    - the preset and clear inputs are not activated simultaneously,

    - the setup time of 6 ns from the J and K inputs to the rising clock edge is observed,

    - the hold time of 2 ns for the J and K inputs after the rising clock edge is observed and

    - the minimum pulse width of 5 ns on each of the clock, preset and clear inputs is observed.

    Write a behavioral architecture body for the flipflop and a test bench that exercises the statements in the entity declaration.

31. [❸ 5.4] Define entity interfaces for a microprocessor, a ROM, a RAM, a parallel I/O controller, a serial I/O controller, an interrupt controller and a clock genera-

tor. Use instances of these entities and an instance of the address decoder described in Exercise 22 to develop a structural model of a microcomputer system.

32. [❸ 5.4] Develop a structural model of a 16-bit carry-look-ahead adder, using instances of the 4-bit adder described in Exercise 28. You will need to develop a carry-look-ahead generator with the following interface:

```
entity carry_look_ahead_generator is
    port ( p0, p1, p2, p3, g0, g1, g2, g3 : in bit;
           c_in : in bit;  c1, c2, c3 : out bit );
end entity carry_look_ahead_generator
```

The carry-look-ahead generator is connected to the 4-bit adders as shown in Figure 5-30. It calculates the carry output signals using the generate, propagate and carry inputs in the same way that the 4-bit counters calculate their internal carry signals.

33. [❹ 5.3] Develop a behavioral model for a household burglar alarm. The alarm has inputs for eight sensors, each of which is normally '0'. When an intruder is detected, one of the sensors changes to '1'. There is an additional input from a key-switch and an output to a siren. When the key-switch input is '0', the alarm is disabled and the siren output is '0'. When the key-switch input changes to '1', there is a 30 s delay before the alarm is enabled. Once enabled, detection of an intruder starts another 30 s delay, after which time the siren output is set to '1'. If the key-switch input changes back to '0', the alarm is immediately disabled.

34. [❹ 5.3] In his book *Structured Computer Organization*, Tanenbaum describes the use of a Hamming code for error detection and correction of 16-bit data ([38], pages 44–48). Develop behavioral models for a Hamming code generator and for an error detector and corrector. Devise a test bench that allows you to introduce single-bit errors into the encoded data, to verify that the error corrector works properly.

FIGURE 5-30

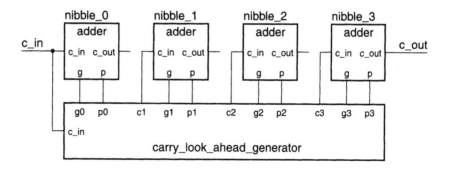

Connections between a carry-look-ahead generator and adders.

35. [❹ 5.3] Develop a behavioral model of a 4K × 8-bit serial-input/output RAM. The device has a chip-enable input **ce**, a serial clock **clk**, a data input **d_in** and a data output **d_out**. When **ce** is '1', the data input is sampled on 23 successive rising clock edges to form the 23 bits of a command string. A string of the form

$$\text{"1 } A_{11}\ A_{10}\ \ldots\ A_0\ 0\ 1\ D_7\ D_6\ \ldots\ D_0\text{"}$$

is a write command, in which the bits A_i are the address and the bits Dj are the data to be written. A string of the form

$$\text{"1 } A_{11}\ A_{10}\ \ldots\ A_0\ 1\ 1\ X\ X\ X\ X\ X\ X\ X\ X\text{"}$$

is a read command, in which the bits denoted by X are ignored. The RAM produces the successive bits of read data synchronously with the last eight rising clock edges of the command.

36. [❹ 5.3/5.4] Develop a model of a device to count the number of cars in a parking lot. The lot has a gate through which only one car at a time may enter or leave. There are two pairs, labeled A and B, each comprising a LED and a photodetector, mounted on the gate as shown in Figure 5-31. Each detector produces a '1' output when a car obscures the corresponding LED. When a car enters the yard, the front of the car obscures LED A, then LED B. When the car has advanced sufficiently, LED A becomes visible again, followed by LED B. The process is reversed for a car leaving the lot. Note that a car may partially enter or leave the lot and then reverse.

Your model should include a clocked finite-state machine (FSM) with two inputs, one from each detector, and increment and decrement outputs that pulse to '1' for one clock cycle when a car has totally entered or left the lot. The FSM outputs should drive a three-digit chain of BCD up/down counters, whose outputs are connected to seven-segment decoders.

FIGURE 5-31

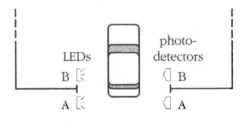

Arrangement of LEDs and photodetectors on a parking lot gate.

chapter six
Analog Modeling Constructs

A model of an analog system consists of the circuit nodes, analog unknowns to be calculated and the characteristic equations that specify analog behavior. In VHDL-AMS, we use terminals to represent the circuit nodes, quantities for the analog unknowns and simultaneous statements for the characteristic equations. In this chapter, we show how we use these features of VHDL-AMS to model analog, mixed-signal and mixed-technology systems.

6.1   **Free Quantities**

In previous chapters we have discussed the use of entities and architectures to represent the elements of the system we are modeling. We have also introduced the types and natures we use to describe the allowable values that objects may hold and have discussed the sequential statements we use to describe behavior within processes. In Chapter 5 we focused on the use of entities and architectures for describing digital behavior and structure. In this chapter we turn our attention to the VHDL-AMS features used in entities and architectures to describe behavior and structure of analog, mixed-signal and mixed-technology systems.

We introduced quantities for analog modeling in Chapter 1. There are three kinds of quantity in VHDL-AMS: free, branch and source quantities. A free quantity is an analog-valued object that can be used in signal-flow modeling. A branch quantity is similar, but is specifically used to model conservative energy systems. We return to branch quantities and their association with terminals in Section 6.2. A source quantity is used for frequency and noise modeling, which we discuss in Chapter 13.

A free quantity can be defined in an architecture body using a *quantity declaration*. The syntax rule for a free quantity declaration is

> free_quantity_declaration ⇐
>   **quantity** identifier ⦃ , ⚬⚬⚬ ⦄ : subtype_indication ⟦ := expression ⟧ ;

This declaration names one or more quantities, specifies their types and optionally provides an initial value to be used for the quantities. The type of a quantity must be either a floating-point type or a composite type whose scalar elements are all floating-point types. As a simple example, we can declare a subtype for charge and use this subtype to declare a free quantity as follows:

```
subtype charge is real tolerance "default_charge";
quantity capacitor_charge : charge;
```

We can use this quantity in equations without adhering to conservative energy laws. This is useful in modeling signal-flow behaviors or when modeling a subset of the physical phenomena associated with a given energy domain. For example, we can relate the **capacitor_charge** quantity to a quantity representing capacitor voltage in the equation

```
capacitor_charge == capacitor_voltage * capacitance;
```

The tolerance group of a scalar free quantity is the tolerance group of its subtype. In the example above, the tolerance was specified in the subtype declaration. Recall that we can also specify a tolerance as part of a subtype indication. This allows us to declare a particular quantity with a tolerance specialized to that quantity alone, for example:

```
quantity engine_power : real tolerance "approximate_power";
```

The syntax rule for a free quantity declaration shows that we can include an expression for the initial value of the quantity. For example:

quantity I_sense : current := 0.15;   *-- initial value is 150mA*

If we include an initial value expression, the value must be of the quantity's type. So for a scalar quantity, the value must be a floating-point value, and for a composite quantity, the value must be of the composite type. For example, in the composite quantity declaration

quantity amplifier_gains : real_vector (3 **downto** 0) := (1.0, 1.0, 1.0, 0.5);

the initial value expression is an array aggregate of four elements to match the constrained **real_vector** type specified for the quantity. In the absence of an initial value expression a default initial value is used. For a scalar quantity, the default initial value is 0.0, and for a composite quantity, the default initial value is an aggregate with 0.0 for each scalar element.

Example Suppose we wish to model a two-input analog multiplier system. Each input is amplified separately, then the amplified signals are multiplied to produce the output. We declare free quantities for the inputs, output and intermediate quantities and constants for the gains as follows:

```
quantity input1, input2, output : real;
quantity amplified_input1, amplified_input2 : real;

constant gain1 : real := 2.0;
constant gain2 : real := 4.0;
```

We model the amplification and multiplication behavior with the following simultaneous statements:

```
amplified_input1 == input1 * gain1;
amplified_input2 == input2 * gain2;
output == amplified_input1 * amplified_input2;
```

Note that we could dispense with the intermediate quantities **amplified_input1** and **amplified_input2** by combining all of the multiplications into one simultaneous statement, as follows:

```
output == input1 * gain1 * input2 * gain2;
```

However, including the additional free quantities allows us to use a simulator to view the amplified value of each input signal. It is common practice to add such quantities to gain additional insight into system behavior.

Quantity Ports

In Chapter 5 we saw how signal ports can be included in an entity declaration for digital models. In a similar way, we can include quantity ports in an entity declaration for analog models. Furthermore, we can include a mixture of signal and quantity ports for mixed-signal and mixed-technology models. This is shown by an extended syntax rule for a port interface list:

interface_list ⇐
    ([**signal**] identifier { , ∘∘∘ } : [mode] subtype_indication
                     [:= expression]
     | **quantity** identifier { , ∘∘∘ } : [**in** | **out**] subtype_indication
                     [:= expression]
) { ; ∘∘∘ }

This rule shows that a quantity port is declared in much the same way as a signal port, except that the keyword **quantity** is not optional and the mode can only be **in** or **out**. If we omit the mode specification, the default mode is **in**, indicating an input quantity port. The rules for the type and the initial value expression for a quantity port are the same as those for a free quantity, namely, that the type must be a floating-point type (or a composite type with floating-point elements) and the expression, if included, must be of this type. Indeed, just as a signal port is treated as a signal within an architecture body corresponding to the entity, a quantity port is treated as a free quantity with an architecture body. Hence, quantity ports allow us to represent interconnections between entity instances using non-conservative modeling techniques.

Example   We can write an abstract signal-flow model of the negative-feedback control system shown in Figure 6-1. The entity declaration, shown in Figure 6-2, uses quantity ports for the inputs and output. The architecture body, also shown in the figure, includes a simultaneous statement that relates the output voltage to the difference between the target and feedback input voltages.

FIGURE 6-1

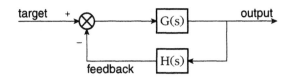

A negative-feedback control system.

FIGURE 6-2

```
library ieee_proposed;  use ieee_proposed.electrical_systems.all;
entity control_system is
    port ( quantity feedback, target : in voltage;
            quantity output : out voltage );
end entity control_system;
```

```
architecture simple_feedback of control_system is
    constant gain : real := 2.0;
begin
    output == gain * ( target − feedback );
end architecture simple_feedback;
```

A model of the feedback control system.

Example   Another common application for quantity ports is modeling the impact of temperature on the behavior of circuitry without including a detailed model of thermal behavior. By including a quantity port, we are able to provide the temperature as an input to the electrical model. For example, an entity declaration for a temperature-dependent resistor is

```
library ieee_proposed;
use ieee_proposed.electrical_systems.all;
use ieee_proposed.thermal_systems.all;

entity temperature_dependent_resistor is
    port ( terminal n1, n2 : electrical;
            quantity temp : in temperature );
end entity temperature_dependent_resistor;
```

A simple model of temperature dependence reduces the nominal resistance linearly with increases in temperature. We express this in the following architecture body:

```
architecture linear_approx of temperature_dependent_resistor is
    constant resistance_at_0 : real := 1.0E6;
    constant resistance_drop_per_kelvin : real := 100.0;
    quantity resistance : real;
    quantity V across I through n1 to n2;
begin
    resistance == resistance_at_0 − temp * resistance_drop_per_kelvin;
    V == I * resistance;
end architecture linear_approx;
```

The architecture body declares a free quantity, **resistance**, to represent the temperature-dependent value of the resistor. The first simultaneous statement in the architecture body relates the resistance to the value of the quantity port **temp**. The architecture body also declares branch quantities, **V** and **I**, as we saw in Chapter 1. The second simultaneous statement relates the quantities using Ohm's law with the temperature-dependent resistance.

6.2   Terminals and Branch Quantities

In Chapter 1 we introduced *terminals* as the VHDL-AMS feature for representing the physical connection points or circuit nodes of a system. Recall that terminals are declared to be of various natures, which represent different energy domains of a system. We also introduced branch quantities as the VHDL-AMS feature for accessing the effort and flow aspects of terminal. In this chapter, we explore these concepts in detail.

Terminal Declarations

Let us start with the syntax rule for a terminal declaration and then show some examples. The syntax rule is

    terminal_declaration ⇐
        terminal identifier {, ... } : subnature_indication ;

A terminal declaration can appear as a declarative item before the keyword **begin** in an architecture body. The declaration names one or more terminal objects of a particular nature. The nature of a terminal determines the across and through types for the terminal, which represent the effort and flow aspects of the energy domain for the terminal.

To illustrate declaration of terminals, consider the following example:

    subtype voltage **is** real **tolerance** "low_voltage";
    subtype current **is** real **tolerance** "low_current";
    nature electrical **is** voltage **across** current **through** electrical_ref **reference**;
    terminal anode, cathode : electrical;

The subtype and nature declarations model the electrical energy domain, as we have seen. The terminal declaration then names two terminals, **anode** and **cathode**, each of which is of the **electrical** nature. The across type associated with the terminals is **voltage** and the through type is **current**. The terminal **electrical_ref**, created implicitly by the nature declaration, is the reference terminal for **anode** and **cathode**.

We can declare terminals of other non-electrical natures in the same way. For example, we can declare a radiant energy nature and terminals for a light bulb and a light-emitting diode as follows:

subtype illuminance **is** real **tolerance** "default_illuminance";
subtype optic_flux **is** real **tolerance** "default_optic_flux";
nature radiant **is** illuminance **across** optic_flux **through** radiant_ref **reference**;
terminal light_bulb, light_emitting_diode : radiant;

All of the terminals in the examples above are scalar terminals, since their natures are scalar. We saw in Chapter 4 that we can declare composite natures and composite terminals of composite natures. We consider each scalar subelement of a composite terminal to be a scalar terminal. For example, if we declare electrical_vector as follows:

nature electrical_vector **is array** (natural **range** <>) **of** electrical;
terminal a_bus : electrical_vector(1 **to** 8);

then the composite terminal **a_bus** consists of eight scalar terminals, **a_bus(1)** to **a_bus(8)**, each with the scalar across type **voltage** and the scalar through type **current**.

Branch Quantity Declarations

In order to refer to the across and through aspects of terminals, we need to declare branch quantities between terminals. We then use the branch quantities in equations in the model. In addition, energy conservation laws relate the branch quantities associated with each terminal. Branch quantities can be defined in an architecture body using a *branch quantity declaration*. The syntax rules for a branch quantity declaration are

branch_quantity_declaration ⇐
    quantity ⟦ across_aspect ⟧ ⟦ through_aspect ⟧ terminal_aspect ;

across_aspect ⇐
    identifier ⟨ , ... ⟩ ⟦ **tolerance** *string*_expression ⟧ ⟦ := expression ⟧ **across**

through_aspect ⇐
    identifier ⟨ , ... ⟩ ⟦ **tolerance** *string*_expression ⟧ ⟦ := expression ⟧ **through**

terminal_aspect ⇐
    *plus_terminal*_name ⟦ **to** *minus_terminal*_name ⟧

These syntax rules are quite involved, so we first show a number of examples and use them to illustrate some important points about branch quantity declarations. Suppose we have two electrical terminals declared as

terminal anode, cathode : electrical;

We can declare branch quantities between these terminals as follows:

quantity battery_voltage **across** battery_current **through** anode **to** cathode;
quantity leakage_voltage **across** leakage_current **through** anode;

The quantities defined by these declarations are illustrated in Figure 6-3.

The syntax rules show that a branch quantity declaration defines

- a *branch* between two terminals. This is defined by the terminal aspect of the declaration. If we include both the plus-terminal and minus-terminal names, the branch is between the two named terminals. This is illustrated by the branch between **anode** and **cathode** in the example. If we omit the minus-terminal name, the branch is between the plus terminal and the reference terminal of the plus terminal's nature. This is illustrated by the branch between anode and the **electrical_ref** terminal in the example.

- one or more *across quantities*. These are quantities that represent the difference in effort between the terminals of the branch. Effort is represented by the across type of the terminals' nature (**voltage** in the example). Thus **battery_voltage** is the difference between the voltages of the **anode** and **cathode** terminals, and **leakage_voltage** is the difference between the voltages of the **anode** and **electrical_ref** terminals.

- one or more *through quantities*. These are quantities that represent the flow through the branch between the terminals. Flow is represented by the through type of the terminals' nature (**current** in the example). Thus **battery_current** is the current flowing from **anode** to **cathode**, and **leakage_current** is the current flowing from **anode** to **electrical_ref**.

In a model of an analog system, we write equations that relate the values of the branch quantities that we declare. Furthermore, as we have mentioned, energy conservation laws apply at terminals. So if several branches defined in branch quantity declarations share a terminal, the effort aspects of the branch ends connected to the terminal are all constrained to be equal, and the sum of the flows in the branches connected to the terminal is constrained to be zero. In the electrical domain, these constraints are expressed as Kirchoff's laws. The job of the analog solver is (in a

FIGURE 6-3

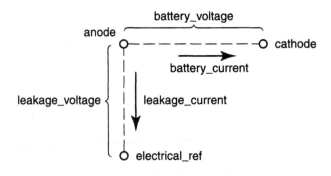

Branch quantities between terminals.

simplified sense) to find values for the branch quantities that satisfy both the equations we provide and the conservation laws.

Returning to the syntax rule for a branch quantity declaration, we see that the across aspect and the through aspect are both optional. This means that we can declare just an across quantity or just a through quantity. For example, given the radiant terminals declared earlier, we can declare branch quantities:

> **quantity** light_illuminance **across** light_bulb;
> **quantity** LED_flux **through** light_emitting_diode;

Note that we cannot omit both the across and through aspects, since that would amount to a quantity declaration that declares no quantities.

Another point to notice about branch quantity declarations is that they permit parallel branches. If we list more than one name in the across aspect or the through aspect, the names each refer to separate branches between the terminals. For example, given two electrical terminals **n1** and **n2**, the declaration

> **quantity** voltage_drop **across**
>   inductive_current, capacitive_current, resistive_current **through**
>   n1 **to** n2;

defines a single across quantity, but three parallel through quantities for the inductive, capacitive and resistive current flows between the terminals. This allows us then to relate the voltage drop to the separate aspects of current flow with three separate equations using the different quantities.

Example   Figure 6-4 illustrates a capacitor with resistive leakage effects. We can model this in VHDL-AMS by declaring terminals for the circuit nodes **p1** and **p2** and branch quantities for the voltage drops and currents, as follows:

> **terminal** p1, p2 : electrical;
> **quantity** vcap **across** icap, ileak **through** p1 **to** p2;

The across quantity **vcap** represents the voltage across both the capacitor and the leakage resistance. The two through quantities **icap** and **ileak** represent the parallel current flows through the capacitor and leakage resistance, respectively. As Figure 6-4 illustrates, the total current flow through the model is the sum of the two branch currents.

We express the behavior of the capacitor with leakage using two simultaneous statements:

> icap == cap * vcap'dot;
>
> ileak == vcap / rleak;

The first of these statements relates the current through the capacitor to the derivative of the voltage quantity. (We discuss the 'dot attribute that yields the

FIGURE 6-4

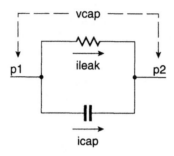

A capacitor with resistive leakage.

derivative of a quantity in detail in Section 6.3.) The second statement expresses Ohm's law, relating the current through the leakage resistor to the voltage quantity.

The examples we considered above illustrate branch quantities between terminals of scalar natures. We saw earlier that terminals can also be of composite natures. There are two cases that arise when we declare branch quantities between such terminals. First, one terminal may be composite and the other scalar. In this case, the scalar subelements of the composite terminal must be of the same nature as the nature of the scalar terminal. For example, given the nature and terminal declarations

> **nature** electrical_vector **is array** (natural **range** <>) **of** electrical;
> **terminal** a_bus : electrical_vector(1 **to** 8);
> **terminal** signal_ground : electrical;

we can declare branch quantities as follows:

> **quantity** bus_drops **across** bus_currents **through** a_bus **to** signal_ground;

Here, the terminal **a_bus** is composite, with scalar subelements of **electrical** nature. The terminal **signal_ground** is scalar with **electrical** nature. Thus, we can declare branch quantities between the terminals, as shown in Figure 6-5. The across quantity **bus_drops** is an array of eight voltage elements, **bus_drops(1)** to **bus_drops(8)**, each of which is a scalar across quantity from an element of the **a_bus** terminal to the **signal_ground** terminal. Similarly, the through quantity **bus_currents** is an array of eight current elements, **bus_currents(1)** to **bus_currents(8)**, each of which is a scalar through quantity between an element of the **a_bus** terminal to the **signal_ground** terminal. We can refer to the composite quantity and to the individual quantity elements in equations in the model.

FIGURE 6·5

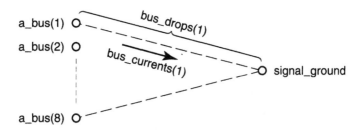

Branch quantities between a composite terminal and a scalar terminal.

Example   Figure 6-6 shows a summing circuit that produces a weighted sum of the voltages on a four-element analog bus. The summer makes use of four resistors that share a common terminal.

We can model the terminals and branch quantities for the resistor package as follows:

terminal p1 : electrical_vector(0 **to** 3);
terminal p2 : electrical;

quantity v **across** i **through** p1 to p2;

Since **p1** is an array terminal, the quantities **v** and **i** are also arrays.   If we assume that the resistors are contained in the same physical package, they are subject to the same temperature effects. We declare constants for the resistance values, the temperature coefficients and the circuit temperatures:

constant tc1 : real := 1.0e–3;   *-- Linear temperature coefficient*
constant tc2 : real := 1.0e–6;   *-- Second–order temperature coefficient*
constant temp : real := 27.0;   *-- Ambient temperature*
constant tnom : real := 50.0;   *-- Nominal temperature*
constant res : real_vector := (1.0e3, 2.0e3, 4.0e3, 8.0e3);   *-- Nominal resistances*

FIGURE 6·6

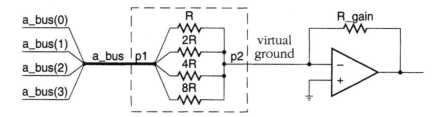

A summer circuit for an analog bus using a package of four resistors.

The temperature effects can be combined to produce a factor by which the resistance varies from its nominal value:

constant res_factor : real := (1.0 + tc1*(temp−tnom) + tc2*(temp−tnom)**2);

We can now write equations that relate the elements of the voltage quantity v and the elements of the current quantity i:

v(0) == i(0) * res(0) * res_factor;
v(1) == i(1) * res(1) * res_factor;
v(2) == i(2) * res(2) * res_factor;
v(3) == i(3) * res(3) * res_factor;

The second case of branch quantities interconnecting composite terminals is the case of both terminals being composite. In this case, the terminals must be of the same nature and have matching elements. The branches are then between the matching elements of the two terminals. For example, given terminals declared as follows:

terminal a_bus : electrical_vector(1 **to** 8);
terminal b_bus : electrical_vector(8 **downto** 1);

we can declare branch quantities as follows:

quantity a_to_b_drops **across** a_to_b_currents **through** a_bus **to** b_bus;

In this example, **a_bus** and **b_bus** each have eight scalar subelements. Thus, the quantity **a_to_b_drops** has eight voltage elements across matching elements of the terminals, and the quantity **a_to_b_currents** has eight current elements between matching elements of the terminals. These are illustrated in Figure 6-7.

FIGURE 6·7

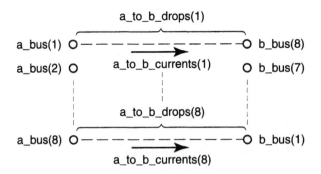

Branch quantities between two composite terminals.

Important points to note from this example are that elements of the terminals match according to their left-to-right position, not according to their array indices, and that the branch quantities take their indices from the plus terminal.

We are not limited to array quantities between array terminals. In general, the terminals can be of any composite nature. The branch quantities then take on a type determined by the structure of the plus terminal's nature. For example, if we declare a record nature and two terminals as follows:

```
nature electrical_bus is
    record
        strobe: electrical;
        databus : electrical_vector(0 to 7);
    end record;
terminal t1, t2 : electrical_bus;
```

we can declare a composite quantity for the voltages:

```
quantity bus_voltages across t1 to t2;
```

Here, **bus_voltages** is a record with a voltage element named **strobe** and an element named **databus** that is an array of eight voltages indexed from 0 to 7.

Example A variation of the resistor package described in the example on page 197 has separate terminal elements for both sides of each resistor, as shown in Figure 6-8. In this case, we model the terminals and branch quantities for the resistor package as follows:

```
terminal p1, p2 : electrical_vector(0 to 3);
quantity v across i through p1 to p2;
```

Here, since p1 and p2 are both array terminals of the same size and nature, the quantities v and i are arrays. We can express the temperature-dependent behavior

FIGURE 6-8

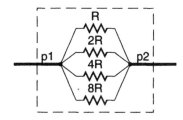

A resistor package with separate terminal elements for both sides of each resistor.

of the resistors using the same constant declarations and equations as shown in the previous example.

In VHDL-AMS, all quantities belong to tolerance groups, which are used by the analog solver to determine how accurately to compute solutions. When we declare branch quantities, the tolerance group is, by default, determined by the nature or subnature of the terminals of the branch. However, as the syntax rules for branch quantity declarations show, we can explicitly specify the tolerance group for the across or through quantities. This allows us to specialize the tolerance for those quantities. For example, the declaration

> **quantity** battery_voltage **tolerance** "battery_tolerance" **across**
>   battery_current **tolerance** "battery_tolerance" **through** anode **to** cathode;

specifies that the tolerance group "battery_tolerance" be used for the two branch quantities instead of the default tolerance specified for the **voltage** and **current** types of the **electrical** nature.

The final feature of branch quantity declarations to consider is specification of initial values. The syntax rules show that we can include expressions for initial values in each of the across and through aspects of a branch quantity declaration. These expressions serve the same purpose as initial value expressions for free quantities and follow the same rules. So the type of each expression must match the type of the corresponding quantity, and in the absence of an expression, a default value of 0.0 (or an aggregate of zero values for composite quantities) is used. For example,

> **quantity** battery_volts := 5.0 **across**
>   battery_amps := 0.0 **through**
>   anode **to** cathode;

specifies that the analog solver should use initial values of 5.0 for the **voltage** quantity battery_volts and 0.0 for the **current** quantity battery_amps.

Terminal Ports

We now come to the third kind of port that can be included in an entity declaration, namely, terminal ports. The extended syntax rule for a port interface list is

> interface_list ⇐
>   ([**signal**] identifier { , ... } : [mode] subtype_indication
>   [:= expression]
> | **quantity** identifier { , ... } : [**in** | **out**] subtype_indication
>   [:= expression]
> | **terminal** identifier { , ... } : subnature_indication
>   ) { ; ... }

This rule shows that a terminal port is declared in much the same way as a signal or quantity port. The differences are that the keyword **terminal** is required, we cannot specify a mode or initial value expression and we specify a nature or subnature rather than a type. For example, we can declare an entity with terminal ports to model a battery:

```
library ieee_proposed;  use ieee_proposed.electrical_systems.all;

entity battery is
    port ( terminal anode, cathode : electrical );
end entity battery;
```

This entity has two ports, **anode** and **cathode**, that are of nature **electrical**.

We can mix different kinds of ports within an entity's interface list. For example, an entity for a mixed-signal model of an analog-to-digital converter may have both signal and terminal ports:

```
library ieee_proposed;  use ieee_proposed.electrical_systems.all;

entity ADC is
    port ( terminal a : electrical;
           signal d : out bit );
end entity ADC;
```

Similarly, we can include terminal ports representing different energy domains within a given interface list. For example, we can write an entity declaration for a mixed electrical/thermal model of a diode, including self-heating effects, as

```
library ieee_proposed;
use ieee_proposed.electrical_systems.all, ieee_proposed.thermal_systems.all;

entity diode_thermal is
    port ( terminal p, m : electrical;
           terminal j : thermal );
end entity diode_thermal;
```

Analogously with other kinds of ports, a terminal port is treated as a terminal with an architecture body. Terminal ports allow us to represent interconnections between entity instances using conservative modeling techniques. We will see how this works when we consider analog structural descriptions in Section 6.5.

6.3 Attributes of Terminals and Quantities

As we saw in previous chapters, we can use attributes to find information about types, natures and signals in a VHDL-AMS model. There are a number of predefined attributes for terminals and quantities, and we now consider them and their use.

Attributes of Terminals

There are two predefined attributes for terminals. Given a terminal T, these attributes are

T'reference   An across branch quantity from T to the reference terminal of the nature of T.

T'contribution   A through quantity measuring the amount "flowing through" the terminal T.

The 'reference attribute serves as a convenient way to refer to the effort applied at a terminal. It saves us having to declare a branch quantity for the terminal. For example, given an electrical terminal declared as

terminal bias_node : electrical;

we can specify that the voltage remain constant with the simultaneous statement

bias_node'reference == 0.5;

The 'contribution attribute refers to the flow out of the terminal into through-branch quantities declared with T as an end and into any terminal ports with which T is associated. If the terminal T is a terminal port that is associated with some terminal T1 in a port map, the quantity T'contribution is the contribution by T to the total flow out of T1. On the other hand, if T is a terminal or a terminal port that is unassociated, the energy conservation laws require that T'contribution be zero. We will return to contribution quantities in more detail in Chapter 7 when we discuss design elaboration and design hierarchies in more detail.

Attributes of Quantities

VHDL-AMS provides a number of predefined attributes of quantities. These attributes, together with simultaneous statements of various forms, are the most important features of VHDL-AMS for behavioral analog and mixed-signal modeling. Given a quantity Q, the attributes are

Q'tolerance   A string that is the tolerance group of the scalar quantity Q.

Q'above(E)   A Boolean signal that is true if the value of Q is greater than the value of the expression E, otherwise false.

Q'delayed(T)   A quantity that is the value of Q delayed by time T.

Q'dot   A quantity that is the derivative with respect to time of the quantity Q.

Q'integ   A quantity that is the integral with respect to time of the quantity Q.

Q'slew(max_rising_slope, max_falling_slope)
> A quantity whose value follows that of **Q**, but whose derivative with respect to time is limited by the specified slopes.

Q'ztf(num, den , t, initial_delay)
> A quantity that is the *z*-domain transfer function of **Q**.

Q'ltf(num, den)   A quantity that is the Laplace-domain transfer function of **Q**.

Q'zoh(t, initial_delay)
> A quantity that is a sampled (zero-order hold) version of **Q**.

The last three of these attributes, **'ztf**, **'ltf** and **'zoh**, are commonly used in frequency-domain modeling. We will discuss them in Chapter 13.

The Tolerance Attribute

The **'tolerance** attribute allows us to declare a number of quantities with the same tolerance group without repeating the tolerance string as a literal in several places in a model. The quantity to which the **'tolerance** attribute is applied must be a scalar quantity. To illustrate the use of this attribute, consider a nature declared as

> **subnature** accurate_electrical **is** electrical
> **tolerance** "accurate_voltage" **across** "accurate_current" **through**;

and terminals declared as

> **terminal** n1, n2 : accurate_electrical;

We can declare branch quantities between the terminals:

> **quantity** n1_n2_voltage **across** n1_n2_current **through** n1 **to** n2;

These quantities take their tolerance group from the across and through types of the nature **accurate_electrical**. If we now wish to declare further quantities with the same tolerance group, we can use the **'tolerance** attribute, as follows:

> **quantity** internal_voltage : voltage **tolerance** n1_n2_voltage'tolerance;
> **quantity** internal_current : current **tolerance** n1_n2_current'tolerance;

Subsequently, if we need to change the tolerance group string, we only need to modify the model in one place, the nature declaration. This makes the model much more maintainable.

The Above Attribute

In examples in Chapter 1, we saw how we can use the **'above** attribute to perform basic analog-to-digital conversion. Now that we have discussed the details of digital modeling, we are in a position to review the 'above attribute in more detail. This attribute can be applied to any scalar quantity **Q** and takes a parameter that is an expression of the same type as **Q**. The result is a Boolean signal that is true when the value of the quantity is greater than the expression value and false otherwise. The expression need not be static, so the threshold level can vary with time. For example, the expression could involve the value of a variable, a signal or another quantity.

Since the 'above attribute yields a signal, we can use events on the signal to cause a process to resume from a wait statement. This is the most common way to synchronize the analog and digital portions of a mixed-signal model.

Example   We can use the 'above attribute as the basis for a simple comparator, shown in Figure 6-9. The entity declaration has an analog terminal port **a** and a digital output signal port **d**. The architecture declares a constant for the reference voltage and a branch quantity for the voltage across the input terminal. The process compares the value of the input voltage with a threshold of half the reference voltage, and sets the output signal to '1' or '0' as a result. It then waits until the signal denoted by the 'above attribute changes, indicating that the input voltage has crossed the threshold in either direction. The process then repeats and changes the output signal accordingly.

FIGURE 6-9

```
library ieee;  use ieee.std_logic_1164.all;
library ieee_proposed;  use ieee_proposed.electrical_systems.all;

entity comparator is
    port ( terminal a : electrical;
            signal d : out std_ulogic );
end entity comparator;
```

```
architecture ideal of comparator is
    constant ref_voltage : real := 5.0;
    quantity vin across a;
begin
    comparator_behavior : process is
    begin
        if vin > ref_voltage / 2.0 then
            d <= '1' after 5 ns;
        else
            d <= '0' after 5 ns;
        end if;
        wait on vin'above(ref_voltage / 2.0);
    end process comparator_behavior;
end architecture ideal;
```

An entity declaration and architecture body for a comparator with a constant threshold.

Note that, in this example, the threshold level is a constant value. We can revise the model to include an additional input terminal for the reference source, as shown in Figure 6-10. The only difference in the architecture body is that the constant is replaced by a branch quantity for the voltage across the reference source. In this model, when the process waits, it can be resumed by either or both of the input voltage or the reference voltage changing so that the input moves above or below the reference.

FIGURE 6-10

```
library ieee;  use ieee.std_logic_1164.all;
library ieee_proposed;  use ieee_proposed.electrical_systems.all;

entity variable_comparator is
    port ( terminal a : electrical;
           terminal ref : electrical;
           signal d : out std_ulogic );
end entity variable_comparator;
```

```
architecture ideal of variable_comparator is
    quantity v_ref across ref;
    quantity vin across a;
begin
    comparator_behavior : process is
    begin
        if vin > v_ref then
            d <= '1' after 5 ns;
        else
            d <= '0' after 5 ns;
        end if;
        wait on vin'above(v_ref / 2.0);
    end process comparator_behavior;
end architecture ideal;
```

An entity declaration and architecture body for a comparator with a variable threshold.

An important point to note when using the 'above attribute is that the comparison between the quantity value and the threshold expression value is a floating-point comparison. As we mentioned in Chapter 2, floating-point numbers are an approximate representation of mathematical real numbers. Whenever we use floating-point numbers, we should be aware that comparisons are not exact. Hence, the test of whether the quantity value is above the threshold value is actually performed as a test of whether the quantity value has passed the threshold value by some "sufficiently large" amount. The precise criterion for "sufficiently large" is implementation dependent, giving simulator vendors some scope for trade-off between simulation speed and accuracy. As a consequence, different simulators operating on different host computers may exhibit slightly different behavior when simulating the same models.

The Delayed Attribute

The attribute Q'delayed(T) denotes a quantity with the value of quantity Q delayed by time T. The quantity can be of any type that is legal for a quantity, and the time parameter must be a static expression yielding a non-negative real number. Thus, the amount of the delay must be fixed. We can omit the time parameter, writing just Q'delayed, in which case a default delay of 0.0 is used.

Example   We can use the 'delayed attribute to create an abstract model of a transmission line or delay element. This approach is similar to the transport delay mechanism we discussed in Chapter 5, but applies to analog quantities instead of digital signals. To revisit the transmission line model in Section 5.3, we can provide an analog version as shown in Figure 6-11. The output voltage follows the input voltage delayed by 2.5 ns and attenuated by a factor of 0.8. Note that we must express the delay as a floating-point number of seconds, not as the value **2.5 ns** of the physical type **time**, since the 'delayed attribute requires a parameter of type **real**.

FIGURE 6-11

```
library ieee_proposed;  use ieee_proposed.electrical_systems.all;
entity transmission_line is
    port ( quantity vin : in voltage;
           quantity vout : out voltage);
end entity transmission_line;
```

```
architecture abstract of transmission_line is
    constant propagation_time : real := 2.5E-9;
    constant attenuation : real := 0.8;
begin
    vout == attenuation * vin'delayed(propagation_time);
end architecture abstract;
```

A model of an analog transmission line with attenuation and delay.

The Dot Attribute

The behavior of many analog systems can be modeled using differential equations. Examples in the electrical domain include capacitors and inductors. In the mechanical domain, Newton's laws of motion lead to differential equations governing velocity and acceleration. VHDL-AMS provides us with the 'dot attribute to express derivatives. Given a scalar quantity **Q**, the attribute **Q'dot** is a quantity with the same type as **Q** whose value is the derivative of **Q** with respect to time. The name of the 'dot attribute derives from the alternative notation used in classical mathematics and physics for derivatives with respect to time:

$$\dot{Q} \equiv \frac{dQ}{dt} \qquad \ddot{Q} \equiv \frac{d^2Q}{dt^2}$$

Example   Figure 6-12 shows a model of an ideal inductor. The architecture body declares branch quantities for the voltage and current between the two terminals. The simultaneous statement expresses the differential equation $V = LdI/dt$.

FIGURE 6-12

```
library ieee_proposed;  use ieee_proposed.electrical_systems.all;
entity inductor is
    port (terminal n1, n2: electrical);
end entity inductor;
```

```
architecture ideal of inductor is
    constant L: inductance := 0.5;
    quantity branch_voltage across branch_current through n1 to n2;
begin
    branch_voltage == L* branch_current'dot;
end architecture ideal;
```

A model of an ideal inductor.

We can also apply the 'dot attribute to a quantity **Q** of composite type. In this case, the result quantity is of the same type as **Q**, with each scalar subelement being the derivative of the corresponding scalar subelement of **Q**. For example, given the following declarations:

```
terminal bus_a_end, bus_b_end : electrical_vector(15 downto 0);
quantity bus_currents through bus_a_end to bus_b_end;
```

The quantity **bus_currents'dot** is a quantity of 16 current derivatives with element 15 being the derivative of **bus_currents(15)**, element 14 being the derivative of **bus_currents(14)** and so on.

The 'dot attribute provides the first derivative of a quantity, but some behaviors require expression of second or higher derivatives. In such cases, we can apply the 'dot attribute several times in succession to obtain the required derivative. For example, Q'dot'dot is the second derivative of Q.

Example Suppose we wish to model a mechanical system in which a force is applied to a piston to move it. Newton's second law of motion states that the force is equal to the product of the piston mass and the acceleration produced. We can express the acceleration as the second derivative of the displacement. This behavior is described in the piston model in Figure 6-13.

FIGURE 6-13

```
library ieee_proposed;  use ieee_proposed.mechanical_systems.all;
entity piston is
    port ( terminal motion : translational );
end entity piston;
```

```
architecture simple of piston is
    constant mass : real := 10.0;
    quantity resultant_displacement across applied_force through motion;
begin
    applied_force == mass * resultant_displacement'dot'dot;
end architecture simple;
```

A piston model expressing mechanical behavior using Newton's second law of motion.

The Integ Attribute

If we wish to express differential equations in integral form, we can use the 'integ attribute. Given a scalar quantity Q, the attribute Q'integ is a quantity with the same type as Q whose value is the definite integral of Q with respect to time from the initial time 0.0 to the time at which the attribute is evaluated. Thus, the value of Q'integ at some simulation time t is given by

$$\text{Q'integ} = \int_{0.0}^{t} Q$$

We can also apply the 'integ attribute to a quantity Q of composite type. In this case, the result quantity is of the same type as Q, with each scalar subelement being the integral of the corresponding scalar subelement of **Q**. This is analogous to the way in which the 'dot attribute works for composite quantities.

Example   We can revise the inductor model on page 207 to express the differential equation in integral form, as shown in Figure 6-14. In the simultaneous statement, we have simply integrated both sides and rearranged the original equation. The behavior exhibited by the two models should be identical, within the limits of accuracy of the analog solver.

FIGURE 6-14

```
library ieee_proposed;  use ieee_proposed.electrical_systems.all;
entity inductor is
    port (terminal n1, n2: electrical);
end entity inductor;
```

```
architecture integral_form of inductor is
    constant L: inductance := 0.5;
    quantity branch_voltage across branch_current through n1 to n2;
begin
    branch_current == branch_voltage'integ / L;
end architecture integral_form;
```

A model of an ideal inductor.

Example   We can use the 'integ and 'dot attributes together in a mechanical model, shown in Figure 6-15, of a mass connected to a spring and a dashpot. The mass has an external attachment point represented by the terminal port of the entity. Newton's second law describes the acceleration of the mass as a function of the total force acting on the mass. There is an external driving force, represented by the through branch quantity of the external attachment terminal. The spring exerts an opposing force that is proportional to the displacement of the mass (the across branch quantity of the external attachment terminal), and the dashpot exerts an opposing force that is proportional to the velocity. Thus, the total force is the applied force less the spring force and the dashpot force.

The architecture body declares constants for the mass, the spring stiffness and the dashpot damping factor, and a free quantity for the velocity of the mass. The initial value of the velocity is 0.0, since no explicit initialization is given. The first simultaneous statement equates the position to the time integral of the velocity. The second simultaneous statement equates the force given by Newton's law (the product of mass and acceleration) with the total force acting on the mass. This simultaneous statement also includes a specification of a tolerance group using the 'tolerance attribute of the **velocity** quantity. We will discuss the need for the

FIGURE 6-15

```
library ieee_proposed;  use ieee_proposed.mechanical_systems.all;
entity moving_mass is
    port ( terminal external_attachment : translational );
end entity moving_mass;
```

```
architecture behavioral of moving_mass is
    constant mass : real := 10.0;
    constant stiffness : real := 2.0;
    constant damping : real := 5.0;
    quantity position across driving_force through external_attachment;
    quantity velocity : real;
begin
    position == velocity'integ;
    mass * velocity'dot == driving_force – stiffness * velocity'integ – damping * velocity
        tolerance velocity'tolerance;
end architecture behavioral;
```

A mechanical model of a mass connected to a spring and dashpot.

tolerance specification in this example when we discuss simultaneous statements in detail in Section 6.4.

The Slew Attribute

The 'slew attribute allows us to produce a quantity whose slew rate (that is, its time derivative) is limited to a specified range. The attribute allows us to represent the inertial effects we see in physical systems due to parasitic effects. It provides analog modeling capabilities related to the use of the inertial delay mechanism for signal assignment in digital models.

The attribute Q'slew takes two parameters, max_rising_slope, which must be a positive real value, and max_falling_slope, which must be a negative real value. The result is a quantity that follows Q provided the derivative of Q remains between the parameter values. If, on the other hand, Q's derivative exceeds max_rising_slope, then the quantity Q'slew trails Q with derivative max_rising_slope. Eventually, when Q stops changing so quickly and Q'slew has "caught up" with Q, Q'slew resumes following Q. Similar but opposite behavior applies when Q's derivative falls below the negative value max_falling_slope. The operation of the 'slew attribute is illustrated in Figure 6-16, which shows the values of a quantity Q and the quantity Q'slew(1.0, –2.0).

The parameters of the 'slew attribute are optional. If we omit the max_falling_slope parameter, it is assumed to be the negative of max_rising_slope. For example, Q'slew(1.5) has both rising and falling slopes limited to 1.5. If we omit both parameters, the slope limits are effectively infinite. Thus, Q'slew with neither parameter specified follows Q exactly.

FIGURE 6-16

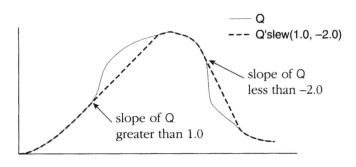

The behavior of a quantity Q'slew(1.0, –2.0) *tracking the quantity* Q.

Example   Figure 6-17 shows a model of an ideal opamp with slew-rate limiting. The opamp is modeled as a simple two-input gain device. (We discuss a more realistic opamp model in Chapter 13.) In this model, the quantity **v_amplified** represents the un-limited product of the gain and the input voltage. The **'slew** attribute is applied to this quantity to determine the output voltage. The attribute parameters specify both rising and falling slew-rate limiting of 1.0×10^6 V/s (1 V/µs).

FIGURE 6-17

```
library ieee_proposed;  use ieee_proposed.electrical_systems.all;
entity opamp is
    port ( terminal plus_in, minus_in, output : electrical );
end entity opamp;
```

```
architecture slew_limited of opamp is
    constant gain : real := 50.0;
    quantity v_in across plus_in to minus_in;
    quantity v_out across i_out through output;
    quantity v_amplified : voltage;
begin
    v_amplified == gain * v_in;

    v_out == v_amplified'slew(1.0e6,–1.0e6);
end architecture slew_limited;
```

A model of a slew-rate-limited opamp.

We can apply the **'slew** attribute not only to scalar quantities, but also to composite quantities. In that case, the result quantity is of the same type as the composite quantity, with each element following the corresponding element of the composite quantity. Each element is individually slew-rate limited.

Example   The previous example presented a model of a slew-rate-limited opamp. We can revise this model to describe a quad opamp: four opamps fabricated together as a single module, illustrated in Figure 6-18. We represent the ports and quantities using arrays, as shown in Figure 6-19. Since the terminal ports are arrays, the across and through branch quantities are also arrays. We declare **v_amplified** as an array quantity and provide equations for each element. (In Chapter 17 we will show how we can generate the equations for the elements without having to write them out individually.) The composite output is determined by applying the **'slew** attribute to the composite **v_amplified** quantity. Note that we need a type conversion for **v_out**, since its type is a different array type from the **real_vector** type of **v_amplified**. The type of **v_out** is the across type of the nature **electrical_vector**. That type is implicitly declared as a distinct, anonymous array type. Even though it has real-valued elements, the fact that it is a separate array type means that it is not directly compatible with **real_vector**. The type conversion avoids this incompatibility.

FIGURE 6·18

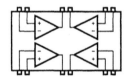

A quad-opamp module.

FIGURE 6·19

```
library ieee_proposed;  use ieee_proposed.electrical_systems.all;
entity quad_opamp is
    port ( terminal plus_in, minus_in, output : electrical_vector(1 to 4) );
end entity quad_opamp;

--------------------------------------------------------------

architecture slew_limited of quad_opamp is
    constant gain : real := 50.0;
    quantity v_in across plus_in to minus_in;
    quantity v_out across i_out through output;
    quantity v_amplified : real_vector(1 to 4);
```

```
begin
    v_amplified(1) == gain * v_in(1);
    v_amplified(2) == gain * v_in(2);
    v_amplified(3) == gain * v_in(3);
    v_amplified(4) == gain * v_in(4);
    real_vector(v_out) == v_amplified'slew(1.0e6,-1.0e6);
end architecture slew_limited;
```

A model of a slew-rate-limited quad opamp.

Quantity Attributes of Signals

In Chapter 5 we mentioned the following attributes of signals:

S'ramp(t_rise, t_fall)   A quantity that follows the value of S with specified rise and fall times.

S'slew(rising_slope, falling_slope)   A quantity that follows the value of S with specified rising and falling slopes.

These attributes yield quantities that depend on the changing values of signals. Thus, they serve as the interface between the digital and analog parts of a mixed-signal model.

The Ramp Attribute

The 'ramp attribute can be applied to any signal S of a floating-point type. The attribute takes two parameters, t_rise and t_fall, which must be non-negative real values. The result is a quantity that follows the value of S. When S changes, S'ramp changes linearly from the old value of S to the new value. If the new value is greater than the old value, the change occurs over an interval of time specified by t_rise. If the new value is less than the old value, the change occurs over an interval specified by t_fall. If a further event happens on S before the quantity has reached its final value, the quantity changes from its value at the time of change on S to the new value of S over a time specified by t_rise or t_fall, depending on the direction of change. The operation of the 'ramp attribute is illustrated in Figure 6-20, which shows the values of a signal S and the quantity S'ramp(1.0, -2.0).

The parameters of the 'ramp attribute are optional. If we omit the t_fall parameter, it is assumed to be the same as t_rise. For example, ramp(1.5) specifies 1.5 for both the rising and falling times. If we omit both parameters, the rise and fall times are both 0.0. Thus, ramp with neither parameter specified follows S exactly.

FIGURE 6-20

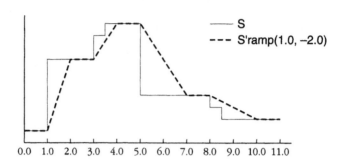

The behavior of a quantity S'ramp(1.0, –2.0) *tracking the signal* S.

Example We can use the 'ramp attribute of a signal when we need to convert from a digital to an analog view of the signal, for example, to model detailed transmission-line effects. The model shown in Figure 6-21 converts a bit-valued signal input to an electrical output. The architecture body declares constants for voltage levels corresponding to high and low signal values. It also declares an intermediate real-valued signal v_in. The concurrent signal assignment statement converts from the standard-logic input to a real value. The simultaneous statement then uses the 'ramp attribute applied to this signal to determine the output voltage. When the signal v_in changes, the 'ramp attribute transforms the step discontinuity to a linear transition between voltage values, in this case, occurring over an interval of 1 ns. Without this transformation, the analog solver would not be able to converge upon a solution for the analog system.

FIGURE 6-21

```
library ieee_proposed;  use ieee_proposed.electrical_systems.all;
entity bit_to_analog is
     port ( d : in bit;
              terminal a : electrical );
end entity bit_to_analog;

--------------------------------------------------------------

architecture ideal of bit_to_analog is
     constant v_low : real := 0.0;
     constant v_high : real := 5.0;
     signal v_in : real := 0.0;
     quantity v_out across i_out through a to electrical_ref;
begin
```

```
        v_in <= v_high when d = '1' else v_low;
        v_out == v_in'ramp(1.0e–9);
end architecture ideal;
```

A digital-to-analog converter for a standard-logic signal.

We can apply the 'ramp attribute not only to scalar signals, but also to composite signals. In that case, the result quantity is of the same type as the composite signal, with each element changing in response to events on the corresponding element of the composite signal.

The Slew Attribute

The 'slew attribute is similar to the 'ramp attribute and can be applied to any signal S of a floating-point type. However, instead of specifying rise and fall times, we specify rising and falling slopes. In this respect, it is similar to the 'slew attribute applied to a quantity. The difference is that the slopes specified for S'slew are the exact slopes of change of the result quantity, whereas the slopes specified for Q'slew are the maximum slopes of change.

The attribute S'slew takes two parameters, max_rising_slope, which must be a positive real value, and max_falling_slope, which must be a negative real value. The result is a quantity that follows the value of S. When S changes, S'slew changes linearly from the old value of S to the new value. If the new value is greater than the old value, the change occurs with slope specified by rising_slope. If the new value is less than the old value, the change occurs with slope specified by falling_slope. If a further event happens on S before the quantity has reached its final value, the quantity changes from its value at the time of change on S to the new value of S with slope specified by rising_slope or falling_slope, depending on the direction of change. The operation of the 'slew attribute is illustrated in Figure 6-22, which shows the values of a signal S and the quantity S'slew(1.0, –2.0).

FIGURE 6-22

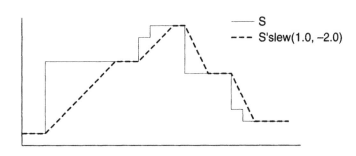

--- S
- - - S'slew(1.0, –2.0)

The behavior of a quantity S'slew(1.0, –2.0) *tracking the signal* S.

The parameters of the 'slew attribute are optional. If we omit the falling_slope parameter, it is assumed to be the negative of rising_slope. For example, S'slew(1.5) has both rising and falling slopes of 1.5. If we omit both parameters, the slope limits are effectively infinite. Thus, S'slew with neither parameter specified follows S exactly.

Example   We can refine the previous example to convert a standard-logic signal instead of a bit-valued signal to an analog quantity. Figure 6-23 shows the model. In this case, the architecture declares an additional constant for a voltage corresponding to an unknown input value. If we were to use the 'ramp attribute, as before, we would see different transition slopes on the output depending on the starting and finishing voltages. Using the 'slew attribute instead allows us to specify the slopes independent of the starting and finishing levels. In this example, the rising slope is 2 V/ns and the falling slope is 1 V/ns.

FIGURE 6-23

```
library ieee;  use ieee.std_logic_1164.all;
library ieee_proposed;  use ieee_proposed.electrical_systems.all;

entity std_logic_to_analog is
    port ( d : in std_logic;
            terminal a : electrical );
end entity std_logic_to_analog;
```

```
architecture ideal of std_logic_to_analog is
    constant v_low : real := 0.0;
    constant v_high : real := 5.0;
    constant v_unknown : real := 2.0;
    signal v_in : real := 0.0;
    quantity v_out across i_out through a to electrical_ref;
begin
    v_in <= v_high when d = '1' or d = 'H' else
            v_low when d = '0' or d = 'L' else
            v_unknown;

    v_out == v_in'slew(2.0e+9, –1.0e+9);

end architecture ideal;
```

A digital-to-analog converter for a standard-logic signal.

We can apply the 'slew attribute not only to scalar signals, but also to composite signals. In that case, the result quantity is of the same type as the composite signal, with each element changing in response to events on the corresponding element of the composite signal.

Signal Initialization

When we use the 'ramp or 'slew attribute of a signal, we need to ensure we properly initialize the signal. The signal must be of a floating-point type, so we usually declare it to be of the predefined type real. Recall that for variables and signals of floating-point types, the default initial value is the leftmost value in the range of the type. For real, the leftmost value, real'left, is a very large negative number (approximately -1.8×10^{308}). Once the model starts executing, a process will normally assign a more reasonable value to the signal.

The problem is that the 'ramp and 'slew quantities are initialized to the same value as the signal. Once the signal is updated to its "more reasonable" value, the 'ramp or 'slew quantity must change to meet the new value. In the case of the 'ramp attribute, the quantity changes from the extreme negative value to the new value in the specified time, resulting in an excessive rate of change for the signal. For example, if the signal s changes from real'left to 0.0, the quantity s'ramp(1.0E–6) will change with a slope of approximately 1.8×10^{314}. In the case of the 'slew attribute, the quantity changes from the extreme negative value to the new value with the specified slew rate. Since the range of change is so great, the time to make the transition will be extreme. For example, given the same signal change just described, s'slew(1.0E+6) will take approximately 1.8×10^{302} seconds to reach the new value. For all practical purposes, the quantity is stuck at a negative extreme.

We can avoid these problems simply by initializing the signal to a reasonable value. Usually 0.0 is appropriate. The most common scenario is to declare the signal in an architecture body and to drive it from within a process that is also declared in the architecture body. In this scenario, we can initialize the signal simply with an initial value expression in its declaration. The examples in Figures 6-21 and 6-23 illustrate this approach. In some cases, the architecture body might drive the signal by associating it with an out mode port of a component instance. In such cases, the initial value expression of the signal declaration is not used. Instead, the initial value of the out mode port is used within the instantiated entity to initialize the driver for the port, and the port's value then becomes the initial value for the signal. The approach to adopt then is to include an initial value expression in the port.

6.4 **Simultaneous Statements**

We use simultaneous statements in VHDL-AMS to express the equations that govern the analog behavior of a model. The simultaneous statements express explicit differential and algebraic equations that, together with implicit equations derived from the model structure and interconnections, constrain the values of quantities in a model. Simultaneous statements can appear anywhere a concurrent statement is allowed. This is shown by an augmented syntax rule for architecture bodies:

architecture_body ⇐
    architecture identifier **of** *entity*_name **is**
        { block_declarative_item }

```
        begin
            { concurrent_statement ▯ simultaneous_statement }
        end [ architecture ] [ identifier ] ;
```

Thus, we can use simultaneous statements along with processes to express both analog and digital behavior within an architecture body. The simultaneous statements contain expressions, as we have seen in other VHDL-AMS statements, but the results of expressions in simultaneous statements are interpreted differently. They are used to constrain the values of quantities rather than to provide new values for objects.

There are five kinds of simultaneous statement in VHDL-AMS: simple simultaneous statements, simultaneous if statements, simultaneous case statements, simultaneous null statements and simultaneous procedural statements. We discuss the first four kinds of simultaneous statement in this section; we defer simultaneous procedural statements until Chapter 9, where we discuss subprograms.

Simple Simultaneous Statement

The first kind of simultaneous statement, the simple simultaneous statement, specifies expressions used by the analog solver to constrain the values of quantities. We have seen several examples of simple simultaneous statements in preceding examples. The syntax rule is

```
simple_simultaneous_statement ⇐
    [ label : ] simple_expression == simple_expression [ tolerance
string_expression ] ;
```

The optional label allows us to identify the statement. We will discuss labeled statements in Chapter 22. The two simple expressions follow the rules we discussed in Section 2.6. They must both produce values of the same floating-point type, or of a composite type with floating-point scalar subelements. The expressions can refer to literals, constants, signals and quantities, but at least one quantity must be referred to in each simultaneous statement. The analog solver ensures that, at each analog solution point, quantities take on values that ensure the expressions on each side of the "==" sign are equal. Equality is determined within the bounds of the tolerance group that applies to the simultaneous statement. We will see shortly how this tolerance group is determined.

As an example, we can express Ohm's law using a simple simultaneous statement. Given declarations for the two terminals of a resistor and for branch quantities as follows:

```
terminal p, m : electrical;
quantity v across i through p to m;
```

and a constant R representing the resistance in ohms, we express the relationship between the quantities with the simple simultaneous statement

```
v == i * R;
```

This specifies that the values for the quantities v and i determined by the analog solver must be such that the voltage is always equal to the product of the current and the resistance.

An analogous formulation arises in the mechanical domain. Hooke's law describes the relationship between the force applied to an elastic element, such as a spring, and the displacement produced. Thus, given declarations

```
terminal node1, node2 : translational;
quantity d across f through node1 to node2;
```

and a constant k representing the spring constant, the relationship is expressed by the simple simultaneous statement

```
f == d * k;
```

These two examples show simple simultaneous statements involving scalar quantities. We can also write simultaneous statements involving composite quantities. In such cases, the results of the two expressions must have corresponding scalar elements. The analog solver finds values for the composite quantities that ensure corresponding elements of the expression results are equal. To illustrate, consider the use of Ohm's law to model the resistive drops across wires of a bus. Recall our earlier example, in which we declared a record nature to model the bus structure:

```
nature electrical_bus is
     record
          strobe: electrical;
          databus : electrical_vector(0 to 7);
     end record;
```

We can declare terminals for the ends of the bus and quantities for the voltage drops and currents as follows:

```
terminal bus_end1, bus_end2 : electrical_bus;
quantity bus_v across bus_i through bus_end1 to bus_end2;
```

We can then use these branch quantities in a simple simultaneous statement as we saw above:

```
bus_v == bus_i * R;
```

This formulation is equivalent to the collection of simple simultaneous statements:

```
bus_v.strobe == bus_i.strobe * R;
bus_v.databus(0) == bus_i.databus(0) * R;
bus_v.databus(1) == bus_i.databus(1) * R;
```

```
...
bus_v.databus(7) == bus_i.databus(7) * R;
```

The analog solver uses the tolerance group associated with a simple simultaneous statement to determine how accurately to compute the expression values. The tolerance group depends on the form of the expressions. If one of them just names a quantity without involving computation using operators or functions, the tolerance group of the named quantity is used. If both expressions are of this simple form, the one on the left-hand side of the "==" sign takes priority. In our example above, expressing Ohm's law using the simultaneous statement

```
v == i * R;
```

the left-hand expression just names the quantity v, so the tolerance group of v is used to determine accuracy of computation. On the other hand, if we write the statement as

```
v / R == i;
```

the left-hand expression involves an operator, but the right-hand expression is just a quantity name, so the tolerance group of i is used.

Note that, in the case of composite quantities, an element named using array indexing or slicing or record selection is also a quantity. Thus, in the case of the simultaneous statements

```
bus_v.strobe == bus_i.strobe * R;
bus_v.databus(0) == bus_i.databus(0) * R;
```

the left-hand expressions are just quantity names, so their tolerance groups are used.

If neither expression in a simple simultaneous statement is just the name of a quantity, the analog solver cannot determine from the expressions what tolerance group to use. In that case, we must include a tolerance clause in the statement. For example, the following statement without a tolerance clause is illegal:

```
i1 * R1 == i2 * R2;   -- illegal
```

since both expressions involve operators acting on quantity values. To fix this, we simply provide a tolerance aspect as follows:

```
i1 * R1 == i2 * R2 tolerance "current_tolerance";
```

One application of the 'tolerance attribute we discussed in Section 6.3 is to provide the tolerance group for a simple simultaneous statement. For example, if we wish to use the tolerance group for the quantity i2, we can rewrite the above statement as

```
i1 * R1 == i2 * R2 tolerance i2'tolerance;
```

We can include a tolerance clause in a simple simultaneous statement whose expressions just name quantities. In that case, the tolerance group we specify is used instead of that of the quantities. For example, had we written our statement of Ohm's law as

v == i * R **tolerance** i'tolerance;

the tolerance group of i is used instead of that of v.

Simultaneous If Statement

If the analog behavior of a system varies depending on a set of conditions, we can use the simultaneous if statement. This statement is similar to the sequential if statement we considered in Chapter 3. The simultaneous if statement selects one of a number of enclosed simultaneous statements depending on the value of one or more conditions. The enclosed statements that are selected at any time determine the analog behavior at that time. The syntax rule for a simultaneous if statement is

> simultaneous_if_statement ⇐
>   ⟦ *if*_label : ⟧
>   **if** *boolean*_expression **use**
>   ⟨ simultaneous_statement ⟩
>   ⟨ **elsif** *boolean*_expression **use**
>   ⟨ simultaneous_statement ⟩ ⟩
>   ⟦ **else**
>   ⟨ simultaneous_statement ⟩ ⟧
>   **end use** ⟦ *if*_label ⟧ ;

The optional label allows us to identify the statement. We will discuss labeled statements in Chapter 22. The syntax is very similar to that of a sequential if statement; the **use** keywords distinguish the simultaneous if statement from the sequential form. Evaluation of a simultaneous if statement starts with evaluation of the first condition (the Boolean expression after the **if** keyword). If that condition is true, the simultaneous statement after the first **use** keyword is selected. If the condition is false and there is one or more **elsif** clauses, successive conditions are evaluated until one is found to be true. The simultaneous statement after the first true condition is selected. If no true condition is found and there is an **else** clause, the simultaneous statement after the **else** keyword is selected. Finally, if no true condition is found and there is no **else** clause, the simultaneous if statement does not contribute to the analog behavior at the time of evaluation.

Example   Consider the ideal operational amplifier in Figure 6-17. Suppose we would like to add power pins and model the voltage limiting from the power rails. In normal operation, the output voltage is the product of the gain and the input voltage. If the output voltage would be greater than the positive supply voltage, we use the positive supply voltage as the output voltage instead. Similarly, if the output voltage would be less than the negative supply voltage, we use that supply voltage. This behavior is modeled in Figure 6-24. Depending on the value of the supply voltages, the input voltage and the gain factor, the appropriate simultaneous statement is selected by the simultaneous if statement in the architecture body. The break statement immediately after the simultaneous if statement is required to deal with the discontinuity that results from changing simultaneous statements. We discuss discontinuities and break statements in Section 6.6.

FIGURE 6-24

```
library ieee_proposed;  use ieee_proposed.electrical_systems.all;
entity opamp is
    port ( terminal positive_supply, negative_supply : electrical;
           terminal plus_in, minus_in, output : electrical );
end entity opamp;
```

```
architecture saturating of opamp is
    constant gain : real := 50.0;
    quantity v_pos across positive_supply;
    quantity v_neg across negative_supply;
    quantity v_in across plus_in to minus_in;
    quantity v_out across i_out through output;
    quantity v_amplified : voltage;
begin
    if v_in'above(v_pos / gain) use
        v_amplified == v_pos;
    elsif not v_in'above(v_neg / gain) use
        v_amplified == v_neg;
    else
        v_amplified == gain * v_in;
    end use;
    break on v_in'above(v_pos/gain), v_in'above(v_neg/gain);
    v_out == v_amplified'slew(1.0e6,–1.0e6);
end architecture saturating;
```

A model of a saturating opamp using a simultaneous if statement.

An important point to note in the above example is the way we expressed the conditions to be tested in the simultaneous if statement using the 'above attribute. We might have been tempted to write the conditions using a relational operator, as follows:

```
if v_in * gain > v_pos use          -- incorrect
    v_amplified == v_pos;
elsif v_in * gain < v_neg use       -- incorrect
    v_amplified == v_neg;
else
    v_amplified == gain * v_in;
end use;
```

The problem with this approach relates to the discontinuity introduced by the change of equation that occurs when the amplifier saturates. We discuss discontinuities and the need for break statements in more detail later in this chapter. Here we cover a related modeling guideline that applies to simultaneous if statements that introduce discontinuities.

The important point to note about our example is that the condition involves a quantity v_in that is changing at the time of the discontinuity. In this example, the discontinuity actually arises in the derivative of the quantity v_amplified, but it is the fact of any discontinuity arising from the simultaneous if statement under discussion that is relevant. If we were to express the conditions using a relational operator, VHDL-AMS does not guarantee at what time steps the analog solver will attempt to compute values for the quantities in the model, including v_in, v_amplified and their derivatives. The solver may attempt to compute values at or near the time of the discontinuity, and thus may not be able to converge upon a solution. We can avoid this problem by using the 'above attribute applied to the varying quantity in the condition, as we did in the example. Doing so ensures that the analog solver will be invoked at the beginning of the interval following the discontinuity and will use the equation determined by the condition value. While this approach may not be strictly necessary in all cases, depending on the precise form of the equations, it is the safest approach. Thus, we advocate it as a modeling style. Note that we can quite safely compare quantities using relational operators within processes, since quantity values do not change during each resumption and execution of a process. Similarly, we can compare signal values using relational operators in a simultaneous if statement, since signal values must be stable during the interval between discontinuities.

Returning now to the syntax rule for a simultaneous if statement, we see that the statements enclosed within the alternatives can be any of the simultaneous statements we describe in this section. Thus, for example, we can nest simultaneous if statements within a simultaneous if statement.

Example   An NMOS transistor can be either forward or reverse biased in a circuit. In each case, there are three operating regions: cutoff, saturation and linear operation. Which region the transistor operates in depends on the voltages at the gate and the drain. The relationships between the voltages and the drain-to-source current vary between the three regions, and in two cases involve the transistor's transconductance parameter k. We can represent this varying behavior using a simultaneous if statement to select between forward and reverse biasing, and within each alternative, using a nested simultaneous if statement to select the appropriate equations for the operating region. The simultaneous statements are

```
if vds'above(0.0) use   -- transistor is forward biased
    if not vgs'above(threshold_voltage) use   -- cutoff region
        ids == 0.0;
    elsif vds'above(vgs – threshold_voltage) use   -- saturation region
        ids == 0.5 * k * (vgs – threshold_voltage)**2;
    else   -- linear/triode region
        ids == k * (vgs – threshold_voltage – 0.5*vds) * vds;
    end use;
else   -- transistor is reverse biased
    if not vgd 'above(threshold_voltage) use   -- cutoff region
        ids == 0.0;
    elsif vsd'above(vgd – threshold_voltage) use   -- saturation region
        ids == –0.5 * k * (vgd – threshold_voltage)**2;
    else   -- linear/triode region
        ids == –k * (vgd – threshold_voltage – 0.5*vsd) * vsd;
    end use;
end use;
```

As the syntax rule for a simultaneous if statement shows, each alternative can enclose more than just one simultaneous statement. When such an alternative is selected, all of the enclosed statements contribute to the behavior of the system at that time. For example, we can model a current switch that alternates between charging and discharging a capacitor to generate a sawtooth waveform using the following simultaneous if statement:

```
if charging use
    i_charge == ( v_plus – v_cap ) / r_charge;
    i_discharge == 0.0;
else
    i_charge == 0.0;
    i_discharge == ( v_cap – v_minus ) / r_discharge;
end use;
```

Simultaneous Case Statement

A simultaneous case statement is similar to the sequential case statement we discussed in Chapter 3, in that it selects one of a number of alternatives based on the value of an expression.   In a simultaneous case statement, the alternatives each enclose one or more simultaneous statements, as shown by the syntax rule

```
simultaneous_case_statement ⇐
    ⟦ case_label : ⟧
    case expression use
        ⦃ when choices => ⦃ simultaneous_statement ⦄ ⦄
```

$\{ \dots \}$
end case ⟦ *case*_label ⟧ ;

choices ⇐ ⟨ simple_expression ⫾ discrete_range ⫾ **others** ⟩ ⟨⟨ ⫾ ... ⟩⟩

The optional label allows us to identify the statement. We will discuss labeled statements in Chapter 22. The syntax is very similar to that of a sequential case statement; the **use** keywords distinguish the simultaneous case statement from the sequential form. The expression of the simultaneous case statement and each of the choices in the alternatives must follow the same rules as a sequential case statement described in Section 3.2. As a reminder, the rules are

- the selector expression must produce a value of a discrete type, or a type that is a one-dimensional array of characters (for example, a character-string or bit-string type),

- all possible values of the selector expression must be covered by one and only one choice,

- the values in the choices must be locally static and

- if the **others** choice is used it must be in the last alternative and must be the only choice in that alternative.

Evaluation of a simultaneous case statement first involves evaluation of the selector expression. Then the resulting value is compared with each of the choices. The simultaneous statements corresponding to the matching choices are selected to determine the analog behavior of the system at the current time.

As with the simultaneous if statement, we can write an arbitrary number of simultaneous statements of any kind in each alternative. This includes writing nested case statements, if statements or any other form of simultaneous statements in the alternatives.

Example Let us return to the model of an NMOS transistor from page 223. Suppose we declare the following types to represent the biasing and operating regions of the transistor and signals of the types

```
type biases is (forward, reverse);
type regions is (cutoff, saturation, linear);

signal bias : biases;
signal region : regions;
```

We can use the following nested simultaneous case statements to model the transistor behavior:

```
case bias use
    when forward =>
        case region use
```

```
                    when cutoff =>
                        ids == 0.0;
                    when saturation =>
                        ids == 0.5 * k * (vgs – threshold_voltage)**2;
                    when linear =>
                        ids == k * (vgs – threshold_voltage – 0.5*vds) * vds;
                end case;
            when reverse =>
                case region use
                    when cutoff =>
                        ids == 0.0;
                    when saturation =>
                        ids == –0.5 * k * (vgd – threshold_voltage)**2;
                    when linear =>
                        ids == –k * (vgd – threshold_voltage – 0.5*vsd) * vsd;
                end case;
        end case;
```

One potential problem to be aware of when modeling analog behavior using simultaneous case statements is that we cannot use the value of a quantity as the selector expression, since quantities are of floating-point types, which are not discrete types. For example, the following attempt at writing a simultaneous case statement is wrong:

```
quantity v : voltage;
...

case v use   –– illegal
    when 0.0 to 0.6 =>
        ...;
    when 0.6 to 2.7 =>
        ...;
    when others =>
        ...;
end case;
```

This fails for two reasons. First, the selector expression is of a floating-point type, and second, the choice ranges are not discrete ranges. In situations like this, the correct way to express the behavior is using a simultaneous if statement. We can rewrite the above illegal example as follows:

```
if v'above(0.0) and not v'above(0.6) use
    ...

elsif v'above(0.6) and not v'above(2.7) use
    ...
```

else

   ...

end use;

Simultaneous Null Statement

As we discussed in Section 3.3 where we introduced sequential null statements, we sometimes wish to indicate explicitly that no action is to be performed. Similar circumstances may arise in analog models using simultaneous statements. In such cases, we can use a simultaneous null statement. The syntax rule is

simultaneous_null_statement ⇐ ⟦ label : ⟧ **null** ;

The optional label allows us to identify the statement. We will discuss labeled statements in Chapter 22. We write a simultaneous statement simply as follows:

null;

We must be careful when we use a simultaneous null statement to be sure that we provide enough equations for the analog solver to be able to find solutions for all of the unknown quantities in a model. The problem we must keep in mind is that, if we include a simultaneous null statement in an alternative of a simultaneous if or case statement, when that alternative is selected, the number of equations contributed by the if or case statement is reduced. We need to ensure that enough equations are provided elsewhere in the model to compensate. We will discuss the requirements for the number of equations in Chapter 7.

Example   As with the sequential null statement, we may include a simultaneous null statement if we have not yet determined what equation to use in particular cases. For example, in a model of a resistor, we can use an enumerated type to indicate which of a set of effects are to be reflected in the model. The ideal case simply reflects Ohm's law, while other cases include more detailed physical effects such as resistor heating. The following VHDL-AMS statements indicate that the detailed model of the resistor is not complete, so a simultaneous null statement is used as a placeholder.

```
if modeling_mode = ideal use
    v == i * R;
else
    null;   -- still need to include resistor with thermal effects!
end use;
```

6.5   **Analog Structural Descriptions**

In Section 5.4 we described component instantiation statements in structural models and saw how to associate signals with signal ports. We can instantiate entities with quantity and terminal ports in the same way. We simply write a component instantiation statement naming the entity. In the port map, we can associate branch or free quantities with quantity ports, and terminals with terminal ports. We can use positional or named association, just as we did for signal ports. For example, suppose we declare the following terminals and a quantity in an architecture body:

> **terminal** bridge1, bridge2 : electrical;
> **quantity** ambient : temperature;

Then we can instantiate the temperature-dependent resistor entity described on page 191 in a component instantiation statement:

> resistor1 : **entity** work.temperature_dependent_resistor(linear_approx)
>   **port map** (n1 => bridge1, n2 => bridge2, temp => ambient);

In our discussion of digital structural descriptions, we mentioned that a component instantiation statement has the effect of creating a copy of the entity with the architecture body substituted for the instance. In the example above, the simultaneous statements are copied with the terminals **bridge1** and **bridge2** associated with the terminal ports **n1** and **n2**, and the quantity **ambient** associated with **temp**. When the analog solver computes solutions, it will use the value of **ambient** as the quantity value in the equations. It will treat the terminal **bridge1** and the terminal port **n1** as equipotential regions, with the current branch from **n1** contributing to the total current flowing from **bridge1**. It will treat **bridge2** and **n2** similarly. We will return to this in Chapter 7 when we discuss elaboration of a model in more detail.

Example   We can implement an inverting integrator using an operational amplifier, a resistor and a capacitor as shown in Figure 6-25.

FIGURE 6-25

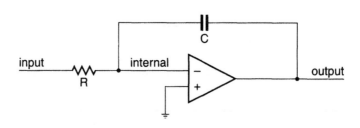

A circuit for an inverting integrator.

To describe this circuit in VHDL-AMS, we can use component models that we have described in previous examples. Models for an ideal resistor and for a capacitor with resistive leakage are shown again in Figure 6-26. We use the opamp model from Figure 6-17.

The entity declaration and architecture body for the inverting integrator are shown in Figure 6-27. The architecture body includes component instantiation statements to include the circuit elements.

FIGURE 6-26

```
library ieee_proposed;  use ieee_proposed.electrical_systems.all;

entity resistor is
    port ( terminal node1, node2 : electrical );
end entity resistor;

architecture ideal of resistor is
    constant R : real := 1000.0;
    quantity v across i through node1 to node2;
begin
    v == i * R;
end architecture ideal;
```

```
library ieee_proposed;  use ieee_proposed.electrical_systems.all;

entity capacitor is
    port ( terminal node1, node2 : electrical );
end entity capacitor;

architecture leakage of capacitor is
    constant c : real := 1.0E-6;
    constant r_leak : real := 10.0E6;
    quantity v_cap across i_cap, i_leak through node1 to node2;
begin
    i_cap == c * v_cap'dot;
    i_leak == v_cap / r_leak;
end architecture leakage;
```

A resistor and a capacitor model for use in the integrator circuit.

FIGURE 6-27

```
library ieee_proposed;  use ieee_proposed.electrical_systems.all;

entity inverting_integrator is
    port ( terminal input, output : electrical );
end entity inverting_integrator;
```

```
architecture structural of inverting_integrator is
    terminal internal : electrical;
begin
    r1 : entity work.resistor(ideal)
        port map ( node1 => input, node2 => internal ) ;
    c1 : entity work.capacitor(leakage)
        port map ( node1 => internal, node2 => output );
    amp : entity work.opamp(slew_limited)
        port map ( plus_in => electrical_ref, minus_in => internal,
                        output => output );

end architecture structural;
```

An entity declaration and structural architecture body for an inverting integrator.

In Section 5.4 we examined a number of aspects of port maps in component instantiation statements, including subelement association, association of expressions with ports and use of the keyword **open** to leave a port unassociated. These aspects also apply to port maps for quantity and terminal ports. Thus, we can use subelement association to associate separate quantities or terminals with individual elements of composite quantity ports or terminal ports, respectively. We can provide an expression whose value is to be used for a quantity port, but not for a terminal port. If we include a default value expression in an input quantity port declaration and use the keyword **open** to leave the port unassociated, the default value is used as the initial value of the quantity. We illustrate these possibilities with some examples.

Example   Given the following type and nature:

```
type illuminance_vector is array ( natural range <> ) of illuminance;
nature electrical_vector is array ( natural range <> ) of electrical;
```

We can declare an entity for a seven-segment light-emitting diode (LED):

```
entity seven_segment_led is
    port ( terminal segment_anodes : electrical_vector ( 1 to 7 );
            terminal common_cathode : electrical;
            quantity segment_illuminances : out illuminance_vector ( 1 to 7 ) );
    end entity seven_segment_led;
```

An instance of this entity used for the hours digit of a 12-hour clock only displays the digit 1. Thus only the segments with indices 2 and 3 are driven by the clock control circuit. The anodes of the other segments are unused. Similarly, only the optical outputs for segments 2 and 3 are used. We use subelement association to connect the ports that require connection. Since we cannot leave the other port elements open using subelement association, we associate them with dummy terminal and quantity elements. Given the following terminal and quantity declarations in the architecture body of the clock system:

```
terminal hour_anode_2, hour_anode_3 : electrical;
terminal anodes_unused : electrical_vector(1 to 5);
terminal hour_display_source_2, hour_display_source_3 : radiant;
quantity hour_illuminance_2 across hour_display_source_2;
quantity hour_illuminance_3 across hour_display_source_3;
quantity illuminances_unused : illuminance_vector(1 to 5);
```

the component instantiation statement is

```
hour_digit : entity work.seven_segment_led(basic_optics)
    port map ( segment_anodes(2) => hour_anode_2,
               segment_anodes(3) => hour_anode_3,
               segment_anodes(1) => anodes_unused(1),
               segment_anodes(4 to 7) => anodes_unused(2 to 5),
               common_cathode => electrical_ref,
               segment_illuminances(2) => hour_illuminance_2,
               segment_illuminances(3) => hour_illuminance_3,
               segment_illuminances(1) => illuminances_unused(1),
               segment_illuminances(4 to 7) => illuminances_unused(2 to 5) );
```

Example We can write an entity declaration for an analog-to-digital converter with a reference voltage input as follows:

```
library ieee_proposed;  use ieee_proposed.electrical_systems.all;
entity adc_with_ref is
    port ( quantity v_in : in voltage;
           signal d_out : out bit;
           quantity v_ref : in voltage := 1.0 );
end entity adc_with_ref;
```

The quantity port v_ref has a default value of 1.0. If we leave this port unassociated in an instance of the entity, the default value is used. For example:

```
default_adc : entity work.adc_with_ref(signal_flow)
    port map ( sensor_in, sensor_data_out );
```

Here, the reference voltage port is omitted from the port map, so it remains unassociated.

Alternatively, we can associate an expression with the reference port to model the port being tied to a fixed voltage:

```
fixed_adc : entity work.adc_with_ref(signal_flow)
    port map ( sensor_in, sensor_data_out, v_ref => v_supply / 2.0 );
```

When we discussed the syntax rules for quantity ports in Section 6.1, we saw that we can declare the mode of a quantity port to be either **in** or **out**. We also mentioned that a quantity port of an entity is treated as a free quantity within an architecture of the entity. This suggests that we should be able to associate a quantity port of an enclosing entity with a quantity port of an instantiated entity. Indeed, if we refer back to Figures 1-13 and 1-17, we see an example: the **gain** port of the **adc** entity is associated with the **g** port of the component instance **amp**. The only restrictions on associations of quantities with quantity ports are

- we may not associate an **in** port of an enclosing entity with an **out** port of a component instance, and

- we may not associate a quantity with more than one component-instance **out** port.

6.6   Discontinuities and Break Statements

When modeling continuously valued systems, at times we find it necessary to introduce discontinuous behaviors. This happens particularly in mixed-signal systems where a process representing a digital part of the system changes the operating conditions of an analog part. We can indicate a discontinuity by using a *break statement*. Each time a break statement executes, it signals to the analog solver that a discontinuity has occurred at the current simulation time. The analog solver in a VHDL-AMS simulator can solve model equations for quantities that are piecewise continuous, provided we indicate the occurrence of discontinuities with break statements and, if necessary, provide new initial conditions at discontinuities. Usually, discontinuities occur when one or more digital signals change value. However, the converse is not true. There may be events on digital signals that do not cause discontinuities in analog quantities, particularly in mixed-signal systems that are predominantly digital. If the simulator were to assume that all digital events produced discontinuities, simulation would be very inefficient and slow. Hence, VHDL-AMS requires us to use break statements to explicitly indicate the occurrence of discontinuities. This is a relatively small price to pay for significant improvements in simulation efficiency.

There are two forms of break statement: a sequential break statement that we can include in a process, and a concurrent break statement. We examine the sequential form first. The syntax rule is

break_statement ⇐
    〚 label : 〛 **break** 〚 break_element 〚 , ... 〛 〛 〚 **when** *boolean*_expression 〛 ;

break_element ⇐ 〚 **for** *quantity*_name **use** 〛 *quantity*_name => expression

Given the number of options in the statement, we will start by examining simple forms and progress to more involved forms. The optional label is used to identify the statement. We discuss labeled statements in Chapter 22. The simplest form of break statement includes just the keyword **break**, omitting any quantity names and the condition, for example:

break;

This simply causes the analog solver to determine a new analog solution starting from the current quantity values. We typically use this form of break statement in a process after changing the values of signals that are used elsewhere in simultaneous statements to determine analog quantity values.

Example   We can construct a simple resettable timer using the circuit shown in Figure 6-28. A low pulse on the trigger_n input sets the flipflop, causing the output q to go high and the clamp transistor to be turned off. The external capacitor then charges through the external resistor. When the voltage reaches half the supply voltage, the comparator resets the flipflop. The flipflop can also be reset by the **reset** input before the timer has completed its cycle.

Figure 6-29 shows a behavioral model of the resettable timer. The connection to the external resistor and capacitor is provided by the rc_ext terminal port. The architecture body declares branch quantities for the voltage across the terminal and the current flowing from the terminal through the clamp transistor. It also declares constants for the on and off resistances of the transistor and a signal q_n for the internal control connection to the transistor.

The simultaneous if statement models the behavior of the clamp transistor. It expresses Ohm's law using either the on or the off resistance for the transistor, depending on the value of the signal q_n. Whenever this value changes, discontinuities arise in the voltage and current quantities due to different equations being used.

FIGURE 6-28

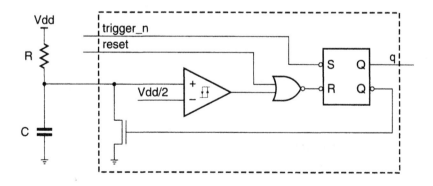

A circuit for a resettable timer.

The process **timer_state** is sensitive to the **trigger_n** and **reset** digital inputs and to the capacitor voltage crossing a threshold at half the supply voltage. When the process resumes, it tests whether it must reset or set the flipflop state. The process **clamp_change** is sensitive to changes on the q_n signal. These changes are the ones that cause discontinuities in the analog quantities, so the **clamp_change** process executes a break statement to invoke the analog solver.

FIGURE 6-29

```
library ieee;  use ieee.std_logic_1164.all;
library ieee_proposed;  use ieee_proposed.electrical_systems.all;
entity timer is
    port ( signal trigger_n, reset : in std_ulogic;  signal q : out std_ulogic;
        terminal rc_ext : electrical );;
end entity timer;
```

```
architecture behavioral of timer is
    constant half_vdd : real := 2.5;
    constant clamp_on_resistance : real := 0.01;
    constant clamp_off_resistance : real := 10.0E6;
    quantity v_rc_ext across i_clamp through rc_ext to electrical_ref;
    signal q_n : std_ulogic := '1';
begin
    if q_n = '1' use
        i_clamp == v_rc_ext / clamp_on_resistance;
    else
        i_clamp == v_rc_ext / clamp_off_resistance;
    end use;
    timer_state : process ( trigger_n, reset, v_rc_ext'above(half_vdd) ) is
    begin
        if reset = '1' or reset = 'H' or v_rc_ext > half_vdd then
            q <= '0';  q_n <= '1';
        elsif trigger_n = '0' or trigger_n = 'L' then
            q <= '1';  q_n <= '0';
        end if;
    end process timer_state;

    clamp_change : process ( q_n ) is
    begin
        break;
    end process clamp_change;
end architecture behavioral;
```

A model of the resettable timer.

In the example above, we placed the break statement in a separate process that is sensitive to changes on the signal q_n that causes discontinuities. We might be tempted to place break statements in the process after the assignments to q_n, as follows:

```
...
if reset = '1' or reset = 'H' or v_rc_ext > half_vdd then
    q <= '0'; q_n <= '1';
    break;
elsif trigger_n = '0' or trigger_n = 'L' then
    q <= '1'; q_n <= '0';
    break;
end if;
...
```

We can show that the break statement would be executed prematurely. First, consider what would happen if we were to change the assignments to include some delay, for example,

```
q_n <= '1' after 20 ns;
break;
```

The signal assignment statement schedules a transaction for q_n at a time 20 ns into the future and then the break statement executes immediately. The break statement causes the analog solver to be executed, even though the signal still has its old value and no discontinuity has yet occurred. When the transaction is eventually performed and the signal does change, causing a discontinuity, the analog solver is not invoked. Hence, the revised model is erroneous.

This problem arises even without adding delay to the assignment. If we write

```
q_n <= '1';
break;
```

the signal assignment still schedules the transaction for q_n in the future. Recall from our discussion of delta cycles in Chapter 5 that the signal is not updated until the next simulation cycle. Meanwhile, statements within the process continue executing until the process suspends. In this example, the break statement is executed immediately after the transaction is scheduled. As we shall see when we discuss the simulation cycle in more detail in Chapter 7, the analog solver is invoked before signals are updated. Hence the signal q_n still has its old value, and the discontinuity has not yet occurred when the analog solver is invoked.

This problem is not a limitation of VHDL-AMS. We just need to be aware of it and adopt an appropriate modeling style if we wish to use sequential break statements in processes. We should avoid placing a break statement immediately after the signal assignment statements that cause a discontinuity to occur. Instead, we should place the break statement in a separate process that is sensitive to the signals or conditions that cause the discontinuity. That way, the analog solver is only invoked after the discontinuity has arisen. An alternative approach that can be used in many models is to use a concurrent break statement, which we will describe shortly. As we will see, a concurrent break statement embodies the modeling style we suggest.

In some models, we write equations involving the derivative of a quantity and expect the analog solver to determine values for the quantity itself. The analog solver effectively calculates values for the quantity over successive time steps in such a way as to ensure that the derivative of the quantity satisfies our equations. When a step discontinuity occurs in the quantity, the history of quantity values before the discontinuity cannot be used to determine the derivative for satisfying the equations. In these circumstances, we must use a break statement and supply a new value for the quantity whose derivative is mentioned in an equation. We do so using a break statement that includes a break element naming a quantity and providing a new value for that quantity.

Example   To illustrate, suppose we are developing a behavioral model of a one-shot timer that uses the charging of a capacitor through a resistor to determine the time interval. A simultaneous statement relates the capacitor charge current to the derivative of the capacitor voltage

    i_cap == capacitance * v_cap'dot;

A process modeling the digital behavior of the timer discharges the capacitor by re-initializing the capacitor voltage to 0.0:

```
trigger_reset : process (trigger) is
begin
    if trigger = '1' then
        break v_cap => 0.0;
    end if;
end process trigger_reset;
```

When the process resumes in response to a **trigger** event, it executes the break statement with **v_cap** as the break quantity. If **trigger** is '1', the statement indicates a discontinuity to the analog solver and provides a new initial value for **v_cap**. The solver uses this value in its computation of subsequent values of **v_cap** and of **v_cap**'dot.

Recall that the syntax for a break element is

break_element ⇐ ⟦ **for** *quantity*_name **use** ⟧ *quantity*_name => expression

The quantity between the **for** and **use** keywords is called the *selector quantity*, for reasons we will return to shortly, and the quantity immediately before the "=>" symbol is called the *break quantity*. In most practical models, as in the above example, we do not need to include the optional part. In such cases, the break quantity also serves as the selector quantity.

The reason for drawing the distinction is that VHDL-AMS has some rules governing the selector quantity. In general, the selector quantity must be either a quantity q whose derivative q'dot appears in a simultaneous statement, or a quantity of the form q'integ. In the above example, the break quantity v_cap is also the selector quantity. It conforms to the first alternative, since the model mentions v_cap'dot in a simultaneous statement. To illustrate the second alternative, consider a model of a mechanical system that includes an equation expressing Newton's second law of motion:

```
applied_force == mass * acceleration;
```

If we wish to model a perfectly elastic collision that results in a reversal of velocity, we can use a break statement that names the integral of acceleration as the break quantity:

```
break acceleration'integ => - acceleration'integ;
```

Again, the break quantity is also the selector quantity, and it is the integral of the acceleration quantity.

The syntax rules for a break statement show that we can specify new values for several break quantities by listing them as separate break elements, for example,

```
break vx => 0.0, vy => 0.0;
```

The syntax rules also show that we can include a condition after the keyword **when**. When a conditional break statement is executed and the condition is true, the discontinuity occurs. Any new values specified for break quantities are applied and the analog solver calculates a new solution. If, on the other hand, the condition is false when the conditional break statement is executed, the statement has no effect. Thus, we can think of a conditional break statement as a succinct notation for an unconditional break statement enclosed in an if statement. For example, we can rewrite the trigger_reset process in the example above as

```
trigger_reset : process (trigger) is
begin
    break v_cap => 0.0 when trigger = '1';
end process trigger_reset;
```

Example   Consider the behavior of a ball that bounces on the ground with perfect elasticity and suffers resistance as it travels through the air. Each time it bounces, its speed reverses. The model in Figure 6-30, based on a model by Christen et al. [9], uses a break statement to model this discontinuity. The simultaneous if statement in the architecture body selects alternate equations of motion depending on whether the ball is rising or falling, since air resistance increases the deceleration when the ball is rising but decreases acceleration when the ball is falling. The process

FIGURE 6·30

```
library ieee_proposed;  use ieee_proposed.mechanical_systems.all;
entity ball is
end entity ball;
```

```
architecture bouncer of ball is
    quantity v : velocity := 0.0;
    quantity s : displacement := 10.0;
    constant g : real := 9.81;
    constant air_res : real := 0.1;
begin
    if v'above(0.0) use
        v'dot == –g – v**2*air_res;
    else
        v'dot == –g + v**2*air_res;
    end use;

    reversal_tester : process is
    begin
        wait on s'above(0.0);
        break v => –v when s < 0.0;
    end process reversal_tester;

    s'dot == v;
end architecture bouncer;
```

A model of a bouncing ball.

reversal_tester resumes whenever the ball reaches the ground. The break statement reverses the velocity when the displacement falls instantaneously below zero.

Let us now return to the distinction between the selector quantity and the break quantity in a break element. In some cases we may need to specify a new value for a break quantity q1 at a discontinuity in a model that does not mention q1'dot in a simultaneous statement. This can occur where the model relates some other quantity q2 to q1 and includes q2'dot in a simultaneous statement. We need to indicate that the new value is supplied for q1 in order for the analog solver to be able to compute values for q2 and q2'dot after the discontinuity. The mechanism for doing so is to specify q2 as a *selector quantity* distinct from the break quantity q1. Recall that the syntax rule for a break element in a break statement is

break_element ⇐ 〚 **for** *quantity*_name **use** 〛 *quantity*_name => expression

We include the optional part, naming the selector quantity between the keywords **for** and **use** and naming the break quantity immediately before the "=>" symbol. In this case, the rule governing the selector quantity applies just to the selector quantity that we name, and not to the separate break quantity. Thus, it is the distinct selector quantity that must be either a quantity q whose derivative q'dot appears in a simultaneous statement, or a quantity of the form q'integ.

Example Consider again the one-shot timer model described on page 236. Suppose we wish to model not only the current and voltage, but also the charge accumulated on the capacitor. Simultaneous statements expressing the relationships are

```
charge == capacitance * v_cap;
i_cap == charge'dot;
```

As in the previous example, the process discharges the capacitor by re-initializing the capacitor voltage to 0.0. However, in this model, the derivative of the voltage quantity is not mentioned in the simultaneous statements. Instead, it is the charge quantity whose derivative depends indirectly on the new value of the voltage. Thus, we name the charge quantity as the selector quantity. We name the voltage quantity as the break quantity and supply a new value for it at the discontinuity. The revised process is

```
trigger_reset : process (trigger) is
begin
    if trigger = '1' then
        break for charge use v_cap => 0.0;
    end if;
end process trigger_reset;
```

As with the previous example, we can combine the condition into the break statement as follows:

```
trigger_reset : process (trigger) is
begin
    break for charge use v_cap => 0.0 when trigger = '1';
end process trigger_reset;
```

Concurrent Break Statements

VHDL-AMS also provides a concurrent break statement to indicate discontinuities in a model. As with several other concurrent statements that we saw in Chapter 5, a concurrent break statement is equivalent to a process containing the sequential form of the statement. The syntax rule is

concurrent_break_statement ⇐
   ⟦ label : ⟧
   break ⟦ break_element ⦃ , ... ⦄ ⟧
      ⟦ **on** signal_name ⦃ , ... ⦄ ⟧
      ⟦ **when** *boolean*_expression ⟧ ;

As in the sequential break statement, the syntax rule for the break elements is

break_element ⇐ ⟦ **for** *quantity*_name **use** ⟧ *quantity*_name => expression

A concurrent break statement is a shorthand notation for a process containing a sequential break statement with the same break elements and condition clause. The sequential break statement is followed by a wait statement. If the concurrent break statement includes a sensitivity clause (a list of signal names after the **on** keyword), the wait statement in the equivalent process contains the same sensitivity clause. For example, the concurrent break statement

discharge_cap : **break** cap_charge => 0.0
                    on clk **when** discharge = '1' **and** clk = '1';

is equivalent to the process

discharge_cap : **process is**
begin
    break cap_charge => 0.0 **when** discharge = '1' **and** clk = '1';
    wait on clk;
end process discharge_cap;

If the concurrent break statement does not contain a sensitivity clause, the wait statement in the equivalent process is just sensitive to the signals named in the condition of the concurrent break statement. For example, we could replace the **trigger_reset** process in the example above with the concurrent break statement

trigger_reset : **break for** charge **use** v_cap => 0.0 **when** trigger = '1';

since this statement is equivalent to

trigger_reset : **process is**
begin
    break for charge **use** v_cap => 0.0 **when** trigger = '1';
    wait on trigger;
end process trigger_reset;

which in turn is equivalent to the process shown in the example.

Example　Figure 6-31 shows a model of an analog switch with digital control. When the control input is high, the switch is closed, shorting the terminals together. When the control input is low or unknown, the switch is open and no current flows between the terminals. The architecture body includes a concurrent break statement to deal with the discontinuities in the voltage and current quantities arising from changes in the switch state.

FIGURE 6-31

```
library ieee;  use ieee.std_logic_1164.all;
library ieee_proposed;  use ieee_proposed.electrical_systems.all;

entity analog_switch is
    port ( terminal n1, n2 : electrical;
            signal control : in std_ulogic );
end entity analog_switch;
```

```
architecture ideal of analog_switch is
    quantity v across i through n1 to n2;
begin
    if control = '1' or control = 'H' use
        v == 0.0;
    else
        i == 0.0;
    end use;

    break on control;
end architecture ideal;
```

A model of a digitally controlled analog switch.

If the concurrent break statement does not contain a sensitivity clause and the condition does not refer to any signals or is omitted, the wait statement in the equivalent process reduces to an indefinite wait. For example, the concurrent break statement

```
useless_break : break q => new_q when q < 0.0 or q > 3.0;
```

where q is the name of a quantity, is equivalent to the process

```
useless_break : process is
begin
    break q => new_q when q < 0.0 or q > 3.0;
```

```
        wait;
    end process useless_break;
```

This process indicates a discontinuity at the start of a simulation (when the analog solver is invoked anyway), and then waits indefinitely. Thus, for a concurrent break statement to be effective, it must include either a sensitivity clause or mention one or more signals in a condition clause. Recall that the 'above attribute yields a signal, so the above concurrent break statement could be correctly rewritten as

```
correct_break : break q => new_q on q'above(0.0), q'above(3.0)
    when q < 0.0 or q > 3.0;
```

Example   Figure 6-32 shows a pendulum with a flexible arm swinging from a pivot point. Below and to one side of the pivot there is an interfering pin that constrains the swing of the pendulum. When the arm reaches the pin, its length is effectively shortened by the distance between the pivot point and the pin.

Figure 6-33 shows a VHDL-AMS model of the pendulum. Since we are modeling a closed system, there are no ports in the entity declaration. The model uses the math_real package, which provides declarations of the sin function and the constant math_pi for the value of π. The architecture body declares a number of constants that represent the physical properties of the system. The quantity phi represents the angular displacement of the pendulum arm from vertical. When the pendulum is hanging from the pivot, this angle is measured from the pivot. When the arm hits the pin, the angle is transferred and is measured from the pin. The quantity current_length represents the free length of the arm upon which the mass is swinging.

FIGURE 6-32

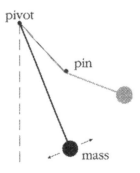

A pendulum with a flexible arm that is limited by a pin.

FIGURE 6-33

```
library ieee;  use ieee.math_real.all;
entity pendulum is
end entity pendulum;
```

```
architecture constrained of pendulum is
    constant mass : real := 10.0;
    constant arm_length : real := 5.0;
    constant pin_angle : real := 0.25 * math_pi;
    constant pin_distance : real := 2.5;
    constant damping : real := 1.0;
    constant gravity : real := 9.81;
    constant short_length : real := arm_length – pin_distance;
    quantity phi : real := –0.5*math_pi;
    quantity current_length : real := arm_length;
begin
    if phi'above(pin_angle) use
        current_length == short_length;
    else
        current_length == arm_length;
    end use;
    break phi'dot => phi'dot * arm_length/short_length
        when phi'above(pin_angle);

    break phi'dot => phi'dot * short_length/arm_length
        when not phi'above(pin_angle);

    mass * current_length * phi'dot'dot
        == – mass * gravity * sin(phi) – damping * current_length * phi'dot;
end architecture constrained;
```

A model of the constrained pendulum.

The simultaneous if statement expresses the fact that the free length of the arm changes when the arm hits the pin. If the arm angle is greater than that of the pin from the pivot, the arm is shortened to the value **short_length**; otherwise, the arm has its full length. The interference of the pin produces a discontinuity, so we have two concurrent break statements in the model. The first break statement applies when the arm angle exceeds that of the pin from the pivot, causing the arm to be shortened. In order for angular momentum in the system to be conserved, the angular velocity of the pendulum is increased by the same factor with which the arm is shortened. Angular velocity is the derivative of the angle, so the break statement applies the scaled value of the derivative as the new value of the derivative quantity. The second break statement applies when the arm angle falls below that of the pin from the pivot. It reduces the angular velocity by the factor with which the arm is lengthened. The last statement in the architecture body equates the torque acting on the arm to the sum of the torques produced by gravity acting on the mass and by damping in the system.

6.7 Step Limit Specifications

Since quantities in an analog model are continuous functions of time, there are an infinite number of quantity values in any given time interval. An analog solver in a VHDL-AMS simulator approximates the quantity values by solving the model equations at a finite number of time steps. The solution at each time step is called an *analog solution point*. In order to give tool vendors some flexibility, the VHDL-AMS language definition does not specify the details of how the analog solver computes analog solution points. In particular, the definition does not specify the times and frequency with which analog solution points are computed. Simulator vendors may use whatever techniques they consider appropriate to achieve high performance and accuracy.

For some models, however, we may wish to ensure that analog solution points will occur within some time window or with some minimum frequency. We can accomplish this in VHDL-AMS using a *step limit specification*. The syntax is

step_limit_specification ⇐
    limit ⟦ *quantity*_name ⦃ , ... ⦄ ▯ **others** ▯ **all** ⟧ : type_mark **with** *real*_expression ;

A step limit specification allows us to identify one or more quantities by their names and type, and to specify the maximum interval between analog solution points for those quantities. The step limit specification must appear in the same list of declarations as the quantity declarations to which it refers. The real-valued expression in the step limit specification is the maximum number of seconds between analog solution points. For example, if we have a mechanical quantity representing displacement, we can limit the interval between analog solution points for the quantity to be no more than 1 ms as follows:

```
quantity d : displacement;
limit d : displacement with 0.001;
```

Note that the step limit specification specifies only a *maximum* time step for use by the analog solver. If the solver determines that it needs to use a smaller step size to achieve sufficient accuracy in the computation, the specified step limit has no effect. Thus, we cannot specify a minimum step size. That is left to the simulation implementer as part of the trade-off between efficiency and accuracy.

Example   Figure 6-34 shows an entity declaration and architecture body for a triangle-wave-form generator that we can use in a test bench. The architecture body includes a process that generates a square-wave signal alternating between the values 0.0 and 1.0. The frequency, 10 kHz, is specified by the constant **freq**, and the period is the reciprocal of the frequency. The simultaneous statement uses the 'ramp attribute to generate the triangle-waveform quantity **v** from the square-wave signal. We include a step limit specification for **v** to ensure that at least 10 analog solution points are calculated for **v** in each period of the waveform.

FIGURE 6-34

```
library ieee_proposed;  use ieee_proposed.electrical_systems.all;

entity triangle_waveform is
    port ( terminal pos, neg : electrical );
end entity triangle_waveform;

--------------------------------------------------------------

architecture ideal of triangle_waveform is
    constant freq : real := 10_000.0;   -- in Hz
    constant period : real := 1.0 / freq;
    constant amplitude : voltage := 5.0;
    constant offset : voltage := 0.0;
    signal square_wave : real := 0.0;
    quantity v across i through pos to neg;
    limit v : voltage with period / 10.0;
begin
    process is
        variable state : bit := '0';
    begin
        if state = '1' then
            square_wave <= 1.0;
        else
            square_wave <= 0.0;
        end if;
        state := not state;
        wait for period / 2.0;
    end process;
    v == offset + amplitude * square_wave'ramp(period / 2.0);
end architecture ideal;
```

A model of a triangle-waveform generator.

The syntax rule for step limit specifications shows that we can name more than one quantity. So if we declare the following quantities in an architecture body:

quantity drive_shaft_av, axle_av, wheel_av : angular_velocity;

we can specify the same step limit for all of them as follows:

limit drive_shaft_av, axle_av, wheel_av : angular_velocity **with** 0.01;

If these are the only quantities of the type **angular_velocity** in the architecture body, we can use the keyword **all** to identify them rather than listing them individually, for example,

limit all : angular_velocity **with** 0.01;

The **all** keyword identifies all of the quantities of the specified type declared in the same list of declarations as the specification. If we include a step limit specification using the keyword **all** for a particular type, it must be the only step limit specification in the declaration list referring to that type and must follow all quantity declarations for that type in the list.

Another way to identify quantities is to use the **others** keyword. We can provide some step limit specifications that explicitly name quantities, then follow them with a specification using **others** to identify all remaining quantities of a particular type. For example,

quantity input, preamp_out, mixer_out, agc_out : voltage;
limit input, preamp_out : voltage **with** 1.0E–9;
limit others : voltage **with** 1.0E–7;

In this case, the first specification applies to the quantities **input** and **preamp_out**, and the second specification applies to the quantities **mixer_out** and **agc_out**. If we include a step limit specification using the keyword **others** for a particular type, it must follow all other step limit specifications for the type in the list and must follow all quantity declarations for that type in the list.

We can use step limit specifications for quantities of composite type and for elements of composite quantities. We simply need to ensure that the type we provide in the specification matches the type of the quantity or element, for example,

terminal bus1 : electrical_vector(1 **to** 8);
terminal bus2 : electrical_vector(1 **to** 8);
quantity v_bus **across** bus1 **to** bus2;
limit v_bus : voltage_vector **with** 1.0E–3;

We complete our discussion of step limit specifications with some notes of caution. First, we can only apply the specifications to quantities that we explicitly declare, namely, free quantities and branch quantities. We cannot apply step limit specifications to implicit quantities defined using attributes, such as the 'across, 'through, 'ramp and 'slew attributes. If we really need to define step limits for such quantities, we would have to explicitly declare intermediate quantities, equate them to the implicit quantities and specify step limits for the intermediate quantities.

The second limitation is that, since we can only name quantities explicitly declared in the same list of declarations as the step limit specification, we cannot name quantity ports of an entity. Again, we would have to use explicitly declared intermediate quantities to circumvent this limitation.

The final point to note is that use of step limit specifications in a model can affect performance of a simulation. The specifications provide us with some capability to control the times at which analog solution points are computed. That, in turn, can help us control the accuracy of the solver and ensure that analog solution points will be found frequently enough for us to understand the system being modeled. However, the simulation time increases with the additional solution points. Thus, we should use care to specify step limits only when they are needed. Even then, we should make the step limit as large as possible to maximize performance. We should expect simulator vendors to include guidelines for using step limit specifications as part of their product documentation.

6.8 Mixed-Signal Descriptions

Mixed-signal systems include interacting digital and analog subsystems. The digital portions of the system are modeled using variables, signals and processes that execute at discrete time steps. The analog portions of the system are modeled using terminals, quantities and simultaneous statements that represent continuous behavior. In this section, we consider the VHDL-AMS mechanisms that support interaction between the digital and analog portions of the system.

A wide variety of applications require mixed-signal modeling capabilities to accurately represent the system behavior. Digital designs sometimes require mixed-signal modeling of high-performance components for which the digital modeling abstraction is not adequate. Since digital systems are really abstractions of well-behaved analog systems, we can use mixed-signal modeling to explore portions of digital-system behavior in more detail. Other systems are explicitly mixed signal with separate digital and analog parts. For example, chip sets for cellular phones comprise digital signal processors, analog transceivers and converters between the analog and digital portions. Other examples include the sense amplifiers used in memories, input/output pads for chips and clock generation circuitry.

When we wish to simulate a mixed-signal system described in VHDL-AMS, we must consider the mechanism that exchanges data between the digital simulation kernel and the analog solver. Let us first consider the exchange of data from the analog domain to the digital domain.

Analog-to-Digital Conversion

There are two aspects of the exchange of data from the analog domain to the digital domain: the translation of continuous-valued quantities to digital signals or variables and the timing of the data exchange. The first aspect is dealt with simply by using the value of an analog quantity in an expression in the digital part of a model, and the second aspect relies on the same event mechanism that is used for digital timing. As part of the definition of the simulation cycle, which will discuss in Chapter 7, the values of quantities are well defined when processes are resumed. Hence processes and concurrent statements can use quantity values in the same way as they use values of other objects simply by naming quantities in expressions. Analog values can be read in the digital domain at discrete time points, for example, at clock edges or in response to other digital events.

Example   The following process statement is an abstract model of an analog-to-digital converter that samples the values of the quantity **q** at every rising edge of a clock signal:

```
sampler : process ( clock ) is
    constant num_levels : real := 64.0;
    constant max_val : real := 5.0;
begin
    if clock = '1' then
        sample <= integer(q * num_levels / max_val) after 5 ns;
    end if;
end process sampler;
```

The quantity **q** varies between 0.0 and the value **max_val**. The expression in the signal assignment statement scales the value of **q** to an integer between 0 and num_levels. The statement then assigns the result to the signal **sample**.

Example   If we wish to compute the running average value of a quantity at each rising clock edge, we can use the following process. This process integrates the input by computing the sum of the sampled values of **q** and places the result in **total**. The result is then divided by the number of samples to compute the running average.

```
compute_running_average : process (clock) is
    variable num_samples : integer := 0;
    variable total : real := 0.0;
    variable running_average : real := 0.0;
begin
    if clock = '1' then
        total := total + q;
        num_samples := num_samples + 1;
        running_average := total / real(num_samples);
```

```
        average <= running_average after 5 ns;
    end if;
end process compute_running_average;
```

VHDL-AMS also allows us to trigger a digital event based on changes in analog quantities using the 'above attribute, which we described in Section 6.3. Recall that this attribute Q'above(E) yields a Boolean signal, and that the transition of the quantity Q above or below the value of the expression E causes an event on the signal. Both the event, which can be used to trigger process execution, and the level value of Q, which indicates on which side of the threshold the quantity value lies, are useful in mixed-signal models. In particular, we can use the attribute in the sensitivity list of a process or a wait statement to cause the process to execute in response to time-dependent conditions on quantities.

Example The following process converts a quantity v_in to a standard-logic signal data. If v_in is below v_il, the process sets data to '0'; if v_in is above v_ih, the process sets data to '1'; otherwise, the process sets data to the unknown value 'X'. The process is sensitive to threshold crossings at v_il and v_ih. It uses the value of the quantity v_in in an if expression to determine the output value.

```
analog_to_std_logic : process (v_in'above(v_il), v_in'above(v_ih)) is
begin
    if not v_in'above(v_il) then
        data <= '0';
    elsif v_in'above(v_ih) then
        data <= '1';
    else
        data <= 'X';
    end if;
end process analog_to_std_logic;
```

Example Figure 6-35 shows a model of a comparator with hysteresis. The output bit is initially '0'. When the voltage on the plus_in terminal rises above that on the minus_in terminal by a margin of 0.2 V, the output changes to '1'. The voltage on plus_in must then fall below that on minus_in by 0.2 V before the output changes back to '0'. The process in the architecture body implements this behavior by maintaining a variable, threshold, that changes as the comparator state changes. After changing state, the process waits on the signal v_in'above(threshold). A change on this signal indicates that the input voltage has crossed the threshold.

FIGURE 6-35

```
library ieee;  use ieee.std_logic_1164.all;
library IEEE_proposed;  use IEEE_proposed.electrical_systems.all;
entity comparator is
    port ( terminal plus_in, minus_in : electrical;
           signal output : out std_ulogic );
end entity comparator;
```

```
architecture hysteresis of comparator is
    constant threshold_margin : real := 0.2;
    quantity v_in across plus_in to minus_in;
begin
    comp_behavior : process is
        variable threshold : real := threshold_margin;
    begin
        if v_in > threshold then
            output <= '1' after 10 ns;
            threshold := –threshold_margin;
        else
            output <= '0' after 10 ns;
            threshold := threshold_margin;
        end if;
        wait on v_in'above(threshold);
    end process comp_behavior;
end architecture hysteresis;
```

A model of a comparator with hysteresis.

Digital-to-Analog Conversion

In the exchange of information from the digital to the analog domain, we are also concerned with both the translation of data values and the timing of the data exchange. We will first consider the data translation. The objects containing data values in the digital domain are signals and variables. We can refer to the values of signals in equations in simultaneous statements. However, we cannot use variable values in this way. We can only use the values of variables within processes, which do not directly affect analog behavior. The definition of the simulation cycle ensures that signals can only change values at discrete time points in response to events. Consequently, their values must be constant in the time intervals between events. Since the simulator does not process digital events while the analog solver is active, the values of signals remain constant during the computation of an analog solution point. The signal values are effectively treated as constants that, through the equations, constrain the values of quantities for the analog solution being computed by the solver.

Example The following simple simultaneous statement illustrates digital-to-analog conversion:

```
analog_voltage == real(digital_level) / real(num_levels) * max_voltage;
```

Here, we assume **digital_level** is an integer-valued signal that varies between 0 and **num_levels**. The expression scales the value to a real number between 0.0 and **max_voltage**. The result is equated to the quantity **analog_voltage**, which represents the maximum voltage available from the supply. The problem introduced by this example is that the discrete changes in the value of **digital_level** produce discontinuities in the value of **analog_voltage**. Each time the analog solver is invoked, it computes a new value for the quantity **analog_voltage** that assumes the value of **digital_level** will remain constant. The solver is not able to determine in advance when the next change will occur on **digital_level**. For this reason, the digital part of the model must use a break statement at each change on **digital_level** to invoke the analog solver to compute a new value for the quantity.

We can deal with the problems of discontinuities and discrete-valued signals by using the 'ramp and 'slew attributes described in Section 6.3. Each of these attributes implicitly provides the effect of break statements where necessary to invoke the analog solver to handle discontinuities. So we could rewrite the above example as

```
real_digital_level <= real(digital_level);
analog_voltage == real_digital_level'ramp(1.0E-6) / real(num_levels) * max_voltage;
```

We first convert the integer value of **digital_level** to a real value and assign it to a real-valued signal. We then use the 'ramp attribute in the simultaneous statement that equates the quantity **analog_voltage** to the scaled digital signal level. The reason for doing the integer-to-real conversion to an intermediate signal is that the 'ramp attribute must operate on a real-valued signal.

Example Figure 6-36 shows a behavioral model of a digital-to-analog converter. The input signal **bus_in** is interpreted as a binary fraction between 0.0 and $1.0 - 2^{-12}$. The voltage on the terminal **analog_out** ranges between 0.0 and the value of the constant **v_max**, defined in the architecture body. Each time the value of **bus_in** changes, the process **convert** is resumed. It converts the input value to an integer value, scales it to a real value between 0.0 and **v_max** and assigns the result to the signal **s_out**. The simultaneous statement in the architecture body uses the 'slew attribute to produce the resulting voltage output with a slew rate of 1 V/μs.

FIGURE 6-36

```
library ieee;  use ieee.std_logic_1164.all;
library ieee_proposed;  use ieee_proposed.electrical_systems.all;
entity dac_12_bit is
     port ( signal  bus_in : in std_ulogic_vector (11 downto 0);
             terminal analog_out :  electrical );;
end entity dac_12_bit;
```

```
architecture behavioral of dac_12_bit is
     constant v_max : real := 3.3;
     signal s_out : real := 0.0;
     quantity v_out across i_out through analog_out to electrical_ref;
begin
     convert : process ( bus_in ) is
         variable sum : natural;
     begin
         sum := 0;
         for i in bus_in'range loop
             sum := sum * 2 + boolean'pos( bus_in(i) = '1' or bus_in(i) = 'H' );
         end loop;
         s_out <= v_max * real(sum) / real(2**12 – 1);
     end process convert;

     v_out == s_out'ramp(1.0E–6);
end architecture behavioral;
```

A behavioral model of a digital-to-analog converter.

We mentioned timing of data transfer as an important aspect of digital-to-analog interaction. There is a potential problem that we need to be aware of if we need to model system timing with high fidelity. Suppose we use a digital signal as an abstraction of a continuously varying system property, and at some stage need to convert the signal to an analog quantity to model detailed electrical effects. We have seen how we can use the 'ramp or 'slew attribute to achieve the conversion.

Consider a change in a system property that is approximated by a linear ramp starting at time T, as shown in Figure 6-37. The ramp crosses a threshold at time $T + t_r/2$. We represent the property in abstract form by a signal S of type bit, with the value '0' representing property values below the threshold and '1' representing property values above the threshold. Thus, the event on the signal corresponding to the property change occurs at time $T + t_r/2$. When we convert from the signal to a quantity using the S'ramp(t_r) attribute, the quantity starts rising at $T + t_r/2$ and does not reach the threshold until time $T + t_r$. Thus, the transition in the quantity lags the

FIGURE 6-37

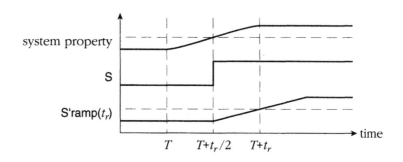

The time lag resulting from conversion of a digital signal that is an abstraction of a continuously varying property to an analog quantity.

transition of the original system property by $t_r/2$. In order to avoid this effect, we would have to start the transition in the quantity before the event on the signal so that the quantity would reach the threshold in time for the event. This would require the analog solver to "look into the digital future" in some sense. While this is possible in principle, it would significantly complicate the implementation of the simulator and would provide a means for introducing temporal paradoxes into models. Hence VHDL-AMS does not provide such a feature. We need to be aware that models such as that described in Figure 6-37 have an inherent time lag built into the modeling abstraction.

6.9 Mixed-Technology Descriptions

Although many users of VHDL-AMS may only be interested in analog and mixed-signal electrical systems, the language also supports a broad range of other energy domains. By defining an appropriate nature, subtypes for branch quantities and tolerance groups, we can describe any energy domain that exhibits energy conservation analogously to electrical systems. To help in creating a common VHDL-AMS modeling framework, a collection of commonly used energy domains is described as a suite of packages in preparation for IEEE standardization. We discuss the packages in Chapter 10. In this section, we discuss techniques for modeling mixed-technology systems using VHDL-AMS.

One application of mixed-technology modeling is to integrate secondary physical effects into the system model. For example, the behavior of electrical and electronic systems can depend significantly on thermal effects, so an integrated model representing both the electrical and thermal energy domains provides greater fidelity. Systems engineers in particular must consider a wide variety of concurrent engineering issues during system development, and the unified modeling capability of VHDL-AMS enables much better coupling between domains. With the increasing complexity of systems on silicon, multiple-domain modeling addresses important design challenges.

Another application of mixed-technology modeling is for systems that bring together components from different domains. Mixed-technology, or mechatronic, systems are common in telecommunications, automotive, aerospace and biomedical areas, just to name a few. The ability to assemble systems with components from various domains, such as electrical, microelectromechanical (MEMS), microfluidic and optical, is becoming more common. VHDL-AMS provides mixed-technology designers with a powerful tool for modeling components and their interactions in multiple energy domains.

The VHDL-AMS language constructs we have discussed thus far allow us to model mixed-technology systems. Signals, variables, and processes represent discrete-time components of the system, and natures describe the various energy domains. The terminals and quantities represent the nodes and continuously valued unknowns of the system. We use simultaneous statements to specify the equations that represent continuous behavior. The simulation cycle includes digital event processing and an analog solver to determine discrete and continuous behavior.

When we are modeling multiple energy domains, there are some issues we need to consider. First, recall that terminals are defined to be of a nature, which represents the energy domain of the terminals. In a mixed-technology system, it is illegal to define branch quantities between terminals of different natures. This restriction is included in VHDL-AMS to prevent us from inadvertently expressing physically unrealizable systems. For example, it does not make sense to talk about the difference in effort between an electrical and an optical terminal, since the effort aspect of one terminal is a voltage, and the effort aspect of the other is a luminance. Similarly, it does not make sense to talk about the flow from an electrical terminal to an optical terminal, since current flows from the electrical terminal and optic flux flows from the optical terminal. For the same reasons, it is illegal for a terminal associated with a terminal port to be of a different nature from that of the port. These rules help to prevent logical errors in our models and force us to craft explicit descriptions of the coupling between quantities of different energy domains. We express the couplings using equations that relate the effort and flow quantities of terminals of different natures.

Example Let us consider the example of a diode to illustrate how we can improve the fidelity of a model of an electrical system by including the thermal effects. The threshold voltage of a semiconductor junction depends on the junction temperature. The model in Figure 6-38 describes the operation of a P-N junction under forward biasing. The entity declaration includes electrical terminal ports for the electrical connections to the diode and a thermal terminal port to represent the temperature and heat flow through the junction. The electrical nature is defined in the package **electrical_systems**, and the thermal nature in **thermal_systems**. Declarations from the other packages are used in the architecture body. The package **energy_systems** provides constant definitions for Boltzmann's constant, **K**, and the charge of an electron, **Q**. The package **math_real** provides a definition for the exponential function, **exp**. We will describe these packages in more detail in Chapter 10.

FIGURE 6-38

```
library ieee, ieee_proposed;
use ieee.math_real.all;
use ieee_proposed.energy_systems.all;
use ieee_proposed.electrical_systems.all;
use ieee_proposed.thermal_systems.all;
entity diode is
    port ( terminal p, m : electrical;
            terminal j : thermal );
end entity diode;
```

```
architecture one of diode is
    constant area : real := 1.0e-3;
    constant Dn : real := 30.0;          -- electron diffusion coefficient
    constant Dp : real := 15.0;          -- hole diffusion coefficient
    constant np : real := 6.77e-5;       -- minority charge density
    constant pn : real := 6.77e-6;       -- minority charge density
    constant Ln : real := 5.47e-6;       -- diffusion length for electrons
    constant Lp : real := 12.25e-6;      -- diffusion length for holes
    quantity v across id through p to m;
    quantity vt : voltage := 1.0;        -- threshold voltage
    quantity temp across power through j;
begin
    vt == temp * K / Q;
    id == Q * area * (Dp * (pn / Lp) + Dn * (np / Ln)) * (exp(v / vt) − 1.0);
    power == v * id;
end architecture one;
```

A model of a forward-biased diode with thermal effects.

In the architecture body, simultaneous statements relate the quantities in different energy domains. The first statement relates the threshold voltage of the diode, **vt**, to the temperature, **temp**. This in turn is used in the second statement to model the diode current, **id**. The voltage and the current are used in the third statement to compute the power flowing across the junction. It is this power that heats the diode.

Note that if we were dealing with a light-emitting diode, we could also model the escape of photons into the radiant energy domain, which would reduce the thermal power generated. In contrast, using a simulator such as SPICE for the self-heating diode would require a number of simulation runs to assess the impact of temperature. Hence, we see that the ability to model interactions between energy domains in VHDL-AMS provides a powerful way to evaluate their effects.

Another issue that we need to be aware of in mixed-technology modeling is the dimensionality of equations. Simultaneous statements relating energy domains include expressions involving branch quantities of terminals. The quantities are of floating-point types, allowing us to combine their values using arithmetic operators. Unfortunately, there is no checking that the operations we express are dimensionally correct. For example, if we declare the following terminals and quantities:

```
terminal plus, minus : electrical;
quantity v across i through plus to minus;

terminal shaft : rotational_v;
quantity applied_torque through shaft;
```

we could write the following simultaneous statement:

```
applied_torque == v * i;
```

While this is legal VHDL-AMS, it does not make physical sense. The left-hand side of the equation is a torque, expressed in newton-meters, whereas the right-hand side is a power (the product of a voltage and a current), expressed in watts.

We could avoid this potential trap by defining separate types for each physical property, but then we would have to define separate operators for all of the combinations of types. This would become very unwieldy. Thus, the standard natures are defined using **real** types. As designers, we need to take care that our models reflect physically realizable systems.

Exercises

1. [❶ 6.1] Write a declaration for a free quantity named **control_voltage** of subtype **voltage** with a tolerance group "control_voltage_tolerance" and an initial value of 3.5 V.

2. [❶ 6.1/6.2] Write an entity declaration for a spring with two translational terminal ports and a quantity input port with temperature subtype.

3. [❶ 6.2] Write a terminal declaration for circuit nodes **node1** and **node2** of electrical nature. Write a quantity declaration for an across quantity **v_circuit** and a through quantity **i_circuit** between the circuit nodes.

4. [❶ 6.2] Write an entity declaration for a voltage supply with two electrical terminal ports **vdd_positive** and **vdd_negative**.

5. [❶ 6.2] Write an entity declaration for a spring with terminal ports of translational nature.

6. [❶ 6.2] Write a terminal declaration for an array of 36 temperature sensors, numbered 1 to 36. Write composite branch quantity declarations for the temperatures of all of the sensors and for the heat flows through sensors 13 to 24.

7. [❶ 6.2] Write an array terminal declaration for the six pistons of an engine. Use a translational mechanical nature for the pistons.

8. [❶ 6.2] Write a composite quantity declaration for the branch quantities **position** and **stroke_force** for the piston composite terminal of Exercise 7.

9. [❶ 6.2] Rewrite the declaration of Exercise 7 as a record terminal.

10. [❶ 6.3] Declare a terminal named **hard_stop** of a translation mechanical nature. Write a simultaneous statement that uses the **'reference** attribute of the terminal to fix the hard stop's position at 0.2 m.

11. [❶ 6.3] Write a declaration for a free quantity **v_amplified** of subtype **voltage** with the same tolerance group as a quantity **v_in**.

12. [❶ 6.3] Write a signal assignment statement that assigns to a bit-valued signal **temp_ok** the value '0' if a quantity **sensor_temp** is above 303 K (30°C), or '1' otherwise.

13. [❶ 6.3] Write a simultaneous statement that describes a mechanical system consisting of a mass attached to a spring and a damper. The equation is

$$F = m\frac{d^2x}{dt^2} + d\frac{dx}{dt} + kx$$

where F is the force applied to the system, m is the mass, x is the displacement of the mass, d is the damper viscosity and k is the spring constant.

14. [❶ 6.3] Write a simultaneous statement that equates the position of a servo-actuator shaft to the integral of the shaft velocity. Assume that the shaft is initially at position 0.25 m.

15. [❶ 6.3] Write an expression that uses the **'slew** attribute to produce a slew rate–limited version of a quantity **v_out** with rising slope limited to 0.6 V/μs and falling slope limited to 1.2 V/μs.

16. [❶ 6.4] Assuming quantities **v_res** and **i_res**, and a constant **r_res**, give a simple simultaneous statement to represent Ohm's law with **"high_accuracy"** as the tolerance group.

17. [❶ 6.4] The compression x of a spring from its free length L_f can be described by the equation $F = kx$, where F is the applied force compressing the spring and k is the spring constant. However, when the spring is fully compressed ($x = L_f - L_c$) or fully extended ($x = L_f - L_e$), no further compression occurs as additional force is applied. Write a simultaneous if statement that models this behavior. Remember to use the **'above** attribute in the conditions rather than simply using relational operators.

18. [❶ 6.6] Write the concurrent break statement that must accompany the simultaneous if statement of Exercise 17 to handle the first-derivative discontinuity that arises when the spring is fully compressed or extended.

19. [❶ 6.7] Assuming we have a free quantity q of type **vflow_rate**, write a step limit specification of 10 ms for q.

20. [❶ 6.8] Suppose the quantity q, sampled by the **sampler** process in the example on page 248, has the following values on successive clock edges: 0.0, 1.5, 2.0, 4.5, 3.0. What is the sequence of values assigned to the signal **sample**?

21. [❶ 6.8] Suppose a quantity q rises across a threshold of 2.5 at time 20 μs. Given the statements

    s <= 5.0 **when** q'above(2.5) **else** 0.0;
    q1 == s'ramp(2.0E–6);

    at what time would the quantity q1 cross the same threshold?

22. [❷ 6.3] Write an entity and architecture for a pressure threshold detector. Assume the detector has a fluidic terminal port and an output signal port of type **bit**. If the pressure at the input terminal exceeds 1.5 kPa, then the signal should output a '1'. Otherwise, the signal should output a '0'.

23. [❷ 6.3] Write a model of an ideal analog delay element. The entity should have terminals of electrical nature named **input** and **output**. The **input voltage** should be the same as the **output voltage**, but delayed by 5 ns. Use the 'delayed attribute.

24. [❷ 6.3] Write a model of an actuator for controlling an airplane flap. The actuator should have a terminal port of electrical nature for control and a terminal port of rotational nature to represent the angular position of the flap. Assume the input voltage ranges from –12 V to 12 V, and the resulting flap angle ranges linearly with the input voltage from –π/4 to π/4. Use the 'slew attribute to bound the movement of the actuator, with a maximum rising slope of 0.5 rad/s and a maximum falling slope of –0.5 rad/s.

25. [❷ 6.8] Revise the flap actuator model of Exercise 24 to have a signal port from control instead of an electrical terminal port. The control port is of type **real** and ranges from –12.0 to 12.0.

26. [❷ 6.4] Write an architecture for the voltage supply for the entity of Exercise 4. Assume the voltage supply has a constant output of 12 V. Use a simple simultaneous statement to express the voltage drop across the terminal ports of the voltage supply.

27. [❷ 6.4/6.6] Write a model of the transmission for a truck. Assume the inputs to the transmission are a terminal **driving** of **rotational_v** nature and a signal **gear** of an enumerated type with values **first**, **second**, **third** and **fourth**. The output of the transmission is a terminal **output** of **rotational_v** nature. Using a simultaneous case statement with **gear** as the selector, model the output angular velocity as the product of a gear constant and the input angular velocity.

28. [❷ 6.4/6.6] Write a model of a pump that has interface terminals **node1** and **node2** of fluidic nature and an input signal **pump_control**. The branch through quantity between **node1** and **node2** is named **chemical_throughput**. The **pump_control** signal may have values **off**, **low** and **high**. If the pump is **off**, **chemical_throughput** is 0.0; if the pump is **low**, **chemical_throughput** is 25.0; if the pump is **high**, **chemical_throughput** is 250.0.

29. [❷ 6.5] Develop a structural model for a passive band-pass filter using the inductor model from Figure 6-12 and the resistor and capacitor models from Figure 6-26. The components are simply connected in series between the input and output terminals.

30. [❷ 6.5] Design a structural implementation of the moving mass model given in Figure 6-15. To accomplish this, create independent mass, spring and dashpot models.

31. [❸ 6.2] Write a behavioral model of a capacitor, including leakage resistance and equivalent series resistance effects.

32. [❸ 6.3] Develop a Proportional-Integral-Derivative (PID) model for a control system.

33. [❸ 6.3] Using the 'dot attribute, add a 5 Hz pole to the opamp model illustrated in Figure 6-17.

34. [❸ 6.5] Develop a structural 12-bit A/D converter model using the following behavioral models:

   - a 12-bit successive-approximation register (create this model),

   - a 12-bit digital latch (create this model),

   - the 12-bit D/A converter from Figure 6-36, and

   - the comparator from Figure 6-9.

35. [❹ 6.8] Develop a model of a transistor using the Ebers-Moll model. See [19] for more information on the Ebers-Moll model of a transistor.

36. [❹ 6.9] Develop a model of a microelectromechanical accelerometer.

37. [❹] Develop a 10-channel data acquisition system with 10 MB of digital data storage capacity. Allow each channel to be triggered externally, as well as a mode in which all channels can be synchronously triggered.

chapter seven

Design Processing

A VHDL-AMS description of a design is usually used to simulate the design and perhaps to synthesize the hardware. This involves processing the description using computer-based tools to create a simulation program to run or a hardware net-list to build. Both simulation and synthesis require two preparatory steps: analysis and elaboration. Simulation then involves executing the elaborated model, whereas synthesis involves creating a net-list of primitive circuit elements that perform the same function as the elaborated model. In this section, we look at the analysis, elaboration and execution operations introduced in Chapter 1.

7.1   **Analysis**

The first step in processing a design is to analyze the VHDL-AMS descriptions. A correct description must conform to the rules of syntax and semantics that we have discussed at length. An *analyzer* is a tool that verifies this. If a description fails to meet a rule, the analyzer provides a message indicating the location of the problem and which rule was broken. We can then correct the error and retry the analysis. Another task performed by the analyzer in most VHDL-AMS systems is to translate the description into an internal form more easily processed by the remaining tools. Whether such a translation is done or not, the analyzer places each successfully analyzed description into a *design library*.

A complete VHDL-AMS description usually consists of a number of entity declarations and their corresponding architecture bodies. Each of these is called a *design unit*. Organizing a design as a hierarchy of modules, rather than as one large flat design, is good engineering practice. It makes the description much easier to understand and manage.

The analyzer analyzes each design unit separately and places the internal form into the library as a *library unit*. If a unit being analyzed uses another unit, the analyzer extracts information about the other unit from the library, to check that the unit is used correctly. For example, if an architecture body instantiates an entity, the analyzer needs to check the number, mode and type or nature of ports of the entity to make sure it is instantiated correctly. To do this, it requires that the entity be previously analyzed and stored in the library. Thus, we see that there are dependency relations between library units in a complete description that enforce an order of analysis of the original design units.

To clarify this point, we divide design units into *primary units,* which include entity declarations, and *secondary units,* which include architecture bodies. There are other kinds of design units in each class, which we come to in later chapters. A primary unit defines the external view or interface to a module, whereas a secondary unit describes an implementation of the module. Thus the secondary unit depends on the corresponding primary unit and must be analyzed after the primary unit has been analyzed. In addition, a library unit may draw upon the facilities defined in some other primary unit, as in the case of an architecture body instantiating some other entity. In this case, there is a further dependency between the secondary unit and the referenced primary unit. Thus we may build up a network of dependencies of units upon primary units. Analysis must be done in such an order that a unit is analyzed before any of its dependents. Furthermore, whenever we change and reanalyze a primary unit, all of the dependent units must also be reanalyzed. Note, however, that there is no way in which any unit can be dependent upon a secondary unit; that is what makes a secondary unit "secondary." This may seem rather complicated, and indeed, in a large design, the dependency relations can form a complex network. For this reason, most VHDL-AMS systems include tools to manage the dependencies, automatically reanalyzing units where necessary to ensure that an outdated unit is never used.

Example   Let us consider a design for a sensor that measures fluid flow, integrates the flow to determine the volume of fluid delivered and triggers a change on a digital signal when the volume reaches a specified level. Figure 7-1 shows a schematic for the system. The inverting integrator transforms the measurement of flow to a measurement of volume. Initially, the integrator output is at 0 V, causing the comparator output to be high. As the fluid flows and adds to the volume delivered, the integrator output voltage goes negative. When it fall below the reference voltage, the comparator output goes low. The integrator is reset by taking the reset input high and then low again. The two flipflops synchronize the comparator output with a clock signal. This reduces the chance of the output changing while it is being read. Two flipflops are used to avoid the metastability problems that can arise in flipflops when the input signal changes while being sampled.

In order to develop a structural model of this system, we need models for the components. We can extend the inverting integrator model from Figure 6-27 by adding a digitally controlled analog switch to discharge the capacitor, as shown in Figure 7-2. For this subsystem, we can use the opamp model from Figure 6-17, the capacitor and resistor models from Figure 6-26 and the analog switch model

FIGURE 7-1

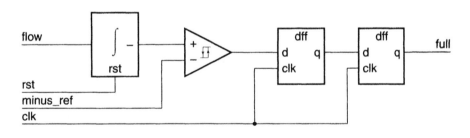

Schematic for a fluid volume-level sensor.

FIGURE 7-2

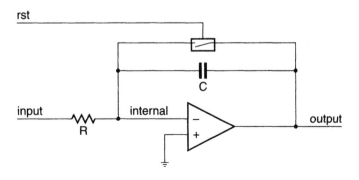

The inverting integrator, revised to include a switch that resets the output.

from Figure 6-31. The revised integrator model is shown in Figure 7-3. For the comparator, we can use the model from Figure 6-35. For the synchronizer flip-flop, we can use the model shown in Figure 7-4. A structural model of the complete volume-level sensor is shown in Figure 7-5.

FIGURE 7-3

```
library ieee;  use ieee.std_logic_1164.all;
library ieee_proposed;  use ieee_proposed.electrical_systems.all;

entity inverting_integrator is
    port ( terminal input, output : electrical;
            signal rst : in std_ulogic );;
end entity inverting_integrator;
```
```
architecture structural of inverting_integrator is
    terminal internal : electrical;
begin
    r1 : entity work.resistor(ideal)
        port map ( node1 => input, node2 => internal);
    c1 : entity work.capacitor(leakage)
        port map ( node1 => internal, node2 => output );
    amp : entity work.opamp(slew_limited)
        port map ( plus_in => electrical_ref, minus_in => internal,
                    output => output);
    switch : entity work.analog_switch(ideal)
        port map ( n1 => internal, n2 => output, control => rst );
end architecture structural;
```

The revised model for the inverting integrator.

FIGURE 7-4

```
library ieee;  use ieee.std_logic_1164.all;

entity dff is
    port ( signal d, clk : in std_ulogic;  q : out std_ulogic );
end entity dff;
```
```
architecture behav of dff is
begin
    storage : process ( clk ) is
    begin
        if clk'event and (clk = '1' or clk = 'H') then
```

```
            q <= d after 5 ns;
        end if;
    end process storage;
end architecture behav;
```

A behavioral model of the D-flipflop used for synchronization.

FIGURE 7-5

```
library ieee;  use ieee.std_logic_1164.all;
library ieee_proposed;  use ieee_proposed.electrical_systems.all;
entity volume_sensor is
    port ( terminal flow, minus_ref : electrical;
           signal clk, rst : in std_ulogic;
           signal full : out std_ulogic );
end entity volume_sensor;
```

```
architecture structural of volume_sensor is
    terminal minus_volume : electrical;
    signal async_full, sync1_full : std_ulogic;
begin
    int : entity work.inverting_integrator(structural)
        port map ( input => flow, output => minus_volume, rst => rst );
    comp : entity work.comparator(hysteresis)
        port map ( plus_in => minus_volume, minus_in => minus_ref,
                   output => async_full );
    sync1 : entity work.dff(behav)
        port map ( d => async_full, clk => clk, q => sync1_full );
    sync2 : entity work.dff(behav)
        port map ( d => sync1_full, clk => clk, q => full );
end architecture structural;
```

A structural model of the volume-level sensor system.

Given these design units, the network of dependencies is shown in Figure 7-6. A possible order of compilation for this set of design units is

```
entity analog_switch
architecture ideal of analog_switch

entity resistor
architecture ideal of resistor
```

FIGURE 7·6

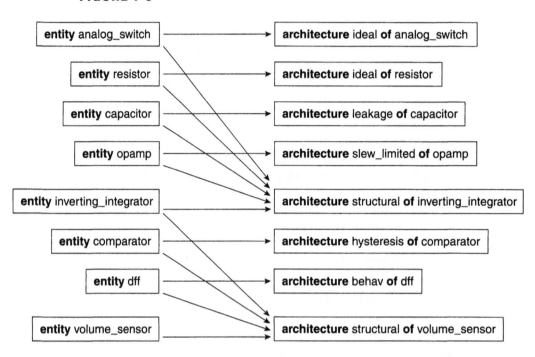

The dependency network for the volume_sensor *module. The arrows point from a primary unit to a dependent secondary unit.*

entity capacitor
architecture leakage of capacitor

entity opamp
architecture slew_limited of opamp

entity inverting_integrator
architecture structural of inverting_integrator

entity comparator
architecture hysteresis of comparator

entity dff
architecture behav of dff

entity volume_sensor
architecture structural of volume_sensor

In this order, each primary unit is analyzed immediately before its corresponding secondary unit, and each primary unit is analyzed before any secondary unit that instantiates it. We could also analyze all of the entity declarations first, then analyze the architecture bodies in arbitrary order.

Design Libraries, Library Clauses and Use Clauses

So far, we have not actually said what a design library is, other than that it is where library units are stored. Indeed, this is all that is defined by the VHDL-AMS language specification, since to go further is to enter into the domain of the host operating system under which the VHDL-AMS tools are run. Some systems may use a database to store analyzed units, whereas others may simply use a directory in the host file system as the design library. The documentation for each VHDL-AMS tool suite indicates what we need to know about how the suite deals with design libraries.

A VHDL-AMS tool suite must also provide some means of using a number of separate design libraries. When a design is analyzed, we nominate one of the libraries as the *working library,* and the analyzed design is stored in this library. We use the special library name **work** in our VHDL-AMS models to refer to the current working library. We have seen examples of this in this chapter's component instantiation statements, in which a previously analyzed entity is instantiated in an architecture body.

If we need to access library units stored in other libraries, we refer to the libraries as *resource libraries.* We do this by including a *library clause* immediately preceding a design unit that accesses the resource libraries. The syntax rule for a library clause is

library_clause ⇐ **library** identifier { , ... } ;

The identifiers are used by the analyzer and the host operating system to locate the design libraries, so that the units contained in them can be used in the description being analyzed. The exact way that the identifiers are used varies between different tool suites and is not defined by the VHDL-AMS language specification. Note that we do not need to include the library name **work** in a library clause; the current working library is automatically available.

Example   Suppose we are working on part of a large design project code-named Wasp, and we are using standard parts supplied by Widget Designs, Inc. Our system administrator has loaded the design library for the Widget cells in a directory called /local/widget/parts in our workstation file system, and our project leader has set up another design library in /projects/wasp/lib for some in-house parts we need to use. We consult the manual for our VHDL-AMS analyzer and use operating system commands to set up the appropriate mapping from the identifiers widget_parts and wasp_lib to these library directories. We can then instantiate entities from these libraries, along with entities we have previously analyzed, into our own working library, as shown in Figure 7-7.

FIGURE 7-7

```
library widget_parts, wasp_lib;
architecture component_based of active_filter is
    -- declaration of signals, terminals, quantities, etc
```

(continued on page 268)

(continued from page 267)

...

begin

    R1 : **entity** wasp_lib.resistor
        port map (node1 => input, node2 => node2);

    C1 : **entity** widget_parts.capacitor
        port map (node1 => node3, node2 => ground);

    Amp1 : **entity** work.LF353_opamp
        port map (plus => node4, minus => node7, output => node15,
                   pos_supply => Vdd, neg_supply => Vss);

    -- other component instantiations

    ...

end architecture component_based;

An outline of a library unit referring to entities from the resource libraries widget_parts *and* wasp_lib.

If we need to make frequent reference to library units from a design library, we can include a *use clause* in our model to avoid having to write the library name each time. The simplified syntax rules are

use_clause ⇐ **use** selected_name ⟨ , ... ⟩ ;

selected_name ⇐ name . ⟨ identifier ▯ **all** ⟩

If we include a use clause with a library name as the prefix of the selected name (preceding the dot), and a library unit name from the library as the suffix (after the dot), the library unit is made *directly visible*. This means that subsequent references in the model to the library unit need not prefix the library unit name with the library name. For example, we might precede the architecture body in the previous example with the following library and use clauses:

library widget_parts, wasp_lib;

use widget_parts.capacitor;

This makes **capacitor** directly visible within the architecture body, so we can omit the library name when referring to it in component instantiations; for example,

    C1 : **entity** capacitor
        port map (node1 => node3, node2 => ground);

If we include the keyword **all** in a use clause, all of the library units within the named library are made directly visible. For example, if we wanted to make all of the

Wasp project library units directly visible, we might precede a library unit with the use clause

use wasp_lib.**all**;

Care should be taken when using this form of use clause with several libraries at once. If two libraries contain library units with the same name, VHDL-AMS avoids ambiguity by making neither of them directly visible. The solution is either to use the full selected name to refer to the particular library unit required, or to include in use clauses only those library units really needed in a model.

Use clauses can also be included to make names from packages directly visible. We will return to this idea when we discuss packages in detail in Chapter 10.

7.2 Elaboration

Once all of the units in a design hierarchy have been analyzed, the design hierarchy can be *elaborated*. The effect of elaboration is to "flesh out" the hierarchy, producing a collection of processes interconnected by *nets* and a collection of *characteristic expressions*. This is done by substituting the contents of an architecture body for every instantiation of its corresponding entity. Each net in the elaborated design consists of a signal and the ports of the substituted architecture bodies to which the signal is connected. (Recall that a signal port of an entity is treated as a signal within a corresponding architecture body.) The characteristic expressions of a model form a set of simultaneous equations that must be solved to determine values for the quantities in the model. Some of the characteristic expressions, the *structural set*, are formed during elaboration from the declarations of terminals and quantities and from associations of terminals and quantities in port maps. Other characteristic expressions are formed during execution of the model. Let us outline how elaboration proceeds, illustrating it step by step with an example.

Elaboration is a recursive operation, started at the topmost entity in a design hierarchy. We use the **volume_sensor** example from Figure 7-5 as our topmost entity. The first step is to create the ports of the entity. Next, an architecture body corresponding to the entity is chosen. If we do not explicitly specify which architecture body to choose, the most recently analyzed architecture body is used. For this illustration, we use the architecture **structural**. This architecture body is then elaborated, first by creating and initializing any signals, quantities and terminals that it declares, then by elaborating each of the concurrent and simultaneous statements in its body. Figure 7-8 shows the **volume_sensor** design with the signals and terminals created; this architecture body does not include any quantities.

The concurrent statements in the **structural** architecture are all component instantiation statements. Each of them is elaborated by creating new instances of the ports specified by the instantiated entity. The signal ports of the component instances are joined into the nets represented by the signals with which they are associated.

Next, the internal structure of the specified architecture body of the instantiated entity is copied in place of the component instance, as shown in Figure 7-9. The

FIGURE 7-8

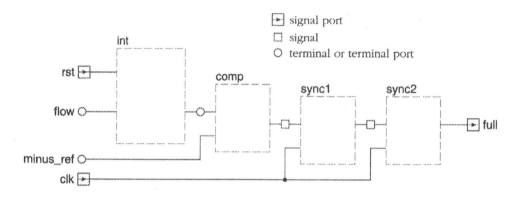

The first stage of elaboration of the **volume_sensor** *entity. The ports have been created, the* **architecture** structural *selected and the signals and terminals of the architecture created.*

FIGURE 7-9

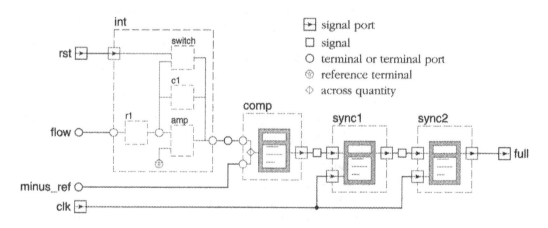

The volume sensor design further elaborated. Behavioral architectures, consisting of just processes, have been substituted for instances of the **comparator** *and* dff *entities. A structural architecture has been substituted for the instance of the* **inverting_integrator** *entity.*

architectures substituted for the instances of the **comparator** and dff entities are both behavioral, consisting of processes that sense the input ports and make assignments to the output ports. Hence elaboration is complete for these architectures. However, the architecture **structural**, substituted for the instance of **inverting_integrator**, contains further component instances. Hence it is elaborated in turn, producing the structure shown in Figure 7-10. We have now reached a stage where we have a collection of nets comprising signals and ports, a collection of terminals and quantities, processes

FIGURE 7-10

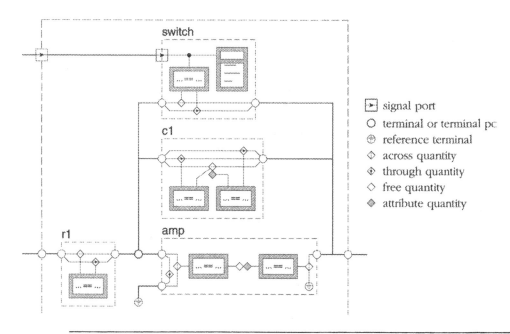

The inverting integrator within the volume sensor structure elaborated down to architectures that consist only of simultaneous statements.

that sense the nets and quantities and drive the nets, and simultaneous statements that relate values of quantities.

Each process statement in the design is elaborated by creating new instances of the variables it declares and by creating a driver for each of the signals for which it has signal assignment statements. The drivers are joined to the nets containing the signals they drive. For example, the **comp_behavior** process within **comp** has a driver for the port **output**, which is part of the net based on the signal **async_full**.

The final phase of elaboration is formation of the structural set of characteristic expressions. These expressions arise as a consequence of the declaration of branch quantities in architectures and the association of quantities and terminals with ports of instantiated entities. We can think of the characteristic expressions as stating constraints that must be satisfied by the analog solver. The structural set of characteristic expressions is defined by the following rules. Where the design includes composite terminals and quantities, the rules apply to the scalar subelements of the composite objects.

1. Where a quantity is associated with a quantity port of a component instance, the values of quantity and the quantity port are equal.

2. Where a terminal is associated with a terminal port of a component instance, the values of the reference quantities of the terminal and the terminal port are equal. (Recall from Section 6.3 that the reference quantity of a terminal is the effort ap-

plied at the terminal, and that we can refer to it using the 'reference attribute.) This rule captures the effort aspect of energy conservation laws that requires connected nodes to be equipotential. For example, in the electrical domain, Kirchoff's voltage law requires connected nodes to have equal voltages.

3. The value of an across branch quantity is the difference between the reference quantities of the plus and minus quantities of the branch. This rule captures the definition of an across branch quantity.

4. The value of the contribution quantity of a terminal is equal to the value of the terminal's contribution expression.

5. The value of a root terminal's contribution expression is equal to 0.0.

These last two rules capture the flow aspect of energy conservation laws and require some explanation. Recall that we briefly outlined the contribution quantity of a terminal in Section 6.3 and indicated that we can refer to the contribution quantity by applying the 'contribution attribute to the terminal. We need to identify the various flows into and out of a terminal, to take account of the hierarchical interconnection of terminals, and to ensure that the net flow over a terminal hierarchy is zero. We use the ideas of contribution expressions and contribution quantities to describe this, starting with the simplest case.

Suppose a terminal port **Tb** is declared in an entity declaration as follows:

```
entity bottom is
    port ( terminal Tb : electrical; ... );
end entity bottom;
```

Within an architecture body **bottom_arch**, **Tb** serves as the plus terminal for through branch quantities i_b1 and i_b2 and as the minus terminal for through branch quantities i_b3 and i_b4. **Tb** is not associated in port maps with any terminal ports of component instances within **bottom_arch**. Declarations for the branch quantities in the architecture body are

```
quantity ... i_b1 through Tb to ...;
quantity ... i_b2 through Tb to ...;
quantity ... i_b3 through ... to Tb;
quantity ... i_b4 through ... to Tb;
```

Figure 7-11 shows the through branches represented by these declarations. In this case, we define the contribution expression of the terminal **Tb** to be the sum of the values of the through quantities with **Tb** as the plus terminal, less the sum of the values of the through quantities with **Tb** as the minus terminal. The contribution expression is the net flow out of the terminal. Rule 4 above specifies that the contribution quantity of **Tb** is equal to the contribution expression, thus

Tb'contribution = (i_b1 + i_b2) − (i_b3 + i_b4)

FIGURE 7-11

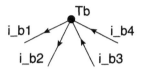

A terminal port that serves as the plus and minus terminal of through branch quantities, but is not associated with terminal ports of component instances.

Now suppose the entity bottom is instantiated in a larger design, as follows:

terminal T : electrical;
quantity ... i_t1, i_t2 **through** T **to** ...;
quantity ... i_t3 **through** ... **to** T;
...

comp1 : **entity** work.bottom(bottom_arch)
    port map (Tb => T, ...);
comp2 : **entity** work.other_ent(other_arch)
    port map (Tx => T, ...);

In this case, there is a terminal T that is the plus terminal for the through quantities i_t1 and i_t2, the minus terminal for the through quantity i_t3, and is associated with the terminal ports Tb of component comp1 and Tx of component comp2. The branch flows are shown in Figure 7-12. Since we have added terminal-port connections in this case, we need to add the net flow out of each terminal port to the contribution expression for the terminal T. Since the net flow out of a terminal port is represented by the contribution expression for that port, and rule 4 equates that with the contribution quantity of the port, we can just include the contribution quantities of Tb and Tx in the contribution expression of T. Thus

$$T'contribution = (\ i\_t1 + i\_t2 \ ) - (\ i\_t3 \ ) + (\ Tb'contribution + Tx'contribution \ )$$

FIGURE 7-12

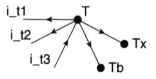

A terminal that serves as the plus and minus quantities of through branch quantities and is also associated with terminal ports of component instances.

Finally, we consider the fact that the terminal T is not a terminal port. There is no "higher-level" terminal associated with T, so we call T a *root terminal*. (A terminal port that is left unassociated when its entity is instantiated in a design is also a root terminal.) The contribution expression of this terminal represents the entire net flow out of the terminal. The flow aspect of energy conservation laws requires this net flow to be zero. This requirement is captured by rule 5 above. In the case of the electrical domain, rule 5 captures Kirchoff's current law.

The mechanism of forming contribution expressions and contribution quantities is a means of hierarchically determining the net flow out of a node. Association of a terminal with one or more terminal ports effectively merges the terminal and ports into a single circuit node, as illustrated in Figure 7-13. The advantage of calculating the contributions hierarchically is that it allows us to use the 'contribution attribute to identify the contributions made locally by a given entity. Monitoring the value of 'contribution in a simulation can help us track down unexpected behavior in a design. For example, if we observe an unexpectedly large current in a branch of a complex design, we may be able to monitor the contributions to the circuit node to locate the source of the current.

Once all of the component instances and all of the resulting processes have been elaborated and the structural set of characteristic expressions has been determined, elaboration of the design hierarchy is complete. We now have a fully fleshed-out version of the design, consisting of a number of process instances with nets connecting them, a collection of simultaneous statements and the structural set of characteristic expressions. Note that there are several distinct instances of some of the processes and simultaneous statements, one for each use of an entity containing the process or simultaneous statement. Each process instance has its own distinct version of the process variables. Each net in the elaborated design consists of a signal, a collection of signal ports associated with it and a driver within a process instance.

FIGURE 7-13

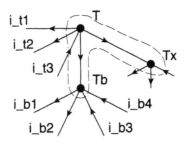

The circuit node represented by a terminal and its associated terminal ports.

Requirements for Solvability

We mentioned at the start of this section that the characteristic expressions of a model form a set of simultaneous equations that are solved by the analog solver. The unknowns in the equations are the quantities explicitly declared in the model and the implicit quantities, such as those defined by 'dot, 'integ and other attributes, that are mentioned in simultaneous statements. The structural set of characteristic equations is derived from the model during elaboration. Other characteristic expressions, called the *explicit set*, are derived from the simultaneous statements in the model. In order for the complete set of simultaneous equations to be solvable, there must be sufficient equations. Furthermore, quantities defined in the model must appear in equations, either by appearing in simultaneous statements or by virtue of the way they are declared or associated with ports. We briefly outline here the rules in VHDL-AMS that ensure that the equations are solvable.

The first rule for ensuring solvability relates to the number of equations in a model. In each architecture of an entity, we start by counting the number of free quantities, through quantities and **out** mode quantity ports in the entity declaration. Next, we subtract the number of quantities associated with **out** mode quantity ports in port maps of component instances within the architecture. *The result must be equal to the number of simultaneous statements in the architecture.*

Note that when we are counting quantities and simultaneous statements, we must count scalar elements. Recall that we can think of a composite quantity or quantity port as being equivalent to a collection of scalar quantities. Similarly, when we write a simultaneous statement equating expressions of composite type, it is equivalent to writing a collection of expressions equating corresponding scalar elements of the expression values.

Example   We might attempt to write a model of a battery as follows:

```
entity battery is
    port ( terminal plus, minus : electrical );
end entity battery;

architecture wrong of battery is
    constant v_nominal : real := 9.0;
    quantity v across plus to minus;
begin
    v == v_nominal;
end architecture wrong;
```

Our reasoning might be that a battery is ideally a constant voltage source, so we simply need to equate the voltage across the terminals to a constant value. The problem with this model, however, is that it does not conform to the rule for the number of simultaneous statements. There are no free quantities, no through quantities, no **out** mode quantity ports and no component instantiations associating quantities with **out** mode ports. So the number of simultaneous statements should be zero. Since we clearly need to provide one simultaneous statement, we need to add to the model to increase the quantity count. An appropriate solution is to declare a through quantity for the battery current, as follows:

```
architecture correct of battery is
    constant v_nominal : real := 9.0;
    quantity v across i through plus to minus;
begin
    v == v_nominal;
end architecture correct;
```

In some of the earlier examples, for example, the model in Figure 6-21, we also declared through quantities that we have not mentioned in simultaneous statements, in order to ensure a match with the number of simultaneous statements.

When we use simultaneous if statements or simultaneous case statements in a model, we need to ensure that the correct number of equations is maintained in all alternatives. Consider, for example, the simultaneous if statement

```
if clamp = '1' use
    v1 == 5.0;
    v2 == 0.0;
else
    v1 == v2;
end use;
```

If the condition is true, there are two simultaneous statements affecting the analog behavior, whereas if the condition is false, only one simultaneous statement affects the behavior. Usually this form of model would be incorrect, since the number of equations would vary from time to time during simulation. The rule stated above requires that the number of equations matches the counted quantities all of the time. The only way the simultaneous if statement shown here could be correct is if there is another simultaneous if statement that effectively relies on the same condition and also changes the number of equations to compensate.

A similar problem can occur with simultaneous null statements in a model. Recall from Chapter 6 that a simultaneous null statement does not provide any equations for the model. So when we are counting simultaneous statements to see if we have the correct number, we should exclude simultaneous null statements from the count. If we include a simultaneous null statement in an alternative of a case statement, as we described in Section 6.4, we need to ensure that the reduction in the number of equations when that alternative is selected is offset by an increase in the number of equations elsewhere in the architecture. This difficulty perhaps makes simultaneous null statements less useful than they might otherwise be.

The second rule for ensuring solvability relates to the use of quantities in simultaneous statements. *Any free quantities declared in an architecture body and any* **out** *mode quantity port that is left unassociated in any instance of the entity must appear in a simultaneous statement in the architecture.* Without this rule, there would be insufficient equations to make the complete model solvable. As we mentioned when describing rules for creating the structural set of characteristic expressions, across quantities and through quantities occur implicitly in that set. Hence they need not necessarily appear in simultaneous statements if the behavior of the system being modeled does not require them to appear.

The two rules described above are necessary conditions for solvability of a model and can be readily checked by a simulator. However, they are not sufficient conditions. A model might conform to the rules, yet not be solvable. Two further requirements are that the equations defined by the simultaneous statements be linearly independent and non-contradictory. If the equations are linearly dependent, there is insufficient information in them to constrain the unknown quantities to unique values. Thus, there would be an infinite number of solutions to the system of equations. On the other hand, if the equations are contradictory, there are no solutions. In either case, the VHDL-AMS model is deemed to be erroneous. Unfortunately, checking for linear dependence and contradiction is not as simple as checking the other rules outlined above. A simulator may not be able to report the error until it attempts to solve the equations during the course of a simulation.

7.3 Execution

Now that we have an elaborated design hierarchy, we can execute it to simulate operation of the system it describes. Much of our previous discussion of VHDL-AMS statements was in terms of what happens when they are executed, so we do not go over statement execution again here. Instead, we concentrate on the simulation algorithm and the analog solver introduced in Chapter 1. We will focus on time-domain simulation in this chapter, and defer consideration of the details of frequency-domain simulation to Chapter 13.

Recall that the simulation algorithm consists of an initialization phase followed by a repeated simulation cycle. The simulator keeps a clock to measure out the passage of simulation time. In the initialization phase, the simulation time is set to zero. Each driver is initialized to drive its signal with the initial value declared for the signal or the default value for the signal if no initial value was declared. The driving values are used to determine the actual values of the signals.

Next, signals and quantities defined by attributes are initialized based on the assumption that the declared signals and quantities to which the attributes are applied have held their initial value for an infinite time before simulation starts. For example, given a signal s, the attributes s'delayed, s'ramp and s'slew are initialized to the value of s. Similarly, given a quantity q, the attributes q'delayed and q'slew are initialized to the value of q. Other quantities defined by attributes, such as q'dot and q'integ, are initialized to 0.0. The attribute q'above(e) is initialized to true if the initial value of q is greater than the value of the expression e, or false otherwise.

After the objects are initialized, each of the process instances in the design is started and executes the sequential statements in its body. We usually write a model so that at least some of these initial statements schedule some transactions to get the simulation under way, then suspend by executing a wait statement. When all of the process instances have suspended, initialization is complete and the simulator can start the first simulation cycle.

At the beginning of each simulation cycle, the analog solver is executed. It uses the characteristic expressions of the model to calculate a sequence of analog solution points, each consisting of the values of all of the quantities used in the model. The analog solution points are spaced at intervals in simulation time, starting from the time of the current simulation cycle. The finishing time for the sequence is the earliest of

- the earliest time at which a transaction is scheduled on a signal driver,

- the earliest time at which a process has a timeout scheduled, or

- the earliest time at which the value of a quantity to which the 'above attribute is applied crosses the threshold specified in the attribute.

The finishing point is the next time at which some signal value changes or some process must resume. VHDL-AMS does not specify how many analog solution points must be computed in the sequence, except that a step limit specification in the model can constrain the maximum interval between them. In general, a simulator will calculate as many analog solution points as it needs to achieve some implementation-dependent accuracy.

Once the analog solver has completed, the current simulation time is advanced to the finishing time of the sequence described above. All of the transactions scheduled for this time are performed, updating the corresponding signals and possibly causing events on those signals. Next, all process instances that are sensitive to any of these events are resumed. In addition, process instances whose timeout expires at the current simulation time are resumed during this step. All of these processes execute their sequential statements, possibly scheduling more transactions or timeouts, and eventually suspend again by executing wait statements. When they have all suspended, the simulation cycle is done and the next cycle can start. If the next earliest time of a transaction scheduled on a driver or a scheduled process timeout is the same as the current simulation time, the next simulation cycle will be a delta cycle, as described in Chapter 5. If there are no more transactions or timeouts scheduled, or if simulation time reaches **time'high** (the largest representable time value), the simulation is complete.

The first simulation cycle and any delta cycles that follow it at simulation time zero are special. They are used to determine the *quiescent state*, or "DC operating point," of the system being simulated. We briefly mentioned in Chapter 2 that VHDL-AMS provides a predefined signal called **domain** of the type **domain_type**. These are defined as follows:

    type domain_type **is** (quiescent_domain, time_domain, frequency_domain);
    signal domain : domain_type := quiescent_domain;

The **domain** signal is initialized to **quiescent_domain** during elaboration of a model and has this value during initialization and all of the simulation cycles at time zero. The idea is that during these cycles the simulation determines the starting state for the system. The simulator uses a number of additional characteristic expressions, called the *quiescent state augmentation set*, during the initial simulation cycles to help it converge upon the quiescent state of the system. The equations represented by the expressions embody the assumption that all quantities in the system have been constant for an infinite time before simulation starts. The equations constrain all derivatives to be zero. So if the model refers to **q'dot** for some quantity **q**, **q'dot** is constrained to equal zero during the initial cycles. Similarly, if the model refers to **q'integ**, the quantity **q** itself is constrained to equal zero, corresponding to the initial value of **q'integ** being zero. In addition, any quantity **q'delayed** is constrained to equal the initial value of **q**.

When the system has reached equilibrium at time zero, the system is at its quiescent state. The simulator then discontinues use of the quiescent state augmentation set and assigns either **time_domain** or **frequency_domain** to the **domain** signal, depending on the kind of simulation we wish to perform. (The means by which we specify which kind of simulation to perform is not specified in VHDL-AMS; we should consult the documentation for each simulator.) After assigning to the **domain** signal, the simulator resets the time of the next simulation cycle to zero, and continues normally. A model can respond to the change on the **domain** signal and modify its behavior accordingly.

In our discussion of VHDL-AMS simulation, we have indicated that the analog solver must solve various sets of differential and algebraic equations (DAEs) that represent the behavior of the modeled system. We have deliberately avoided specifying how the simulator solves the equation, except to say that some form of iterative numerical technique is used. The VHDL-AMS language standard does not specify any particular techniques to be used, leaving that decision to the implementors of simulators. As system designers, we need only be concerned that a simulator implements the language correctly and with adequate performance and accuracy. While we may be interested in looking "under the hood" of simulators to learn about the solution techniques used, that topic is beyond the scope of this book. There are several resources that the interested reader can refer to. The book by Cooper [10] offers a gentle introduction to the mathematics involved in the solution of DAEs and provides some worked examples. Pillage et al. [31] provide a more complete treatment of circuit simulation methods. Fjeldly et al. [13] discuss device and circuit simulation, particularly oriented toward SPICE. The book by Kielkowski [23] goes into more detail of techniques used in SPICE simulators and is a good reference on integration methods and the likely causes of convergence and other errors.

Describing the operation of a simulator as we have done is a little like setting a play in a theater without any seats—nobody is there to watch it, so what's the point! In reality, a simulator is part of a suite of VHDL-AMS tools and provides us with various means to control and monitor the progress of the simulation. Typical simulators allow us to step through the model one line at a time or to set breakpoints, causing the simulation to stop when a line of the model is executed, a signal is assigned a particular value, or an analog solution point is computed. They usually provide commands to display the value of signals, quantities and variables. Most simulators also provide a graphical waveform display of the history of signal and quantity values similar to a logic analyzer or oscilloscope display, and allow storage and subsequent redisplay of the history for later analysis. It is these facilities that make the simulation useful. Unfortunately, since there is a great deal of variation between the facilities provided by different simulators, it is not practical to go into any detail in this book. Similarly, the convergence and performance properties of the analog solver within the VHDL-AMS simulator will vary based on the specific implementation. Simulator vendors usually provide training documentation and lab courses that explain how to use the facilities provided by their products.

Exercises

1. [❶ 7.1] The example on page 263 shows one possible order of analysis of the design units in the volume sensor. Show two other possible orders of analysis.

2. [❶ 7.1] Write a context clause that makes the resource libraries **company_lib** and **project_lib** accessible and that makes directly visible the entities **in_pad** and **out_pad** from **company_lib** and all entities from **project_lib**.

3. [❶ 7.2] Draw a diagram similar to Figure 7-13 showing the circuit node represented by the terminal **minus_volume** and all associated terminal ports in the volume sensor model.

4. [❷ 7.2] Try applying a VHDL-AMS analyzer to the erroneous battery model from the example on page 275 to see what error message (if any) it issues. You might find it helpful to remember the message in case it arises for other models that you develop.

chapter eight

Case Study 1: Mixed-Signal Focus

With a contribution by Scott Cooper,
Mentor Graphics Corporation

This first case study introduces the radio-controlled airplane system that will be thoroughly analyzed throughout the five case studies presented in this book. In this case study we focus on the encoding, transmission and decoding of the analog throttle and rudder command signals as they make their way to their respective end effectors. This portion of the system constitutes the "command and control" electronics for the airplane. We emphasize analog-to-digital (A/D) and digital-to-analog (D/A) signal conversions to illustrate mixed-signal modeling with VHDL-AMS.

8.1   System Overview

As noted in the Preface, the case studies revolve around a radio-controlled (RC) electric airplane system. The case studies illustrate the capabilities of the VHDL-AMS modeling language and include both mixed-signal and mixed-technology models. They also encompass several VHDL-AMS language features and embody clear guidelines for systems design and analysis. Figure 8-1 shows the system design for the RC airplane, with the command and control system highlighted by dashed boxes.

8.2   Command and Control System Design

The command and control system electronics constitute much of the overall system. The radio frequency (RF) block, the servos and throttle/rudder mechanics and the 42 V power converter will be discussed in separate case studies. Figure 8-2 illustrates the command and control system in more detail. It is composed of four primary functional sections: analog control (the control stick blocks); digitization and encoding (the digitize/encode block); decoding and pulse-width generation (the decode/PW block); and pulse-width-to-analog voltage conversion (the PW/analog blocks).

VHDL is well established as a digital modeling language and is sufficient for the strictly digital models in the command and control system. However, since we are dealing with VHDL-AMS, we will focus on the mixed-signal models used in this design. Source-code files for the complete model are provided on the companion CD for this book.

FIGURE 8-1

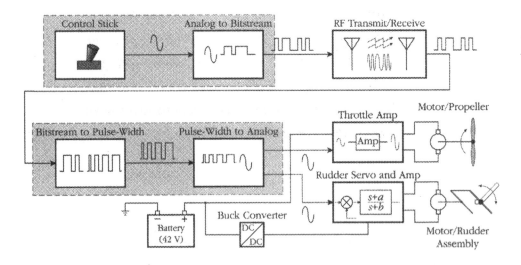

RC airplane system diagram with command and control blocks highlighted.

FIGURE 8-2

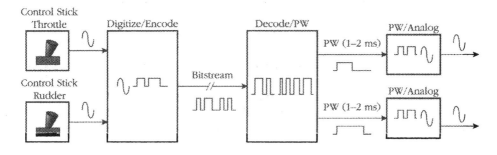

Command and control system: analog command input to discrete analog servo command.

Control Sticks

The speed and direction of the airplane are controlled by throttle and rudder control sticks, respectively. The control sticks output continuous analog signals whose values are derived from the position of a mechanical lever with which the operator controls the airplane. In an RC airplane system there is typically a single lever. When moved vertically, the lever controls the throttle and hence the speed of the plane. When moved horizontally, the lever controls the tail-wing rudder position. For simplicity, these two functions are shown independently in Figure 8-2, each with a separate lever.

The outputs of the control stick vary from 0 V to 4.8 V. For the throttle (propeller, or "prop") control, the control lever center position corresponds to 2.4 V on the output, which rotates the propeller at approximately one-half of its maximum speed. Moving the lever "down" or toward the operator reduces the voltage, and therefore the prop speed; moving the lever "up" or away from the operator increases the voltage and also the prop speed.

The rudder lever center position corresponds to straight-ahead flight. Moving the rudder control lever right commands the rudder to pivot counterclockwise about its axis, forcing the plane to move right; moving the lever left commands the rudder to pivot clockwise, causing the plane to move left.

Digitize/Encode Block

The primary purpose of the encoder block is to sample the analog outputs of the two control sticks every 20 ms and convert them into 10-bit serialized digital strings.

In communications systems, the process of digitizing analog signals and formatting them for transmission in this manner is referred to as pulse-code modulation (PCM). This block also time-multiplexes each data channel using time-division multiplexing (TDM). The result is a single bitstream containing all of the data to be sent to the receiver.

Data is organized in the bitstream as a collection of frames, each of which is 20 ms in duration. Each frame consists of up to 8 channels, each about 2 ms in duration. Frame synchronization and error detection information are also encoded into the bitstream prior to transmission. The analog-to-digital conversion, bitstream construction and overall timing are controlled by a local state machine.

For the purpose of this case study, the encoder output bitstream is sent to the input of the decoder block. In the full airplane system, it is sent via the RF transmit and receive blocks. The bitstream data rate is between 6000 and 7000 bits/s. The minimum allowable data rate for this system is (8 channels) × (16 bits/channel) / (20 ms frame length) = 6400 bits/s. The meaningful data for the system is contained in the first three channels of the frame: synchronization, throttle and rudder; the other channels are unused. Each channel is 16 bits: 10 data bits, 1 start bit and 1 parity bit. Additionally, 4 zero bits are added to the end of each channel to provide clear channel separation when we view waveforms.

An example of the encoder output bitstream is shown in Figure 8-3. The synchronization channel consists of 12 bits of alternating 1 and 0 bits. This information is used by the decoder to determine when valid data is about to be received. Actual throttle and rudder information is contained in channels 1 and 2, respectively.

The encoder circuit, shown in Figure 8-4, works as follows. First, the 12-bit sync pattern is generated in the TDM_encoder block, latched into a parallel-to-serial shift register and shifted out serially. An additional 4 zero bits are also shifted out to complete the 16-bit channel. Next, the actual command data is generated. The analog throttle and rudder signals connect to the inputs of a two-input analog switch. The switch is first set to pass the analog throttle signal through to an A/D converter. This signal is digitized into 10 bits, which are presented to the TDM_encoder block to be encoded in 16 bits of channel data. The analog switch then toggles to the rudder command signal so that it can be digitized and encoded in the same way.

The TDM_encoder block is illustrated in Figure 8-5. The encoder takes the 10-bit digitized signal and adds a start bit and parity bit, resulting in 12 bits of data. The parity bit allows a single-bit error between the transmitter and receiver to be detected for each channel. If an error is detected at the receiver, the channel will not be updated. Instead, it will continue to use its previous data. The 12 bits from the parity generator are latched into the parallel-to-serial shift register and shifted out serially, again followed by 4 zero bits.

FIGURE 8-3

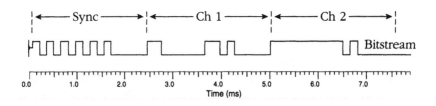

Serial digital bitstream containing synchronization, throttle and rudder data.

FIGURE 8-4

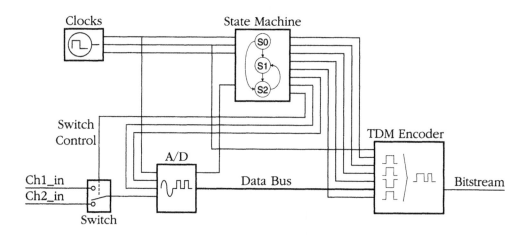

Schematic representation of the encoder circuit.

FIGURE 8-5

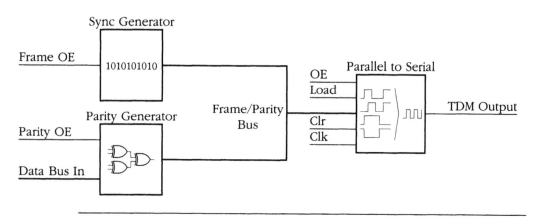

Schematic representation of TDM_encoder block.

Analog Switch

The two-input analog switch model is shown in Figure 8-6. A logic 0 on the digital control pin **sw_state** causes the resistance between terminals **p_in1** and **p_out** to equal the value of **r_closed**, and the resistance between terminals **p_in2** and **p_out** to equal the value of **r_open**. Since **r_closed** is typically defined as a very small value and **r_open** as a very large value, the effect is to allow current to flow from **p_in1** to **p_out** and to prevent current flowing from **p_in2** to **p_out**. The reverse occurs when a logic 1 is present on the digital control pin.

FIGURE 8-6

```
library ieee;  use ieee.std_logic_1164.all;
library ieee_proposed;  use ieee_proposed.electrical_systems.all;
entity switch_dig_2in is
    port ( sw_state : in std_ulogic;                 -- Digital control input
           terminal p_in1, p_in2, p_out : electrical );  -- Analog output
end entity switch_dig_2in;
```

```
architecture ideal of switch_dig_2in is
    constant r_open : resistance := 1.0e6;       -- Open switch resistance
    constant r_closed : resistance := 0.001;     -- Closed switch resistance
    constant trans_time : real := 0.00001;       -- Transition time to each position

    signal r_sig1 : resistance := r_closed;      -- Closed switch resistance variable
    signal r_sig2 : resistance := r_open;        -- Open switch resistance variable

    quantity v1 across i1 through p_in1 to p_out;  -- V & I for in1 to out
    quantity v2 across i2 through p_in2 to p_out;  -- V & I for in2 to out
    quantity r1 : resistance;      -- Time–varying resistance for in1 to out
    quantity r2 : resistance;      -- Time–varying resistance for in2 to out
begin
    process (sw_state) is   -- Sensitivity to digital control input
    begin
        if sw_state = '0' or sw_state = 'L' then       -- Close sig1, open sig2
            r_sig1 <= r_closed;
            r_sig2 <= r_open;
        elsif sw_state = '1' or sw_state = 'H' then    -- Open sig1, close sig2
            r_sig1 <= r_open;
            r_sig2 <= r_closed;
        end if;
    end process;
    r1 == r_sig1'ramp(trans_time, trans_time);   -- Ensure resistance continuity
    r2 == r_sig2'ramp(trans_time, trans_time);   -- Ensure resistance continuity

    v1 == r1 * i1;      -- Apply Ohm's law to in1
    v2 == r2 * i2;      -- Apply Ohm's law to in2
end architecture ideal;
```

Digitally controlled, two-input analog switch model.

The process is sensitive to the digital signal **sw_state** and assigns the values r_open and r_closed to the signals r_sig1 and r_sig2, representing the switch resistance values, as the switch changes state. The simultaneous statements equate the analog quantities r1 and r2 to the switch resistance values, with the 'ramp attributes ensuring analog continuity. The quantities are then used to determine switch voltage and current values using Ohm's law.

Analog-to-Digital Converter

The analog-to-digital (A/D) converter uses a successive approximation algorithm controlled by the encoder state machine. The converter divides the conversion operation into two functional steps: input (reading the analog input data) and convert (testing the input voltage and setting the resulting bit values in a temporary array and putting the result data on the output pins). These steps are represented by values of an enumeration type and are implemented by a case statement in a process, outlined in Figure 8-7.

For the input step, the converter waits for the **start** signal to be asserted. It then samples the analog input **Vin** and initializes variables used for the convert step. It also resets the "end of conversion" condition and changes the converter state to **convert**, ready for the second step.

For the convert step, the converter waits for the next clock cycle, and then compares the sampled analog input value to the threshold value for the most-significant bit. If the input is greater than the threshold, the converter sets the most-significant bit of a logic vector to '1' and reduces the sampled input value by the amount of the threshold. Otherwise, the converter sets the bit to '0' and leaves the sampled input value unchanged. This step is then repeated for each of the remaining bits. When the least-significant bit is determined, the converter sets the **eoc** signal to '1', indicating the "end of conversion" condition, and drives the logic vector value onto the data output bus. Finally, it resets the state variable to **input**, ready for the next conversion operation.

FIGURE 8-7

```
library ieee;  use ieee.std_logic_1164.all;
library ieee_proposed;  use ieee_proposed.electrical_systems.all;

entity a2d_nbit is
     port ( signal start : in std_ulogic;                    -- Start signal
            signal clk : in std_ulogic;                      -- Strobe clock
            terminal ain : electrical;                       -- Analog input terminal
            signal eoc : out std_ulogic := '0';              -- End of conversion pin
            signal dout : out std_ulogic_vector(9 downto 0) );   -- Digital output signal
end entity a2d_nbit;
```

```
architecture sar of a2d_nbit is
     constant Vmax : real := 5.0;        -- ADC's maximum range
     constant delay : time := 10 us;     -- ADC's conversion time
```

(continued on page 288)

(continued from page 287)

```
type states is (input, convert);        -- Two states of A2D Conversion
constant bit_range : integer := 9;      -- Bit range for dtmp and dout
quantity Vin across Iin through ain to electrical_ref;  -- ADC's input branch
begin
    sa_adc: process is
        variable thresh : real := Vmax;      -- Threshold to test input voltage against
        variable Vtmp : real := Vin;         -- Snapshot of input voltage
                                             -- when conversion starts
        variable dtmp : std_ulogic_vector(bit_range downto 0); -- Temp. output data
        variable status : states := input;   -- Begin with "input" case
        variable bit_cnt : integer := bit_range;
    begin
        case status is
            when input =>            -- Read input voltages when start goes high
                wait on start until start = '1' or start = 'H';
                bit_cnt := bit_range;   -- Reset bit_cnt for conversion
                thresh := Vmax;
                Vtmp := Vin;            -- Variable to hold input comparison voltage
                eoc <= '0';             -- Reset end of conversion
                status := convert;      -- Go to convert state
            when convert =>          -- Begin successive approximation conversion
                wait on clk until clk = '1' or clk = 'H';
                thresh := thresh / 2.0;         -- Get value of MSB
                if Vtmp > thresh then
                    dtmp(bit_cnt) := '1';       -- Store '1' in dtmp variable vector
                    Vtmp := Vtmp - thresh;      -- Prepare for next comparison
                else
                    dtmp(bit_cnt) := '0';       -- Store '0' in dtmp variable vector
                end if;
                if bit_cnt > 0 then
                    bit_cnt := bit_cnt - 1;  -- Decrement the bit count
                else
                    dout <= dtmp;            -- Put contents of dtmp on output pins
                    eoc <= '1' after delay;  -- Signal end of conversion
                    status := input;         -- Go to input state
                end if;
        end case;
    end process sa_adc;

    Iin == 0.0;    -- Ideal input draws no current
end architecture sar;
```

Partial listing of analog-to-digital converter model.

Encoder State Machine

All of the encoder timing and data transmission is controlled by a synchronous state machine. The state diagram is shown in Figure 8-8. When the system is first reset, all state values are initialized. Next, the sync pattern is latched into the parallel-to-serial shift register (**p2s_load := 1**), then the state machine waits 16 bitstream clock cycles for the data (12 sync bits and 4 zero bits) to be shifted out serially. After 16 clock cycles (**ser_done = 1**), the A/D is instructed to start converting the throttle voltage (**ch1**). When the conversion is complete (**a2d_eoc = 1**), the digitized data is sent to the parallel-to-serial shift register. Then 16 further clock cycles pass as the data is shifted serially out. Once all bits have shifted, the process is repeated for the rudder command voltage (**ch2**). The entire sequence repeats at approximately 20 ms intervals. The VHDL-AMS model for the encoder state machine is included on the companion CD.

FIGURE 8-8

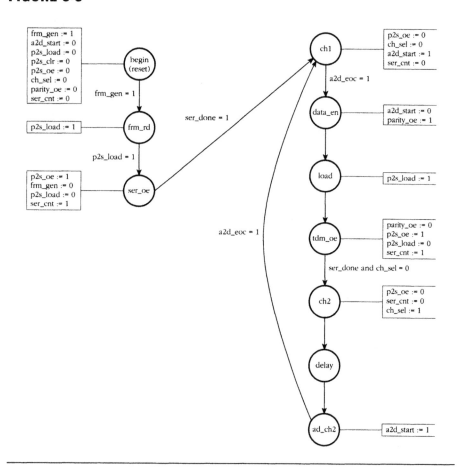

State diagram controller for the encoder block.

Decoder/Pulse-Width Block

As the RC airplane field has grown over the last few decades, many system standards have been adopted. One such standard specifies a "servo module," or "servo," which is interchangeable between airplanes. A servo is typically commanded by a voltage pulse that varies from about 1 ms to 2 ms in width. The decoder/pulse-width (PW) block in our design decodes the incoming bitstream data and generates the pulse-width servo command.

The decoder/PW block receives an asynchronous TDM digital bitstream from the encoder block via the RF transmit/receive block. The data is synchronously extracted from the TDM bitstream and converted into parallel words representing the original digitized control-stick information. These words are used in conjunction with a digital counter to generate a proportional analog pulse width for each channel driving the servos. All synchronization, decoding and pulse-width generation is controlled by another local state machine.

The decoder/PW block outputs analog pulse-width information for each channel to drive a dedicated servo. The pulse-width voltage level is 4.8 V. The pulse output is updated at 20 ms intervals (50 Hz), with the pulse width varying from 1 ms to 2 ms in response to operator commands. Typical output waveforms for this block are illustrated in Figure 8-9.

The varying pulse-width waveforms are generated by the circuitry shown in Figure 8-10. This circuit accepts the digital bitstream generated by the encoder block. Under control of the local state machine, the TDM decoder divides the bitstream into its constituent channels. For each channel, the data bits are presented to one input of a digital comparator. The other input of the comparator is driven by a counter. As the data is latched into the comparator, a clock starts incrementing the counter, and the comparator's output is set high. When the counter output matches the latched channel value, the comparator output goes low. The width of the comparator's output pulse is proportional to the time taken for the counter's output to reach the data value.

Pulse-Width/Analog Converter

The PW/analog converter blocks convert the analog pulse-width information from the decoder/PW block into analog voltage signals to drive the throttle and rudder servo-control loops. The incoming pulses are converted into digital words (again using digital counters), and these words are transformed into their analog equivalents using

FIGURE 8-9

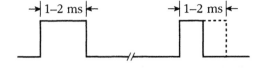

Variable pulse-width outputs that drive the servos.

FIGURE 8-10

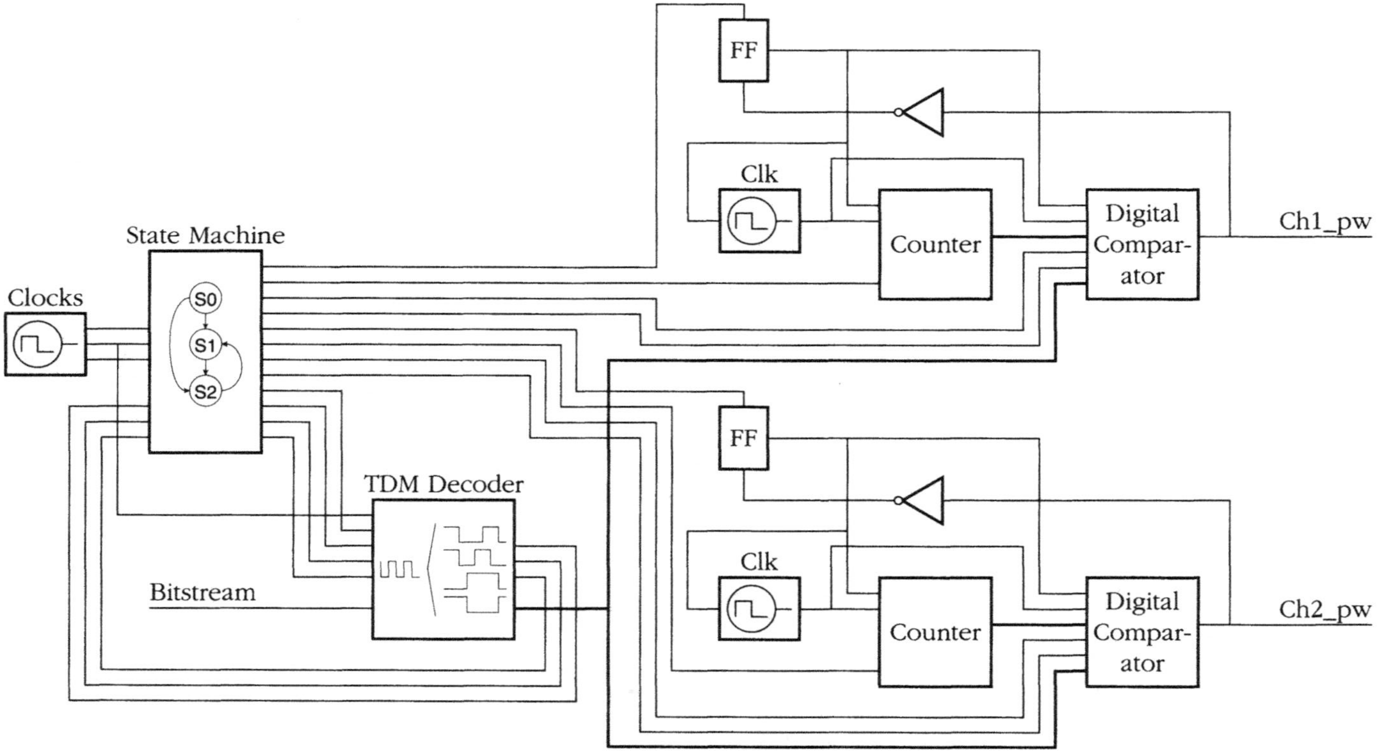

Schematic representation of the decoder block.

digital-to-analog (D/A) converters. While the conversion from digital words to a pulse-width signal and back again might seem redundant, it allows us to conform to the pulse-width standard for servo control. The conversion to the pulse-width signal is logically part of the radio receiver, whereas the conversion from the pulse-width signal to a servo-control voltage is part of a standard subsystem for RC airplanes.

This conversion from pulse-width to discrete analog values is performed by the circuitry shown in Figure 8-11. This circuit takes the varying pulse-width input and uses it to control the **enable** pins on a counter and its clock. This counter is fed directly into a D/A converter that produces the proportional analog voltage level.

Digital-to-Analog Converter

Nearly all of the components in the PW/analog block of Figure 8-11 are digital. The exception is the D/A converter, which is a mixed-signal component. A VHDL-AMS model for it is shown in Figure 8-12. The converter reads the input bits one at a time, starting with the most-significant bit. For each bit, the converter determines the corresponding voltage value by repeatedly dividing the reference voltage (**delt_v**) by two. If an input bit is high, the corresponding voltage is added into **v_sum**; if it is low, no voltage is added. After testing all of the input bits, the converter sets the signal **sum_out** to the value of the summed voltage in **v_sum**. The converter determines the output voltage, **vout**, using the 'ramp attribute applied to the signal **sum_out**. This is the step where the digital-to-analog transition is made. The 'ramp attribute ensures that **vout** has finite, continuous transitions from one level to another.

The overall control stick to D/A output voltage relationships for the throttle and rudder are shown in Figure 8-13. The analog throttle and rudder commands issued from the control sticks are reproduced in discrete analog form to command the servo-control loops in the airplane. The analog values are updated with every frame at 20 ms intervals.

FIGURE 8-11

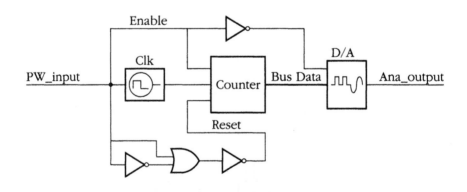

Circuit that converts variable pulse-width information into discrete analog voltages.

FIGURE 8-12

```
library ieee;  use ieee.std_logic_1164.all;
library ieee_proposed;  use ieee_proposed.electrical_systems.all;
entity dac_10_bit is
    port ( signal bus_in : in std_ulogic_vector(9 downto 0);
        signal clk : in std_ulogic;
        terminal analog_out :  electrical );
end entity dac_10_bit;

--------------------------------------------------------------

architecture behavioral of dac_10_bit is
    constant v_max : real := 5.0;
    signal s_out : real := 0.0;
    quantity v_out across i_out through analog_out to electrical_ref;
begin
    convert : process is
        variable v_sum : real;
        variable delta_v : real;
    begin
        wait until clk'event and (clk = '1' or clk = 'H');
        v_sum  := 0.0;
        delta_v  := v_max;
        for i in bus_in'range loop
            delta_v  := delta_v / 2.0;
            if bus_in(i) = '1' or bus_in(i) = 'H' then
                v_sum := v_sum + delta_v;
            end if;
        end loop;
        s_out <= v_sum;
    end process convert;

    v_out == s_out'ramp(100.0E-9);
end architecture behavioral;
```

Listing of digital-to-analog converter.

FIGURE 8-13

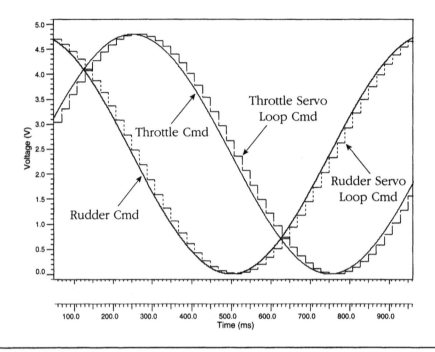

Analog input to digitized analog output of the complete system.

8.3   Design Trade-Off Analysis

In the previous section we developed a model of the encoding and decoding of analog information from the control sticks. In order to maintain RC airplane conventions, we transform the command data in many ways. In the transmitter we transform from analog input commands to parallel digital bits, then to serial bits and then to a multiplexed serial bitstream. In the receiver on the airplane we transform from the serial bitstream back to parallel digital bits, then to voltage pulses of varying widths, then back to parallel digital bits and finally to analog values that drive the servo-control loops. We can use simulation to verify that the data is successfully propagated from the analog control sticks to the servo-control loop inputs.

In this trade-off analysis we investigate the effects of A/D and D/A bit resolution on the airplane's rudder signal. We then look at another potential source of accuracy loss in the system. The accuracy required for an RC airplane system is difficult to define precisely. This is not because the accuracy of the system is difficult to measure. Rather, it is due to the subjective nature of the effects on the user's flying experience. With increased system accuracy, the person controlling the airplane will generally experience a smoother, more intuitive link between the control stick and the plane movement.

Converter Accuracy

Prior to determining the overall accuracy of the RC airplane system, we will analyze a test circuit, shown in Figure 8-14, to familiarize ourselves with A/D and D/A conversion principles. In this test circuit, a pulse source drives the analog input of the A/D model shown in Figure 8-7. After the conversion time, the end-of-conversion signal **eoc** goes high. This signal is transformed into a short pulse that drives the latch pin on the D/A. As a result, an analog signal is converted to a digital word and then back to an analog signal.

We use the circuit to simulate the accuracy effects of changing the number of bits of resolution in the A/D and D/A components. For these tests, we use a ramp waveform that changes from 0 V to 9.5 V in 600 ms. We chose the 9.5 V amplitude because it represents nearly the full range that the converters must resolve (±4.8 V). We chose the 600 ms ramp time to meet a tracking specification discussed in the second case study in Chapter 14.

We first run a series of tests to illustrate the effects of bit resolution on overall converter accuracy. Figure 8-15 illustrates the quantized D/A outputs for bit resolutions ranging from 5 to 10 bits. The continuous analog signal is the input ramp, and the quantized signals consist of the D/A output signals for six simulation runs, each with a different bit-resolution setting. These signals are overlaid on one another. The digital signal at the bottom of the figure drives the A/D's start-conversion pin.

We can see from Figure 8-15 that there is progressively more error between the analog input ramp voltage and the D/A output as the converter bit resolution is decreased. The error is quantified in Figure 8-16, which shows the quantization error for a specific sample of the input ramp. The ramp was sampled at about 285 ms, indicated by the leftmost vertical line. This time coincides with the rising edge of the A/D start-conversion command. The analog voltage that was sampled has an amplitude of 4.49 V. If we were to examine the measured values with more significant digits, we would see that the D/A generates a 2.3 mV error with 10 bits of converter resolution, and a 292 mV error with 5 bits of resolution. The calculated maximum

FIGURE 8-14

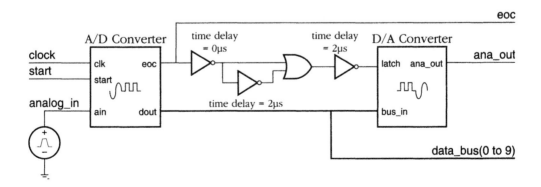

Test circuit for A/D and D/A accuracy comparisons.

FIGURE 8·15

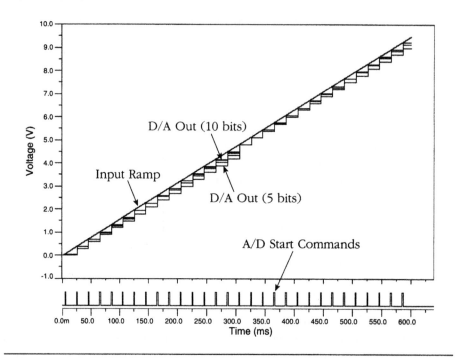

Effects of bit resolution on converter accuracy (lower bits).

error (the quantization error) for a 10-bit converter is $FSR/2^{10}$, where FSR is the full-scale range of the converter. For our converter, $FSR = 9.6$ V, which gives a quantization error of 9.6 V/1024 = 9.4 mV. This puts our measured error well within margin. Using the same approach for 5 bits of converter resolution, the calculated quantization error is 9.6 V/32 = 300 mV, which is just greater than the measured value of 292 mV. How close the measurements come to the calculated maximum values depends on how close to a bit threshold the analog sample is taken.

While we are mainly concerned with the effects of the less-significant A/D and D/A bits in our trade-off analysis, it is also worth noting the effects that the more-significant bits have on the system. Figure 8-17 shows the D/A output waveforms resulting from reducing the number of bits below five. The figure illustrates that reduced bit resolution becomes a serious operational factor for the RC airplane. We see that not only is the controller smoothness sacrificed with decreasing accuracy, but ultimately the ability to effectively control the plane is lost. The response of the plane becomes coarser and coarser until the rudder effectively operates in only two positions.

System Analysis

Now that we have a general idea of what to expect from our A/D and D/A converters, let us assume that in the course of system development, we start with 8 bits of

FIGURE 8-16

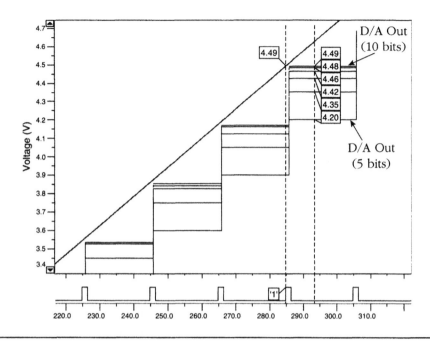

Measured effects of bit resolution on converter accuracy (lower bits).

converter resolution. From the previous analysis of converter accuracy, we can calculate the quantization error for an 8-bit system to be 9.6 V/256 = 37.5 mV. We would therefore expect this value to represent the greatest difference between any sampled analog voltage value and its quantized counterpart. Simulation results for the rudder channel with 8 bits of converter resolution are illustrated in Figure 8-18. There are two pairs of measurements illustrated in this figure. The left vertical line of each pair measures the input ramp signal at the time the A/D converter samples it; the right vertical line of each pair represents the quantized value that corresponds to the sampled value. Measurements taken throughout the illustrated range of data show a maximum conversion error of 34.5 mV, which is within the quantization error limit. This is as expected and indicates that the system accuracy is acceptable.

Now suppose we wish to increase the converter bit resolution to 10 bits, in order to have a "smoother" feeling system. We make the change and re-run the analysis. The simulation results are given in Figure 8-19. From our previous calculations, we would expect a maximum quantization error of 9.4 mV. However, the measurement illustrated in the figure reveals a problem. The ramp input voltage is sampled at 1.0095 V and the resulting quantized voltage is 0.9938 V. The difference is 15.7 mV, which is larger than the calculated quantization error. We need to determine the cause of this unacceptable error.

Thus far we have confined our accuracy analysis to the A/D and D/A converters themselves. However, there is another data conversion that we have neglected: the digital command to analog pulse-width conversion. Recall from the description of

FIGURE 8·17

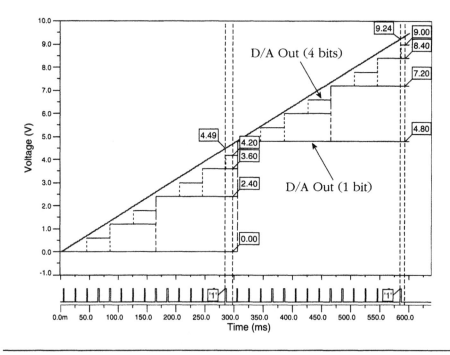

Effects of bit resolution on converter accuracy (upper bits).

Figure 8-10 that the digital command to pulse-width conversion circuitry employs a digital counter/comparator. The pulse width is determined by measuring how many clock cycles it takes for a counter's output to match the digitized command word.

The relationship between pulse width and clock frequency is analogous to the relationship between voltage level and bit resolution: the more clock cycles used to make up the pulse width, the greater the accuracy. Since we are representing up to 1 ms of time with the clock, an 8-bit system would require a clock cycle every 1 ms/256, which is approximately 4 μs (a frequency of 250 kHz). For a 10-bit system, however, we must decrease the period to 1 ms/1024, which is approximately 1 μs (a frequency of 1 MHz). The problem we have observed results from providing 10 bits of A/D and D/A converter resolution, but only 8 bits of digital-command to pulse-width conversion resolution.

We now re-simulate the system with 10 bits of converter resolution, but this time we use a 1 μs clock period for the digital-command to pulse-width converter circuitry. Figure 8-20 shows the revised measurements. We now have an acceptable error measurement of 6.4 mV between the sampled voltage of 1.0095 V and the quantized voltage of 1.0031 V. This analysis underscores the value of simulating multiple subsystems together as an integrated system, rather than in isolation from one another.

FIGURE 8-18

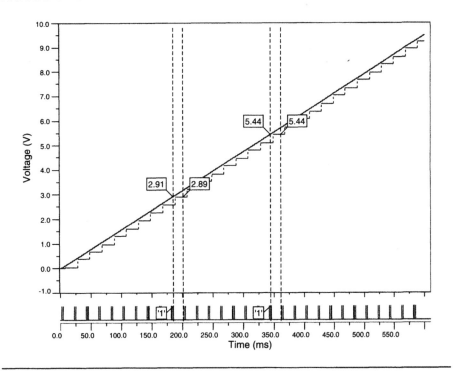

Rudder channel input versus output with 8 bits of converter resolution.

Exercises

1. [❶ 8.2] How can the digitally controlled switch model of Figure 8-6 be modified to use asymmetrical open/close and close/open transition times?

2. [❶ 8.2] In the D/A model shown in Figure 8-12, why is it necessary to have the variable v_sum, the signal s_out and the quantity vout? They all represent essentially the same data, namely, the sum of the voltage contributions for each bit. Can they be combined using this model topology?

3. [❷ 8.2] When the input to the digitally controlled switch model in Figure 8-6 changes state, the switch resistance varies linearly from the open to closed and closed positions. Revise the model so that the switch resistance varies exponentially from one position to the other. The change in resistance over time, $R(t)$, from R_1 to R_2 starting at time t_1 is given by

$$R(t - t_1) = R_2 + (R_1 - R_2)e^{-k(t - t_1)}$$

where $k = 1.0 \times 10^6$.

FIGURE 8·19

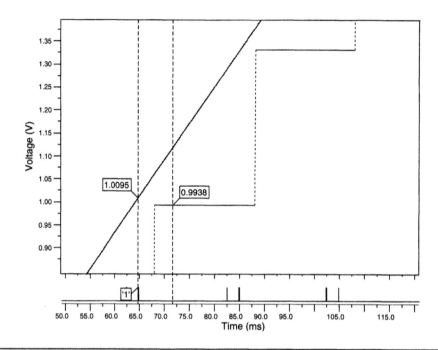

Rudder channel input versus output with 10 bits of converter resolution.

4. [❸ 8.2] Develop a structural model of a successive-approximation A/D converter using a sample-and-hold device, a D/A converter, a shift register, a state machine and any other digital parts you need. Develop behavioral models for the parts and a test bench to test your design using a VHDL-AMS simulator.

5. [❹] One issue that we have not addressed in the case study design is synchronization of the clock used to encode data in the transmitter with the clock used to decode data in the receiver. The encoded bitstream is shown in Figure 8-3. Recall that the first frame contains a synchronization word, consisting of 12 bits alternating between one and zero followed by 4 zero bits. Develop a model of the bitstream decoder that detects the arrival of a synchronization frame. The decoder should be driven by a clock that is four times the data bit rate. When the decoder detects a synchronization frame, it should reset an output clock for use in sampling the data in subsequent frames. The leading edge of the output clock should occur in the middle of each bit in the bitstream.

Develop a test bench to verify that your model correctly synchronizes to the incoming bitstream and recovers the data. Explore the effects of drift and jitter between the transmit and receive clocks. How sensitive is your design to these variations?

FIGURE 8-20

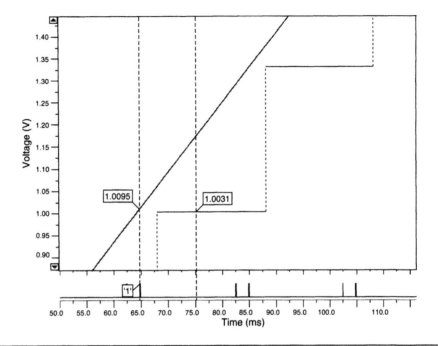

Rudder channel input versus output with 10 bits of converter resolution and 1 μs pulse-width clock.

chapter nine

Subprograms

When we write complex behavioral models it is useful to divide the code into sections, each dealing with a relatively self-contained part of the behavior. VHDL-AMS provides a subprogram facility to let us do this. In this chapter, we look at the two kinds of subprograms: procedures *and* functions. *The difference between the two is that a procedure encapsulates a collection of sequential statements that are executed for their effect, whereas a function encapsulates a collection of statements that compute a result. Thus a procedure is a generalization of a statement, whereas a function is a generalization of an expression. Also in this chapter we examine* simultaneous procedural statements, *which are related to functions but are used to express analog behavior.*

9.1 Procedures

We start our discussion of subprograms with procedures. There are two aspects to using procedures in a model: first the procedure is declared, then elsewhere the procedure is *called*. The syntax rule for a procedure declaration is

> subprogram_body ⟸
>   **procedure** identifier ⟦ (*parameter*_interface_list) ⟧ **is**
>   ⦃ subprogram_declarative_part ⦄
>   **begin**
>   ⦃ sequential_statement ⦄
>   **end** ⟦ **procedure** ⟧ ⟦ identifier ⟧ ;

For now we will just look at procedures without the parameter list part; we will come back to parameters in the next section.

The *identifier* in a procedure declaration names the procedure. The name may be repeated at the end of the procedure declaration. The sequential statements in the body of a procedure implement the algorithm that the procedure is to perform and can include any of the sequential statements that we have seen in previous chapters. A procedure can declare items in its declarative part for use in the statements in the procedure body. The declarations can include types, subtypes, constants, variables and nested subprogram declarations. The items declared are not accessible outside of the procedure; we say they are *local* to the procedure.

Example   Figure 9-1 is a declaration for a procedure that calculates an average of a collection of data values stored in an array called **samples** and assigns the result to a variable called **average**. This procedure has a local variable **total** for accumulating the sum of array elements. Unlike variables in processes, procedure local variables are created anew and initialized each time the procedure is called.

FIGURE 9-1

```
procedure average_samples is
    variable total : real := 0.0;
begin
    assert samples'length > 0 severity failure;
    for index in samples'range loop
        total := total + samples(index);
    end loop;
    average := total / real(samples'length);
end procedure average_samples;
```

A declaration for a procedure to average a number of values.

The actions of a procedure are invoked by a *procedure call* statement, which is yet another VHDL-AMS sequential statement. A procedure with no parameters is called simply by writing its name, as shown by the syntax rule

procedure_call_statement ⇐ ⟦ label : ⟧ *procedure*_name ;

The optional label allows us to identify the procedure call statement. We will discuss labeled statements in Chapter 22. As an example, we might include the following statement in a process:

average_samples;

The effect of this statement is to invoke the procedure **average_samples**. This involves creating and initializing a new instance of the local variable **total**, then executing the statements in the body of the procedure. When the last statement in the procedure is completed, we say the procedure *returns;* that is, the thread of control of statement execution returns to the process from which the procedure was called, and the next statement in the process after the call is executed.

We can write a procedure declaration in the declarative part of an architecture body or a process. We can also declare procedures within other procedures, but we will leave that until a later section. If a procedure is included in an architecture body's declarative part, it can be called from within any of the processes in the architecture body. On the other hand, declaring a procedure within a process hides it away from use by other processes.

Example   The outline in Figure 9-2 illustrates a procedure defined within a process. The procedure **do_arith_op** encapsulates an algorithm for arithmetic operations on two values, producing a result and a flag indicating whether the result is zero. It has a variable **result**, which it uses within the sequential statements that implement the algorithm. The statements also use the signals and other objects declared in the architecture body. The process **alu** invokes **do_arith_op** with a procedure call statement. The advantage of separating the statements for arithmetic operations into a procedure in this example is that it simplifies the body of the **alu** process.

FIGURE 9-2

```
architecture rtl of control_processor is
    type func_code is (add, subtract);
    signal op1, op2, dest : integer;
    signal Z_flag : boolean;
    signal func : func_code;
    ...
begin
```

(continued on page 306)

(continued from page 305)

```
alu : process is
    procedure do_arith_op is
        variable result : integer;
    begin
        case func is
            when add =>
                result := op1 + op2;
            when subtract =>
                result := op1 – op2;
        end case;
        dest <= result after Tpd;
        Z_flag <= result = 0 after Tpd;
    end procedure do_arith_op;
begin
    ...
    do_arith_op;
    ...
end process alu;

...

end architecture rtl;
```

An outline of an architecture body with a process containing a procedure. The procedure encapsulates part of the behavior of the process and is invoked by the procedure call statement within the process.

Another important use of procedures arises when some action needs to be performed several times at different places in a model. Instead of writing several copies of the statements to perform the action, the statements can be encapsulated in a procedure, which is then called from each place.

Example   Figure 9-3 shows an outline of a process taken from a behavioral model of a CPU. The process fetches instructions from memory and interprets them. Since the actions required to fetch an instruction and to fetch a data word are identical, the process encapsulates them in a procedure, **read_memory**. The procedure copies the address from the memory address register to the address bus, sets the read signal to '1', then activates the request signal. When the memory responds, the procedure copies the data from the data bus signal to the memory data register and acknowledges to the memory by setting the request signal back to '0'. When the memory has completed its operation, the procedure returns.

The procedure is called in two places within the process. First, it is called to fetch an instruction. The process copies the program counter into the memory address register and calls the procedure. When the procedure returns, the pro-

FIGURE 9-3

```
instruction_interpreter : process is
    variable mem_address_reg, mem_data_reg,
            prog_counter, instr_reg, accumulator, index_reg : word;
    ...
    procedure read_memory is
    begin
        address_bus <= mem_address_reg;
        mem_read <= '1';
        mem_request <= '1';
        wait until mem_ready = '1';
        mem_data_reg := data_bus_in;
        mem_request <= '0';
        wait until mem_ready = '0';
    end procedure read_memory;
begin
    ...   -- initialization
    loop
        -- fetch next instruction
        mem_address_reg := prog_counter;
        read_memory;              -- call procedure
        instr_reg := mem_data_reg;
        ...
        case opcode is
            ...
            when load_mem =>
                mem_address_reg := index_reg + displacement;
                read_memory;     -- call procedure
                accumulator := mem_data_reg;
            ...
        end case;
    end loop;
end process instruction_interpreter;
```

An outline of an instruction interpreter process from a CPU model. The procedure read_memory *is called from two places.*

cess copies the data from the memory data register, placed there by the procedure, to the instruction register. The second call to the procedure takes place when a "load memory" instruction is executed. The process sets the memory address register using the values of the index register and some displacement, then calls the memory read procedure to perform the read operation. When it returns, the process copies the data to the accumulator.

Since a procedure call is a form of sequential statement and a procedure body implements an algorithm using sequential statements, there is no reason why one procedure cannot call another procedure. In this case, control is passed from the calling procedure to the called procedure to execute its statements. When the called procedure returns, the calling procedure carries on executing statements until it returns to its caller.

Example   The process outlined in Figure 9-4 is a control sequencer for a register-transfer-level model of a CPU. It sequences the activation of control signals with a two-phase clock on signals **phase1** and **phase2**. The process contains two procedures, **control_write_back** and **control_arith_op**, that encapsulate parts of the control algorithm. The process calls **control_arith_op** when an arithmetic operation must be performed. This procedure sequences the control signals for the source and destination operand registers in the data path. It then calls **control_write_back**, which sequences the control signals for the register file in the data path, to write the value from the destination register. When this procedure is completed, it returns to the first procedure, which then returns to the process.

FIGURE 9-4

```
control_sequencer : process is
    procedure control_write_back is
    begin
        wait until phase1 = '1';
        reg_file_write_en <= '1';
        wait until phase2 = '0';
        reg_file_write_en <= '0';
    end procedure control_write_back;

    procedure control_arith_op is
    begin
        wait until phase1 = '1';
        A_reg_out_en <= '1';
        B_reg_out_en <= '1';
        wait until phase1 = '0';
        A_reg_out_en <= '0';
        B_reg_out_en <= '0';
        wait until phase2 = '1';
        C_reg_load_en <= '1';
        wait until phase2 = '0';
        C_reg_load_en <= '0';
        control_write_back;-- call procedure
    end procedure control_arith_op;

    ...
begin
    ...
```

control_arith_op;-- *call procedure*

...

end process control_sequencer;

An outline of a control sequencer processor for a register-transfer-level model of a CPU. The process contains procedures that encapsulate parts of the control algorithm. The process calls these procedures, which may in turn call other procedures.

Return Statement in a Procedure

In all of the examples above, the procedures completed execution of the statements in their bodies before returning. Sometimes it is useful to be able to return from the middle of a procedure, for example, as a way of handling an exceptional condition. We can do this using a *return* statement, described by the simplified syntax rule

return_statement ⇐ ⟦ label : ⟧ **return** ;

The optional label allows us to identify the return statement. We will discuss labeled statements in Chapter 22. The effect of the return statement, when executed in a procedure, is that the procedure is immediately terminated and control is transferred back to the caller.

Example Figure 9-5 is a revised version of the instruction interpreter process from Figure 9-3. The procedure to read from memory is revised to check for the reset signal becoming active during a read operation. If it does, the procedure returns immediately, aborting the operation in progress. The process then exits the fetch/execute loop and starts the process body again, reinitializing its state and output signals.

FIGURE 9-5

instruction_interpreter : **process is**

 ...

 procedure read_memory **is**
 begin
  address_bus <= mem_address_reg;
  mem_read <= '1';
  mem_request <= '1';
  wait until mem_ready = '1' **or** reset = '1';

(continued on page 310)

(continued from page 309)

```
        if reset = '1' then
            return;
        end if;
        mem_data_reg := data_bus_in;
        mem_request <= '0';
        wait until mem_ready = '0';
    end procedure read_memory;
begin
    ...   -- initialization
    loop
        ...
        read_memory;
        exit when reset = '1';

        ...
    end loop;
end process instruction_interpreter;
```

A revised instruction interpreter process. The read memory procedure now checks for the reset signal becoming active.

9.2 Procedure Parameters

Now that we have looked at the basics of procedures, we will discuss procedures that include parameters. A *parameterized procedure* is much more general in that it can perform its algorithm using different data objects or values each time it is called. The idea is that the caller passes parameters to the procedure as part of the procedure call, and the procedure then executes its statements using the parameters.

When we write a parameterized procedure, we include information in the *parameter interface list* (or *parameter list*, for short) about the parameters to be passed to the procedure. The syntax rule for a procedure declaration on page 304 shows where the parameter list fits in. Following is the syntax rule for a parameter list:

interface_list ⇐
    (⟦ **constant** ▯ **variable** ▯ **signal** ⟧
        identifier ⦃ , ₒₒₒ ⦄ : ⟦ mode ⟧ subtype_indication
                                   ⟦ := *static*_expression ⟧) ⦃ ; ₒₒₒ ⦄

mode ⇐ **in** ▯ **out** ▯ **inout**

As we can see, it is similar to the port interface list used in declaring entities. The main difference is that a parameter interface list may not include quantities or terminals. The similarity is not coincidental, since both forms of interface list specify information about objects upon which the user and the implementation must agree. In the case of a procedure, the user is the caller of the procedure, and the implementation is the body of statements within the procedure. The objects defined in the parameter list are called the *formal parameters* of the procedure. We can think of them as placeholders that stand for the *actual parameters,* which are to be supplied by the caller when it calls the procedure. Since the syntax rule for a parameter list is quite complex, let us start with some simple examples and work up from them.

Example   First, let's rewrite the procedure do_arith_op, from Figure 9-2, so that the function code is passed as a parameter. The new version is shown in Figure 9-6. In the parameter interface list we have identified one formal parameter named **op**. This name is used in the statements in the procedure to refer to the value that will be passed as an actual parameter when the procedure is called. The mode of the formal parameter is **in**, indicating that it is used to pass information into the procedure from the caller. This means that the statements in the procedure can use the value but cannot modify it. In the parameter list we have specified the type of the parameter as func_code. This indicates that the operations performed on the value in the statements must be appropriate for a value of this type, and that the caller may only pass a value of this type as an actual parameter.

Now that we have parameterized the procedure, we can call it from different places passing different function codes each time. For example, a call at one place might be

    do_arith_op (add);

The procedure call simply includes the actual parameter value in parentheses. In this case we pass the literal value **add** as the actual parameter. At another place in the model we might pass the value of the signal **func** shown in the model in Figure 9-2:

    do_arith_op (func);

In this example, we have specified the mode of the formal parameter as **in**. Note that the syntax rule for a parameter list indicates that the mode is an optional part. If we leave it out, mode **in** is assumed, so we could have written the procedure as

    procedure do_arith_op (op : func_code) **is** ...

While this is equally correct, it's not a bad idea to include the mode specification for **in** parameters, to make our intention explicitly clear.

FIGURE 9·6

```
procedure do_arith_op ( op : in func_code ) is
    variable result : integer;
begin
    case op is
        when add =>
            result := op1 + op2;
        when subtract =>
            result := op1 – op2;
    end case;
    dest  <=  result after Tpd;
    Z_flag  <=  result = 0 after Tpd;
end procedure do_arith_op;
```

A procedure to perform an arithmetic operation, parameterized by the kind of operation.

The syntax rule for a parameter list also shows us that we can specify the *class* of a formal parameter, namely, whether it is a constant, a variable or a signal within the procedure. If the mode of the parameter is **in**, the class is assumed to be *constant*, since a constant is an object that cannot be updated by assignment. It is just a quirk of VHDL-AMS that we can specify both **constant** and **in**, even though to do so is redundant. Usually we simply leave out the keyword **constant**, relying on the mode to make our intentions clear. (The exceptions are parameters of access types, discussed in Chapter 20, and file types, discussed in Chapter 21.) For an **in** mode constant-class parameter, we write an expression as the actual parameter. The value of this expression must be of the type specified in the parameter list. The value is passed to the procedure for use in the statements in its body.

Let us now turn to formal parameters of mode **out**. Such a parameter lets us transfer information out from the procedure back to the caller. Here is an example, before we delve into the details.

Example The procedure in Figure 9-7 performs addition of two unsigned numbers represented as bit vectors of type **word32**, which we assume is defined elsewhere. The procedure has two **in** mode parameters **a** and **b**, allowing the caller to pass two bit-vector values. The procedure uses these values to calculate the sum and overflow flag. Within the procedure, the two **out** mode parameters, **result** and **overflow**, appear as variables. The procedure performs variable assignments to update their values, thus transferring information back to the caller.

FIGURE 9-7

```
procedure addu ( a, b : in word32;
                       result : out word32;  overflow : out boolean ) is
    variable sum : word32;
    variable carry : bit := '0';
begin
    for index in sum'reverse_range loop
        sum(index) := a(index) xor b(index) xor carry;
        carry := ( a(index) and b(index) ) or ( carry and ( a(index) xor b(index) ) );
    end loop;
    result := sum;
    overflow := carry = '1';
end procedure addu;
```

A procedure to add two bit vectors representing unsigned integers.

A call to this procedure may appear as follows:

```
variable PC, next_PC : word32;
variable overflow_flag : boolean;
...
addu ( PC, X"0000_0004", next_PC, overflow_flag);
```

In this procedure call statement, the first two actual parameters are expressions, whose values are passed in through the formal parameters a and b. The third and fourth actual parameters are the names of variables. When the procedure returns, the values assigned by the procedure to the formal parameters result and overflow are used to update the variables next_PC and overflow_flag.

In the above example, the **out** mode parameters are of the class *variable*. Since this class is assumed for **out** parameters, we usually leave out the class specification **variable**, although it may be included if we wish to state the class explicitly. We will come back to signal-class parameters in a moment. The mode **out** indicates that the only way the procedure may use the formal parameters is to update them by variable assignment to transfer information back to the caller. It may not read the values of the parameters, as it can with **in** mode parameters. For an **out** mode, variable-class parameter, the caller must supply a variable as an actual parameter. Both the actual parameter and the value returned must be of the type specified in the parameter list.

The third mode we can specify for formal parameters is **inout**, which is a combination of **in** and **out** modes. It is used for objects that are to be both read and updated by a procedure. As with **out** parameters, they are assumed to be of class variable if the class is not explicitly stated. For **inout** mode variable parameters, the caller supplies a variable as an actual parameter. The value of this variable is used to initialize the formal parameter, which may then be used in the statements of the procedure. The procedure may also perform variable assignments to update the formal parameter. When the procedure returns, the value of the formal parameter is copied back to the actual parameter variable, transferring information back to the caller.

Example   The procedure in Figure 9-8 negates a number represented as a bit vector, using the "complement and add one" method. Since **a** is an **inout** mode parameter, we can refer to its value in expressions in the procedure body. (This differs from the parameter **result** in the **addu** procedure of the previous example.) We might include the following call to this procedure in a model:

```
variable op1 : word32;
...
negate ( op1 );
```

This uses the value of **op1** to initialize the formal parameter **a**. The procedure body is then executed, updating **a**, and when it returns, the final value of **a** is copied back into **op1**.

FIGURE 9-8

```
procedure negate ( a : inout word32 ) is
    variable carry_in : bit := '1';
    variable carry_out : bit;
begin
    a := not a;
    for index in a'reverse_range loop
        carry_out := a(index) and carry_in;
        a(index) := a(index) xor carry_in;
        carry_in := carry_out;
    end loop;
end procedure negate;
```

A procedure to negate an integer represented by a bit vector.

Signal Parameters

The third class of object that we can specify for formal parameters is *signal,* which indicates that the algorithm performed by the procedure involves a signal passed by the caller. A signal parameter can be of any of the modes **in**, **out** or **inout**. The way that signal parameters work is somewhat different from constant and variable parameters, so it is worth spending a bit of time understanding them.

When a caller passes a signal as a parameter of mode **in**, instead of passing the value of the signal, it passes the signal object itself. Any reference to the formal parameter within the procedure is exactly like a reference to the actual signal itself. A consequence of this is that if the procedure executes a wait statement, the signal value may be different after the wait statement completes and the procedure resumes. This behavior differs from that of constant parameters of mode **in**, which have the same value for the whole of the procedure.

Example   Suppose we wish to model the receiver part of a network interface. It receives fixed-length packets of data on the signal rx_data. The data is synchronized with changes, from '0' to '1', of the clock signal rx_clock. Figure 9-9 is an outline of part of the model.

FIGURE 9-9

```
architecture behavioral of receiver is
    ...    -- type declarations, etc
    signal recovered_data : bit;
    signal recovered_clock : bit;

    ...

    procedure receive_packet ( signal rx_data : in bit;
                               signal rx_clock : in bit;
                               data_buffer : out packet_array ) is
    begin
        for index in packet_index_range loop
            wait until rx_clock = '1';
            data_buffer(index) := rx_data;
        end loop;
    end procedure receive_packet;

begin
    packet_assembler : process is
        variable packet : packet_array;
    begin
        ...
        receive_packet ( recovered_data, recovered_clock, packet );
        ...
    end process packet_assembler;

    ...

end architecture behavioral;
```

An outline of a model of a network receiver, including a procedure with signal parameters of mode **in**.

During execution of the model, the process **packet_assembler** calls the procedure **receive_packet**, passing the signals **recovered_data** and **recovered_clock** as actual parameters. We can think of the procedure as executing "on behalf of" the process. When it reaches the wait statement, it is really the calling process that suspends. The wait statement mentions **rx_clock**, and since this stands for **recovered_clock**, the process is sensitive to changes on **recovered_clock** while it is suspended. Each time it resumes, it reads the current value of **rx_data** (which represents the actual signal **recovered_data**) and stores it in an element of the array parameter **data_buffer**.

Now let's look at signal parameters of mode **out**. In this case, the caller must name a signal as the actual parameter, and the procedure is passed a reference to the driver for the signal. When the procedure performs a signal assignment statement on the formal parameter, the transactions are scheduled on the driver for the actual signal parameter. In Chapter 5, we said that a process that contains a signal assignment statement contains a driver for the target signal, and that an ordinary signal may only have one driver. When such a signal is passed as an actual **out** mode parameter, there is still only the one driver. We can think of the signal assignments within the procedure as being performed on behalf of the process that calls the procedure.

Example   Figure 9-10 is an outline of an architecture body for a signal generator. The procedure **generate_pulse_train** has **in** mode constant parameters that specify the characteristics of a pulse train and an **out** mode signal parameter on which it generates the required pulse train. The process **raw_signal_generator** calls the procedure, supplying **raw_signal** as the actual signal parameter for **s**. A reference to the driver for **raw_signal** is passed to the procedure, and transactions are generated on it.

FIGURE 9-10

```
library ieee;  use ieee.std_logic_1164.all;
architecture top_level of signal_generator is
    signal raw_signal : std_ulogic;
    ...
    procedure generate_pulse_train ( width, separation : in delay_length;
                                     number : in natural;
                                     signal s : out std_ulogic ) is
begin
    for count in 1 to number loop
        s <= '1', '0' after width;
        wait for width + separation;
    end loop;
end procedure generate_pulse_train;
```

```
begin

    raw_signal_generator : process is
    begin
        …
        generate_pulse_train ( width => period / 2,
                               separation => period – period / 2,
                               number => pulse_count,
                               s => raw_signal );
        …
    end process raw_signal_generator;
    …
end architecture top_level;
```

An outline of a model for a signal generator, including a pulse generator procedure with an **out** *mode signal parameter.*

An incidental point to note is the way we have specified the actual value for the **separation** parameter in the procedure call. This ensures that the sum of the **width** and **separation** values is exactly equal to **period**, even if **period** is not an even multiple of the time resolution limit. This illustrates an approach sometimes called "defensive programming," in which we try to ensure that the model works correctly in all possible circumstances.

As with variable-class parameters, we can also have a signal-class parameter of mode **inout**. When the procedure is called, both the signal and a reference to its driver are passed to the procedure. The statements within it can read the signal value, include it in sensitivity lists in wait statements, query its attributes and schedule transactions using signal assignment statements.

A final point to note about signal parameters relates to procedures declared immediately within an architecture body. The target of any signal assignment statements within such a procedure must be a signal parameter, rather than a direct reference to a signal declared in the enclosing architecture body. The reason for this restriction is that the procedure may be called by more than one process within the architecture body. Each process that performs assignments on a signal has a driver for the signal. Without the restriction, we would not be able to tell easily by looking at the model where the drivers for the signal were located. The restriction makes the model more comprehensible and hence easier to maintain.

Default Values

The one remaining part of a procedure parameter list that we have yet to discuss is the optional default value expression, shown in the syntax rule on page 310. Note that we can only specify a default value for a formal parameter of mode **in**, and the parameter must be of the class constant or variable. If we include a default value in a parameter specification, we have the option of omitting an actual value when the procedure is called. We can either use the keyword **open** in place of an actual parameter value or, if the actual value would be at the end of the parameter list, simply leave it out. If we omit an actual value, the default value is used instead.

Example   Figure 9-11 is a procedure that increments an unsigned integer represented as a bit vector. The amount to increment by is specified by the second parameter, which has a default value of the bit-vector representation of 1.

If we have a variable count declared to be of type word32, we can call the procedure to increment it by 4, as follows:

```
increment(count, X"0000_0004");
```

If we want to increment the variable by 1, we can make use of the default value for the second parameter and call the procedure without specifying an actual value to increment by, as follows:

```
increment(count);
```

This call is equivalent to

```
increment(count, by => open);
```

FIGURE 9-11

```
procedure increment ( a : inout word32;  by : in word32 := X"0000_0001" ) is
    variable sum : word32;
    variable carry : bit := '0';
begin
    for index in a'reverse_range loop
        sum(index) := a(index) xor by(index) xor carry;
        carry := ( a(index) and by(index) ) or ( carry and ( a(index) xor by(index) ) );
    end loop;
    a := sum;
end procedure increment;
```

A procedure to increment a bit vector representing an unsigned integer.

Unconstrained Array Parameters

In Chapter 4 we described unconstrained array types, in which the index range of the array was left unspecified using the "box" ("<>") notation. For such a type, we constrain the index bounds when we create an object, such as a variable or a signal. Another use of an unconstrained array type is as the type of a formal parameter to procedure. This use allows us to write a procedure in a general way, so that it can operate on array values of any size or with any range of index values. When we call the procedure and provide a constrained array as the actual parameter, the index bounds of the actual array are used as the bounds of the formal array parameter. Let us look at an example to show how unconstrained array parameters work.

Example   Figure 9-12 is a procedure that finds the index of the first bit set to '1' in a bit vector. The formal parameter v is of type **bit_vector**, which is an unconstrained array type. Note that in writing this procedure, we do not explicitly refer to the index bounds of the formal parameter v, since they are not known. Instead, we use the 'range attribute.

When the procedure is executed, the formal parameters stand for the actual parameters provided by the caller. So if we call this procedure as follows:

```
variable int_req : bit_vector (7 downto 0);
variable top_priority : natural;
variable int_pending : boolean;
…
find_first_set ( int_req, int_pending, top_priority );
```

FIGURE 9-12

```
procedure find_first_set ( v : in bit_vector;
                           found : out boolean;
                           first_set_index : out natural ) is
begin
    for index in v'range loop
        if v(index) = '1' then
            found := true;
            first_set_index := index;
            return;
        end if;
    end loop;
    found := false;
end procedure find_first_set;
```

A procedure to find the first set bit in a bit vector.

v'range returns the range 7 **downto** 0, which is used to ensure that the loop parameter **index** iterates over the correct index values for v. If we make a different call:

```
variable free_block_map : bit_vector(0 to block_count–1);
variable first_free_block : natural;
variable free_block_found : boolean;
    ...
find_first_set ( free_block_map, free_block_found, first_free_block );
```

v'range returns the index range of the array **free_block_map**, since that is the actual parameter corresponding to v.

When we have formal parameters that are of array types, either constrained or unconstrained, we can use any of the array attributes mentioned in Chapter 4 to refer to the index bounds and range of the actual parameters. We can use the attribute values to define new local constants or variables whose index bounds and ranges depend on those of the parameters. The local objects are created anew each time the procedure is called.

Example The procedure in Figure 9-13 has two bit-vector parameters, which it assumes represent signed integer values in two's-complement form. It performs an arithmetic comparison of the numbers. It operates by taking temporary copies of each of the bit-vector parameters, inverting the sign bits and performing a lexical comparison using the built-in "<" operator. This is equivalent to an arithmetic comparison of the original numbers. Note that the temporary variables are declared to be of the same size as the parameters by using the 'range attribute, and the sign bits (the leftmost bits) are indexed using the 'left attribute.

FIGURE 9-13

```
procedure bv_lt ( bv1, bv2 : in bit_vector;  result : out boolean ) is
    variable tmp1 : bit_vector(bv1'range) := bv1;
    variable tmp2 : bit_vector(bv2'range) := bv2;
begin
    tmp1(tmp1'left) := not tmp1(tmp1'left);
    tmp2(tmp2'left) := not tmp2(tmp2'left);
    result :=  tmp1 < tmp2;
end procedure bv_lt;
```

A procedure to compare two bit vectors representing two's-complement signed integers.

Summary of Procedure Parameters

Let us now summarize all that we have seen in specifying and using parameters for procedures. The syntax rule on page 310 shows that we can specify five aspects of each formal parameter. First, we may specify the class of object, which determines how the formal parameter appears within the procedure, namely, as a constant, a variable or a signal. Quantities and terminals may not serve as formal parameters for a procedure. Second, we give a name to the formal parameter so that it can be referred to in the procedure body. Third, we may specify the mode, **in**, **out** or **inout**, which determines the direction in which information is passed between the caller and the procedure, and hence whether the procedure can read or assign to the formal parameter. Fourth, we must specify the type or subtype of the formal parameter, which restricts the type of actual parameters that can be provided by the caller. This is important as a means of preventing inadvertent misuse of the procedure. Fifth, we may include a default value, giving a value to be used if the caller does not provide an actual parameter. These five aspects clearly define the interface between the procedure and its callers, allowing us to partition a complex behavioral model into sections and concentrate on each section without being distracted by other details.

Once we have encapsulated some operations in a procedure, we can then call that procedure from different parts of a model, providing actual parameters to specialize the operation at each call. The syntax rule for a procedure call is

procedure_call_statement ⇐
    ⟦ label : ⟧ *procedure*_name ⟦ (*parameter*_association_list) ⟧ ;

This is a sequential statement, and so it may be used in a process or inside of another subprogram body. If the procedure has formal parameters, the call can specify actual parameters to associate with the formal parameters. The actual associated with a constant-class formal is the value of an expression. The actual associated with a variable-class formal must be a variable, and the actual associated with a signal-class formal must be a signal. The simplified syntax rule for the parameter association list is

parameter_association_list ⇐
    ⟨ ⟦ *parameter*_name => ⟧
        expression ▯ *signal*_name ▯ *variable*_name ▯ **open** ⟩ ⟨ , … ⟩

This is in fact the same syntax rule that applies to port maps in component instantiations, seen in Chapter 5. Most of what we said there also applies to procedure parameter association lists. For example, we can use positional association in the procedure call by providing one actual parameter for each formal parameter in the order listed in the procedure declaration. Alternatively, we can use named association by identifying explicitly which formal corresponds to which actual parameter in the call. In this case, the parameters can be in any order. Also, we can use a mix of positional and named association, provided all of the positional parameters come first in the call.

Example   Suppose we have a procedure declared as

```
procedure p ( f1 : in t1;  f2 : in t2;  f3 : out t3;  f4 : in t4 := v4 ) is
begin
    ...
end procedure p;
```

We could call this procedure, providing actual parameters in a number of ways, including

```
p ( val1, val2, var3, val4 );
p ( f1 => val1, f2 => val2, f4 => val4, f3 => var3 );
p ( val1, val2, f4 => open, f3 => var3 );
p ( val1, val2, var3 );
```

9.3   Concurrent Procedure Call Statements

In Chapter 5 we saw that VHDL-AMS provides concurrent signal assignment statements and concurrent assertions as shorthand notations for commonly used kinds of processes. Now that we have looked at procedures and procedure call statements, we can introduce another shorthand notation, the *concurrent procedure call statement*. As its name implies, it is short for a process whose body contains a sequential procedure call statement. The syntax rule is

concurrent_procedure_call_statement ⇐
    〚 label : 〛 *procedure*_name 〚 (*parameter*_association_list) 〛 ;

This looks identical to an ordinary sequential procedure call, but the difference is that it appears as a concurrent statement, rather than as a sequential statement. A concurrent procedure call is exactly equivalent to a process that contains a sequential procedure call to the same procedure with the same actual parameters. For example, a concurrent procedure call of the form

```
call_proc : p ( s1, s2, val1 );
```

where s1 and s2 are signals and val1 is a constant, is equivalent to the process

```
call_proc : process is
begin
    p ( s1, s2, val1 );
    wait on s1, s2;
end process call_proc;
```

This also shows that the equivalent process contains a wait statement, whose sensitivity clause includes the signals mentioned in the actual parameter list. This is useful, since it results in the procedure being called again whenever the signal values change. Note that only signals associated with **in** mode or **inout** mode parameters are included in the sensitivity list. It would not make sense to include signals associated with **out** mode parameters, since the procedure never reads them but only assigns to them.

Example We can write a procedure that checks setup timing of a data signal with respect to a clock signal, as shown in Figure 9-14. When the procedure is called, it tests to see if there is a rising edge on the clock signal, and if so, checks that the data signal has not changed within the setup time interval. We can invoke this procedure using a concurrent procedure call, for example:

```
check_ready_setup : check_setup ( data => ready, clock => phi2,
                                   Tsu => Tsu_rdy_clk );
```

The procedure is called whenever either of the signals in the actual parameter list, **ready** or **phi2**, changes value. When the procedure returns, the concurrent procedure call statement suspends until the next event on either signal. The advantage of using a concurrent procedure call like this is twofold. First, we can write a suite of commonly used checking procedures and reuse them whenever we need to include a check in a model. This is potentially a great improvement in productivity. Second, the statement that invokes the check is more compact and readily understandable than the equivalent process written in-line.

FIGURE 9-14

```
procedure check_setup ( signal data, clock : in bit;
                                  constant Tsu : in time ) is
begin
    if clock'event and clock = '1' then
        assert data'last_event >= Tsu
            report "setup time violation" severity error;
    end if;
end procedure check_setup;
```

A procedure to check setup timing of a data signal.

Another point to note about concurrent procedure calls is that if there are no signals associated with **in** mode or **inout** mode parameters, the wait statement in the equivalent process does not have a sensitivity clause. If the procedure ever returns, the process suspends indefinitely. This may be useful if we only want the procedure to be called once at startup time. On the other hand, we may write the procedure so that it never returns. If we include wait statements within a loop in the procedure, it behaves somewhat like a process itself. The advantage of this is that we can declare a procedure that performs some commonly needed behavior and then invoke one or more instances of it using concurrent procedure call statements.

Example   The procedure in Figure 9-15 generates a periodic clock waveform on a signal passed as a parameter. The **in** mode constant parameters specify the shape of a clock waveform. The procedure waits for the initial phase delay, then loops indefinitely, scheduling a new rising and falling transition on the clock signal parameter on each iteration. It never returns to its caller. We can use this procedure to generate a two-phase non-overlapping pair of clock signals, as follows:

```
signal phi1, phi2 : std_ulogic := '0';
...
gen_phi1 : generate_clock ( phi1, Tperiod => 50 ns, Tpulse => 20 ns,
                                   Tphase => 0 ns );
gen_phi2 : generate_clock ( phi2, Tperiod => 50 ns, Tpulse => 20 ns,
                                   Tphase => 25 ns );
```

Each of these calls represents a process that calls the procedure, which then executes the clock generation loop on behalf of its parent process. The advantage of this approach is that we only had to write the loop once in a general-purpose procedure. Also, we have made the model more compact and understandable.

FIGURE 9-15

```
procedure generate_clock ( signal clk : out std_ulogic;
                                   constant Tperiod, Tpulse, Tphase : in time ) is
begin
    wait for Tphase;
    loop
        clk <= '1', '0' after Tpulse;
        wait for Tperiod;
    end loop;
end procedure generate_clock;
```

A procedure that generates a clock waveform on a signal.

9.4 **Functions**

Let us now turn our attention to the second kind of subprogram in VHDL-AMS: *functions*. We can think of a function as a generalization of expressions. The expressions that we described in Chapter 2 combined values with operators to produce new values. A function is a way of defining a new operation that can be used in expressions. We define how the new operation works by writing a collection of sequential statements that calculate the result. The syntax rule for a function declaration is very similar to that for a procedure declaration:

subprogram_body ⇐
    ⟦ **pure** ∣ **impure** ⟧
    function identifier ⟦ (*parameter*_interface_list) ⟧ **return** type_mark **is**
        ❴ subprogram_declarative_item ❵
    begin
        ❴ sequential_statement ❵
    end ⟦ **function** ⟧ ⟦ identifier ⟧ ;

The identifier in the declaration names the function. It may be repeated at the end of the declaration. Unlike a procedure subprogram, a function calculates and returns a result that can be used in an expression. The function declaration specifies the type of the result after the keyword **return**. The parameter list of a function takes the same form as that for a procedure, with two restrictions. First, the parameters of a function may not be of the class variable. If the class is not explicitly mentioned, it is assumed to be constant. Second, the mode of each parameter must be **in**. If the mode is not explicitly specified, it is assumed to be **in**. We come to the reasons for these restrictions in a moment. Like a procedure, a function can declare local items in its declarative part for use in the statements in the function body.

A function passes the result of its computation back to its caller using a return statement, given by the syntax rule

return_statement ⇐ ⟦ label : ⟧ **return** expression ;

The optional label allows us to identify the return statement. We will discuss labeled statements in Chapter 22. The form described by this syntax rule differs from the return statement in a procedure subprogram in that it includes an expression to provide the function result. Furthermore, a function must include at least one return statement of this form, and possibly more. The first to be executed causes the function to complete and return its result to the caller. A function cannot simply run into the end of the function body, since to do so would not provide a way of specifying a result to pass back to the caller.

A function call looks exactly like a procedure call. The syntax rule is

function_call ⇐ *function*_name ⟦ (*parameter*_association_list) ⟧

The difference is that a function call is part of an expression, rather than being a sequential statement on its own, like a procedure call.

Example Figure 9-16 is a simple function that calculates whether a value is within given bounds and returns a result limited to those bounds. A call to this function might be included in a variable assignment statement, as follows:

new_temperature := limited (current_temperature + increment, 10.0, 100.0);

In this statement, the expression on the right-hand side of the assignment consists of just the function call, and the result returned is assigned to the variable new_temperature. However, we might also use the result of a function call in further computation, for example:

new_motor_speed := old_motor_speed
                    + scale_factor * limited (error, −10.0, +10.0);

FIGURE 9-16

```
function limited ( value, min, max : real ) return real is
begin
    if value > max then
        return max;
    elsif value < min then
        return min;
    else
        return value;
    end if;
end function limited;
```

A function to limit a value to specified bounds.

Example The function in Figure 9-17 determines the number represented in binary by a bit-vector value. The algorithm scans the bit vector from the most-significant end. For each bit, it multiplies the previously accumulated value by two and then adds in the integer value of the bit. The accumulated value is then used as the result of the function, passed back to the caller by the return statement.

As an example of using this function, consider a model for a read-only memory, which represents the stored data as an array of bit vectors, as follows:

```
type rom_array is array (natural range 0 to rom_size−1)
                    of bit_vector(0 to word_size−1);
variable rom_data : rom_array;
```

If the model has an address port that is a bit vector, we can use the function to convert the address to a natural value to index the ROM data array, as follows:

FIGURE 9-17

```
function bv_to_natural ( bv : in bit_vector ) return natural is
    variable result : natural := 0;
begin
    for index in bv'range loop
        result := result * 2 + bit'pos(bv(index));
    end loop;
    return result;
end function bv_to_natural;
```

A function that converts the binary representation of an unsigned number to a numeric value.

```
data <= rom_data ( bv_to_natural(address) ) after Taccess;
```

Functional Modeling

In Chapter 5 we looked at concurrent signal assignment statements for functional modeling of designs. We can use functions in VHDL-AMS to help us write functional models more expressively by defining a function that encapsulates the data transformation to be performed and then calling the function in a concurrent signal assignment statement. For example, given a declaration of a function to add two bit vectors:

```
function bv_add ( bv1, bv2 : in bit_vector ) return bit_vector is
begin
    ...
end function bv_add;
```

and signals declared in an architecture body:

```
signal source1, source2, sum : bit_vector(0 to 31);
```

we can write a concurrent signal assignment statement as follows:

```
adder : sum <= bv_add(source1, source2) after T_delay_adder;
```

Pure and Impure Functions

Let us now return to the reason for the restrictions on the class and mode of function formal parameters stated above. These restrictions are in keeping with our idea that a function is a generalized form of operator. If we pass the same values to an operator, such as the addition operator, in different expressions, we expect the operator to return the same result each time. By restricting the formal parameters of a function in the way described above, we go part of the way to ensuring the same property for function calls. One additional restriction we need to make is that the function may not refer to any variables or signals declared by its parents, that is, by any process, subprogram or architecture body in which the function declaration is nested. Otherwise the variables or signals might change values between calls to the function, thus influencing the result of the function. We call a function that makes no such reference a *pure* function. We can explicitly declare a function to be pure by including the keyword **pure** in its definition, as shown by the syntax rule on page 325. If we leave it out, the function is assumed to be pure. Both of the above examples of function declarations are pure functions.

On the other hand, we may deliberately relax the restriction about a function referencing its parents' variables or signals by including the keyword **impure** in the function declaration. This is a warning to any caller of the function that it might produce different results on different calls, even when passed the same actual parameter values.

Example   Many network protocols require a sequence number in the packet header so that they can handle packets getting out of order during transmission. We can use an impure function to generate sequence numbers when creating packets in a behavioral model of a network interface. Figure 9-18 is an outline of a process that represents the output side of the network interface.

In this model, the process has a variable **next_seq_number**, used by the function **generate_seq_number** to determine the return value each time it is called. The function has the side effect of incrementing this variable, thus changing the value to be returned on the next call. Because of the reference to the variable in the function's parent, the function must be declared to be impure. The advantage of writing the function this way lies in the expressive power of its call. The function call is simply part of an expression, in this case yielding an element in a record aggregate of type **pkt_header**. Writing it this way makes the process body more compact and easily understandable.

FIGURE 9-18

```
network_driver : process is
    constant seq_modulo : natural := 2**5;
    subtype seq_number is natural range 0 to seq_modulo-1;
    variable next_seq_number : seq_number := 0;
    ...
    impure function generate_seq_number return seq_number is
        variable number : seq_number;
    begin
        number := next_seq_number;
        next_seq_number := (next_seq_number + 1) mod seq_modulo;
        return number;
    end function generate_seq_number;
```

```
begin   -- network_driver
    ...
    new_header := pkt_header'( dest => target_host_id,
                              src => my_host_id,
                              pkt_type => control_pkt,
                              seq => generate_seq_number );

    ...
end process network_driver;
```

An outline of a network driver process, including an impure function to calculate sequence numbers for network packets.

Functions in Simultaneous Statements

We have seen that a function evaluates statements to compute a value for use in an expression. We can invoke functions in the expressions on either side of the "==" symbol in simultaneous statements, provided the functions exhibit appropriate behavior. First, we must ensure that the functions are pure. The reason for this is that the analog solver might evaluate the expressions that invoke the functions several times during calculation of an analog solution point. The solver requires that the expressions be *cycle pure;* that is, each time the expressions are evaluated with the same values for any quantities they reference, they yield the same value. For expressions that invoke functions, if the functions are pure, then the expressions are cycle pure.

Example   Suppose we define a function to multiply a real vector by a scalar value as follows:

```
function vector_multiply ( p : real_vector;  r : real ) return real_vector is
    variable result : real_vector(p'range);
begin
    for index in p'range loop
        result(index) := p(index) * r;
    end loop;
    return result;
end function vector_multiply;
```

We can use the function in a simultaneous statement that multiplies an array quantity representing a point in space by the value of a scale factor quantity. The declarations are

```
quantity scale_factor : real;
quantity source_position, scaled_position : real_vector(1 to 3);
```

and the simultaneous statement that invokes the function is

```
        scaled_position == vector_multiply ( source_position, scale_factor );
```

The second aspect of using functions in simultaneous statements relates to discontinuities. In the above example, provided the quantities passed as arguments to the function **vector_multiply** are continuous, the function result is also continuous. In general, however, a function could compute a result in such a way that a discontinuity would arise, even if the arguments are continuous quantities. For example, suppose we use the function **limited** from Figure 9-16 in a simultaneous statement to model output limiting in an amplifier, as follows:

```
        v_amplified == limited ( gain * v_in, v_neg, v_pos );
```

A discontinuity would be introduced when the product of the gain and the quantity v_in is limited to v_neg or v_pos. The discontinuity would arise from the change in the way the function computes the result, depending on the conditions in the if statement within the function body. This is analogous to the discontinuities introduced when a simultaneous if statement changes equations, and the same considerations relating to convergence in the analog solver apply. In our discussion of discontinuities and simultaneous if statements in Section 6.4, we advocated a modeling style that uses the **'above** attribute in the conditions of a simultaneous if statement. However, when we embed the test in a function body, we no longer make reference to the quantity in the condition. Instead, we pass the current value of the quantity to the function invocation, and so cannot apply the **'above** attribute. For these reasons, we extend our modeling guideline to suggest that only functions that are continuous and that have continuous first derivatives be used in simultaneous statements. When such a function is applied to a quantity that is continuous with respect to time, the function result is also continuous with respect to time.

The Function Now

VHDL-AMS provides a predefined function, **now**, that returns the current simulation time when it is called. Because VHDL-AMS is a mixed-signal modeling language supporting both continuous-time analog behavior and discrete-time digital behavior, there are in fact two versions of the function **now**. One version returns the time as a discrete value of type **delay_length**, and the other version returns the time as a continuous value of type **real**. (We will see in Section 9.6 when we discuss subprogram overloading how we can have multiple versions of a subprogram.) The discrete-time function is defined as

impure function now **return** delay_length;

Unlike its definition in VHDL, **now** is defined to be an impure function in VHDL-AMS. Recall that the type **delay_length** is a predefined subtype of the physical type **time**, constrained to non-negative time values. The function **now** is often used to check that the inputs to a model obey the required timing constraints.

Example Figure 9-19 is a process that checks the clock and data inputs of an edge-triggered flipflop for adherence to the minimum hold time constraint, Thold_d_clk. When the clock signal changes to '1', the process saves the current simulation time in the variable last_clk_edge_time. Because the variable is declared to be of the discrete type time, the discrete version of the function now is used. When the data input changes, the process tests whether the current simulation time has advanced beyond the time of the last clock edge by at least the minimum hold time, and reports an error if it has not.

FIGURE 9-19

```
hold_time_checker : process ( clk, d ) is
    variable last_clk_edge_time : time := 0 fs;
begin
    if clk'event and clk = '1' then
        last_clk_edge_time := now;
    end if;
    if d'event then
        assert now - last_clk_edge_time >= Thold_d_clk
            report "hold time violation";
    end if;
end process hold_time_checker;
```

A process that checks for data hold time after clock rising edges for an edge-triggered flipflop.

Let us now consider accessing the simulation time as a continuous value. We do this using the version of the function now defined as

impure function now **return** real;

This function is cycle pure, and so can be used in time-dependent continuous expressions that are evaluated during the execution of the analog solver.

Example Figure 9-20 shows a model of a sinusoidal voltage source. The simultaneous statement in the architecture body invokes the sin function declared in the package math_real in the library ieee. This function is used to compute a mathematical function of the simulation time, determined using the continuous version of the function now. Each time the analog solver is invoked to compute an analog solution point, the simulation time for that solution point is returned by the function now.

FIGURE 9-20

```
library ieee_proposed;  use ieee_proposed.electrical_systems.all;
library ieee;  use ieee.math_real.all;

entity v_source is
    port ( terminal p, m : electrical );
end entity v_source;
```

```
architecture source_sine of v_source is
    constant ampl : real := 1.0;
    constant freq : real := 60.0;
    quantity v across i through p to m;
begin
    v == ampl * sin(2.0 * math_pi * freq * now);
end architecture source_sine;
```

A model of a sinusoidal voltage source.

Example   Figure 9-21 shows a behavioral model of a frequency detector. It produces a voltage on its output terminal that is proportional to the frequency of the waveform on its input terminal. The process **detect** is sensitive to the input voltage crossing a threshold. On each rising transition, the process calculates the waveform period as the difference between the current time and the time of the previous transition. The variable t_previous representing the time of the previous transition is initialized to real'low, effectively indicating an infinite time before the start of simulation. The process divides the period into the scale factor to determine the instantaneous frequency and assigns the result to the signal **freq**. It then updates t_previous with the current time ready for the next transition. The simultaneous statement uses the 'ramp attribute to convert the frequency signal into the output quantity.

FIGURE 9-21

```
library ieee;  use ieee.math_real.all;
library ieee_proposed;  use ieee_proposed.electrical_systems.all;

entity freq_detect is
    port ( terminal input : electrical;
            terminal freq_out : electrical );
end entity freq_detect;
```

```
architecture threshold_crossing of freq_detect is
```

```
        quantity v_in across input to electrical_ref;
        quantity v_out across i_out through freq_out to electrical_ref;
        signal freq : real := 0.0;
        constant threshold : real := 0.0;
        constant scale_factor : real := 1.0e–6;
begin
        detect: process ( v_in'above(threshold) ) is
            variable t_previous : real := real'low;
        begin
            if v_in > threshold then
                freq <= scale_factor / ( now – t_previous );
                t_previous := now;
            end if;
        end process detect;

        v_out == freq'ramp(1.0e–9, 1.0e–9);

end threshold_crossing;
```

A model of a frequency detector.

9.5 Simultaneous Procedural Statements

We now consider another modeling facility provided by VHDL-AMS, the *simultaneous procedural statement*, or *procedural* for short, which allows us to express analog behavior using sequential statements. The name might lead us to think of procedurals as another form of subprogram akin to procedures, but that would be a misapprehension. In fact, procedurals are closer to functions than procedures, but are a form of simultaneous statement that we include in an architecture body. Unlike procedures and functions, procedurals are declared in a declarative part of a model and are not invoked using a calling mechanism. The name "procedural" derives from the procedural modeling style, in which we represent a computation as a sequence of steps to be performed. Contrast this with the declarative modeling style embodied in other simultaneous statements, where we express equalities that constrain quantities, without indicating directly how the quantities might be computed.

The syntax rule for a procedural is

```
simultaneous_procedural_statement ⇐
    [ procedural_label : ]
        procedural [ is ]
            { procedural_declarative_part }
        begin
            { sequential_statement }
        end procedural [ procedural_label ] ;
```

The label may be used to identify the procedural. We will discuss labeled statements in Chapter 22. The label may be repeated at the end of the procedural. The sequential statements in the body of a procedural express the required analog behavior. They can include any of the sequential statements that we have seen in previous chapters, with some exceptions that we will return to later. A procedural can also declare local items in its declarative part for use in the sequential statements, including types, subtypes, constants, variables and subprogram declarations. The items declared within a procedural are not accessible outside of the procedural.

A procedural describes analog behavior by computing new values for quantities from the current value of quantities. The computation is expressed as a sequence of statements and can make use of the local variables declared in the procedural. The statements can refer to quantities declared in the enclosing architecture body. The procedural treats the quantities like variables, using their values in expressions and updating them using variable assignment statements.

Example   Figure 9-22 shows a model of a mixer whose output voltage is a weighted sum of its input voltages. The inputs are represented by an array terminal port. The architecture body declares branch quantities for the inputs and output and a vector of weight values. The procedural **apply_weights** iterates through the input voltage elements, multiplying each by the corresponding weight and accumulating the products in the local variable **sum**. It then assigns the result to the output quantity v_out.

FIGURE 9-22

```
library ieee_proposed;  use ieee_proposed.electrical_systems.all;
entity mixer is
    port ( terminal inputs : electrical_vector(1 to 8);
            terminal output : electrical );
end entity mixer;
```

```
architecture weighted of mixer is
    quantity v_in across inputs;
    quantity v_out across i_out through output;
    constant gains : real_vector(1 to 8)
        := ( 0.01, 0.04, 0.15, 0.30, 0.03, 0.15, 0.04, 0.01 );
begin
    apply_weights : procedural is
        variable sum : real := 0.0;
    begin
        for index in v_in'range loop
            sum := sum + v_in(index) * gains(index);
        end loop;
```

```
        v_out := sum;
      end procedural apply_weights;
  end architecture weighted;
```

A model for a weighted summing mixer.

We mentioned earlier that procedurals are related to functions. Exploring this relationship will help us understand how procedurals work, how we can use them in models and why some restrictions apply.

The fact that the procedural in the above example refers to values of the quantity v_in and assigns to the quantity **v_out** indicates that it describes a relationship between the quantities. The procedural is equivalent to a function that is passed the values of the quantities referenced by the procedural. The body of the function is derived from the statements in the procedural, and the result of the function is the collection of quantity values assigned to within the procedural. The function is invoked by the analog solver as part of the process of calculating an analog solution point. Within the function, the quantities referenced by the procedural are treated like variables that are initialized using the quantity values passed as parameters. The variables are updated using variable assignment statements. When execution of the statements completes, the final values of the assigned variables are returned and used as the value of the corresponding quantities for the analog solution point. Thus, the procedural in the above example has the same effect as a simultaneous statement that equates the quantity **v_out** to the computed weighted sum of the elements of **v_in**.

The equivalence of a procedural to a function explains the restrictions on the statements that we can include in a procedural body. As in functions, we cannot include wait, break or signal assignment statements in a procedural. Furthermore, since a procedural is equivalent to a pure function, it cannot refer to signals or variables declared in an enclosing architecture body, although it can refer to externally declared constants. Finally, a procedural can include a return statement, but the value returned is restricted to be a collection of the values of quantities assigned to within the procedural. The quantities must be listed in the same order in which their assignments occur in the procedural's statements. If we were to revise the statements in such a way as to alter the order of assignment, we would need to make a corresponding revision to the return statements in the procedural. Since the use of return statements in procedurals is so restricted and difficult to manage, we advocate avoiding their use. A model requiring a return statement in the middle of a procedural would be clearer and easier to maintain if the procedural were replaced with a function declaration and a simultaneous statement that invoked the function.

Example The diagram shown in Figure 9-23 represents a motor system comprising three one-pole low-pass filter blocks. The first filter represents the motor's electrical time constant, the second filter represents the motor's mechanical time constant and the lower block represents a filtered feedback element such as a tachometer.

FIGURE 9-23

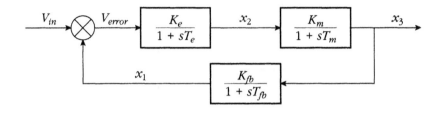

Block diagram for a motor system.

We can represent this system using state-space formulation methods. The equation is

$$
\begin{bmatrix} \dot{x}_1 \\ \dot{x}_2 \\ \dot{x}_3 \end{bmatrix} = \begin{bmatrix} \dfrac{-1}{T_{fb}} & 0 & \dfrac{K_{fb}}{T_{fb}} \\ \dfrac{-K_e}{T_e} & \dfrac{-1}{T_e} & 0 \\ 0 & \dfrac{K_m}{T_m} & \dfrac{-1}{T_m} \end{bmatrix} \begin{bmatrix} x_1 \\ x_2 \\ x_3 \end{bmatrix} + \begin{bmatrix} 0 \\ \dfrac{K_e}{T_e} \\ 0 \end{bmatrix} u
$$

Figure 9-24 shows a VHDL-AMS model of the motor system. The ports **vp** and **vm** are the input terminals, and the three-element port **px** represents the three system output terminals. The branch quantity **v_in** declared in the architecture body is the input voltage to the system, and the branch quantity **x** contains the three output voltages. The architecture body also declares a number of constants for the motor properties and uses them to initialize the coefficient matrix.

FIGURE 9-24

```
library ieee_proposed; use ieee_proposed.electrical_systems.all;
entity motor_system is
    port ( terminal vp, vm : electrical;
           terminal px : electrical_vector(1 to 3) );
end entity motor_system;

----------------------------------------------------------------

architecture state_space of motor_system is
    quantity v_in across vp to vm;
    quantity x across i_x through px to electrical_ref;
    constant Tfb : real := 0.001;
    constant Kfb : real := 1.0;
```

```
constant Te : real := 0.001;
constant Ke : real := 1.0;
constant Tm : real := 0.1;
constant Km : real := 1.0;
type real_matrix is array (1 to 3, 1 to 3) of real;
constant c : real_matrix := ( ( -1.0/Tfb, 0.0, Kfb/Tfb ),
                              ( -Ke/Te, -1.0/Te, 0.0 ),
                              ( 0.0, Km/Tm, -1.0/Tm ) );
begin
    state_eqn : procedural is
        variable sum : real_vector(1 to 3) := (0.0, 0.0, 0.0);
    begin
        for i in 1 to 3 loop
            for j in 1 to 3 loop
                sum(i) := sum(i) + c(i, j) * x(j);
            end loop;
        end loop;
        x(1)'dot := sum(1);
        x(2)'dot := sum(2) + (Ke/Te)*v_in;
        x(3)'dot := sum(3);
    end procedural state_eqn;
end architecture state_space;
```

A model of a motor system based on a state-space formulation.

The procedural in the architecture body implements the motor system behavior. It is invoked by the analog solver when determining an analog solution point. The variable **sum** is a local variable used only during the invocation of the procedural. Its value is not retained for subsequent invocations. The statements in the procedural multiply the coefficient matrix by the vector of output quantities to determine the vector of output derivatives. After the for loops, the final statements add the input term to the second element of the derivative vector.

To understand how this procedural works, recall that the quantities referred to in the procedural are treated like variables, initialized to the quantity values when the procedural is invoked. The statements in the procedural example assign to the variables corresponding to the quantities x(1)'dot, x(2)'dot and x(3)'dot. Upon completion of the procedural, the final values of the variables are used as the values for the quantities x(1)'dot, x(2)'dot and x(3)'dot in the analog solution point.

9.6 **Overloading**

When we are writing subprograms, it is a good idea to choose names for our subprograms that indicate what operations they perform, to make it easier for a reader to understand our models. This raises the question of how to name two subprograms that perform the same kind of operation but on parameters of different types. For example, we might wish to write two procedures to increment variables holding numeric values, but in some cases the values are represented as type **integer**, and in other cases they are represented using type **bit_vector**. Ideally, since both procedures perform the same operation, we would like to give them the same name, such as **increment**. But if we did that, would we be able to tell them apart when we wanted to call them? Recall that VHDL-AMS strictly enforces the type rules, so we have to refer to the right procedure depending on the type of the variable we wish to increment.

Fortunately, VHDL-AMS allows us to define subprograms in this way, using a technique called *overloading* of subprogram names. We can define two distinct subprograms with the same name but with different numbers or types of formal parameters. When we call one of them, the number and types of the actual parameters we supply in the call are used to determine which subprogram to invoke. It is the context of the call that determines how to resolve the apparent ambiguity. We have already seen overloading applied to identifiers used as literals in enumeration types (see Chapter 2). We saw that if two enumeration types included the same identifier, the context of use in a model is used to determine which type is meant.

The precise rules used to disambiguate a subprogram call when the subprogram name is overloaded are quite complex, so we will not enumerate them all here. Fortunately, they are sufficiently complete to sort out most situations that arise in practice. Instead, we look at some examples to show how overloading of procedures and functions works in straightforward cases. First, here are some procedure outlines for the increment operation described above:

```
procedure increment ( a : inout integer;   n : in integer := 1 ) is ...
procedure increment ( a : inout bit_vector;  n : in bit_vector := B"1" ) is ...
procedure increment ( a : inout bit_vector;  n : in integer := 1 ) is ...
```

Suppose we also have some variables declared as follows:

```
variable count_int : integer := 2;
variable count_bv : bit_vector (15 downto 0) := X"0002";
```

If we write a procedure call using count_int as the first actual parameter, it is clear that we are referring to the first procedure, since it is the only one whose first formal parameter is an integer. Both of the following calls can be disambiguated in this way:

```
increment ( count_int, 2 );
increment ( count_int );
```

Similarly, both of the next two calls can be sorted out:

```
increment ( count_bv, X"0002");
increment ( count_bv, 1 );
```

The first call refers to the second procedure, since the actual parameters are both bit vectors. Similarly, the second call refers to the third procedure, since the actual parameters are a bit vector and an integer. Problems arise, however, if we try to make a call as follows:

```
increment ( count_bv );
```

This could equally well be a call to either the second or the third procedure, both of which have default values for the second formal parameter. Since it is not possible to determine which procedure is meant, a VHDL-AMS analyzer rejects such a call as an error.

Overloading Operator Symbols

When we introduced function subprograms in Section 9.4, we described them as a generalization of operators used in expressions, such as "+", "–", **and, or** and so on. Looking at this the other way around, we could say that the predefined operators are specialized functions, with a convenient notation for calling them. In fact, this is exactly what they are. Furthermore, since each of the operators can be applied to values of various types, we see that the functions they represent are overloaded, so the operand types determine the particular version of each operator used in an expression.

Given that we can define our own types in VHDL-AMS, it would be convenient if we could extend the predefined operators to work with these types. For example, if we are using bit vectors to model integers using two's-complement notation, we would like to use the addition operator to add two bit vectors in this form. Fortunately, VHDL-AMS provides a way for us to define new functions using the operator symbols as names. The extended syntax rules for subprogram declarations are shown in Appendix E. Our bit-vector addition function can be declared as

```
function "+" ( left, right : in bit_vector ) return bit_vector is
begin
    ...
end function "+";
```

We can then call this function using the infix "+" operator with bit-vector operands, for example:

```
variable addr_reg : bit_vector(31 downto 0);
...
addr_reg := addr_reg + X"0000_0004";
```

Operators denoted by reserved words can be overloaded in the same way. For example, we can declare a bit-vector absolute-value function as

```
function "abs" ( right : in bit_vector ) return bit_vector is
begin
    …
end function "abs";
```

We can use this operator with a bit-vector operand, for example:

```
variable accumulator : bit_vector(31 downto 0);
    …
accumulator := abs accumulator;
```

We can overload any of the operator symbols shown in Figure 2-6. One important point to note, however, is that overloaded versions of the logical operators **and**, **nand**, **or** and **nor** are not evaluated in the short-circuit manner described in Chapter 2. For any type of operands other than **bit** and **boolean**, both operands are evaluated first, then passed to the function.

Example   The std_logic_1164 package defines functions for logical operators applied to values of type **std_ulogic** and **std_ulogic_vector**. We can use them in functional models to write Boolean equations that represent the behavior of a design. For example, Figure 9-25 describes a block of logic that controls an input/output register in a microcontroller system. The architecture body describes the behavior in terms of Boolean equations. Its concurrent signal assignment statements use the logical operators **and** and **not**, referring to the overloaded functions defined in the std_logic_1164 package.

FIGURE 9-25

```
library ieee;  use ieee.std_logic_1164.all;
entity reg_ctrl is
    port ( reg_addr_decoded, rd, wr, io_en, cpu_clk : in std_ulogic;
           reg_rd, reg_wr : out std_ulogic );
end entity reg_ctrl;
```

```
architecture bool_eqn of reg_ctrl is
begin
    rd_ctrl : reg_rd <= reg_addr_decoded and rd and io_en;
    rw_ctrl : reg_wr <= reg_addr_decoded and wr and io_en and not cpu_clk;
end architecture bool_eqn;
```

An entity and architecture body for a logic block that controls operation of a register.

9.7   **Visibility of Declarations**

The last topic we need to discuss in relation to subprograms is the use of names declared within a model. We have seen that names of types, constants, variables and other items defined in a subprogram can be used in that subprogram. Also, in the case of procedures and impure functions, names declared in an enclosing process, subprogram or architecture body can also be used. The question we must answer is: What are the limits of use of each name?

To answer this question, we introduce the idea of the *visibility* of a declaration, which is the region of the text of a model in which it is possible to refer to the declared name. We have seen that architecture bodies, processes and subprograms are each divided into two parts: a declarative part and a body of statements. A name declared in a declarative part is visible from the end of the declaration itself down to the end of the corresponding statement part. Within this area we can refer to the declared name. Before the declaration, within it and beyond the end of the statement part, we cannot refer to the name because it is not visible.

Example   Figure 9-26 shows an outline of an architecture body of a model. It contains a number of declarations, including some procedure declarations. The visibility of each of the declarations is indicated. The first item to be declared is the type t; its visibility extends to the end of the architecture body. Thus it can be referred in other declarations, such as the variable declarations. The second declaration is the signal s; its visibility likewise extends to the end of the architecture body. So the assignment within procedure p1 is valid. The third and final declaration in the declarative part of the architecture body is that of the procedure p1, whose visibility extends to the end of the architecture body, allowing it to be called in either of the processes. It includes a local variable, v1, whose visibility extends only to the end of p1. This means it can be referred to in p1, as shown in the signal assignment statement, but neither process can refer to it.

In the statement part of the architecture body, we have two process statements, proc1 and proc2. The first includes a local variable declaration, v2, whose visibility extends to the end of the process body. Hence we can refer to v2 in the process body and in the procedure p2 declared within the process. The visibility of p2 likewise extends to the end of the body of proc1, allowing us to call p2 within proc1. The procedure p2 includes a local variable declaration, v3, whose visibility extends to the end of the statement part of p2. Hence we can refer to v3 in the statement part of p2. However, we cannot refer to v3 in the statement part of proc1, since it is not visible in that part of the model.

Finally, we come to the second process, proc2. The only items we can refer to here are those declared in the architecture body declarative part, namely, t, s and p1. We cannot call the procedure p2 within proc2, since it is local to proc1.

FIGURE 9-26

```
architecture arch of ent is                                        t
    type t is ...;      ─────────────────────────────────────┐
    signal s : t;       ───────────────────────────────┐ s   │
    procedure p1 ( ... ) is  ──────────────────┐ p1     │     │
        variable v1 : t;  ──────────┐ v1        │        │     │
    begin                           │           │        │     │
        v1 := s;                    │           │        │     │
    end procedure p1;   ────────────┘           │        │     │
begin  ── arch                                  │        │     │
    proc1 : process is                          │        │     │
        variable v2 : t;  ──────────────┐ v2    │        │     │
        procedure p2 ( ... ) is  ───────┐ p2    │        │     │
            variable v3 : t;  ────┐ v3   │       │        │     │
        begin                     │      │       │        │     │
            p1 ( v2, v3, ... );   │      │       │        │     │
        end procedure p2;   ──────┘      │       │        │     │
    begin  ── proc1                      │       │        │     │
        p2 ( v2, ... );                  │       │        │     │
    end process proc1;   ────────────────┘       │        │     │
    proc2 : process is                           │        │     │
        ...                                      │        │     │
    begin  ── proc2                              │        │     │
        p1 ( ... );                              │        │     │
    end process proc2;                           │        │     │
end architecture arch;   ────────────────────────┘────────┘─────┘
```

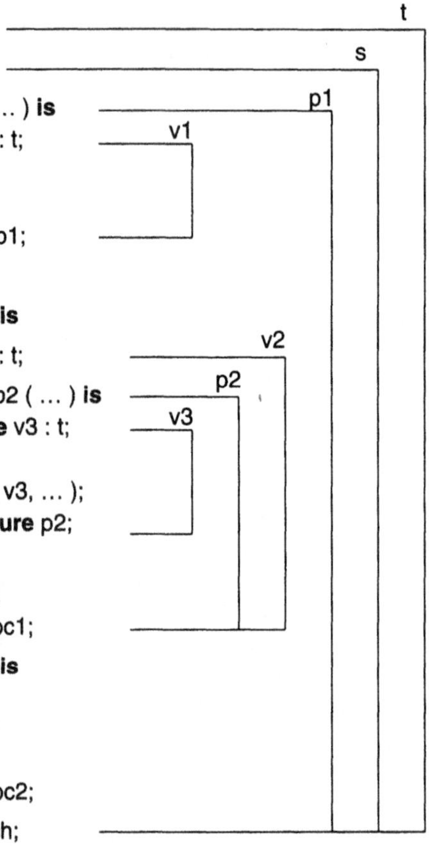

An outline of an architecture body, showing the visibility of declared names within it.

One point we mentioned earlier about subprograms but did not go into in detail was that we can include nested subprogram declarations within the declarative part of a subprogram. This means we can have local procedures and functions within a procedure or a function. In such cases, the simple rule for the visibility of a declaration still applies, so any items declared within an outer procedure before the declaration of a nested procedure can be referred to inside the nested procedure.

Example   Figure 9-27 is an outline of an architecture of a cache memory for a computer system. The entity interface includes ports named mem_addr, mem_ready, mem_ack and mem_data_in. The process behavior contains a procedure, read_block, which reads a block of data from main memory on a cache miss. It has the local variables memory_address_reg and memory_data_reg. Nested inside of this procedure

FIGURE 9-27

```
architecture behavioral of cache is
begin
    behavior : process is
        ...
        procedure read_block( start_address : natural; entry : out cache_block ) is
            variable memory_address_reg : natural;
            variable memory_data_reg : word;

            procedure read_memory_word is
            begin
                mem_addr <= memory_address_reg;
                mem_read <= '1';
                wait until mem_ack = '1';
                memory_data_reg := mem_data_in;
                mem_read <= '0';
                wait until mem_ack = '0';
            end procedure read_memory_word;
        begin   -- read_block
            for offset in 0 to block_size – 1 loop
                memory_address_reg := start_address + offset;
                read_memory_word;
                entry(offset) := memory_data_reg;
            end loop;
        end procedure read_block;
    begin   -- behavior
        ...
        read_block( miss_base_address, data_store(entry_index) );
        ...
    end process behavior;
end architecture behavioral;
```

An outline of a behavioral architecture of a cache memory.

is another procedure, **read_memory_word**, which reads a single word of data from memory. It uses the value placed in **memory_address_reg** by the outer procedure and leaves the data read from memory in **memory_data_reg**.

Now let us consider a model in which we have one subprogram nested inside of another, and each declares an item with the same name as the other, as shown in Figure 9-28. Here, the first variable **v** is visible within all of the procedure **p2** and the statement body of **p1**. However, because **p2** declares its own local variable called **v**, the variable belonging to **p1** is not *directly visible* where **p2**'s **v** is visible. We say the

---

FIGURE 9-28

```
procedure p1 is                          v
    variable v : integer;      ————————
    procedure p2 is                v
        variable v : integer;  ————
    begin   —— p2
        ...
        v := v + 1;
        ...
    end procedure p2;          ————
begin   —— p1
    ...
    v := 2 * v;
    ...
end procedure p1;             ————
```

Nested procedures showing hiding of names. The declaration of v *in* p2 *hides the variable* v *declared in* p1.

inner variable declaration *hides* the outer declaration, since it declares the same name. Hence the addition within **p2** applies to the local variable **v** of **p2** and does not affect the variable **v** of **p1**. If we need to refer to an item that is visible but hidden, we can use a selected name. For example, within **p2** in Figure 9-28, we can use the name **p1.v** to refer to the variable **v** declared in **p1**. Although the outer declaration is not directly visible, it is *visible by selection*. An important point to note about using a selected name in this way is that it can only be used within the construct containing the declaration. Thus, in Figure 9-28, we can only refer to **p1.v** within **p1**. We cannot use the name **p1.v** to "peek inside" of **p1** from places outside of **p1**.

The idea of hiding is not restricted to variable declarations within nested procedures. Indeed, it applies in any case where we have one declarative part nested within another, and an item is declared with the same name in each declarative part in such a way that the rules for resolving overloaded names are unable to distinguish between them. The advantage of having inner declarations hide outer declarations, as opposed to the alternative of simply disallowing an inner declaration with the same name, is that it allows us to write local procedures and processes without having to know the names of all items declared at outer levels. This is certainly beneficial when writing large models. In practice, if we are reading a model and need to check the use of a name in a statement against its declaration, we only need to look at successively enclosing declarative parts until we find a declaration of the name, and that is the declaration that applies.

Exercises

1. **[❶ 9.2]** Write parameter specifications for the following constant-class parameters:

   - an integer, operand1,
   - a bit vector, tag, indexed from 31 down to 16, and
   - a Boolean, trace, with default value false.

2. **[❶ 9.2]** Write parameter specifications for the following variable-class parameters:

   - a real number, average, used to pass data back from a procedure, and
   - a string, identifier, modified by a procedure.

3. **[❶ 9.2]** Write parameter specifications for the following signal-class parameters:

   - a bit signal, clk, to be assigned to by a procedure, and
   - an unconstrained standard-logic vector signal, data_in, whose value is to be read by a procedure.

4. **[❶ 9.2]** Given the following procedure declaration:

   ```
   procedure stimulate ( signal target : out bit_vector;
                         delay : in delay_length := 1 ns;
                         cycles : in natural := 1 ) is ...
   ```

   write procedure calls using a signal s as the actual parameter for target and using the following values for the other parameters:

   - delay = 5 ns, cycles = 3,
   - delay = 10 ns, cycles = 1 and
   - delay = 1 ns, cycles = 15.

5. **[❶ 9.3]** Suppose we have a procedure declared as

   ```
   procedure shuffle_bytes ( signal d_in : in std_ulogic_vector(0 to 15);
                             signal d_out : out std_ulogic_vector(0 to 15);
                             signal shuffle_control : in std_ulogic;
                             prop_delay : delay_length ) is ...
   ```

   Write the equivalent process for the following concurrent procedure call:

   ```
   swapper : shuffle_bytes ( ext_data, int_data, swap_control, Tpd_swap );
   ```

6. **[❶ 9.4]** Suppose we have a function declared as

   ```
   function approx_log_2 ( a : in bit_vector ) return positive is ...
   ```

that calculates the minimum number of bits needed to represent a binary-encoded number. Write a variable assignment statement that calculates the minimum number of bits needed to represent the product of two numbers in the variables **multiplicand** and **multiplier** and assigns the result to the variable **product_size**.

7. [❶ 9.4] Write an assertion statement that verifies that the current simulation time has not exceeded 20 ms.

8. [❶ 9.4] Write a simultaneous statement to model the voltage on a capacitor as it charges up to a supply voltage through a resistor. The voltage is given by the equation

$$V_{cap} = V_{supply}\left(1 - e^{\frac{-t}{RC}}\right)$$

9. [❶ 9.5] The example on page 329 includes a simultaneous statement that scales a point by a scale factor. Rewrite the statement as a procedural that performs the multiplication using the algorithm from the function **vector_multiply**.

10. [❶ 9.6] Given the declarations of the three procedures named **increment** and the variables **count_int** and **count_bv** shown on page 338, which of the three procedures, if any, is referred to by each of the following procedure calls?

```
increment ( count_bv, –1 );
increment ( count_int );
increment ( count_int, B"1" );
increment ( count_bv, 16#10# );
```

11. [❶ 9.7] Show the parts of the following model in which each of the declared items is visible:

```
architecture behavioral of computer_system is
    signal internal_data : bit_vector(31 downto 0);
    interpreter : process is
        variable opcode : bit_vector(5 downto 0);
        procedure do_write is
            variable aligned_address : natural;
        begin
            ...
        end procedure do_write;
    begin
        ...
    end process interpreter;
end architecture behavioral;
```

12. [❷ 9.1] Write a procedure that calculates the sum of squares of elements of an array variable **deviations**. The elements are real numbers. Your procedure should store the result in a real variable **sum_of_squares**.

13. [❷ 9.1] Write a procedure that generates a 1 μs pulse every 20 μs on a signal **syn_clk**. When the signal **reset** changes to '1', the procedure should immediately set **syn_clk** to '0' and return.

14. [❷ 9.2] Write a procedure called **align_address** that aligns a binary encoded address in a bit-vector variable parameter. The procedure has a second parameter that indicates the alignment size. If the size is 1, the address is unchanged. If the size is 2, the address is rounded to a multiple of 2 by clearing the least-significant bit. If the size is 4, two bits are cleared, and if the size is 8, three bits are cleared. The default alignment size is 4.

15. [❷ 9.2/9.3] Write a procedure that checks the hold time of a data signal with respect to rising edges of a clock signal. Both signals are of the IEEE standard-logic type. The signals and the hold time are parameters of the procedure. The procedure is invoked by a concurrent procedure call.

16. [❷ 9.2/9.3] Write a procedure, to be invoked by a concurrent procedure call, that assigns successive natural numbers to a signal at regular intervals. The signal and the interval between numbers are parameters of the procedure.

17. [❷ 9.4] Write a function, **weaken**, that maps a standard-logic value to the same value, but with weak drive strength. Thus, '0' and 'L' are mapped to 'L', '1' and 'H' are mapped to 'H', 'X' and 'W' are mapped to 'W' and all other values are unchanged.

18. [❷ 9.4] Write a function, returning a Boolean result, that tests whether a standard-logic signal currently has a valid edge. A valid edge is defined to be a transition from '0' or 'L' to '1' or 'H' or vice versa. Other transitions, such as 'X' to '1', are not valid.

19. [❷ 9.4] Write two functions, one to find the maximum value in an array of integers and the other to find the minimum value.

20. [❷ 9.4] Write an entity declaration for a voltage supply with two electrical terminal ports. Write an architecture body that generates a sinusoidal supply voltage with an amplitude of 12 V and a frequency of 60 Hz.

21. [❷ 9.4] We can describe the relationship between the voltage across a diode (v) and the current flowing through it (i) using the equations

$$i = \begin{cases} 10^{-3} \times v & \text{if } v \le 0 \\ 10^{-3} \times v + 3.075 \times 10^{5} \times v^{4} & \text{if } 0 < v \le 0.933 \\ 10^{6} \times (v - 0.7) + 0.7 \times 10^{-3} & \text{if } 0.933 < v \end{cases}$$

This relationship is continuous and has a continuous first derivative with respect to v. Write a model of a diode that includes a function declaration that evaluates the equations. The function should have a parameter representing a voltage and should return the current. Use the function in a simultaneous statement to model the diode behavior.

22. [❷ 9.6] Write overloaded versions of the logical operators to operate on integer operands. The operators should treat the value 0 as logical falsehood and any non-zero value as logical truth.

23. [❸ 9.2] Write a procedure called **scan_results** with an **in** mode bit-vector signal parameter **results**, and **out** mode variable parameters **majority_value** of type **bit**, **majority_count** of type **natural** and **tie** of type **boolean**. The procedure counts the occurrences of '0' and '1' values in **results**. It sets **majority_value** to the most frequently occurring value, **majority_count** to the number of occurrences and **tie** to true if there are an equal number of occurrences of '0' and '1'.

24. [❸ 9.2/9.3] Write a procedure that stimulates a bit-vector signal passed as a parameter. The procedure assigns to the signal a sequence of all possible bit-vector values. The first value is assigned to the signal immediately, then subsequent values are assigned at intervals specified by a second parameter. After the last value is assigned, the procedure returns.

25. [❸ 9.2/9.3] Write a passive procedure that checks that setup and hold times for a data signal with respect to rising edges of a clock signal are observed. The signals and the setup and hold times are parameters of the procedure. Include a concurrent procedure call to the procedure in the statement part of a D-flipflop entity.

26. [❸ 9.4] Write a function that calculates the cosine of a real number, using the series

$$\cos\theta = 1 - \frac{\theta^2}{2!} + \frac{\theta^4}{4!} - \frac{\theta^6}{6!} + \dots$$

Next, write a second function that returns a cosine table of the following type:

type table **is array** (0 **to** 1023) **of** real;

Element i of the table has the value $\cos(i\pi/2048)$. Finally, develop a behavioral model of a cosine lookup ROM. The architecture body should include a constant of type **table**, initialized using a call to the second function.

chapter ten

Packages and Use Clauses

Packages in VHDL-AMS provide an important way of organizing the data and subprograms declared in a model. In this chapter, we describe the basics of packages and show how they may be used. We also look at several predefined and standard packages, which provide types, natures and operators for use in VHDL-AMS models.

10.1 **Package Declarations**

A VHDL-AMS package is simply a way of grouping a collection of related declarations that serve a common purpose. They might be a set of subprograms that provide operations on a particular type of data, or they might just be the set of declarations needed to model a particular design. The important thing is that they can be collected together into a separate design unit that can be worked on independently and reused in different parts of a model.

Another important aspect of packages is that they separate the external view of the items they declare from the implementation of those items. The external view is specified in a *package declaration,* whereas the implementation is defined in a separate *package body.* We will look at package declaration first and return to the package body shortly.

The syntax rule for writing a package declaration is

package_declaration ⇐
    package identifier **is**
        { package_declarative_item }
    end [**package**] [identifier] ;

The identifier provides a name for the package, which we can use elsewhere in a model to refer to the package. Inside the package declaration we write a collection of declarations, including type, subtype, nature, subnature, constant, signal, terminal and subprogram declarations, as well as several other kinds of declarations that we see in later chapters. These are the declarations that are provided to the users of the package. The advantage of placing them in a package is that they do not clutter up other parts of a model, and they can be shared within and between models without having to rewrite them. Figure 10-1 is a simple example of a package declaration.

FIGURE 10-1

```
package cpu_types is
    constant word_size : positive := 16;
    constant address_size : positive := 24;
    subtype word is bit_vector(word_size – 1 downto 0);
    subtype address is bit_vector(address_size – 1 downto 0);
    type status_value is ( halted, idle, fetch, mem_read, mem_write,
                           io_read, io_write, int_ack );
end package cpu_types;
```

A package that declares some useful constants and types for a CPU model.

A package is another form of design unit, along with entity declarations and architecture bodies. It is separately analyzed and is placed into the working library as a library unit by the analyzer. From there, other library units can refer to an item declared in the package using the *selected name* of the item. The selected name is formed by writing the library name, then the package name and then the name of the item, all separated by dots; for example:

```
work.cpu_types.status_value
```

Example Suppose the cpu_types package, shown in Figure 10-1, has been analyzed and placed into the work library. We might make use of the declared items when modeling an address decoder to go with a CPU. The entity declaration and architecture body of the decoder are shown in Figure 10-2.

FIGURE 10-2

```
entity address_decoder is
    port ( addr : in work.cpu_types.address;
           status : in work.cpu_types.status_value;
           mem_sel, int_sel, io_sel : out bit );
end entity address_decoder;
```

```
architecture functional of address_decoder is
    constant mem_low : work.cpu_types.address := X"000000";
    constant mem_high : work.cpu_types.address := X"EFFFFF";
    constant io_low : work.cpu_types.address := X"F00000";
    constant io_high : work.cpu_types.address := X"FFFFFF";
begin
    mem_decoder :
        mem_sel <= '1' when ( work.cpu_types."="(status, work.cpu_types.fetch)
                        or work.cpu_types."="(status, work.cpu_types.mem_read)
                        or work.cpu_types."="(status, work.cpu_types.mem_write) )
                        and addr >= mem_low and addr <= mem_high else
                    '0';
    int_decoder :
        int_sel <= '1' when work.cpu_types."="(status, work.cpu_types.int_ack) else
                    '0';
    io_decoder :
        io_sel <= '1' when ( work.cpu_types."="(status, work.cpu_types.io_read)
                        or work.cpu_types."="(status, work.cpu_types.io_write) )
                        and addr >= io_low and addr <= io_high else
                    '0';
end architecture functional;
```

An entity and architecture body for an address decoder, using items declared in the cpu_types *package.*

Note that we have to use selected names to refer to the subtype **address**, the type **status_value**, the enumeration literals of **status_value** and the implicitly declared = operator, defined in the package **cpu_types**. This is because they are not directly visible within the entity declaration and architecture body. We will see later in this chapter how a use clause can help us avoid long selected names. If we needed to type-qualify the enumeration literals, we would use selected names for both the type name and the literal name; for example:

```
work.cpu_types.status_value'(work.cpu_types.fetch)
```

We have seen that a package, when analyzed, is placed into the working library. Items in the package can be accessed by other library units using selected names starting with **work**. However, if we are writing a package of generally useful declarations, we may wish to place them into a different library, such as a project library, where they can be accessed by other designers. Different VHDL-AMS tool suites provide different ways of specifying the library into which a library unit is placed. We must consult the documentation for a particular product to find out what to do. However, once the package has been included in a resource library, we can refer to items declared in it using selected names, starting with the resource library name. As an example, we might consider the IEEE standard-logic package, which must be placed in a resource library called **ieee**. We can refer to the types declared in that package, for example:

```
variable stored_state : ieee.std_logic_1164.std_ulogic;
```

One kind of declaration we can include in a package declaration is a signal declaration. This gives us a way of defining a signal, such as a master clock or reset signal, that is global to a whole design, instead of being restricted to a single architecture body. Any module that needs to refer to the global signal simply names it using the selected name as described above. This avoids the clutter of having to specify the signal as a port in each entity that uses it, making the model a little less complex. However, it does mean that a module can affect the overall behavior of a system by means other than through its ports, namely, by assigning to global signals. This effectively means that part of the module's interface is implicit, rather than being specified in the port map of the entity. As a matter of style, global signals declared in packages should be used sparingly, and their use should be clearly documented with comments in the model.

We can also include declarations of global terminals in a package declaration. In the electrical domain, global terminals can be useful for power and ground terminals and for a terminal representing the substrate of an integrated circuit. We might then use these terminals to model effects such as ground bounce and switching noise. Using global terminals in an analog model can provide the same benefits as using global signals in a digital model, but the same disadvantages also apply. Thus we should use global terminals only in rare cases. Note that we cannot declare quantities in a package declaration. The reason for this restriction in the language is to simplify the rules governing solvability of the system of equations expressed in a model.

Example   The package shown in Figure 10-3 declares two clock signals and analog supply and ground terminals for use within an integrated circuit design for an input/output interface controller. The top-level architecture of the controller circuit is outlined in Figure 10-4. The instance of the **phase_locked_clock_gen** entity uses the **ref_clock** port of the circuit to generate the two-phase clock waveforms on the global clock signals. Similarly, the instance of the **regulator** entity generates the global analog power supplies from the external supply input. The architecture also includes an instance of an entity that sequences bus operations using the bus control signals and generates internal register control signals, and an instance of an analog output interface entity that provides an analog output from the integrated circuit. The architecture body for the sequencer is outlined in Figure 10-5. It creates an instance of a register entity and connects the global clock signals to its clock input ports. The architecture body for the analog output interface is shown in Figure 10-6. It similarly creates an instance of a digital-to-analog converter entity and connects the global analog power supply terminals to the converter's power supply terminal ports.

FIGURE 10-3

```
library ieee;  use ieee.std_logic_1164.all;
library ieee_proposed;  use ieee_proposed.electrical_systems.all;
package clock_power_pkg is
    constant Tpw : delay_length := 4 ns;
    signal clock_phase1, clock_phase2 : std_ulogic;
    terminal analog_plus_supply, analog_ground : electrical;
end package clock_power_pkg;
```

A package that declares global clock signals.

FIGURE 10-4

```
library ieee;  use ieee.std_logic_1164.all;
entity io_controller is
    port ( signal ref_clock : in std_ulogic;
            terminal ext_supply, ext_ground : electrical; ... );
end entity io_controller;
```

```
architecture top_level of io_controller is
```

(continued on page 354)

(continued from page 353)

...

begin

    internal_clock_gen : **entity** work.phase_locked_clock_gen(std_cell)
        port map (ref_clock => ref_clock,
               phi1 => work.clock_power_pkg.clock_phase1,
               phi2 => work.clock_power_pkg.clock_phase2);

    internal_analog_regulator : **entity** work.regulator(device_level)
        port map (plus_in => ext_supply, minus_in => ext_ground,
               plus_out => work.clock_power_pkg.analog_plus_supply,
               minus_out => work.clock_power_pkg.analog_ground);

    the_bus_sequencer : **entity** work.bus_sequencer(fsm)
        port map (rd, wr, sel, width, burst, addr(3 **downto** 0), ready,
               control_reg_wr, status_reg_rd, data_fifo_wr, data_fifo_rd,
               analog_out_wr_0, ...);

    analog_output_interface_0 : **entity** work.analog_output_interface(structural)
        port map (analog_out_wr_0, internal_data(7 **downto** 0), analog_out_0);

   ...

end architecture top_level;

An outline of the entity and architecture body for the input/output controller integrated circuit. The architecture body uses the master clock signals and the global analog supply terminals.

FIGURE 10-5

architecture fsm **of** bus_sequencer **is**
    -- This architecture implements the sequencer as a finite-state machine.
    -- NOTE: it uses the clock signals from clock_power_pkg to synchronize the fsm.
    signal next_state_vector : ...;
begin
    bus_sequencer_state_register : **entity** work.state_register(std_cell)
        port map (phi1 => work.clock_power_pkg.clock_phase1,
               phi2 => work.clock_power_pkg.clock_phase2,
               next_state => next_state_vector,
               ...);

   ...

end architecture fsm;

An outline of the architecture body for the bus sequencer of the input/output controller circuit.

FIGURE 10-6

```
architecture structural of analog_output_interface is
    -- This architecture implements the interface as a register connected to a DAC.
    -- NOTE: it uses the analog power supply terminals from clock_power_pkg
    -- to supply the DAC.
    signal register_out : ...;
begin
    ...
    dac : entity work.analog_interface_dac(macroblock)
        port map ( d_in => register_out, output => analog_out,
                   plus_supply => work.clock_power_pkg.analog_plus_supply,
                   minus_supply => work.clock_power_pkg.analog_ground );
end architecture structural;
```

An outline of the architecture body for the analog output interface of the input/output controller circuit.

Subprograms in Package Declarations

Another kind of declaration that may be included in a package declaration is a subprogram declaration—either a procedure or a function declaration. This ability allows us to write subprograms that implement useful operations and to call them from a number of different modules. An important use of this feature is to declare subprograms that operate on values of a type declared by the package. This gives us a way of conceptually extending VHDL-AMS with new types and operations, so-called *abstract data types,* a topic we return to in Chapter 20.

An important aspect of declaring a subprogram in a package declaration is that we only write the header of the subprogram, that is, the part that includes the name and the interface list defining the parameters (and result type for functions). We leave out the body of the subprogram. The reason for this is that the package declaration, as we mentioned earlier, provides only the external view of the items it declares, leaving the implementation of the items to the package body. For items such as types, natures, signals and terminals, the complete definition is needed in the external view. However, for subprograms, we need only know the information contained in the header to be able to call the subprogram. As users of a subprogram, we need not be concerned with how it achieves its effect or calculates its result. This is an example of a general principle called *information hiding:* making an interface visible but hiding the details of implementation. To illustrate this idea, suppose we have a package declaration that defines a bit-vector subtype:

```
subtype word32 is bit_vector(31 downto 0);
```

We can include in the package a procedure to do addition on **word32** values that represent signed integers. The procedure declaration in the package declaration is

```
procedure add ( a, b : in word32;
                    result : out word32;  overflow : out boolean );
```

Note that we do not include the keyword **is** or any of the local declarations or statements needed to perform the addition. These are deferred to the package body. All we include is the description of the formal parameters of the procedure. Similarly, we might include a function to perform an arithmetic comparison of two **word32** values:

```
function "<" ( a, b : in word32 ) return boolean;
```

Again, we omit the local declarations and statements, simply specifying the formal parameters and the result type of the function.

Constants in Package Declarations

Just as we can apply the principle of information hiding to subprograms declared in a package, we can also apply it to constants declared in a package. The external view of a constant is just its name and type. We need to know these in order to use it, but we do not actually need to know its value. This may seem strange at first, but if we recall that the idea of introducing constant declarations in the first place was to avoid scattering literal values throughout a model, it makes more sense. We defer specifying the value of a constant declared in a package by omitting the initialization expression, for example:

```
constant max_buffer_size : positive;
```

This defines the constant to be a positive integer value. However, since we cannot see the actual value, we are not tempted to write the value as an integer literal in a model that uses the package. The specification of the actual value is deferred to the package body, where it is not visible to a model that uses the package. Given the above deferred constant in a package declaration, the corresponding package body must include the full constant declaration, for example:

```
constant max_buffer_size : positive := 4096;
```

Note that we do not have to defer the value in a constant declaration—it is optional.

Example   We can extend the package specification from Figure 10-1, declaring useful types for a CPU model, by including declarations related to opcode processing. The revised package is shown in Figure 10-7. It includes a subtype that represents an opcode value, a function to extract an opcode from an instruction word and a number of constants representing the opcodes for different instructions.

Figure 10-8 shows a behavioral model of a CPU that uses these declarations. The instruction set interpreter process declares a variable of the **opcode** type and uses the **extract_opcode** function to extract the bits representing the opcode from the fetched instruction word. It then uses the constants from the package as choices in a case statement to decode and execute the instruction specified by the opcode.

Note that since the constants are used as choices in the case statement, they must be locally static. If we had deferred the values of the constants to the package body, their value would not be known when the case statement was analyzed. This is why we included the constant values in the package declaration. In general, the value of a deferred constant is not locally static.

FIGURE 10-7

```
package cpu_types is

    constant word_size : positive := 16;
    constant address_size : positive := 24;

    subtype word is bit_vector(word_size – 1 downto 0);
    subtype address is bit_vector(address_size – 1 downto 0);

    type status_value is ( halted, idle, fetch, mem_read, mem_write,
                           io_read, io_write, int_ack );

    subtype opcode is bit_vector(5 downto 0);

    function extract_opcode ( instr_word : word ) return opcode;

    constant op_nop : opcode := "000000";
    constant op_breq : opcode := "000001";
    constant op_brne : opcode := "000010";
    constant op_add : opcode := "000011";
    ...

end package cpu_types;
```

A revised version of the package used in a CPU model.

FIGURE 10-8

```
architecture behavioral of cpu is
begin

    interpreter : process is

        variable instr_reg : work.cpu_types.word;
        variable instr_opcode : work.cpu_types.opcode;
```

(continued on page 358)

(continued from page 357)

```
        begin
            ...  -- initialize
        loop
                ...   -- fetch instruction
                instr_opcode := work.cpu_types.extract_opcode ( instr_reg );
                case instr_opcode is
                    when work.cpu_types.op_nop => null;
                    when work.cpu_types.op_breq => ...

                    ...
                end case;
            end loop;
        end process interpreter;
    end architecture behavioral;
```

An outline of a CPU model that uses items declared in the revised **cpu_types** *package.*

10.2 Package Bodies

Now that we have seen how to define the interface to a package, we can turn to the package body. Each package declaration that includes subprogram declarations or deferred constant declarations must have a corresponding package body to fill in the missing details. However, if a package declaration only includes other kinds of declarations, such as types, natures, signals, terminals or fully specified constants, no package body is necessary. The syntax rule for a package body is similar to that for the interface, but with the inclusion of the keyword **body**:

package_body ⇐
    package body identifier **is**
        ⟦ package_body_declarative_item ⟧
    end ⟦ **package body** ⟧ ⟦ identifier ⟧ ;

The items declared in a package body must include the full declarations of all subprograms defined in the corresponding package declaration. These full declarations must include the subprogram headers exactly as they are written in the package declaration, to ensure that the implementation *conforms* with the interface. This means that the names, types, modes and default values of each of the formal parameters must be repeated exactly. There are only two variations allowed. First, a numeric literal may be written differently, for example, in a different base, provided it has the same value. Second, a simple name consisting just of an identifier may be replaced by a selected name, provided it refers to the same item. While this conformance requirement might seem an imposition at first, in practice it is not. Any reasonable text editor used to create a VHDL-AMS model allows the header to be copied from the package declaration with little difficulty. Similarly, a deferred constant defined in a package declaration must have its value specified by repeating the declaration in the package body, this time filling in the initialization expression as in a full constant declaration.

In addition to the full declarations of items deferred from the package declaration, a package body may include declarations of additional types, subtypes, constants and subprograms. These items are used to implement the subprograms defined in the package declaration. Note that the items declared in the package declaration cannot be declared again in the body (apart from subprograms and deferred constants, as described above), since they are automatically visible in the body. Furthermore, the package body cannot include declarations of additional natures, subnatures, terminals or signals. These declarations may only be included in the interface declaration of a package.

Example Figure 10-9 shows outlines of a package declaration and a package body declaring overloaded versions of arithmetic operators for bit-vector values. The functions treat bit vectors as representing signed integers in binary form. Only the function headers are included in the package declaration. The package body contains the full function bodies. It also includes a function, mult_unsigned, not defined in the package declaration. It is used internally in the package body to implement the signed multiplication operator.

FIGURE 10-9

```
package bit_vector_signed_arithmetic is
    function "+" ( bv1, bv2 : bit_vector ) return bit_vector;
    function "–" ( bv : bit_vector ) return bit_vector;
    function "*" ( bv1, bv2 : bit_vector ) return bit_vector;
    ...
end package bit_vector_signed_arithmetic;
```

```
package body bit_vector_signed_arithmetic is
    function "+" ( bv1, bv2 : bit_vector ) return bit_vector is ...
    function "–" ( bv : bit_vector ) return bit_vector is ...
    function mult_unsigned ( bv1, bv2 : bit_vector ) return bit_vector is
        ...
    begin
        ...
    end function mult_unsigned;
    function "*" ( bv1, bv2 : bit_vector ) return bit_vector is
    begin
        if bv1(bv1'left) = '0' and bv2(bv2'left) = '0' then
```

(continued on page 360)

(continued from page 359)

```
            return mult_unsigned(bv1, bv2);
        elsif bv1(bv1'left) = '0' and bv2(bv2'left) = '1' then
            return −mult_unsigned(bv1, −bv2);
        elsif bv1(bv1'left) = '1' and bv2(bv2'left) = '0' then
            return −mult_unsigned(−bv1, bv2);
        else
            return mult_unsigned(−bv1, −bv2);
        end if;
    end function "*";

    …

end package body bit_vector_signed_arithmetic;
```

An outline of a package declaration and body that define signed arithmetic functions on integers represented as bit vectors.

One final point to mention on the topic of packages relates to the order of analysis. We mentioned before that a package is a separate design unit that is analyzed separately from other design units, such as entity declarations and architecture bodies. In fact, a package declaration and its corresponding package body are each separate design units; hence they may be analyzed separately. A package declaration is a primary design unit, and a package body is a secondary design unit. The package body depends on information defined in the package declaration, so the declaration must be analyzed first. Furthermore, the declaration must be analyzed before any other design unit that refers to an item defined by the package. Once the declaration has been analyzed, it does not matter when the body is analyzed in relation to units that use the package, provided it is analyzed before the model is elaborated. In a large suite of models, the dependency relationships can get quite complex, and a correct order of analysis can be difficult to find. A good VHDL-AMS tool suite will provide some degree of automating this process by working out the dependency relationships and analyzing those units needed to build a particular target unit to simulate or synthesize.

10.3 Use Clauses

We have seen how we can refer to an item provided by a package by writing its selected name, for example, work.cpu_types.status_value. This name refers to the item status_value in the package cpu_types stored in the library work. If we need to refer to this object in many places in a model, having to write the library name and package name becomes tedious and can obscure the intent of the model. We saw in Chapter 5 that we can write a *use clause* to make a library unit directly visible in a model, allowing us to omit the library name when referring to the library unit. Since an analyzed package is a library unit, use clauses also apply to making packages directly visible. So we could precede a model with a use clause referring to the package defined in the example in Figure 10-1:

use work.cpu_types;

This use clause allows us to write declarations in our model more simply, for example:

variable data_word : cpu_types.word;
variable next_address : cpu_types.address;

In fact, the use clause is more general than this usage indicates and allows us to make any name from a library or package directly visible. Let us look at the full syntax rule for a use clause, then discuss some of the possibilities.

use_clause ⇐ **use** selected_name 〔 , ₀₀₀ 〕 ;

selected_name ⇐ name . 〔 identifier 〖 character_literal 〖 operator_symbol 〖 **all** 〕

The syntax rule for names, shown in Appendix E, includes the possibility of a name itself being either a selected name or a simple identifier. If we make these substitutions in the above syntax rule, we see that a selected name can be of the form

identifier . identifier . 〔 identifier 〖 character_literal 〖 operator_symbol 〖 **all** 〕

One possibility is that the first identifier is a library name, and the second is the name of a package within the library. This form allows us to refer directly to items within a package without having to use the full selected name. For example, we can simplify the above declarations even further by rewriting the use clause as

use work.cpu_types.word, work.cpu_types.address;

The declarations can then be written as

variable data_word : word;
variable next_address : address;

We can place a use clause in any declarative part in a model. One way to think of a use clause is that it "imports" the names of the listed items into the part of the model containing the use clause, so that they can be used without writing the library or package name. The names become directly visible after the use clause, according to the same visibility rules that we discussed in Chapter 9.

The syntax rule for a use clause shows that we can write the keyword **all** instead of the name of a particular item to import from a package. This form is very useful, as it is a shorthand way of importing all of the names defined in the interface of a package. For example, if we are using one of the proposed IEEE standard nature packages as the basis for the terminals and quantities in a design, it is often convenient to import everything from the package. For example, we can import all of the contents of the electrical systems package with a use clause as follows:

use ieee_proposed.electrical_systems.**all**;

This use clause means that the model imports all of the names defined in the package electrical_systems residing in the library ieee_proposed. This explains the "magic" that we have used in previous chapters when we needed to model data using the standard natures. The keyword **all** can be included for any package where we want to import all of the declarations from the package into a model.

Example   Figure 10-10 is a revised version of the architecture body outlined in Figure 10-8. It includes a use clause referring to items declared in the cpu_types package. This makes the rest of the model considerably less cluttered and easier to read. The use clause is included within the declarative part of the instruction set interpreter process. Thus the names "imported" from the package are directly visible in the rest of the declarative part and in the body of the process.

FIGURE 10-10

```
architecture behavioral of cpu is
begin
    interpreter : process is
        use work.cpu_types.all;
        variable instr_reg : word;
        variable instr_opcode : opcode;
    begin
        ...   -- initialize
        loop
            ...   -- fetch instruction
            instr_opcode := extract_opcode ( instr_reg );
            case instr_opcode is
                when op_nop => null;
                when op_breq => ...
                ...
            end case;
        end loop;
    end process interpreter;
end architecture behavioral;
```

A revised outline of a CPU model, including a use clause to refer to items from the cpu_types *package.*

One final point to clarify about use clauses before looking at an extended example is the way in which they may be included at the beginning of a design unit, as well as in declarative parts within a library unit. We have seen in Chapter 7 how we may include library and use clauses at the head of a design unit, such as an entity interface or architecture body. This area of a design unit is called its *context clause*. In fact, this is probably the most common place for including use clauses. The names imported here are made directly visible throughout the design unit. For example, if we want to use the IEEE standard-logic type **std_ulogic** in the declaration of an entity, we might write the design unit as follows:

```
library ieee;  use ieee.std_logic_1164.std_ulogic;

entity logic_block is
    port ( a, b : in std_ulogic;
             y, z : out std_ulogic );
end entity logic_block;
```

The library clause and the use clause together form the context clause for the entity declaration in this example. The library clause makes the contents of the library accessible to the model, and the use clause imports the type name **std_ulogic** declared in the package **std_logic_1164** in the library **ieee**. By including the use clause in the context clause of the entity declaration, the **std_ulogic** type name is available when declaring the ports of the entity.

The names imported by a use clause in this way are made directly visible in the entire design unit after the use clause. In addition, if the design unit is a primary unit (such as an entity declaration or a package declaration), the visibility is extended to any corresponding secondary unit. Thus, if we include a use clause in the primary unit, we do not need to repeat it in the secondary unit, as the names are automatically visible there.

10.4 The Predefined Package Standard

In previous chapters, we have introduced numerous predefined types and operators. We can use them in our VHDL-AMS models without having to write type declarations or subprogram definitions for them. These predefined items all come from a special package called **standard**, located in a special design library called **std**. A full listing of the **standard** package is included for reference in Appendix B.

Because nearly every model we write needs to make use of the contents of this library and package, as well as the library **work**, VHDL-AMS includes an implicit context clause of the form

```
library std, work;  use std.standard.all;
```

at the beginning of each design unit. Hence we can refer to the simple names of the predefined items without having to resort to their selected names. In the occasional case where we need to distinguish a reference to a predefined operator from an overloaded version, we can use a selected name, for example:

```
result := std.standard."<" ( a, b );
```

Example A package that provides signed arithmetic operations on integers represented as bit vectors might include a relational operator, defined as shown in Figure 10-11. The function negates the sign bit of each operand, then compares the resultant bit vectors using the predefined relational operator from the package **standard**. The full selected name for the predefined operator is necessary to distinguish it from the function being defined. If the return expression were written as "**tmp1 < tmp2**", it would refer to the function in which it occurs, creating a circular definition.

FIGURE 10-11

```
function "<" ( a, b : bit_vector ) return boolean is
    variable tmp1 : bit_vector(a'range) := a;
    variable tmp2 : bit_vector(b'range) := b;
begin
    tmp1(tmp1'left) := not tmp1(tmp1'left);
    tmp2(tmp2'left) := not tmp2(tmp2'left);
    return std.standard."<" ( tmp1, tmp2 );
end function "<";
```

An operator function for comparing two bit vectors representing signed integers.

10.5 IEEE Standard Packages

When we design models, we can define types and operations using the built-in facilities of VHDL-AMS. However, the IEEE has published standards for packages that define commonly used data types and operations. Using these standards can save us development time. Furthermore, many tool vendors provide optimized implementations of the standard packages, so using them makes our simulations run faster. In this section, we outline the types and operations defined in the IEEE standard packages. Complete details of the package declarations are included in Appendix C. Each of these packages is included in a library called **ieee**. Hence, to use one of the packages in a design, we name the library **ieee** in a library clause, and name the required package in a use clause. We have seen examples of how to do this for the IEEE standard package std_logic_1164; the same applies for the other IEEE standard packages.

Std_Logic_1164 Multivalue Logic System

The IEEE standard package std_logic_1164 defines types and operations for models that need to deal with strong, weak and high-impedance strengths, and with unknown values. We have already described most of the types and operations in previous chapters and seen their use in examples. For completeness, we draw the information together in this section.

The types declared in **std_logic_1164** are

std_ulogic	The basic multivalued enumeration type (see page 56)
std_ulogic_vector	Array of **std_ulogic** elements (see page 121)
std_logic	Resolved multivalued enumeration type (see Section 15.2)
std_logic_vector	Array of **std_logic** elements (see Section 15.2)

In addition, the package declares the subtypes **X01**, **X01Z**, **UX01** and **UX01Z** for cases where we do not need to distinguish between strong and weak driving strengths. Each of these subtypes includes just the values listed in the subtype name.

The operations provided by the **std_logic_1164** package include overloaded versions of the logical operators **and**, **nand**, **or**, **nor**, **xor**, **xnor** and **not**, operating on values of each of the scalar and vector types and subtypes listed above. In addition, the package declares a number of functions for conversion between values of different types. In the following lists, the parameter **b** represents a bit value or bit vector, the parameter **s** represents a standard logic value or standard logic vector, and the parameter **x** represents a value of any of these types.

To_bit(s,xmap)	Convert to a bit value
To_bitvector(s, xmap)	Convert to a bit vector

In these two functions, the parameter **xmap** is a bit value that is used in the result when a bit to be converted is other than '0', '1', 'L' or 'H'.

To_StdULogic(b)	Convert to a standard logic value
To_StdLogicVector(x)	Convert to a **std_logic_vector**
To_StdULogicVector(x)	Convert to a **std_ulogic_vector**
To_X01(x)	Strip strength
To_X01Z(x)	Strip strength
To_UX01(x)	Strip strength

The strength-stripping functions remove the driving strength information from the parameter value. **To_X01** converts 'U', 'X', 'Z', 'W' and '–' elements to 'X'. **To_X01Z** is similar, but leaves 'Z' elements intact. **To_UX01** is similar to **To_X01**, but leaves 'U' elements intact.

Finally, the **std_logic_1164** package contains the following utility functions.

rising_edge(s)	True when there is a rising edge on **s**, false otherwise
falling_edge(s)	True when there is a falling edge on **s**, false otherwise

is_X(s)   True if **s** contains an unknown value, false otherwise

The edge-detection functions detect changes between low and high values on a scalar signal, irrespective of the driving strengths of the values. The functions are true only during the simulation cycles on which such events occur. The unknown-detection function determines whether there is a 'U', 'X', 'Z' or 'W' value in the scalar or vector value **s**.

Standard VHDL Synthesis Packages

The IEEE standard packages numeric_bit and numeric_std define arithmetic operations on integers represented using vectors of bit and std_logic elements, respectively. Most digital synthesis tools accept models that use these types and operations for numeric computations. For more information on this standard and the topic of digital synthesis of VHDL models, see *The Designer's Guide to VHDL, 2nd Edition*.

Standard VHDL Mathematical Packages

The IEEE standard packages math_real and math_complex define constants and mathematical functions on real and complex numbers, respectively.

Real Number Mathematical Package

The constants defined in math_real are listed in Figure 10-12. The functions, their operand types and meanings are listed in Figure 10-13. In the figure, the parameters **x** and **y** are of type **real**, and the parameter n is of type **integer**.

In addition to the functions listed in Figure 10-13, the math_real package defines the procedure uniform as follows:

procedure uniform (**variable** seed1, seed2 : **inout** positive;
                    variable x : **out** real);

This procedure generates successive values between 0.0 and 1.0 (exclusive) in a pseudo-random number sequence. The variables **seed1** and **seed2** store the state of the generator and are modified by each call to the procedure. **Seed1** must be initialized to a value between 1 and 2,147,483,562, and **seed2** to a value between 1 and 2,147,483,398, before the first call to **uniform**.

FIGURE 10-12

Constant	Value	Constant	Value
math_e	e	math_log_of_2	$\ln 2$
math_1_over_e	$1/e$	math_log_of_10	$\ln 10$
math_pi	π	math_log2_of_e	$\log_2 e$
math_2_pi	2π	math_log10_of_e	$\log_{10} e$
math_1_over_pi	$1/\pi$	math_sqrt_2	$\sqrt{2}$
math_pi_over_2	$\pi/2$	math_1_over_sqrt_2	$1/\sqrt{2}$
math_pi_over_3	$\pi/3$	math_sqrt_pi	$\sqrt{\pi}$
math_pi_over_4	$\pi/4$	math_deg_to_rad	$2\pi/360$
math_3_pi_over_2	$3\pi/2$	math_rad_to_deg	$360/2\pi$

Constants defined in the package math_real.

FIGURE 10-13

Function	Meaning	Function	Meaning
ceil(x)	Ceiling of x (least integer $\geq x$)	sign(x)	Sign of x (-1.0, 0.0 or $+1.0$)
floor(x)	Floor of x (greatest integer $\leq x$)	"mod"(x, y)	Floating-point modulus of x/y
round(x)	x rounded to nearest integer value (ties rounded away from 0.0)	realmax(x, y)	Greater of x and y
trunc(x)	x truncated toward 0.0	realmin(x, y)	Lesser of x and y
sqrt(x)	$\sqrt{x}$	log(x)	$\ln x$
cbrt(x)	$\sqrt[3]{x}$	log2(x)	$\log_2 x$
"**"(n, y)	n^y	log10(x)	$\log_{10} x$
"**"(x, y)	x^y	log(x, y)	$\log_y x$
exp(x)	e^x		

(continued on page 368)

(continued from page 367)

Function	Meaning	Function	Meaning
sin(x)	sin x (x in radians)	arcsin(x)	arcsin x
cos(x)	cos x (x in radians)	arccos(x)	arccos x
tan(x)	tan x (x in radians)	arctan(x)	arctan x
		arctan(y, x)	arctan of point (x, y)
sinh(x)	sinh x	arcsinh(x)	arcsinh x
cosh(x)	cosh x	arccosh(x)	arccosh x
tanh(x)	tanh x	arctanh(x)	arctanh x

Functions defined in the package math_real.

Example Suppose we need to test a structural implementation of an ALU, whose entity is declared as follows:

```
use ieee.numeric_bit.all;
subtype ALU_func is unsigned(3 downto 0);
subtype data_word is unsigned(15 downto 0);
...
entity ALU is
    port ( a, b : in data_word;  func : in ALU_func;
             result : out data_word;  carry : out bit );
end entity ALU;
```

We can devise a test bench that stimulates an instance of the ALU with randomly generated data and function-code inputs. The test-bench architecture body is outlined in Figure 10-14. The stimulus process generates new random stimuli for the ALU input signals every 100 ns. The process generates three random numbers in the range (0.0, 1.0) in the variables a_real, b_real and func_real. It then scales these values to get numbers in the range (−0.5, 65,635.5) for the data values and (−0.5, 15.5) for the function code value. These are rounded and converted to unsigned bit vectors for assignment to the ALU input signals.

FIGURE 10-14

```
architecture random_test of test_ALU is
    use ieee.numeric_bit.all;
    use ieee.math_real.uniform;
    signal a, b, result : data_word;
    signal func : ALU_func;
```

```
       signal carry : bit;
begin
    dut : entity work.ALU(structural)
        port map ( a, b, func, result, carry );
    stimulus : process is
        variable seed1, seed2 : positive := 1;
        variable a_real, b_real, func_real : real;
    begin
        wait for 100 ns;
        uniform ( seed1, seed2, a_real );
        uniform ( seed1, seed2, b_real );
        uniform ( seed1, seed2, func_real );

        a <= to_unsigned( natural(a_real * real(2**integer'(data_word'length)) – 0.5),
                    data_word'length );
        b <= to_unsigned( natural(b_real * real(2**integer'(data_word'length)) – 0.5),
                    data_word'length );
        func <= to_unsigned( natural(func_real
                                    * real(2**integer'(ALU_func'length)) – 0.5),
                        ALU_func'length );
    end process stimulus;

    ...   -- verification process to check result and carry
end architecture random_test;
```

An architecture body for a random-stimulus test bench for the ALU.

Complex Number Mathematical Package

The math_complex package deals with complex numbers represented in Cartesian and polar form. The package defines types for these representations, as follows:

```
type complex is record
        re : real;              -- real part
        im : real;              -- imaginary part
    end record;
subtype positive_real is real range 0.0 to real'high;
subtype principal_value is real range –math_pi to math_pi;

type complex_polar is record
        mag : positive_real;        -- magnitude
        arg : principal_value;      -- angle in radians; –math_pi is illegal
    end record;
```

The constants defined in math_complex are

math_cbase_1	$1.0 + j0.0$
math_cbase_j	$0.0 + j1.0$
math_czero	$0.0 + j0.0$

The package defines a number of overloaded operators, listed in Figure 10-15. The curly braces indicate that for each operator to the left of the brace, there are overloaded versions for all combinations of types to the right of the brace. Thus, there are six overloaded versions of each of the "+", "−", "*" and "/" operators.

Overloaded versions of "=" and "/=" are necessary for numbers in polar form, since two complex numbers are equal if their magnitudes are both 0.0, even if their arguments are different. The predefined equality and inequality operators do not have this behavior. No overloaded versions of these operators are required for Cartesian form, since the predefined operators behave correctly.

In addition to the operators, the **math_complex** package defines a number of mathematical functions, listed in Figure 10-16. In the figure, the parameters **x** and **y** are real, the parameter **c** is complex, the parameter **p** is complex_polar, and the parameter **z** is either complex or complex_polar.

FIGURE 10-15

Operator	Operation	Left operand	Right operand	Result
=	equality	complex_polar	complex_polar	boolean
/=	inequality	complex_polar	complex_polar	boolean
abs	magnitude		complex	positive_real
			complex_polar	positive_real
−	negation		complex	complex
			complex_polar	complex_polar
+	addition	complex	complex	complex
−	subtraction	real	complex	complex
*	multiplication	complex	real	complex
/	division	complex_polar	complex_polar	complex_polar
		real	complex_polar	complex_polar
		complex_polar	real	complex_polar

Overloaded operators defined in math_complex.

FIGURE 10-16

Function	Result type	Meaning
cmplx(x, y)	complex	$x + jy$
get_principal_value(x)	principal_value	$x + 2\pi k$ for some k, such that $-\pi < \text{result} \le \pi$
complex_to_polar(c)	complex_polar	c in polar form
polar_to_complex(p)	complex	p in Cartesian form
arg(z)	principal_value	$\arg(z)$ in radians
conj(z)	same as z	complex conjugate of z
sqrt(z)	same as z	$\sqrt{z}$
exp(z)	same as z	e^z
log(z)	same as z	$\ln z$
log2(z)	same as z	$\log_2 z$
log10(z)	same as z	$\log_{10} z$
log(z, y)	same as z	$\log_y z$
sin(z)	same as z	$\sin z$
cos(z)	same as z	$\cos z$
sinh(z)	same as z	$\sinh z$
cosh(z)	same as z	$\cosh z$

Functions defined in the package math_complex.

Proposed Standard Analog Packages

As we have seen, VHDL-AMS can be used for modeling systems from a number of energy domains. In order to improve model portability and designer productivity, the VHDL-AMS language development team is also developing a set of packages for various energy domains. Throughout this book, we use the name ieee_proposed for the library in which these packages are held. Once they have been officially approved by the IEEE, the packages will be found in the ieee library. Designers should be aware that, until then, the packages are subject to change.

The set of packages in the ieee_proposed library includes the package energy_systems, which contains declarations of a number of important constants associated with various energy domains, as well as constants and subtypes that are common to all domains. The subtypes are

energy, energy_vector   Energy (joules)

power, power_vector   Power (watts)

periodicity, periodicity_vector   Periodicity, or angular frequency (radian/sec)

The package defines constants representing unit multipliers, shown in Figure 10-17, and a number of natural constants, shown in Figure 10-18. Lastly, the package defines an attribute **symbol** of type **string** that we can use to annotate a subtype with its physical units. We will describe annotation using attributes in Chapter 22.

The packages supporting specific energy domains are shown in Figure 10-19. Each package defines a number of subtypes for physical quantities, one or more natures, an array nature type for each scalar nature and in some cases an alternate name for the reference terminal of a nature. To use one of the packages in a design, we name the library **ieee_proposed** in a library clause and name the required package in a use clause.

FIGURE 10-17

yocto	10^{-24}	nano	10^{-9}	deka	10^{+1}	tera	10^{+12}
zepto	10^{-21}	micro	10^{-6}	hecto	10^{+2}	peta	10^{+15}
atto	10^{-18}	milli	10^{-3}	kilo	10^{+3}	exa	10^{+18}
femto	10^{-15}	centi	10^{-2}	mega	10^{+6}	zetta	10^{+21}
pico	10^{-12}	denci	10^{-1}	giga	10^{+9}	yotta	10^{+24}

Constants for metric multipliers defined in the energy_systems *package.*

FIGURE 10-18

Constant	Value	Physical meaning
eps0	$8.854187817 \times 10^{-12}$ F/m	Permittivity of vacuum (farad/meter)
mu0	$4.0 \times 10^{-7} . \pi$ H/m	Permeability of vacuum (henry/meter)
q	$1.602176462 \times 10^{-19}$ C	Electron charge (coulomb)
k	$1.3806503 \times 10^{-23}$ J/K	Boltzmann constant (joules/kelvin)
grav	9.80665 m/s^2	Acceleration due to gravity (meter/second^2)
ctok	273.15	Conversion between kelvin and °C
eps_si	11.7	Relative permittivity of silicon
eps_sio2	3.9	Relative permittivity of silicon dioxide
e_si	$190.0 \times 10^{+9}$ Pa	Young's modulus for silicon (pascal)
e_sio2	$73.0 \times 10^{+9}$ Pa	Young's modulus for silicon dioxide (pascal)
nu_si	0.28	Poisson's ratio for silicon

Constants for physical quantities defined in the energy_systems *package.*

FIGURE 10-19

Subtype	Vector subtype	Unit	Nature	Across type	Through type	Reference terminal	Vector nature
Package electrical_systems							
voltage	voltage_vector	volt	electrical	voltage	current	electrical_ref (alias ground)	electrical_vector
current	current_vector	ampere					
charge	charge_vector	coulomb	magnetic	mmf	flux	magnetic_ref	magnetic_vector
resistance	resistance_vector	ohm					
capacitance	capacitance_vector	farad					
mmf	mmf_vector	ampere-turn					
flux	flux_vector	weber					
inductance	inductance_vector	henry					
Package mechanical_systems							
displacement	displacement_vector	meter	translational	displacement	force	translational_ref (alias anchor)	translational_vector
force	force_vector	newton					
velocity	velocity_vector	meter/second	translational_v	velocity	force	translational_v_ref	translational_v_vector
acceleration	acceleration_vector	meter/second^2	rotational	angle	torque	rotational_ref	rotational_vector
mass	mass_vector	kilogram	rotational_v	angular_velocity	torque	rotational_v_ref	rotational_v_vector
stiffness	stiffness_vector	newton/meter					
damping	damping_vector	newton-second/meter					
angle	angle_vector	radian					
torque	torque_vector	newton-meter					

(continued on page 374)

(continued from page 373)

Subtype	Vector subtype	Unit	Nature	Across type	Through type	Reference terminal	Vector nature
angular_velocity	angular_velocity_vector	radian/second					
angular_accel	angular_accel_vector	radians/second^2					
mmoment_i	mmoment_i_vector	kilogram-meter^2					
Package fluidic_systems							
pressure	pressure_vector	pascal	fluidic	pressure	vflow_rate	fluidic_ref	fluidic_vector
vflow_rate	vflow_rate_vector	meter^3/second					
volume	volume_vector	meter^3					
density	density_vector	kilogram/meter^3					
viscosity	viscosity_vector	newton-second/meter^2					
fresistance	fresistance_vector	newton-second/meter^5					
fcapacitance	fcapacitance_vector	meter^5/newton					
inertance	inertance_vector	newton-second^2/meter^5					
Package thermal_systems							
temperature	temperature_vector	kelvin	thermal	temperature	heat_flow	thermal_ref	thermal_vector
heat_flow	heat_flow_vector	joule/second					
Package radiant_systems							
illuminance	illuminance_vector	candela	radiant	illuminance	optic_flux	radiant_ref	radiant_vector
optic_flux	optic_flux_vector	lumen					

Subtypes and natures defined in the proposed standard packages for various modeling domains.

Exercises

1. [❶ 10.1] Write a package declaration for use in a model of an engine management system. The package contains declarations of a mechanical rotational-nature terminal, **engine_crankshaft**; a constant, **peak_rpm**, with a value of 6000 revolutions per minute (RPM); and an enumeration type, **gear**, with values representing first, second, third, fourth and reverse gears. Assuming the package is analyzed and stored in the current working library, write selected names for each of the items declared in the package.

2. [❶ 10.1] Write a declaration for a procedure that increments an integer, as the procedure declaration would appear in a package declaration.

3. [❶ 10.1] Write a declaration for a function that tests whether an integer is odd, as the function declaration would appear in a package declaration.

4. [❶ 10.1] Write a deferred constant declaration for the real constant $e = 2.71828$.

5. [❶ 10.2] Is a package body required for the package declaration described in Exercise 1?

6. [❶ 10.3] Write a use clause that makes the **engine_crankshaft** type from the package described in Exercise 1 directly visible.

7. [❶ 10.3] Write a context clause that makes a library **DSP_lib** accessible and that makes an entity **systolic_FFT** and all items declared in a package **DSP_types** in the library directly visible.

8. [❷ 10.4] Integers can be represented in *signed magnitude* form, in which the leftmost bit represents the sign ('0' for non-negative, '1' for negative), and the remaining bits are the absolute value of the number, represented in binary. If we wish to compare bit vectors containing numbers in signed magnitude form, we cannot use the predefined relational operators directly. We must first transform each number as follows: if the number is negative, complement all bits; if the number is non-negative, complement only the sign bit. Write a comparison function, overloading the operator "<", to compare signed-magnitude bit vectors using this method.

9. [❸ 10.1/10.2] Develop a package declaration and body that provide operations for dealing with time-of-day values. The package defines a time-of-day value as a record containing hours, minutes and seconds since midnight and provides deferred constants representing midnight and midday. The operations provided by the package are

   • comparison ("<", ">", "<=" and ">="),

   • addition of a time-of-day value and a number of seconds to yield a time-of-day result and

   • subtraction of two time-of-day values to yield a number-of-seconds result.

10. [❸ 10.1/10.2] Develop a package declaration and body to provide operations on character strings representing identifiers. An outline of the package declaration is

```
package identifier_pkg is

    subtype identifier is string(1 to 15);

    constant max_table_size : integer := 50;
    subtype table_index is integer range 1 to max_table_size;
    type table is array (table_index) of identifier;

    ...

end package identifier_pkg;
```

The package also declares a procedure to convert alphabetic characters in a string to lowercase and a procedure to search for an occurrence of a given identifier in a table. The search procedure has two **out** mode parameters: a Boolean value indicating whether the sought string is in the table and a **table_index** value indicating its position, if present.

chapter eleven

Aliases

Since the main purpose of a model written in VHDL-AMS is to describe a hardware design, it should be made as easy as possible to read and understand. In this chapter, we introduce aliases as a means of making a model clearer. As in everyday use, an alias is simply an alternate name for something. We see how we can use aliases in VHDL-AMS for both data objects and other kinds of items that do not represent data in a model.

11.1 **Aliases for Data Objects**

If we have a model that includes a data object, such as a constant, a variable, a signal, a quantity, a terminal or, as we see in a later chapter, a file, we can declare an alias for the object with an *alias declaration*. A simplified syntax rule for this is

alias_declaration ⇐ **alias** identifier **is** name ;

An alias declaration in this form simply defines an alternate identifier to refer to the named data object. We can refer to the object using the new identifier, treating it as being of the type or nature specified in the original object's declaration. Operations we perform using the alias are actually applied to the original object. (The only exceptions are reading the 'simple_name, 'path_name and 'instance_name attributes and the attributes that provide information about the index ranges of an array. In these cases, the attributes refer to the alias name rather than the original object's name.)

Example   One use of alias declarations is to define simple names for objects imported from packages. Suppose, for example, that we need to use objects from two different packages, **alu_types** and **io_types**, and that each declares a constant named **data_width**, possibly with different values. If we include use clauses for these packages in our model, as follows:

use work.alu_types.**all**, work.io_types.**all**;

neither of the versions of **data_width** becomes directly visible, since they have the same name. Hence we would have to refer to them as **work.alu_types.data_width** and **work.io_types.data_width**. However, we can avoid this long notation simply by introducing two alias declarations into our model, as shown in the architecture body outlined in Figure 11-1.

FIGURE 11-1

```
library ieee;  use ieee.std_logic_1164.all;
use work.alu_types.all, work.io_types.all;
architecture structural of controller_system is
    alias alu_data_width is work.alu_types.data_width;
    alias io_data_width is work.io_types.data_width;
    signal alu_in1, alu_in2,
           alu_result : std_logic_vector(0 to alu_data_width – 1);
    signal  io_data : std_logic_vector(0 to io_data_width – 1);
    ...
```

```
begin
    ...
end architecture structural;
```

An outline of an architecture body that aliases objects imported from two packages.

Example When we define a nature for modeling in an analog domain, we often use the reference terminal to declare branch quantities. The proposed standard packages for various domains define natures that specify reference terminals. Some of the packages also define aliases for reference terminals, listed in Figure 10-19. For example, the electrical_systems package includes the alias declaration

```
    alias ground is electrical_ref;
```

and the mechanical_systems package includes the alias declaration

```
    alias anchor is translational_ref;
```

We can make our models clearer by using these aliases, since their names are more intuitive than the standardized names used in the nature definitions. Figure 11-2 shows an outline of an architecture body for an earth leakage safety switch that uses the packages for the electrical and mechanical domains. It declares across quantities representing differences in efforts between terminal ports and the corresponding reference terminals identified by their aliases **ground** and anchor.

FIGURE 11-2

```
library ieee_proposed;
use ieee_proposed.electrical_systems.all, ieee_proposed.mechanical_systems.all;
architecture basic of safety_switch is
    quantity neutral_potential across neutral to ground;
    quantity relay_position across relay_actuator to anchor;
    ...
begin
    ...
end architecture basic;
```

An outline of an architecture body that refers to object aliases.

As well as denoting a whole data object, an alias can denote a single element from a composite data object, such as a record or an array. We write the element name, including a record element selector or an array index, as the name to be aliased. For example, given the following declarations of types and a variable:

```
type register_array is array (0 to 15) of bit_vector(31 downto 0);
type register_set is record
        general_purpose_registers : register_array;
        program_counter : bit_vector(31 downto 0);
        program_status : bit_vector(31 downto 0);
    end record;
variable CPU_registers : register_set;
```

we can declare aliases for the record elements:

```
alias PSW is CPU_registers.program_status;
alias PC is CPU_registers.program_counter;
alias GPR is CPU_registers.general_purpose_registers;
```

We can also declare aliases for individual registers in the register array, for example:

```
alias SP is CPU_registers.general_purpose_registers(15);
```

Similarly, we can declare aliases for the elements of a record nature. If we have a composite record nature declared as

```
nature electrical_bus is
    record
        strobe : electrical;
        databus : electrical_vector(0 to 7);
    end record;
terminal ebus : electrical_bus;
quantity bus_voltages across ebus to ground;
```

then we can define aliases for the record elements as follows:

```
alias e_strobe is bus_voltages.strobe;
alias e_data is bus_voltages.databus;
```

The name that we are aliasing can itself be an alias. Hence the alias declaration for SP can be written using the alias name GPR:

```
alias SP is GPR(15);
```

An alias can also be used to denote a slice of a one-dimensional array. For example, given the above declaration for **CPU_registers**, we can declare an alias for part of the program status register:

alias interrupt_level **is** PSW(30 **downto** 26);

This declares interrupt_level to denote a bit vector, with indices from 30 down to 26, being part of the bit vector denoted by **PSW**. In general, if we declare an alias for an array slice in this way, the alias denotes an array with index range and direction determined by the slice.

In many cases, it would be convenient to use an alias to take a slightly different view of the array being aliased. For example, we would like to view the interrupt_level alias as a bit vector indexed from four down to zero. We can do this by using an extended form of alias declaration, described by the following syntax rule:

alias_declaration ⇐ **alias** identifier
                          ⟦ : ⟨ subtype_indication ⟦ subnature_indication ⟩ ⟧ **is** name ;

This shows that we can indicate the subtype or subnature for the alias. The subtype or subnature determines how we view the original object that the alias denotes. We can include a subtype or subnature indication in aliases for scalar objects, but the bounds and direction specified must be the same as those of the original object. Hence this only serves as a form of documentation, to restate the type or nature information for the object. We can also include an unconstrained array type name as the alias subtype when aliasing an array object or slice. In this case the index bounds and direction come from the original object. Similarly, we can include an unconstrained array subnature name as the alias subnature when aliasing an array object or slice. However, when we declare an alias for an array or for an array slice, we can use the subtype or subnature indication to specify different index bounds and direction from the original object. The base type of the subtype indication must be the same as the base type of the original object, or the base nature of the subnature indication must be the same as the base nature of the original object. (This means that the subtype indication must refer to an array type with the same element and index types as the original object, or the subnature indication must refer to an array nature with the same element natures and index types as the original object.) Furthermore, there must be the same number of elements in the alias subtype or subnature and the original object. Elements in the alias denote the corresponding elements in the actual object in left-to-right order. For example, if we were to declare the alias interrupt_level as follows:

alias interrupt_level : bit_vector(4 **downto** 0) **is** PSW(30 **downto** 26);

then interrupt_level(4) would denote **PSW(30)**, interrupt_level(3) would denote **PSW(29)**, and so on.

Example   When we write subprograms that take parameters of unconstrained array types or natures, the index bounds and direction of the parameter are not known until actual array objects are passed as arguments during a call. Without this knowledge, the body of the subprogram is difficult to write. For example, suppose we need to implement a function to perform addition on two bit vectors that represent two's-complement, signed integers. The function specification is

>   function "+" (bv1, bv2 : bit_vector) **return** bit_vector;

When the function is called it is possible that the first argument is indexed from 0 to 15, while the other argument is indexed from 31 down to 8. We must check that the arguments are of the same size and then index them in a loop running from the rightmost bit to the leftmost. The different ranges, directions and sizes make this difficult.

We can use aliases to make the task easier by viewing the objects as arrays with the same leftmost index and direction. The subprogram body is shown in Figure 11-3. The alias declarations create views of the bit-vector arguments, indexed from one up to their length. The function, after checking that the arguments are of the same length, can then use the same index values for corresponding elements of the two arguments and the result.

FIGURE 11-3

```
function "+" ( bv1, bv2 : bit_vector ) return bit_vector is
    alias norm1 : bit_vector(1 to bv1'length) is bv1;
    alias norm2 : bit_vector(1 to bv2'length) is bv2;

    variable result : bit_vector(1 to bv1'length);
    variable carry : bit := '0';
begin
    if bv1'length /= bv2'length then
        report "arguments of different length" severity failure;
    else
        for index in norm1'reverse_range loop
            result(index) := norm1(index) xor norm2(index) xor carry;
            carry := ( norm1(index) and norm2(index) )
                        or ( carry and ( norm1(index) or norm2(index) ) );
        end loop;
    end if;
    return result;
end function "+";
```

A function that performs addition on two bit vectors representing signed integers.

11.2 **Aliases for Non-Data Items**

We saw in the previous section that we can declare aliases for data objects such as constants, variables, signals, terminals and quantities. We can also declare aliases for other named items that do not represent stored data, such as types, natures, subprograms, packages, entities and so on. In fact, the only kinds of items for which we cannot declare aliases are labels, loop parameters and generate parameters (see Chapter 17). The syntax rule for alias declarations for non-data items is

> alias_declaration ⇐
>   **alias** ⟦ identifier ⧵ character_literal ⧵ operator_symbol ⟧
>   **is** name ⟦ signature ⟧ ;

We can use character literals as aliases for enumeration literals, and operator symbols as aliases for function subprograms. We will return to the optional signature part shortly.

If we define an alias for a type, we can use the alias in any context where the original type name can be used. Furthermore, all of the predefined operations for values of the original type can be used without being declared. For example, if we define an alias:

> **alias** binary_string **is** bit_vector;

we can declare objects to be of type **binary_string** and perform bit-vector operations on them; for example:

> **variable** s1, s2 : binary_string(0 **to** 7);
> ...
> s1 := s1 **and not** s2;

Declaring an alias for a type is different from declaring a new type. In the latter case, new overloaded versions of the operators would have to be declared. The alias, on the other hand, is simply another name for the existing type. Similarly, we can define an alias for a nature to provide another name for the existing nature.

If we define an alias for an enumeration type, all of the enumeration literals of the original type are available for use. We do not need to define aliases for the literals, nor use fully selected names. For example, if a package **system_types** declares an enumeration type as follows:

> **type** system_status **is** (idle, active, overloaded);

and a model defines an alias for this type:

> **alias** status_type **is** work.system_types.system_status;

the model can simply refer to the literals **idle**, **active** and **overloaded**, instead of **work.system_types.overloaded** and so on. Similarly, if we declare an alias for a physical type, all of the unit names are available for use without aliasing or selection.

The optional signature part in an alias declaration is only used in aliases for subprograms and enumeration literals. These items can be overloaded, so it is possible that the name alone is not sufficient to identify which item is being aliased. The signature serves to identify one item uniquely. The syntax rule for a signature is

signature ⇐ [⟦ type_mark ⟨ , ... ⟩ ⟧ ⟦ **return** type_mark ⟧]

Note that the outer square bracket symbols ("[...]") are a required part of the signature, whereas the hollow square brackets ("⟦ ... ⟧") are part of the EBNF syntax and indicate optional parts of the signature.

When we declare an alias for a subprogram, the signature identifies which overloaded version of the subprogram name is aliased. The signature lists the types of each of the subprogram's parameters, in the same order that they appear in the subprogram's declaration. For example, if a package **arithmetic_ops** declares two procedures as follows:

procedure increment (bv : **inout** bit_vector; by : **in** integer := 1);

procedure increment (int : **inout** integer; by : **in** integer := 1);

we can declare aliases for the procedures as follows:

alias bv_increment **is** work.arithmetic_ops.increment [bit_vector, integer];

alias int_increment **is** work.arithmetic_ops.increment [integer, integer];

If the subprogram is a function, the signature also includes the type of the return value, after the keyword **return**. For example, we might alias the operator symbols "*", "+" and "−" to the bit operators **and**, **or** and **not**, as follows:

alias "*" **is** "and" [bit, bit **return** bit];

alias "+" **is** "or" [bit, bit **return** bit];

alias "−" **is** "not" [bit **return** bit];

We would then be able to express Boolean equations using these operators. For example, given bit signals **s**, **a**, **b** and **c**, we could write

s <= a * b + (−a) * c;

Note that when we alias an operator symbol to a function, the function overloads the operator symbol, so it must have the correct number of parameters for the operator. A binary operator symbol must be aliased to a function with two parameters, and a unary operator symbol must be aliased to a function with one parameter.

If we wish to alias an individual literal of an enumeration type, we must deal with the possibility that the literal may belong to several different enumeration types. We can use a signature to distinguish one particular meaning by noting that an enumeration literal is equivalent to a function with no parameters that returns a value of the enumeration type. For example, when we write the enumeration literal '1', we can think of this as a call to a function with no parameters, returning a value of type **bit**. We can write an alias for this literal as follows:

alias high **is** std.standard.'1' [**return** bit];

The signature distinguishes the literal as being of type **bit**, rather than of any other character type. Note that a selected name is required for a character literal, since a character literal by itself is not a syntactically valid name.

Example   One useful application of aliases for non-data items is to compose a package by collecting together a number of items declared in other packages. Figure 11-4 shows such a package for use in a DMA controller design. The package defines aliases for two types imported from the **cpu_types** package and for a function imported from a package that provides bit-vector arithmetic operations.

The DMA controller architecture body outlined in Figure 11-5 imports the aliases from the utility package. The reference to the name **word** denotes the type originally defined in the package **cpu_types**, and the operator "+" denotes the bit-vector operator originally defined in the package bit_vector_unsigned_arithmetic.

FIGURE 11-4

```
package DMA_controller_types_and_utilities is
    alias word is work.cpu_types.word;
    alias status_value is work.cpu_types.status_value;
    alias "+" is work.bit_vector_unsigned_arithmetic."+"
                        [ bit_vector, bit_vector return bit_vector ];
    ...
end package DMA_controller_types_and_utilities;
```

A utility package for a DMA controller design, collecting together items imported from other packages.

FIGURE 11-5

```
architecture behavioral of DMA_controller is
    use work.DMA_controller_types_and_utilities.all;
begin
    behavior : process is
```

(continued on page 386)

(continued from page 385)

```
        variable address_reg0, address_reg1 : word;
        variable count_reg0, count_reg1 : word;
        ...
    begin
        ...
        address_reg0 := address_reg0 + X"0000_0004";
        ...
    end process behavior;
end architecture behavioral;
```

An outline of the architecture body for the DMA controller that makes use of the aliases defined in the utility package.

Exercises

1. [❶ 11.1] Given the following declarations:

    ```
    subtype byte is bit_vector(0 to 7);
    type data_array is array (0 to 31) of byte;
    type network_packet is record
            source, dest, flags : byte;
            payload : data_array;
            checksum : byte;
        end record network_packet;
    variable received_packet : network_packet;
    ```

    write alias declarations for the individual elements of the variable.

2. [❶ 11.1] Given the following declarations:

    ```
    nature FET is record
            source : electrical;
            drain : electrical;
            gate : electrical;
            substrate : electrical;
        end record FET;
    terminal M1 : FET;
    ```

    write alias declarations for the individual elements of the terminal.

3. [❶ 11.1] The layout of information within the **flags** element of a network packet described in Exercise 1 is shown in Figure 11-6. Write alias declarations for the individual fields of the **flags** element of the **received_packet** variable. The aliases

FIGURE 11-6

0	1	2	3	4	5	6	7
AK	ACKNO			SEQNO			UD

The layout of information within a network packet.

for the ACKNO and SEQNO fields should view the fields as bit vectors indexed from two down to zero.

4. [❶ 11.2] Write an alias declaration that defines the name **cons** as an alias for the predefined operation "**&**" with a character left argument, a string right argument and a string result. Use the alias in a report statement that reports the string constructed from the value of the variable **grade_char** concatenated to the string "–grade".

5. [❷ 11.1] Develop a behavioral model of a bit-reversing module with the following entity interface:

    ```
    entity reverser is
        port ( d_in : in std_ulogic_vector;
               d_out : out std_ulogic_vector );
    end entity reverser;
    ```

    When the entity is instantiated, the actual signals must be of the same length, but may differ in their index bounds and directions. The output is the input delayed by 500 ps using transport delay, and with the bits in reverse order from left to right.

6. [❷ 11.1] Develop a behavioral model of a reversing module with the following entity interface:

    ```
    entity e_reverser is
        port ( terminal input : electrical_vector;
               terminal output : electrical_vector );
    end entity e_reverser;
    ```

    When the entity is instantiated, the actual terminal arrays must be of the same length, but may differ in their index bounds and directions. The output terminal elements are connected to the input terminal elements in reverse order from left to right.

chapter twelve
Generic Constants

The models that we have used as examples in preceding chapters all have fixed behavior and structure. In many respects, this is a limitation, and we would like to be able to write more general, or generic, models. VHDL-AMS provides us with a mechanism, called generics, *for writing parameterized models. We discuss generics in this chapter and show how they may be used to write families of models with varying behavior and structure.*

12.1 **Parameterizing Behavior**

We can write a generic entity by including a *generic interface list* in its declaration that defines the *formal generic constants* that parameterize the entity. The extended syntax rule for entity declarations including generics is

> entity_declaration ⇐
>   **entity** identifier **is**
>   〚 **generic** (*generic*_interface_list) ; 〛
>   〚 **port** (*port*_interface_list) ; 〛
>   ⦃ entity_declarative_item ⦄
>   〚 **begin**
>   ⦃ concurrent_assertion_statement
>   ⎮ *passive*_concurrent_procedure_call_statement
>   ⎮ *passive*_process_statement ⦄ 〛
>   **end** 〚 **entity** 〛 〚 identifier 〛 ;

The difference between this and the simpler rule we have seen before is the inclusion of the optional generic interface list before the port interface list. The generic interface list is like any other interface list, but with the restriction that we can only include constant-class objects, which must be of mode **in**. Since these are the defaults for a generic interface list, we can use a simplified syntax rule:

> generic_interface_list ⇐
>   ⦇ identifier ⦃ , ࣴ ⦄ : subtype_indication 〚 := expression 〛 ⦈
>   ⦃ ; ࣴ ⦄

A simple example of an entity declaration including a generic interface list is

```
entity and2 is
    generic ( Tpd : time );
    port ( a, b : in bit; y : out bit );
end entity and2;
```

This entity includes one generic constant, **Tpd**, of the predefined type **time**. The value of this generic constant may be used within the entity statements and any architecture body corresponding to the entity. In this example the intention is that the generic constant specify the propagation delay for the module, so the value should be used in a signal assignment statement as the delay. An architecture body that does this is

```
architecture simple of and2 is
begin
    and2_function :
        y <= a and b after Tpd;
end architecture simple;
```

Another simple example of an entity declaration including a generic interface list is

entity resistor **is**
    generic (resistance : real);
    port (**terminal** pos, neg : electrical);
end entity resistor;

This entity includes one generic constant, **resistance**, of type **real**. An architecture body that uses the resistance to model the resistor behavior using Ohm's law is

architecture simple **of** resistor **is**
    quantity v **across** i **through** pos **to** neg;
begin
    v == i * resistance;
end architecture simple;

The visibility of a generic constant extends from the end of the generic interface list to the end of the entity declaration and extends into any architecture body corresponding to the entity declaration.

A generic constant is given an actual value when the entity is used in a component instantiation statement. We do this by including a *generic map*, as shown by the extended syntax rule for component instantiations:

component_instantiation_statement ⇐
    *instantiation*_label :
        entity *entity*_name 〚 (*architecture*_identifier) 〛
        〚 **generic map** (*generic*_association_list) 〛
        〚 **port map** (*port*_association_list) 〛 ;

The generic association list is like other forms of association lists, but since generic constants are always of class constant, the actual arguments we supply must be expressions. Thus the simplified syntax rule for a generic association list is

generic_association_list ⇐
    (〚 *generic*_name => 〛 (expression I **open**)) { , ... }

To illustrate this, let us look at a component instantiation statement that uses the and2 entity shown above:

gate1 : **entity** work.and2(simple)
    generic map (Tpd => 2 ns)
    port map (a => sig1, b => sig2, y => sig_out);

The generic map specifies that this instance of the **and2** module uses the value 2 ns for the generic constant **Tpd**; that is, the instance has a propagation delay of 2 ns.

We might include another component instantiation statement using **and2** in the same design but with a different actual value for **Tpd** in its generic map, for example:

```
gate2 : entity work.and2(simple)
    generic map ( Tpd => 3 ns )
    port map ( a => a1,  b => b1,  y => sig1 );
```

When the design is elaborated we have two processes, one corresponding to the instance **gate1** of **and2**, which uses the value 2 ns for **Tpd**, and another corresponding to the instance **gate2** of **and2**, which uses the value 3 ns.

In the same way, we can instantiate different resistor components and use the generic map mechanism to assign a specific resistance value to each one. Hence, the use of generic constants allows us to create a set of generally useful components and instantiate them with the appropriate generic constant values.

Example   As the syntax rule for the generic interface list shows, we may define a number of generic constants of different types and include default values for them. A more involved example is shown in Figure 12-1. In this example, the generic interface list includes a list of two generic constants that parameterize the propagation delay of the module and a Boolean generic constant, **debug**, with a default value of false. The intention of this last generic constant is to allow a design that instantiates this entity to activate some debugging operation. This operation might take the form of report statements within if statements that test the value of debug.

FIGURE 12-1

```
entity control_unit is
    generic ( Tpd_clk_out, Tpw_clk : delay_length;
            debug : boolean := false );
    port ( clk : in bit;
            ready : in bit;
            control1, control2 : out bit );
end entity control_unit;
```

An entity declaration for a block of sequential control logic, including generic constants that parameterize its behavior.

We have the same flexibility in writing a generic map as we have in other association lists. We can use positional association, named association or a combination of both. We can omit actual values for generic constants that have default expressions, or we may explicitly use the default value by writing the keyword **open** in the generic map. To illustrate these possibilities, here are three different ways of writing a generic map for the control_unit entity:

generic map (200 ps, 1500 ps, false)

generic map (Tpd_clk_out => 200 ps, Tpw_clk => 1500 ps)

generic map (200 ps, 1500 ps, debug => **open**)

Example   Consider once again the resettable timer we introduced in Section 6.6. The model from Figure 6-29 is revised in Figure 12-2 to include generic constants for the threshold voltage and the on and off resistances of the switch that discharges the capacitor. The values of the generic constants are used in the architecture body.

FIGURE 12-2

```
library ieee;  use ieee.std_logic_1164.all;
library ieee_proposed;  use ieee_proposed.electrical_systems.all;
entity timer is
    generic ( threshold : real;
                clamp_on_resistance, clamp_off_resistance : real );
    port ( signal trigger_n, reset : in std_ulogic;  signal q : out std_ulogic;
        terminal rc_ext : electrical );
end entity timer;

-------------------------------------------------------

architecture behavioral of timer is
    quantity v_rc_ext across i_clamp through rc_ext to electrical_ref;
    signal q_n : std_ulogic := '1';
begin
    if q_n = '1' use
        i_clamp == v_rc_ext / clamp_on_resistance;
    else
        i_clamp == v_rc_ext / clamp_off_resistance;
    end use;
    timer_state : process ( trigger_n, reset, v_rc_ext'above(threshold) ) is
    begin
        if reset = '1' or reset = 'H' or v_rc_ext > threshold then
            q <= '0';  q_n <= '1';
        elsif trigger_n = '0' or trigger_n = 'L' then
            q <= '1';  q_n <= '0';
        end if;
    end process timer_state;

    break on q_n;
end architecture behavioral;
```

A revised entity and architecture body for a resettable timer, including generic constants.

The entity might be instantiated as follows, with actual values for the generic constants specified in the generic map:

```
interval_timer : entity work.timer(behavioral)
    generic map ( threshold => 2.5,
                        clamp_on_resistance => 0.01,
                        clamp_off_resistance => 10.0E+6 )
    port map ( trigger_n => start_n, reset => reset, q => time_out,
                        rc_ext => interval_rc );
```

12.2 Parameterizing Structure

The second main use of generic constants in entities is to parameterize their structure. We can use the value of a generic constant to specify the size of an array port. To see why this is useful, let us look at an entity declaration for a register. A register entity that uses an unconstrained array type for its input and output ports can be declared as

```
entity reg is
    port ( d : in bit_vector;  q : out bit_vector;  ... );
end entity reg;
```

While this is a perfectly legal entity declaration, it does not include the constraint that the input and output ports d and q should be of the same size. Thus we could write a component instantiation as follows:

```
signal small_data : bit_vector(0 to 7);
signal large_data : bit_vector(0 to 15);
...
problem_reg : entity work.reg
    port map ( d => small_data,  q => large_data, ... );
```

The model is analyzed and elaborated without the error being detected. It is only when the register tries to assign a small bit vector to a target bit vector of a larger size that the error is detected. We can avoid this problem by including a generic constant in the entity declaration to parameterize the size of the ports. We use the generic constant in constraints in the port declarations. To illustrate, here is the register entity declaration rewritten:

```
entity reg is
    generic ( width : positive );
    port ( d : in bit_vector(0 to width − 1);
              q : out bit_vector(0 to width − 1);
```

```
        ... );
end entity reg;
```

In this declaration we require that the user of the register specify the desired port width for each instance. The entity then uses the width value as a constraint on both the input and output ports, rather than allowing their size to be determined by the signals associated with the ports. A component instantiation using this entity might appear as follows:

```
signal in_data, out_data : bit_vector(0 to bus_size − 1);
...

ok_reg : entity work.reg
    generic map ( width => bus_size )
    port map ( d => in_data,  q => out_data, ... );
```

If the signals used as actual ports in the instantiation were of different sizes, the analyzer would signal the error early in the design process, making it easier to correct. As a matter of style, whenever the sizes of different array ports of an entity are related, generic constants should be considered to enforce the constraint.

Example   A complete model for the register, including the entity declaration and an architecture body, is shown in Figure 12-3. The generic constant is used to constrain the widths of the data input and output ports in the entity declaration. It is also used in the architecture body to determine the size of the constant bit vector **zero**. This bit vector is the value assigned to the register output when it is reset, so it must be of the same size as the register port.

We can create instances of the register entity in a design, each possibly having different-sized ports. For example:

```
word_reg : entity work.reg(behavioral)
    generic map ( width => 32 )
    port map ( ... );
```

creates an instance with 32-bit-wide ports. In the same design, we might include another instance, as follows:

```
subtype state_vector is bit_vector(1 to 5);
...

state_reg : entity work.reg(behavioral)
    generic map ( width => state_vector'length )
    port map ( ... );
```

This register instance has 5-bit-wide ports, wide eno h to store values of the subtype state_vector.

FIGURE 12-3

```
entity reg is
    generic ( width : positive );
    port ( d :  in  bit_vector(0 to width − 1);
           q :  out  bit_vector(0 to width − 1);
           clk, reset : in bit );
end entity reg;
```

```
architecture behavioral of reg is
begin
    behavior : process (clk, reset) is
        constant zero : bit_vector(0 to width − 1) := (others => '0');
    begin
        if reset = '1' then
            q <= zero;
        elsif clk'event and clk = '1' then
            q <= d;
        end if;
    end process behavior;
end architecture behavioral;
```

An entity and architecture body for a register with parameterized port size.

The use of generic constants to constrain the size of an array port does not just apply to signal ports. We can also use generic constants to constrain the size of array quantity and terminal ports.

Example Figure 12-4 shows a model of a multiple-opamp module in which the number of opamps is specified by the generic constant **size**. The entity has two terminal ports of the composite nature **electrical_vector**, both constrained using **size**. The generic **gains** is a real vector intended to have one gain value per opamp. However, since VHDL-AMS does not permit us to refer to the value of a generic constant in the same generic list as it is defined, we cannot use **size** to constrain the vector gains. Instead, we leave it unconstrained and include a concurrent assertion statement in the architecture body to ensure that the actual gains-vector value supplied on instantiation is of the correct size. The architecture body includes a procedural to amplify each input voltage quantity by the corresponding gain to determine each output voltage quantity.

FIGURE 12-4

```
library ieee_proposed;  use ieee_proposed.electrical_systems.all;
entity multiple_opamp is
    generic ( size : positive;
                    gains : real_vector );
    port ( terminal inputs, outputs : electrical_vector(1 to size) );
end entity multiple_opamp;

--------------------------------------------------------

architecture ideal of multiple_opamp is

    quantity v_in across i_in through inputs to electrical_ref;
    quantity v_out across outputs to electrical_ref;
    alias gains_alias : real_vector(1 to size) is gains;
begin
    assert gains'length = size
        report "gains vector size differs from input/output size";

    amplify : procedural is
    begin
        for index in 1 to size loop
            v_out(index) := v_in(index) * gains_alias(index);
        end loop;
    end procedural amplify;
end architecture ideal;
```

A model of a multiple-opamp module using a generic constant to specify the number of opamps.

We can instantiate the multiple-opamp entity to provide eight opamps all with unity gain as follows:

```
constant num_sensors : positive := 8;
terminal sensors_raw,
            sensors_buffered : electrical_vector(num_sensors – 1 downto 0);
    ...
buf_amps : entity work.multiple_opamp(ideal)
    generic map ( size => num_sensors,
                    gains => real_vector'(num_sensors – 1 downto 0 => 1.0) )
    port map ( sensors_raw, sensors_buffered );
```

The elements of the actual terminals are associated left to right with the elements of the terminal ports.

Exercises

1. [❶ 12.1] Add to the following entity interface a generic clause defining generic constants Tpw_clk_h and Tpw_clk_l that specify the minimum clock pulse width timing. Both generic constants have a default value of 3 ns.

    ```
    entity flipflop is
         port ( clk, d : in bit;  q, q_n : out bit );
    end entity flipflop;
    ```

2. [❶ 12.1] Add to the following entity interface a generic clause defining generic constants r_nom, temp, W and L that specify the nominal resistance, the temperature, the channel width and the length of a resistor. The generic constants have default values of 1000.0 Ω, 298.0 K, 0.0 m and 0.0 m, respectively.

    ```
    entity resistor is
         port ( terminal node1, node2 : electrical );
    end entity resistor;
    ```

3. [❶ 12.1] Write a component instantiation statement that instantiates the following entity from the current working library. The actual value for the generic constant should be 10 ns, and the clk signal should be associated with a signal called master_clk.

    ```
    entity clock_generator is
         generic ( period : delay_length );
         port ( clk : out std_ulogic );
    end entity clock_generator;
    ```

4. [❶ 12.2] Following is an incomplete entity interface that uses a generic constant to specify the sizes of the standard-logic vector input and output ports. Complete the interface by filling in the types of the ports.

    ```
    entity adder is
         generic ( data_length : positive );
         port ( a, b : in ...;  sum : out ... );
    end entity adder;
    ```

5. [❶ 12.2] A system has an 8-bit data bus declared as

    ```
    signal data_out : bit_vector(7 downto 0);
    ```

    Write a component instantiation statement that instantiates the **reg** entity defined in Figure 12-3 to implement a 4-bit control register. The register data input connects to the rightmost four bits of **data_out**, the clk input to io_write, the reset input to io_reset and the data output bits to control signals io_en, io_int_en, io_dir and io_mode.

6. [❷ 12.1] Develop a behavioral model of a D-latch with separate generic constants for specifying the following propagation delays:

    *   rising data input to rising data output,

- falling data input to falling data output,

- rising enable input to rising data output and

- rising enable input to falling data output.

7. [❷ 12.1] Develop a behavioral model of a counter with output of type **natural** and clock and reset inputs of type **bit**. The counter has a Boolean generic constant, **trace_reset**. When this is true, the counter reports a trace message each time the reset input is activated.

8. [❷ 12.2] Develop a behavioral model of the adder described in Exercise 4.

9. [❷ 12.2] Develop a behavioral model of a capacitor with a generic constant for capacitance.

10. [❷ 12.2] Develop a behavioral model of a spring with a generic constant for the spring constant.

11. [❷ 12.2] Develop a behavioral model of a multiplexer with n select inputs, 2^n data inputs and one data output.

12. [❷ 12.2] Develop a behavioral model of an operational amplifier with terminals for the positive and negative inputs, high and low supply rails and an output. The amplifier should have its gain and input impedance specified by generic constants.

13. [❸] Develop a behavioral model of a RAM with generic constants governing the read access time, minimum write time, the address port width and the data port width.

chapter thirteen

Frequency and Transfer Function Modeling

Frequency modeling and noise analysis are very important when describing analog and mixed-signal systems. The ability to specify transfer functions in the frequency domain is also quite useful in modeling systems. In this chapter we look at the mechanisms provided by VHDL-AMS for modeling spectral and noise sources as well as for transfer functions in the frequency domain.

13.1 Frequency-Based Modeling

Although the discussions thus far in this book have focused on time-based modeling and simulation with VHDL-AMS, we can also represent frequency domain concepts in VHDL-AMS. In this chapter, we focus on modeling frequency-based views of a system and the interaction between time-based and frequency-based views. We start with small-signal frequency simulation to calculate the frequency response of a system over a range of frequencies. Next, we consider capabilities in VHDL-AMS for modeling noise. Finally, we discuss VHDL-AMS support for Laplace and Z transfer functions in the frequency domain.

As all engineering students learn during their undergraduate studies, frequency is an important aspect of a system's behavior. In electrical systems, we often see filters that pass or amplify certain frequency ranges and attenuate others. Mechanical systems often have resonant frequencies for oscillation. Control systems often employ feedback in which frequency-related issues are key aspects of the system behavior. Because the focus of this book is the VHDL-AMS language and its use, we will not discuss the area of signals and systems in detail. Readers seeking additional information on this area should seek out the standard texts used in junior- and senior-level courses. Books such as the one by Oppenheim, Willsky and Nawab [30] are particularly helpful. Before we discuss the frequency modeling aspects of VHDL-AMS, let us recall some of the most important considerations in representing signals and the frequency domain.

We often characterize the frequency aspects of a signal using a sum of sinusoidal waveforms with different frequencies and magnitudes, as in a Fourier series representation of a signal. Because any periodic function can be represented using an infinite series of sinusoids, the Fourier series of a signal is constructed based on a fundamental frequency ω_0 and the infinite summation of sinusoids with frequency $n\omega_0$. Recall that each of these sinusoids has its own magnitude and phase.

Because of the notion of superposition in linear circuits, we can characterize the response of a system to a periodic input consisting of a sum of sinusoids by first computing the response for each of the constituent sinusoidal waveforms. The system response is found by then summing each of the resulting outputs. We define the collection of all of the sinusoidal components of a signal to be its spectrum. The superposition principle, when applied in conjunction with the spectral components of an input signal, enables us to find the response of a system to an input signal. Hence, for a linear circuit excited by a sinusoidal stimulus, all of the branch voltages and currents in the circuit are also sinusoidal with the same frequency as the stimulus. Of course, the magnitudes and phases of the voltages and currents may be scaled and shifted, respectively. Using superposition and an infinite series of sinusoidal stimuli, we can apply any periodic input signal and ascertain its output.

Because we so often encounter sinusoidal inputs, engineers often represent the sinusoids as equivalent complex numbers using Euler's identity. A *phasor* is a shorthand for a sinusoid that provides a frequency domain representation of the sinusoid. The following are equivalent for linear systems:

Time domain: $v(t) = M\cos(\omega t + \phi)$

Frequency domain (phasor): $V(j\omega) = Me^{j\phi}$

VHDL-AMS provides the ability to characterize transfer functions in the frequency domain. Given an input signal, the transfer functions describe the output as a function of the magnitude and frequency of the input sinusoids. If we view the input signal as a sum of sinusoids (which we can think of as a set of phasors), the transfer functions produce an output that is the superposition of each of the input sinusoids. We will discuss the details of how to express these transfer functions in VHDL-AMS later in this chapter.

Note that VHDL-AMS does not provide a Laplace or Fourier transform mechanism to translate between the time and frequency domains. Rather, the Laplace and Z transfer functions provide a mechanism for expressing system behavior as a function of frequency, even when the system simulation proceeds in the time domain throughout.

Before we consider transfer functions in detail, let us first consider small-signal frequency modeling for our system. In essence, we are considering small changes in the across and through quantities (such as voltage and current) superimposed on a DC operating point. As we consider small-signal frequency modeling, an important consideration to remember for continuous simulations is the execution time. In particular, the mathematical formulation used for the model has significant impact on the execution time, and even on our general ability to find a solution. In order to reduce small-signal frequency simulation execution time and the likelihood of solvability issues, simulators often use a linearized form of the circuit at the DC operating point. VHDL-AMS defines linearized forms for use in small-signal frequency and noise simulation to allow us to use superposition.

Intuitively, a linearized form of an expression is simply one in which the characteristic expressions that describe system behavior are substituted with linear expressions. Thus, any nonlinear models for system behavior are replaced by a linear expression that is the slope of the curve at the operating point. In general, the linear form has much better properties with respect to execution time and solvability than the nonlinear form. The specific linear model for the system depends on the current operating point, so we must find the operating point before substituting the linear form.

Example Consider the current/voltage (I/V) curve of a diode characterized by the nonlinear relationship illustrated in Figure 13-1. Although it appears as one continuous nonlinear curve, we can think of the diode transfer function as consisting of multiple regions of operation.

Now let us assume we wish to perform a small-signal AC analysis on the diode. We first obtain an operating point. For this example, suppose the operating point is (V_1, I_1) in the forward-biased region of the diode. We perform the actual AC analysis on a linear segment, the slope of which matches that of the forward-biased region. Figure 13-2 illustrates this AC linearized "model" of the diode at the given operating point. The linear segment used for the analysis is shown in bold superimposed on the I/V curve.

FIGURE 13·1

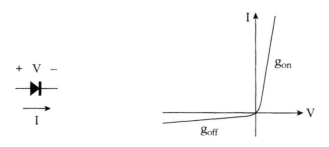

Diode symbol (left) and nonlinear transfer function (right).

FIGURE 13·2

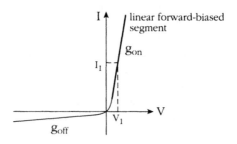

Nonlinear diode transfer function with linear segment emphasized.

For systems described in VHDL-AMS, the simulator determines the linear segments that represent a given model for AC analysis. We do not explicitly specify this information in the VHDL-AMS model itself.

Recall that in Chapter 2 we introduced the predefined VHDL-AMS type domain_type, which is used to specify the kind of analysis being performed by a simulator. As a reminder, the type is defined as

type domain_type **is** (quiescent_domain, time_domain, frequency_domain);

We discussed quiescent and time domain simulation in Chapter 7. We now turn to frequency domain simulation. The simulator uses the predefined signal domain of type domain_type during the simulation cycle to determine the type of operations the simulator must perform. The domain signal takes on the value quiescent_domain in the first delta cycles of a simulation during which a quiescent point (also known as the operating point, Q point or DC bias point) is computed. For time-based simulations, the domain signal is subsequently updated to time_domain, and the simulation proceeds as we discussed in Chapter 7. For small-signal frequency-based simulations, the domain signal is updated to frequency_domain, and the simulation proceeds as we discuss below.

Having computed the quiescent point, the simulator builds the small-signal model by replacing each explicit characteristic expression by its linear form for small-signal frequency domain calculations and small-signal noise calculations. (We discuss noise in the next section.) Additionally, the simulator replaces the implicit characteristic expressions of the model. The implicit characteristic expressions related to quantities of the form Q'dot, Q'integ and Q'delayed(T) are replaced by their respective forms after performing a Fourier transform. In some cases, the simulator must also replace the implicit characteristic expression corresponding to some source quantities; this will be discussed below. We note that nothing needs to be done to the other implicit characteristic expressions, such as the implicit structural characteristic equations that ensure conservation of energy. Because they are linear, their linearized form is identical to their original form.

With the small-signal frequency simulation model prepared, we can now sweep across a range of frequency values to determine the spectral behavior of the system. As we sweep across frequencies, we can observe the frequency response of the system to inputs at different frequencies. With a stimulus comprised of a set of sinusoids at different frequencies, we can then employ the frequency response information gathered from the frequency sweeps to understand the system behavior at an operating point. For readers interested in the underlying details of spectral analysis and simulation, the book by Pillage [31] is an excellent reference for additional information on small-signal frequency domain analysis.

Spectral Source Quantities

We now consider the VHDL-AMS mechanism to specify the energy sources in the frequency domain for our system. For small-signal frequency simulations, a VHDL-AMS simulator makes use of spectral sources that we specify in our model as *spectral source quantities*. The spectral source quantities are stimuli for the frequency domain simulations. Recall that a sinusoidal signal can be characterized by the equation

$$v(t) = M\cos(\omega t + \phi)$$

A spectral source quantity declaration allows us to specify a quantity in this form. The simulator chooses values for the frequency ω, and we specify values for the magnitude M and the phase ϕ in the declaration. During frequency simulation, the simulator includes characteristic equations derived from the spectral source declarations in the frequency domain augmentation set.

A spectral source quantity declaration is a new form of quantity declaration. The simplified syntax rules are

quantity_declaration ⇐
    quantity identifier ⦃ , ... ⦄ : subtype_indication source_aspect ;

source_aspect ⇐
    spectrum *magnitude*_simple_expression , *phase*_simple_expression

The subtype indication serves the same purpose as in a free quantity declaration, namely, to indicate the type of values that the source quantity can take on. It must be a floating-point type or a composite type whose scalar elements are of a floating-point type. The new part of the declaration is the source aspect, in which we write expressions to specify the magnitude and phase of the source quantity. For example, the declaration

    quantity spec_source : real **spectrum** 2.5, math_pi / 2.0;

defines a spectral source named **spec_source** that has a magnitude of 2.5 and a phase of $\pi/2$. This corresponds to the sinusoidal input

$$v(t) = 2.5\cos(\omega t + \pi/2)$$

The magnitude and phase expressions in a spectral source quantity declaration must be of the same type as the source quantity. This ensures that there are magnitude and phase values corresponding to each scalar element of the source quantity. Furthermore, the expressions are not required to be static, so they can refer to quantities and signals defined in the model.

It is important to note that source quantities are only useful for small-signal frequency analyses. During computation of the quiescent point and in time domain simulation, the value of a source quantity is constrained to be zero. This allows us to add a source quantity as a term in an expression or equation with no effect except in small-signal simulation. There, its effect is as expected, due to the substitution of the linearized form and the corresponding calculations to obtain small-signal results.

Example Suppose we wish to provide a voltage source as a stimulus for a system. The voltage source should allow us to find the frequency response of the system during frequency simulations, but act as a DC source for other simulations. We can simply define the voltage source as shown in Figure 13-3. The generic constants specify the DC voltage, AC magnitude in volts and the AC phase in degrees. The phase expression in the spectral source quantity declaration converts the phase generic constant to radians per second. The simultaneous if statement selects between a constant output voltage for quiescent and time simulation, and an AC output voltage for frequency simulation.

FIGURE 13-3

```
library ieee;  use ieee.math_real.all;
library ieee_proposed;  use ieee_proposed.electrical_systems.all;
entity v_source is
     generic ( DC : voltage := 1.0;          -- output peak amplitude
                    ac_mag : voltage := 1.0;      -- AC magnitude
                    ac_phase : real := 0.0 );     -- AC phase [degree]
          port ( terminal pos, neg : electrical );
end entity v_source;
```

```
architecture behavior of v_source is
     quantity vout across iout through pos to neg;
     -- declare quantity in frequency domain for AC analysis
     quantity ac_spec : real spectrum ac_mag, math_2_pi*ac_phase/360.0;
begin
     if domain = quiescent_domain or domain = time_domain use
          vout == DC;
     else
          vout == ac_spec;   -- used for frequency (AC) analysis
     end use;
end architecture behavior;
```

A model of a voltage source with DC behavior for quiescent and time simulation and AC behavior for frequency simulation.

In order for us to be able to specify a frequency-dependent spectrum, VHDL-AMS provides the predefined function **frequency**, defined as

function frequency **return** real;

As the simulator sweeps across the frequency spectrum during frequency simulation, the frequency function returns the simulation frequency at each point in the sweep. We can use the function in the magnitude and phase expressions of a spectral source quantity declaration to make the magnitude and phase of the source dependent on the frequency. Indeed, we can only refer to the frequency function in source quantity declarations. In any other place in a model, such as in a simultaneous statement, it is illegal to refer to the function.

As an example, suppose we have a function **inverse_exp** that returns the value of $10.0e^{-2 \times 10^{-6}x}$ when given a parameter x. We can use the function in a spectral source quantity declaration as follows:

quantity source1 : real **spectrum** inverse_exp(frequency), math_pi / 4.0;

This results in a small-signal sinusoidal input of the following form:

$$v(t) = 10.0e^{-2 \times 10^{-6}\omega}\cos(\omega t + \pi/4)$$

As mentioned above, we can also make the phase a function of the frequency. For example, we might declare a quantity whose phase varies linearly with frequency as follows:

quantity source2 : real **spectrum** 5.0, 1.0E–6 * frequency / math_pi;

Example   Suppose we wish to provide a voltage source similar to the one described above, but that is constrained to a specified range of frequencies. The revised model is shown in Figure 13-4. The generics min_freq and max_freq specify the bounds of the frequency range in radians per second. The function g within the architecture body returns 1.0 if its argument is within the frequency range and 0.0 otherwise. The spectral source quantity declaration uses the function g, passing it the simulation frequency, and scaling the source magnitude by the result. Thus, the source has the specified magnitude within the frequency range of interest and a magnitude of zero outside that range.

FIGURE 13-4

```
library ieee;  use ieee.math_real.all;
library ieee_proposed;  use ieee_proposed.electrical_systems.all;

entity v_source is
    generic ( DC : voltage := 1.0;         -- output peak amplitude
              min_freq : real := 10.0;     -- minimum frequency for spectral source
              max_freq : real := 1.0e4;    -- maximum frequency for spectral source
              ac_mag : voltage := 1.0;     -- AC magnitude
              ac_phase : real := 0.0 );    -- AC phase [degree]
    port ( terminal pos, neg : electrical );
end entity v_source;
```

```
architecture behavior of v_source is
    function g (freq : real) return real is
    begin
        if (freq > min_freq and freq < max_freq) then
            return 1.0;
        else
            return 0.0;
        end if;
    end function g;
```

```
        quantity vout across iout through pos to neg;
        -- declare quantity in frequency domain for AC analysis
        quantity ac_spec : real spectrum ac_mag*g(frequency),
                                        math_2_pi*ac_phase/360.0;
    begin
        if domain = quiescent_domain or domain = time_domain use
            vout == DC;
        else
            vout == ac_spec;   -- used for frequency (AC) analysis
        end use;
    end architecture behavior;
```

A voltage source whose magnitude is non-zero only within a specified frequency range.

13.2 Noise Modeling

When we model the behavior of a system, we often need to analyze the impact of device-generated noise in a circuit or the system's sensitivity to input noise. VHDL-AMS provides a second form of source quantity, a noise source quantity, to allow us to perform noise analysis. The complete syntax rules for a source quantity declaration are

quantity_declaration ⇐
    quantity identifier ⟦ , ₀₀₀ ⟧ : subtype_indication source_aspect ;

source_aspect ⇐
    spectrum *magnitude*_simple_expression , *phase*_simple_expression
    ⟦ **noise** *power*_simple_expression

These rules show that there are two kinds of source quantities in VHDL-AMS: spectral sources and noise sources, distinguished by the form of the source aspect used in the declaration. We discussed spectral sources in Section 13.1. Both kinds of source quantity provide stimulus for small-signal frequency domain simulation. In the case of a noise source quantity declaration, the expression after the keyword **noise** specifies the power of the noise source. The expression must be of the same type as the noise source quantity, to ensure that there are scalar power elements corresponding to each scalar element of the quantity. The expression is evaluated at each frequency point in the frequency sweep during frequency simulation to determine the power level of the source quantity at that frequency. The power expression is not required to be static, so it can refer to the values of quantities and signals in the model.

As with spectral source quantities, noise source quantities are only useful for small-signal frequency analyses. During computation of the quiescent point and in time domain simulation, both spectral and noise source quantities are constrained to be zero. During frequency simulation, however, the effects of the noise source quantities are computed at each frequency in the frequency sweep. The simulator computes the effect of each noise source individually at each frequency by evaluating the noise power expression and allowing the noise quantity to take on a value that is the square root of the power. The model equations are then solved with the single noise quantity having its effect. The simulator can then sum the effects on quantities in the model affected by each of the noise sources to obtain the aggregate noise effect.

One common kind of noise is thermal noise, which arises due to the random thermal motion of electrons. Thermal noise is highly dependent on the temperature of the resistor or active device, but does not depend on the presence of an electric field. (See reference [19] or [22] for an excellent treatment of noise in circuits.) We can model thermal noise in a resistor using a noise source quantity declared as

> **quantity** thermal_noise_source : real **noise** 4.0 * k_Boltzmann * temp * res;

This noise source quantity introduces white noise with a power based on the temperature. We can include this quantity in our model by adding it to the resistive voltage drop in a simultaneous statement:

> resistor_voltage == resistor_current * res + thermal_noise_source;

Note that the noise is white because it does not depend on the frequency. To produce shaped noise we can use the predefined **frequency** function that we discussed in Section 13.1. When modeling transistors, we may have a power gain function of the form $G(f)$ to model the frequency dependence of the noise. Based on this, we can define a frequency-dependent noise source as follows:

> **quantity** shaped_noise_source : real **noise** k_noise * temp * G(frequency);

Another common kind of noise is flicker noise, especially for channel current [24]. The flicker noise is dependent on the frequency of the transistor.

> **quantity** flicker_noise_source : real **noise** k_flicker * ids**af / frequency;

Using these forms of noise source quantities, we can consider the effect of various noise sources in our system. Using superposition, the overall effects of noise on system operation can then be determined. Of course, this depends on the noise sources being independent, which is generally true for circuit noise sources.

Example Let us consider a MOS (metal oxide semiconductor) transistor and the effect of thermal and flicker noise on its operation. The channel under a MOS gate is resistive, and therefore exhibits thermal noise. MOS transistors also exhibit flicker noise due to surface states trapping and releasing current carriers. These two noise sources can be combined into one noise generator as discussed in [19]. The model shown in Figure 13-5 describes the behavior of a MOS transistor including the effects of both thermal and flicker noise.

FIGURE 13-5

```
library ieee;  use ieee.math_real.all;
library ieee_proposed;  use ieee_proposed.electrical_systems.all;
entity NMOS_transistor is
     generic ( Cgs : real := 1.0e–6;        -- gate to source capacitance
               Cgd : real := 1.0e–6;        -- gate to drain capacitance
               gm : real := 5.0e–4;         -- transconductance
               temp : real := 1.0;          -- termperature
               Ro : real := 500.0e3;        -- ro resistance
               af : real := 1.0;            -- flicker noise exponent constant
               k_flicker : real := 1.0 );   -- flicker noise constant
     port ( terminal gate, drain, source : electrical );
end entity NMOS_transistor;
```

```
architecture noisy of NMOS_transistor is
     quantity vgs across igs through gate to source;
     quantity vds across ids through drain to source;
     quantity vsd across source to drain;
     quantity vgd across igd through gate to drain;
     constant threshold_voltage : voltage := 1.0;
     constant k : real := 1.0e–5;
     -- declare quantity in frequency domain for AC analysis
     quantity MOS_noise_source : real noise
                              4.0*K*temp/Ro +           -- thermal noise
                              k_flicker*ids**af/frequency;   -- flicker noise
begin
     if domain = quiescent_domain or domain = time_domain use
          if vds >= 0.0 use   -- transistor is forward biased
               if vgs < threshold_voltage use   -- cutoff region
                    ids == 0.0;
               elsif vds > vgs – threshold_voltage use   -- saturation region
                    ids == 0.5 * k * (vgs – threshold_voltage)**2;
               else   -- linear/triode region
                    ids == k * (vgs – threshold_voltage – 0.5*vds) * vds;
               end use;
          else   -- transistor is reverse biased
               if vgd < threshold_voltage use   -- cutoff region
                    ids == 0.0;
               elsif vsd > vgd – threshold_voltage use   -- saturation region
                    ids == –0.5 * k * (vgd – threshold_voltage)**2;
               else   -- linear/triode region
                    ids == –k * (vgd – threshold_voltage – 0.5*vsd) * vsd;
```

(continued on page 412)

(continued from page 411)

```
              end use;
          end use;
          igs == 0.0;
          igd == 0.0;
      else   -- noise and frequency model
          igs == Cgs*vgs'dot;
          igd == Cgd*vgd'dot;
          ids == gm*vgs + vds/Ro + MOS_noise_source;
      end use;
  end architecture noisy;
```

A model of a MOS transistor that exhibits thermal and flicker noise effects.

Using this model, we can perform small-signal noise calculations for MOS transistors that include both the thermal and flicker noise effects. When performing quiescent or time-based simulations, the model performs as discussed in Chapter 6.

13.3 Laplace Transfer Functions

Quite often it is convenient to specify system functionality in terms of continuous transfer functions in the frequency domain. The Laplace transfer function implements a ratio of two polynomials in the Laplace operator s. In the time domain, this corresponds to a linear ordinary differential equation with constant coefficients.

In VHDL-AMS the Laplace transfer function is provided by the 'ltf attribute. Given any scalar quantity **Q**, the attribute Q'ltf(num, den) yields a quantity whose type is the the base type of **Q** and whose value is the Laplace transform of **Q**. The numerator and denominator polynomials, **num** and **den**, respectively, are specified as **real_vector** arrays, with the requirement that the first element of the denominator array must not be 0.0. The numerator and denominator polynomial vectors must be constant to permit an analytical transformation of the resulting characteristic expressions into the frequency domain.

The numerator and denominator represent the frequency response of the transfer function. By examining the numerator to find what values of s result in a zero value, we can determine the zeros of the transfer function. Similarly, we can examine the denominator to find what values of s result in a zero value to find the poles of the transfer function. When we plot the poles and zeros, we can determine a number of important aspects of the system. The poles of the transfer function yield the roots of the natural response of the system, or the natural frequencies of the system. For a complete treatment of poles and zeros, as well as their implications on system behavior, a text on signals and systems or on control systems would be helpful. Good examples include Ogata [28]; Oppenheim, Willsky and Nawab [30]; and D'Azzo and Houpis [11].

To illustrate modeling using transfer functions, we will examine several models of a low-pass filter circuit. We will start with a simple structural model, then consider behavioral models expressed using differential equations and Laplace transfer functions.

Example Figure 13-6 shows a simple R-C (resistor/capacitor) circuit for a low-pass filter. For this filter, we select the desired –3 dB gain frequency and then calculate the values of R and C that place a pole f_p at that frequency. For example, suppose we want the –3 dB gain frequency to occur at 10 Hz (62.83 rad/s). We calculate the values of R and C as follows:

$$\tau_p = 1/f_p = 1/62.83 = 15.9 \text{ ms}$$
$$\tau_p = RC$$

If we let $C = 1 \text{ μF}$, then $R = \tau_p/C = 15.9 \text{ ms}/1 \text{ μF} = 15.9 \text{ kΩ}$.

Figure 13-7 shows a structural model of the filter. In this implementation, we simply instantiate and connect existing models for a resistor and capacitor. We provide values for the generic constants based on the calculations shown above.

FIGURE 13-6

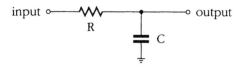

Schematic representation of R-C low-pass filter.

FIGURE 13-7

```
library ieee_proposed;  use ieee_proposed.electrical_systems.all;
entity lowpass is
    port ( terminal input : electrical;
            terminal output : electrical );
end entity lowpass;
```

```
architecture RC of lowpass is
begin
```

(continued on page 414)

(continued from page 413)

    R : **entity** work.resistor(ideal)
        generic map (res => 15.9e3)
        port map (p1 => input, p2 => output);

    C : **entity** work.capacitor(ideal)
        generic map (cap => 1.0e–6)
        port map (p1 => output, p2 => electrical_ref);

end architecture RC;

Low-pass filter implemented as the structural combination of a resistor and capacitor.

The frequency and time domain simulation results for the structural R-C model are illustrated in Figure 13-8. The frequency domain response results from driving the filter with a spectral source quantity as described in Section 13.1. The time domain response results from driving the filter with a 100 Hz, 5 V peak-to-peak sine wave. As we would expect, the frequency domain response shows a voltage drop of –3 dB at 10 Hz. The time domain sine wave has an amplitude of 0.5 V,

---

FIGURE 13-8

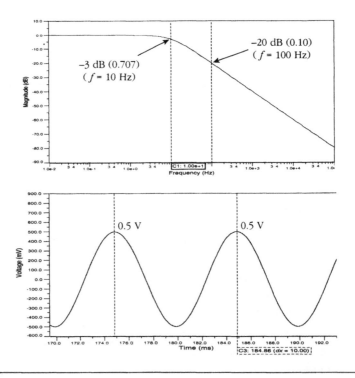

R-C low-pass filter simulation results.

which is expected for a 5 V, 100 Hz signal passing through a single-pole 10 Hz low-pass filter.

Example   We will now derive a behavioral model of the R-C filter circuit, expressed in terms of differential equations. We can determine the voltage transfer function by treating the circuit as a voltage divider as shown in the following equation:

$$\frac{v_{out}}{v_{in}} = \frac{Z_C}{R + Z_C} = \frac{\dfrac{1}{sC}}{R + \dfrac{1}{sC}} \tag{13-1}$$

where Z_C is the impedance of the capacitor. Multiplying both the numerator and denominator by sC results in

$$\frac{v_{out}}{v_{in}} = \frac{1}{RCs + 1} \tag{13-2}$$

This is the defining equation for the single-pole low-pass filter implemented with a resistor and capacitor. If we recall that

$$\tau_p = RC \tag{13-3}$$

where τ_p can be interpreted as "the time constant of the pole," Equation 13-2 can be expressed more generally as

$$\frac{v_{out}}{v_{in}} = \frac{1}{1 + s\tau_p} \tag{13-4}$$

We can easily implement Equation 13-4 in VHDL-AMS with either the 'dot or 'integ attributes. For this example we will use the 'dot attribute. A straightforward way in which to create a model is to transform Equation 13-4 in two steps. First, we simplify the equation. It is often helpful to solve for one quantity in the equation in terms of other quantities (although this is not strictly required). It is also advisable to avoid division as much as possible, particularly by anything whose value can change during the simulation. Second we substitute d/dt for s.

With these two steps in mind, we rearrange Equation 13-4 into the following form:

$$v_{in} = v_{out} + \tau_p \times \frac{dv_{out}}{dt} \tag{13-5}$$

Since we know that the derivative function d/dt can be implemented in VHDL-AMS models using the 'dot attribute, we can summarize the relationship between s, d/dt and 'dot as follows:

$s \rightarrow d/dt \rightarrow$ 'dot

A VHDL-AMS model that directly implements Equation 13-5 is shown in Figure 13-9. The frequency and time domain simulation results for this filter implementation are illustrated in Figure 13-10. These results were obtained using the same spectral source and sine wave stimuli that were used for the structural model in the previous example.

The filter model illustrated in Figure 13-9 specifies the low-pass response directly with the time constant τ_p. However, the filter would more likely be referred to as a "10 Hz low-pass filter" since the pole location f_p (–3 dB gain frequency) is specified as 10 Hz. In order to allow the model user to specify the filter's frequency response in hertz, yet still use the 'dot attribute in the model's equation, we could revise the model to define f_p as a constant and derive τ_p as follows:

```
constant fp : real := 10.0;          -- filter pole in hertz
constant wp : real := math_2_pi * fp;   -- filter pole in rad/s
constant tp : real := 1.0 / wp;      -- filter time constant
```

FIGURE 13-9

```
library ieee_proposed;  use ieee_proposed.electrical_systems.all;

entity lowpass is
    port ( terminal input : electrical;
           terminal output : electrical );
end entity lowpass;
```

```
architecture dot of lowpass is

    quantity vin across input to electrical_ref;
    quantity vout across iout through output to electrical_ref;
    constant tp : real := 15.9e–3;   -- filter time constant

begin

    vin == vout + tp * vout'dot;

end architecture dot;
```

Low-pass filter model using the 'dot attribute.

FIGURE 13-10

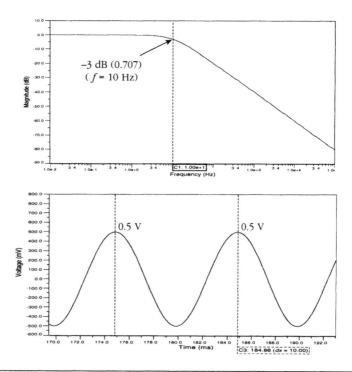

Frequency and time domain responses of low-pass filter implemented with 'dot.

The Laplace transfer function attribute gives an alternative way to express the systems of equations. Integration and differentiation are represented in the *s*-domain by multiplication and division by *s*, respectively. For common circuit components, we use impedances ($Z = R$ for resistors, $Z = 1/sC$ for capacitors and $Z = sL$ for inductors) when manipulating equations involving phasors. Of course, mechanical systems and systems in other energy domains have equivalent mappings to impedances.

Example   Recall the fundamental equation for the R-C filter topology as given in Equation 13-2.

$$\frac{v_{out}}{v_{in}} = \frac{1}{RCs + 1} \tag{13-6}$$

As we described the relationship between RC and τ_p in Equation 13-3, we can likewise express the relationship between RC and the pole frequency ω_p as follows:

$$w_p = \frac{1}{RC} \tag{13-7}$$

where ω_p specifies the filter pole location in rad/s. Equation 13-6 can now be expressed more generally as shown in Equation 13-8.

$$\frac{v_{out}}{v_{in}} = \frac{1}{1 + \dfrac{s}{\omega_p}} \tag{13-8}$$

If we now multiply Equation 13-8 through by ω_p, we have the following form:

$$\frac{v_{out}}{v_{in}} = \frac{\omega_p}{s + \omega_p} \tag{13-9}$$

We can use Equation 13-9 as the basis for the VHDL-AMS implementation of the filter using the 'ltf attribute, as shown in Figure 13-11. Because this model is implemented with the frequency-based 'ltf attribute, conversion from the filter pole location to an equivalent time constant is not required. The characteristic filter equation is also expressed in a more economical and intuitive manner with the 'ltf implementation.

The frequency and time domain responses for this filter implementation are illustrated in Figure 13-12. Inspection of the waveforms shows that they are equivalent to the waveforms given in Figure 13-10.

FIGURE 13-11

```
library ieee_proposed;  use ieee_proposed.electrical_systems.all;
library ieee;  use ieee.math_real.all;

entity lowpass is
    port ( terminal input : electrical;
           terminal output : electrical );
end entity lowpass;
```

```
architecture ltf of lowpass is
    quantity vin across input to electrical_ref;
    quantity vout across iout through output to electrical_ref;
    constant wp : real := 10.0 * math_2_pi;      -- pole in rad/s
    constant num : real_vector := (0 => wp);      -- numerator in s
    constant den : real_vector := (wp, 1.0);      -- denominator in s
begin
```

```
                vout == vin'ltf(num, den);

        end architecture ltf;
```

Low-pass filter model using the 'ltf attribute.

FIGURE 13-12

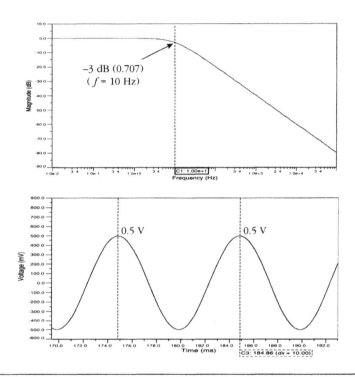

Frequency and time domain responses of low-pass filter implemented with 'ltf.

Use of the 'ltf attribute is not confined to small systems. In fact, as models become larger, the reasons for using the 'ltf attribute instead of the 'dot attribute become more compelling. It is far easier to derive and implement a higher-order transfer function as a simple ratio of *s*-domain polynomials than it is to derive the equivalent differential equations for the function. The following example illustrates the advantage of the 'ltf attribute over the 'dot attribute for a second-order model.

Example   Let us now reconsider the ideal opamp model introduced in Chapter 6. The model listing for the opamp is reproduced in Figure 13-13 for convenience. This opamp is actually modeled as a two-input electrical gain device, without any bandwidth limitations.

FIGURE 13-13

```
library ieee_proposed; use ieee_proposed.electrical_systems.all;
entity opamp is
    port ( terminal plus_in, minus_in, output : electrical );
end entity opamp;
```

```
architecture slew_limited of opamp is
    constant gain : real := 50.0;
    quantity v_in across plus_in to minus_in;
    quantity v_out across i_out through output;
    quantity v_amplified : voltage;
begin
    v_amplified == gain * v_in;

    v_out == v_amplified'slew(1.0e6,-1.0e6);
end architecture slew_limited;
```

Ideal opamp model without frequency response characteristics.

Due to the ideal nature of this model, it will not properly function at typical opamp gain values. One reason for this is that the model has no intrinsic frequency limiting. A more realistic opamp implementation would include the frequency response and other characteristics of an actual opamp device. Opamps can be modeled at various levels of complexity, with offset voltages and currents, power pins, input and output impedance and many other real-world behaviors. However, in this example, we simply extend the opamp model, representing it as a two-pole device with the frequency response characteristics shown in Figure 13-14. To keep the model as straighforward as possible, we do not include slew-rate limiting.

FIGURE 13-14

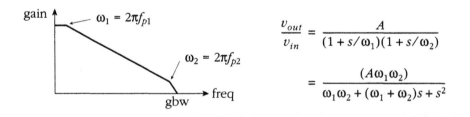

$$\frac{v_{out}}{v_{in}} = \frac{A}{(1 + s/\omega_1)(1 + s/\omega_2)}$$

$$= \frac{(A\omega_1\omega_2)}{\omega_1\omega_2 + (\omega_1 + \omega_2)s + s^2}$$

Two-pole opamp transfer function in the frequency domain.

Figure 13-15 shows the entity declaration and two architecture bodies for the revised opamp model. One architecture uses the 'dot attribute and the other uses the 'ltf attribute. We can see from the **dot** architecture that even a second-order equation can be fairly complicated when implemented in this manner. Contrast this to the **ltf** architecture, where the model equations are both easier to derive and to implement.

FIGURE 13-15

```
library ieee; use ieee.math_real.all;
library ieee_proposed; use ieee_proposed.electrical_systems.all;
entity opamp_2pole is
    port ( terminal in_pos, in_neg, output : electrical );
end entity opamp_2pole;
```

```
architecture dot of opamp_2pole is
    constant A : real := 1.0e6;              -- open loop gain
    constant fp1 : real := 5.0;             -- first pole
    constant fp2 : real := 9.0e5;           -- second pole
    constant tp1 : real := 1.0 / (fp1 * math_2_pi);   -- first time constant
    constant tp2 : real := 1.0 / (fp2 * math_2_pi);   -- second time constant
    quantity v_in across in_pos to in_neg;
    quantity v_out across i_out through output;
begin
    v_in == (tp1 * tp2) * v_out'dot'dot / A + (tp1 + tp2) * v_out'dot / A + v_out / A;
end architecture dot;
```

```
architecture ltf of opamp_2pole is
    constant A : real := 1.0e6;              -- open loop gain
    constant fp1 : real := 5.0;             -- first pole (Hz)
    constant fp2 : real := 9.0e5;           -- second pole (Hz)
    constant wp1 : real := fp1 * math_2_pi;     -- first pole (rad/s)
    constant wp2 : real := fp2 * math_2_pi;     -- second pole (rad/s)
    constant num : real_vector := (0 => wp1 * wp2 * A);
    constant den : real_vector := (wp1 * wp2, wp1 + wp2, 1.0);
    quantity v_in across in_pos to in_neg;
    quantity v_out across i_out through output;
begin
    v_out == v_in'ltf(num, den);
end architecture ltf;
```

Opamp with two poles implemented with the 'dot and 'ltf attributes.

With some simple additions to either of these architectures, we can develop a more useful opamp model. Figure 13-16 illustrates a revised version of the ltf architecture with generic constants for gain and pole frequencies, as well as for input and output resistance.

FIGURE 13-16

```
library ieee;  use ieee.math_real.all;
library ieee_proposed;  use ieee_proposed.electrical_systems.all;
entity opamp_2pole_res is
    generic ( A : real := 1.0e6;        -- open loop gain
              rin : real := 1.0e6;       -- input resistance
              rout : real := 100.0;      -- output resistance
              fp1 : real := 5.0;         -- first pole
              fp2 : real := 9.0e5 );     -- second pole
    port ( terminal in_pos, in_neg, output : electrical );
end entity opamp_2pole_res;
```

```
architecture ltf of opamp_2pole_res is
    constant wp1 : real := fp1 * math_2_pi;
    constant wp2 : real := fp2 * math_2_pi;
    constant num : real_vector := (0 => wp1 * wp2 * A);
    constant den : real_vector := (wp1 * wp2, wp1 + wp2, 1.0);
    quantity v_in across i_in through in_pos to in_neg;
    quantity v_out across i_out through output;
begin
    i_in  == v_in / rin;   -- input current
    v_out == v_in'ltf(num, den) + i_out * rout;
end architecture ltf;
```

Opamp model using 'ltf with input and output resistance.

As the previous examples show, the Laplace transfer function representation of a system is equivalent to its differential equation representation, but is often easier to derive and implement. In our VHDL-AMS models, we can express the differential equations directly using simultaneous statements, or we can express them using a Laplace transfer function. Alternatively, we can describe the system structurally using a set of interconnected component instances and rely on the elaborator of a VHDL-AMS simulator to create an equivalent set of characteristic equations.

13.4 **Discrete Transfer Functions and Sampling**

In the previous section, we examined use of the Laplace transform, which is a continuous transfer function. In many systems, it is also important to be able to model systems using discrete transfer functions. VHDL-AMS provides three quantity attributes, 'zoh, 'ztf and 'delayed, to support this modeling activity. The 'zoh and 'ztf attributes are used specifically for discrete modeling, while 'delayed is a general-purpose delay attribute. We examined the 'delayed attribute in Chapter 6.

Zero-Order Hold (ZOH)

The 'zoh attribute acts essentially as a sample-hold function. It allows for the periodic sampling of a quantity, the value of which is held between samples. The attribute is a useful primitive whose behavior cannot otherwise be described using the VHDL-AMS language; hence it is provided as an attribute built into the language. Given a quantity Q, the attribute Q'zoh(T, initial_delay) yields a quantity that is the value of Q sampled at the time given by initial_delay and at intervals of T thereafter. The quantity Q can be of any type, and the result of the attribute is of the same type as Q. The sampling interval is a static expression of type **real**, provided its value is greater than 0.0. Similarly, the initial delay is a static expression of type **real**, provided its value is non-negative. We can omit the initial delay expressions, writing Q'zoh(T), in which case the first sample is taken at time 0.0, after the quiescent state has been determined.

Example Let us consider again the continuous low-pass filter that we implemented using the 'ltf attribute in Section 13.3. The governing equation for this model implementation was

$$\frac{v_{out}}{v_{in}} = \frac{\omega_p}{s + \omega_p} \tag{13-10}$$

We can describe a discrete approximation of this filter with a z-domain transfer function. To create this approximation, we need to perform a conversion between the Laplace operator s and the z-domain operator z^{-1}. A popular conversion technique is known as the *bilinear transform*. To implement this transform, we substitute the right-hand side of the following equation for each occurrence of s in the equation to be transformed:

$$s = \frac{2}{T}\left(\frac{1 - z^{-1}}{1 + z^{-1}}\right) \tag{13-11}$$

If we replace s in Equation 13-10 with the right-hand expression from Equation 13-11, we generate a new equation that directly describes the filter in z-domain transfer function form:

$$\frac{v_{out}}{v_{in}} = \frac{T\omega_p z^0 + T\omega_p z^{-1}}{(T\omega_p + 2)z^0 + (T\omega_p - 2)z^{-1}} \tag{13-12}$$

We will use Equation 13-12 in our model implementation, since it lends itself to automatic calculation of the coefficients based on the sampling period and filter pole location. A more general expression for the z-domain version of the low-pass filter is given in Equation 13-13:

$$\frac{v_{out}}{v_{in}} = \frac{n_0 + n_1 z^{-1}}{d_0 + d_1 z^{-1}} \tag{13-13}$$

The VHDL-AMS implementation of the filter with 'zoh and 'delay involves two steps. First, we sample the continuous input quantity at discrete points in time using the 'zoh attribute. Then we implement the z-domain delay, z^{-1}, as needed using the 'delayed attribute. A model developed using this approach is illustrated in Figure 13-17. The continuous input quantity vin is sampled using 'zoh to produce the discrete vin_sampled quantity. The model equations are derived by introducing clock-cycle delayed quantities for vin (vin_zm1) and vout (vout_zm1). With these quantities, the describing equation is algebraically solved for vout. The coefficients n_0, n_1, n_2 and n_3 from Equation 13-13 map to the model constants n0, n1, d0 and d1, respectively. Detailed derivation of z-domain coefficients is

FIGURE 13-17

```
library ieee;  use ieee.math_real.all;
library ieee_proposed;  use ieee_proposed.electrical_systems.all;

entity lowpass is
    generic ( fp : real := 10.0;        -- pole in Hz for 'zoh, 'delayed
              Fsmp : real := 10.0e3 );  -- sample frequency for 'zoh, 'delayed
    port ( terminal input : electrical;
           terminal output: electrical );
end entity lowpass;

------------------------------------------------------------------

architecture z_minus_1 of lowpass is

    quantity vin across input to electrical_ref;
    quantity vout across iout through output to electrical_ref;
```

```
      quantity vin_sampled : real;              -- discrete sample of input quantity
      quantity vin_zm1, vout_zm1 : real;        -- z**-1
      constant Tsmp : real := 1.0 / Fsmp;       -- sample period
      constant wp : real := fp * math_2_pi;     -- pole in rad/s
      constant n0 : real := Tsmp * wp;          -- z0 numerator coefficient
      constant n1 : real := Tsmp * wp;          -- z-1 numerator coefficient
      constant d0 : real := Tsmp * wp + 2.0;    -- z0 denominator coefficient
      constant d1 : real := Tsmp * wp - 2.0;    -- z-1 denominator coefficient
begin
      vin_sampled  == vin'zoh(Tsmp);

      vin_zm1  == vin_sampled'delayed(Tsmp);

      vout_zm1 == vout'delayed(Tsmp);

      vout == vin_sampled * n0 / d0 + n1 * vin_zm1 / d0 - d1 * vout_zm1 / d0;
end z_minus_1;
```

Z-domain low-pass filter model using the 'zoh and 'delayed attributes.

FIGURE 13-18

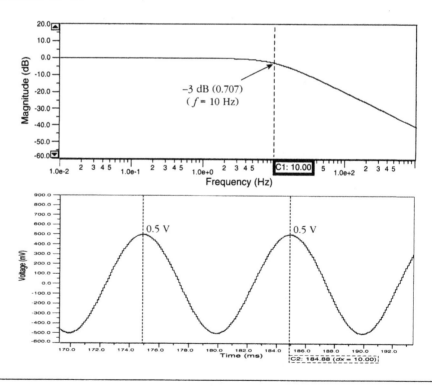

Frequency and time domain responses of the low-pass filter implemented using the 'zoh and 'delayed attributes.

presented in Case Study 2 in Chapter 14. A good general reference for discrete control systems is Ogata [29].

The frequency and time domain responses for this filter implementation are illustrated in Figure 13-18. Inspection of the waveforms shows that they are functionally equivalent to the waveforms given in Figures 13-8, 13-10 and 13-12.

Z Transfer Function (ZTF)

We saw above that VHDL-AMS provides the 'zoh and 'delayed attributes as primitive mechanisms for z-domain modeling. However, it also combines these capabilities in a single attribute, 'ztf, that we can often use to express a z-domain model more concisely. The 'ztf attribute, or "z-domain transfer function" attribute, implements a ratio of two polynomials in the variable z^{-1}, which represents a delay by a constant T.

Like the Laplace transfer function, the z-domain transfer function is defined as an attribute that yields a quantity. Given any scalar quantity Q, the attribute Q'ztf(num, den, T, initial_delay) yields a quantity whose type is the same as that of Q and whose value is the z-domain transform of Q. The numerator and denominator polynomials, num and den, respectively, are specified as real_vector arrays, with the requirement that the first element of the denominator array must not be 0.0. The numerator and denominator polynomial vectors must be constant, to permit an analytical transformation of the resulting characteristic expressions into the frequency domain. The quantity Q is sampled at the time given by initial_delay and at intervals of T thereafter. As with the 'zoh attribute, the sampling-interval expression must be static and yield a positive real value, and the initial-delay expression must be static and yield a non-negative real value. We can omit the initial-delay expressions, writing Q'ztf(num, den, T), in which case the first sample is taken at time 0.0, after the quiescent state has been determined.

Example   We return once again to the low-pass filter example. We can implement Equation 13-12 directly in a model using the 'ztf attribute, as illustrated in Figure 13-19. This model describes the numerator and denominator coefficients in ascending powers of z^{-1} (descending powers of z). This is a much more

---

FIGURE 13-19

```
library ieee;  use ieee.math_real.all;
library ieee_proposed;  use ieee_proposed.electrical_systems.all;

entity lowpass is
    generic ( fp : real := 10.0;          -- pole in Hz for 'ztf
              Fsmp : real := 10.0e3);     -- sample frequency for 'ztf
    port ( terminal input: electrical;
           terminal output: electrical );
end entity lowpass;
```

```
architecture ztf of lowpass is
    quantity vin across input to electrical_ref;
    quantity vout across iout through output to electrical_ref;
    constant Tsmp : real := 1.0 / Fsmp;        -- sample period
    constant wp : real := fp * math_2_pi;      -- pole in rad/s
    constant n0 : real := Tsmp * wp;           -- z0 numerator coefficient (a)
    constant n1 : real := Tsmp * wp;           -- z-1 numerator coefficient (b)
    constant d0 : real := Tsmp * wp + 2.0;     -- z0 denominator coefficient (c)
    constant d1 : real := Tsmp * wp - 2.0;     -- z-1 denominator coefficient (d)
    constant num : real_vector := (n0, n1);
    constant den : real_vector := (d0, d1);
begin
    vout == vin'ztf(num, den, Tsmp);
end ztf;
```

Z-domain low-pass filter model using the 'ztf attribute.

FIGURE 13-20

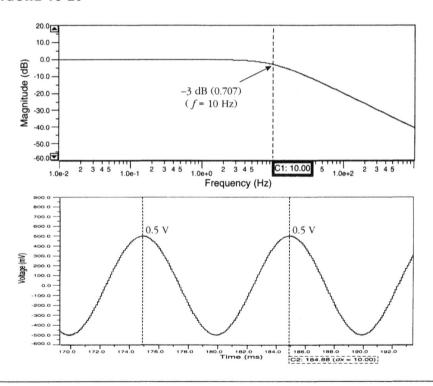

Frequency and time domain responses of the low-pass filter implemented using the 'ztf at-tribute.

straightforward and intuitive filter implementation than that shown in Figure 13-17, as no intermediate quantities need to be defined and the coefficients of Equation 13-12 map directly to those given in the model.

The frequency and time domain responses for this model implementation are illustrated in Figure 13-20. They appear as we would expect based on the previous simulation results we have seen.

Summary of Transfer Function Attributes

We have now discussed the relationships and differences between the 'dot, 'ltf, 'zoh and 'ztf attributes. Figure 13-21 summarizes the use of the attributes in the low-pass filter models and provides a comparison with the structural R-C implementation.

Figure 13-22 collects together the various implementations of the low-pass filter discussed in this chapter, with some minor enhancements. The structural architecture has been modified to automatically calculate the resistance value from the constant capacitance value and the filter pole frequency specified as a generic constant. The other architectures have all been modified to allow the user to specify the filter gain.

FIGURE 13-21

	Analytical relationship	*Language representation*	*Relationship with filter frequency, f_p*
Circuit elements		Netlist equations formulated by elaboration	$RC = \dfrac{1}{2\pi f_p}$
Differential equations	$\dfrac{v_{out}}{v_{in}} = \dfrac{1}{1 + s\tau_p}$	vin == vout + tp*vout'dot	$\tau_p = \dfrac{1}{2\pi f_p}$
Laplace transfer function	$\dfrac{v_{out}}{v_{in}} = \dfrac{\omega_p}{s + \omega_p}$	vout == vin'lft(num, den)	$\omega_p = 2\pi f_p$
Direct z^{-1}	$\dfrac{v_{out}}{v_{in}} = \dfrac{T\omega_p z^0 + T\omega_p z^{-1}}{(T\omega_p + 2)z^0 + (T\omega_p - 2)z^{-1}}$	vout == vin_sampled*n0/d0 + n1*vin_zm1/d0 - d1*vout_zm1/d0	$\omega_p = 2\pi f_p$
z-domain transfer function	$\dfrac{v_{out}}{v_{in}} = \dfrac{T\omega_p z^0 + T\omega_p z^{-1}}{(T\omega_p + 2)z^0 + (T\omega_p - 2)z^{-1}}$	vout == vin'Ztf(num,den,Tsmp)	$\omega_p = 2\pi f_p$

Relationships between transfer function attributes.

FIGURE 13-22

```
library ieee;  use ieee.math_real.all;
library ieee_proposed;  use ieee_proposed.electrical_systems.all;
entity lowpass is
    generic ( gain : real := 1.0;       -- gain for 'dot, 'ltf, and 'ztf
              fp : real := 10.0;        -- pole in Hz for 'dot, 'ltf, and 'ztf
              Fsmp : real := 10.0e3 );  -- sample frequency for ztf
        port ( terminal input: electrical;
               terminal output: electrical );
end entity lowpass;
```

```
architecture RC of lowpass is
    constant cap : real := 1.0e-6;
    constant res : real := 1.0 / (math_2_pi * cap * fp);
begin
    assert false
        report "gain is ignored in architecture RC" severity note;
    assert false
        report "Fsmp is not used in architecture RC" severity note;
    R : entity work.resistor(ideal)
        generic map( res => res )
        port map( p1 => input, p2 => output );
    C : entity work.capacitor(ideal)
        generic map( cap => cap )
        port map( p1 => output, p2 => electrical_ref );
end architecture RC;
```

```
architecture dot of lowpass is
    quantity vin across input to electrical_ref;
    quantity vout across iout through output to electrical_ref;
    constant wp : real := fp * math_2_pi;    -- pole in rad/s
    constant tp : real := 1.0 / wp;          -- time constant
begin
    assert false
        report "Fsmp is not used in architecture dot" severity note;
    vin == (vout + tp * vout'dot) / gain;
end architecture dot;
```

(continued on page 430)

(continued from page 429)

```
architecture ltf of lowpass is
    quantity vin across input to electrical_ref;
    quantity vout across iout through output to electrical_ref;
    constant wp : real := fp * math_2_pi;    -- pole in rad/s
    constant num : real_vector := (0 => wp);
    constant den : real_vector := (wp, 1.0);
begin
    assert false
        report "Fsmp is not used in architecture ltf" severity note;
    vout == gain*vin'ltf(num, den);
end architecture ltf;
```

```
architecture z_minus_1 of lowpass is
    quantity vin across input to electrical_ref;
    quantity vout across iout through output to electrical_ref;
    quantity vin_sampled : real;              -- sampled input
    quantity vin_zm1, vout_zm1 : real;        -- z**-1
    constant Tsmp : real := 1.0 / Fsmp;       -- sample period
    constant wp : real := fp * math_2_pi;     -- pole in rad/s
    constant n0 : real := Tsmp * wp;          -- z0 numerator coefficient
    constant n1 : real := Tsmp * wp;          -- z-1 numerator coefficient
    constant d0 : real := Tsmp * wp + 2.0;    -- z0 denominator coefficient
    constant d1 : real := Tsmp * wp - 2.0;    -- z-1 denominator coefficient
begin
    vin_sampled  == gain*vin'zoh(Tsmp);

    vin_zm1  == vin_sampled'delayed(Tsmp);

    vout_zm1 == vout'delayed(Tsmp);

    vout == vin_sampled * n0 / d0 + n1 * vin_zm1 / d0 - d1 * vout_zm1 / d0;
end z_minus_1;
```

```
architecture ztf of lowpass is
    quantity vin across input to electrical_ref;
    quantity vout across iout through output to electrical_ref;
    constant Tsmp : real := 1.0 / Fsmp;       -- sample period
    constant wp : real := fp * math_2_pi;     -- pole in rad/s
    constant n0 : real := Tsmp * wp;          -- z0 numerator coefficient
    constant n1 : real := Tsmp * wp;          -- z-1 numerator coefficient
    constant d0 : real := Tsmp * wp + 2.0;    -- z0 denominator coefficient
    constant d1 : real := Tsmp * wp - 2.0;    -- z-1 denominator coefficient
    constant num : real_vector := (n0, n1);
    constant den : real_vector := (d0, d1);
```

```
begin
    vout == gain*vin'ztf(num, den, Tsmp);
end ztf;
```

Multiple-architecture filter model.

Z-Domain Sampling

While we have implemented a low-pass filter as a discrete model in the z-domain, there is another important issue we must take into account. Discrete-sampled system development requires careful consideration of the sample frequency. A z-domain filter's response approximates its continuous counterpart only if the sample rate is high enough.

We now discuss how we can analyze the selection of sampling frequency in both the time and frequency domains using the 'ztf attribute. The ability to analyze a z-domain model in the frequency domain is extremely useful. When the design is further implemented as a real-time system, small-signal frequency analysis is no longer possible.

Example   In this example we use the low-pass filter model implemented with 'ztf to illustrate the waveform corruption that occurs as the sampling frequency is reduced from 10 kHz to 100 Hz. This corruption is shown in both the time and frequency domains.

The time domain simulation results are illustrated in Figure 13-23. These results show the effects of sample rate on the filter's accuracy when filtering a 100 Hz sine wave. The waveforms illustrate the time domain effects of decreasing the sample rate from 10 kHz to 100 Hz. A 10 kHz sample rate yields a digitized signal that closely approximates an ideal continuous sine wave. As the sample rate is decreased to 1 kHz, the discrete states that make up the sine wave become much larger, resulting in much less accuracy. As the sample rate is further decreased to 100 Hz, the discrete steps lose all useful information from the sine wave. Note the similarity between this discussion and that presented in the trade-off analysis of Case Study 1 in Chapter 8. Here, an insufficient sampling frequency has a similar effect to an insufficient number of bits in A/D or D/A conversion.

Not only does insufficient sampling frequency cause a lack of filter resolution, it can also produce other erratic results. In order to determine the range of frequencies that can be correctly filtered by the low-pass filter for a given sample rate, we can perform small-signal AC analyses and see where the results begin to lose coherence.

The Nyquist criterion [27] mandates that we sample an analog signal at twice the highest frequency we expect to encounter. Failure to do so can cause aliasing, which produces unwanted frequencies within the range we wish to sample. These unwanted frequency components occur at the difference between the input and sampling frequencies, and produce erroneous sampled waveforms. To

FIGURE 13-23

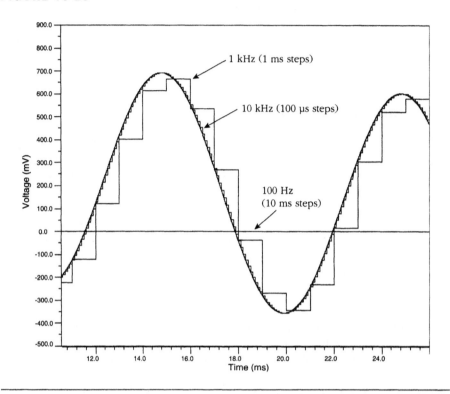

Time domain response for various sample rates.

overcome aliasing, many sampling systems employ anti-aliasing filters that limit the highest frequency sampled to at least satisfy the Nyquist criterion.

In Figure 13-24, the low-pass filter is simulated in the frequency domain at the same three sample rates used for the time domain analysis. There are four waveforms illustrated in the figure. The top waveform shows the continuous ('dot and 'ltf) responses; the remaining waveforms show the 'ztf responses for sample rates of 10 kHz, 1 kHz and 100 Hz, respectively. The waveforms demonstrate that the frequency domain response becomes corrupted as a function of decreasing sampling rate. For a sampling rate of 10 kHz, the filter output is corrupted at about 5 kHz, which is half of the sample frequency and is the limit set by the Nyquist criterion. Similarly, for sampling rates of 1 kHz and 100 Hz, the filter output is corrupted at 500 Hz and 50 Hz, respectively. Again this is consistent with the Nyquist criterion. Also note from the bottom waveform that, even though the filter pole is located at 10 Hz, it is still affected by the 100 Hz sample rate. Whereas there should be a gain of −3 dB at 10 Hz, the low sampling frequency causes a further 0.3 dB attenuation.

FIGURE 13-24

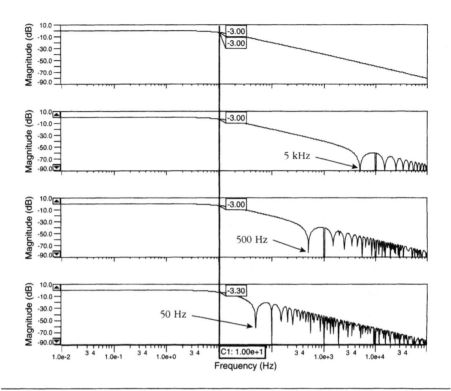

Frequency domain response as a function of various sample rates.

Exercises

1. [● 13.3] What is the relationship between *s* and 'dot?

2. [● 13.3] What is the primary advantage of the 'ltf attribute over the 'dot attribute?

3. [● 13.3] When is it not a good idea to use 'ltf rather than 'dot?

4. [● 13.4] Give two approaches that can be used to ensure aliasing problems will not arise in a sampled system.

5. [● 13.4] What is an advantage of using the 'zoh or 'ztf attributes instead of implementing a model that literally samples the continuous data with a clocked sample hold?

6. [● 13.4] What is the function of the 'zoh attribute?

7. [● 13.4] What two VHDL-AMS attributes does the 'ztf attribute automatically incorporate?

8. [❶ 13.4] Aside from the previous question, what is the benefit of simulating a sampled data system?

9. [❶ 13.4] Why is sample rate important for sampled systems?

10. [❶ 13.4] What is a benefit of implementing a discrete system rather than a continuous system?

11. [❶ 13.4] What fundamentally happens when a quantity is sampled using the 'zoh attribute?

12. [❷ 13.1] Write a structural VHDL-AMS model for a low-pass filter and provide a small-signal frequency source using a spectral source quantity.

13. [❷ 13.1] Write a structural VHDL-AMS model for a high-pass filter and provide a small-signal frequency source using a spectral source quantity.

14. [❷ 13.1] Write a structural VHDL-AMS model for a notch filter and provide a small-signal frequency source using a spectral source quantity.

15. [❷ 13.2] Write a model for a resistor with thermal noise.

16. [❷ 13.2] Write a model for a diode with thermal noise.

17. [❷ 13.2] Write a model for a diode with shot noise.

18. [❷ 13.2] Write a model for a zener diode with avalanche noise.

19. [❷ 13.3] Create a low-pass filter model like that illustrated in Figure 13-9 using the 'dot attribute such that vout is isolated on the left-hand side of the simultaneous equation.

20. [❷ 13.3] Simulate the low-pass filter of your choice with three different input sinewave frequencies. Also run an AC analysis on the same filter. Explain in detail the correlation between the time domain responses and the frequency domain response.

21. [❷ 13.3] Give a Laplace transfer function for a high-pass filter.

22. [❷ 13.3] Create a high-pass filter model using a 'dot architecture and a 'ltf architecture.

23. [❷ 13.3] Add input and output resistance characteristics to the 'dot opamp architecture illustrated in Figure 13-15.

24. [❷ 13.3] Add voltage offset characteristics to the opamp model illustrated in Figure 13-16.

25. [❷ 13.4] The z-domain low-pass filter architectures from Figure 13-22 first calculate the z-domain coefficients for the model, and then implement them. Modify the model so that the calculated values of the z-domain coefficients will be displayed to the user.

26. [❷ 13.4] Implement a z-domain model in which a real clock/sample-hold is used. What happens when this model is simulated with a small-signal frequency analysis?

27. [❷ 13.4] Create a z-domain model for a high-pass filter. (Hint: see Chapter 14 for z-domain coefficient determination.)

28. [❷ 13.4] Create a z-domain model for a second-order notch filter. (Hint: see Chapter 14 for z-domain coefficient determination.)

29. [❷ 13.4] Write a VHDL-AMS model to find the frequency response for the following z-domain transfer functions:

$$H(z)) = \frac{(z+1)^2}{z(z+0.5)(z-0.5)}$$

$$H(z) = \frac{(z+1)^4}{z^2(z+0.5)(z-0.5)}$$

30. [❸ 13.2] Write a model for a bipolar transistor with thermal, shot and flicker noise.

31. [❸ 13.2] Write a model for an operational amplifier with thermal, shot and flicker noise.

32. [❸ 13.3] Create a band-pass filter model with a 'dot architecture and a 'ltf architecture.

33. [❸ 13.3] Create a PID control system using the 'ltf attribute.

34. [❸ 13.4] Create a flash analog-to-digital converter. Use the 'zoh attribute in the model.

35. [❸ 13.4] Create a PID control system using a combination of the 'zoh and 'delayed attributes.

36. [❸ 13.4] Create a PID control system using the 'ztf attribute.

37. [❹ 13.3] Write a VHDL-AMS model for an aircraft longitudinal control system (see the text by Friedland [17] for more information).

38. [❹ 13.3] Write a VHDL-AMS model for an aircraft lateral axis control system (see the text by Friedland for more information).

39. [❹ 13.3] Create an opamp model with the following characteristics: two poles, input/output resistance, input offset voltage, input offset current, power supply voltage and current limiting, slew-rate limiting, and common-mode rejection ratio (CMRR).

40. [❹ 13.4] Assume we have a black box whose analog output we wish to digitize and store. Create a test bench and supporting models that automatically determine the minimum sample rate that can be used to accurately reproduce the black box outputs.

41. [❹ 13.4] Write a VHDL-AMS model for an antilock brake digital control system.

chapter fourteen

Case Study 2: Mixed-Technology Focus

With a contribution by Scott Cooper,
Mentor Graphics Corporation

This case study highlights VHDL-AMS as a mixed-technology, mixed-domain modeling language by focusing on the RC airplane rudder and servo control system (rudder system). We first implement the rudder system exclusively in the s-domain. After verifying top-level system requirements, we then refine most of the system to use conservation-based electromechanical components in which we model true physical characteristics of the system. Finally, we realize the servo compensator in the z-domain, so that it can be implemented as software rather than hardware.

14.1 **Rudder System Overview**

As noted in the Preface, the case studies revolve around a radio-controlled (RC) electric airplane system. This case study focuses on the rudder along with its servo controller, collectively referred to as the rudder system. Figure 14-1 shows the system diagram for the RC airplane system, with the rudder system indicated by the dashed box.

The RC airplane system is controlled with two channels, one for the propeller speed and the other for the rudder position. In a simple two-channel airplane system, the rudder controls the direction of the airplane. More advanced, multichannel airplanes control direction with ailerons, which cause the plane to bank in the desired direction. Since a simple two-channel plane has no ailerons to bank the plane, the rudder itself, in conjunction with dihedral wing design (where the tips of the wings are at a higher elevation than their base), causes the plane to bank left or right in response to rudder movement. This is similar to riding a bicycle: it is a combination of banking the bicycle and turning the handle bars that produces a turn.

The rudder system portions of the RC airplane system are shown in Figure 14-2. Control of the rudder is established with a closed-loop servo system. The servo accepts analog positioning commands from the PW/analog block (see Chapter 8) and drives a DC motor and connected gearbox. The gearbox is integrated into the motor symbol in Figure 14-2. The rudder is positioned by connecting a "control horn" mounted on the gearbox to a separate control horn mounted on the rudder. The control horns are used to transfer the angular displacement of the gearbox to the rudder through a translational linkage. As the gearbox turns, torque and angular position are translated through the linkage into force and translational position, which are trans-

FIGURE 14-1

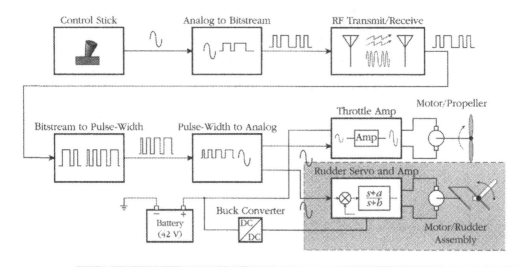

RC airplane system diagram with rudder block highlighted.

FIGURE 14-2

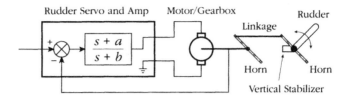

Servo controller and mechanical rudder.

ferred to the rudder and translated back into torque and angular position. This causes the rudder to rotate about a pivot point attached to the vertical stabilizer (so-called because its position remains fixed parallel to the oncoming air, helping to stabilize the plane's flight). As the rudder pivots, airflow is manipulated to control the airplane direction. The servo loop is closed with position feedback from a potentiometer mounted on the motor gearbox.

Rudder System Specifications and Development

We will design the rudder system to meet the following five specifications:

- Rudder deflection angle = ±60° (±1.05 radians)

- Rudder speed (0° to 60°) ≤ 300 ms (with 0.2 Nm load at maximum angle)

- Torque at gearbox ≥ 0.7 Nm (99 oz-in)

- Servo loop error (at steady state with ramp input) ≤ 1%

- Servo loop phase margin ≥ 35°

We will develop the rudder system in three stages. First, we will describe and analyze it as a collection of Laplace transfer function building blocks (commonly referred to as "*s*-domain" models). This implementation will allow us to determine whether the overall servo loop accuracy and phase margin requirements are met. We discuss this design in Section 14.2.

Second, we will replace all of the *s*-domain models with their mixed-technology counterparts (with the exception of the servo loop components). We will also add in the control horn and translational linkage components, which are not included in the *s*-domain implementation. This gives us a complete system modeled as a combination of *s*-domain models (for the servo functions) and mixed-technology models (for the rudder and associated parts). We discuss this design in Section 14.3.

Third, we will replace the *s*-domain servo compensator with its *z*-domain counterpart. We discuss and analyze this *z*-domain implementation in detail in Section 14.4.

14.2 S-Domain Implementation

There are many advantages to using a versatile mixed-technology modeling language like VHDL-AMS. One major advantage is the freedom it allows to describe a system at the appropriate level of abstraction for any particular phase of the design and manufacturing process. At the beginning of a new design, for example, a high-level behavioral representation of a system may be sufficient to verify the overall design topology and subsystem interfaces. As the design progresses, we can add extra detail and complexity to the high-level models, or we can replace them with lower-level models.

In this section, we use Laplace transfer function models for each component to determine the overall design topology and verify high-level specifications. These *s*-domain models allow us to postpone mixed-technology considerations, such as the interface between connection points of different energy domains. For example, we can postpone consideration of connecting electrical outputs to mechanical inputs. This is possible because the inputs and outputs of *s*-domain models are defined as real quantities that do not have through or across aspects.

Figure 14-3 shows an example of an *s*-domain gain model. The ports are specified as directional quantities of subtype real. Since the ports are quantities rather than terminals, conservation laws are not applied to them (that is, there are no across and through definitions associated with the quantity ports). Since conservation laws are not enforced at each node of an *s*-domain design, such systems typically have shorter simulation run times that equivalent technology-based systems.

A disadvantage of *s*-domain modeling in VHDL-AMS is the inability to integrate *s*-domain models into mixed-technology structural designs. The drawback is that each "parent" block must have the same kinds of ports as its "child" block. This would pose a problem, for example, if we want a high-level *s*-domain block to contain an electrical block. In this case, it would be best to change the "parent" *s*-domain quantity ports to electrical terminals.

FIGURE 14-3

```
entity gain is
    generic ( k : real := 1.0 );   -- gain multiplier
    port ( quantity input : in real;
        quantity output : out real );
end entity gain;
```

```
architecture simple of gain is
begin
    output == k * input;
end architecture simple;
```

S-domain gain model.

Figure 14-4 shows how we can readily implement the gain model of Figure 14-3 with electrical terminal ports instead of quantity ports. Since the electrical reference for the terminal ports (electrical_ref) is declared in the electrical_systems package, we can define the voltage branches internally and implement the model with just two ports.

Despite the difficulties associated with integrating *s*-domain and conservative models into multitechnology designs, *s*-domain modeling techniques remain a good starting point for system design. Thus we take this approach to design the rudder system. Our first attempt at developing an *s*-domain model for the rudder system is shown in Figure 14-5. The control horns and translational linkage are not included in this representation. The four functional parts are the servo controller, the motor model, the gearbox and the rudder load. In the remainder of this section, we describe these parts in detail and analyze their performance as a composite system.

Servo Controller

We can model the rudder system as a closed-loop position controller, or servo. A positioning command is sent to a two-input summing junction, which feeds into a servo gain block and signal limiter. The limiter ensures that no more than 4.8 V (the plane's power-supply limit) is available to drive the motor. The loop is closed by scaling and inverting the position output and feeding it back to the summing junction. We will examine two models from the servo implementation: the summer and limiter.

FIGURE 14-4

```
library ieee_proposed;  use ieee_proposed.electrical_systems.all;

entity gain_e is
    generic ( k : real := 1.0);   -- gain multiplier
    port ( terminal input : electrical;
            terminal output : electrical );
end entity gain_e;
```

```
architecture simple of gain_e is

    quantity vin across input to electrical_ref;
    quantity vout across iout through output to electrical_ref;

begin

    vout == k * vin;

end architecture simple;
```

Electrical-domain gain model.

FIGURE 14-5

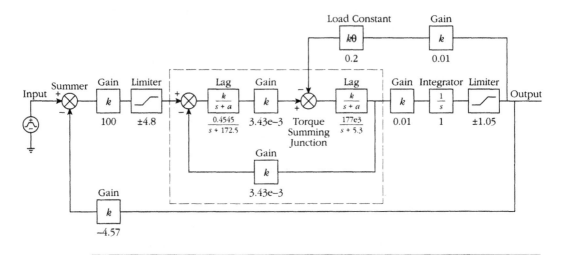

S-domain representation of the rudder system. The dashed box outlines the motor.

Two-Input Summer Model

The two-input summer algebraically sums the values presented on its inputs. In the servo, these values have opposite signs by design, so the summer actually works as a differencer. The summer model is illustrated in Figure 14-6. This model simply takes the values on the inputs, multiplies them by gain values and sums the products together. The inputs and output are real quantities, which implies that conservation laws do not apply to them.

FIGURE 14-6

```
entity sum2 is
     generic ( k1, k2 : real := 1.0 );    -- optional gain multipliers
     port ( quantity in1, in2 : in real;
          quantity output : out real );
end entity sum2;
```

```
architecture simple of sum2 is
begin
     output == k1 * in1 + k2 * in2;    -- sum of inputs (with optional gain)
end architecture simple;
```

S-domain two-input summer model.

Limiter Model

There are two limiter blocks in the design. The first limiter is designed to limit the overall error signal to the power-supply voltage level, 4.8 V. The second limiter is used to model the mechanical stop that prevents the gear shaft from rotating beyond a ±60° arc. The block is set to limit any input signal to ±1.05 radians, which corresponds to ±60°.

The limiter blocks are implemented as shown in Figure 14-7. This model works as follows. If the input quantity is greater than the user-specified limit, limit_high, the output is held at limit_high. A small slope is introduced to the otherwise flat limited quantity in order to assist with simulation convergence. (It helps keep the solution algorithm from getting lost on quantities with zero slope.) A similar approach is used to limit input quantities less than limit_low. The break statement is required to notify the simulator that a first-derivative discontinuity occurs at the points where limiting occurs. The simulator uses this information to reset the analog solver whenever such discontinuities occur.

FIGURE 14-7

```
entity limiter is
    generic ( limit_high : real := 4.8;      -- upper limit
              limit_low : real := -4.8 );    -- lower limit
    port ( quantity input : in real;
           quantity output : out real);
end entity limiter;

architecture simple of limiter is
    constant slope : real := 1.0e-4;
begin
    if input > limit_high use     -- upper limit exceeded, so limit input signal
        output == limit_high + slope*(input - limit_high);
    elsif input < limit_low use   -- lower limit exceeded, so limit input signal
        output == limit_low + slope*(input - limit_low);
    else                          -- no limit exceeded, so pass input signal as is
        output == input;
    end use;

    break on input'above(limit_high), input'above(limit_low);
end architecture simple;
```

S-domain limiter model.

Motor Model

The servo drives the motor, enclosed in the dashed box in Figure 14-5. The motor implementation was chosen so that load torque (resulting from air pushing against the rudder) can be directly subtracted from the generated torque. This is accomplished by representing the motor as a collection of blocks that isolate the generated motor torque. Once the torque generator for the motor is isolated, a summing junction is inserted so that external torque contributions (positive or negative) can be summed in with the torque generated by the motor.

The s-domain motor model is illustrated in Figure 14-8. This motor model accounts for the electrical and mechanical time constants of the motor and is configured to allow load torque to be summed directly into it. The forward gain block performs the current-to-torque conversion, and the feedback gain block accounts for generated back-EMF.

FIGURE 14-8

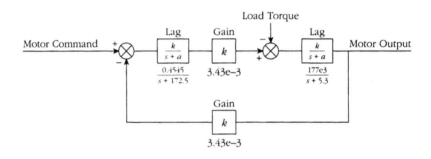

S-domain motor model implementation.

The values used for this motor model are derived from vendor-supplied motor parameters for a standard DC servo motor. Its specifications are

$R = 2.2\ \Omega$	armature winding resistance
$L = 2.03\ \text{mH}$	armature winding inductance
$J = 168\ \text{kg/m}^2$	shaft inertia
$k_T = 3.43\ \text{mNm/A}$	torque (motor) constant
$k_E = 3.43\ \text{mV/rad/s}$	voltage (back-EMF) constant
$B = 5.63\ \mu\text{Nm/rad/s}$	viscous damping factor

The motor model depicted in Figure 14-8 is composed essentially of lag and gain blocks. The lag blocks represent the motor's electrical and mechanical time constants, and the gain blocks represent the torque and voltage constants. The lag block parameters can be determined using the following equations:

$$\tau_e = \frac{L}{R} \tag{14-1}$$

where τ_e is the electrical time constant, and

$$\tau_m = \frac{J}{B} \tag{14-2}$$

where τ_m is the mechanical time constant. Since these time constants will be implemented using a model that accepts frequency rather than time parameters, we express the time constants as pole positions as follows:

$$p = -\frac{1}{\tau} \tag{14-3}$$

where p is the pole position in rad/s.

To determine the actual pole values for this motor, we use the motor specifications along with Equations 14-1 through 14-3. The electrical pole is calculated at 1.08 krad/s (172.5 Hz), and the mechanical pole is calculated at 33.5 rad/s (5.3 Hz).

To complete the motor model definition, the values of the gain throughout the motor implementation must also be determined. The dedicated gain blocks are both set to 3.43×10^{-3}, which corresponds to the voltage and torque constants for the motor. The electrical lag block has a DC gain of 0.4545, which is calculated by solving the following transfer function with $s = 0$:

$$T(s)_e = \frac{1}{sL + R} \tag{14-4}$$

The mechanical lag block has a DC gain of 177.6×10^3, which is calculated by solving the following transfer function with $s = 0$:

$$T(s)_m = \frac{1}{sJ + B} \tag{14-5}$$

Lag Model

The VHDL-AMS lag model implementation is given in Figure 14-9. This is essentially the same as the low-pass filter model extensively discussed in Chapter 13, with the exception that the ports are defined as quantities, rather than terminals. The ieee.math_real library is included to allow use of the predefined constant, math_2_pi, which is used to convert from frequencies specified in hertz to rad/s.

FIGURE 14-9

```
entity lpf_1 is
    generic ( fp : real;              -- pole freq in hertz
              gain : real := 1.0 );   -- filter gain
    port ( quantity input : in real;
           quantity output : out real);
end entity lpf_1;
```

```
library ieee;  use ieee.math_real.all;

architecture simple of lpf_1 is
    constant wp : real := math_2_pi*fp;
    constant num : real_vector := (0 => wp * gain);   -- "0 =>" is needed to give
                                                      -- vector index when only
                                                      -- a single element is used.
    constant den : real_vector := (wp, 1.0);
begin
    output == input'ltf(num, den);
end architecture simple;
```

S-domain lag filter model.

The core of the model is fairly simple to implement in VHDL-AMS using the Laplace transform attribute, 'ltf. In this case, the denominator is specified as "(wp, 1.0)", which is the description of a first-order system in ascending powers of s. The numerator of the transfer function is specified as "(0 => wp*gain)", which automatically normalizes the overall gain of the model to the user-specified gain parameter.

Gearbox

The gearbox consists of gain, integrator and limiter blocks. The integrator is required because the motor produces a velocity signal on its output shaft. The velocity quantity must be converted to a position quantity before it can be summed with the input position command. On a physical gearbox of this type, a potentiometer is mounted directly to the gearbox shaft, implicitly integrating the output signal. The additional limiter is provided to model mechanical hard stops in the system, which limit the gearbox shaft movement to ±60° (±1.05 radians). We use the limiter described in Figure 14-7.

Gain Model

The purpose of the mechanical gearbox in this design is to magnify the motor torque at the expense of motor velocity. In this instance, a 100:1 gear ratio was chosen, meaning that the rated motor torque will be amplified by a factor of 100, and the rated motor velocity will be reduced by the same amount. In the *s*-domain, the gear is modeled simply as a gain block, as illustrated previously in Figure 14-3, with a gain of 0.01. The equation for the block is

```
output == k * input;
```

where k is the gear ratio.

Integrator Model

The purpose of the integrator block is to convert the angular velocity output of the gearbox into a proportional angular position. This is done so that the signal that is fed back into the loop summer is the angular position, which is ultimately what we are trying to control at the rudder. Its transfer function is implemented in VHDL-AMS as

```
output == k * input'integ;
```

where k is an optional gain factor, and the predefined attribute 'integ is used for integration.

Rudder Load

In order to produce the appropriate load torque, the gearbox output angle is fed to the motor's internal torque summing junction through two blocks. The first block reduces the rudder angle by the gear ratio, resulting in the effective motor angle, and the second block represents a mechanical spring. The spring model produces a load torque that is dependent on the rudder deflection angle: as the angle increases, the torque also increases. We discuss the detailed characteristics of this model in Section 14.3.

The load torque produced by the spring model is subtracted from the generated motor torque to model the effects of the load on the motor. Because the load torque is directly subtracted from the motor in this manner, the actual control horns and rudder assembly are not required in the analysis of the servo loop in the *s*-domain.

S-Domain System Performance

We will test the *s*-domain system to ensure it meets three of the specifications noted previously:

- Rudder speed (0° to 60°) ≤ 300 ms (with 0.2 Nm load at maximum angle)
- Servo loop error (at steady state with ramp input) ≤ 1%
- Servo loop phase margin ≥ 35°

To test the system against the requirements, we first measure how closely the rudder system of Figure 14-5 follows an input command that ramps from 0 V to 4.8 V in 300 ms, and then increase the system gain if necessary to increase the accuracy. This system gain will be modified at the gain block located just after the servo position summing junction.

Three simulations were run with gains of 1, 10 and 100. The resulting responses to a ramp input are given in Figure 14-10. There are two *y*-axes so that the input ramp voltage (0 V to 4.8 V) can be superimposed on the output ramp positions (0 to 1.05 radians) measured at the output of the gearbox. The figure shows that with a gain of 1, there appears to be a large error between the input ramp and the gearbox output response. The waveform generated with a gain of 10 shows less error, but still does not appear to meet the 1% steady-state error specification. The waveform generated with a gain of 100 matches the input signal better, but we cannot tell how precisely it matches.

We can quantitatively determine how well each of these waveforms tracks the input ramp by dividing the system error signal by the commanded input signal at steady state. The error signal, measured at the output of the position loop summing junction shown in Figure 14-5, is presented for each of the gain scenarios in Figure 14-11.

For the steady-state error measurements, we pick a location around 4 V on the input ramp. As shown in the figure, a gain of 1 produces 2.27/4.06 = 56% error relative to the input signal at the indicated time; a gain of 10 results in 0.34/4.06 = 8.3%

FIGURE 14-10

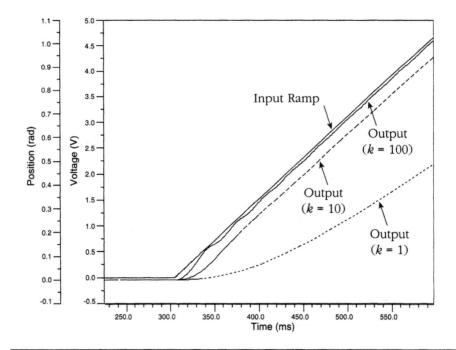

Comparison of rudder response to ramp input with servo gains of 1, 10 and 100.

FIGURE 14-11

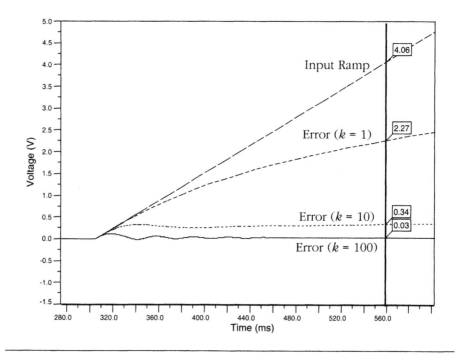

Voltage (V) vs Time (ms)

Input Ramp

Error (k = 1)   2.27

Error (k = 10)   0.34

Error (k = 100)   0.03

4.06

Error signals for servo gains of 1, 10 and 100.

error; and a gain of 100 results in 0.034/4.06 = 0.83% error. Of all these gain values, only a gain of 100 satisfies our 1% error specification.

We have now satisfied two of the three specifications: the system can move full scale in 300 ms or less, and it can do so with less than 1% error at steady state. However, now that we have an appropriate value of gain for the system, we must still ensure that the system has adequate phase margin at this gain value to be stable. The phase margin is measured for the system with a gain of 100, and the results are illustrated in Figure 14-12.

As shown in the figure, a gain value of 100 results in an underdamped system with an unacceptable phase margin of 7.6°. We therefore need to add some form of compensation to restore adequate phase margin to the design while maintaining the necessary tracking accuracy.

In order to determine what form of compensation serves us best, it helps to understand the major factors that influence the loop's phase margin. In this case, we have a motor with poles located at 5.3 Hz and 172 Hz. We also have an integrator at the origin. The relationship between system gain and its effects on pole locations can be conveniently illustrated with root locus techniques. The migration of poles as a function of gain in this system is shown in Figure 14-13.

This diagram (not drawn to scale) illustrates the movement of the three dominant system poles as a function of servo gain. These poles are located at 0 Hz, 5.3 Hz and 172 Hz. The bold "×" marks at the arrow tails indicate the starting location of the

FIGURE 14-12

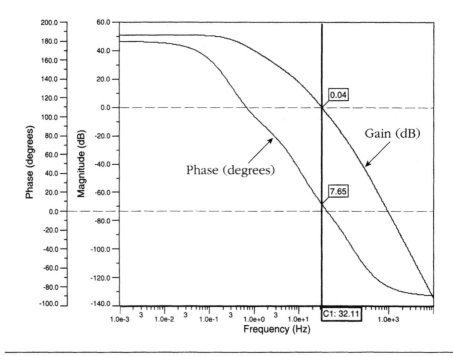

Phase margin with servo gain of 100.

FIGURE 14-13

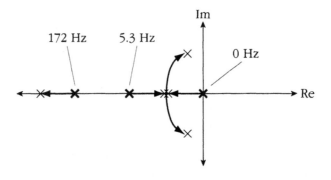

System pole migration as a function of system gain.

poles, and the lighter "×" marks at the arrow heads indicate the poles at various positions as the servo gain is increased. Of particular interest is the way in which the integrator pole (0 Hz) and the motor mechanical time constant pole (5.3 Hz) interact. As servo gain is increased, these poles combine to form a complex conjugate pole pair that quickly migrates to the right-hand plane. This pole migration is the cause of the low phase margin at a gain of 100.

We insert a lead-lag compensator between the gain and limiter blocks in Figure 14-5 in an attempt to increase the phase margin. Since this system has poles at 0 Hz and at 5.3 Hz, we insert a zero between these poles. The idea is to draw the integrator pole away from the imaginary axis. We place the zero at 5 Hz. The location of the lag (pole) of the compensator is not critical, as long as it is far enough away from the imaginary axis to avoid introducing problems itself. We place the pole at 2000 Hz. The new system response is illustrated in Figure 14-14.

As seen in the diagram, the 5 Hz zero of the lead-lag compensator acts to draw the pole at the origin to it, where the pole terminates. (Again, the diagram is not drawn to scale.) The 5.3 Hz motor pole then moves left on the real axis until meeting with the 172 Hz motor electrical pole. While these poles still form a complex conjugate pole pair, they do not border the imaginary axis when the gain reaches 100, and the system is stable as a result.

The system with the compensator is shown in Figure 14-15. The newly inserted compensator block is outlined with a dashed box. The open-loop response of the system with the pole-zero compensator is illustrated in Figure 14-16. The compensated system has a 44° phase margin, which meets the system specifications. The performance of the overall system, including compensation, in response to a ramp input is illustrated in Figure 14-17. The figure shows that the output of the compensated system tracks the input very well, particularly at steady state. This also shows that the output can still ramp from null to full deflection in 300 ms, as required by the specifications.

Lead-Lag Compensator Model

The servo compensator is necessary to achieve the desired accuracy in the closed-loop system, without the system becoming unstable. This trade-off between accuracy and stability is common in closed-loop control systems, and as we have seen, simulation technology is well suited to deal with it.

FIGURE 14-14

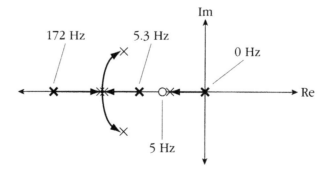

System pole migration with compensator zero.

FIGURE 14-15

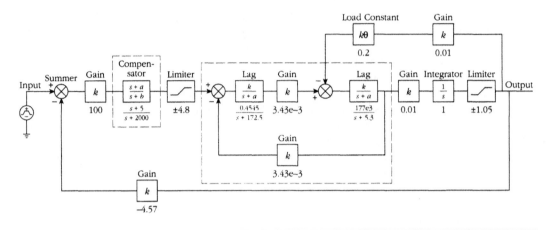

S-domain implementation with lead-lag compensator.

FIGURE 14-16

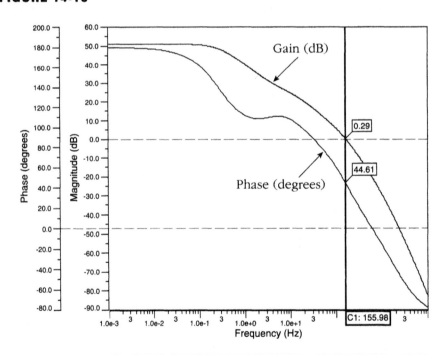

Open-loop response with lead-lag compensator.

FIGURE 14-17

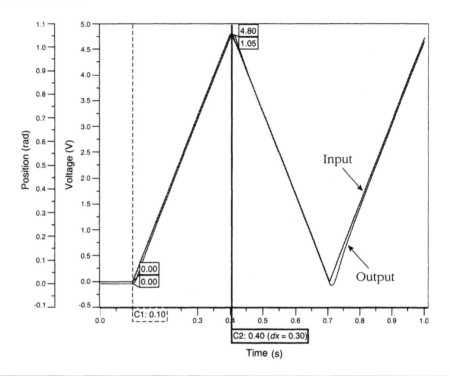

S-domain system response with final gain and compensator values.

The VHDL-AMS compensator model is shown in Figure 14-18. Like the lag filter model, the lead-lag compensator is modeled using the predefined attribute 'ltf. The multiplier, k, can be used to normalize the gain of the model. In this case, f1 = 5, and f2 = 2000, which makes the non-normalized gain at DC equal to $5/2000 = 2.5 \times 10^{-3}$. In order to normalize the gain to 1, the gain factor, k, is therefore set to 2000/5 = 400. The ieee.math_real package is included in the model because the predefined constant math_2_pi is used to convert input frequencies in hertz to rad/s.

FIGURE 14-18

```
library ieee;  use ieee.math_real.all;

entity lead_lag is
        generic ( k : real := 400.0;      -- gain multiplier
                  f1 : real := 5.0;       -- break frequency (zero)
                  f2 : real := 2000.0);   -- break frequency (pole)
          port ( quantity input : in real;
                 quantity output : out real);
end entity lead_lag;
```

(continued on page 454)

(continued from page 453)

```
architecture simple of lead_lag is
    constant num : real_vector := (f1 * math_2_pi, 1.0);
    constant den : real_vector := (f2 * math_2_pi, 1.0);
begin
    output == k * input'ltf(num, den);
end architecture simple;
```

S-domain lead-lag compensator model.

14.3 Mixed Mechanical/*S*-Domain Implementation

The *s*-domain representation provides an excellent starting point for the design and analysis of the rudder system. We are able to determine the necessary servo gain as well as compensator component values. Next, we step down a level of abstraction into the details of mechanical and electromechanical systems. We do this for a number of reasons, but primarily because the *s*-domain only deals with abstract quantities (real numbers) that are propagated from one model to the next. A physical system, on the other hand, is subject to the laws of conservation, and developing a conservation-based simulation model allows us to more accurately represent the physical system.

We saw one limitation of the *s*-domain modeling approach with the motor model. In order to subtract load torque from the system, we need a motor topology that allows the torque to be subtracted directly from the motor's generated torque. This results in an accurate, although cumbersome and complex, *s*-domain motor model. In the mixed-technology domain, such steps prove unnecessary due to the nature of conservation-based models.

The mixed-technology representation of the rudder system is shown in Figure 14-19. The entire chain of components, with the exception of the servo, is connected with terminals that have both across and through quantities. This means that conservation laws are enforced at each node, and the actual load torque effects at the rudder are propagated back to the motor, as is the case in a real physical system.

This system spans three technologies: *s*-domain (servo/amplifier); electrical (motor input, position feedback); and mechanical (motor output, gearbox, mechanical hard stop, control horns, translational linkage and rudder). The system consists of five functional pieces: servo/amplifier, DC motor, gearbox, control horn assembly and rudder. We discuss each of these pieces in this section.

FIGURE 14-19

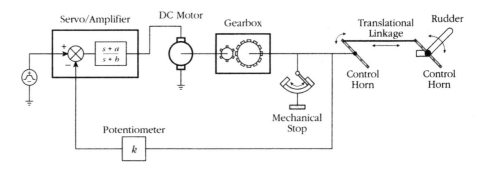

Mixed-technology representation of the rudder system.

Servo/Amplifier

The rudder servo block contains the familiar compensator design, illustrated as a hierarchical block in Figure 14-20.

Motor Model

The electromechanical motor model is shown in Figure 14-21. This model differs quite significantly from that implemented in the s-domain. First, since the motor is an electromechanical device, both the **electrical_systems** and **mechanical_systems** packages are referenced in the model. Also, in this motor representation, the motor's electrical and mechanical conservation laws are explicitly expressed in the model's equations.

FIGURE 14-20

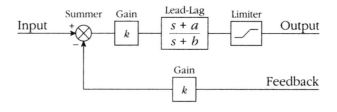

Rudder servo compensator block.

FIGURE 14-21

```
library ieee_proposed;
use ieee_proposed.mechanical_systems.all;
use ieee_proposed.electrical_systems.all;
entity DC_Motor is
    generic ( r_wind : resistance;   -- motor winding resistance [ohm]
              kt : real;             -- torque coefficient [N*m/amp]
              l : inductance;        -- winding inductance [henrys]
              d : real;              -- damping coefficient [N*m/(rad/sec)]
              j : mmoment_i );       -- moment of inertia [kg*meter**2]
    port ( terminal p1, p2 : electrical;
           terminal shaft_rotv : rotational_v);
end entity DC_Motor;

------------------------------------------------------------

architecture basic of DC_Motor is
    quantity v across i through p1 to p2;
    quantity w across torq through shaft_rotv to rotational_v_ref;
begin
    torq == -1.0 * kt * i + d * w + j * w'dot;
    v == kt * w + i * r_wind + l * i'dot;
end architecture basic;
```

Mixed-technology DC motor model.

The torque equation for the model,

$$T = -K_T i + D\omega + J\frac{d\omega}{dt} \tag{14-6}$$

describes the net torque production of the motor as the difference between the generated torque ($K_T i$) and the torque losses, $D\omega$ (viscous damping loss) and $Jd\omega/dt$ (inertial losses). Similarly, the electrical equation for the model,

$$V = K_T\omega + Ri + L\frac{di}{dt} \tag{14-7}$$

illustrates that the input voltage is equal to the sum of the back-EMF ($K_T\omega$), the motor's winding resistance voltage drop (Ri) and the winding inductance voltage drop (Ldi/dt). Note that $K_T = K_E$ when SI units are used in the motor definition.

Gearbox

The gearbox consists of two models: the gear ratio model and the mechanical hard stop model. The mechanical gear model is illustrated in Figure 14-22. Where the *s*-domain gearbox was modeled as a simple gain block, the mechanical domain gearbox is modeled such that as the torque (through variable) is multiplied by the gear ratio, the velocity (across variable) is divided by the same amount. This ensures conservation of mechanical power. Also, since the input velocity is integrated, this model acts as both a gearbox and integrator. Hence, a separate integration block is not required in the overall system, as the gearbox model intrinsically converts the input velocity to an output position.

The mechanical hard stop model, shown in Figure 14-23, is used to approximate a physical boundary in a system. The mechanical stop model allows normal system operation as long as the angle between the ports is within the stop limits, **ang_min** and **ang_max** (±1.05 radians in this system). When a limit is exceeded, an amount of torque is generated to drive the angle back to the limit. The mechanical stiffness of the stop is controlled by the **k_top** parameter, and the inelastic properties of a collision with the hard stop are specified with the **damp_stop** parameter.

In the *s*-domain system discussed in Section 14.2, a limiter was used to model the effect of the hard stop. A drawback to the simple limiter approach is that if the system dwells at a limit for any length of time, the limiter operates by restricting its output to ±1.05. However, the input to the limiter is the output of an integrator, which continues ramping while the limiter is restricting its output. When the input to the integrator

---

FIGURE 14-22

```
library ieee_proposed;  use ieee_proposed.mechanical_systems.all;
entity gear_rv_r is
      generic ( ratio : real := 1.0 );    -- gear ratio (revs of shaft2 for 1 rev of shaft1)
                                          -- note: can be negative, if shaft polarity changes
      port ( terminal rotv1 : rotational_v;  -- rotational velocity terminal
             terminal rot2 : rotational );    -- rotational angle terminal
end entity gear_rv_r;
```

```
architecture ideal of gear_rv_r is

      quantity w1 across torq_vel through rotv1 to rotational_v_ref;
      quantity theta across torq_ang through rot2 to rotational_ref;
begin
      theta  == ratio * w1'integ;        -- output is angle (integral of w1)
      torq_vel == -1.0 * torq_ang * ratio;  -- input torque as function of output angle
end architecture ideal;
```

Mechanical gear model.

FIGURE 14-23

```
library ieee_proposed;  use ieee_proposed.mechanical_systems.all;
entity stop_r is
    generic ( k_stop : real := 1.0e6;
                ang_max : real := 1.05;
                ang_min : real := -1.05;
                damp_stop : real := 1.0e2 );
    port ( terminal ang1, ang2 : rotational );
end entity stop_r;
```

```
architecture ideal of stop_r is
    quantity velocity : velocity;
    quantity ang across trq through ang1 to ang2;
begin
    velocity == ang'dot;
    if ang > ang_max use      -- Hit upper stop, generate opposing torque
        trq == k_stop * (ang - ang_max) + (damp_stop * velocity);
    elsif ang > ang_min use   -- Between stops, no opposing torque
        trq   == 0.0;
    else                       -- Hit lower stop, generate opposing torque
        trq   == k_stop * (ang - ang_min) + (damp_stop * velocity);
    end use;
    break on ang'above(ang_min), ang'above(ang_max);
end architecture ideal;
```

Mechanical stop model.

comes out of the limiting region, the output of the integrator takes some time to ramp down, resulting in a delay before normal operation may resume.

We can overcome this problem either by creating a limiting integrator, or by using a mechanical stop model as we have done here. For the mechanical stop model, there is no ramping up of an integrator since the excess torque is in effect "canceled" by the stop model when a limit is reached.

Control Horn Assembly

Now that we are working with conservation-based models, it is a simple matter to include the control horn assembly that we omitted from the s-domain analyses. A control horn is a device that converts between rotational and translational movement, and vice versa. The gearbox control horn converts the rotational shaft position of the gearbox into a translational shaft position. The rudder control horn performs the opposite function, transforming the translational position back to an angular position at the rudder. This subsystem is shown in Figure 14-24.

FIGURE 14-24

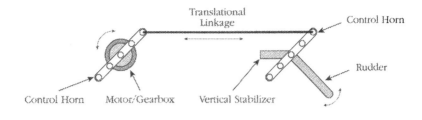

Gearbox and rudder control horn configuration.

Mechanical energy is transferred from the motor and gearbox to the rudder as follows. As the gearbox control horn rotates clockwise, the translational linkage "pushes" the rudder control horn, which then also rotates clockwise. As the gearbox control horn rotates counterclockwise, the translational linkage "pulls" the rudder control horn, which then rotates counterclockwise. The reverse is also true: as air pushes against the rudder, the resulting torque is passed through the rudder control horn, through the translational linkage, through the gearbox control horn and ultimately back to the motor.

This example illustrates an advantage of conservation-based models over *s*-domain models. Since conservation laws are enforced at each terminal, proper torque/angle relationships are maintained naturally throughout the system. Compare this with the *s*-domain implementation, where we had to specifically model the motor in such a way as to allow load torque to be subtracted from the generated torque.

The relationship between the gearbox control horn and translational linkage is modeled as

$$out_x = R\sin(in_\phi) \tag{14-8}$$

where

out_x =   horizontal displacement of control horn

R =   radius of the gearbox control horn (center of rotation to linkage connection point)

in_ϕ =   horn rotation angle

For example, if the horn radius is 1 inch (2.54 cm), and it is rotated a full 60°, then the horizontal displacement of the linkage rod would be 0.866 inches (2.2 cm).

The reverse situation occurs at the rudder control horn: the translational input displacement must be translated back into angular displacement to ensure correct rudder movement. This relationship is modeled as

$$out_\phi = arc\sin\left(\frac{in_x}{R}\right) \qquad (14\text{-}9)$$

where

out_ϕ =   angular displacement of rudder

R =   radius of the rudder control horn (center of rotation to linkage connection point)

in_x =   horizontal displacement of horn

These models prove especially useful when determining the effects of changing the radius for either the control or rudder horn.

Rudder Model

When the rudder is placed in its center position, it is parallel to the oncoming air (like the vertical stabilizer), which allows the plane to fly straight ahead. In this position, no load torque is produced by the rudder. As the rudder is rotated, the force of the oncoming air creates a torque along the rudder's connecting axis that is proportional to the angle of rotation. For this reason, the rudder is modeled as a mechanical spring using the following relation:

$$T = k(\theta_1 - \theta_0) \qquad (14\text{-}10)$$

where

T = torque produced at rudder's connecting axis by oncoming air

k = spring constant (set equal to the maximum torque value, 0.2 Nm)

θ_1 = rudder rotation angle

θ_2 = rudder rotational reference angle

Modeled as a spring, the rudder produces a torque that is proportional to its angle of rotation. Since the torque available to drive the load is 100 times that produced by the motor (due to the gearbox), the load torque is reduced by 100 prior to being subtracted from the motor torque. The maximum torque is produced for either ±60° rotation limit.

When implemented as a mixed-technology system, the simulation waveforms appear as shown in Figure 14-25. The simulation results are nearly identical to those given in Figure 14-17 for the *s*-domain system implementation.

FIGURE 14-25

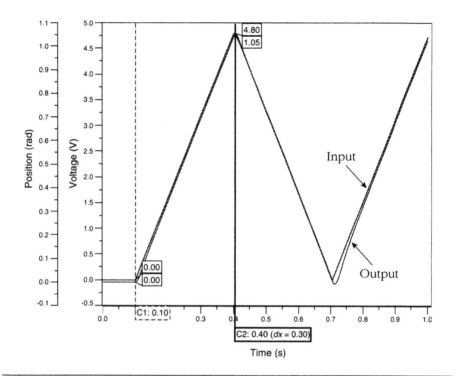

Time (s)

Mixed-technology system response.

14.4 **Design Trade-Off Analysis**

Thus far we have used a "top-down" design methodology to create and analyze the rudder system. We started with an *s*-domain representation of the entire system in order to meet some high-level requirements, such as error response to an input ramp and loop stability. We then substituted actual mechanical and electromechanical models for their *s*-domain counterparts in order to get a true conservation-based implementation of the system. We showed that both implementations accurately describe the system behavior and discussed some advantages and disadvantages of each approach.

In today's design environment, many analog and digital functions are being designed in software or firmware to be implemented with a microprocessor or programmable logic device. In fact, the majority of the circuitry discussed for the command and control functions of an electric airplane are typically implemented with a programmable gate array (PGA) or similar type device. It usually makes good sense from a reliability and maintenance standpoint to incorporate as much of the system electronics into such a device as possible.

In the trade-off analysis in this section, we will work toward three goals. First, we will derive the z-domain equivalent model for the lead-lag compensator using the methods discussed in Chapter 13. Second, we will determine an acceptable clock speed for the compensator that maintains system error and stability requirements. Third, we will create difference equations based on our z-domain work, so that we may implement the compensator as software code.

The servo design of Figure 14-20 with z-domain compensator is illustrated in Figure 14-26. The servo is identical to that used for the previous implementations, except that the lead-lag compensator block is now based in the z-domain.

One of the useful predefined attributes in VHDL-AMS is the '**ztf** attribute. Similar to the '**ltf** attribute, '**ztf** allows a z-domain transfer function to be specified in ascending powers of z^{-1}. The compensator implementation using the '**ztf** attribute is illustrated in Figure 14-27. The model simply employs the '**ztf** attribute to implement the z-domain transfer function specified with the coefficients **a1**, **a2**, **b1** and **b2**. In this example, a sampling clock period of 100 µs is used, along with a system-normalizing gain of 400 (the same gain used with the s-domain compensator).

FIGURE 14-26

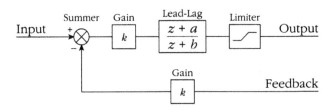

Servo circuit with z-domain compensator.

FIGURE 14-27

```
entity lead_lag_ztf is
    generic ( a1 : real := 2.003140;
              a2 : real := -1.996860;
              b1 : real := 3.250000;
              b2 : real := -0.750000;
              k : real := 400.0;          -- normalizing gain
              tsampl : real := 0.1e-3;    -- sample period
              init_delay : real := 0.0 ); -- optional delay
    port ( quantity input : in real;
           quantity output : out real );
end entity lead_lag_ztf;
```

```
architecture simple of lead_lag_ztf is
    constant num: real_vector := (a1, a2);
    constant den: real_vector := (b1, b2);
begin
    output == k * input'ztf(num, den, tsampl, init_delay);   -- implement
                                                             -- transfer function
end architecture simple;
```

Compensator implemented in the z-domain with 'ztf attribute.

Deriving Z-Domain Coefficients

In order to use the z-domain model of Figure 14-27, we must first determine the co-efficients for the transfer function. Since we have validated the s-domain compensator, we can perform a bilinear transform on the s-domain transfer function to generate a z-domain equivalent transfer function. The s-domain transfer function is

$$\frac{Y(s)}{X(s)} = k\frac{s + \omega_z}{s + \omega_p} \tag{14-11}$$

The bilinear transform (without prewarping) requires substituting the following expression for every occurrence of s in Equation 14-11:

$$\frac{2}{T}\left(\frac{1 - z^{-1}}{1 + z^{-1}}\right) \tag{14-12}$$

Performing the substitution and simplifying results:

$$\frac{Y(Z)}{X(Z)} = k\frac{2 + T\omega_z + (T\omega_z - 2)z^{-1}}{2 + T\omega_p + (T\omega_p - 2)z^{-1}} \tag{14-13}$$

Substituting $T = 100$ μs, $\omega_z = 31.4$ rad/s (5 Hz) and $\omega_p = 12.56 \times 10^3$ rad/s (2000 Hz):

$$\frac{Y(Z)}{X(Z)} = k\frac{2.003140 - 1.996860z^{-1}}{3.250000 - 0.750000z^{-1}} \tag{14-14}$$

The results of simulating the system with these coefficients, as well as recalculated coefficients for clock periods of 5 ms and 1 ms, are shown in Figure 14-28. The

FIGURE 14-28

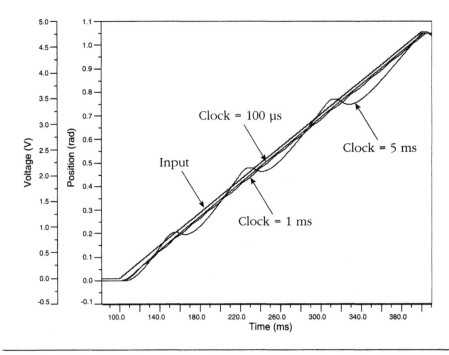

Input/output simulation results with various clock periods.

waveforms with clocks of 100 µs and 1 ms follow the input ramp fairly well, while the waveform from the 5 ms clock clearly shows tracking error and possibly also indicates problems with stability.

It is difficult to quantify the effects of the clock period just by looking at the system output. It is easier to see the effects by observing the servo error signal that results from the various clock periods. The error waveforms are given in Figure 14-29. Both the 5 ms and 1 ms clock period settings result in unacceptable system error. (The measurement is taken when the input ramp signal equals 4 V.) Furthermore, both the 5 ms and 1 ms clocks result in sustained oscillations, making the system much less stable. The 100 µs clock produces a stable error signal, nearly identical to that produced by the *s*-domain compensator implementation.

Implement Compensator as Difference Equations

Now that we have successfully implemented the compensator in the *z*-domain and have established that a 100 µs clock period produces acceptable accuracy and stability, we can take the final step required to implement the lead-lag compensator as software code. This involves simply converting the *z*-domain transfer function into difference equations. The *z*-domain lead-lag filter implemented as difference equations is given in Figure 14-30.

FIGURE 14-29

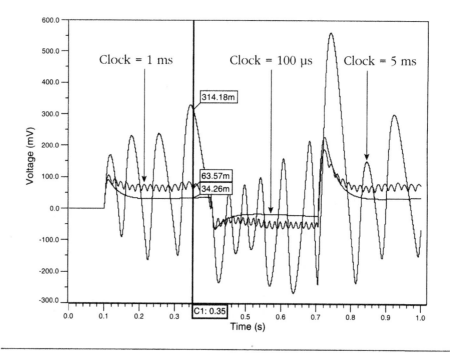

System error as a function of clock period.

To calculate the difference equations, we solve the *z*-domain transfer function from Equation 14-14 for *Y*(*z*). Changing to difference equation notation by substituting **k** for **z**, we have:

$$Y(k) = 0.6163507X(k) - 0.6144184X(k-1) + 0.2307692Y(k-1) \qquad (14\text{-}15)$$

where

$X(k)$	= input at current clock
$X(k-1)$	= input at previous clock
$Y(k)$	= output at current clock
$Y(k-1)$	= output at previous clock

Essentially, this model works in the same way that software code would work in a synchronous real-time control system: every time a system clock occurs, the applicable code is sequentially executed. In the case of the model in Figure 14-30, the statements in the body of the process **proc** are executed each clock cycle. The variables **zi_dly1** and **zo_dly1** represent the previous clock's input and output values, respectively. **Z_new** is the actual output value, which is presented on the output port

FIGURE 14-30

```
library ieee;  use ieee.std_logic_1164.all;

entity lead_lag_diff is
      port ( signal clk : in std_logic;   -- clock
              quantity input : in real;
              quantity output : out real );
end entity lead_lag_diff;

--------------------------------------------------------

architecture bhv of lead_lag_diff is
      constant k : real := 400.0;   -- normalize gain
      signal z_out : real := 0.0;
begin
      proc : process (clk)
          variable zi_dly1 : real := 0.0;   -- input delayed 1 clk cycle
          variable zo_dly1 : real := 0.0;   -- output delayed 1 clk cycle
          variable z_new : real := 0.0;     -- new output value this clk cycle
      begin
          zo_dly1 := z_out;      -- store previous output value
          z_new := 0.6163507 * input - 0.6144184 * zi_dly1 + 0.2307692 * zo_dly1;
          zi_dly1 := input;      -- store previous input value
          z_out <= z_new;
      end process;
      output == k * z_out'ramp(100.0e-9);   -- ensure continuous transitions on output
end bhv;
```

Difference equation lead-lag compensator model.

as real quantity **output**. The 'ramp attribute is used in the simultaneous statement to ensure that **output** is continuous.

While we have concentrated on the lead-lag compensator alone, the entire servo could be described using sequential statements within a single process. This approach would allow the complex algorithms to be debugged with a VHDL-AMS simulator. Alternatively, actual software code fragments expressed in a programming language such as C could be executed as foreign subprograms to the VHDL-AMS model, allowing them to be verified directly prior to building actual hardware.

The results of the simulations for the difference-equation-based model of Figure 14-30 are given in Figure 14-31. Once again, these simulation results are virtually identical to the *s*-domain results illustrated in Figure 14-17 and the mixed-technology results given in Figure 14-25.

As a final verification, each of the systems discussed in this chapter is driven with a 1 Hz sine wave, and the results illustrated in Figure 14-32. All three system implementations behave as expected, underscoring the ability of VHDL-AMS to effectively handle multiple system representations.

FIGURE 14-31

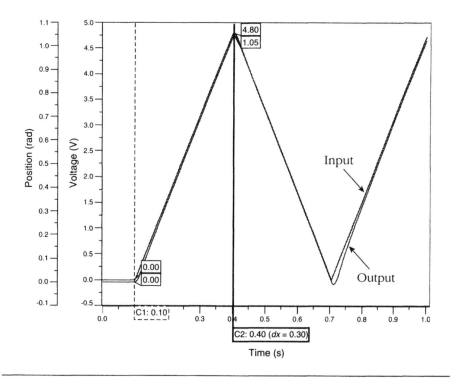

Difference equation system outputs to ramp input.

Exercises

1. [● 14.2] What is the significance of using quantity ports in *s*-domain models rather than terminals?

2. [● 14.2] What is the function of the **break on** statement in the limiter model listed in Figure 14-7?

3. [● 14.2] Referring to the electrical gain model illustrated in Figure 14-4, what is the significance of not specifying a through variable for the **input** terminal?

4. [● 14.3] In the DC motor model illustrated in Figure 14-21, the generated torque, kt*i, is multiplied by –1 in the torque equation. Why?

5. [● 14.3] In the gear model listed in Figure 14-22, the input port, rot1, is declared as subtype **rotational_v**, and the output port, rot2, is declared as subtype **rotational**. Why are they different?

6. [● 14.3] In Figure 14-30, why is vo_dly1 updated before z_new is calculated, and vi_dly1 updated after z_new is calculated?

FIGURE 14-32

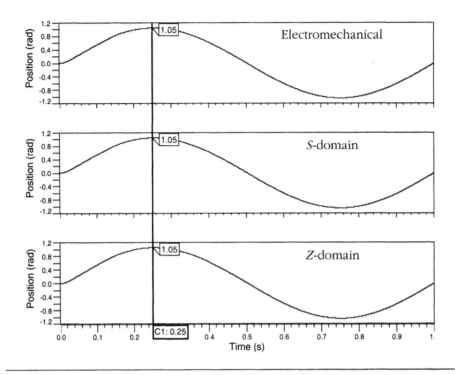

Responses for electromechanical, s-*domain and* z-*domain implementations.*

7. [❶ 14.3] Write entity port declarations for both the gearbox control horn and the rudder control horn.

8. [❶ 14.4] Why is the 'ramp attribute used in the **lead_lag_diff** model shown in Figure 14-30?

9. [❷ 14.2] How could the lead-lag compensator from Figure 14-18 be modified to have electrical inputs and outputs rather than real quantities? Can it still be a two-pin device?

10. [❷ 14.3] Rewrite the gear model of Figure 14-22 without the intrinsic integration so that it produces angular velocity at the output port.

11. [❷ 14.3] Create a feedback potentiometer model that produces a variable resistance as a function of rotational shaft position.

12. [❸ 14.2] Create a limiting integrator model.

13. [❹ 14.4] Implement the entire rudder servo block from Figure 14-26 in the z-domain.

chapter fifteen

Resolved Signals

Throughout the previous chapters we have studiously avoided considering the case of multiple output ports connecting one signal. The problem that arises in such a case is determining the final value of the signal when multiple sources drive it. In this chapter we discuss resolved signals, *the mechanism provided by VHDL-AMS for modeling such cases.*

15.1 **Basic Resolved Signals**

If we consider a real digital system with two outputs driving one signal, we can fairly readily determine the resulting value based on some analog circuit theory. The signal is driven to some intermediate state, depending on the drive capacities of the conflicting drivers. This intermediate state may or may not represent a valid logic state. While we can readily develop an analog circuit model for this behavior using the analog modeling features of VHDL-AMS, we can also stay in the digital domain and model the behavior at a higher level of abstraction. Usually we only connect digital outputs in a design if at most one is active at a time, and the rest are in some high-impedance state. In this case, the resulting value should be the driving value of the single active output. In addition, we include some form of "pull-up" that determines the value of the signal when all outputs are inactive.

While this simple approach is satisfactory for some models, there are other cases where we need to go further. One of the reasons for simulating a model of a design is to detect errors such as multiple simultaneously active connected outputs. In this case, we need to extend the simple approach to detect such errors. Another problem arises when we are modeling at a higher level of abstraction and are using more complex types. We need to specify what, if anything, it means to connect multiple outputs of an enumeration type together.

The approach taken by VHDL-AMS for digital modeling is a very general one: the language requires the designer to specify precisely what value results from connecting multiple outputs. It does this through *resolved signals,* which are an extension of the basic signals we have used in previous chapters. A resolved signal includes in its definition a function, called the *resolution function,* that is used to calculate the final signal value from the values of all of its sources.

Let us see how this works by developing an example. We can model the values driven by a tristate output using a simple extension to the predefined type **bit**, for example:

type tri_state_logic **is** ('0', '1', 'Z');

The extra value, 'Z', is used by an output to indicate that it is in the high-impedance state. Next, we need to write a function that takes a collection of values of this type, representing the values driven by a number of outputs, and return the resulting value to be applied to the connected signal. For this example, we assume that at most one driver is active ('0' or '1') at a time and that the rest are all driving 'Z'. The difficulty with writing the function is that we should not restrict it to a fixed number of input values. We can avoid this by giving it a single parameter that is an unconstrained array of tri_state_logic values, defined by the type declaration

type tri_state_logic_array **is array** (integer **range** <>) **of** tri_state_logic;

The declaration of the resolution function is shown in Figure 15-1. The final step to making a resolved signal is to declare the signal, as follows:

signal s1 : resolve_tri_state_logic tri_state_logic;

FIGURE 15-1

```
function resolve_tri_state_logic ( values : in tri_state_logic_array )
                                   return tri_state_logic is
    variable result : tri_state_logic := 'Z';
begin
    for index in values'range loop
        if values(index) /= 'Z' then
            result := values(index);
        end if;
    end loop;
    return result;
end function resolve_tri_state_logic;
```

A resolution for resolving multiple values from tristate drivers.

This declaration is almost identical to a normal signal declaration, but with the addition of the resolution function name before the signal type. The signal still takes on values from the type **tri_state_logic**, but inclusion of a function name indicates that the signal is a resolved signal, with the named function acting as the resolution function. The fact that **s1** is resolved means that we are allowed to have more than one source for it in the design. (Sources include drivers within processes and output ports of components associated with the signal.) When a transaction is scheduled for the signal, the value is not applied to the signal directly. Instead, the values of all sources connected to the signal, including the new value from the transaction, are formed into an array and passed to the resolution function. The result returned by the function is then applied to the signal as its new value.

Let us look at the syntax rule that describes the VHDL-AMS mechanism we have used in the above example. It is an extension of the rules for the subtype indication, which we first introduced in Chapters 2 and 4. The combined rule is

subtype_indication ⇐
    ⟦ *resolution_function*_name ⟧
    type_mark ⟦ **range** ⟨ *range*_attribute_name
                              ⎮ simple_expression ⟨ **to** ⎮ **downto** ⟩ simple_expression ⟩
            ⎮ (discrete_range ⟨ , ... ⟩) ⟧

This rule shows that a subtype indication can optionally include the name of a function to be used as a resolution function. Given this new rule, we can include a resolution function name anywhere that we specify a type to be used for a signal. For example, we could write a separate subtype declaration that includes a resolution function name, defining a *resolved subtype,* then use this subtype to declare a number of resolved signals, as follows:

subtype resolved_logic **is** resolve_tri_state_logic tri_state_logic;
signal s2, s3 : resolved_logic;

The subtype **resolved_logic** is a resolved subtype of **tri_state_logic**, with **resolve_tri_state_logic** acting as the resolution function. The signals **s2** and **s3** are resolved signals of this subtype. Where a design makes extensive use of resolved signals, it is good practice to define resolved subtypes and use them to declare the signals and ports in the design.

The resolution function for a resolved signal is also invoked to initialize the signal. At the start of a simulation, the drivers for the signal are initialized to the expression included in the signal declaration, or to the default initial value for the signal type if no initialization expression is given. The resolution function is then invoked using these driver values to determine the initial value for the signal. In this way, the signal always has a properly resolved value, right from the start of the simulation.

Let us now return to the tristate logic type we introduced earlier. In the previous example, we assumed that at most one driver is '0' or '1' at a time. In a more realistic model, we need to deal with the possibility of driver conflicts, in which one source drives a resolved signal with the value '0' and another drives it with the value '1'. In some logic families, such driver conflicts cause an indeterminate signal value. We can represent this indeterminate state with a fourth value of the logic type, 'X', often called an *unknown* value. This gives us a complete and consistent *multivalued logic* type, which we can use to describe signal values in a design in more detail than we can using just bit values.

Example   Figure 15-2 shows a package interface and the corresponding package body for the four-state multivalued logic type. The constant **resolution_table** is a lookup table used to determine the value resulting from two source contributions to a signal of the resolved logic type. The resolution function uses this table, indexing it with each element of the array passed to the function. If any source contributes 'X', or if there are two sources with conflicting '0' and '1' contributions, the result is 'X'. If one or more sources are '0' and the remainder 'Z', the result is '0'. Similarly, if one or more sources are '1' and the remainder 'Z', the result is '1'. If all sources are 'Z', the result is 'Z'. The lookup table is a compact way of representing this set of rules.

FIGURE 15-2

```
package MVL4 is
    type MVL4_ulogic is ('X', '0', '1', 'Z');    -- unresolved logic type
    type MVL4_ulogic_vector is array (natural range <>) of MVL4_ulogic;
    function resolve_MVL4 ( contribution : MVL4_ulogic_vector )
                          return MVL4_ulogic;
    subtype MVL4_logic is resolve_MVL4 MVL4_ulogic;
end package MVL4;
```

```
package body MVL4 is
    type table is array (MVL4_ulogic, MVL4_ulogic) of MVL4_ulogic;
```

```
        constant resolution_table : table :=
            -- 'X'    '0'    '1'    'Z'
            -- --------------
            (( 'X',   'X',   'X',   'X' ),    -- 'X'
             ( 'X',   '0',   'X',   '0' ),    -- '0'
             ( 'X',   'X',   '1',   '1' ),    -- '1'
             ( 'X',   '0',   '1',   'Z' ));   -- 'Z'
        function resolve_MVL4 ( contribution : MVL4_ulogic_vector )
                            return MVL4_ulogic is
            variable result : MVL4_ulogic := 'Z';
        begin
            for index in contribution'range loop
                result := resolution_table(result, contribution(index));
            end loop;
            return result;
        end function resolve_MVL4;
    end package body MVL4;
```

A package interface and body for a four-state multivalued and resolved logic subtype.

We can use this package in a design for a tristate buffer. The entity declaration and a behavioral architecture body are shown in Figure 15-3. The buffer drives the value 'Z' on its output when it is disabled. It copies the input to the output when it is enabled and the input is a proper logic level ('0' or '1'). If either the input or the enable port is not a proper logic level, the buffer drives the unknown value on its output.

FIGURE 15-3

```
use work.MVL4.all;
entity tri_state_buffer is
    port ( a, enable : in MVL4_ulogic;  y : out MVL4_ulogic );
end entity tri_state_buffer;
```

```
architecture behavioral of tri_state_buffer is
begin
    y <= 'Z' when enable = '0' else
         a  when enable = '1' and (a = '0' or a = '1') else
         'X';
end architecture behavioral;
```

An entity and behavioral architecture body for a tristate buffer.

Figure 15-4 shows the outline of an architecture body that uses the tristate buffer. The signal **selected_val** is a resolved signal of the multivalued logic type. It is driven by the two buffer output ports. The resolution function for the signal is used to determine the final value of the signal whenever a new transaction is applied to either of the buffer outputs.

FIGURE 15-4

```
use work.MVL4.all;

architecture gate_level of misc_logic is
    signal src1, src1_enable : MVL4_ulogic;
    signal src2, src2_enable : MVL4_ulogic;
    signal selected_val : MVL4_logic;

    ...

begin
    src1_buffer : entity work.tri_state_buffer(behavioral)
        port map ( a => src1, enable => src1_enable, y => selected_val );

    src2_buffer : entity work.tri_state_buffer(behavioral)
        port map ( a => src2, enable => src2_enable, y => selected_val );

    ...

end architecture gate_level;
```

An outline of an architecture body that uses the tristate buffer. The output ports of the two instances of the buffer form two sources for the resolved signal **selected_val**.

Composite Resolved Subtypes

The above examples have all shown resolved subtypes of scalar enumeration types. In fact, VHDL-AMS's resolution mechanism is more general. We can use it to define a resolved subtype of any type that we can legally use as the type of a signal. Thus, we can define resolved integer subtypes, resolved composite subtypes and others. In the latter case, the resolution function is passed an array of composite values and must determine the final composite value to be applied to the signal.

Example   Figure 15-5 shows a package interface and body that define a resolved array sub-type. Each element of an array value of this subtype can be 'X', '0', '1' or 'Z'. The unresolved type **uword** is a 32-element array of these values. The resolution function has an unconstrained array parameter consisting of elements of type **uword**. The function uses the lookup table to resolve corresponding elements from each of the contributing sources and produces a 32-element array result. The subtype **word** is the final resolved array subtype.

FIGURE 15-5

```
package words is
    type X01Z is ('X', '0', '1', 'Z');
    type uword is array (0 to 31) of X01Z;
    type uword_vector is array (natural range <>) of uword;
    function resolve_word ( contribution : uword_vector ) return uword;
    subtype word is resolve_word uword;
end package words;
```

```
package body words is
    type table is array (X01Z, X01Z) of X01Z;
    constant resolution_table : table :=
        -- 'X'   '0'   '1'   'Z'
        -- --------------
        (( 'X',  'X',  'X',  'X' ),      -- 'X'
         ( 'X',  '0',  'X',  '0' ),      -- '0'
         ( 'X',  'X',  '1',  '1' ),      -- '1'
         ( 'X',  '0',  '1',  'Z' ) );    -- 'Z'
    function resolve_word ( contribution : uword_vector ) return uword is
        variable result : uword := (others => 'Z');
    begin
        for index in contribution'range loop
            for element in uword'range loop
                result(element) :=
                    resolution_table( result(element), contribution(index)(element) );
            end loop;
        end loop;
        return result;
    end function resolve_word;
end package body words;
```

A package interface and body for a resolved array subtype.

We can use these types to declare array ports in entity declarations and re-solved array signals with multiple sources. Figure 15-6 shows outlines of a CPU entity and a memory entity, which have bidirectional data ports of the unresolved array type. The architecture body for a computer system, also outlined in Figure 15-6, declares a signal of the resolved subtype and connects it to the data ports of the instances of the CPU and memory.

FIGURE 15-6

```
use work.words.all;
entity cpu is
    port ( address : out uword;  data : inout uword; ... );
end entity cpu;
```

```
use work.words.all;
entity memory is
    port ( address : in uword;  data : inout uword; ... );
end entity memory;
```

```
architecture top_level of computer_system is

    use work.words.all;

    signal address : uword;
    signal data : word;

    ...

begin

    the_cpu : entity work.cpu(behavioral)
        port map ( address, data, ... );

    the_memory : entity work.memory(behavioral)
        port map ( address, data, ... );

    ...

end architecture top_level;
```

An outline of a CPU and memory entity with resolved array ports, and an architecture body for a computer system that uses the CPU and memory.

A resolved composite subtype works well provided every source for a resolved signal of the subtype is connected to every element of the signal. For the subtype shown in the example, every source must be a 32-element array and must connect to all 32 elements of the data signal. However, in a realistic computer system, sources are not always connected in this way. For example, we may wish to connect an 8-bit-wide device to the low-order eight bits of a 32-bit-wide data bus. We might attempt to express such a connection in a component instantiation statement, as follows:

```
boot_rom : entity work.ROM(behavioral)
    port map ( a => address, d => data(24 to 31), ... );   -- illegal
```

If we add this statement to the architecture body in Figure 15-6, we have two sources for elements 0 to 23 of the data signal and three for elements 24 to 31. A problem arises when resolving the signal, since we are unable to construct an array containing the contributions from the sources. For this reason, VHDL-AMS does not allow us to write such a description; it is illegal.

The solution to this problem is to describe the data signal as an array of resolved elements, rather than as a resolved array of elements. We can declare an array type whose elements are values of the **MVL4_logic** type, shown in Figure 15-2. The array type declaration is

type MVL4_logic_vector **is array** (natural **range** <>) **of** MVL4_logic;

This approach has the added advantage that the array type is unconstrained, so we can use it to create signals of different widths, each element of which is resolved. An important point to note, however, is that the type **MVL4_logic_vector** is distinct from the type **MVL4_ulogic_vector**, since they are defined by separate type declarations. Neither is a subtype of the other. Hence we cannot legally associate a signal of type **MVL4_logic_vector** with a port of type **MVL4_ulogic_vector**, or a signal of type **MVL4_ulogic_vector** with a port of type **MVL4_logic_vector**. One solution is to identify all ports that may need to be associated with a signal of the resolved type and to declare them to be of the resolved type. This avoids the type mismatch that would otherwise occur. We illustrate this approach in the following example. Another solution is to use type conversions in the port maps. We will discuss type conversions in association lists in Chapter 24.

Example   Let us assume that the type **MVL4_logic_vector** described above has been added to the package **MVL4**. Figure 15-7 shows entity declarations for a ROM entity and a single in-line memory module (SIMM), using the **MVL4_logic_vector** type for their data ports. The data port of the SIMM is 32 bits wide, whereas the data port of the ROM is only 8 bits wide.

FIGURE 15-7

```
use work.MVL4.all;
entity ROM is
    port ( a : in MVL4_ulogic_vector(15 downto 0);
           d : inout MVL4_logic_vector(7 downto 0);
           rd : in MVL4_ulogic );
end entity ROM;
```

(continued on page 478)

(continued from page 477)

```
use work.MVL4.all;
entity SIMM is
    port ( a : in MVL4_ulogic_vector(9 downto 0);
            d : inout MVL4_logic_vector(31 downto 0);
            ras, cas, we, cs : in MVL4_ulogic );
end entity SIMM;
```

```
architecture detailed of memory_subsystem is
    signal internal_data : MVL4_logic_vector(31 downto 0);
    ...
begin
    boot_ROM : entity work.ROM(behavioral)
        port map ( a => internal_addr(15 downto 0),
                    d => internal_data(7 downto 0),
                    rd => ROM_select );
    main_mem : entity work.SIMM(behavioral)
        port map ( a => main_mem_addr, d => internal_data, ... );
    ...
end architecture detailed;
```

Entity declarations for memory modules whose data ports are arrays of resolved elements, and an outline of an architecture body that uses these entities.

Figure 15-7 also shows an outline of an architecture body that uses these two entities. It declares a signal, **internal_data**, of the **MVL4_logic_vector** type, representing 32 individually resolved elements. The SIMM entity is instantiated with its data port connected to all 32 internal data elements. The ROM entity is instantiated with its data port connected to the rightmost eight elements of the internal data signal. When any of these elements is resolved, the resolution function is passed contributions from the corresponding elements of the SIMM and ROM data ports. When any of the remaining elements of the internal data signal are resolved, they have one less contribution, since they are not connected to any element of the ROM data port.

Summary of Resolved Subtypes

At this point, let us summarize the important points about resolved signals and their resolution functions. Resolved signals of resolved subtypes are the only means by which we may connect a number of sources together, since we need a resolution function to determine the final value of the signal or port from the contributing values. The resolution function must take a single parameter that is a one-dimensional unconstrained array of values of the signal type, and must return a value of the signal type. The index type of the array does not matter, so long as it contains enough index values for the largest possible collection of sources connected together. For example, an array type declared as follows is inadequate if the resolved signal has five sources:

```
type small_int is range 1 to 4;
type small_array is array (small_int range <>) of ... ;
```

The resolution function must be a pure function; that is, it must not have any side effects. This requirement is a safety measure to ensure that the function always returns a predictable value for a given set of source values. Furthermore, since the source values may be passed in any order within the array, the function should be commutative; that is, its result should be independent of the order of the values. When the design is simulated, the resolution function is called whenever any of the resolved signal's sources is active. The function is passed an array of all of the current source values, and the result it returns is used to update the signal value. When the design is synthesized, the resolution function specifies the way in which the synthesized hardware should combine values from multiple sources for a resolved signal.

15.2 IEEE Std_Logic_1164 Resolved Subtypes

In previous chapters we have used the IEEE standard multivalued logic package, std_logic_1164. We are now in a position to describe all of the items provided by the package, including the resolved subtypes and operators. The intent of the IEEE standard is that the multivalued logic subtypes defined in the package be used for models that must be interchanged between designers. The full package interface is included for reference in Appendix C. First, recall that the package provides the basic type std_ulogic, defined as

```
type std_ulogic is ('U', 'X', '0', '1', 'Z', 'W', 'L', 'H', '–');
```

and an array type std_ulogic_vector, defined as

```
type std_ulogic_vector is array ( natural range <> ) of std_ulogic;
```

We have not mentioned it before, but the "u" in "ulogic" stands for unresolved. These types serve as the basis for the declaration of the resolved subtype std_logic, defined as follows:

```
function resolved ( s : std_ulogic_vector ) return std_ulogic;
subtype std_logic is resolved std_ulogic;
```

The standard-logic package also declares an array type of standard-logic elements, analogous to the bit_vector type, for use in declaring array signals:

```
type std_logic_vector is array ( natural range <>) of std_logic;
```

The IEEE standard recommends that models use the subtype **std_logic** and the type **std_logic_vector** instead of the unresolved types **std_ulogic** and **std_ulogic_vector**, even if a signal has only one source. The reason is that simulation vendors are expected to optimize simulation of models using the resolved subtype, but need not optimize use of the unresolved type. The disadvantage of this approach is that it prevents detection of erroneous designs in which multiple sources are inadvertently connected to a signal that should have only one source. Nevertheless, if we are to conform to the standard practice, we should use the resolved logic type. We will conform to the standard in the subsequent examples in this book.

The standard defines the resolution function **resolved** as shown in Figure 15-8. VHDL and VHDL-AMS tools are allowed to provide built-in implementations of this function to improve performance. The function uses the constant **resolution_table** to resolve the driving values. If there is only one driving value, the function returns that value unchanged. If the function is passed an empty array, it returns the value 'Z'. (The circumstances under which a resolution function may be invoked with an empty array will be covered in Chapter 19.) The value of **resolution_table** shows exactly what is meant by "forcing" driving values ('X', '0' and '1') and "weak" driving values ('W', 'L' and 'H'). If one driver of a resolved signal drives a forcing value and another drives a weak value, the forcing value dominates. On the other hand, if both drivers drive different values with the same strength, the result is the unknown value of that strength ('X' or 'W'). The high-impedance value, 'Z', is dominated by forcing and weak values. If a "don't care" value ('–') is to be resolved with any other value, the result is the unknown value 'X'. The interpretation of the "don't care" value is that the model has not made a choice about its output state. Finally, if an "uninitialized" value ('U') is to be resolved with any other value, the result is 'U', indicating that the model has not properly initialized all outputs.

In addition to this multivalued logic subtype, the package **std_logic_1164** declares a number of subtypes for more restricted multivalued logic modeling. The subtype declarations are

```
subtype X01 is resolved std_ulogic range 'X' to '1';        -- ('X','0','1')
subtype X01Z is resolved std_ulogic range 'X' to 'Z';       -- ('X','0','1','Z')
subtype UX01 is resolved std_ulogic range 'U' to '1';       -- ('U','X','0','1')
subtype UX01Z is resolved std_ulogic range 'U' to 'Z';      -- ('U','X','0','1','Z')
```

Each of these is a closed subtype; that is, the result of resolving values in each case is a value within the range of the subtype. The subtype **X01Z** corresponds to the type MVL4 we introduced in Figure 15-2.

The standard-logic package provides overloaded forms of the logical operators **and**, **nand**, **or**, **nor**, **xor**, **xnor** and **not** for standard-logic values and vectors, returning values in the range 'U', 'X', '0' or '1'. In addition, there are functions to convert between values of the full standard-logic type, the subtypes shown above and the predefined bit and bit-vector types. These are all listed in Appendix C.

FIGURE 15-8

```
type stdlogic_table is array (std_ulogic, std_ulogic) of std_ulogic;
constant resolution_table : stdlogic_table :=
    -- ------------------------------------------------
    --   'U', 'X', '0', '1', 'Z', 'W', 'L', 'H', '-'
    -- ------------------------------------------------
    ((  'U', 'U', 'U', 'U', 'U', 'U', 'U', 'U', 'U' ),   -- 'U'
     (  'U', 'X', 'X', 'X', 'X', 'X', 'X', 'X', 'X' ),   -- 'X'
     (  'U', 'X', '0', 'X', '0', '0', '0', '0', 'X' ),   -- '0'
     (  'U', 'X', 'X', '1', '1', '1', '1', '1', 'X' ),   -- '1'
     (  'U', 'X', '0', '1', 'Z', 'W', 'L', 'H', 'X' ),   -- 'Z'
     (  'U', 'X', '0', '1', 'W', 'W', 'W', 'W', 'X' ),   -- 'W'
     (  'U', 'X', '0', '1', 'L', 'W', 'L', 'W', 'X' ),   -- 'L'
     (  'U', 'X', '0', '1', 'H', 'W', 'W', 'H', 'X' ),   -- 'H'
     (  'U', 'X', 'X', 'X', 'X', 'X', 'X', 'X', 'X' )    -- '-'
    );
function resolved ( s : std_ulogic_vector ) return std_ulogic is
    variable result : std_ulogic := 'Z';   -- weakest state default
begin
    if s'length = 1 then
        return s(s'low);
    else
        for i in s'range loop
            result := resolution_table(result, s(i));
        end loop;
    end if;
    return result;
end function resolved;
```

The definition of the resolution function **resolved**.

15.3 **Resolved Signals and Ports**

In the previous discussion of resolved signals, we have limited ourselves to the simple case where a number of drivers or output ports of component instances drive a signal. Any input port connected to the resolved signal gets the final resolved value as the port value when a transaction is performed. We now look in more detail at the case of ports of mode **inout** being connected to a resolved signal. The question to answer here is, What value is seen by the input side of such a port? Is it the value driven by the component instance or the final value of the resolved signal connected to the port? In fact, it is the latter. An **inout** port models a connection in which the driver contributes to the associated signal's value, and the input side of the component senses the actual signal rather than using the driving value.

Example   Some asynchronous bus protocols use a distributed synchronization mechanism based on a wired-and control signal. This is a single signal driven by each module using active-low open-collector or open-drain drivers and pulled up by the bus terminator. If a number of modules on the bus need to wait until all are ready to proceed with some operation, they use the control signal as follows. Initially, all modules drive the signal to the '0' state. When each is ready to proceed, it turns off its driver ('Z') and monitors the control signal. So long as any module is not yet ready, the signal remains at '0'. When all modules are ready, the bus terminator pulls the signal up to the '1' state. All modules sense this change and proceed with the operation.

Figure 15-9 shows an entity declaration for a bus module that has a port of the unresolved type **std_ulogic** for connection to such a synchronization control signal. The architecture body for a system comprising several such modules is also outlined. The control signal is pulled up by a concurrent signal assignment statement, which acts as a source with a constant driving value of 'H'. This is a value having a weak strength, which is overridden by any other source that drives '0'. It can pull the signal high only when all other sources drive 'Z'.

FIGURE 15-9

```
library ieee;  use ieee.std_logic_1164.all;

entity bus_module is
    port ( synch : inout std_ulogic;  ... );
end entity bus_module;
```

```
architecture top_level of bus_based_system is

    signal synch_control : std_logic;

    ...

begin

    synch_control_pull_up : synch_control <= 'H';

    bus_module_1 : entity work.bus_module(behavioral)
        port map ( synch => synch_control, ... );

    bus_module_2 : entity work.bus_module(behavioral)
        port map ( synch => synch_control, ... );

    ...

end architecture top_level;
```

An entity declaration for a bus module that uses a wired-and synchronization signal, and an architecture body that instantiates the entity, connecting the synchronization port to a resolved signal.

Figure 15-10 shows an outline of a behavioral architecture body for the bus module. Each instance initially drives its synchronization port with '0'. This value is passed up through the port and used as the contribution to the resolved signal from the entity instance. When an instance is ready to proceed with its operation, it changes its driving value to 'Z', modeling an open-collector or open-drain driver being turned off. The process then suspends until the value seen on the synchronization port changes to 'H'. If other instances are still driving '0', their contributions dominate, and the value of the signal stays '0'. When all other instances eventually change their contributions to 'Z', the value 'H' contributed by the pull-up statement dominates, and the value of the signal changes to 'H'. This value is passed back down through the ports of each instance, and the processes all resume.

FIGURE 15-10

```
architecture behavioral of bus_module is
begin
    behavior : process is
        ...
    begin
        synch <= '0' after Tdelay_synch;
        ...
        -- ready to start operation
        synch <= 'Z' after Tdelay_synch;
        wait until synch = 'H';
        -- proceed with operation
        ...
    end process behavior;
end architecture behavioral;
```

An outline of a behavioral architecture body for a bus module, showing use of the synchronization control port.

Resolved Ports

Just as a signal declared with a signal declaration can be of a resolved subtype, so too can a port declared in an interface list of an entity. This is consistent with all that we have said about ports appearing just like signals to an architecture body. Thus if the architecture body contains a number of processes that must drive a port or a number of component instances that must connect outputs to a port, the port must be resolved. The final value driven by the resolved port is determined by resolving all of the sources within the architecture body. For example, we might declare an entity with a resolved port as follows:

```
library ieee;  use ieee.std_logic_1164.all;
entity IO_section is
    port ( data_ack : inout std_logic;  ... );
end entity IO_section;
```

The architecture body corresponding to this entity might instantiate a number of I/O controller components, each with their data acknowledge ports connected to the **data_ack** port of the entity. Each time any of the controllers updates its data acknowledge port, the standard-logic resolution function is invoked. It determines the driving value for the **data_ack** port by resolving the driving values from all controllers.

If it happens that the actual signal associated with a resolved port in an enclosing architecture body is itself a resolved signal, then the signal's resolution function will be called separately after the port's resolution function has determined the port's driving value. Note that the signal in the enclosing architecture body may use a different resolution function from the connected port, although in practice, most designs use the one function for resolution of all signals of a given subtype.

An extension of the above scenario is a design in which there are several levels of hierarchy, with a process nested at the deepest level generating a value to be passed out through resolved ports to a signal at the top level. At each level, a resolution function is called to determine the driving value of the port at that level. The value finally determined for the signal at the top level is called the *effective value* of the signal. It is passed back down the hierarchy of ports as the effective value of each **in** mode or **inout** mode port. This value is used on the input side of each port.

Example   Figure 15-11 shows the hierarchical organization for a single-board computer system, consisting of a frame buffer for a video display, an input/output controller section, a CPU/memory section and a bus expansion block. These are all sources for the resolved data bus signal. The CPU/memory section in turn comprises a memory block and a CPU/cache block. Both of these act as sources for the data port, so it must be a resolved port. The cache has two sections, both of which act as sources for the data port of the CPU/cache block. Hence, this port must also be resolved.

Let us consider the case of one of the cache sections updating its data port. The new driving value is resolved with the current driving value from the other cache section to determine the driving value of the CPU/cache block data port. This result is then resolved with the current driving value of the memory block to determine the driving value of the CPU/memory section. Next, this driving value is resolved with the current driving values of the other top-level sections to determine the effective value of the data bus signal. The final step involves propagating this signal value back down the hierarchy for use as the effective value of each of the data ports. Thus, a module that reads the value of its data port will see the final resolved value of the data bus signal. This value is not necessarily the same as the driving value it contributes.

FIGURE 15-11

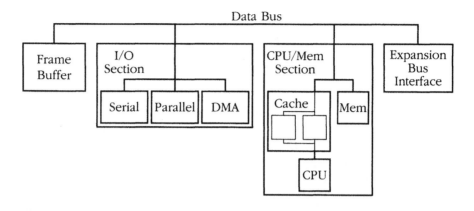

A hierarchical block diagram of a single-board computer system, showing the hierarchical connections of the resolved data bus ports to the data bus signal.

Driving Value Attribute

Since the value seen on a signal or on an **inout** mode port may be different from the value driven by a process, VHDL-AMS provides an attribute, 'driving_value, that allows the process to read the value it contributes to the prefix signal. For example, if a process has a driver for a resolved signal **s**, it may be driving **s** with the value 'Z' from a previously executed signal assignment statement, but the resolution function for **s** may have given it the value '0'. The process can refer to **s**'driving_value to retrieve the value 'Z'. Note that a process can only use this attribute to determine its own contribution to a signal; it cannot directly find out another process's contribution.

15.4 **Resolved Signal Parameters**

Let us now return to the topic of subprograms with signal parameters and see how they behave in the presence of resolved signals. Recall that when a procedure with an **out** mode signal parameter is called, the procedure is passed a reference to the caller's driver for the actual signal. Any signal assignment statements performed within the procedure body are actually performed on the caller's driver. If the actual signal parameter is a resolved signal, the values assigned by the procedure are used to resolve the signal value. No resolution takes place within the procedure. In fact, the procedure need not be aware that the actual signal is resolved.

In the case of an **in** mode signal parameter to a function or procedure, a reference to the actual signal parameter is passed when the subprogram is called, and the subprogram uses the actual value of the signal. If the signal is resolved, the subprogram sees the value determined after resolution. In the case of an **inout** signal parameter, a procedure is passed references to both the signal and its driver, and no resolution is performed internally to the procedure.

Example   We can encapsulate the distributed synchronization protocol described in the example on page 482 in a set of procedures, each with a single signal parameter, as shown in Figure 15-12. Suppose a process uses a resolved signal **barrier** of subtype **std_logic** to synchronize with other processes. Figure 15-13 shows how the process might use the procedures to implement the protocol.

The process has a driver for **barrier**, since the procedure calls associate the signal as an actual parameter with formal parameters of mode **out** and **inout**. A reference to this driver is passed to init_synchronize, which assigns the value '0' on behalf of the process. This value is used in the resolution of **barrier**. When the process is ready to start its synchronized operation, it calls **begin_synchronize**, passing references to its driver for **barrier** and to the actual signal itself. The procedure uses the driver to assign the value 'Z' on behalf of the process and then waits until the actual signal changes to 'H'. When the transaction on the driver matures, its value is resolved with other contributions from other processes and the result applied to the signal. This final value is used by the wait statement in the procedure to determine whether to resume the calling process. If the value is 'H', the process resumes, the procedure returns to the caller and the operation goes ahead. When the process completes the operation, it calls **end_synchronize** to reset **barrier** back to '0'.

FIGURE 15-12

```
procedure init_synchronize ( signal synch : out std_logic ) is
begin
    synch <= '0';
end procedure init_synchronize;

procedure begin_synchronize ( signal synch : inout std_logic;
                              Tdelay : in delay_length := 0 fs ) is
begin
    synch <= 'Z' after Tdelay;
    wait until synch = 'H';
end procedure begin_synchronize;

procedure end_synchronize ( signal synch : inout std_logic;
                            Tdelay : in delay_length := 0 fs ) is
begin
    synch <= '0' after Tdelay;
    wait until synch = '0';
end procedure end_synchronize;
```

Three procedures that encapsulate the distributed synchronization operation.

FIGURE 15-13

```
synchronized_module : process is
    ...
begin
    init_synchronize(barrier);
    ...
    loop
        ...
        begin_synchronize(barrier);
        ...    -- perform operation, synchronized with other processes
        end_synchronize(barrier);
        ...
    end loop;
end process synchronized_module;
```

An outline of a process that uses the distributed synchronization protocol procedures, with a resolved control signal barrier.

Exercises

1. [● 15.1] Suppose there are four drivers connected to a resolved signal that uses the resolution function shown in Figure 15-1. What is the resolved value of the signal if the four drivers contribute these values:

    (a) 'Z', '1', 'Z', 'Z'?

    (b) '0', 'Z', 'Z, '0'?

    (c) 'Z', '1', 'Z', '0'?

2. [● 15.1] Rewrite the following resolved signal declaration as a subtype declaration followed by a signal declaration using the subtype.

    signal synch_control : wired_and tri_state_logic := '0';

3. [● 15.1] What is the initial value of the following signal of the type MVL4_logic defined in Figure 15-2? How is that value derived?

    signal int_req : MVL4_logic;

4. [● 15.1] Does the result of the resolution function defined in Figure 15-2 depend on the order of contributions from drivers in the array passed to the function?

5. [● 15.1] Suppose we define a resolved array subtype, **byte**, in the same way that the type **word** is defined in Figure 15-5, but with 8 elements in the array type in-

stead of 32. We then declare a signal of type **byte** with three drivers. What is the resolved value of the signal if the three drivers contribute these values:

(a) "ZZZZZZZZ", "ZZZZ0011", "ZZZZZZZZ"?

(b) "XXXXZZZZ", "ZZZZZZZZ", "00000011"?

(c) "00110011", "ZZZZZZZZ", "ZZZZ1111"?

6. [❶ 15.1] Suppose a signal is declared as

    signal data_bus : MVL4_logic_vector(0 **to** 15);

where MVL4_logic_vector is as described on page 477, and the following signal assignments are each executed in different processes:

    data_bus <= "ZZZZZZZZZZZZZZZZ";
    data_bus(0 **to** 7) <= "XXXXZZZZ";
    data_bus(8 **to** 15) <= "00111100";

What is the resolved signal value after all of the transactions have been performed?

7. [❶ 15.2] Suppose there are four drivers connected to a signal of type **std_logic**. What is the resolved value of the signal if the four drivers contribute these values:

(a) 'Z', '0', 'Z', 'H'?

(b) 'H', 'Z', 'W', '0'?

(c) 'Z', 'W', 'L', 'H'?

(d) 'U', '0', 'Z', '1'?

(e) 'Z', 'Z', 'Z', '–'?

8. [❶ 15.3] Figure 15-14 is a timing diagram for the system with two bus modules using the wired-and synchronization signal described in Figure 15-9. The diagram shows the driving values contributed by each of the bus modules to the synch_control signal. Complete the diagram by drawing the resolved waveform for synch_control. Indicate the times at which each bus module proceeds with its internal operation, as described in Figure 15-10.

9. [❶ 15.3] Suppose all of the modules in the hierarchy of Figure 15-11 use resolved ports for their data connections. If the Mem, Cache, Serial and DMA modules all update their data drivers in the same simulation cycle, how many times is the resolution function invoked to determine the final resolved values of the data signals?

10. [❶ 15.3] Suppose a process in a model drives a bidirectional port **synch_T** of type **std_logic**. Write a signal assignment statement that inverts the process's contribution to the port.

FIGURE 15-14

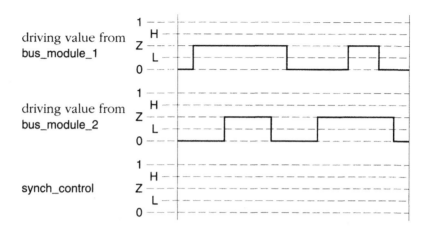

Timing diagram for wired-and synchronization.

11. [❷ 15.1] Develop a model that includes two processes, each of which drives a signal of the type **MVL4_logic** described in Figure 15-2. Experiment with your simulator to see if it allows you to trace the invocation and execution of the resolution function.

12. [❷ 15.2] Develop a model of an inverter with an open-collector output of type **std_logic**, and a model of a pull-up resistor that drives its single **std_logic** port with the value 'H'. Test the models in a test bench that connects the outputs of a number of inverter instances to a signal of type **std_logic**, pulled up with a resistor instance. Verify that the circuit implements the active-low wired-or operation.

13. [❷ 15.2] Develop a behavioral model of an 8-bit-wide bidirectional transceiver, such as the 74245 family of components. The transceiver has two bidirectional data ports, **a** and **b**, an active-low output-enable port, **oe_n**, and a direction port, **dir**. When **oe_n** is low and **dir** is low, data is received from **b** to **a**. When **oe_n** is low and **dir** is high, data is transmitted from **a** to **b**. When **oe_n** is high, both **a** and **b** are high impedance. Assume a propagation delay of 5 ns for all output changes.

14. [❷ 15.2] Many combinatorial logic functions can be implemented in integrated circuits using pass transistors acting as switches. While a pass transistor is, in principle, a bidirectional device, for many circuits it is sufficient to model it as a unidirectional device. Develop a model of a unidirectional pass transistor switch, with an input port, an output port and an enable port, all of type **std_logic**. When the enable input is 'H' or '1', the input value is passed to the output, but with weak drive strength. When the enable input is 'L' or '0', the output is high impedance. If the enable input is at an unknown level, the output is unknown, except that its drive strength is weak.

15. [❸ 15.2] Develop a behavioral model of a tristate buffer with data input, data output and enable ports, all of type std_logic. The propagation time from data input to data output when the buffer is enabled is 4 ns. The turn-on delay from the enable port is 3 ns, and the turn-off delay is 3.5 ns. Use the buffer and any other necessary gate models in a structural model of the 8-bit transceiver described in Exercise 13.

16. [❸ 15.2] Use the unidirectional pass transistor model of Exercise 14 in a structural model of a four-input multiplexer. The multiplexer has select inputs s0 and s1. Pass transistors are used to construct the multiplexer as shown in Figure 15-15.

17. [❸ 15.2] Develop a model of a distributed priority arbiter for a shared bus in a multiprocessor computer system. Each bus requester has a request priority, R, between 0 and 31, with 0 indicating the most urgent request and 31 indicating no request. Priorities are binary-encoded using 5-bit vectors, with bit 4 being the most-significant bit and bit 0 being the least-significant bit. The standard-logic values 'H' and '1' both represent the binary digit 1, and the standard-logic value '0' represents the binary digit 0. All requesters can drive and sense a 5-bit arbitration bus, A, which is pulled up to 'H' by the bus terminator. The requesters each use A and their own priority to compute the minimum of all priorities by comparing the binary digits of priorities as follows. For each bit position i:

- if $(R_{4...i+1} = A_{4...i+1})$ and $(R_i = 0)$: drive A_i with '0' after T_{pd}
- if $(R_{4...i+1} \neq A_{4...i+1})$ or $(R_i = 1)$: drive A_i with 'Z' after T_{pd}

T_{pd} is the propagation delay between sensing a value on A and driving a resulting value on A. When the value on A has stabilized, it is the minimum of all request priorities. The requester with $R = A$ wins the arbitration. If you are not convinced that the distributed minimization scheme operates as required, trace its execution for various combinations of priority values.

FIGURE 15·15

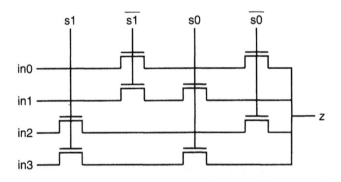

A multiplexer constructed of pass transistors.

18. [❹] Develop a behavioral model of a telephone keypad controller. The controller has outputs c1 to c3 and inputs r1 to r4, connected to the 12 switches of a touch-tone telephone as shown in Figure 15-16.

Each key in the keypad is a single-pole switch that shorts the row signal to the column signal when the key is pressed. Due to the mechanical construction of the switch, "switch bounce" occurs when the key is pressed. Several intermittent contacts are made between the signals over a period of up to 5 ms, before a sustained contact is made. Bounce also occurs when the key is released. Several intermittent contacts may occur over the same period before sustained release is achieved.

The keypad controller scans the keypad by setting each of the column signals to '0' in turn. While a given column signal is '0', the controller examines each of the row inputs. If a row input is 'H', the switch between the column and the row is open. If the row input is '0', the switch is closed. The entire keypad is scanned once every millisecond.

The controller generates a set of column outputs c1_out to c3_out and a set of row outputs r1_out to r4_out. A valid switch closure is indicated by exactly one column output and exactly one row output going to '1' at the same time. The controller filters out spurious switch closures due to switch bounce and ignores multiple concurrent switch closures.

19. [❹] The IEEE standard-logic type models two drive strengths: forcing and weak. This is insufficient to model detailed operation of circuits at the switch level. For example, in circuits that store a charge on the gate terminal of a MOS transistor, we need to distinguish the weaker capacitive drive strength of the stored value from the resistive strength of a value transmitted through a pass transistor.

FIGURE 15-16

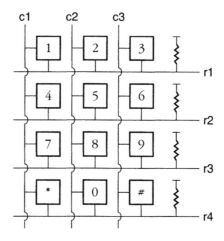

Keypad switch connections for a touch-tone telephone.

Develop a package that defines a resolved type similar to **std_logic**, with forcing, resistive and capacitive strengths for 0, 1 and unknown values.

20. [❹] Exercise 19 describes a logic type that incorporates three drive strengths. If we need to model switch level circuits in finer detail, we can extend the type to deal with an arbitrary number of drive strengths. Each time a signal is transmitted through a pass transistor, its drive strength is diminished. We can model this by representing a logic value as a record containing the bit value ('0', '1' or unknown) and an integer representing the strength. We use 0 to represent power-supply strength and a positive integer n to represent the strength of a signal after being transmitted through n pass transistors from the power supply. A normal driver has strength 1, to reflect the fact that it derives the driving value by turning on a transistor connected to one or the other power supply rail. (This scheme is described by Smith and Acosta in [35].)

Develop a package that defines a resolved type based on this scheme. Include functions for separating the bit value and strength components of a combined value, for constructing a combined value from separate bit value and strength components and for weakening the strength component of a combined value. Use the package to model a pass transistor component. Then use the pass transistor in a model of an eight-input multiplexer similar to the four-input multiplexer of Exercise 16.

21. [❹] Self-timed asynchronous systems use handshaking to synchronize operation of interacting modules. In such systems, it is sometimes necessary to synchronize a number of modules at a *rendezvous*. Each module waits until all modules are ready to perform an operation. When all are ready, the operation commences. A scheme for rendezvous synchronization of a number of modules using three wired-and control signals was first proposed by Sutherland et al. for the TRIMOS-BUS [37] and was subsequently adopted for use in the arbitration protocol of the IEEE Futurebus [21].

Develop a high-level model of a system that uses the three-wire synchronization scheme. You should include a package to support your model. The package should include a type definition for a record containing the three synchronization wires and a pair of procedures, one to wait for a rendezvous and another to leave the rendezvous after completion of the operation. The procedures should have a bidirectional signal parameter for the three-wire record and should determine the state of the synchronization protocol from the parameter value.

chapter sixteen

Components and Configurations

In Chapters 5 and 6 we saw how to write entity declarations and architecture bodies that describe the structure of a system. Within an architecture body, we can write component instantiation statements that describe instances of an entity and connect signals, quantities and terminals to the ports of the instances. This simple approach to building a hierarchical design works well if we know in advance all the details of the entities we want to use. However, that is not always the case, especially in a large design project. In this chapter we introduce an alternative way of describing the hierarchical structure of a design that affords significantly more flexibility at the cost of a little more effort in managing the design.

16.1 **Components**

The first thing we need to do to describe an interconnection of subsystems in a design is to describe the different kinds of components used. We have seen how to do this by writing entity declarations for each of the subsystems. Each entity declaration is a separate design unit and has corresponding architecture bodies that describe implementations. An alternative approach is to write *component declarations* in the declarative part of an architecture body or package interface. We can then create *instances* of the components within the statement part of the architecture body.

Component Declarations

A component declaration simply specifies the external interface to the component in terms of generic constants and ports. We do not need to describe any corresponding implementation, since all we are interested in is how the component is connected in the current level of the design hierarchy. This makes the architecture completely self-contained, since it does not depend on any other library units except its corresponding entity interface. Let us look at the syntax rule that governs how we write a component declaration.

```
component_declaration ⇐
    component identifier [ is ]
        [ generic ( generic_interface_list ) ; ]
        [ port ( port_interface_list ) ; ]
    end component [ identifier ] ;
```

A simple example of a component declaration that follows this syntax rule is

```
component nfet is
    generic ( Vt : real;
                transconductance : real );
    port ( terminal gate, drain, source : electrical );
end component nfet;
```

This declaration defines a component type that represents an NMOS field effect transistor with gate, drain and source terminal ports. It also has generic constants for parameterizing the threshold voltage and transconductance.

Note the similarity between a component declaration and an entity declaration. This similarity is not accidental, since they both serve to define the external interface to a module. Although there is a very close relationship between components and entities, in fact they embody two different concepts. This may be a source of confusion to newcomers to VHDL-AMS. Nevertheless, the flexibility afforded by having the two different constructs is a powerful feature of VHDL-AMS, so we will work through it carefully in this section and try to make the distinction clear.

One way of thinking about the difference between an entity declaration and a component declaration is to think of the modules being defined as having different levels of "reality." An entity declaration defines a "real" module: something that ulti-mately will have a physical manifestation. For example, it may represent a circuit board in a rack, a packaged integrated circuit or a standard cell included in a piece of silicon. An entity declaration is a separate design unit that may be separately analyzed and placed into a design library. A component declaration, on the other hand, defines a "virtual," or "idealized," module that is included within an architecture body. It is as though we are saying, "For this architecture body, we assume there is a module as defined by this component declaration, since such a module meets our needs exactly." We specify the names, natures, types and modes of the ports on the virtual module (the component) and proceed to lay out the structure of the design using this idealized view.

Of course, we do not make these assumptions about modules arbitrarily. One possibility is that we know what real modules are available and customize the virtual reality based on that knowledge. The advantage here is that the idealization cushions us from the irrelevant details of the real module, making the design easier to manage. Another possibility is that we are working "top down" and will later use the idealized module as the specification for a real module. Either way, eventually a link has to be made between an instance of a virtual component and a real entity so that the design can be constructed. In the rest of this section, we look at how to use components in an architecture body, then come back to the question of the binding between com-ponent instances and entities.

Component Instantiation

If a component declaration defines a kind of module, then a component instantiation specifies a usage of the module in a design. We have seen how we can instantiate an entity directly using a component instantiation statement within an architecture body. Let us now look at an alternative syntax rule that shows how we can instantiate a declared component:

component_instantiation_statement ⇐
    *instantiation*_label :
        ⟦ **component** ⟧ *component*_name
        ⟦ **generic map** (*generic*_association_list) ⟧
        ⟦ **port map** (*port*_association_list) ⟧ ;

This syntax rule shows us that we may simply name a component declared in the ar-chitecture body and, if required, provide actual values for the generic constants and actual signals, quantities and terminals to connect to the ports. The label is required to identify the component instance.

Example   We can construct a circuit for an opamp using MOSFET transistors. (See, for ex-ample, Gray et al. [19].) Figure 16-1 shows an entity declaration and an outline of an architecture body for a structural opamp model. The architecture body uses the NMOS transistor component shown on page 494. Note that all we have done here is specify the structure of this level of the design hierarchy, without having

---

FIGURE 16-1

```
library ieee_proposed;  use ieee_proposed.electrical_systems.all;
entity opamp is
    port ( terminal plus_in, minus_in, output, vdd, vss, gnd : electrical );
end entity opamp;
```

```
architecture struct of opamp is
    component nfet is
        generic ( Vt : real;
                    transconductance : real );
        port ( terminal gate, drain, source : electrical );
    end component nfet;

    terminal int_1, int_2, int_3, ... : electrical;
begin
    m1 : component nfet
        generic map ( Vt => 0.026, transconductance => 1.0 )
        port map ( gate => plus_in, drain => int_1, source => int_2 );

    m2 : component nfet
        generic map ( Vt => 0.026, transconductance => 1.0 )
        port map ( gate => minus_in, drain => int_1, source => int_3 );

    -- other component instances
    ...

end architecture struct;
```

An entity declaration and architecture body for an opamp using a component declaration for an NMOS transistor.

indicated how the NMOS transistor is implemented. We will see how that may be done in the remainder of this chapter.

Packaging Components

Let us now turn to the issue of design management for large projects and see how we can make management of large libraries of entities easier using packages and components. Usually, work on a large design is partitioned among several designers, each responsible for implementing one or more entities that are used in the complete system. Each entity may need to have some associated types and natures defined in a utility package, so that entity ports can be declared using those types and natures. When the entity is used, other designers will need component declarations to instantiate components that will eventually be bound to the entity. It makes good sense to include a component declaration in the utility package, along with the types, natures and other related items. This means that users of the entity do not need to rewrite the declarations, thus avoiding a potential source of errors and misunderstanding.

Example   Suppose we are responsible for designing a hydraulic valve for use in automotive applications. We can write a package specification that defines the interface to be used in the rest of the design, as outlined in Figure 16-2. The component declaration in this package corresponds to our entity declaration for the valve, shown in Figure 16-3. When designers working on an automotive system need to instantiate the valve, they only need to import the items in the package, rather than rewriting all of the declarations. Figure 16-4 shows an outline of a design that does this.

FIGURE 16-2

```
library ieee_proposed;
use ieee_proposed.fluidic_systems.all, ieee_proposed.mechanical_systems.all;

package automotive_valve_defs is

    subnature valve_fluidic is fluidic
        tolerance "valve_pressure" across "valve_vflow_rate" through;

    subnature valve_translational is translational
        tolerance "valve_displacement" across "valve_force" through;

    ...   -- other useful declarations

    component automotive_valve is
        port ( terminal p1, p2 : valve_fluidic;
                terminal control : valve_translational );
    end component automotive_valve;

end package automotive_valve_defs;
```

An outline of a package declaration containing useful definitions for an automotive hydraulic valve.

FIGURE 16-3

```
use work.automotive_valve_defs.all;

entity automotive_valve is
    port ( terminal p1, p2 : valve_fluidic;
            terminal control : valve_translational );
end entity automotive_valve;
```

An entity declaration for the hydraulic valve.

FIGURE 16-4

```
architecture structure of brake_system is
    use work.automotive_valve_defs.all;
    ...  -- declarations of other components, terminals, etc
begin
    pedal_valve : component automotive_valve
        port map ( p1 => master_reservoir,
                   p2 => brake_line,
                   control => brake_pedal );
    ...  -- other component instances
end architecture structure;
```

An outline of an architecture body that uses the hydraulic valve definitions package and instantiates the component defined in it.

16.2 Configuring Component Instances

Once we have described the structure of one level of a design using components and component instantiations, we still need to flesh out the hierarchical implementation for each component instance. We can do this by writing a *configuration declaration* for the design. In it, we specify which real entity interface and corresponding architecture body should be used for each of the component instances. This is called *binding* the component instances to design entities. Note that we do not specify any binding information for a component instantiation statement that directly instantiates an entity, since the entity and architecture body are specified explicitly in the component instantiation statement. Thus our discussion in this section only applies to instantiations of declared components.

Basic Configuration Declarations

We start by looking at a simplified set of syntax rules for configuration declarations, as the full set of rules is rather complicated. The simplest case arises when the entities to which component instances are bound are implemented with behavioral architectures. In this case, there is only one level of the hierarchy to flesh out. The simplified syntax rules are

```
configuration_declaration ⇐
    configuration identifier of entity_name is
        for architecture_name
            {   for component_specification
```

binding_indication ;
      end for ; ⟧
    end for ;
  end ⟦ **configuration** ⟧ ⟦ identifier ⟧ ;

component_specification ⟸
  (*instantiation*_label ⟨ , ... ⟩ ⏐ **others** ⏐ **all**) : *component*_name

binding_indication ⟸ **use entity** *entity*_name ⟦ (*architecture*_identifier) ⟧

The identifier given in the configuration declaration identifies this particular spec-ification for fleshing out the hierarchy of the named entity. There may be other con-figuration declarations, with different names, for the same entity. Within the configuration declaration we write the name of the particular architecture body to work with (included after the first **for** keyword), since there may be several corre-sponding to the entity. We then include the binding information for each component instance within the architecture body. The syntax rule shows that we can identify a component instance by its label and its component name, as used in the component instantiation in the architecture body. We bind it by specifying an entity name and a corresponding architecture body name. For example, we might bind instances m1 and m2 of the component nfet as follows:

```
for m1, m2 : nfet
    use entity work.bulk_cmos_nfet(basic);
end for;
```

This indicates that the instances are each to be bound to the design entity bulk_cmos_nfet, found in the current working library, and that the architecture body basic corresponding to that entity should be used as the implementation of the in-stances.

Note that since we can identify each component instance individually, we have the opportunity to bind different instances of a given component to different entity/architecture pairs. After we have specified bindings for some of the instances in a design, we can use the keyword **others** to bind any remaining instances of a given component type to a given entity/architecture pair. Alternatively, if all instances of a particular component type are to have the same binding, we can use the keyword **all** instead of naming individual instances. The syntax rules also show that the architec-ture name corresponding to the entity is optional. If it is omitted, a default binding takes place when the design is elaborated. The component instance is bound to whichever architecture body for the named entity has been most recently analyzed at the time of elaboration. A further possibility is that we omit bindings for one or more component instances in the design. In this case, the default binding rule attempts to find an entity with the same name as the component. The entity must be located in the same design library as the design unit in which the instantiated component is de-clared. If no entity is found, the component instance remains unbound (see "Deferred Component Binding," on page 512). Relying on the default binding rules to locate and bind the right entity can make a design difficult to understand and reduces portability. The safest approach is to ensure that we bind all component instances explicitly.

A configuration declaration is a primary design unit, and as such, may be separately analyzed and placed into the working design library as a library unit. If it contains sufficient binding information so that the full design hierarchy is fleshed out down to behavioral architectures, the configuration may be used as the target unit of a simulation. The design is elaborated by substituting instances of the specified architecture bodies for bound component instances in the way described in Chapter 7. The only difference is that when component declarations are instantiated, the configuration must be consulted to find the appropriate architecture body to substitute.

Example Let us look at a sample configuration declaration that binds the component instances in the opamp model of Figure 16-1. Suppose we have a resource library for a project, **cmos_lib**, that contains the basic design entities that we need to use. Our configuration declaration might be written as shown in Figure 16-5.

The library clause preceding the design unit is required to locate the resource library containing the entities we need. The use clause following it makes the entity names we require directly visible in the configuration declaration. The configuration is called **opamp_mosfets** and selects the architecture **struct** of the **opamp** entity. Within this architecture, we single out the instances m1 and m2 of the **nfet** component and bind them to the entity **bulk_cmos_nfet** with architecture **detailed**. This shows how we can give special treatment to particular component instances when configuring bindings. We bind all remaining instances of the **nfet** component to the **bulk_cmos_nfet** entity using the **basic** architecture.

FIGURE 16-5

```
library cmos_lib;
use cmos_lib.bulk_cmos_nfet;

configuration opamp_mosfets of opamp is
    for struct   -- architecture of opamp
        for m1, m2 : nfet
            use entity bulk_cmos_nfet(detailed);
        end for;
        for others : nfet
            use entity bulk_cmos_nfet(basic);
        end for;

        ...
    end for;   -- end of architecture struct
end configuration opamp_mosfets;
```

A configuration declaration for an opamp model.

Configuring Multiple Levels of Hierarchy

In the previous section, we saw how to write a configuration declaration for a design in which the instantiated components are bound to behavioral architecture bodies. Most realistic designs, however, have deeper hierarchical structure. The components at the top level have architecture bodies that, in turn, contain component instances that must be configured. The architecture bodies bound to these second-level components may also contain component instances, and so on. In order to deal with configuring these more complex hierarchies, we need to use an alternative form of binding indication in the configuration declaration. The alternative syntax rule is

binding_indication ⇐ **use configuration** *configuration*_name

This form of binding indication for a component instance allows us to bind to a preconfigured entity/architecture pair simply by naming the configuration declaration for the entity. For example, a component instance of **opamp** with the label **voltage_amp** might be bound in a configuration declaration as follows:

for voltage_amp : opamp
    use configuration work.opamp_mosfets;
end for;

Example   Figure 16-6 shows an entity declaration and an outline of a structural architecture body for a notch filter. The architecture body includes a component declaration for an opamp and two instances of the component. (See Franco [16] for details of the circuit.)

    We can configure this implementation of the notch filter with the configuration declaration shown in Figure 16-7. This configuration specifies that each instance of the **simple_opamp** component is bound using the information in the configuration declaration named **opamp_mosfets** in the current design library, shown in Figure 16-5. That configuration in turn specifies the entity to use (opamp), a corresponding architecture body (**struct**) and the bindings for each component instance in that architecture body. Thus the two configuration declarations combine to fully configure the design hierarchy down to the device level.

FIGURE 16-6

```
library ieee_proposed;  use ieee_proposed.electrical_systems.all;
entity notch_filter is
    port ( terminal input, output, vdd, vss, gnd : electrical );
end entity notch_filter;
```

- -

(continued on page 502)

(continued from page 501)

```
architecture opamp_based of notch_filter is
    component simple_opamp is
        port ( terminal plus_in, minus_in, output, vdd, vss, gnd : electrical );
    end component simple_opamp;
        ...
    terminal opamp1_in, opamp1_out, opamp2_in, ... : electrical;
begin
    opamp1 : component simple_opamp
        port map ( plus_in => gnd, minus_in => opamp1_in, output => opamp1_out,
                       vdd => vdd, vss => vss, gnd => gnd );

        opamp2 : component simple_opamp
            port map ( plus_in => gnd, minus_in => opamp2_in, output => output,
                           vdd => vdd, vss => vss, gnd => gnd );
    -- other component instances
        ...

end architecture opamp_based;
```

An entity declaration and architecture body for a notch filter, using a component representing an opamp.

FIGURE 16-7

```
configuration notch_filter_down_to_device_level of notch_filter is
    for opamp_based
        for all : simple_opamp
            use configuration work.opamp_mosfets;
        end for;
        ...   -- bindings for other component instances
    end for;   -- end of architecture opamp_based
end configuration notch_filter_down_to_device_level;
```

A configuration declaration for the notch filter.

The example above shows how we can use separate configuration declarations for each level of a design hierarchy. As a matter of style this is good practice, since it prevents the configuration declarations themselves from becoming too complex. The alternative approach is to configure an entity and its hierarchy fully within the one configuration declaration. We look at how this may be done, as some models from other designers may take this approach. While this approach is valid VHDL-

AMS, we recommend the practice of splitting up the configuration information into separate configuration declarations corresponding to the entities used in the design hierarchy.

To see how to configure multiple levels within one declaration, we need to look at a more complex form of syntax rule for configuration declarations. In fact, we need to split the rule into two parts, so that we can write a recursive syntax rule.

configuration_declaration ⇐
    configuration identifier **of** *entity*_name **is**
        block_configuration
    end ⟦ **configuration** ⟧ ⟦ identifier ⟧ ;

block_configuration ⇐
    for *architecture*_name
        ⟅   **for** component_specification
            binding_indication ;
            ⟦ block_configuration ⟧
        end for ; ⟆
    end for ;

The rule for a block configuration indicates how to write the configuration information for an architecture body and its inner component instances. (The reason for the name "block configuration" in the second rule is that it applies to block statements as well as architecture bodies. We discuss block statements in Chapter 19. Note that we have included an extra part after the binding indication for a component instance. If the architecture that we bind to an instance also contains component instances, we can nest further configuration information for that architecture inside the enclosing block configuration.

Example   We can write a configuration declaration equivalent to that in Figure 16-7 but containing all of the configuration information for the entire hierarchy, as shown in Figure 16-8. The difference between this configuration declaration and the one in Figure 16-7 is that the binding indication for instances of simple_opamp directly refers to the entity opamp and the architecture body struct, rather than using a separate configuration for the entity. The configuration then includes all of the binding information for component instances within struct. This relatively simple example shows how difficult it can be to read nested configuration declarations. Separate configuration declarations are easier to understand and provide more flexibility for managing alternative compositions of a design hierarchy.

FIGURE 16-8

```
library cmos_lib; use cmos_lib.bulk_cmos_nfet;
configuration full of notch_filter is
```

(continued on page 504)

(continued from page 503)

```
for opamp_based  -- architecture of notch_filter
    for all : simple_opamp
        use entity work.opamp(struct);
        for struct  -- architecture of opamp
            for m1, m2 : nfet
                use entity bulk_cmos_nfet(detailed);
            end for;
            for others : nfet
                use entity bulk_cmos_nfet(basic);
            end for;

            ...

        end for;  -- end of architecture struct
    end for;
    ...  -- bindings for other component instances
end for;  -- end of architecture opamp_based
end configuration full;
```

An alternate configuration declaration for the notch filter.

Direct Instantiation of Configured Entities

As we have seen, a configuration declaration specifies the design hierarchy for a design entity. We can make direct use of a fully configured design entity within an architecture body by writing a component instantiation statement that directly names the configuration. The alternative syntax rule for component instantiation statements that expresses this possibility is

component_instantiation_statement ⇐
    *instantiation*_label :
        configuration *configuration*_name
        ⟦ **generic map** (*generic*_association_list) ⟧
        ⟦ **port map** (*port*_association_list) ⟧ ;

The configuration named in the statement includes a specification of an entity and a corresponding architecture body to use. We can include generic and port maps in the component instantiation to provide actual values for any generic constants of the entity and actual signals to connect to the ports of the entity. This is much like instantiating the entity directly, but with all of the configuration information for its implementation included.

Example Figure 16-9 shows an outline of an architecture body that directly instantiates the notch-filter entity. The component instantiation statement labeled left_pilot_filter refers to the configuration notch_filter_down_to_device_level, shown in Figure 16-7. That configuration, in turn, specifies the notch-filter entity and architecture to use.

FIGURE 16-9

```
architecture top_level of fm_radio is
    terminal left_decoded, left_filtered : electrical;
    terminal right_decoded, right_filtered : electrical;
    ...
begin
    left_pilot_filter : configuration work.notch_filter_down_to_device_level
        port map ( input => left_decoded, output => left_filtered,
                   vdd => vdd, vss => vss, gnd => gnd );

    ...

end architecture top_level;
```

An outline of an architecture body that directly instantiates the configured notch-filter entity.

Generic and Port Maps in Configurations

We now turn to a very powerful and important aspect of component configurations: the inclusion of generic maps and port maps in the binding indications. This facility provides a great deal of flexibility when binding component instances to design entities. However, the ideas behind the facility are somewhat difficult to grasp on first encounter, so we will work through them carefully. First, let us look at an extended syntax rule for a binding indication that shows how generic and port maps can be included:

```
binding_indication ⇐
    use ( entity entity_name [ ( architecture_identifier ) ]
          | configuration configuration_name )
    [ generic map ( generic_association_list ) ]
    [ port map ( port_association_list ) ]
```

This rule indicates that after specifying the entity to which to bind (either directly or by naming a configuration), we may include a generic map or a port map or both. We show how this facility may be used by starting with some simple examples illustrating the more common uses. We then proceed to the general case.

One of the most important uses of this facility is to separate the specification of generic constants used for timing from the structure of a design. We can write component declarations in a structural description without including generic constants for timing. Later, when we bind each component instance to an entity in a configuration declaration, we can specify the timing values by supplying actual values for the generic constants of the bound entities.

Example   Suppose we are designing an integrated circuit for a sensor input interface, and we wish to use the analog-to-digital converter whose entity declaration is shown in Figure 16-10. We can write a component declaration for the converter without including the generic constants used for timing, as shown in the architecture body outlined in Figure 16-11. This component represents a virtual module that has all of the structural characteristics we need, but ignores timing. The component instantiation statement specifies a value for the port-width generic constant, but does not specify any timing parameters.

FIGURE 16-10

```
library ieee;  use ieee.std_logic_1164.all;
library ieee_proposed;  use ieee_proposed.electrical_systems.all;

entity successive_approx_adc is
    generic ( t_setup, t_hold, t_pd : delay_length;
              width : positive );
    port ( terminal analog_in : electrical;
           signal clock : in std_logic;
           signal start : in std_logic;
           signal eoc : out std_logic;
           signal data_out : out std_logic_vector(0 to width – 1) );
end entity successive_approx_adc;
```

An entity declaration for an analog-to-digital converter, including generic constants for timing and port width.

FIGURE 16-11

```
architecture structural of sensor_interface is

    component adc is
        generic ( width : positive );
        port ( terminal analog_in : electrical;
               signal clock : in std_logic;
               signal start : in std_logic;
               signal eoc : out std_logic;
               signal data_out : out std_logic_vector(0 to width – 1) );
    end component adc;
```

```
    ...
begin
    sensor_adc : component adc
        generic map ( width => sensor_data'length )
        port map ( analog_in => sensor_input,
                   clock => clk,
                   start => start_conversion,
                   eoc => end_conversion,
                   data_out => sensor_data );
    ...

end architecture structural;
```

An outline of a structural architecture body of a sensor interface design, using an idealized representation of the analog-to-digital converter module.

Since we are operating in the real world, we cannot ignore timing forever. Ultimately the values for the timing parameters will be determined from the physical layout of the integrated circuit. Meanwhile, during the design phase, we can use estimates for their values. When we write a configuration declaration for our design, we can configure the component instance as shown in Figure 16-12, supplying the estimates in a generic map. Note that we also need to specify a value for the **width** generic of the bound entity. In this example, we supply the value of the **width** generic of the component instance. We discuss this in more detail on page 510.

When we simulate the design, the estimated values for the generic constants are used by the real design entity to which the component instance is bound. Later, when the integrated circuit has been laid out, we can substitute, or *back*

FIGURE 16-12

```
configuration sensor_interface_with_timing of sensor_interface is
    for structural
        for sensor_adc : adc
            use entity work.successive_approx_adc(struct)
                generic map ( t_setup => 200 ps, t_hold => 150 ps, t_pd => 150 ps,
                              width => width );
        end for;
        ...
    end for;
end configuration sensor_interface_with_timing;
```

A configuration for the sensor interface circuit, supplying values for the timing parameters of the analog-to-digital converter instance.

annotate, the actual timing values in the configuration declaration without having to modify the architecture body of the model. We can then resimulate to obtain test vectors for the circuit that take account of the real timing.

Another important use of generic and port maps in a configuration declaration arises when the entity to which we want to bind a component instance has different names for generic constants and ports. The maps in the binding indication can be used to make the link between component generics and ports on the one hand, and entity generics and ports on the other. Furthermore, the entity may have additional generics or ports beyond those of the component instance. In this case, the maps can be used to associate actual values, signals, quantities or terminals from the architecture body with the additional generics or ports.

Example   Suppose we need to use a two-input-to-four-output decoder in a design, as shown in the outline of an architecture body in Figure 16-13. The component declaration for the decoder represents a virtual module that meets our needs exactly.

Now suppose we check in our library of entities for a real module to use for this instance and find a three-input-to-eight-output decoder. The entity declaration is shown in Figure 16-14. We could make use of this entity in our design if we could adapt to the different generic and port names and tie the unused ports to appropriate values. The configuration declaration in Figure 16-15 shows how this may be done. The generic map in the binding indication specifies the correspondence between entity generics and component generics. In this case, the component generic **prop_delay** is to be used for both entity generics. The port map in the binding indication similarly specifies which entity ports correspond to which component ports. Where the entity has extra ports, we can specify how those ports are to be connected. In this design, **s2** is tied to '0', **enable** is tied to '1', and the remaining ports are left unassociated (specified by the keyword **open**).

FIGURE 16-13

```
architecture structure of computer_system is
    component decoder_2_to_4 is
        generic ( prop_delay : delay_length );
        port ( in0, in1 : in bit;
                out0, out1, out2, out3 : out bit );
    end component decoder_2_to_4;

    ...

begin
    interface_decoder : component decoder_2_to_4
        generic map ( prop_delay => 4 ns )
        port map ( in0 => addr(4), in1 => addr(5),
```

```
                       out0 => interface_a_select, out1 => interface_b_select,
                       out2 => interface_c_select, out3 => interface_d_select );

    ...

end architecture structure;
```

An outline of an architecture body for a computer system, using a four-output decoder component.

FIGURE 16-14

```
entity decoder_3_to_8 is
    generic ( Tpd_01, Tpd_10 : delay_length );
    port ( s0, s1, s2 : in bit;
            enable : in bit;
            y0, y1, y2, y3, y4, y5, y6, y7 : out bit );
end entity decoder_3_to_8;
```

An entity declaration for the real decoder module.

FIGURE 16-15

```
configuration computer_structure of computer_system is
    for structure

        for interface_decoder : decoder_2_to_4
            use entity work.decoder_3_to_8(basic)
            generic map ( Tpd_01 => prop_delay, Tpd_10 => prop_delay )
            port map ( s0 => in0, s1 => in1, s2 => '0',
                        enable => '1',
                        y0 => out0, y1 => out1, y2 => out2, y3 => out3,
                        y4 => open, y5 => open, y6 => open, y7 => open );
        end for;

        ...

    end for;
end configuration computer_structure;
```

A configuration declaration for the computer system design, showing how the decoder component instance is bound to the real decoder entity.

The two preceding examples illustrate the most common uses of generic maps and port maps in configuration declarations. We now look at the general mechanism that underlies these examples, so that we can understand its use in more complex cases. We use the terms *local generics* and *local ports* to refer to the generics and ports of a component. Also, in keeping with previous discussions, we use the terms *formal generics* and *formal ports* to refer to the generics and ports of the entity to which the instance is bound.

When we write a component instantiation statement with a generic map and a port map, these maps associate actual values, signals, quantities and terminals with the *local* generics and ports of the component instance. Recall that the component is just a virtual module used as a template for a real module, so at this stage we have just made connections to the template. Next, we write a configuration declaration that binds the component instance to a real entity. The generic and port maps in the binding indication associate actual values, signals, quantities and terminals with the *formal* generics and ports of the entity. These actuals may be the locals from the component instance, or they may be values, signals, quantities and terminals from the architecture body containing the component instance. Figure 16-16 illustrates the mappings. It is this two-stage association mechanism that makes configurations so powerful in mapping a design to real modules.

Figure 16-16 shows that the actuals supplied in the configuration declaration may be local generics or ports from the component instance. This is the case for the formal generics **Tpd_01** and **Tpd_10** and for the formal ports **s0**, **s1**, **y0**, **y1**, **y2** and **y3** in Figure 16-15. Every local generic and port of the component instance must be

FIGURE 16-16

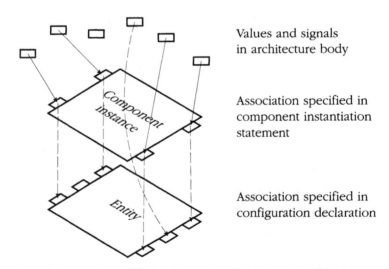

Values and signals
in architecture body

Association specified in
component instantiation
statement

Association specified in
configuration declaration

The generic and port maps in the component instantiation and the configuration declaration define a two-stage association. Values and signals in the architecture body are associated, via the local generics and ports, with the formal generics and ports of the bound entity.

associated with a formal generic or port, respectively; otherwise the design is in error. The figure also shows that the configuration declaration may supply values, signals, quantities or terminals from the architecture body. Furthermore, they may be any other values, signals, quantities or terminals visible at the point of the component instantiation statement, such as the literals '0' and '1' shown in the example. Note that while it is legal to associate a signal in the architecture body with a formal port of the entity, it is not good practice to do so. This effectively modifies the structure of the circuit, making the overall design much more difficult to understand and manage. For example, in the configuration in Figure 16-15, had we associated the formal port **s2** with the signal **addr(6)** instead of the literal value '0', the operation of the circuit would be substantially altered.

The preceding examples show how we can use generic and port maps in binding indications to deal with differences between the component and the entity in the number and names of generics and ports. However, if the component and entity have similar interfaces, we can rely on a *default binding* rule. This rule is used automatically if we omit the generic map or the port map in a binding indication, as we did in the earlier examples in this section. The default rule causes each local generic or port of the component to be associated with a formal generic or port of the same name in the entity interface. If the entity interface includes further formal generics or ports, they remain open. If the entity does not include a formal with the same name as one of the locals, the design is in error. So, for example, if we declare a component as

```
component nand3 is
    port ( a, b, c : in bit := '1';  y : out bit );
end component nand3;
```

and instantiate it as

```
gate1 : component nand3
    port map ( a => s1, b => s2, c => open, y => s3 );
```

then attempt to bind to an entity declared as

```
entity nand2 is
    port ( a, b : in bit := '1';  y : out bit );
end entity nand2;
```

with a component configuration

```
for gate1 : nand3
    use entity work.nand2(basic);
end for;
```

an error occurs. The reason for the error is that there is no formal port named **c** to associate with the local port of that name. The default rule requires that such a correspondence be found, even though the local port is unconnected in the architecture body.

Deferred Component Binding

We have seen that we can specify the binding for a component instance either by naming an entity and a corresponding architecture body, or by naming a configuration. A third option is to leave the component instance unbound and to defer binding it until later in the design cycle. The syntax rule for a binding indication that expresses this option is

binding_indication ⇐ **use open**

If we use this form of binding indication to leave a component instance unbound, we cannot include a generic map or port map. This makes sense: since there is no entity, there are no formal generics or ports with which to associate actual values, signals, quantities or terminals.

A scenario in which we may wish to defer binding arises in complex designs that can be partially simulated before all subsystems are complete. We can write an architecture body for the system, including component declarations and instances as placeholders for the subsystems. Initially, we write a configuration declaration that defers bindings of the subsystems. Then, as the design of each subsystem is completed, the corresponding component configuration is updated to bind to the new entity. At intermediate stages it may be possible to simulate the system with some of the components unbound. The effect of the deferred bindings is simply to leave the corresponding ports unassociated when the design is elaborated. Thus the inputs to the unbound modules are not used, and the outputs remain undriven.

Example   Figure 16-17 shows an outline of a structural architecture for a single-board computer system. The design includes all of the components needed to construct the system, including a CPU, main memory and a serial interface. However, if we have not yet designed an entity and architecture body for the serial interface, we cannot bind the component instance for the interface. Instead, we must leave it unbound, as shown in the configuration declaration in Figure 16-18. We can proceed to simulate the design, using the implementations of the CPU and main memory, provided we do not try to exercise the serial interface. If the processor were to try to access registers in the serial interface, it would get no response. Since there is no entity bound to the component instance representing the interface, there is nothing to drive the data or other signals connected to the instance.

FIGURE 16-17

```
architecture structural of single_board_computer is
    ...   -- type and signal declarations
    component processor is
        port ( clk : in bit;  a_d : inout word; ... );
    end component processor;
```

```
        component memory is
            port ( addr : in bit_vector(25 downto 0); ... );
        end component memory;

        component serial_interface is
            port ( clk : in bit;  address : in bit_vector(3 downto 0); ... );
        end component serial_interface;

    begin

        cpu : component processor
            port map ( clk => sys_clk, a_d => cpu_a_d, ... );

        main_memory : component memory
            port map ( addr => latched_addr(25 downto 0), ... );

        serial_interface_a : component serial_interface
            port map ( clk => sys_clk, address => latched_addr(3 downto 0), ... );

        ...

    end architecture structural;
```

An outline of an architecture body for a single-board computer, including component declarations and instances for the CPU, main memory and a serial interface controller.

FIGURE 16-18

```
library chips;

configuration intermediate of single_board_computer is
    for structural
        for cpu : processor
            use entity chips.XYZ3000_cpu(full_function)
            port map ( clock => clk, addr_data => a_d, ... );
        end for;

        for main_memory : memory
            use entity work.memory_array(behavioral);
        end for;

        for all : serial_interface
            use open;
        end for;

        ...

    end for;
end configuration intermediate;
```

A configuration declaration for the single-board computer, in which the serial interface is left unbound.

16.3 **Configuration Specifications**

We complete this chapter with a discussion of *configuration specifications*. These provide a way of including binding information for component instances in the same architecture body as the instances themselves, as opposed to separating the information out into a configuration declaration. If we know the interface of the entity and want to use it "as is," we can instantiate it directly, without having to write a corresponding component declaration. The main remaining use of configuration specifications is to bind a known entity to component instances in cases where our idealized module is different from the entity. Using a component declaration to describe the idealized module may make the design easier to understand. The syntax rule for a configuration specification is

> configuration_specification ⇐
>   **for** component_specification
>   binding_indication ;

A configuration specification is similar to a component configuration without the keywords **end for**, so we need to take care not to confuse the two. The component specification and binding indication are written in exactly the same way in both cases. However, a configuration specification does not provide an opportunity to configure the internal structure of the architecture to which the component instance is bound. That must be done in a separate configuration declaration. If we write a configuration specification for a component instance, it must be included in the declarative part of the architecture body or block that directly contains the component instance.

The effect of a configuration specification in an architecture body is exactly the same as if the binding indication had been included in a configuration declaration. Thus, we can bind a component instance to a design entity, and we can specify the mapping between the local generics and ports of the component instance and the formal generics and ports of the entity.

Example   Suppose we need to include a two-input nand gate in a model, but our library only provides a three-input nand gate, declared as

> **entity** nand3 **is**
>   **port** (a, b, c : **in** bit; y : **out** bit);
> **end entity** nand3;

We can write our model using a component declaration to show that we really would prefer a two-input gate, and include a configuration specification to handle the difference in interfaces between the component instance and the entity. The architecture is shown in Figure 16-19.

FIGURE 16-19

```
library gate_lib;
architecture ideal of logic_block is
    component nand2 is
        port ( in1, in2 : in bit;  result : out bit );
    end component nand2;
    for all : nand2
        use entity gate_lib.nand3(behavioral)
        port map ( a => in1, b => in2, c => '1', y => result );
    ...   -- other declarations
begin
    gate1 : component nand2
        port map ( in1 => s1, in2 => s2, result => s3 );
    ...   -- other concurrent statements
end architecture ideal;
```

An outline of an architecture body that uses an idealized nand-gate component, and a con-figuration specification for the component instance.

Incremental Binding

We have now seen that there are two places where we can specify the mapping be-tween the local generics and ports of a component instance and the formal generics and ports of the bound entity. The mappings can be specified either in a configura-tion specification or in a separate configuration declaration. We must now consider the possibility of having two binding indications for a given component instance, one in each of these places. VHDL-AMS does, in fact, allow this. The first binding indi-cation, in the configuration specification in the architecture body, is called the *primary* binding indication. The second binding indication, in the configuration declaration, is called an *incremental* binding indication. The primary binding indication must at least specify the entity or configuration to which the instance is bound and may also include generic and port maps. If there is a primary binding indication, the incremen-tal binding indication can either repeat the entity part exactly as specified in the pri-mary binding indication, or it can omit the entity part. The full syntax rule for a binding indication allows for the entity part to be omitted in this case (see Appendix E). The incremental binding indication can also include generic and port maps, and the associations in them override those made in the primary binding indi-cation, with some restrictions. An incremental binding indication must include at least one of the entity part, a port map or a generic map, since it must not be empty. We look at the various possibilities for incremental binding, with some examples.

The first possibility is that the primary binding indication for a component instance leaves some of the formal generics or ports of the entity unassociated. In this case, the incremental binding indication can "fill in the gaps" by associating actual values, signals, quantities and terminals with the unassociated generics and ports.

Example Figure 16-20 shows an architecture body for the control section of a processor, including a register component to store flag bits. The configuration specification binds the register component instance to the register entity shown in Figure 16-21. This entity has additional formal generics t_setup, t_hold and t_pd for timing parameters, and an additional port, reset_n. Since the component declaration does not include corresponding local generics and ports, and the configuration specification does not specify values or signals for the formal generics and ports, they are left open in the architecture body.

FIGURE 16-20

```
architecture structural of control_section is
    component reg is
        generic ( width : positive );
        port ( clk : in std_logic;
               d : in std_logic_vector(0 to width – 1);
               q : out std_logic_vector(0 to width – 1) );
    end component reg;

    for flag_reg : reg
        use entity work.reg(gate_level)
        port map ( clock => clk, data_in => d, data_out => q );

    ...

begin

    flag_reg : component reg
        generic map ( width => 3 )
        port map ( clk => clock_phase1,
                   d(0) => zero_result, d(1) => neg_result,
                   d(2) => overflow_result,
                   q(0) => zero_flag, q(1) => neg_flag,
                   q(2) => overflow_flag );

    ...

end architecture structural;
```

An architecture body of a processor control section, using an idealized representation of a register module. The configuration specification binds the component instance to the real register entity.

FIGURE 16-21

```
library ieee;  use ieee.std_logic_1164.all;
entity reg is
    generic ( t_setup, t_hold, t_pd : delay_length;
                width : positive );
    port ( clock : in std_logic;
           reset_n : in std_logic := 'H';
           data_in : in std_logic_vector(0 to width – 1);
           data_out : out std_logic_vector(0 to width – 1) );
end entity reg;
```

The entity declaration for the register used in the control section.

The configuration declaration for the design, shown in Figure 16-22, contains an incremental binding indication for the register component instance. It does not specify an entity/architecture pair, since that was specified in the primary binding indication. It does, however, include a generic map, filling in values for the formal generics that were left open by the primary binding indication. The generic map also associates the value of the local generic **width** with the formal generic **width**. The port map in the incremental binding indication associates the literal value '1' with the formal port **reset_n**.

FIGURE 16-22

```
configuration controller_with_timing of control_section is
    for structural
        for flag_reg : reg
            generic map ( t_setup => 200 ps, t_hold => 150 ps,
                            t_pd => 150 ps, width => width )
            port map ( reset_n => '1' );
        end for;

        ...



    end for;
end configuration controller_with_timing;
```

A configuration for the controller circuit, supplying values for the timing parameters of the register instance.

The second possibility is that the primary binding indication associates actual values with the formal generics of the entity bound to the component instance. In this case, the incremental binding indication can include new associations for these formal generics, overriding the associations in the primary binding indication. This may be useful in the back-annotation stage of design processing. Estimates for values of generics controlling propagation delay can be included in the primary binding indication and the design simulated before doing physical layout. Later, when actual delay values have been calculated from the physical layout, they can be included in incremental binding indications in a configuration declaration without having to modify the architecture body in any way.

Example Figure 16-23 shows an outline of an architecture body for the interlock control logic of a pipelined processor. It declares a nor-gate component with a generic constant for the input port width, but with no generics for timing parameters. The architecture includes a configuration specification for the instance of the gate component, which binds it to a nor-gate entity that does include timing generics. The generic map in the configuration specification supplies estimates of the timing as actual values for the generics.

FIGURE 16-23

```
architecture detailed_timing of interlock_control is

    component nor_gate is
        generic ( input_width : positive );
        port ( input : in std_logic_vector(0 to input_width – 1);
               output : out std_logic );
    end component nor_gate;

    for ex_interlock_gate : nor_gate
        use entity cell_lib.nor_gate(primitive)
        generic map ( width => input_width,
                      Tpd01 => 250 ps, Tpd10 => 200 ps );   –– estimates
    ...

begin

    ex_interlock_gate : component nor_gate
        generic map ( input_width => 2 )
        port map ( input(0) => reg_access_hazard,
                   input(1) => load_hazard,
                   output => stall_ex_n);

    ...

end architecture detailed_timing;
```

An architecture body for the interlock control logic of a processor.

This model can be simulated with these estimates by configuring it as shown at the top of Figure 16-24. Since there is no further configuration information supplied for the nor-gate instance, the estimated timing values are used. After the design has been laid out and the real timing values have been determined, the configuration declaration can be updated as shown at the bottom of Figure 16-24. An incremental binding indication has been added, supplying the new values for the timing generics. When the design is simulated with this updated configuration, these new values override the estimates specified in the primary binding indication in the architecture body.

FIGURE 16-24

configuration interlock_control_with_estimates **of** interlock_control **is**
    for detailed_timing
    end for;

    ...

end configuration interlock_control_with_estimates;

----

configuration interlock_control_with_actual **of** interlock_control **is**
    for detailed_timing
        for ex_interlock_gate : nor_gate
            generic map (Tpd01 => 320 ps, Tpd10 => 230 ps);
        end for;

        ...

    end for;
end configuration interlock_control_with_actual;

Two versions of a configuration declaration for the interlock control logic.

The third possibility to consider is that the primary binding indication associates actual signals with the formal ports of the entity. In this case, the incremental binding indication cannot override the associations, since to do so would modify the structure of the design.

The final case that arises is one in which a component instantiation associates actual values, signals, quantities and terminals with local generics and ports, but the primary binding indication does not explicitly associate actual values, signals, quantities or terminals with formal generics or ports of the same name. In this case, the default binding rule normally causes the local generics to be associated with formal generics of the same name and local ports to be associated with formal ports of the same name. However, we can preempt this default rule by supplying alternative associations for the formal generics and ports in the incremental binding indication.

Example   Figure 16-25 outlines an architecture body for a block of miscellaneous logic. It includes a component declaration for a three-input nand gate and an instance of the component with an actual value supplied for a local timing generic. The primary binding indication binds the instance to a three-input nand gate entity, but does not specify the mappings between the local generic and ports and the formal generic and ports.

The configuration declaration for this design shown in Figure 16-26 overrides the default mapping. It supplies an actual value for the formal timing generic **Tpd**, instead of using the value of the local generic of that name. It maps the local port c onto the formal port a, and the local port a onto the formal port c. The local ports b and y map onto the formal ports of the same names.

FIGURE 16-25

```
architecture gate_level of misc_logic is
    component nand3 is
        generic ( Tpd : delay_length );
        port ( a, b, c : in bit;  y : out bit );
    end component nand3;

    for all : nand3
        use entity project_lib.nand3(basic);

    ...

begin
    gate1 : component nand3
        generic map ( Tpd => 2 ns )
        port map ( a => sig1, b => sig2, c => sig3, y => out_sig );

    ...

end architecture gate_level;
```

An architecture body for a block of logic.

FIGURE 16-26

```
configuration misc_logic_reconfigured of misc_logic is
    for gate_level
        for gate1 : nand3
            generic map ( Tpd => 1.6 ns )
            port map ( a => c, c => a, b => b, y => y );
        end for;
    end for;
```

end configuration misc_logic_reconfigured;

A configuration declaration for the logic block.

Exercises

1. **[❶ 16.1]** List some of the differences between an entity declaration and a component declaration.

2. **[❶ 16.1]** Write a component declaration for a binary magnitude comparitor, with two standard-logic vector data inputs, **a** and **b**, whose length is specified by a generic constant, and two standard-logic outputs indicating whether **a** = **b** and **a** < **b**. The component also includes a generic constant for the propagation delay.

3. **[❶ 16.1]** Write a component instantiation statement that instantiates the magnitude comparitor described in Exercise 2. The data inputs are connected to signals **current_position** and **upper_limit**, the output indicating whether **a** < **b** is connected to **position_ok** and the remaining output is open. The propagation delay of the instance is 12 ns.

4. **[❶ 16.1]** Write a package declaration that defines a subtype of natural numbers representable in eight bits and a component declaration for an adder that adds values of the subtype.

5. **[❶ 16.1]** Write a package declaration that defines component declarations for a resistor, capacitor and operational amplifier.

6. **[❶ 16.1]** Write a model for an active low-pass filter using components from the package in Exercise 5. The circuit is shown in Figure 16-27.

FIGURE 16-27

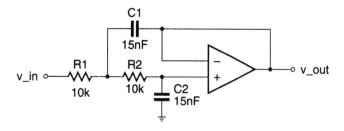

A circuit for an active low-pass filter.

7. [❶ 16.1] Write a package that defines component declarations for nMOS and pMOS field-effect transistors. The component declarations should each include a temperature quantity port for modeling of thermal effects.

8. [❶ 16.2] Suppose we have an architecture body for a digital filter, outlined as follows:

```
architecture register_transfer of digital_filter is
    ...
    component multiplier is
        port ( ... );
    end component multiplier;
begin
    coeff_1_multiplier : component multiplier
        port map ( ... );
    ...
end architecture register_transfer;
```

Write a configuration declaration that binds the multiplier component instance to a multiplier entity called fixed_point_mult from the library dsp_lib, using the architecture algorithmic.

9. [❶ 16.2] Suppose the library dsp_lib referred to in Exercise 8 includes a configuration of the fixed_point_mult entity called fixed_point_mult_std_cell. Write an alternative configuration declaration for the filter described in Exercise 8, binding the multiplier instance using the fixed_point_mult_std_cell configuration.

10. [❶ 16.2] Modify the outline of the filter architecture body described in Exercise 8 to directly instantiate the fixed_point_mult_std_cell configuration described in Exercise 9, rather than using the multiplier component.

11. [❶ 16.2] Suppose we declare and instantiate a multiplexer component in an architecture body as follows:

```
component multiplexer is
    port ( s, d0, d1 : in bit; z : out bit );
end component multiplexer;

    ...

serial_data_mux : component multiplexer
    port map ( s => serial_source_select,
               d0 => rx_data_0, d1 => rx_data_1,
               z => internal_rx_data );
```

Write a binding indication that binds the component instance to the following entity in the current working library, using the most recently analyzed architecture and specifying a value of 3.5 ns for the propagation delay.

```
entity multiplexer is
    generic ( Tpd : delay_length := 3 ns );
```

```
        port ( s, d0, d1 : in bit; z : out bit );
    end entity multiplexer;
```

12. [❶ 16.2] Draw a diagram, based on Figure 16-16, that shows the mapping between entity ports and generics, component ports and generics and other values in the configured computer system model of Figure 16-15.

13. [❶ 16.2] Suppose we have an entity **nand4** with the following interface in a library gate_lib:

```
    entity nand4 is
        generic ( Tpd_01, Tpd_10 : delay_length := 2 ns );
        port ( a, b, c, d : in bit := '1';  y : out bit );
    end entity nand4;
```

We bind the entity to the component instance **gate1** described on page 511 using the following component configuration:

```
    for gate1 : nand3
        use entity get_lib.nand4(basic);
    end for;
```

Write the generic and port maps that comprise the default binding indication used in this configuration.

14. [❶ 16.2] Write a configuration for the active filter from Exercise 6 that binds component instances to entities named **resistor**, **capacitor** and **opamp** in library ideal_lib. Use an architecture named **ideal** for each entity.

15. [❶ 16.2] Suppose we have an architecture body for an active filter, outlined as follows:

```
    architecture structural of active_filter is
        ...
        component opamp is
            port ( ... );
        end component opamp;
    begin
        opamp1 : component opamp
            port map ( ... );
        ...
    end architecture structural;
```

Write a configuration declaration that binds the opamp component instance to a opamp entity called **uA741_opamp** from the library **bipolar**, using the architecture **behavioral**.

16. [❶ 16.2] Suppose the library **bipolar** referred to in Exercise 15 includes a configuration of the uA741_opamp entity called discrete_uA741_opamp. Write an alternative configuration declaration for the filter described in Exercise 15, binding the opamp instance using the discrete_uA741_opamp configuration.

17. [❶ 16.2] Modify the outline of the filter architecture body described in Exercise 15 to directly instantiate the discrete_uA741_opamp configuration described in Exercise 16, rather than using the opamp component.

18. [❶ 16.3] Rewrite the component configuration information in Figure 16-15 as a configuration specification for inclusion in the computer system architecture body.

19. [❶ 16.3] Assuming that the computer system referred to in Exercise 18 includes the configuration specification, write a configuration declaration that includes an incremental binding indication, specifying values of 4.3 ns and 3.8 ns for the entity generics Tpd_01 and Tpd_10, respectively.

20. [❷ 16.1] Develop a structural model of a 32-bit bidirectional transceiver, implemented using a component based on the 8-bit transceiver described in Exercise 13 in Chapter 15.

21. [❷ 16.1] Develop a structural model for an 8-bit serial-in/parallel-out shift register, assuming you have available a 4-bit serial-in/parallel-out shift register. Include a component declaration for the 4-bit register, and instantiate it as required for the 8-bit register. The 4-bit register has a positive-edge-triggered clock input, an active-low asynchronous reset input, a serial data input and four parallel data outputs.

22. [❷ 16.1] Develop a package of component declarations for two-input gates and an inverter, corresponding to the logical operators in VHDL-AMS. Each component has ports of type bit and generic constants for rising output and falling output propagation delays.

23. [❷ 16.1] Develop structural models for CMOS two-input nand, two-input nor and inverter gates using the components from the package in Exercise 7 to include thermal effects.

24. [❷ 16.1/16.2] Develop a structural model for a full-adder circuit. The architecture body should include component declarations for two-input nand, two-input nor and inverter gates with electrical terminal ports only. Write a configuration declaration for the adder, binding the CMOS gate models from Exercise 23 to the gate component instances in the adder. The configuration declaration should map the temperature inputs of the gate entities to the constant value 300 K to model a constant ambient temperature.

25. [❷ 16.2] Develop a configuration declaration for the 32-bit transceiver described in Exercise 20 that binds each instance of the 8-bit transceiver component to the 8-bit transceiver entity.

26. [❷ 16.2] Develop a behavioral model of a 4-bit shift register that implements the component interface described in Exercise 21. Write a configuration declaration for the 8-bit shift register, binding the component instances to the 4-bit shift register entity.

27. [❷ 16.2] Suppose we wish to use an XYZ1234A automotive valve in the brake system described in Figure 16-4. The entity interface for the XYZ1234A is

```
use work.automotive_valve_defs.all;

entity XYZ1234A is
    generic ( max_control : real := 0.01;
              valve_area : real := 2.0E-4 );
    port ( terminal fluid_in, fluid_out : valve_fluidic;
           terminal control_spool : valve_translational );
end entity XYZ1234A;
```

Write a configuration declaration that binds the **automotive_valve** component instance to the XYZ1234A entity, using the most recently compiled architecture, setting the generic **max_control** to 0.02 and using the default value for the **valve_area** generic.

28. [❷ 16.1/16.2] Use the package described in Exercise 22 to develop a structural model of a full adder, described by the Boolean equations

$$S = (A \oplus B) \oplus C_{in}$$
$$C_{out} = A \cdot B + (A \oplus B) \cdot C_{in}$$

Write behavioral models of entities corresponding to each of the gate components and a configuration declaration that binds each component instance in the full adder to the appropriate gate entity.

29. [❸ 16.1] Develop a structural model of a CMOS RAM bit cell using the components from the package in Exercise 4 and the MOSFET package declared in Exercise 7.

30. [❸ 16.2] Develop a structural model of a 4-bit adder using instances of a full-adder component. Write a configuration declaration that binds each instance of the full-adder component, using the configuration declaration described in Exercise 28. For comparison, write an alternative configuration declaration that fully configures the 4-bit adder hierarchy without using the configuration declaration described in Exercise 28.

31. [❸ 16.2] Develop a behavioral model of a RAM with bit-vector address, data-in and data-out ports. The size of the ports should be constrained by generics in the entity interface. Next, develop a test bench that includes a component declaration for the RAM without the generics and with fixed-sized address and data ports. Write a configuration declaration for the test bench that binds the RAM entity to the RAM component instance, using the component local port sizes to determine values for the entity formal generics.

32. [❸ 16.3] The majority function of three inputs can be described by the Boolean equation

$$M(a, b, c) = a \cdot b \cdot c + a \cdot b \cdot \bar{c} + a \cdot \bar{b} \cdot c + \bar{a} \cdot b \cdot c$$

Develop a structural model of a three-input majority circuit, using inverter, and-gate and or-gate components with standard-logic inputs and outputs. Also develop behavioral models for the inverter and gates, including generic constants in the interfaces to specify propagation delays for rising and falling output transitions. Include configuration specifications in the structural model to bind the component instances to the entities. The configuration specifications should include estimated propagation delays of 2 ns for all gates.

Next, develop a configuration declaration for the majority circuit that includes incremental bindings to override the estimated delays with actual propagation delays as shown below.

	rising-output delay	falling-output delay
inverter	1.8 ns	1.7 ns
and gate	2.3 ns	1.9 ns
or gate	2.2 ns	2.0 ns

33. [❹ 16.1] Develop a structural model of a RAM with bit-vector address, data-in and data-out ports consistent with the RAM in Exercise 31 using the RAM bit cells from Exercise 29.

34. [❹ 16.1] Write a package of components for MEMS primitive elements including beams, springs, dampers and masses. Develop a structural model for a MEMS accelerometer using the components.

35. [❹] Develop a suite of models of a digital stopwatch circuit. The circuit has three inputs: a 100 kHz clock, a start/stop switch input and a lap/reset switch input. The two switch inputs are normally high and are pulled low when an external push-button switch is pressed. The circuit has outputs to drive an external seven-segment display of minutes, seconds and hundredths of seconds, formatted as shown in the margin. There is a single output to drive the minutes (') and seconds (") indicators. When an output is high, the corresponding segment or indicator is visible. When the output is low, the segment or indicator is blank. The stopwatch circuit contains a time counter that counts minutes, seconds and hundredths of seconds.

The stopwatch counter is initially reset to 00'00"00, with the display showing the counter time and the minute and second indicators on. In this state, pressing the start/stop button starts counting, with the display showing the counter time. Pressing the start/stop button again stops counting. Successive presses of start/stop continue or stop counting, with the display showing the counter time. If the lap/reset button is pressed while the counter is stopped and the display is showing the counter time, the counter is reset to 00'00"00. If the lap/reset button is pressed while the counter is running, the display freezes the time at which the lap/reset button was pressed, the counter continues running and the minutes and seconds indicators flash at a 1 Hz rate to indicate that the counter is still running. If the start/stop button is pressed, the counter stops, the minutes and seconds indicators stop flashing and the displayed time is unchanged. Successive presses of start/stop continue or stop counting, with the displayed time unchanged and the minutes and seconds indicators flashing when the counter is running. Pressing the lap/reset button while the display is frozen causes it to return to displaying the current counter time, whether the counter is running or stopped.

The first model in your suite should be a behavioral model. Test your behavioral model by writing a test bench for it. You should write a configuration declaration for the test bench that binds the unit under test to the behavioral stopwatch model. Next, refine your stopwatch model to a structural design, including a control sequencer, registers, counters, decoders and other components as required. Develop behavioral models corresponding to each of these components, and write a configuration for the stopwatch that binds the behavioral models to the component instances. Revise the test-bench configuration to use the structural model, and compare its operation with that of the behavioral model. Continue this process of refinement by implementing the control sequencer as a finite-state machine with next-state logic and a state register and by implementing the other components using successively lower-level components down to the level of flip-flops and gates. At each stage, develop configuration declarations to bind entities to component instances, and test the complete model using the test bench.

chapter seventeen

Generate Statements

Many digital systems can be implemented as regular iterative compositions of subsystems. Memories are a good example, being composed of a rectangular array of storage cells. Indeed, VLSI designers prefer to find such implementations, as they make it easier to produce a compact, area-efficient layout, thus reducing cost. If a design can be expressed as a repetition of some subsystem, we should be able to describe the subsystem once, then describe how it is to be repeatedly instantiated, rather than describe each instantiation individually. In this chapter, we look at the VHDL-AMS facility that allows us to generate such regular structures.

17.1 **Generating Iterative Structures**

We have seen how we can describe the implementation of a subsystem using simultaneous statements, as well as concurrent statements such as processes and component instantiations. If we want to replicate a subsystem, we can use a *generate statement*. This is a concurrent statement containing further concurrent and simultaneous statements that are to be replicated. Generate statements are particularly useful if the number of times we want to replicate the concurrent statements is not fixed but is determined, for example, from the value of a generic constant. The syntax rule for writing iterative generate statements is

> generate_statement ⇐
>   *generate*_label :
>   **for** identifier **in** discrete_range **generate**
>   ⟦ { block_declarative_item }
>   **begin** ⟧
>   { concurrent_statement ǀ simultaneous_statement }
>   **end generate** ⟦ *generate*_label ⟧ ;

The generate label is required to identify the generated structure. The header of the generate statement looks very similar to that of a for loop and indeed serves a similar purpose. The discrete range specifies a set of values, and for each value, the block declarative items and concurrent and simultaneous statements are replicated once. Within each replication, the value from the range is given by the identifier, called the *generate parameter*. It appears as a constant, with a type that is the base type of the discrete range. We can specify the discrete range using the same notations that we used in for loops. As a reminder, here is the syntax rule for a discrete range:

> discrete_range ⇐
>   *discrete*_subtype_indication
>   ǀ *range*_attribute_name
>   ǀ simple_expression ⟦ **to** ǀ **downto** ⟧ simple_expression

We can include declarations in the generate statement, as shown by the syntax rule. The kinds of items we can declare here are the same kinds that we can declare in the declarative part of the architecture body, including constants, types, subtypes, natures, subnatures, subprograms, signals, quantities and terminals. These items are replicated once for each copy of the set of concurrent and simultaneous statements and are local to that copy. Note that the syntax rule for a generate statement requires us to include the keyword **begin** if we include any declarations. However, if we have no declarations, we may omit the keyword.

Example   We can implement a bar-graph display by replicating a cell consisting of a light-emitting diode (LED) and a current-limiting resistor, as shown in Figure 17-1. Figure 17-2 shows an entity declaration for such a display. The generic constant **width** specifies the number of segments in the bar-graph display and is used to determine the size of the **anodes** port. The **common_cathode** port represents the common connection of the LED cathodes. The architecture body implements this register in terms of a resistor component and an LED component for each segment.

FIGURE 17-1

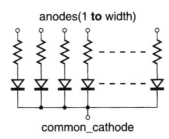

anodes(1 **to** width)

common_cathode

An LED bar-graph display circuit.

FIGURE 17-2

```
library ieee_proposed; use ieee_proposed.electrical_systems.all;
entity led_bar_display is
    generic ( width : positive );
    port ( terminal anodes : electrical_vector(1 to width);
           terminal common_cathode : electrical );
end entity led_bar_display;
```

```
architecture device_level of led_bar_display is
    component resistor is
        port ( terminal p1, p2 : electrical );
    end component resistor;
    component led is
        port ( terminal anode, cathode : electrical );
    end component led;
begin
    device_array : for segment in 1 to width generate
        terminal led_anode : electrical;
    begin
        limiting_resistor : component resistor
            port map ( p1 => anodes(segment), p2 => led_anode );
```

(continued on page 532)

(continued from page 531)

```
        segment_led : component led
            port map ( anode => led_anode, cathode => common_cathode );
    end generate device_array;
end architecture device_level;
```

An entity and architecture body for an LED bar-graph display, based on iterative instanti-
ation of a resistor and an LED.

The generate statement in this structural architecture body replicates the component instantiations labeled limiting_resistor and segment_led, with the number of
copies being determined by width. For each copy, the generate parameter
segment_index takes on successive values from 1 to width. This value is used within each copy to determine which element of the anodes port is connected to the
resistor. Within each copy there is also a local terminal called led_anode, which
connects the resistor to the anode terminal of the LED.

Example   We can use generate statements to describe analog behavioral models by replicating simultaneous statements. Figure 17-3 shows a model of a resistor pack
comprising a number of resistors bonded to a common substrate. The resistances
are specified by a generic constant of type real_vector, whose length determines
the number of resistors in the pack. The temperature quantity port is used to determine the effective resistances, based on the resistances at 298 K and the temperature coefficient.

FIGURE 17-3

```
library ieee_proposed;
use ieee_proposed.electrical_systems.all, ieee_proposed.thermal_systems.all;

entity resistor_pack is
    generic ( resistances_at_298K : real_vector;
            temperature_coeff : real := 0.0 );
    port ( terminal p1, p2 : electrical_vector(1 to resistances_at_298K'length);
        quantity package_temp : in temperature );
end entity resistor_pack;

--------------------------------------------------------

architecture coupled of resistor_pack is

    quantity v across i through p1 to p2;
    quantity effective_resistance : real_vector(1 to resistances_at_298K'length);
begin
```

```
resistor_array : for index in 1 to resistances_at_298K'length generate
    effective_resistance(index)
        == resistances_at_298K(index)
            + ( package_temp – 298.0 ) * temperature_coeff;
    v(index ) == i(index) * effective_resistance(index);
end generate resistor_array;
end architecture coupled;
```

A model of a pack of temperature-dependent resistors.

The architecture body declares array branch quantities for the resistors' voltages and currents, and an array free quantity for the temperature-dependent effective resistances. The generate statement replicates the simultaneous statements for each resistor in the pack. The first simultaneous statement relates the effective resistance to the temperature, and the second simultaneous statement relates the resistor's voltage and current using Ohm's law.

Example   We can also use generate statements to describe digital behavioral models, in which behavioral elements implemented using process statements are replicated. Suppose we are modeling part of a graphics transformation pipeline in which a stream of points representing vertices in a scene is to be transformed by matrix multiplication. The equation describing the transformation is

$$
\begin{bmatrix} p_1' \\ p_2' \\ p_3' \end{bmatrix} = \begin{bmatrix} a_{11} & a_{12} & a_{13} \\ a_{21} & a_{22} & a_{23} \\ a_{31} & a_{32} & a_{33} \end{bmatrix} \begin{bmatrix} p_1 \\ p_2 \\ p_3 \end{bmatrix}
$$

where $[p_1, p_2, p_3]$ is the input point to the pipeline stage, and $[p_1', p_2', p_3']$ is the transformed output three clock cycles later. We can implement the transformation with three identical cells, each producing one result element. The equation is

$$
p_i' = a_{i1} \cdot p_1 + a_{i2} \cdot p_2 + a_{i3} \cdot p_3, \qquad i = 1, 2, 3
$$

An outline of the architecture body implementing the pipeline with this stage is shown in Figure 17-4. The generate statement replicates the process statement three times, once for each element of the transformed point signal. Each copy of the process uses its value of the generate parameter i to index the appropriate elements of the point and transformation matrix signals.

FIGURE 17-4

```
architecture behavioral of graphics_engine is
    type point is array (1 to 3) of real;
    type transformation_matrix is array (1 to 3, 1 to 3) of real;

    signal p, transformed_p : point;
    signal a : transformation_matrix;
    signal clock : bit;

    ...

begin
    transform_stage : for i in 1 to 3 generate
    begin

        cross_product_transform : process is
            variable result1, result2, result3 : real := 0.0;
        begin
            wait until clock = '1';
            transformed_p(i) <= result3;
            result3 := result2;
            result2 := result1;
            result1 :=  a(i, 1) * p(1) + a(i, 2) * p(2) + a(i, 3) * p(3);
        end process cross_product_transform;

    end generate transform_stage;


    ...   -- other stages in the pipeline, etc
end architecture behavioral;
```

A behavioral architecture body for a graphics transformation pipeline.

If we need to describe a regular two-dimensional structure, we can use nested generate statements. Nesting of generate statements is allowed in VHDL-AMS, since a generate statement is a kind of concurrent statement, and generate statements contain concurrent statements. Usually we write nested generate statements so that the outer statement creates the rows of the structure, and the inner statement creates the elements within each row. Of course, this is purely a convention relating to the way we might draw such a regular structure graphically. However, the convention does help to design and understand such structures.

Example   We can use nested generate statements to describe a memory array, constructed from 4-bit-wide dynamic memory (DRAM) circuits. Each DRAM stores 4M words (4×2^{20} words) of four bits each. We can construct a 16M × 32-bit memory array by generating a 4 × 8 array of DRAM circuits. An outline of the architecture body containing the memory array is shown in Figure 17-5, and a schematic diagram is shown in Figure 17-6.

FIGURE 17-5

```
architecture chip_level of memory_board is
    component DRAM is
        port ( a :  in std_logic_vector(0 to 10);
               d :  inout std_logic_vector(0 to 3);
               cs, we, ras, cas : in std_logic );
    end component DRAM;
    signal buffered_address : std_logic_vector(0 to 10);
    signal DRAM_data : std_logic_vector(0 to 31);
    signal bank_select : std_logic_vector(0 to 3);
    signal buffered_we, buffered_ras, buffered_cas : std_logic;
    ...  -- other declarations
begin
    bank_array : for bank_index in 0 to 3 generate
    begin
        nibble_array : for nibble_index in 0 to 7 generate
            constant data_lo : natural := nibble_index * 4;
            constant data_hi : natural := nibble_index * 4 + 3;
        begin
            a_DRAM : component DRAM
                port map ( a => buffered_address,
                           d => DRAM_data(data_lo to data_hi),
                           cs => bank_select(bank_index),  we => buffered_we,
                           ras => buffered_ras,  cas => buffered_cas );
        end generate nibble_array;
    end generate bank_array;
    ...  -- other component instances, etc
end architecture chip_level;
```

An architecture body for a memory board, using nested generate statements to create a two-dimensional array of memory chips.

FIGURE 17-6

buffered_address, buffered_we, buffered_ras, buffered_cas

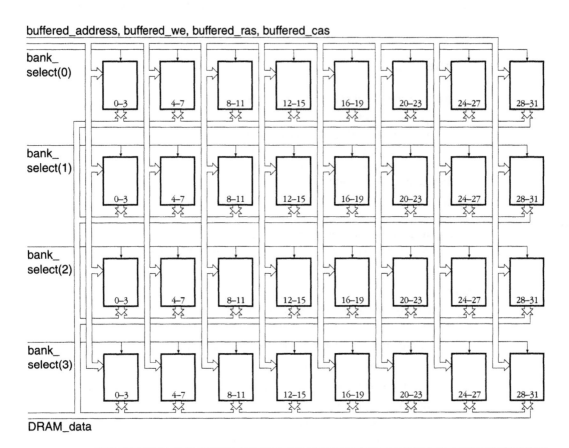

DRAM_data

A schematic for a 16M × 32-bit memory array composed of 4M × 4-bit DRAM circuits.

17.2 Conditionally Generating Structures

In the examples in the previous section, each cell in an iterative structure was connected identically. In some designs, however, there are particular cells that need to be treated differently. This often occurs where cells are connected to their neighbors. The cells at each end do not have neighbors on both sides, but instead are connected to signals, quantities, terminals or ports in the enclosing architecture body. We can deal with these special cases within an iterative structure using a *conditional generate statement*. The syntax rule is

    generate_statement ⇐
        *generate*_label :

if *boolean*_expression **generate**
    〖 〘 block_declarative_item 〙
begin 〗
        〘 concurrent_statement 〡 simultaneous_statement 〙
end generate 〖 *generate*_label 〗 ;

This is just like the iterative generate statement, except that we specify a Boolean expression instead of a range of values to control how the concurrent and simultaneous statements are copied in the design. If the condition is true, the declarations and statements in the generate statement are included in the design. On the other hand, if the condition is false, they are omitted. We can refer to the values of generic constants or the generate parameter of an enclosing iterative generate statement in the control expression of a conditional generate statement. The generate label is required to identify the structure that is generated if the condition is true.

Example   We can construct a Manchester carry chain from NMOS and PMOS transistors as shown in Figure 17-7. Although this is a digital circuit, we can model it using analog terminals and detailed transistor components in order to study the detailed electrical behavior. The circuit includes a subcircuit that is repeated once per bit, plus a variation of the subcircuit for the carry input.

The entity declaration is shown at the top of Figure 17-8. The generic constant n specifies the length of the carry chain. The terminal clk is the analog representation of the digital clock; c_in is the carry input; c_out is the carry output; p is the carry propagate array; g is the carry generate array; and vdd and vss are the power supply terminals.

The architecture contains component declarations for the NMOS and PMOS transistors used in the circuit and a terminal declaration for the intermediate negative carry nodes. The iterative generate statement makes instances of the

FIGURE 17-7

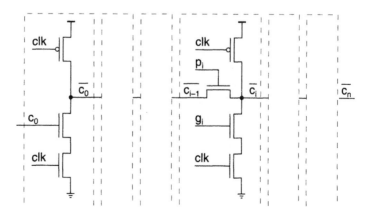

A Manchester carry chain circuit composed of NMOS and PMOS transistors.

FIGURE 17-8

```
library ieee_proposed;  use ieee_proposed.electrical_systems.all;
entity carry_chain is
    generic ( n : positive );
    port ( terminal clk, c_in, c_out, vdd, vss : electrical;
            terminal p, g : electrical_vector (1 to n) );
end entity carry_chain;
```

```
architecture device_level of carry_chain is
    component nmos is
        port ( terminal gate, source, drain : electrical );
    end component nmos;

    component pmos is
        port ( terminal gate, source, drain : electrical );
    end component pmos;

    terminal c_neg : electrical_vector(0 to n-1);
begin
    bit_array : for index in 0 to n generate
        terminal clk_pulldown_drain : electrical;
    begin
        clk_pulldown : component nmos
            port map ( clk, vss, clk_pulldown_drain );

        bit_0 : if index = 0 generate
        begin
            clk_precharge : component pmos
                port map ( clk, c_neg(index), vdd );
            g_pulldown : component nmos
                port map ( c_in, clk_pulldown_drain, c_neg(index) );
        end generate bit_0;

        middle_bit : if index /= 0 and index /= n generate
        begin
            clk_precharge : component pmos
                port map ( clk, c_neg(index), vdd );
            g_pulldown : component nmos
                port map ( g(index), clk_pulldown_drain, c_neg(index) );
            p_pass : component nmos
                port map ( p(index), c_neg(index - 1), c_neg(index) );
        end generate middle_bit;

        bit_n : if index = n generate
        begin
            clk_precharge : component pmos
                port map ( clk, c_out, vdd );
```

```
      g_pulldown : component nmos
          port map ( g(index), clk_pulldown_drain, c_out );
      p_pass : component nmos
          port map ( p(index), c_neg(index – 1), c_out );
  end generate bit_n;

end generate bit_array;

end architecture device_level;
```

An entity and architecture body for a Manchester carry chain.

transistors for the carry input (index = 0) and for each bit from 1 to n. It includes a terminal declaration for the internal node between the bottom two transistors in each cell. Within the iterative generate statement, conditional generate statements are used to treat the input cell and the output cell differently from the middle cells. The condition "index = 0" identifies the input cell, which takes its input from the c_in port, omitting the pass transistor. The second conditional generate statement identifies the middle cells that have their input and output terminals connected to neighboring cells. Finally, the condition "index = n" identifies the output cell, which connects its output to the c_out port. In each of the port maps, the generate parameter index is used to connect the appropriate element of the p, g and c_neg array terminals.

Another important use of conditional generate statements is to conditionally include or omit part of a design, usually depending on the value of a generic constant. A good example is the inclusion or otherwise of *instrumentation:* additional processes or component instances that trace or debug the operation of a design during simulation. When the design is sufficiently tested, a generic constant can be changed to exclude the instrumentation so that it does not slow down a large simulation and is not included if the design is synthesized.

Example Suppose we wish to measure the relative frequencies of instruction fetches, data reads and data writes made by a CPU accessing memory in a computer system. This information may be important when considering how to optimize a design to improve performance. An entity declaration for the computer system is

```
entity computer_system is
    generic ( instrumented : boolean := false );
    port ( ... );
end entity computer_system;
```

The generic constant instrumented is used to determine whether to include the instrumentation to measure relative frequencies of each kind of memory access. An outline of the architecture body is shown in Figure 17-9. The signals ifetch_freq, write_freq and read_freq and the process access_monitor are only included in the design if the generic constant **instrumented** is true. The process resumes each time the CPU requests access to the memory and keeps count of the number of each kind of access, as well as the total access count. It uses these values to update the relative frequencies. We can trace these signals using our simulator to see how the relative frequencies converge over the lifetime of a simulation.

FIGURE 17-9

```
architecture block_level of computer_system is
    ...   -- type and component declarations for cpu and memory, etc
    signal clock : bit;           -- the system clock
    signal mem_req : bit;         -- cpu access request to memory
    signal ifetch : bit;          -- indicates access is to fetch an instruction
    signal write : bit;           -- indicates access is a write
    ...                           -- other signal declarations
begin
    ...   -- component instances for cpu and memory, etc
    instrumentation : if instrumented generate
        signal ifetch_freq, write_freq, read_freq : real := 0.0;
    begin
        access_monitor : process is
            variable access_count, ifetch_count,
                    write_count, read_count : natural := 0;
        begin
            wait until mem_req = '1';
            if ifetch = '1' then
                ifetch_count := ifetch_count + 1;
            elsif write = '1' then
                write_count := write_count + 1;
            else
                read_count := read_count + 1;
            end if;
            access_count := access_count + 1;
            ifetch_freq <= real(ifetch_count) / real(access_count);
            write_freq <= real(write_count) / real(access_count);
            read_freq <= real(read_count) / real(access_count);
        end process access_monitor;
    end generate instrumentation;
end architecture block_level;
```

An instrumented architecture body for a computer system.

We can control whether the instrumentation is included or not when we write a configuration declaration for the design. To include the instrumentation, we configure an instance of the computer system as follows:

```
for system_under_test : computer_system
    use entity work.computer_system(block_level)
    generic map ( instrumented => true )
    ...
end for;
```

To exclude the instrumentation, we change the value of the generic constant in the generic map to false.

Recursive Structures

A more unusual application of conditional generate statements arises when describing recursive hardware structures, such as tree structures. We can write a description of a recursive structure using a recursive model, that is, one in which an architecture of an entity creates an instance of that same entity. We enclose the recursive instantiation in a conditional generate statement that determines when to terminate the recursion.

Example   Clock-signal distribution can be a problem in a large integrated circuit. We typically have one clock signal that must be distributed to a very large number of components without overloading the clock drivers and without creating too much skew between different parts of the circuit. One solution is to distribute the clock signal using a fanout tree. A simplified binary fanout tree is shown in Figure 17-10. The clock signal feeds two buffers, each of which in turn feeds two buffers, and so on, until we have generated enough buffered clock signals to drive all elements of the circuit. As the diagram shows, we can think of a tree of height 3 as being constructed from two buffers feeding trees of height 2. Similarly, a tree of height 2 is two buffers feeding trees of height 1. A tree of height 1 is two buffers feeding the outputs of the fanout tree. We can think of these output connections as being degenerate trees of height 0. In general, we can say that a tree of height n consists of two buffers feeding trees of height $n - 1$, where $n > 0$.

We can describe this structure in VHDL-AMS by starting with an entity declaration for a fanout tree that includes a generic constant **height** specifying the height of the tree, as shown in Figure 17-11. The entity has one input and 2^{height} outputs. The architecture body uses conditional generate statements that test the value of **height** to see if any subtrees are required. If **height** is zero, the output port of the fanout tree is a vector of length one. The generate statement labeled **degenerate_tree** creates a connection from the input to the single output element. Otherwise, if **height** is greater than zero, the generate statement labeled **compound_tree** creates two buffers and two subtrees of reduced height. The local signals **buffered_input_0** and **buffered_input_1** connect the buffers to the inputs of the subtrees. The outputs of the subtrees are of length $2^{height - 1}$ and are connected to slices of the output port vector of the enclosing tree.

FIGURE 17-10

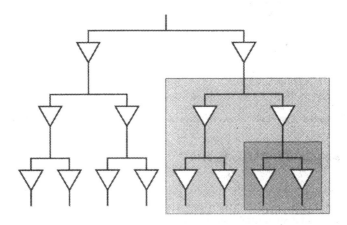

A binary fanout tree for clock distribution. The inner shaded section is a fanout tree of height 1, and the outer shaded section is a tree of height 2. The whole structure is a tree of height 3.

FIGURE 17-11

```
library ieee;  use ieee.std_logic_1164.all;

entity fanout_tree is
    generic ( height : natural );
    port ( input : in std_logic;
            output : out std_logic_vector (0 to 2**height − 1) );
end entity fanout_tree;

-- ---------------------------------------------------------------

architecture recursive of fanout_tree is

begin

    degenerate_tree : if height = 0 generate
    begin
        output(0) <= input;
    end generate degenerate_tree;

    compound_tree : if height > 0 generate
        signal buffered_input_0, buffered_input_1 : std_logic;
    begin
        buf_0 : entity work.buf(basic)
            port map ( a => input, y => buffered_input_0 );
```

```
        subtree_0 : entity work.fanout_tree(recursive)
            generic map ( height => height − 1 )
            port map ( input => buffered_input_0,
                        output => output(0 to 2**(height − 1) − 1) );
        buf_1 : entity work.buf(basic)
            port map ( a => input, y => buffered_input_1 );
        subtree_1 : entity work.fanout_tree(recursive)
            generic map ( height => height − 1 )
            port map ( input => buffered_input_1,
                        output => output(2**(height − 1) to 2**height − 1) );
    end generate compound_tree;
end architecture recursive;
```

An entity and architecture body for a recursive fanout tree model.

This compact description of a relatively complex structure is fleshed out when the design is elaborated. Suppose we instantiate a fanout tree of height 3 in a design:

```
clock_buffer_tree : entity work.fanout_tree(recursive)
    generic map ( height => 3 )
    port map ( input => unbuffered_clock,
                output => buffered_clock_array );
```

In the first stage of elaboration, height has the value 3, so the generate statement compound_tree creates the first two buffers and two instances of the fanout_tree entity with height having the value 2. In each of these instances, the generate statement compound_tree creates two more buffers and two instances of the fanout_tree entity with height having the value 1. Then, in each of these instances, the generate statement compound_tree creates a further two buffers and two instances of the fanout_tree entity with height having the value 0. In these last instances, the condition of the generate statement degenerate_tree is true, so it creates a connection directly from its input to its output. This statement is where the recursion terminates, as there are no further instantiations of the fanout_tree entity within the statement.

17.3 Configuration of Generate Statements

In this section we describe how to write configuration declarations for designs that include generate statements. If a design includes an iterative generate statement, we need to be able to identify individual cells from the iteration in order to configure them. If the design includes a conditional generate statement, we need to be able to include configuration information that is to be used only if the cell is included in the design. In order to handle these cases, we use an extended form of block configuration. We first introduced block configurations in Section 16.2. The syntax rule for the extended form is

block_configuration ⇐
    for ⟨   *architecture*_name
           ⎜ *block_statement*_label
           ⎜ *generate_statement*_label
                      ⟦ (⟨ discrete_range ⎜ *static*_expression ⟩) ⟧ ⟩
        ⦃   block_configuration
        ⎜   **for** component_specification
               ⟦ binding_indication ; ⟧
               ⟦ block_configuration ⟧
            end for ; ⦄
    end for ;

The new part in this rule is the alternative allowing us to configure a generate statement by writing its label. The optional part after the label is only used for iterative generate statements. This part allows us to write either an expression whose value selects a particular cell from the iterative structure or a range of values that select a collection of cells. Once we have identified the generate statement, the remaining configuration information within the block configuration specifies how the concurrent statements within the generated cells are to be configured.

Let us first apply this rule to writing configurations for conditional generate statements. In this case, we simply write the generate statement label in the block configuration and fill in the configuration information for generated component instances. If the generate statement control expression is true when the design is elaborated, the configuration information is used to bind entities to the component instances. On the other hand, if the expression is false, no instances are created, and the configuration information is ignored.

Example   Let us return to our model of a computer system that uses a conditional generate statement to include instrumentation. Recall that the entity declaration was

        entity computer_system **is**
            generic (instrumented : boolean := false);
            port (...);
        end entity computer_system;

Suppose we wish to use a general-purpose bus monitor component that collects statistics on bus transactions between the CPU and the memory. An outline of the revised architecture body is shown in Figure 17-12.

We can write a configuration declaration for the computer system as shown in Figure 17-13. This configuration information may be used when the computer system entity is elaborated. If the value of the generic constant **instrumented** is true, the bus monitor is instantiated. In this case, the information in the block configuration starting with "**for** instrumentation" is used to bind an entity to the bus monitor instance. On the other hand, if instrumented is false, no instance is created, and the configuration information is ignored.

FIGURE 17-12

```
architecture block_level of computer_system is
    ...  -- type and component declarations for cpu and memory, etc.
    signal clock : bit;        -- the system clock
    signal mem_req : bit;      -- cpu access request to memory
    signal ifetch : bit;       -- indicates access is to fetch an instruction
    signal write : bit;        -- indicates access is a write
    ...                        -- other signal declarations
begin
    ...  -- component instances for cpu and memory, etc.
    instrumentation : if instrumented generate
        use work.bus_monitor_pkg;
        signal bus_stats : bus_monitor_pkg.stats_type;
    begin
        cpu_bus_monitor : component bus_monitor_pkg.bus_monitor
            port map ( mem_req, ifetch, write, bus_stats );
    end generate instrumentation;
end architecture block_level;
```

A revised architecture body for the instrumented computer system, including an instance of a bus monitor component in the conditional generate statement.

FIGURE 17-13

```
configuration architectural of computer_system is
    for block_level
        ...  -- component configurations for cpu and memory, etc
        for instrumentation
            for cpu_bus_monitor : bus_monitor_pkg.bus_monitor
                use entity work.bus_monitor(general_purpose)
                    generic map ( verbose => true, dump_stats => true );
            end for;
```

(continued on page 546)

(continued from page 545)

> **end for**;
>
> **end for**;
>
> **end configuration** architectural;

A configuration declaration for the instrumented computer system.

We now turn to configurations for designs including iterative generate statements. The simplest case is a structure in which all cells are to be configured identically. In this case, we just write the generate statement label in the block configuration and include the configuration information to be applied to each cell.

Example   In the LED bar-graph display model in Figure 17-2, each cell consisted of a resistor and an LED component. We can write a configuration declaration for this design as shown in Figure 17-14. The block configuration starting with "**for device_array**" identifies the iterative generate statement labeled **device_array**. Since there is no specification of particular cells within the generated structure, the information in the block configuration is applied to all cells.

FIGURE 17-14

```
library device_lib;
configuration identical_devices of led_bar_display is
    for device_level
        for device_array
            for limiting_resistor : resistor
                use entity device_lib.resistor(ideal);
            end for;
            for segment_led : led
                use entity device_lib.led(ideal);
            end for;
        end for;
    end for;
end configuration identical_devices;
```

A configuration declaration for a bar-graph display module.

Where we have a design that includes nested generate statements to generate a two-dimensional structure, we simply nest block configurations in a configuration declaration.

Example The memory array described in Figure 17-5 is implemented using two nested iterative generate statements. We can write a configuration declaration for the design as shown in Figure 17-15. The block configuration starting with "**for bank_array**" selects the memory array generated by the outer generate statement labelled **bank_array**. Each bank is configured identically, using the inner block configuration starting with "**for nibble_array**". This selects the generate statement that creates a bank of DRAM chips and configures each chip in the bank identically to the rest.

FIGURE 17-15

```
library chip_lib;  use chip_lib.all;
configuration down_to_chips of memory_board is
    for chip_level
        for bank_array
            for nibble_array
                for a_DRAM : DRAM
                    use entity DRAM_4M_by_4(chip_function);
                end for;
            end for;
        end for;
        ...  -- configurations of other component instances
    end for;
end configuration down_to_chips;
```

A configuration declaration for a memory array.

In some designs using iterative generate statements, there may be particular cells or groups of cells that we wish to configure differently from other cells. In these cases we can use an expression or a range of values in parentheses after the generate statement label in the block configuration. The values identify those cells to which the configuration information applies. The rules for specifying the discrete range are the same as those for specifying a discrete range in other contexts.

Example   The Manchester carry chain design shown in Figure 17-8 is composed of cells indexed from 0 to n, each of which includes instances of NMOS and PMOS transistors. Suppose we wish to use ideal transistors for all except the last cell of the carry chain. In the last cell, we wish to use an architecture called **spice-equivalent** for the pass transistor, with the remaining transistors in the cell being ideal. A configuration declaration for the carry chain that achieves this is shown in Figure 17-16.

FIGURE 17-16

```
library device_lib;
configuration last_pass_spice of carry_chain is
    for device_level
        for bit_array ( 0 to n − 1 )
            for bit_0
                for all : nmos
                    use entity device_lib.nmos(ideal);
                end for;
                for all : pmos
                    use entity device_lib.pmos(ideal);
                end for;
            end for;
            for middle_bit
                for all : nmos
                    use entity device_lib.nmos(ideal);
                end for;
                for all : pmos
                    use entity device_lib.pmos(ideal);
                end for;
            end for;
        end for;
        for bit_array ( n )
            for bit_n
                for p_pass : nmos
                    use entity device_lib.nmos(spice_equivalent);
                end for;
                for others : nmos
                    use entity device_lib.nmos(ideal);
                end for;
                for all : pmos
                    use entity device_lib.pmos(ideal);
                end for;
            end for;
```

end for;

  end for;

end configuration last_pass_spice;

A configuration declaration for a shift register.

The first of the block configurations for **bit_array** identifies those cells generated with index values in the range 0 to **n** – 1. In the first of these cells, the control condition of the inner generate statement **bit_0** is true, and the control conditions for **middle_bit** and **bit_n** are false. In the remaining cells, the conditions for **bit_0** and **bit_n** are false, and the condition for **middle_bit** is true. Thus we only need to include inner block configurations for **bit_0** and **middle_bit**. These inner block configurations specify use of the **ideal** architectures for all instances of **nmos** and **pmos**.

The second of the block configurations for **bit_array** singles out the cell generated with index value **n**. This is the cell for which we wish to use a pass transistor with **spice_equivalent** architecture. We know that in this cell the control conditions for **bit_0** and **middle_bit** are false. Hence, we do not need to include nested block configurations for those generate statements. We only include a nested block configuration for the generate statement **bit_n**. In that nested block configuration, we specify use of the **spice_equivalent** architecture for the **p_pass** transistor instance and the **ideal** architectures for the remaining instances.

Exercises

1. [❶ 17.1] Draw a diagram illustrating the circuit described by the following generate statement:

   ```
   synch_delay_line : for stage in 1 to 4 generate
       delay_ff : component d_ff
           port map ( clk => sys_clock,
                      d => delayed_data(stage – 1),
                      q => delayed_data(stage) );
   end generate synch_delay_line;
   ```

2. [❶ 17.1] Write a generate statement that instantiates an inverter component for each element of an input bit-vector signal **data_in** to derive an inverted bit-vector output signal **data_out_n**. Use the index range of **data_in** to determine the number of inverters required, and assume that **data_out_n** has the same index range as **data_in**.

3. [❶ 17.2] Write conditional generate statements that connect a signal **external_clock** directly to a signal **internal_clock** if a Boolean generic constant **positive_clock** is true. If the generic is false, the statements should connect **external_clock** to **internal_clock** via an instance of an inverter component.

4. [❶ 17.3] Write block configurations for the generate statement shown in Exercise 1. The first flipflop (with index 1) should be bound to the entity **d_flipflop** in the library **parts_lib**, using the architecture body **low_input_load**. The remaining flipflops should be bound to the same entity, but use the architecture body **standard_input_load**.

5. [❶ 17.3] Write block configurations for the generate statements described in Exercise 3. The inverter component, if generated, should be bound to the entity **inverter** using the most recently analyzed architecture body in the library **parts_lib**.

6. [❷ 17.1] Develop a structural model for an n-bit-wide two-input multiplexer composed of single-bit-wide two-input multiplexer components. The width n is a generic constant in the entity interface.

7. [❷ 17.1] A first-in/first-out (FIFO) queue can be constructed from the register component shown in Figure 17-17. The bit width of the component is a generic constant in the component interface. The FIFO is constructed by chaining cells together and connecting their **reset** inputs in parallel. The depth of the FIFO is specified by a generic constant in the entity interface. Develop a structural model for a FIFO implemented in this manner.

8. [❷ 17.1] Use a generate statement to develop a model for an n-element diode array with separate connections for the anodes and cathodes.

9. [❷ 17.1] Use a generate statement to develop a model for an n-stage R-2R ladder network as shown in Figure 17-18.

10. [❷ 17.1/17.2] Develop a structural model for a binary ripple counter implemented using D-flipflops as shown in Figure 17-19. The width n is a generic constant in the entity interface.

FIGURE 17-17

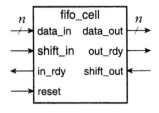

A register component used to construct a FIFO.

FIGURE 17-18

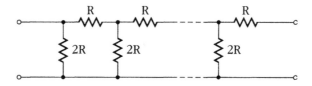

An n-stage R-2R ladder network.

FIGURE 17-19

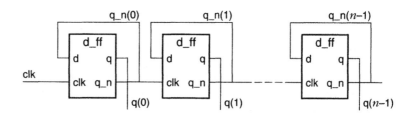

A binary ripple counter.

11. [❷ 17.1/17.2] Develop a structural model for an *n*-bit-wide ripple-carry adder. The least-significant bits are added using a half-adder component, and the remaining bits are added using full-adder components.

12. [❷ 17.2] Develop a model of an *n*-element transmission line, where an element consists of an inductor and capacitor, as shown in Figure 17-20. Use conditional generate statements to account for the source and load components. Include generic constants for the number of elements, the total capacitance and the total inductance. Assign the individual inductance and capacitance values as the total value divided by the number of elements.

FIGURE 17-20

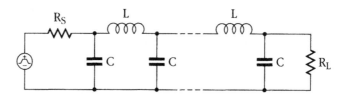

An n-element transmission line model with source and load impedances.

13. [❷ 17.3] Develop a behavioral model for a single-bit-wide two-input multiplexer. Write a configuration declaration for the n-bit-wide multiplexer described in Exercise 6, binding the behavioral implementation to each component instance.

14. [❷ 17.3] Develop a behavioral model for the D-flipflop described in Exercise 10. Write a configuration declaration for the ripple counter, binding the behavioral implementation to each D-flipflop component instance.

15. [❷ 17.3] Develop a behavioral model for a half adder and a full adder. Write a configuration declaration for the ripple-carry adder described in Exercise 11, binding the behavioral models to the component instances.

16. [❸ 17.1/17.2] Exercises 28 and 32 in Chapter 5 describe the components needed to implement a 16-bit carry-look-ahead adder. The same components can be used to implement a 64-bit carry-look-ahead adder as shown in Figure 17-21. The 64-bit addition is split into four identical 16-bit groups, each implemented with a 16-bit carry-look-ahead adder. The carry-look-ahead generator is augmented to include generate and propagate outputs, calculated in the same way as those calculated by each 4-bit adder. An additional carry-look-ahead generator is used to calculate the carry inputs to each 16-bit group. Develop a structural model of a 64-bit carry-look-ahead adder using nested generate statements to describe the two-level iterative structure of the circuit.

17. [❸ 17.2] A circuit to generate the odd-parity function of an 8-bit word is implemented using a tree of exclusive-or gates as shown in Figure 17-22. This structure can be generalized to an input word size of 2^n, implemented using a tree with n levels of gates. Develop a recursive model that describes such a parity generator circuit. The depth of the tree is a generic constant in the entity interface and is used to constrain the size of the input word.

18. [❸ 17.2] Use generate statements to develop a model for an n-bit binary-weighted resistor D/A converter, as shown in Figure 17-23. Make the resistor values a function of the number of bits as shown. Combine the inputs into a digital bus.

FIGURE 17-21

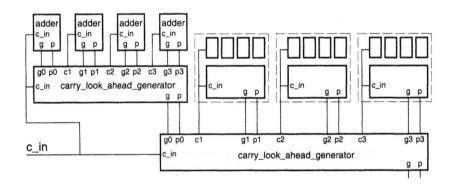

A 64-bit carry-look-ahead adder.

FIGURE 17-22

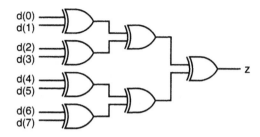

An odd-parity generator implemented using exclusive-or gates.

FIGURE 17-23

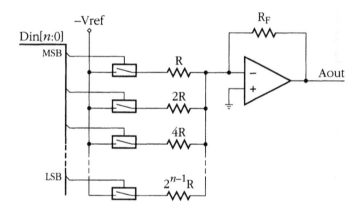

Binary-weighted resistor DAC.

19. [❸ 17.2] Figure 17-24 shows a 3-bit voltage switch decoder used in DAC applications. Develop a mode for an n-bit decoder using recursive generate statements.

20. [❸ 17.3] Develop a behavioral model for the FIFO cell described in Exercise 7. The cell contains storage for one n-bit word of data. When reset, the cell sets in_rdy to '1' and out_rdy to '0', indicating that it contains no data. When **shift_in** changes to '1', the cell latches the input data and makes it available at **data_out**, then sets in_rdy to '0' and out_rdy to '1', indicating that the cell contains data. When **shift_out** changes to '1', the cell sets in_rdy to '1' and out_rdy to '0', indicating that the cell no longer contains data. Write a configuration declaration for the FIFO queue described in Exercise 7, binding the behavioral FIFO cell model to each component instance.

21. [❹] Ward and Halstead, in their book *Computation Structures* ([41], pp. 130–134), describe a combinatorial array multiplier that multiplies two unsigned binary numbers. The multiplier consists of an array of cells, each of which contains an

FIGURE 17-24

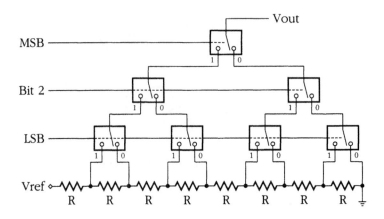

Voltage-switching decoder.

and gate to multiply two operand bits and a full adder to form a partial-product bit, as shown in Figure 17-25.

The cells are connected in the multiplier array as shown in Figure 17-26. Develop a structural model of an *n*-bit × *n*-bit array multiplier, in which the word length *n* is a generic constant in the entity interface. Write a behavioral model of the multiplier cell and a configuration declaration that binds the cell model to each cell component instance in the array multiplier. Next, refine the behavioral cell model to a gate-level model, and revise the configuration declaration to use the refined cell model.

FIGURE 17-25

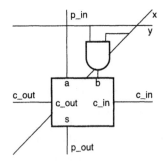

A single-bit multiplier cell.

FIGURE 17-26

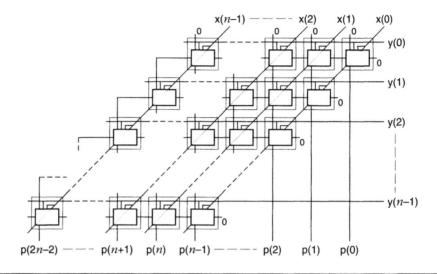

A multiplier array constructed from single-bit multipler cells.

22. [❹] Weste and Eshraghian, in their book *Principles of CMOS VLSI Design: A Systems Perspective* ([42], pp. 384–407), describe a systolic array processor for dynamic time warping (DTW) pattern-matching operations used in speech recognition. Develop a model of the DTW processing element, and use it to implement the systolic array processor.

23. [❹] A hypercube multicomputer consists of a collection of 2^n processing elements (PEs) arranged at the vertices of an n-dimensional cube. Hypercubes with dimensions 1, 2, 3 and 4 are illustrated in Figure 17-27.

Each PE has a unique address, formed by concatenating the index (0 or 1) in each dimension to derive a binary number. Attached to each PE is a message switch with n bidirectional message channels, one in each dimension. The switches are interconnected along the edges of the hypercube. PEs exchange messages by passing them to the attached switches, which route them through the inter-

FIGURE 17-27

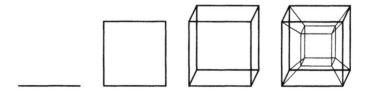

Hypercubes of dimension 1, 2, 3 and 4.

connections from source to destination. A message includes source and destination PE addresses, allowing the switches to determine a route for the message.

The hypercube structure can be described recursively. A hypercube of dimension 1 is simply a line from position 0 to position 1 in the first dimension. A hypercube of dimension n ($n > 1$) is composed of two sub-hypercubes of dimension $n - 1$, one at position 0 in the nth dimension and the other at position 1 in the nth dimension. Each vertex in one sub-hypercube is joined to the vertex with the same address in the other sub-hypercube.

Develop a recursive structural model of an n-dimensional hypercube multicomputer, where the number of dimensions is specified by a generic constant in the entity interface. Your model should include separate component instances for the PEs and the message switches. Also develop behavioral models for the PEs and message switches. The PEs should generate streams of test messages to different destinations to test the switch network. Each switch should implement a simple message-routing algorithm of your devising.

chapter eighteen

Case Study 3:
DC-DC Power Converter

*With a contribution by Tom Egel,
Mentor Graphics Corporation*

This case study illustrates how VHDL-AMS can be used for the detailed design of a DC-DC switching power supply. For the RC airplane system, a step-down converter is required to convert the 42 V battery voltage used to power the propeller motor to the 4.8 V needed for the on-board servo electronics. In this case study we briefly introduce switched-mode power supply theory, and then perform a detailed design of a simple step-down (buck) converter. We discuss averaging techniques that facilitate analysis of the closed-loop system and use VHDL-AMS simulations to perform system-level design trade-offs.

18.1 **Buck Converter Theory and Design**

In this case study, we examine the design of a switching power converter for the RC airplane, outlined in Figure 18-1. Switch-mode power supplies have all but replaced their linear counterparts as the preferred method for converting the supply of DC power from one voltage level to another. This is especially true in today's world of handheld compact electronic systems, where size, weight, efficiency and cost are all critical to the overall system design. All switching supplies use pulse-width modulation (PWM) techniques to achieve efficiency and provide the necessary control of the output voltage as load conditions change. Because of the combination of electronic and magnetic components in a switching power supply, computer simulation plays a vital role in creating a successful design. As we will see, VHDL-AMS is well suited to handle both this mixed-technology aspect and the state-averaging techniques commonly used for the design and analysis of switch-mode power supply systems. For a more complete study on switching power converter theory and design, see Brown [7].

Selecting a Switching Regulator Topology

There are two basic types of PWM switching regulators: forward mode and flyback mode. From these two basic modes, the common topologies are formed. The *buck* (step-down) converter is a forward-mode converter, whereas the *boost* (step-up) and the *buck-boost* (step-up/down) are derivations of the flyback-mode converter. All of these converters have the same four basic elements: a power switch for creating the PWM control waveform, a diode, an inductor and a capacitor. The duty cycle of the

FIGURE 18-1

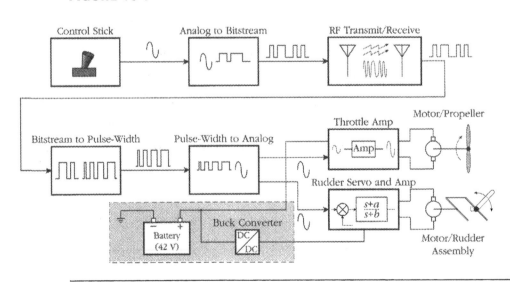

The RC airplane system with the switching power converter outlined.

switch control signal determines how long the switch is closed during any given period and thus can be used to control the amount of energy stored in the inductor. A complete switching power supply also includes a transformer to provide isolation between the input and output and feedback to control the duty cycle of the PWM waveform as load conditions change.

The requirements of our regulator design are shown in Figure 18-2. They indicate that we need to convert a 42 V DC battery input to 4.8 V DC. For this we need to design a forward-mode (buck) converter. The basic topology is shown in Figure 18-3. In the remainder of this section we describe the detailed operation of a buck converter and walk through the design process.

The buck converter shown in Figure 18-3 has two basic modes of operation: continuous mode and discontinuous mode, referring to the current flowing through the inductor (L1). In continuous mode, current is always flowing through L1 whether the switch (SW1) is on or off, while in discontinuous mode the inductor current goes to zero during part of the off time of SW1. Since the frequency response is significantly different between the two modes, it is best to operate in only one of the modes. For this case study, we design the converter to operate only in the continuous mode by sizing the inductor according to the worst-case load conditions to avoid the zero current threshold. Keeping the buck converter operating in continuous mode also simplifies the design and analysis considerably.

FIGURE 18-2

Input Specifications		*Output Specifications*	
V_{in}	42 V DC	V_{out}	4.8 V DC
$F_{switching}$	25 kHz	$V_{out(ripple)}$	< 100 mV p-p
		I_{out}	15 mA to 2 A
		$I_{out(ripple)}$	< 30 mA p-p

Regulator design requirements.

FIGURE 18-3

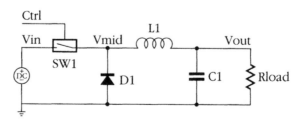

Basic buck converter topology.

In continuous mode, the circuit operates in two states: the on state and the off state, referring to the state of the power switch (SW1) in Figure 18-3. It is common to draw the equivalent circuit for each of these states to aid in the understanding and derive the circuit equations. We can deduce the equivalent circuits from the original circuit. The diode (D1) in a buck converter circuit is sometimes referred to as a *passive switch*, since it also has an on and off state determined by the circuit conditions. During the circuit on state, SW1 is on, D1 is reversed biased (off) and current passes through the inductor to the load. During the circuit off state, SW1 is off, and D1 is forward biased (on), maintaining the forward current through L1. The equivalent circuits for the on state and off state are shown in Figure 18-4.

The amount of energy transferred to the load is controlled by the duty cycle of the switch control waveform. The duty cycle (D) is defined as

$$D = \frac{T_{on}}{T_s} \tag{18-1}$$

where T_s is the total switching period and T_{on} is the amount of time the switch is on. The duty cycle can range from 0.0 to 1.0, but typically falls between 0.05 and 0.95 (5% to 95%). From Equation 18-1 we can derive equations for T_{on} and T_{off}:

$$T_{on} = D \times T_s \tag{18-2}$$

$$T_{off} = (1-D) \times T_s \tag{18-3}$$

FIGURE 18-4

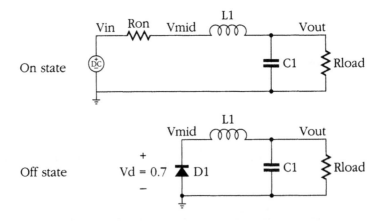

Equivalent circuits for on and off states.

These times are shown in Figure 18-5, which also shows some representative wave-forms for the buck converter operating in continuous mode at steady state with a duty cycle of about 30%.

From Figure 18-5 we see that when the switch is on (**ctrl** signal is high), the inductor current increases while the diode current is zero. When the switch is off, the inductor current decreases and the diode is conducting.

The first step in designing a switching regulator is to select the duty cycle. For the buck converter operating in continuous mode, the following relationship can be used to approximate the duty cycle:

$$V_{out} = V_{in} \times D \qquad (18\text{-}4)$$

From our specifications we can easily calculate the duty cycle required to give the desired output. However, since our desired output is relatively small (4.8 V), we should include the diode voltage drop in the calculation as follows:

$$V_{out} = (V_{in} \times D) - V_d \qquad (18\text{-}5)$$

Solving for D, the equation becomes

FIGURE 18-5

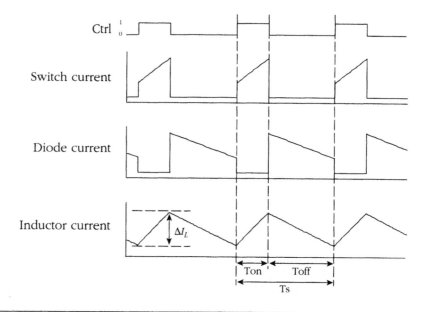

Buck converter continuous-mode steady-state waveforms.

$$D = \frac{V_{out} + V_d}{V_{in}} = \frac{4.8 + 0.7}{42} = 0.131 \qquad (18\text{-}6)$$

From Equations 18-2 and 18-3 we can also calculate the on and off time of the control input. Recall from the power supply requirements that the switching frequency, f_s, is 25 kHz. Thus, $T_s = 1/f_s = 40$ μs. Noting that $T_s = T_{on} + T_{off}$ and substituting in Equations 18-2 and 18-3:

$$T_{on} = 0.131 \times 40 \text{ μs} = 5.24 \text{ μs} \qquad (18\text{-}7)$$

$$T_{off} = (1 - 0.131) \times 40 \text{ μs} = 34.76 \text{ μs} \qquad (18\text{-}8)$$

The next step is to calculate the values for the inductor (L1) and capacitor (C1) in the output filter. For the inductor we use the familiar equation

$$V_L = L \times \frac{dI_L}{dt} \approx L \times \frac{\Delta I_L}{\Delta t} \qquad (18\text{-}9)$$

where V_L is the voltage across the inductor and I_L is the inductor current. The goal here is to select a minimum value for L1 such that the converter operates in continuous mode.

In the output specifications we have a minimum output current of 15 mA. This minimum current level also sets the maximum allowed current ripple, ΔI_L. If the ripple current exceeds 30 mA peak to peak, the inductor current goes to zero during part of the off time, causing the converter to operate in discontinuous mode. This is illustrated in Figure 18-6.

FIGURE 18-6

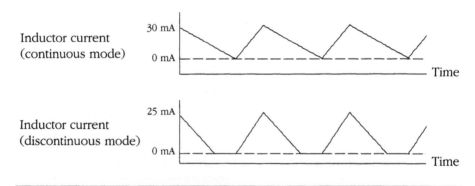

Inductor current for continuous and discontinuous modes.

To calculate the minimum inductance to remain in continuous mode, we can re-arrange Equation 18-9 to solve for L_{min}:

$$
\begin{aligned}
L_{min} &= V_L \times \frac{\Delta t}{\Delta I_{L(max)}} \\[2mm]
&= (V_{in} - V_{out}) \times \frac{T_{on}}{\Delta I_{L(max)}} \\[2mm]
&= (42 - 4.8) \times \frac{5.2 \ \mu s}{30 \ mA} \\[2mm]
&= 6.5 \ mH
\end{aligned}
\qquad (18\text{-}10)
$$

where T_{on} is the on time and $\Delta I_{L(max)}$ is the maximum ripple current. Here we have used the equivalent circuit for the on state shown in Figure 18-4, neglecting the on resistance for the switch. The inductor value calculated guarantees continuous-mode operation as long as the load current does not exceed 15 mA.

The capacitor controls the amount of ripple voltage on the output. The following formula can be used to calculate the minimum capacitance for a buck converter:

$$
C_{min} = \frac{\Delta I_{out}}{8 \times F_s \times \Delta V_{out}} = \frac{30 \ mA}{8 \times 25 \ kHz \times 100 \ mV} = 1.5 \ \mu F
\qquad (18\text{-}11)
$$

Using a capacitor value equal to or greater than this value guarantees the ripple voltage will be below 100 mV. The exact value for the capacitor is not critical and is often up to 10 times the minimum calculated value.

The final step is to calculate the minimum and maximum load resistance. This can easily be determined from the load current and voltage specifications:

$$
R_{Load(min)} = \frac{V_{out}}{I_{out(max)}} = \frac{4.8 \ V}{2 \ A} = 2.4 \ \Omega
\qquad (18\text{-}12)
$$

$$
R_{Load(max)} = \frac{V_{out}}{I_{out(min)}} = \frac{4.8 \ V}{15 \ mA} = 320 \ \Omega
\qquad (18\text{-}13)
$$

The $R_{Load(max)}$ value is critical to ensure the current does not fall below 15 mA and force the circuit into the discontinuous mode.

This completes the design of the basic buck converter. Figure 18-7 shows a struc-tural VHDL-AMS model of the completed open-loop (no feedback) circuit from Figure 18-3. The time domain simulation results of the output voltage and inductor current are shown in Figure 18-8. To simulate this circuit, we need models for the

FIGURE 18-7

```
library ieee;  use ieee.std_logic_1164.all;
library ieee_proposed;  use ieee_proposed.electrical_systems.all;

entity tb_BuckConverter is
    port ( ctrl : std_logic );
end tb_BuckConverter;
```

```
architecture tb_BuckConverter of tb_BuckConverter is

    terminal vin : electrical;
    terminal vmid : electrical;
    terminal vout : electrical;

begin

    L1 : entity work.inductor(ideal)
        generic map ( ind => 6.5e-3 )
        port map ( p1 => vmid, p2 => vout );

    C1 : entity work.capacitor(ideal)
        generic map ( cap => 1.5e-6 )
        port map ( p1 => vout, p2 => electrical_ref );

    VinDC : entity work.v_constant(ideal)
        generic map ( level => 42.0 )
        port map ( pos => vin, neg => electrical_ref );

    RLoad : entity work.resistor(ideal)
        generic map ( res => 2.4 )
        port map ( p1 => vout, p2 => electrical_ref );

    D1 : entity work.diode(ideal)
        port map ( p => electrical_ref, n => vmid );

    sw1 : entity work.switch_dig(ideal)
        port map ( sw_state => ctrl, p2 => vmid, p1 => vin );

end architecture tb_BuckConverter;
```

Structural VHDL-AMS code for a buck converter.

individual components and a test bench that creates the digital control signal with a 13.1% duty cycle (see the exercises at the end of this chapter).

From these results the following measurements verify that the open-loop design meets the specifications:

- $V_{out(avg)}$ = 4.76 V

- $V_{out(ripple)}$ = 50 mV

- $I_{out(avg)}$ = 1.97 A

- $I_{out(ripple)}$ = 30 mA

FIGURE 18-8

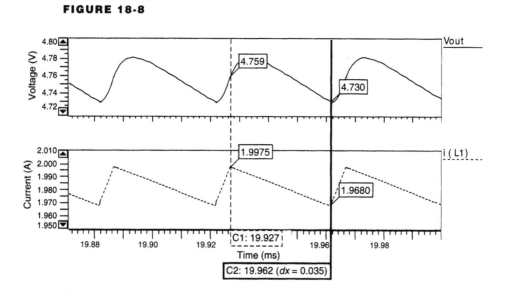

Buck converter open-loop transient simulation results.

18.2 **Modeling with VHDL-AMS**

The next step in the design process is to close the loop and provide compensation to ensure stability as the load conditions change. Before doing this, however, we will examine some of the VHDL-AMS models needed for this design in more detail.

The resistor, capacitor, inductor and diode are elementary electrical components that can be easily modeled using the techniques we saw in Chapter 6. Models written in VHDL-AMS can be as detailed as desired, including numerous effects beyond ideal behavior. However, it is good practice to include only as much detail as is necessary for the analysis being performed. With VHDL-AMS we can write models with varying degrees of detail by creating multiple architectures of an entity. It is important to understand what effects are included in a model (and, equally, what effects are excluded) before using the model in a simulation. This helps us to interpret the simulation results.

Capacitor Model

In previous chapters, we have seen models of an ideal capacitor using the familiar current-voltage relationship:

$$I_C = C \times \frac{dV_C}{dt}$$

(18-14)

where I_C is the current through the capacitor and V_C is the voltage across the capacitor. For switching power supplies it is often necessary to consider the effect of the equivalent series resistance (ESR). If the ESR is too large, it can introduce an unwanted "zero" in the frequency response, which may lead to instability.

We can model this effect in VHDL-AMS by including an additional generic constant, r_esr, in the entity declaration and creating an additional architecture, as shown in Figure 18-9. In this model, the capacitor is an open circuit at DC and uses the user-specified initial voltage v_ic, provided the value is other than **real'low**. This value is the default value for the generic constant and is used to determine whether initialization is required. During time domain simulation, the voltage across the capacitor is reduced by the voltage drop across the equivalent series resistance. The reduced voltage is used in the statement representing Equation 18-14.

Ideal Switch Model

In the final switching power-supply design, the switch component will typically be a power bipolar transistor or power MOSFET. In the early design stages, we may not have determined which particular device to use. However, since we are only using

---

FIGURE 18-9

```
library ieee_proposed;  use ieee_proposed.electrical_systems.all;

entity capacitor is
    generic ( cap : capacitance;
                    r_esr : resistance := 0.0;
                    v_ic : voltage := real'low );
        port ( terminal p1, p2 : electrical );
    end entity capacitor;
```

```
architecture esr of capacitor is
    quantity v across i through p1 to p2;
    quantity vc : voltage;    -- Internal voltage across capacitor
begin
    if domain = quiescent_domain and v_ic /= real'low use
        vc == v_ic;
        i == 0.0;
    else
        vc == v - (i * r_esr);
        i == cap * vc'dot;
    end use;
end architecture esr;
```

Capacitor architecture with equivalent series resistance.

the device as a switch, it will be either on (saturated) or off, so its detailed characteristics are not relevant. We can proceed with simulations of the system using an idealized model of the device.

The switch model shown in Figure 18-10 models the on and off resistance and has a linear transition between the two states. The switch is controlled by the port sw_state, which, in the power-supply system, is connected to the signal ctrl and driven by the 25 kHz clock. This switch model provides sufficient detail for the early design stages, where we are designing the L-C filter and performing load analysis. For more detailed analysis, we could substitute an architecture that provides logarithmic transitions between on and off resistances, or use a SPICE-based model, as described in Appendix A.

FIGURE 18-10

```
library ieee;  use ieee.std_logic_1164.all;
library ieee_proposed;  use ieee_proposed.electrical_systems.all;

entity switch_dig is
    generic ( r_open : resistance := 1.0e6;
              r_closed : resistance := 1.0e-3;
              trans_time : real := 1.0e-9 );
    port ( sw_state : in std_logic;
           terminal p1, p2 : electrical );
end entity switch_dig;
```

```
architecture linear of switch_dig is

    signal r_sig : resistance := r_open;
    quantity v across i through p1 to p2;
    quantity r : resistance;

begin
    -- detect switch state and assign resistance value to r_sig
    DetectState: process (sw_state)
    begin
        if (sw_state'event and sw_state = '0') then
            r_sig <= r_open;
        elsif (sw_state'event and sw_state = '1') then
            r_sig <= r_closed;
        end if;
    end process DetectState;

    r == r_sig'ramp(trans_time, trans_time);
    v == r * i;

end architecture linear;
```

Digitally controlled ideal switch model.

18.3 **Voltage-Mode Control**

As we saw in Section 18.1, the output voltage of the buck regulator is a function of the input voltage and the duty cycle of the switching waveform. Thus, we can adjust the output voltage simply by changing the duty cycle. Pulse-width modulation (PWM) control techniques provide an effective way of doing this. The simplest method for controlling the output voltage level in PWM switching regulators is voltage-mode control. This method involves sensing the output voltage in a closed-loop configuration, comparing to a reference voltage and adjusting the duty cycle of the PWM waveform based on the error signal. In order to do this we need to modify the basic buck converter from Figure 18-3 to provide a voltage control input.

The schematic in Figure 18-11 shows one way to control the duty cycle of the PWM waveform. The control voltage is compared to a sawtooth waveform using a comparator with a digital output. The comparator output is then inverted, and the resulting waveform is used to control the switch.

Examining the simulation results in Figure 18-12, we see that a control voltage of 0.327 V provides a PWM waveform, **sw_ctrl**, with the desired duty cycle of 13.1% calculated in Equation 18-6. This control voltage value was derived from the following relationship:

$$V_{out} = V_{in} \times \frac{V_c}{V_{ramp}} - V_d \qquad (18\text{-}15)$$

where V_c is the control voltage, and V_{ramp} is the amplitude of the sawtooth waveform. Note that this equation is identical to Equation 18-5 with the duty cycle replaced by the ratio V_c/V_{ramp}. Setting V_{ramp} to 2.5 V and solving for V_c, the equation becomes

FIGURE 18-11

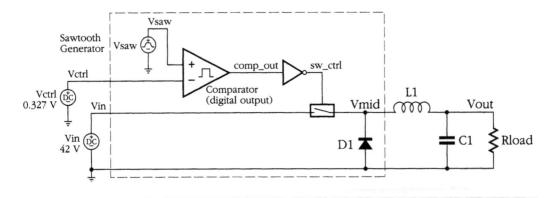

Buck converter with voltage-mode PWM control.

FIGURE 18-12

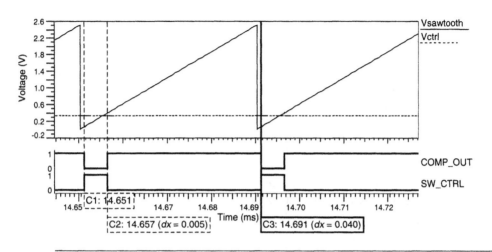

Waveforms illustrating PWM voltage control technique.

$$V_c = V_{ramp} \times \frac{V_{out} + V_d}{V_{in}} = 2.5 \times \frac{4.8 + 0.7}{42} = 0.327 \text{ V} \tag{18-16}$$

Note the resulting digital control signal is the same as that used in the original design, with a duty cycle of 13.1%. In order to simulate this design, we need a few additional elementary models: a pulse waveform generator, an analog comparator with digital output (see Exercise 23) and a simple logic inverter. The simulation results for the buck converter using this PWM control scheme are identical to those shown in Figure 18-8.

18.4 **Averaged Model**

We can replace the switching elements in the switched power supply with a state-averaged model, producing a smooth (averaged) voltage on the output. By replacing the simulation-intensive switching model, the simulation times are significantly reduced. An averaged model also allows us to run a small-signal frequency (AC) analysis and examine the stability of the control loop. Furthermore, it allows us to run a closed-loop time domain analysis and examine how the system responds to sudden changes in load or line conditions. For our buck converter example, we can create an averaged model to replace the circuitry shown within the dashed box in Figure 18-11 (the diode, switch and digital control circuitry). The averaged model for the buck converter operating in continuous mode contains the basic relationship from Equation 18-15 and is shown in Figure 18-13. The simulation results using the averaged model and the switching model are compared in Figure 18-14. Note that the averaged waveforms are a "smooth" approximation of the original waveforms.

FIGURE 18-13

library ieee_proposed; **use** ieee_proposed.electrical_systems.**all**;

entity buck_sw **is**

    generic (Vd : voltage := 0.7;   *-- diode voltage*

              Vramp : voltage := 2.5);   *-- p–p amplitude of ramp voltage*

    port (**terminal** input, output, ref, ctrl: electrical);

end entity buck_sw;

---

architecture average **of** buck_sw **is**

    quantity Vout **across** Iout **through** output **to** ref;

    quantity Vin **across** input **to** ref;

    quantity Vctrl **across** ctrl **to** ref;

begin

    Vout == Vctrl * Vin / Vramp – Vd;   *-- averaged equation*

end architecture average;

Averaged model for buck switching converter.

FIGURE 18-14

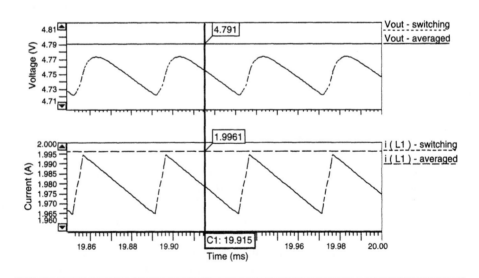

Simulation results for switching and averaged models.

18.5 **Closing the Loop**

At steady state, the output voltage of the power supply is only a function of the input voltage, diode voltage drop and duty cycle, as described earlier and shown in Equation 18-5. DC-DC converters, however are subject to sudden changes in conditions, such as input voltage (line) variations or output load changes. These changes can cause the output voltage to vary outside of the specified limits. To complete the design, we need to provide a feedback mechanism that senses a change in the output voltage and adjusts the duty cycle to bring the voltage back to the desired level.

The schematic for performing these types of analyses is shown in Figure 18-15. The hierarchical block **buck_sw** has replaced the switch, diode and PWM circuitry. This allows us to use either the switching model or the averaged model simply by changing architectures, depending on the type of analysis required. Initially, we use the averaged model shown in Figure 18-13; we will use the switching model later to examine the effects of line and load transients. The load resistor has been replaced by a load model that can be enabled or disabled to provide sudden changes in the load conditions. The two-pole switch between the compensator and the control input allows to use the same circuit for both open-loop and closed-loop simulations. The position of this switch is controlled by a generic parameter that we set prior to running a simulation. Opening the switch breaks the loop so that the control-to-output transfer characteristic can be obtained. This information is useful for designing the compensation. The compensator block compares the output voltage to a reference and generates the appropriate control voltage. The block is introduced in the closed-loop configuration to allow stability analysis. We will discuss these models and the different types of analyses in more detail in the following sections.

FIGURE 18-15

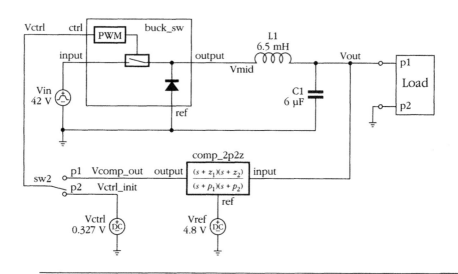

Buck converter with voltage feedback.

Compensation Design

The first step in designing the compensation is to determine the frequency characteristics of the system, commonly referred to as the "control-to-output" transfer characteristic or transfer function. To do this, we remove the load and break the feedback loop, as discussed above. Figure 18-16 shows the model of the switch used to break the feedback loop. When the generic constant **sw_state** is 1, the common terminal **c** is connected to the terminal **p1** with resistance **r_closed** and to **p2** with resistance **r_open**. When **sw_state** is 2, the connections are reversed.

To generate the control-to-output transfer curve, we set **sw_state** to 2. This breaks the loop and connects a voltage source of 0.327 V to the control input. For this analysis, we must also remove the load. While we could do so simply by deleting the load, a more flexible approach is to add an "enable" generic constant. We will return to this approach shortly. To generate the control-to-output transfer function, we need

FIGURE 18-16

```
library ieee_proposed;  use ieee_proposed.electrical_systems.all;
entity sw_LoopCtrl is
    generic ( r_open : resistance := 1.0e6;
              r_closed : resistance := 1.0e–3;
              sw_state : integer range 1 to 2 := 1 );
    port ( terminal c, p1, p2 : electrical );
end entity sw_LoopCtrl;
```

```
architecture ideal of sw_LoopCtrl is
    quantity v1 across i1 through c to p1;
    quantity v2 across i2 through c to p2;
    quantity r1, r2 : resistance;
begin
    sw1 : if sw_state = 1 generate
        r1 == r_closed;
        r2 == r_open;
    end generate sw1;
    sw2 : if sw_state = 2 generate
        r1 == r_open;
        r2 == r_closed;
    end generate sw2;
    v1 == r1 * i1;
    v2 == r2 * i2;
end architecture ideal;
```

Switch model used to break the feedback loop.

to perform a frequency analysis, as we discussed in Chapter 13. We sweep the frequency over a range of interest and use the resulting Bode plot to analyze the magnitude and phase response. The Bode plot of our control-to-output curve using the averaged model is shown in Figure 18-17.

We can use the corner frequencies of the control-to-output curve to determine the placement of the poles and zeros of the compensator design. The curve shows the double pole contributed by the L-C output filter at a frequency of 806 Hz, along with a −40 dB/decade rolloff and a −180° phase shift. This frequency can also be calculated by

$$f_{LC} = \frac{1}{2\pi\sqrt{LC}} = \frac{1}{2\pi\sqrt{6.5 \text{ mH} \times 6 \text{ }\mu\text{F}}} = 805.9 \text{ Hz} \qquad (18\text{-}17)$$

Note that we have substituted a capacitance value of 6 μF for the minimum value of 1.5 μF in order to shift this pole slightly to the left, simplifying the compensator design. The larger capacitor slows the time response, but also decrease the amount of voltage ripple on the output.

The Bode plot also reveals a zero occurring at about 530 kHz. This is due to the 50 mΩ equivalent series resistance of the capacitor and can be calculated by

$$f_{ESR} = \frac{1}{2\pi R_{ESR}C} = \frac{1}{2\pi \times 50 \text{ m}\Omega \times 6 \text{ }\mu\text{F}} = 530.5 \text{ kHz} \qquad (18\text{-}18)$$

FIGURE 18-17

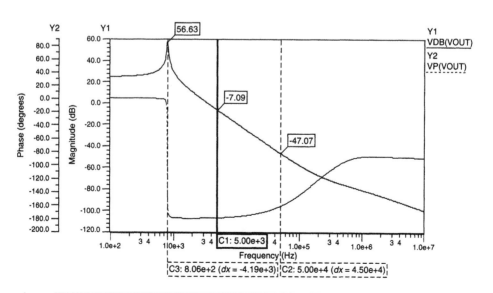

Control-to-output transfer characteristics.

The detailed compensator design is beyond the scope of this book (see [7] and [40]), but generally the compensation should be designed to counteract the poles and zeros in the control-to-output response that may lead to instability. We choose a two-pole, two-zero method here due to the −40 dB/decade rolloff above the L-C poles and the −180° phase lag. Factors to take into account when designing the compensation are the overall desired crossover frequency of the system, f_{xo}, usually selected to be well below the switching frequency (we select $f_{xo} = f_s/5 = 5$ kHz); the gain needed to bring the control-to-output transfer function up to 0 dB at the crossover frequency; and the pole and zero locations. We can see from Figure 18-17 that the required gain is 7.09 dB at 5 kHz. The zeros are typically placed at $f_{LC}/2$ to counteract the L-C filter poles, giving a resulting phase margin of 45°. One pole is placed well beyond the desired crossover frequency ($f_{p1} = 1.5f_{xo} = 7.5$ kHz) to increase the overall bandwidth. The second pole is placed at 531 kHz to compensate for the equivalent series resistance of the filter capacitor.

We can create a behavioral transfer function model containing the desired pole and zero locations and use it in the system simulation until the detailed compensator design is completed. The transfer function we use for the compensation is

$$H(s) = \frac{V_{out}}{V_{in}} = K \times \frac{\left(\frac{s}{z_1} + 1\right)\left(\frac{s}{z_2} + 1\right)}{s \times \left(\frac{s}{p_1} + 1\right)\left(\frac{s}{p_2} + 1\right)} \tag{18-19}$$

where z_1 and z_2 are the zero locations and p_1 and p_2 are the pole locations. We can use the 'ltf attribute to create high-level transfer function models. First the equation must be simplified to the general form

$$H(s) = \frac{\displaystyle\sum_{k=0}^{m} a_k s^k}{\displaystyle\sum_{k=0}^{n} b_k s^k} = \frac{a_0 + a_1 s + a_2 s^2 + \ldots + a_m s^m}{b_0 + b_1 s + b_2 s^2 + \ldots + b_n s^n} \tag{18-20}$$

Simplifying Equation 18-19 to this form gives us the following:

$$\frac{V_{out}}{V_{in}} = K \times \frac{\dfrac{s^2}{z_1 z_2} + s\left(\dfrac{z_1 + z_2}{z_1 z_2}\right) + 1}{\dfrac{s^3}{p_1 p_2} + s^2\left(\dfrac{p_1 + p_2}{p_1 p_2}\right) + s} \tag{18-21}$$

Figure 18-18 shows a model that implements Equation 18-21. A high-level model such as this simulates very quickly and is extremely useful when performing system design trade-offs. Using this model, we can also easily modify the compensator poles and zeros to accommodate any unexpected system design changes that may occur.

The frequency analysis results for the compensator block (**vcomp**) overlaid on top of the original control-to-output transfer curve (**vout**) are shown in Figure 18-19. Again, since we are using very high-level models, we can easily adjust the desired response to accommodate design changes. For example, we could deemphasize the high Q of the L-C filter pole pair by separating the zeros. For now, this response is sufficient to continue with our design until further information becomes available.

FIGURE 18-18

```
library ieee;  use ieee.math_real.all;
library ieee_proposed;  use ieee_proposed.electrical_systems.all;

entity comp_2p2z is
    generic ( gain : real := 100.0;    -- high DC gain for good load regulation
              fp1 : real := 7.5e3;     -- pole location to achieve crossover frequency
              fp2 : real := 531.0e3;   -- pole location to cancel effect of ESR
              fz1 : real := 403.0;     -- zero locations to cancel L-C filter poles
              fz2 : real := 403.0 );
    port ( terminal input, output, ref : electrical );
end entity comp_2p2z;
```

```
architecture ltf of comp_2p2z is
    quantity vin across input to ref;
    quantity vout across iout through output to ref;
    constant wp1 : real := math_2_pi * fp1;    -- Pole freq (in radians)
    constant wp2 : real := math_2_pi * fp2;
    constant wz1 : real := math_2_pi * fz1;    -- Zero freq (in radians)
    constant wz2 : real := math_2_pi * fz2;
    constant num : real_vector := ( 1.0,
                                    (wz1 + wz2) / (wz1 * wz2),
                                    1.0 / (wz1 * wz2) );
    constant den : real_vector := ( 1.0e-9, 1.0,
                                    (wp1 + wp2) / (wp1 * wp2),
                                    1.0 / (wp1 * wp2) );
begin
    vout == -1.0 * gain * vin'ltf(num, den);
end architecture ltf;
```

Behavioral model of the loop compensator.

FIGURE 18-19

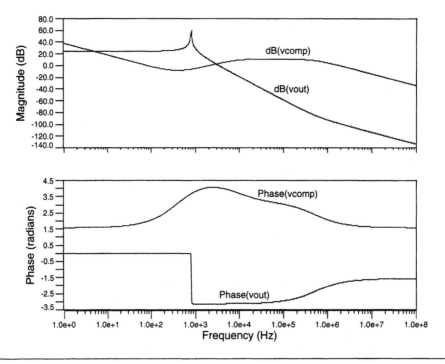

Control-to-output transfer curve and compensator response.

Load Regulation

The next step is to place the compensator into the design shown in Figure 18-15 and run the closed-loop time domain simulation. Before doing this, we need to change the sw_state parameter on **sw2** to 1 to close the loop and connect the output of the compensator to the control input. We also reintroduce the load into the system. To examine how the system responds to a sudden change in load conditions, the original resistor load model is replaced with a load model that changes value at a nominated time. The load model is shown in Figure 18-20. The load is basically a piecewise-linear resistor model with initial resistance **res_init**. At time **t1** the resistance changes to **res1**, and at time **t2** the resistance changes again to **res2**. This allows us to run a time domain simulation and examine the effect of instantaneous load changes on our buck converter. The model also has a generic parameter, **load_enable**, that is used to insert or remove the load depending on the desired analysis.

The simulation results shown in Figure 18-21 arise from an initial resistance of 2.4 Ω changing to 1 Ω at 5 ms, and to 5 Ω at 30 ms. The response shows that the loop is able to recover from the instantaneous change in load conditions, returning the output to the desired 4.8 V.

FIGURE 18-20

```
library ieee_proposed; use ieee_proposed.electrical_systems.all;
entity pwl_load is
    generic ( load_enable : boolean := true;
                res_init : resistance;
                res1 : resistance;
                t1 : time;
                res2 : resistance;
                t2 : time );
    port ( terminal p1, p2 : electrical );
end entity pwl_load;
```

```
architecture ideal of pwl_load is
    quantity v across i through p1 to p2;
    signal res_signal : resistance := res_init;
begin
    load_present : if load_enable generate
        if domain = quiescent_domain or domain = frequency_domain use
            v == i * res_init;
        else
            v == i * res_signal'ramp(1.0e–6, 1.0e–6);
        end use;
        create_event : process is
        begin
            wait for t1;
            res_signal <= res1;
            wait for t2 – t1;
            res_signal <= res2;
            wait;
        end process create_event;
    end generate load_present;
    load_absent : if not load_enable generate
        i == 0.0;
    end generate load_absent;
end architecture ideal;
```

Piecewise-linear load model.

FIGURE 18-21

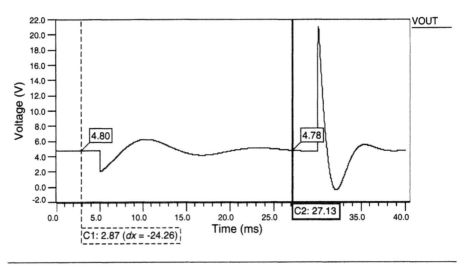

Closed-loop time domain simulation results with changing load conditions.

Line Regulation

We can perform a similar test to examine how the supply responds to a change in input (line) voltage. In the RC airplane system, the 42 V input voltage to the buck converter is also used to power the propeller motor. If there is a sudden change in this voltage, for example, due to a motor stall condition, the converter must be able to continue regulating at 4.8 V. Figure 18-22 shows how the system responds to a sudden droop in the input voltage from 42 V to 30 V. The transient response shows a corresponding droop in the output voltage of about 0.5 V and a recovery time of about 20 ms. These are important system-level performance measurements and will be useful information when integrating the power converter with the rest of the RC airplane system.

18.6 Design Trade-Off Study

Now that we have completed and verified the basic design, we can use VHDL-AMS models and simulation as tools for studying the various design trade-offs. For example, we could study various topology decisions, such as selecting between different converter modes (buck mode versus forward mode), control methods (voltage mode versus current mode) and compensator topologies. We will not go into such a detailed level of design in this case study. Instead, we will consider one particular system design trade-off decision that can be made using high-level models and that can

FIGURE 18-22

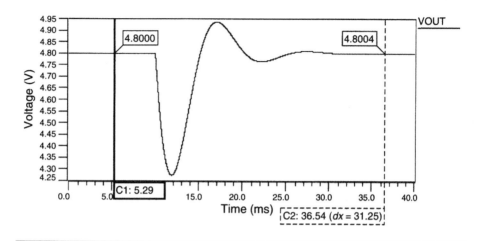

Simulation results of converter output with sudden change in input voltage.

assist in completing the detailed converter design. We will consider the trade-off between the switching frequency and the values for the L-C filter.

As we saw in Equations 18-10 and 18-11, there is an inverse relationship between
the L-C values and the clock frequency. Other factors affect these values as well
(namely, output voltage and current), but the selection of the clock speed is a con-
trollable design parameter and is somewhat arbitrary. The system design challenge is
to find the optimum L-C values and clock speed that meet the overall system requirements. We can use the equations mentioned above to manually calculate different
values for **Lmin** and **Cmin** for given clock frequencies. Alternatively, we can express
the equations in a VHDL-AMS model and use a simulator to calculate the values. An
example of such a model is shown in Figure 18-23. This model contains all the basic
relationships from Equations 18-1 through 18-11. The input parameters (**Vout, Vin, Im-
in, Vripple, Vd**) are generic constants with default values taken from the system specification. The switching frequency is input using a quantity port so that it can be easily
varied during a simulation by a ramped source model. The outputs **Lmin** and **Cmin**
are output quantity ports that can be plotted.

FIGURE 18-23

```
library ieee_proposed;  use ieee_proposed.electrical_systems.all;

entity CalcBuckParams is

    generic ( Vin : voltage range 1.0 to 50.0 := 42.0;      -- input voltage [volts]
              Vout : voltage := 4.8;                         -- output voltage [volts]
              Vd : voltage := 0.7;                           -- diode voltage [volts]
              Imin : current := 15.0e-3;                     -- min output current [amps]
```

(continued on page 580)

(continued from page 579)

```
                    Vripple : voltage range 1.0e–6 to 100.0
                        := 100.0e–3 );              –– output voltage ripple [volts]
        port ( quantity Fsw : in real range 1.0 to 1.0e6
                        := 2.0;                     –– switching frequency [Hz]
            quantity Lmin : out inductance;         –– minimum inductance [henries]
            quantity Cmin : out capacitance );      –– minimum capacitance [farads]
    end entity CalcBuckParams;
```

```
    architecture behavioral of CalcBuckParams is
        constant D : real := (Vout + Vd) / Vin;    –– duty cycle
        quantity Ts : real;                         –– period
        quantity Ton : real;                        –– on time
    begin
            Ts == 1.0 / Fsw;

            Ton == D * Ts;

            Lmin == (Vin – Vout) * Ton / (2.0 * Imin);

            Cmin == (2.0 * Imin) / (8.0 * Fsw * Vripple);
    end architecture behavioral;
```

Model for calculating L and C values for the buck converter.

For the simulation, we use a pulse source with a quantity port output to sweep the input frequency from 25 kHz to 200 kHz. The simulation results are shown in Figure 18-24. Inductance values for switching frequencies of 50 kHz and 100 kHz are highlighted. The results verify the inverse relationship between Lmin and the clock-switching frequency mentioned above and allow us to quickly find the appropriate values for each.

The model could be expanded further to include the poles and zeros for the behavioral compensator model in Figure 18-18 (see Exercise 18). Such a model can be very useful, since many of the circuit parameters are interrelated. For example, changing the switching frequency changes the values for L and C, which also changes the control-to-output transfer curve (see Figure 18-17) by moving the location of the double pole. This changes the compensation requirements and probably affects system performance. Using high-level models, such as the state-averaged model of the switch and the transfer function model for the compensator, we can run system-level simulations very quickly to optimize system performance prior to completing the detailed design.

To illustrate this, we repeated the line regulation test from Figure 18-22, simultaneously varying the L and C values and the pole and zero locations of the compensator according to the values calculated by the model in Figure 18-23. The results are shown in Figure 18-25. Examining this plot closely reveals an inverse relationship between the output voltage droop and settling time as a function of switching frequency.

FIGURE 18-24

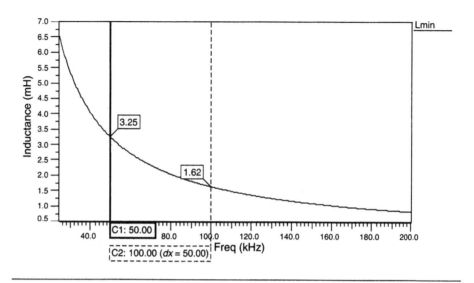

Inductance versus switching frequency.

FIGURE 18-25

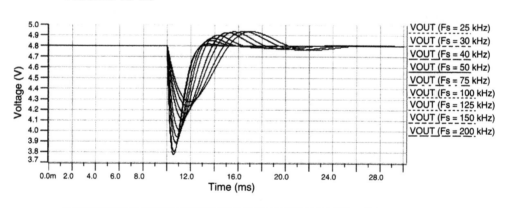

Line regulation for various switching frequencies.

The relationships can be plotted, as shown in Figure 18-26, by performing a series of measurements on the original simulation data. The plot reveals that, as the switching frequency is increased, a definite trade-off exists between maximum voltage droop and the settling time when the system is recovering from a sudden change in the line voltage.

FIGURE 18-26

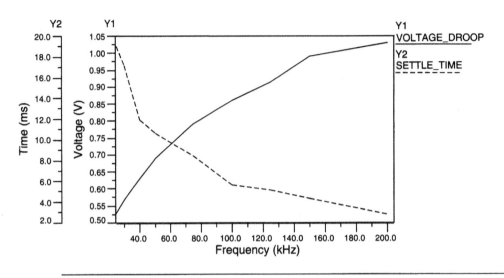

Output voltage droop and settle time measurements.

Exercises

1. [● 18.1] For a buck converter, what is the relationship between input voltage, output voltage and duty cycle?

2. [● 18.1] What topology is be needed to convert 4.8 VDC to 42 VDC?

3. [● 18.1] What is the main purpose of adding a transformer to complete the DC-DC converter design?

4. [● 18.1] How is the operation of the buck converter affected if the load resistance rises above the maximum allowed value?

5. [● 18.2] Why is the ideal switch model sufficient for much of the buck converter design process?

6. [● 18.4] What is the advantage of the averaged model over the switching model when designing a buck converter?

7. [● 18.5] What role does the compensation block play in the buck converter design, and why is it advantageous to use a behavioral model that utilizes the 'ltf attribute?

8. [● 18.5] What is the purpose of the two-pole switch (SW2) in Figure 18-15?

9. [● 18.5] How do you generate the control-to-output transfer curve, and what is it used for?

10. [❶ 18.6] What is the relationship between the L-C values and switching frequency?

11. [❷ 18.2] Create a model for a linear resistor with electrical ports that includes the relationship $v = i \times R$.

12. [❷ 18.2] Add an architecture to the resistor model where the resistance varies linearly with temperature. Hint: Use the equation

$$R_T = R_{nom}(1 + \alpha(T_{env} - 27°C))$$

where R_{nom} is the nominal resistance, α is the linear temperature coefficient and T_{env} is the ambient temperature in °C.

13. [❷ 18.2] Create a model for a linear capacitor with electrical ports that includes the relationship

$$i = v \times \frac{dv}{dt}$$

14. [❷ 18.2] Create a model for a linear inductor with electrical ports that includes the relationship

$$i = L \times \int v dt$$

15. [❷ 18.2] Create a model for a diode with electrical ports that includes the relationship

$$i = i_{sat}(e^{v/v_t} - 1)$$

16. [❷ 18.2] Create a model for a constant (DC) voltage source.

17. [❷ 18.6] Create a pulse source with a quantity port output to test the **CalcBuckParams** model in Figure 18-23.

18. [❷ 18.6] Modify the model in Figure 18-23 to calculate the poles and zeros for the compensator model.

19. [❸ 18.1] Write a test bench with a 25 kHz digital clock to run the structural VHDL-AMS model shown in Figure 18-7, and verify the simulation results.

20. [❸ 18.2] Add an architecture to the capacitor model that includes leakage resistance. Hint: Use a second through variable to define a parallel resistance across the capacitor terminals.

21. [❸ 18.2] Add an architecture to the switch model in Figure 18-10 to provide a logarithmic transition between the on and off resistances.

22. [❸ 18.2] Create a behavioral model for a two-winding transformer with the following equations:

$$v_p = I_p \times R_p + L_p \times \frac{dI_p}{dt} + m \times \frac{dI_s}{dt}$$

$$v_s = I_s \times R_s + L_s \times \frac{dI_s}{dt} + m \times \frac{dI_s}{dt}$$

where the subscript p signifies the primary winding and the subscript s signifies the secondary winding.

23. [❸ 18.3] Write a model for a comparator with electrical input pins and a digital (**std_logic**) output pin for the PWM control method shown in Figure 18-11.

24. [❸ 18.5] Design a detailed (component-level) compensator circuit and compare the simulation results to the behavioral models in Figure 18-18.

25. [❹ 18.4] Modify the averaged model in Figure 18-13 to handle discontinuous mode.

26. [❹ 18.5] Create a model for a complete forward converter that includes a transformer, snubber circuitry and a detailed compensator design.

27. [❹ 18.5] Create a PWL load model where the (time, resistance) pairs are a two-dimensional array of variable length.

28. [❹] Create a battery model that has inputs of voltage and amp-hour ratings with a state-of-charge and voltage-versus-time outputs.

chapter nineteen
Guards and Blocks

In this chapter we look at a number of closely related topics. First, we discuss a new kind of resolved signal called a guarded signal. We see how we can disconnect drivers from such signals. Next, we introduce the idea of blocks in a VHDL-AMS design. We show how blocks and guarded signals work together with guards and guard expressions to cause automatic disconnection of drivers. Finally, we discuss blocks as a mechanism for describing a hierarchical structure within an architecture.

19.1 **Guarded Signals and Disconnection**

In Chapter 15 we saw how we can use resolved signals that include values such as 'Z' for modeling high-impedance outputs. However, if we are modeling at a higher level of abstraction, we may wish to use a more abstract type such as an integer type or a simple bit type to represent signals. In such cases, it is not appropriate to include the high-impedance state as a value, so VHDL-AMS provides us with an alternative approach, using *guarded signals*. These are resolved signals for which we can *disconnect* the drivers; that is, we can cause the drivers to stop contributing values to the resolved signal. We see why these signals are called "guarded" in the next section. First, let us look at the complete syntax rule for a signal declaration, which includes a means of declaring a signal to be guarded.

> signal_declaration ⇐
>   **signal** identifier ⟨ , ... ⟩ : subtype_indication ⟦ **register** ∣ **bus** ⟧
>   ⟦ := expression ⟧ ;

The difference between this rule and the simplified rule we introduced earlier is the inclusion of the option to specify the signal kind as either a *register* signal or a *bus* signal. Note that a guarded signal must be a resolved signal. Hence, the subtype indication in the signal declaration must denote a resolved subtype. Some examples of declarations of guarded signals are

> **signal** interrupt_request : pulled_up bit **bus**;
> **signal** stored_state : resolve_state state_type **register** := init_state;

The difference between the two kinds of guarded signals lies in their behavior when all of their drivers are disconnected. A bus signal uses the resolution function to determine the signal value by passing it an empty array. The bus kind of guarded signal can be used to model a signal that is "pulled up" to some value dependent on the signal type when all drivers are disconnected. A register signal, on the other hand, keeps the resolved value that it had just before the last disconnection. The register kind of guarded signal can be used to model signals with dynamic storage, for example, signals in CMOS logic that store data as charge on transistor gates when all drivers are disconnected. Note that a signal may be neither a register nor a bus signal, in which case it is a regular (unguarded) signal, from which drivers may not be disconnected.

A process can disconnect a driver for a guarded signal by specifying a *null transaction* in a signal assignment statement. As a reminder, the syntax rule we used to introduce a signal assignment was

> signal_assignment_statement ⇐
>   ⟦ label : ⟧ name <= ⟦ delay_mechanism ⟧ waveform ;

The waveform is a sequence of transactions, that is, new values to be applied to the signal after given delays. A more complete syntax rule for waveforms includes null transactions:

waveform ⟸
    ⟦ *value*_expression ⟦ **after** *time*_expression ⟧
      ⟦ **null** ⟦ **after** *time*_expression ⟧ ⟧ ⟨ , ... ⟩

This rule shows that instead of specifying a value in a transaction, we can use the keyword **null** to indicate that the driver should be disconnected after the given delay. When this null transaction matures, the driver ceases to contribute values to the resolution function used to compute the signal's value. Hence the size of the array of values passed as an argument to the resolution function is reduced by one for each driver that currently has a null transaction determining its contribution. When a driver subsequently performs a non-null transaction, it reconnects and contributes the value in the non-null transaction.

Example   Figure 19-1 outlines an architecture body for a computer system consisting of a CPU, a memory and a DMA controller. The architecture body includes a guarded signal of kind bus, write_en, representing a control connection to the memory. The resolution function performs the logical "or" operation of all of the contributing drivers and returns '0' if there are no drivers connected. This result ensures that the memory remains inactive when neither the CPU nor the DMA controller is driving the write_en control signal.

When the process representing the CPU is initialized, it drives write_en with the value '0'. Subsequently, when the DMA controller requests access to the memory by asserting the hold_req signal, the CPU schedules a null transaction on write_en. This transaction removes the CPU's driver from the set of drivers contributing to the resolved value of write_en. Later, when the DMA controller negates hold_req, the CPU reconnects its driver to write_en by scheduling a transaction with the value '0'.

FIGURE 19-1

```
architecture top_level of computer_system is
    function resolve_bits ( bits : bit_vector ) return bit is
        variable result : bit := '0';
    begin
        for index in bits'range loop
            result := result or bits(index);
            exit when result = '1';
        end loop;
        return result;
    end function resolve_bits;
```

(continued on page 588)

(continued from page 587)

```
        signal write_en : resolve_bits bit bus;
        ...
begin
    CPU : process is
        ...
    begin
        write_en <= '0' after Tpd;
        ...
        loop
            wait until clock = '1';
            if hold_req = '1' then
                write_en <= null after Tpd;
                wait on clock until clock = '1' and hold_req = '0';
                write_en <= '0' after Tpd;
            end if;
            ...
        end loop;
    end process CPU;
    ...
end architecture top_level;
```

An outline of an architecture body for a computer system, including a guarded signal of the bus kind and a process representing the CPU that drives the signal.

Example Figure 19-2 shows an outline of a register-transfer-level model of a processor, in which data path elements are modeled by processes. The data path includes two register signals that represent the source operand connections to the ALU. In this design, only one process should drive each of these signals at a time. The resolution function returns the single contributing value.

FIGURE 19-2

```
architecture rtl of processor is
    subtype word is bit_vector(0 to 31);
    type word_vector is array (natural range <>) of word;

    function resolve_unique ( drivers : word_vector ) return word is
    begin
        return drivers(drivers'left);
    end function resolve_unique;

    signal source1, source2 : resolve_unique word register;
    ...
```

```
begin
    source1_reg : process (phase1, source1_reg_out_en, ...) is
        variable stored_value : word;
    begin
        ...
        if source1_reg_out_en = '1' and phase1 = '1' then
            source1 <= stored_value;
        else
            source1 <= null;
        end if;
    end process source1_reg;
    alu : perform_alu_op ( alu_opcode, source1, source2, destination, ... );
    ...

end architecture rtl;
```

An outline of an architecture body for a processor. The source operand buses are register guarded signals driven by processes during phase 1 of a clock cycle. They retain their values during phase 2.

The process **source1_reg** represents one of the data path elements that connects to the **source1** signal. When its output enable signal and the clock phase 1 signal are both '1', the process drives the signal with its stored value. The resolution function is passed an array of one element consisting of this driving value. It is applied to the **source1** signal and is used by the concurrent procedure call representing the ALU. At the end of the clock phase, the process disconnects from **source1** by scheduling a null transaction. Since **source1** is a register signal and all drivers are now disconnected, the resolution function is not called, and **source1** retains its value until some other driver connects. This models a real system in which the operand value is stored as electrical charge on the inputs of transistors in the ALU.

When we are dealing with guarded signals of a composite type such as an array type, it is important to note that within each driver for the signal, all elements must be connected or all must be disconnected. It is not permissible to disconnect some elements using a null transaction and leave other elements connected. The reason for this rule is that the complete composite value from each driver is passed as a contribution to the resolution function. For example, it is not possible to pass just half of a bit vector as an element in the array of values to be resolved. Thus, given a guarded bit-vector signal declared as

```
subtype word is bit_vector(0 to 31);
type word_array is array (integer range <>) of word;
function resolve_words ( words : word_array ) return word;
signal s : resolve_words word bus;
```

we may not write the following signal assignments within one process:

s(0 **to** 15) <= X"003F" **after** T_delay;
s(16 **to** 31) <= **null after** T_delay;

If the design requires that only part of a composite driver be connected at some stages during model execution, then the signal type must be a composite of individually resolved elements, rather than a resolved composite type. This is similar to the requirement we discussed in Chapter 15 on page 477.

In the above examples, we have assumed that a null transaction is scheduled after all previously scheduled transactions have been applied. We have yet to consider how null transactions are scheduled in the general case where there are still transactions pending in the driver. On page 157 in Section 5.3 we described in detail how the list of transactions previously scheduled on a driver is edited when a signal assignment is executed. In particular, when the inertial delay mechanism is used, transactions are deleted if their values differ from that of the newly scheduled transaction. For the purpose of this editing algorithm, a null transaction is deemed to have a value that is different from any value of the signal type. Successive null transactions are deemed to have the same value. So, for example, if a driver for signal **s** has transactions pending as shown at the top of Figure 19-3, and the following signal assignment is executed at time 10 ns:

s <= **reject** 3 ns **inertial null after** 10 ns;

then the resulting list of transactions will be as shown at the bottom of Figure 19-3. The first two transactions are retained because they are scheduled to occur before the

FIGURE 19-3

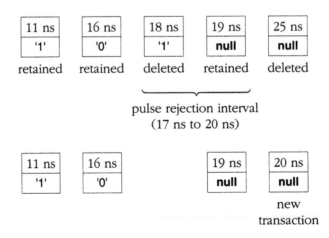

The transactions before (top) and after (bottom) an inertial delay signal assignment involving a null transaction.

pulse rejection interval. The transaction at time 18 ns is deleted, as its value is different from that of the new null transaction. The transaction at 19 ns is retained because it immediately precedes the new null transaction and is deemed to have the same value. The transaction at 25 ns is deleted because it is scheduled to occur later than the new transaction.

The Driving Attribute

In addition to the 'driving_value attribute for signals that we saw in Chapter 15, VHDL-AMS also provides an attribute, 'driving, that is useful with guarded signals. It returns true if the driver in the process referring to the attribute currently has its driver connected to the signal. It returns false if the driver is disconnected. Of course, the attribute 'driving_value should not be used if the driver is disconnected, since there is no driving value in that case. An error will occur if a model tries to do this.

Guarded Ports

Throughout all the examples in this book, we have seen that the signal ports of an entity are treated as signals within an architecture body for that entity. Just as we can have guarded signals, so we can have guarded signal ports as part of an entity's interface. However, there are some important limitations that come about due to the way in which ports are resolved. The main restriction is that guarded quantity and terminal ports are not allowed in VHDL-AMS. Also, a guarded port can only be of the bus kind, not the register kind. A guarded port includes the keyword **bus** in its declaration. For example, given the following declarations to define a resolved subtype **resolved_byte**:

```
subtype byte is bit_vector(0 to 7);
type byte_array is array (integer range <>) of byte;
function resolve ( bytes : byte_array ) return byte;
subtype resolved_byte is resolve byte;
```

we can declare an entity with a guarded port q as follows:

```
entity tri_state_reg is
    port ( d : in resolved_byte;
            q : out resolved_byte bus;
            clock, out_enable : in bit );
end entity tri_state_reg;
```

Since the port q is declared to be a guarded port, a process in an architecture body for tri_state_reg can disconnect from the port by assigning a null transaction. Here is where the behavior is different from what we might first expect. Since the port is of a resolved subtype, it is resolved independently of any external signal associated with it. This means that even if all processes in the architecture for tri_state_reg are disconnected, the resolution function for the port is still invoked to determine the port's value. The port itself does not become disconnected. It continues to contribute its resolved value to the external signal associated with it. While this may seem counter-intuitive, it follows directly from the way resolved signals and ports behave in VHDL-AMS. Hence the entity tri_state_reg declared above does not in fact represent a module that can disconnect its port from an associated signal. There is no mechanism in VHDL-AMS for doing that. While some designers argue that this is a limitation of the language, there are often ways to circumvent the problem. The difficulty mainly arises when modeling at a high level of abstraction. At a lower level, we would use some multivalued logic type that includes a representation of the high-impedance state instead of using disconnection, so the problem does not arise.

Example   Let us look more closely at the tri_state_reg module to see how we can achieve the desired effect. When using tristate logic, we only allow one output to drive a bus at a time. Our solution to the problem lies in writing the resolution function so that it returns an identity value when passed an empty array of contributing values. The identity value, when resolved with any other value, should result in the other value. For bit-vector types, we can resolve values using a logical "or" operation, which has an identity value of a bit vector comprising all '0' bits. The body of the resolution function can be written as shown in Figure 19-4. A behavioral architecture of the tri_state_reg entity can be written as shown in Figure 19-5.

While this description does not actually cause the port q to become disconnected from its associated signal in an instantiating design, it does express the intention of the designer. When the driver in **reg_behavior** disconnects, the resolution function is invoked with an empty array as its argument and returns the value b"0000_0000" as the resolved value for q. This value is then used as the contribution to the associated resolved signal in a design containing an instance of tri_state_reg. If this signal uses the same resolution function, the identity value returned from q will not affect the value returned by another source that is active.

FIGURE 19-4

```
function resolve ( bytes : byte_array ) return byte is
    variable result : byte := b"0000_0000";
begin
    for index in bytes'range loop
        result := result or bytes(index);
    end loop;
    return result;
end function resolve;
```

A resolution function for a resolved bit-vector type.

FIGURE 19-5

```
architecture behavioral of tri_state_reg is
begin
    reg_behavior : process (d, clock, out_enable) is
        variable stored_byte : byte;
    begin
        if clock'event and clock = '1' then
            stored_byte := d;
        end if;
        if out_enable = '1' then
            q <= stored_byte;
        else
            q <= null;
        end if;
    end process reg_behavior;
end architecture behavioral;
```

A behavioral architecture body for a tristate register entity.

Guarded Signal Parameters

In Chapter 9 we saw how we can write subprograms that have signal class parameters. We cannot, however, specify that a signal parameter be a bus signal by adding the keyword **bus** in the parameter list, as we can for ports. Instead, the subprogram uses the kind of the actual signal (bus, register or unguarded) associated with a signal parameter. A procedure can include signal assignment statements that assign null transactions to a formal parameter, but if the actual signal is not a guarded signal, the model is in error. Recall that for signal parameters of mode **out** or **inout**, when the procedure is called, it is passed a reference to the driver for the actual signal. Signal assignments within the procedure schedule transactions onto the driver for the actual signal. If the actual signal is a guarded signal, and the procedure assigns a null transaction to it, the driver that is disconnected is the one in the calling process. When the actual signal is resolved, the subprogram, acting on behalf of the process, does not contribute a value. We can take advantage of this behavior when writing high-level models that include processes that disconnect from bus signals. We can use a subprogram as an abstraction for processes, instead of using component instances.

Example   Suppose we must write a model of a data logger that monitors two byte-wide input ports. The module includes an input register for each port. Both input registers are connected to the data bus of a small microprocessor. The data bus is a guarded signal, and each register, when enabled, connects and drives its stored value. Only one register may connect at a time. The outline of an architecture body for the data logger is shown in Figure 19-6.

The procedure reg, activated by the concurrent procedure calls in the architecture body, encapsulates the behavior for a flow-through register with tristate outputs. In both activations, the signal data_bus is associated with the **out** mode signal parameter q. Since this signal is a guarded signal, the null signal assignment within the procedure is valid. For example, when the activation labeled a_reg executes the null signal assignment, the driver for data_bus in a_reg is disconnected.

FIGURE 19-6

```
architecture high_level of data_logger is
    subtype byte is bit_vector(7 downto 0);
    type byte_array is array (integer range <>) of byte;
    function resolver ( bytes : byte_array ) return byte is
    begin
        if bytes'length > 0 then
            return bytes( bytes'left );
        else
            return X"00";
        end if;
    end function resolver;
    subtype resolved_byte is resolver byte;
    procedure reg ( signal clock, out_enable : in bit;
                    signal d : in byte;
                    signal q : out resolved_byte ) is
        variable stored_byte : byte;
    begin
        loop
            if clock = '1' then
                stored_byte := d;
            end if;
            if out_enable = '1' then
                q <= stored_byte;
            else
                q <= null;
            end if;
            wait on clock, out_enable, d;
        end loop;
    end procedure reg;
    signal data_bus : resolved_byte bus;
    ...
begin
```

```
        a_reg : reg (a_reg_clk, a_reg_read, port_a, data_bus);

        b_reg : reg (b_reg_clk, b_reg_read, port_b, data_bus);

        …

end architecture high_level;
```

An outline of a high-level architecture body of a data logger, using a procedure to encapsulate the behavior of a register process.

19.2 **Blocks and Guarded Signal Assignment**

In this section, we introduce the VHDL-AMS *block* statement. In their most general form, blocks provide a way of partitioning the concurrent and simultaneous statements within an architecture body. However, we start with a simpler form of block statement that relates to guarded signals and return to the more general form in the next section.

A *block statement* is a statement that groups together a number of inner concurrent and simultaneous statements. A simplified syntax rule for block statements is

```
block_statement ⇐
    block_label :
    block 〚 ( guard_expression ) 〛 〚 is 〛
    begin
        〔 concurrent_statement | simultaneous_statement 〕
    end block 〚 block_label 〛 ;
```

The block label is required to identify the block statement. The syntax rule shows that we can write a block statement with an optional Boolean *guard expression*. If the guard expression is present, it must be surrounded by parentheses and appear after the keyword **block**. It is used to determine the value of an implicitly declared signal called **guard**. This signal is only implicitly declared if the guard expression is present. Its visibility extends over the whole of the block statement. Whenever a transaction occurs on any of the signals mentioned in the guard expression, the expression is reevaluated and the **guard** signal is immediately updated. Since the **guard** signal has its value automatically determined, we may not include a source for it in the block. That means we may not write a signal assignment for it, nor use it as an actual signal for an output port of a component instance.

Example Figure 19-7 is an example of a block statement with a guard expression. Since the guard expression is present, there is a **guard** signal implicitly declared within the block. Its value is updated whenever a transaction occurs on either of the signals **reg_sel** or **read**. It is used in the conditional signal assignment statement within the block.

FIGURE 19-7

```
reg_read_selector : block (reg_sel = '1' and read = '1') is
begin
    dbus <= reg0 when guard and reg_addr = '0' else
            reg1 when guard and reg_addr = '1' else
            "ZZZZZZZZ";
end block reg_read_selector;
```

An example of a block statement with a guard expression.

The main use of guard expressions in a block is to control operation of *guarded signal assignments*. These are special forms of the concurrent signal assignments described in Section 5.3. If the target of a concurrent signal assignment is a guarded signal, we must use a guarded signal assignment rather than an ordinary concurrent signal assignment. The extended syntax rules are

conditional_signal_assignment ⇐
    name <= ⟦ **guarded** ⟧ ⟦ delay_mechanism ⟧
              ⦃ waveform **when** *boolean*_expression **else** ⦄
              waveform ⟦ **when** *boolean*_expression ⟧ ;

selected_signal_assignment ⇐
    with expression **select**
        name <= ⟦ **guarded** ⟧ ⟦ delay_mechanism ⟧
              ⦃ waveform **when** choices , ⦄
              waveform **when** choices ;

The difference is the inclusion of the keyword **guarded** after the assignment symbol. This denotes that the signal assignment is to be executed when the **guard** signal changes value. The effect depends on whether the target of the assignment is a guarded signal or an ordinary signal. For a guarded target, if **guard** changes from true to false, the driver for the target is disconnected using a null transaction. When **guard** changes back to true, the assignment is executed again to reconnect the driver.

Example   Figure 19-8 shows an outline of an architecture body for a processor node of a multiprocessor computer. The signal **address_bus** is a guarded bit-vector signal. The block labeled **cache_to_address_buffer** has a guard expression that is true when the cache misses and a block needs to be replaced. The expression is evaluated whenever either **cache_miss** or **dirty** changes value, and the implicit signal **guard** in the block is set to the result. If it is true, the driver in the concurrent signal assignment statement within the block is connected. Any changes in the signals mentioned in the statement cause a new assignment to the target signal **address_bus**. When the guard signal changes to false, the driver in the assignment is disconnected using a null transaction.

FIGURE 19-8

```
architecture dataflow of processor_node is
    signal address_bus : resolve_unique word bus;
    ...
begin
    cache_to_address_buffer : block ( cache_miss = '1' and dirty = '1' ) is
    begin
        address_bus <= guarded
            tag_section0 & set_index & B"0000" when replace_section = '0' else
            tag_section1 & set_index & B"0000";
    end block cache_to_address_buffer;

    snoop_to_address_buffer : block ( snoop_hit = '1' and flag_update = '1' ) is
    begin
        address_bus <= guarded snoop_address(31 downto 4) & B"0000";
    end block snoop_to_address_buffer;

    ...

end architecture dataflow;
```

An outline of an architecture body for a processor node of a multiprocessor computer, showing parts of the cache system that drive addresses onto the address bus.

The block labeled snoop_to_address_buffer also has a guard expression, which is true when an external bus monitor (the "snoop") needs to update flags in the cache. The expression is evaluated when either snoop_hit or flag_update changes. The result is assigned to a separate **guard** signal for this block, used to control a second concurrent signal assignment statement with address_bus as the target. Assuming that the two guard expressions are mutually exclusive, only one of the drivers is connected to address_bus at a time.

If the target of a guarded signal assignment is an ordinary unguarded signal, the driver is not disconnected when **guard** changes to false. Instead, the assignment statement is disabled. No further transactions are scheduled for the target, despite changes that may occur on signals to which the statement is sensitive. Subsequently, when **guard** changes to true, the assignment is executed again and resumes normal operation.

Example   A simple model for a transparent latch can be written using a guarded signal assignment, as shown in Figure 19-9. The architecture body uses a block statement with a guard expression that tests the state of the **enable** signal. When **enable** is '0', the **guard** signal is false, and the guarded signal assignment is disabled. Changes in d are ignored, so q maintains its current value. When **enable** changes

FIGURE 19-9

```
entity latch is
    generic ( width : positive );
    port ( enable : in bit;
            d : in bit_vector(0 to width – 1);
            q : out bit_vector(0 to width – 1) );
end entity latch;
```

```
architecture behavioral of latch is
begin
    transfer_control : block ( enable = '1' ) is
    begin
        q <= guarded d;
    end block transfer_control;
end architecture behavioral;
```

An entity and behavioral architecture body for a transparent latch.

to '1', the guarded signal assignment is enabled and copies the value of d to q. So long as **enable** is '1', changes in d are copied to q.

Explicit Guard Signals

In the preceding examples, the guarded signal assignment statements used the implicitly declared **guard** signal to determine whether the assignment should be executed. As an alternative, we can explicitly declare our own Boolean signal called **guard**. Provided it is visible at the position of a guarded signal assignment, it will be used to control the signal assignment. The advantage of this approach is that we can use a more complex algorithm to control the guard signal, rather than relying on a simple Boolean expression. For example, we might use a separate process to drive **guard**. Whenever **guard** is changed to false, guarded signal assignments are disabled, disconnecting any drivers for guarded signals. When **guard** is changed back to true, the assignments are reenabled.

Example   Suppose we are modeling a computer system that includes a CPU and a DMA controller, among other modules. The DMA controller asserts the signal hold_req when it needs to use the memory address, data and control buses. The CPU completes its current operation, then disables its bus drivers before acknowledging the request. Figure 19-10 shows an outline of the computer system model, including the processes that describe the CPU. The CPU is described by a collection of processes in the block cpu. The address bus is driven by the guarded concurrent

FIGURE 19-10

```
architecture abstract of computer_system is

    ...

    signal address_bus : resolve_word word bus;
    signal hold_req : bit;
    ...

begin
    cpu : block is
        signal guard : boolean := false;
        signal cpu_internal_address : word;
        ...

    begin
        cpu_address_driver:
            address_bus <= guarded cpu_internal_address;
        ...   -- other bus drivers
        controller : process is
            ...
        begin
            ...
            ...   -- determine when to disable cpu bus drivers
            guard <= false;
            wait on clk until hold_req = '0' and clk = '1';
            guard <= true;  -- reenable cpu bus drivers
            ...
        end process controller;
        ...   -- cpu data-path processes
    end block cpu;
    ...   -- blocks for DMA and other modules
end architecture abstract;
```

An outline of a computer system model that uses an explicit guard signal to control guarded signal assignment statements representing bus drivers.

signal assignment labeled **cpu_address_driver**. Since the Boolean signal **guard** is visible at that point, it controls connection of the driver.

The process **controller** describes the control section of the CPU. It monitors the **hold_req** signal and determines when the guard signal should be asserted. The process then waits until the next rising clock edge after **hold_req** is negated before negating the guard signal. In this way, the CPU causes the bus drivers to be connected synchronously with the clock, rather than whenever the request signal changes.

Disconnection Specifications

One aspect of guarded signal assignments for guarded signals that we have not yet dealt with is timing. In the previous examples in this section, we have only shown zero-delay models. If we need to include delays in signal assignments, we should also include a specification of the delay associated with disconnecting a driver in a guarded signal assignment. The problem is that the null transaction that disconnects a driver in this case is not explicitly written in the model. It occurs as a result of the **guard** signal changing to false. The mechanism in VHDL-AMS that we may use if we need to specify a non-zero disconnection delay is a *disconnection specification*. The syntax rule is

> disconnection_specification ⇐
>   **disconnect** ⦇ *signal*_name ⦃ , ... ⦄ ▯ **others** ▯ **all** ⦈ : type_mark
>   **after** *time*_expression ;

A disconnection specification allows us to identify a particular signal or set of signals by name and type, and to specify the delay associated with any null transactions scheduled for the signals. This delay only applies to the implicit null transactions resulting from guarded signal assignments. It does not apply to null transactions we may write explicitly using the keyword **null** in a signal assignment in a process.

A disconnection specification for a guarded signal must appear in the same list of declarations as the signal declaration for the guarded signal. So, for example, we might include the following in the declarative part of an architecture body:

```
signal memory_data_bus : resolved_word bus;
disconnect memory_data_bus : resolved_word after 3 ns;
```

We might then include the following block in the architecture body:

```
mem_write_buffer : block (mem_sel and mem_write) is
begin
    memory_data_bus <=
        guarded reject 2 ns inertial cache_data_bus after 4 ns;
end block mem_write_buffer;
```

This indicates that so long as the guard expression evaluates to true, the value of cache_data_bus will be copied to memory_data_bus with a delay of 4 ns and a pulse rejection interval of 2 ns. When the guard expression changes to false, the driver corresponding to the guarded signal assignment is disconnected with a null transaction. The delay used is 3 ns, as indicated in the disconnection specification, but the pulse rejection limit of 2 ns is still taken from the assignment statement. When the guard expression changes back to true, the assignment is executed again, scheduling a new transaction with 4 ns delay.

If we have a number of guarded signals of the same type in an architecture body, and we wish to use the same disconnection delay for all of them, we can use the **all** keyword in a disconnection specification instead of listing all of the signals. For example, if the following signal declarations are the only ones for guarded signals of type resolved_word:

signal source_bus_1, source_bus_2 : resolved_word **bus**;
signal address_bus : resolved_word **bus**;

we can specify a disconnection delay of 2 ns for all of the signals as follows:

disconnect all : resolved_word **after** 2 ns;

The remaining way of identifying which signals a disconnection specification applies to is with the keyword **others**. This identifies all remaining signals of a given type that are not referred to by previous disconnection specifications. For example, suppose that the signal **address_bus** shown above should have a disconnection delay of 3 ns instead of 2 ns. We could write the disconnection specifications for the set of signals as

disconnect address_bus : resolved_word **after** 3 ns;

disconnect others : resolved_word **after** 2 ns;

If we write a disconnection specification using the keyword **others** in an architecture body, it must appear after any other disconnection specifications referring to signals of the same type and after all declarations of signals of that type. Similarly, if we write a disconnection specification using the keyword **all**, it must be the only disconnection specification referring to signals of the given type and must appear after all declarations of signals of that type.

19.3 **Using Blocks for Structural Modularity**

In the previous section, we introduced block statements and showed how they may be used in conjunction with guarded signals to achieve automatic disconnection of drivers. In this section we look at the use of blocks to partition the concurrent and simultaneous statements within an architecture body. We can think of a block as a way of drawing a line around a collection of concurrent and simultaneous statements and their associated declarations, so that they can be clearly seen as a distinct aspect of a design. The full syntax rule for a block statement is as follows:

```
block_statement ⇐
    block_label :
        block ⟦ ( guard_expression ) ⟧ ⟦ is ⟧
            ⟦ generic ( generic_interface_list ) ;
            ⟦ generic map ( generic_association_list ) ; ⟧ ⟧
            ⟦ port ( port_interface_list ) ;
            ⟦ port map ( port_association_list ) ; ⟧ ⟧
            { block_declarative_item }
```

begin
        {{ concurrent_statement ⌷ simultaneous_statement }}
    end block ⟦ *block*_label ⟧ ;

The block label is required to identify the block statement. The guard expression, as we saw in the previous section, may be used to control guarded signal assignments. If we are only using a block as a means of partitioning a design, we do not need to include a guard expression. The generic and port clauses allow us to define an interface to the block. We return to this shortly.

The declarative part of a block statement allows us to declare items that are local to the block. We can include the same kinds of declarations here as we can in an architecture body, for example, constant, type, subtype, nature, subnature, signal, quantity, terminal and subprogram declarations. Items declared in a block are only visible within that block and cannot be referred to before or after it. However, items declared in the enclosing architecture body remain visible (unless hidden by a local item declared within the block).

Example   To illustrate how blocks can be used for partitioning a design, we develop a model for a sensor input to a digital system, including analog sensor data input, analog-to-digital conversion and digital data output. We can specify the propagation delays as combinations of input delays before the function block and output delays after the conversion block, as shown in Figure 19-11. The entity declaration for this sensor is shown in Figure 19-12.

We can separate the delay and function aspects of the model into separate blocks within the architecture body, as shown in Figure 19-13. The first block, input_port_delay, derives delayed versions of the input ports. These are used in the second block, **AD_conversion**, the zero-delay behavioral implementation of the sensor. This block produces a bit value indicating when the voltage threshold is crossed. The output of the analog-to-digital converter is used in the other block, output_port_delay, to apply the delay between the function block and the output port.

FIGURE 19-11

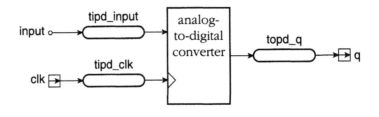

A propagation delay model for a sensor.

FIGURE 19-12

```
library ieee_proposed;  use ieee_proposed.electrical_systems.all;
entity sensor is
        generic ( threshold : real;              -- voltage threshold
                  tipd_clk : delay_length;       -- input prop delay on clk
                  tipd_input : real;             -- input prop delay on sensor input
                  topd_q : delay_length );       -- output prop delay on q
        port ( terminal input : electrical;      -- sensor analog input
               signal clk : in bit;              -- edgeñtriggered clock input
               signal q : out bit );             -- sensor digital output
end entity sensor;
```

An entity declaration for the sensor.

FIGURE 19-13

```
architecture detailed_timing of sensor is
        quantity vin across input;        -- analog input values
        quantity v_delayed : voltage;     -- input voltage delayed
        signal clk_delayed : bit;         -- clk input port delayed
        signal q_int : bit;               -- q output with zero delay
begin
        input_port_delay : block is
        begin
            v_delayed == vin'delayed(tipd_input);
            clk_delayed <= clk'delayed(tipd_clk);
        end block input_port_delay;

        AD_conversion : block is
        begin
            q_int <= '1' when vin'above(threshold) else
                     '0';
        end block AD_conversion;

        output_port_delay : block is
        begin
            q <= q_int'delayed(topd_q);
        end block output_port_delay;
end architecture detailed_timing;
```

An architecture body for the sensor.

Since a block contains a collection of concurrent and simultaneous statements, and a block statement is itself a concurrent statement, it is perfectly legal to nest blocks one inside another. The same visibility rules that we described for subprograms also apply for items declared in nested blocks. However, in practice, we would rarely write a model with nested blocks. If the design hierarchy is that complex, it is better to use separate entities and component instantiation statements to partition the design. The main reason VHDL-AMS allows complex nesting of blocks is that the block structure is used as the underlying mechanism for implementing other VHDL-AMS constructs, such as component instantiation (described in Chapter 16) and generate statements (described in Chapter 17). The language definition defines these constructs in terms of the substitution of blocks containing the contents of the architecture body being instantiated or the contents of the generate statement.

Generics and Ports in Blocks

Another aspect of block statements, also arising from their use as the underlying mechanism for component instantiation, is the possibility of including generic and port interface lists. These allow us to make explicit the interface between the block and its enclosing architecture body or enclosing block. The formal generic constants and ports can be used within the block in exactly the same way that those of an entity are used within a corresponding architecture body. The actual values for generic constants are supplied by a generic map in the block header, and the actuals associated with the formal ports are supplied by a port map. These are all shown in the syntax rule for block statements on page 601. Since this facility is rarely used in actual model writing, we do not dwell on it beyond looking at one simple example.

Example   The architecture body shown in Figure 19-14 contains a block, mux, with generic constant width and ports d0, d1, y and sel. The generic constant is used to constrain the size of the ports. The concurrent signal assignment statements within the block refer to the formal ports of the block and the local objects zero, gated_d0 and gated_d1. The generic map supplies an actual value for width, using the constant sig_width declared in the enclosing architecture body. Similarly, the port map associates the actual signals s1, s2, s3 and sel from the enclosing architecture body with the formal ports of the block.

FIGURE 19-14

```
architecture contrived of example_entity is
    constant sig_width : positive := 16;
    signal s1, s2, s3 : bit_vector (0 to sig_width – 1);
    signal sel : bit;
    ...
begin
```

```
mux : block is
    generic ( width : positive );
    generic map ( width => sig_width );
    port ( d0, d1 : in bit_vector(0 to width – 1);
            y : out bit_vector(0 to width – 1);
            sel : in bit);
    port map ( d0 => s1, d1=> s2, y => s3, sel => sel );

    constant zero : bit_vector(0 to width – 1) := ( others => '0' );
    signal gated_d0, gated_d1 : bit_vector(0 to width – 1);
begin
    gated_d0 <= d0 when sel = '0' else zero;
    gated_d1 <= d1 when sel = '1' else zero;
    y <= gated_d0 or gated_d1;
end block mux;

    ...

end architecture contrived;
```

An outline of an architecture body containing a block with generic constants and ports.

Configuring Designs with Blocks

In Chapter 16 we showed how to configure a design whose hierarchy was formed by instantiating components. We configure an architecture body containing nested block statements in a similar way. When we write configuration declarations for such architecture bodies, the configuration information must mirror the block structure of the architecture body. We introduce a further level of detail in the syntax rules for configuration declarations, showing how to configure architecture bodies containing blocks.

```
configuration_declaration ⇐
    configuration identifier of entity_name is
        block_configuration
    end 〖 configuration 〗〖 identifier 〗 ;

block_configuration ⇐
    for 《 architecture_name ▯ block_statement_label 》
        〔   block_configuration
            ▯   for component_specification
                    〖 binding_indication ; 〗
                    〖 block_configuration 〗
                end for ; 〕
    end for ;
```

The difference here is that we have added a block statement label as an alternative to an architecture name at the point where we specify the region containing concurrent and simultaneous statements. Furthermore, we have allowed a block configuration as an alternative to component configuration information within that region. If we put these together, we can see how to write the configuration information for an architecture body containing block statements. At the top level of the configuration declaration, we write a block configuration naming the architecture body, just as we have done in all of the previous examples. Within it, however, we include block configurations that name and configure each block.

Example   Suppose we need to write a model for an integrated circuit that takes account of propagation delays through input and output pads. The entity declaration and architecture body are shown in Figure 19-15. The architecture body is divided into blocks for input delay, function and output delay. The operation of the circuit is described structurally, as an interconnection of cells within the function block.

FIGURE 19-15

```
entity circuit is
    generic ( inpad_delay, outpad_delay : delay_length );
    port ( in1, in2, in3 : in bit;  out1, out2 : out bit );
end entity circuit;
```

```
architecture with_pad_delays of circuit is
    component subcircuit is
        port ( a, b : in bit;  y1, y2 : out bit );
    end component subcircuit;
    signal delayed_in1, delayed_in2, delayed_in3 : bit;
    signal undelayed_out1, undelayed_out2 : bit;
begin
    input_delays : block is
    begin
        delayed_in1 <= in1 after inpad_delay;
        delayed_in2 <= in2 after inpad_delay;
        delayed_in3 <= in3 after inpad_delay;
    end block input_delays;

    functionality : block is
        signal intermediate : bit;
    begin
        cell1 : component subcircuit
            port map ( delayed_in1, delayed_in2, undelayed_out1, intermediate );
```

```
        cell2 : component subcircuit
              port map ( intermediate, delayed_in3, undelayed_out2, open );
        end block functionality;

        output_delays : block is
        begin
              out1 <= undelayed_out1 after outpad_delay;
              out2 <= undelayed_out2 after outpad_delay;
        end block output_delays;

    end architecture with_pad_delays;
```

An entity and architecture body for a design, partitioned into separate blocks for pad delays and functionality.

A configuration declaration for this design, shown in Figure 19-16, binds the instances of the component subcircuit within the block functionality to an entity real_subcircuit with architecture basic. The block configuration starting with "**for** with_pad_delays" specifies the architecture of circuit that is being configured. Within it, the block configuration starting with "**for** functionality" specifies the configuration of the contents of the block labeled functionality. It, in turn, contains a component configuration for the two component instances. Note that there are no block configurations for the other two blocks in the design, since they do not contain any component instances. They only contain concurrent signal assignment statements, which represent leaf nodes of the design hierarchy.

FIGURE 19-16

```
configuration full of circuit is
    for with_pad_delays   -- configure the architecture
        for functionality   -- configure the block
            for all : subcircuit
                use entity work.real_subcircuit(basic);
            end for;
        end for;
    end for;
end configuration full;
```

A configuration declaration for the partitioned design.

Exercises

1. [● 19.1] Write signal declarations for

   • a bus-kind signal, **serial_bus**, of the resolved subtype **wired_or_bit**, and

   • a register-kind signal, **d_node**, of the resolved subtype **unique_bit**.

2. [● 19.1] A signal **rx_bus** is declared to be a bus-kind signal of type **std_logic**. Trace the value of the signal as transactions from the following two drivers are applied:

   • null, '0' after 10 ns, '1' after 20 ns, '0' after 30 ns, null after 40 ns

   • null, '1' after 35 ns, '0' after 45 ns, null after 55 ns

3. [● 19.1] Repeat Exercise 2, this time assuming **rx_bus** is a register-kind signal that is initialized to 'U'.

4. [● 19.1] Write a signal assignment statement that schedules the value 3 on an integer signal **vote** after 2 μs, then disconnects from the signal after 5 μs.

5. [● 19.1] Suppose a process contains the following signal assignment, executed at time 150 ns:

   > result <= 0 **after** 10 ns, 42 **after** 20 ns, 0 **after** 100 ns, **null after** 120 ns;

   Assuming the driver for **result** is disconnected at time 150 ns, trace the value of **result'driving** resulting from the signal assignment.

6. [● 19.1] If the resolution function in the example on page 592 were modified to perform the logical "and" operation on the contributed values, what should the function return when called with an empty vector argument?

7. [● 19.2] Write a block with a guard expression that is true when a signal **en** is '1' or 'H'. The block should contain a guarded signal assignment that assigns an inverted version of the signal **d_in** to the signal **q_out_n** when the guard expression is true.

8. [● 19.2] Write disconnection specifications that specify

   • a disconnection delay of 3.5 ns for a signal **source1** of type **wired_word**,

   • a disconnection delay of 3.2 ns for other signals of type **wired_word** and

   • a disconnection delay of 2.8 ns for all signals of type **wired_bit**.

9. [● 19.2] Trace the values on the signal **priority** resulting from execution of the following statements. The resolution function for the subtype **resolved_integer** selects the leftmost value from the contributing drivers or returns the value 0 if there are no contributions. Assume that no other drivers for **priority** are connected.

   ```
   signal request : integer := 0;
   signal guard : boolean := false;
   ```

signal priority : resolved_integer **bus** := 0;
disconnect priority : resolved_integer **after** 2 ns;
…

request <= 3 **after** 40 ns, 5 **after** 80 ns, 1 **after** 120 ns;
guard <= true **after** 50 ns, false **after** 100 ns;
priority <= **guarded** request **after** 1 ns;

10. [❶ 19.3] Write a block statement that encapsulates component instantiation statements implementing the circuit shown in Figure 19-17. The signal q_internal, of type **bit**, should be declared local to the block.

11. [❶ 19.3] Write a block configuration for the block statement described in Exercise 10, binding the flipflop component instance to an entity d_flipflop and architecture **basic**, and the inverter component to the entity **inverter** and architecture **basic**. The entities are in the current working library.

12. [❶ 19.3] Write a model for a capacitor with leakage resistance, as shown in Figure 6-4, using block statements for the parallel resistance and capacitance effects.

13. [❶ 19.3] Write a model for a low-pass filter, as shown in Figure 13-6, using block statements for the resistance and capacitance effects.

14. [❷ 19.1] Suppose we declare the following subtypes:

subtype word **is** bit_vector(31 **downto** 0);
…
subtype resolved_word **is** bitwise_or word;

The resolution function performs a bitwise logical "or" operation on the contributing driver values. Write a procedure that encapsulates the behavior of a tristate buffer. The procedure has input signal parameters **oe** of type **bit** and **d** of the subtype **word** and an output signal parameter **z** of type **resolved_word**. When **oe** is '1', the value of **d** is transmitted to **z**. When **oe** is '0', **z** is disconnected. Test the procedure by invoking it with a number of concurrent procedure calls in a test bench.

15. [❷ 19.2] Develop a dataflow model of a latching four-input multiplexer. The multiplexer has four data inputs, two bits of select input, and an enable input. When the enable input is high, the select inputs determine which data input is transmitted to the single data output. When the enable input is low, the value on the data output is latched.

FIGURE 19-17

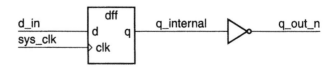

An inverting-register circuit.

16. [❷ 19.2] A dynamic register can be implemented in NMOS technology as shown in Figure 19-18. Develop a dataflow model for this form of register, using guarded signal assignments to model the pass transistors. The signals should be of a resolved subtype of bit, and the signal latched_d should be a register-kind signal.

17. [❷ 19.3] Develop a behavioral model of a three-to-eight decoder with three select inputs, an enable input and eight active-low outputs. The entity interface includes generic constants for

- input propagation delay for the enable input,
- input propagation delay for the select inputs and
- output propagation delay for the outputs.

Write the architecture body with separate blocks for input delays, function and output delays.

18. [❷ 19.3] Create a series R-L-C filter using a block statement for each component function (resistance, inductance and capacitance). The filter may be of any type or configuration.

19. [❷ 19.3] Rewrite the moving mass model from Figure 6-15 using a block statement for each mechanical effect (mass, spring and damping).

20. [❷ 19.3] Rewrite the opamp model from Figure 13-16 using block statements for the input and output resistance effects.

21. [❸ 19.1] Revise the tristate buffer procedure described in Exercise 14 to make it bidirectional. Include an additional input parameter that determines the direction of data transfer.

22. [❸ 19.1] Develop a behavioral model of a read/write memory with a bidirectional data port of the type **resolved_byte**, defined on page 591. The data port should be a bus-kind signal, and the model should use null signal assignments appropriately to indicate when the memory is not supplying data.

23. [❸ 19.2] A 4-bit carry-look-ahead adder can be implemented in CMOS technology with a Manchester carry chain, shown in Figure 19-19. The signal c0 is the carry

---

FIGURE 19-18

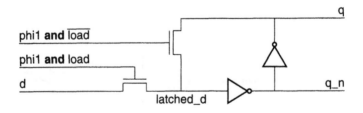

A circuit for a dynamic register.

FIGURE 19-19

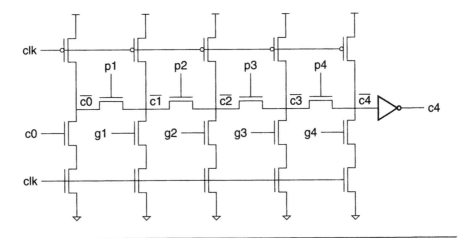

A Manchester carry chain for a carry-look-ahead adder.

input, c4 is the carry output, $\overline{c0}$ to $\overline{c4}$ are active-low intermediate carry signals, g1 to g4 are carry generate signals and p1 to p4 are carry propagate signals. During the low half of a clock cycle, the intermediate carry signals are precharged to '1'. During the high half of the clock cycle, the pass transistors controlled by the generate and propagate signals conditionally discharge the intermediate carry signals, determining their final value. The Boolean equations for the sum, generate and propagate signals are

$$s_i = a_i \oplus b_i \oplus c_{i-1}$$
$$g_i = a_i b_i$$
$$p_i = a_i + b_i$$

Develop a dataflow model of a 4-bit Manchester carry adder, using register-kind signals for the internal carry signals. All signals should be of a resolved-bit type.

24. [❸ 19.2] A 4 × 4 barrel shifter can be constructed from pass transistors as shown in Figure 19-20. The signals i0 to i3 are the inputs, and z0 to z3 are the outputs. The control signal s0 causes input bits to be transmitted to the outputs unshifted, s1 causes them to be shifted by one place, s2 by two places and s3 by three places. The outputs must be precharged to '1' on the first half of a clock cycle, then one of the control signals activated on the second half of the clock cycle. Develop a dataflow model of the barrel shifter, using register-kind signals for the output signals. All signals should be of a resolved-bit type.

FIGURE 19-20

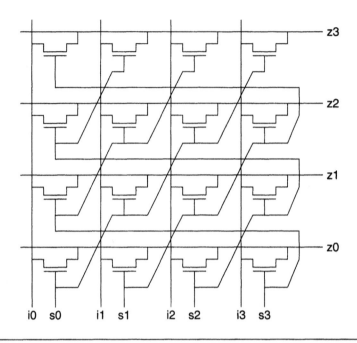

A 4 × 4 barrel shifter.

25. [❸ 19.3] Create a DC motor model that separates the electrical and mechanical governing equations into separate block statements. Use the motor model from Figure 14-21 as a guide.

26. [❸ 19.3] Write a servo amplifier model to replace that given in Figure 14-20. Use block statements for each servo function (summer, gain, lead-lag filter and limiter).

27. [❸ 19.3] Create a single model for the control horn to control-horn transmission path for the rudder system shown in Figure 14-24. Use block statements for the three components (motor control horn, rudder control horn and translational linkage), and use the correct terminal units throughout.

chapter twenty

Access Types and Abstract Data Types

We have seen in previous chapters how we can use variables within processes to create data that is associated with a name. We can write a variable name in a model to read its value in expressions and to update its value in variable assignment statements. In this chapter, we introduce access types as a mechanism in VHDL-AMS for creating and managing unnamed data during a simulation.

20.1 **Access Types**

The scalar and composite data types we are now familiar with can be used to represent either single data items or regular collections of data. However, in some applications, we need to store collections of data whose size is not known in advance. Alternatively, we may need to represent a complex set of relations between individual data objects. In these cases, simple scalar and composite types are not sufficient. Instead, we need to create data objects as they are required during a simulation and to represent the links between these data objects. We do this in VHDL-AMS using *access types*. These are similar to pointer types found in many programming languages. In VHDL-AMS, access types are used mainly in high-level behavioral models and rarely in low-level models.

We start this section with a description of access types, pointers and mechanisms for creating data objects. Then we look at the way in which these mechanisms are used to create linked data structures during a simulation.

Access Type Declarations and Allocators

We can declare an access type using a new form of type definition, given by the syntax rule

access_type_definition ⇐ **access** subtype_indication

We can include such a type definition in a type declaration, for example:

type natural_ptr **is access** natural;

This defines a new type, named **natural_ptr**, representing values that point to data objects of type **natural**. Values of type **natural_ptr** can only point to natural numbers, not to objects of any other type. In general, we can write access type declarations referring to any VHDL-AMS type except file types.

Once we have declared an access type, we can declare a variable of that type within a process or subprogram. For example, we might declare a variable of the type **natural_ptr** shown above:

variable count : natural_ptr;

This declaration creates a variable, called **count**, that may point to a data object of type **natural** stored in memory. Initially, the variable has the value **null**. This is a special pointer value that does not point to any data object and is the default initial value for any access type. We can represent the null pointer variable pictorially as shown in Figure 20-1(a). The box represents the location in memory where the variable **count** is stored. Since it is a named variable, we can label the box with the variable name. Note that we cannot declare constants, signals, quantities or terminals of access types. Variables are the only class of object that may be of an access type.

FIGURE 20-1

(a) *An access variable initialized to* **null**. *(b) A data object created by an allocator expression.* *(c) A pointer returned by an allocator assigned to the access variable.*

Next, we can create a new natural number data object and set **count** to point to it. We do this using an *allocator*, written according to the following syntax rule:

primary ⇐ **new** subtype_indication ▯ **new** qualified_expression

This rule shows that an allocator, written using the keyword **new**, is a kind of primary. Recall that primaries are the basis of VHDL-AMS expressions. The first form of allocator creates a new data object of the specified subtype in memory, initializes it to the default initial value for the subtype and returns a pointer to it. For example, the allocator expression

new natural

creates a natural number data object in memory and initialized to 0 (the leftmost value in the subtype **natural**). The allocator then returns a pointer to the object, as shown in Figure 20-1(b). The box represents the location in memory where the data object is stored, but since it is an unnamed object, there is no label. Instead, the arrow represents the pointer to the object. This is the only way of accessing the object.

The next step is to assign the pointer to the access variable **count**. Since the allocator is an expression that returns the pointer value, we can write it on the right-hand side of a variable assignment statement, as follows:

count := **new** natural;

This statement has the combined effects of creating and initializing the data object and assigning a pointer to it to the variable **count**, as shown in Figure 20-1(c). The pointer overwrites the null pointer previously stored in **count**.

Now that we have an access variable pointing to a data object in memory, we can use and update the value of the object, accessing it via the variable. This use of the variable is the reason for the terms "access type" and "access variable." We access the object using the keyword **all** as a suffix after the access variable name. For example, we can update the object's value as follows:

count.**all** := 10;

and we use its value in an expression:

```
if count.all = 0 then
    …
end if;
```

Note that we need to use the keyword **all** in this way if we wish to use the data object rather than the pointer itself. If we had written the expression "**count = 0**", our VHDL-AMS analyzer would report an error, since the value of **count** is a pointer, not a number, so it cannot be compared with the number 0.

The second form of allocator, shown in the syntax rule on page 615, uses a qualified expression to specify both the subtype and the initial value for the created data object. Recall that the syntax rule for a qualified expression is

qualified_expression ⇐ type_mark ' (expression) ▯ type_mark ' aggregate

Thus, instead of writing the two statements

```
count := new natural;
count.all := 10;
```

we could achieve the same effect with this second form of allocator:

```
count := new natural'(10);
```

The qualified expression can also take the form of an array or record aggregate. For example, if we have a record type and access type declared as

```
type stimulus_record is record
        stimulus_time : time;
        stimulus_value : real_vector(0 to 3);
    end record stimulus_record;
type stimulus_ptr is access stimulus_record;
```

and an access variable declared as

```
variable bus_stimulus : stimulus_ptr;
```

we could create a new stimulus record data object and set **bus_stimulus** to point to it as follows:

```
bus_stimulus := new stimulus_record'( 20 ns, real_vector'(0.0, 5.0, 0.0, 42.0) );
```

The value in the allocator is a qualified record aggregate that specifies both the type of the data object (**stimulus_record**) and the value for each of the record elements. In this case, the stimulus value is itself a **real_vector** array.

Assignment and Equality of Access Values

Let us now look at the effect of assigning one access variable value to another access variable. Suppose we have two access variables declared as follows:

variable count1, count2 : natural_ptr;

and we create data objects and set the variables to point to them:

count1 := **new** natural'(5);
count2 := **new** natural'(10);

The variables and data objects are illustrated in Figure 20-2(a). Next, we perform the following variable assignment:

count2 := count1;

The effect of this assignment is to copy the pointer from count1 into count2, making both access variables point to the same object, as shown in Figure 20-2(b). We can see that this is in fact the case by accessing the object via each of the access variables. For example, if we update the object via count1

count1.**all** := 20;

then the value we get via count2.**all** is 20.

Note that when we copied the pointer from count1 to count2, we overwrote the pointer to the data object 10. The object itself is still stored in memory, but count2 is no longer pointing to it. If we had previously copied the pointer before overwriting it, then we could access the object via that other copy. However, if there is no other pointer to the object, it is inaccessible. This is one of the main differences between named variables and allocated data objects. We can always access a variable by using its name, but an allocated object has no name, so we can only access it via pointers.

FIGURE 20-2

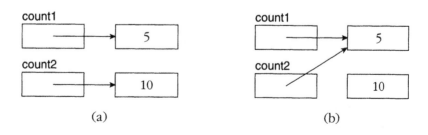

(a)   (b)

The effect of assigning one access variable to another. The two variables point to the same data object.

If there are no pointers to an object, it is lost forever, even though it is still resident in the host computer's memory. We often call such inaccessible objects *garbage*. We return to the topic of dealing with unneeded objects later in this section.

Next, we look at the effect of comparing two access variables using the "=" and "/=" operators. These operators test whether the two pointers point to the same location in memory. For example, after performing the assignment

```
count2 := count1;
```

the expression

```
count1 = count2
```

is true, since, as Figure 20-2(b) shows, the two access variables then point to the same object. However, if we instead set count1 and count2 as follows:

```
count1 := new natural'(30);
count2 := new natural'(30);
```

we create two distinct data objects in memory, each storing the number 30. The variable count1 points to one of them, and count2 points to the other. In this case the result of the equality comparison is false. If we really want to test whether the data objects are equal, as opposed to testing the pointers, we write

```
count1.all = count2.all
```

One very useful pointer comparison is the test for equality with **null**, the special pointer value that does not point to any object. For example, we might write

```
if count1 /= null then
    count1.all := count1.all + 1;
end if;
```

The test in the if statement ensures that we only access the value pointed to by count1 if there is a value to access. If count1 has the value **null**, trying to access count1.all results in an error.

Access Types for Records and Arrays

We have introduced access types in this section by concentrating on access types that point to scalars, in order to keep things simple. However, most models that include access types use them to point to records or arrays. Pointers to records are mainly used for building linked data structures, and pointers to arrays are used if the lengths of the arrays are not known when the model is written. In both cases, we can use a shorthand notation for referring to objects via access variables.

Let us start with records and return to the example shown earlier, in which we had types declared as

```
type stimulus_record is record
        stimulus_time : time;
        stimulus_value : real_vector(0 to 3);
    end record stimulus_record;
type stimulus_ptr is access stimulus_record;
```

We also declared an access variable as

```
variable bus_stimulus : stimulus_ptr;
```

We have seen that we can access a record object pointed to by bus_stimulus using the notation "bus_stimulus.all". If we want to refer to the stimulus_time element, we could write "bus_stimulus.all.stimulus_time". In practice, we usually want to refer either to the pointer itself or to an element of the record, and rarely to the record as a whole. For this reason, VHDL-AMS allows us to write "bus_stimulus.stimulus_time" to refer to the record element. Whenever we select a record element name after an access variable name, we automatically follow the pointer to get to the record.

A similar shorthand notation applies when we use access variables that point to array data objects. For example, suppose we declare types as follows:

```
type coordinate is array (1 to 3) of real;
type coordinate_ptr is access coordinate;
```

and an access variable:

```
variable origin : coordinate_ptr := new coordinate'(0.0, 0.0, 0.0);
```

This last declaration creates the access variable and initializes it to point to an array object initialized with the aggregate value. We can refer to the elements of the array using the notation "origin(1)", "origin(2)" and "origin(3)", instead of having to write "origin.all(1)", and so on. This is similar to accessing elements of records. Whenever we write an array index after an access variable name, we automatically follow the pointer to the array.

One of the advantages of using access types that point to array objects is that we can deal with arrays of mixed lengths. This is in contrast to array variables, which have their length fixed when they are created. For example, if we create an array variable activation_times as follows:

```
type time_array is array (positive range <>) of time;
variable activation_times : time_array(1 to 100);
```

it is fixed at 100 elements for its entire lifetime. On the other hand, we can create an access type that points to data objects of an unconstrained array type, for example:

type time_array_ptr **is access** time_array;

and declare our variable to be a pointer of this type:

variable activation_times : time_array_ptr;

Since the variable points to an array object of an unconstrained type, it may point to different array objects of different lengths during the course of a simulation. However, each array object is constrained. This means that once an array object is created in memory, its length is fixed. We can create an array object using an allocator that includes a qualified aggregate, for example:

activation_times := **new** time_array'(10 us, 15 us, 40 us);

This allocator creates an array object whose length is determined from the length of the aggregate. We can update each of these elements, but we cannot change the size of the array. If we need to add two more elements, we have to create a new array object of length five, with the first three elements being a copy of the elements from the old array. This might be done as follows:

activation_times := **new** time_array'(activation_times.**all**
                                          & time_array'(70 us, 100 us));

The allocator in this assignment creates an array object whose length is determined by the result of the concatenation operation. If we want to create an array object without initializing the values, we write an allocator that names the array type and includes an index constraint. For example, to create an array object of length 10, we might write

activation_times := **new** time_array(1 **to** 10);

20.2 **Linked Data Structures**

Suppose we wish to store a list of values to be used to stimulate a signal during a simulation. One possible approach would be to define an array variable of stimulus values. However, a problem arises if we do not know how large to make the array. If we make it too small, we may run out of space. If we make it too large, we may waste space in the host computer's memory and run out of space for other variables. The alternative approach is to use access types and to create values only as they are needed. The values can be linked together with pointers to form an extensible data structure. There are several possible organizations for linked structures, but we look at one of the simplest, a *linked list,* as an example, showing how it is constructed and manipulated.

A linked list of values that might be used as stimuli for a signal is shown in Figure 20-3. To construct this list, we need to compose each cell from a record that

FIGURE 20-3

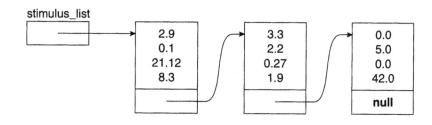

A linked list structure of stimulus records.

has one element for the stimulus value and an extra element for a pointer to the next cell in the list. This pointer must be of an access type used to access record objects. A first attempt to write the type declarations for this structure might be

```
type value_cell is record
        value : real_vector(0 to 3);
        next_cell : value_ptr;
    end record value_cell;
type value_ptr is access value_cell;
```

The problem here is that the definition of **value_cell** uses the name **value_ptr** as the type of one of the elements, but **value_ptr** is not declared until after the declaration of **value_cell**. If we reverse the two type declarations, the same problem arises in the definition of **value_ptr** when it tries to use the name **value_cell**. To solve this "chicken and egg" problem, VHDL-AMS lets us write an *incomplete type declaration* for the record type. The syntax rule is

type_declaration ⟸ **type** identifier ;

An incomplete type declaration simply names the type, indicating that it will be fully defined later. Meanwhile, we can use the type name to declare access types. However, we must complete the definition of the incomplete type before the end of the declarative part in which the incomplete declaration appears. Since we can do this after the access type declaration, we can use the name of the access type within the complete type declaration. Thus, we can rewrite our circular type declarations as

```
type value_cell;
type value_ptr is access value_cell;
type value_cell is record
        value : real_vector(0 to 3);
        next_cell : value_ptr;
    end record value_cell;
```

Next we can declare an access variable to point to the beginning of the list:

variable value_list : value_ptr;

This declaration creates a variable containing a null pointer, as shown in Figure 20-4(a). We can think of this as representing an empty list. Thus, if we need to determine whether a list is empty, we can test the access variable to see whether it is **null**, for example:

if value_list /= **null then**
    ...   -- *do something with the list*
end if;

We can add a cell to the empty list by allocating a new record and assigning the pointer to the access variable, as follows:

value_list := **new** value_cell'(real_vector'(0.0, 5.0, 0.0, 42.0), value_list);

The second element in the aggregate is a copy of the pointer initially stored in value_list. This has the value **null**, so the result of executing the whole statement is as

---

FIGURE 20-4

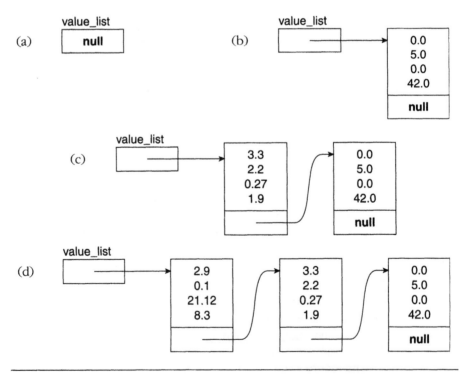

Successive stages in the creation of a list of stimulus values.

shown in Figure 20-4(b). The reason for using the old value of value_list instead of writing in the value **null** is that we can use the same form of statement to add the next cell:

    value_list := **new** value_cell'(real_vector'(3.3, 2.2, 0.27, 1.9), value_list);

The allocator creates a new cell in memory, with the **value** element initialized to real_vector'(3.3, 2.2, 0.27, 1.9) and the next_cell element initialized to a copy of the pointer to the old cell. A pointer to the new cell is then returned and assigned to value_list, as shown in Figure 20-4(c). We can create the third cell in the same way:

    value_list := **new** value_cell'(real_vector'(2.9, 0.1, 21.12, 8.3), value_list);

This assignment produces the final list as shown in Figure 20-4(d). Note that each cell we create is added onto the front of the list.

Now suppose we have a list of stimulus values of arbitrary length, pointed to by our access variable, and we wish to go through the list applying each value to a signal. We can write a loop to traverse the list as follows. We need to make use of a working variable, current_cell, of type value_ptr. The statements to perform this traversal are shown in Figure 20-5.

The first assignment sets current_cell to point to the first cell in the list, as shown in Figure 20-6(a). The first pass through the loop uses the value element of this cell to stimulate the signal, then copies the next_cell element of the cell into the working variable. At the end of the first iteration the working variable points to the next element in the list, as shown in Figure 20-6(b). The loop repeats in this way, with current_cell being advanced from one cell to the next cell in each iteration. In the last iteration, the variable points to the last cell as shown in Figure 20-6(c). The next_cell element of this cell is **null**, and this is copied into current_cell. When the loop test is performed again it evaluates to false, and so the loop terminates.

Another operation we may wish to perform on a list is to search for a particular value. Again, we make use of a working access variable to traverse the list, checking each cell to see if its **value** element matches the value for which we are searching, as shown in Figure 20-7. The test for a null pointer in the loop condition is most important. It guards against the possibility that the sought value is not in the list. If the list terminates with the working variable equal to **null**, we know that the value was not

---

FIGURE 20-5

```
current_cell := value_list;
while current_cell /= null loop
    s <= current_cell.value;
    wait for 10 ns;
    current_cell := current_cell.next_cell;
end loop;
```

Statements to traverse a list of stimulus values.

FIGURE 20·6

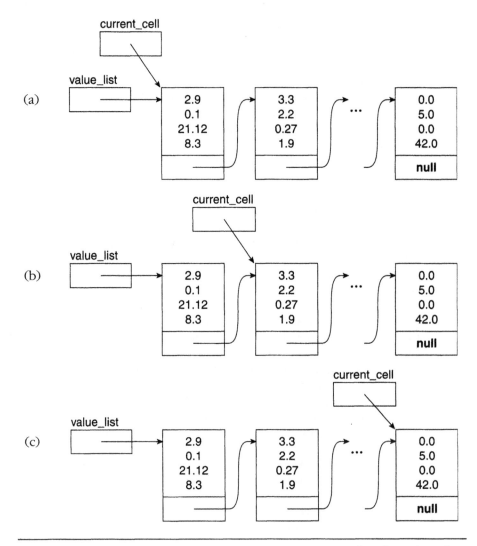

Successive stages in traversing a list of stimulus values.

found, and we can deal with the condition appropriately. Note that the **and** operator in the loop condition is a "short circuit" operator, so the second part of the test will not proceed if current_cell is **null**, not pointing to any list cell.

The linked list data structure is just one of a number of linked data structures that we can construct using access types. Other examples include queues, trees and network structures. We come across some of these in further examples in this chapter and later in the book. However, the field of data structures is much larger than we can hope to cover in a book that focuses on hardware modeling and simulation. Fortunately, there are numerous good textbooks available that discuss data structures at

FIGURE 20-7

```
current_cell := value_list;
while current_cell /= null and current_cell.value /= search_value loop
    current_cell := current_cell.next_cell;
end loop;
assert current_cell /= null
    report "search for value failed";
```

Statements to search for a value in a list of values.

length. Of these, the books that use the Ada programming language are particularly relevant, as VHDL-AMS's access types are based on those of Ada. (See, for example, [12].)

Deallocation and Storage Management

We saw earlier that if we overwrite a pointer to an unnamed data object, we can lose all means of accessing the object, making it "garbage." While this is usually not a problem, if we create too much garbage during a simulation run, the host computer may run out of memory space for allocating new objects. Some computers are able to avoid this problem by periodically scanning memory for inaccessible data and reclaiming the space they occupy, a process called *garbage collection*. However, most computers do not provide this service, so we may have to perform our own storage management.

The mechanism VHDL-AMS provides for us to do this is the implicitly defined procedure **deallocate**. Whenever we declare an access type, VHDL-AMS automatically provides an overloaded version of **deallocate** to handle pointers of that type. For example, if we declare an access type for pointers to objects of type T as follows:

```
type T_ptr is access T;
```

we automatically get a version of **deallocate** declared as

```
procedure deallocate ( P : inout T_ptr );
```

The purpose of this procedure is to reclaim the memory space used by the data object pointed to by the parameter P. When the procedure returns, it sets P to the null pointer, since the object is no longer stored in memory. Note that if P is **null** to start with, the procedure has no effect. Thus, there is no need to test whether a pointer is **null** before passing it to **deallocate**.

Example Suppose we wish to delete cells from our list of stimulus values, shown in the previous example. The first cell in the list is pointed to by the access variable **value_list**. We can delete the first cell and reclaim its storage as follows:

```
cell_to_be_deleted := value_list;
value_list := value_list.next_cell;
deallocate(cell_to_be_deleted);
```

The first statement simply copies the pointer to the first cell into the access variable cell_to_be_deleted, so that we do not lose access to it. The second statement advances the list head to the second cell. The third statement then reclaims the storage used by the first cell. Note that, if we do not need to reclaim the storage for the first cell, we only need to include the second statement.

If we wish to delete the whole list, we can use a loop to repeat these statements for each cell in the list, as follows:

```
while value_list /= null loop
    cell_to_be_deleted := value_list;
    value_list := value_list.next_cell;
    deallocate(cell_to_be_deleted);
end loop;
```

This loop simply repeats the steps needed to delete the cell at the head of the list until the list is empty, indicated by value_list being **null**.

We can use deallocate to reclaim memory space, provided we are sure that no other pointer points to the object being deallocated. It is very important that we keep this condition in mind when using deallocate. If some other pointer points to an object that we deallocate, that pointer is not set to **null**. Instead, it becomes a "dangling" pointer, possibly pointing to some random piece of data in memory or not pointing to a valid memory location at all. If we try to access data via a dangling pointer, the effects are unpredictable, varying from accessing seemingly random data to crashing the simulation run. Thus, we must take the utmost care to avoid this situation when using deallocate. Furthermore, we should document such models very thoroughly, so that other designers using or modifying the models are aware of the potential problems.

20.3 **Abstract Data Types Using Packages**

We mentioned earlier that access types are most commonly used in high-level behavioral models of hardware systems to create complex linked data structures. It is appropriate that we should also take a high-level view of the data structures. To do this, we introduce a term from the discipline of software engineering, *abstract data type* (ADT), and show how ADTs can be implemented in VHDL-AMS. An ADT is a data type, together with a collection of operations for creating and working with data objects of that type. In a strict implementation of an ADT, the data structure underlying the data type is not visible to users of the ADT. The operations provided are the only way of working with data objects, thus preventing incorrect use of the objects. This is the means of enforcing the abstract view of the data type. Unfortunately, VHDL-AMS does not provide a way of hiding the data structure, so we have to rely on conventions and documentation.

The most convenient way to implement an ADT in VHDL-AMS is to use a package. In the package declaration we write the VHDL-AMS type declarations that represent the underlying data structure and declare functions and procedures that perform the ADT operations. We, or other designers, can use these declarations to create data objects and perform operations on them without being concerned about the implementation details of the data structure. Any designer has plenty of other concerns to think about, so the more we can do to ease the task of system modeling, the more productive the designer will be. As implementers of the ADT, we write the details of the operations in the package body. We should make the operations as general as possible, so that we can reuse the ADT in several different designs.

Example   Suppose we are working as part of a team designing a network communications controller. Within the behavioral model, we need to represent a buffer memory in which received bytes of data are stored. Bytes are retrieved from this buffer in the same order that they are written. This is often called a "first in, first out" (FIFO) buffer. Since memory in a real hardware system is not an infinite resource, we specify a bound on the amount of data that can be stored at once.

We write an ADT to provide types and operations for bounded buffers of bytes. The package declaration is shown in Figure 20-8. The parts of the package declaration marked as "private" are details of the concrete implementation of the bounded buffer ADT. A user of the ADT does not need to know about them. However, we need to include them in the package declaration in order to declare the type **bounded_buffer**, which is the type made public. Unfortunately, VHDL-AMS does not provide a way of hiding the types that should be private. Note that the operations **test_empty** and **test_full** are written as procedures rather than functions. We are forced to write them in this way, since function parameters must be objects of constant class, and constants may not be of an access type. Hence, we write the operations as procedures with variable class parameters of mode **in**.

FIGURE 20-8

```
package bounded_buffer_adt is
    subtype byte is bit_vector(0 to 7);
    type bounded_buffer_object;   -- private
    type bounded_buffer is access bounded_buffer_object;
    function new_bounded_buffer ( size : in positive ) return bounded_buffer;
    -- creates a bounded buffer object with 'size' bytes of storage
```

(continued on page 628)

(continued from page 627)

```
procedure test_empty ( variable the_bounded_buffer : in bounded_buffer;
                       is_empty : out boolean );
-- tests whether the bounded buffer is empty (i.e., no data to read)

procedure test_full ( variable the_bounded_buffer : in bounded_buffer;
                      is_full : out boolean );
-- tests whether the bounded buffer is full (i.e., no data can be written)

procedure write ( the_bounded_buffer : inout bounded_buffer;  data : in byte );
-- if the bounded buffer is not full, writes the data
-- if it is full, assertion violation with severity failure

procedure read ( the_bounded_buffer : inout bounded_buffer;  data : out byte );
-- if the bounded buffer is not empty, read the first byte of data
-- if it is empty, assertion violation with severity failure
```

```
-- the following types are private to the ADT

type store_array is array (natural range <>) of byte;

type store_ptr is access store_array;

type bounded_buffer_object is record
        byte_count : natural;
        head_index, tail_index : natural;
        store : store_ptr;
    end record bounded_buffer_object;
end package bounded_buffer_adt;
```

A package declaration for a bounded buffer ADT.

The public information in the package declaration is all that is needed to write a model using bounded buffers. For example, Figure 20-9 shows a process that is part of the network receiver model, using the bounded buffer ADT. This process makes no reference to the implementation details of the bounded buffer. It is written using only the operations provided in the public interface of the package. The advantage of separating out the bounded buffer part of the model into an ADT is that the model is more compact, easier to write and easier to understand.

We can now turn to the implementation details of the bounded buffer ADT. The converse advantage of the separation is that as the implementer of the ADT, we can concentrate on writing it as a compact, well-defined software module. We are not distracted by the code of the models that use bounded buffers. The private types in the package declaration indicate that the concrete implementation of this bounded buffer ADT is as a *circular buffer,* stored in an array of bytes, as shown in Figure 20-10. (We can think of the end of the array as being wrapped around to meet the beginning, forming a circle.) Data is stored in successive bytes in the array, starting from the first element. The record element **tail_index** contains the index of the next free position in the array, and the element **head_index**

FIGURE 20-9

```
receiver : process is
    use work.bounded_buffer_adt.all;
    variable receive_buffer : bounded_buffer := new_bounded_buffer(2048);
    variable buffer_overrun, buffer_underrun : boolean;
    ...
begin
    ...
    test_full(receive_buffer, buffer_overrun);
    if not buffer_overrun then
        write(receive_buffer, received_byte);
    end if;
    ...
    test_empty(receive_buffer, buffer_underrun);
    if not buffer_underrun then
        read(receive_buffer, check_byte);
    end if;
    ...
end process receiver;
```

A process forming part of a network receiver, using the bounded buffer ADT.

contains the index of the first available byte. Each time a new byte is written to the buffer, **tail_index** is incremented, and each time a byte is read, **head_index** is incremented. They are incremented modulo the size of the buffer, so that the space made available when bytes are read is reused for new bytes when the end of the array is reached. The record element **byte_count** keeps track of the number of bytes in the buffer and is used to ensure that the write position does not overtake the read position, and vice versa.

The package body is shown in Figure 20-11. The function **new_bounded-_buffer** allocates a new record object in memory, with the **byte_count**, **head_index** and **tail_index** elements initialized to zero. The **store** element is initialized to a pointer to an array of bytes allocated in memory. The length of this array is determined by the actual parameter passed to the function. The procedure **test_empty** simply tests whether the **byte_count** element of the record object is zero. The procedure **test_full** tests whether **byte_count** is equal to the length of the array used to store data.

The **write** procedure uses an assertion statement to test whether the buffer is full, using the ADT operation **test_full**. It then writes the data byte into the buffer at the tail position and increments the **tail_index** element of the record. The **read** procedure similarly uses an assertion statement to test whether the buffer is empty, using the ADT operation **test_empty**. It then reads the data byte from the head position of the buffer and increments the **head_index** element of the record.

FIGURE 20-10

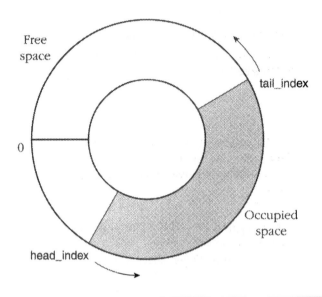

The array used to store data as a circular buffer.

FIGURE 20-11

```
package body bounded_buffer_adt is
    function new_bounded_buffer ( size : in positive ) return bounded_buffer is
    begin
        return new bounded_buffer_object'(
                        byte_count => 0, head_index => 0, tail_index => 0,
                        store => new store_array(0 to size − 1) );
    end function new_bounded_buffer;
    procedure test_empty ( variable the_bounded_buffer : in bounded_buffer;
                        is_empty : out boolean ) is
    begin
        is_empty := the_bounded_buffer.byte_count = 0;
    end procedure test_empty;
    procedure test_full ( variable the_bounded_buffer : in bounded_buffer;
                        is_full : out boolean ) is
    begin
        is_full := the_bounded_buffer.byte_count = the_bounded_buffer.store'length;
    end procedure test_full;
    procedure write ( the_bounded_buffer : inout bounded_buffer;  data : in byte ) is
        variable buffer_full : boolean;
    begin
```

```
        test_full(the_bounded_buffer, buffer_full);
        if buffer_full then
            report "write to full bounded buffer" severity failure;
        else
            the_bounded_buffer.store(the_bounded_buffer.tail_index) := data;
            the_bounded_buffer.tail_index := (the_bounded_buffer.tail_index + 1)
                                    mod the_bounded_buffer.store'length;
            the_bounded_buffer.byte_count := the_bounded_buffer.byte_count + 1;
        end if;
    end procedure write;

    procedure read ( the_bounded_buffer : inout bounded_buffer;  data : out byte ) is
        variable buffer_empty : boolean;
    begin
        test_empty(the_bounded_buffer, buffer_empty);
        if buffer_empty then
            report "read from empty bounded buffer" severity failure;
        else
            data := the_bounded_buffer.store(the_bounded_buffer.head_index);
            the_bounded_buffer.head_index := (the_bounded_buffer.head_index + 1)
                                    mod the_bounded_buffer.store'length;
            the_bounded_buffer.byte_count := the_bounded_buffer.byte_count − 1;
        end if;
    end procedure read;
end package body bounded_buffer_adt;
```

The package body for the bounded buffer ADT implementation.

The advantages of using ADTs in complex behavioral models are overwhelming, but there is one risk that must be borne. As we mentioned before, VHDL-AMS provides no way of hiding the concrete details of the data structure underlying an ADT, as the type declarations must be written in the package declaration. This means that an ADT user can make use of the information to modify the data structures without using the ADT procedures and functions. For example, if an ADT operation simply updates a record element, a user might be tempted to update the record directly and avoid the overhead of a procedure call. However, modern compilers and computers make such "optimizations" unnecessary, and the risk is that the user might inadvertently corrupt the data structure. ADTs in VHDL-AMS require that users avoid such temptations and abide by the contract expressed in the ADT interface. A small amount of self-discipline here will yield significant benefits in the modeling process.

Container ADTs

One good application of ADTs is as "container" or "collection" types. We have seen one such type when we introduced linked data structures. The linked list in that example was a collection of stimulus values. We can organize a linked structure in other ways, depending on how we need to access the objects in the collection. The significant aspect of such structures, however, is that the way we implement them is largely independent of the type of object they contain. For example, adding a new element to a list is done in the same way for a list of integers, a list of records or lists of any other type of object. This indicates that we should look for a way to make a general-purpose list ADT that we can specialize for different types of contained objects.

Unfortunately, VHDL-AMS does not provide a mechanism for parameterizing a package with a type name, so we cannot literally write an ADT for some collection structure and fill in the type of contained object later. However, we can come close to the same effect by writing a template package for the ADT that has a placeholder where the type name for the contained object should be. Each time we need a new kind of collection, we use a text editor to make a copy of the template and fill in the placeholder.

An Ordered-Collection ADT

We can create an ADT that represents an ordered collection of objects. The objects in the collection should have a key that can be used to determine their relative order. The ADT provides operations to insert new objects into a collection, to search for an object with a given key, to traverse the collection and to delete an object. First, Figure 20-12 shows the template for the package declaration defining the ADT. The identifiers enclosed in angle brackets (« ») are template placeholders to be filled in when the package is specialized for a particular type of contained object. The template placeholders «element_type» and «key_type» must be replaced by the names of the element type and key type. The placeholder «key_function» must be replaced by the name of a function that takes an element as a parameter and returns its key value. The placeholder «less_than_function» must be replaced by the name of a function that compares two key values. Note that element_type and key_type may not be access types, since they are used as the types of function parameters.

FIGURE 20-12

```
package «element_type_simple_name»_ordered_collection_adt is
    -- template: fill in the placeholders to specialize for a particular type

    alias element_type is «element_type»;
    alias key_type is «key_type»;
    alias key_of is «key_function» [ element_type return key_type ];
    alias "<" is «less_than_function» [ key_type, key_type return boolean ];

    -- types provided by the package

    type ordered_collection_object;         -- private
    type position_object;                   -- private

    type ordered_collection is access ordered_collection_object;
    type position is access position_object;

    -- operations on ordered collections
```

function new_ordered_collection **return** ordered_collection;
-- *returns an empty ordered collection of element_type values*

procedure insert (c : **inout** ordered_collection; e : **in** element_type);
-- *inserts e into c in position determined by key_of(e)*

procedure get_element (**variable** p : **in** position; e : **out** element_type);
-- *returns the element value at position p in its collection*

procedure test_null_position (**variable** p : **in** position; is_null : **out** boolean);
-- *test whether p refers to no position in its collection*

procedure search (**variable** c : **in** ordered_collection; k : **in** key_type;
                p : **out** position);
-- *searches for an element with key k in c, and returns the position of that*
-- *element, or, if not found, a position for which test_null_position returns true*

procedure find_first (**variable** c : **in** ordered_collection; p : **out** position);
-- *returns the position of the first element of c*

procedure advance (p : **inout** position);
-- *advances p to the next element in its collection,*
-- *or if there are no more, sets p so that test_null_position returns true*

procedure delete (p : **inout** position);
-- *deletes the element at position p from its collection, and advances p*

-- *private types: pretend these are not visible*

type ordered_collection_object **is**
    record
        element : element_type;
        next_element, prev_element : ordered_collection;
    end record ordered_collection_object;

type position_object **is**
    record
        the_collection : ordered_collection;
        current_element : ordered_collection;
    end record position_object;

end package «element_type_simple_name»_ordered_collection_adt;

A template for a package declaration for an ordered-collection ADT.

The ADT provides two types. The first, **ordered_collection**, is the actual collection type itself. The function **new_ordered_collection** returns a value of this type, representing an empty collection. We can add an element into a collection with the **insert** procedure. The second type provided by the ADT, **position**, is a type used to search for objects and to traverse a collection. Since the implementation of the collection is hidden, we are unable to access elements directly. Instead, the ADT provides the **position** type as an abstract form of index. The procedure **get_element** sets the parameter **e** to the value of the element in the collection at a given position. The procedure **test_null_position** tests whether a position value actually refers to an element or not. The procedure **search** sets the parameter **p** to a **position** value, being the position of the first element in the collection with the specified key value. If there is no such element, **p** is assigned a position value that would cause **test_null_position** to return true. The procedures **find_first** and **advance** are used to traverse a collection. We see how this is done shortly when we look at an example of a model that uses the ADT. Finally, the procedure **delete** removes an item at a given position from the collection. After the deletion, the position object refers to the element in the collection following the deleted element.

We can use this ADT to store a collection of stimulus vectors for a design under test. To do this, we must write a package defining the types and functions required by the ADT, as shown in Figure 20-13. Next, we use a text editor to replace the template placeholders in the ADT package declaration. For «element_type_simple_name», we substitute **stimulus_element**; for «element_type», we substitute **work.stimulus-_types.stimulus_element**; for «key_type», we substitute **delay_length**; for «key_function», we substitute **work.stimulus_types.stimulus_key**; and for «less_than_function», we substitute **std.standard."<"**. This creates a specialized version of the ADT package called **stimulus_element_ordered_collection_adt**, which defines types and operations for collections of stimulus elements.

An outline of an architecture body that uses this specialized package is shown in Figure 20-14. The process **stimulus_generation** declares a variable of type **ordered-_collection**, referring to the type provided by the specialized package. The variable initially stores an empty collection. The process starts by inserting a number of stimulus element records into the collection. In a more realistic setting, the stimulus information would be read from a file. However, since we have not yet described file operations in VHDL-AMS, direct insertion by the process serves to illustrate use of the

---

FIGURE 20-13

```
package stimulus_types is
    constant stimulus_vector_length : positive := 4;
    type stimulus_element is record
            application_time : delay_length;
            pattern : real_vector(0 to stimulus_vector_length − 1);
        end record stimulus_element;
    function stimulus_key ( stimulus : stimulus_element ) return delay_length;
end package stimulus_types;

----------------------------------------------------------------

package body stimulus_types is
    function stimulus_key ( stimulus : stimulus_element ) return delay_length is
    begin
        return stimulus.application_time;
    end function stimulus_key;
end package body stimulus_types;
```

A package declaration and body for types and functions representing stimulus information.

FIGURE 20-14

```
architecture initial_test of test_bench is
    use work.stimulus_types.all;
    ...    -- component and signal declarations
begin
    ...    -- instantiate design under test
    stimulus_generation : process is
        use work.stimulus_element_ordered_collection_adt.all;
        variable stimulus_list : ordered_collection := new_ordered_collection;
        variable next_stimulus_position : position;
        variable next_stimulus : stimulus_element;
        variable position_is_null : boolean;
    begin
        insert(stimulus_list, stimulus_element'(0 ns, real_vector'(0.0, 5.0, 0.0, 2.0)));
        insert(stimulus_list, stimulus_element'(200 ns, real_vector'(3.3, 2.1, 0.0, 2.0)));
        insert(stimulus_list, stimulus_element'(300 ns, real_vector'(3.3, 2.1, 1.1, 3.3)));
        insert(stimulus_list, stimulus_element'(50 ns, real_vector'(3.3, 3.3, 2.2, 4.0)));
        insert(stimulus_list, stimulus_element'(60 ns, real_vector'(5.0, 3.3, 4.0, 2.2)));
        ...
        find_first(stimulus_list, next_stimulus_position);
        loop
            test_null_position(next_stimulus_position, position_is_null);
            exit when position_is_null;
            get_element(next_stimulus_position, next_stimulus);
            wait for next_stimulus.application_time - now;
            dut_signals <= next_stimulus.pattern;
            advance(next_stimulus_position);
        end loop;
        wait;
    end process stimulus_generation;
end architecture initial_test;
```

An architecture body that uses the ADT for collections of stimulus elements.

insertion operation. Note that the element need not be inserted in ascending key order. The ADT is responsible for maintaining the order of elements in the collection.

Next, the process applies the stimulus set to signals connected to the design under test. It uses the ADT operation find_first, which returns a position value referring to the first element in the collection. Since we are using the application time of each element as the key, the first element returned is the one with the earliest application time. The process then enters a loop to traverse the entire collection in order. It tests whether the position variable still refers to an element in the collection by using the test_null_position operation. It uses the get_element operation to retrieve the element at the next position and waits until simulation time reaches the element's application time. After assigning the element's pattern to the test signals, it moves the position variable to the next element in the collection using the **advance** procedure. If there are no more elements in the collection, this procedure returns a position value that does not refer to any element in the collection. This value causes the loop to terminate.

We can now turn to the implementation of the ordered-collection ADT. The declarations marked private in the package declaration hint that the collection is implemented using a data structure called a *doubly linked circular list,* illustrated in Figure 20-15. Such a list consists of cells, each storing an element of the collection, a pointer to the next cell in the list and a pointer to the previous cell in the list. As Figure 20-15(a) shows, an empty collection is represented as a list with just a single cell whose pointers point back to the cell itself. This special cell is called the *list header.* Its data element does not form part of the collection, but is included so that the header cell is an object of the same type as other cells in the list. This greatly simplifies the implementation of the ADT operations. Figure 20-15(b) shows a list representing a collection into which two elements have been inserted. The next-element pointer of the last cell points back to the list header, as does the previous-element pointer of the first cell.

The ADT operations for the ordered collection are implemented in the package body shown in Figure 20-16. The function **new_ordered_collection** creates a new list cell, forming the list header for an empty collection. The **element** part of the cell is not explicitly initialized, since its value is never used. The pointer parts of the cell are set to point to the cell itself, and the pointer to the cell is returned as the function result.

FIGURE 20·15

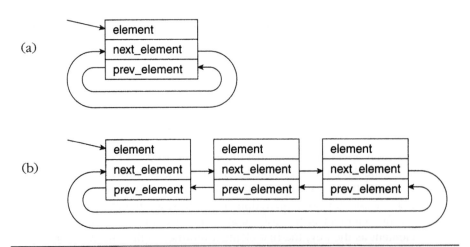

The doubly linked circular list structure used to implement the ordered-collection ADT: (a) an empty list, consisting of just the header, and (b) a list consisting of the header and two inserted elements.

FIGURE 20-16

```
package body «element_type_simple_name»_ordered_collection_adt is
    function new_ordered_collection return ordered_collection is
        variable result : ordered_collection := new ordered_collection_object;
    begin
        result.next_element := result;
        result.prev_element := result;
        return result;
    end function new_ordered_collection;

    procedure insert ( c : inout ordered_collection;  e : in element_type ) is
        variable current_element : ordered_collection := c.next_element;
        variable new_element : ordered_collection;
    begin
        while current_element /= c
            and key_of(current_element.element) < key_of(e) loop
            current_element := current_element.next_element;
        end loop;
        -- insert new element before current_element
        new_element := new ordered_collection_object'(
                                element => e,
                                next_element => current_element,
                                prev_element => current_element.prev_element );
        new_element.next_element.prev_element := new_element;
        new_element.prev_element.next_element := new_element;
    end procedure insert;

    procedure get_element ( variable p : in position;  e : out element_type ) is
    begin
        e := p.current_element.element;
    end procedure get_element;

    procedure test_null_position ( variable p : in position;  is_null : out boolean ) is
    begin
        is_null := p.current_element = p.the_collection;
    end procedure test_null_position;

    procedure search ( variable c : in ordered_collection;  k : in key_type;
                        p : out position ) is
        variable current_element : ordered_collection := c.next_element;
    begin
        while current_element /= c
                and key_of(current_element.element) < k loop
            current_element := current_element.next_element;
        end loop;
        if current_element = c or k < key_of(current_element.element) then
            p := new position_object'(c, c);  -- null position
```

(continued on page 638)

(continued from page 637)

```
        else
            p := new position_object'(c, current_element);
        end if;
    end procedure search;

    procedure find_first ( variable c : in ordered_collection;  p : out position ) is
    begin
        p := new position_object'(c, c.next_element);
    end procedure find_first;

    procedure advance ( p : inout position ) is
        variable is_null : boolean;
    begin
        test_null_position(p, is_null);
        if not is_null then
            p.current_element := p.current_element.next_element;
        end if;
    end procedure advance;

    procedure delete ( p : inout position ) is
        variable is_null : boolean;
    begin
        test_null_position(p, is_null);
        if not is_null then
            p.current_element.next_element.prev_element
                := p.current_element.prev_element;
            p.current_element.prev_element.next_element
                := p.current_element.next_element;
            p.current_element := p.current_element.next_element;
        end if;
    end procedure delete;
end package body «element_type_simple_name»_ordered_collection_adt;
```

The package body for the ordered-collection ADT.

The insert procedure must create a new cell for the list and insert it in the appropriate position, based on the key value of the element. The procedure has a local variable, current_element, that is initialized to the first cell after the list header. The loop then scans from cell to cell until it returns to the header or until it reaches a cell whose element key is not less than that of the new element to be inserted. In either case, the new cell must be inserted immediately before the cell pointed to by current_element. The allocator creates the new cell, sets its element part to the new element value and sets its pointer parts to point to the cells on either side of the new position. The next-element pointer of the previous cell and the previous-element pointer of the next cell are then set to point to the new cell. These pointer manipulations achieve the effect of "splicing" the new cell into position in the list. Note that since the header is a cell of the same type as other list cells, we do not need to make any special cases to insert the new cell at the beginning or end of the list.

The implementation of a position object is shown in Figure 20-17. It contains two parts, one pointing to a collection and the other pointing to a cell in the linked list for that collection. The **get_element** procedure simply returns the value in the **element** part of the cell pointed to by the position object. The **test_null_position** procedure tests whether the cell pointer of the position object points to the list header of the collection. This condition is used to represent a position object that does not refer to any cell in the collection.

The **search** procedure finds a cell whose element part has the same key value as the given key and returns a position object referring to the cell. It compares key values using the "<" function provided when the package is specialized. It starts by setting a pointer variable, **current_element**, to point to the first cell after the list header. It then scans from cell to cell until it returns to the header, or until it reaches a cell whose element key is not less than the given key. If it returns to the header, or if the cell that it reaches contains an element whose key is greater than the given key, then the collection does not contain any cell matching the given key. In this case, the function returns a null position object. (Note the use of the short-circuit **or** operator in the test for this case.) Otherwise the cell reached by the function does match the given key, so the function returns a position object referring to this cell.

The procedure **find_first** returns a position object referring to the first cell after the header cell of the collection passed as a parameter. The **advance** procedure updates a position object by changing its cell pointer part to the next-element part of the cell. This change has the effect of making the position object refer to the next cell in the list.

The final procedure in the package body, **delete**, removes a cell referred to by a position object from a collection (provided the position object does, in fact, refer to a cell). The procedure uses the next-element and previous-element pointers of the cell to access the cells on either side, and updates their pointers to bypass the cell being deleted. It then updates the position object to refer to the cell following the cell being deleted. After these operations, no pointer in the structure points to the original cell

FIGURE 20-17

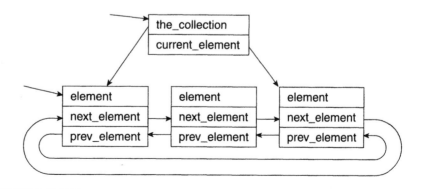

A position object, pointing to the collection list header and a cell in the list.

any longer, so it has become garbage. If storage reclamation were an important consideration on a particular host computer system, the **delete** procedure could be modified to deallocate the cell after it has been unlinked.

Exercises

1. [● 20.1] Write a type declaration for an access type that points to a character data object. Declare a variable of the type, initialized by allocating a character with the value ETX. Write a statement that changes the character value to 'A'.

2. [● 20.1] Identify the error in the following VHDL-AMS fragment:

    ```
    type real_ptr is access real;
    variable r : real_ptr;
    ...
    r := new real;
    r := r + 1.0;
    ```

3. [● 20.1] Draw a diagram showing the pointer variables and the data objects to which they refer after execution of the following VHDL-AMS fragment:

    ```
    type int_ptr is access integer;
    variable a, b, c, d : int_ptr;
    ...
    a := new integer'(1);  b := new integer'(2);
    c := new integer'(3);  d := new integer'(4);
    b := a;  a := b;
    c.all := d.all;
    ```

4. [● 20.1] After execution of the fragment shown in Exercise 3, what is the value of each of the following conditions?

a = b	c = d
a.all = b.all	c.all = d.all

5. [● 20.1] Write a type declaration for an access type that points to a **string** data object. Declare a variable of the type, initialized by allocating a string of four spaces. Write a statement that changes the first character in the string to the character NUL.

6. [● 20.1] The following declarations define a type for complex numbers, an access type referring to the complex number type and three pointer variables:

    ```
    type complex is record
            re, im : real;
        end record complex;
    type complex_ptr is access complex;
    variable x, y, z : complex_ptr;
    ```

Write statements that assign the complex product of the values pointed to by x and y to the data object pointed to by z. The steps required in complex multiplication are given by the following formulas:

$$z_{real} = x_{real} \times y_{real} - x_{imag} \times y_{imag}$$
$$z_{imag} = x_{real} \times y_{imag} + x_{imag} \times y_{real}$$

7. [❶ 20.2] Write type declarations for use in constructing a linked list of message objects. Each message contains a source and destination number (both of type **natural**) and a 256-bit data field. Declare a variable to point to a list of messages, and write a statement to add to the list a message with source number 1, destination number 5 and a data field of all '0' bits.

8. [❶ 20.2] Why is the following fragment to delete the first object in a linked list incorrect?

```
cell_to_be_deleted := value_list;
deallocate(cell_to_be_deleted);
value_list := value_list.next_cell;
```

9. [❶ 20.3] Suppose the variable **test_buffer** is an instance of the bounded buffer ADT described on pages 627 to 629. Write statements that fill the buffer with zero bytes.

10. [❷ 20.2] Figure 20-5 shows statements to traverse a linked list of stimulus values and apply them to a signal. Encapsulate these statements in a procedure with the list pointer and the signal as parameters.

11. [❷ 20.2] The algorithm for traversing a list, encapsulated in a procedure as described in Exercise 10, can be expressed recursively. If the list is empty, the procedure has nothing to do, so it returns. Otherwise, the procedure applies the first stimulus value from the list, waits for the delay, then recursively calls itself with the next cell pointer as the list parameter. Thus, recursive invocation of the procedure replaces the iterative traversal of the list. Rewrite the procedure to use this recursive algorithm.

12. [❷ 20.2] Write a recursive procedure to delete all cells from a linked list pointed to by a parameter of type **value_ptr**. Hint: The procedure should call itself to delete the cells after the first cell, then delete the first cell.

13. [❸ 20.3] The example given in Section 20.3 provides a flexible means of providing analog and digital stimuli to a system under test. Extend the stimulus element record to support both analog and digital stimuli, and extend the test-bench model to apply both digital and analog stimuli to a device under test.

14. [❸ 20.3] Develop an ADT for last-in/first-out stacks of objects. The ADT should be parameterized by the type of object and should provide operations to create a new stack, to test whether a stack is empty, to push an object onto the stack and to pop the top object from the stack and return the object's value.

15. [❸ 20.3] Develop an ADT for first-in/first-out queues of objects. The ADT should be parameterized by the type of object and maximum number of objects allowed in the queue. The operations are to create a new queue, to test whether a queue is empty or full, to add an object to the tail of a queue and to remove an object from the head of a queue and return the object's value. The queue may be implemented as a linked list, as shown in Figure 20-18.

    Use the ADT in a behavioral model of an 8-bit-wide FIFO, based on the behavior described in Exercises 7 and 20 in Chapter 17.

16. [❷ 20.2/20.3] Modify the implementation of the ordered-collection ADT to de-allocate storage when it is no longer used. Note that the procedure **delete** is not the only place in which garbage is created.

17. [❹ 20.3] Develop an alternative implementation of the ordered-collection ADT based on a binary search tree data structure. A binary search tree is a collection of cells, each of which contains a key value, an element and pointers to a left subtree and a right subtree. All cells in the left subtree have key values that are less than that of the parent cell, and all cells in the right subtree have key values that are greater than that of the parent cell. In order to implement the position object and associated operations, the basic tree structure is augmented with pointers from each cell to its parent. Descriptions of algorithms for binary search tree operations can be found in most textbooks on data structures.

FIGURE 20-18

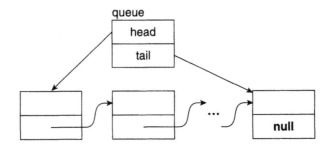

Linked list implementation of a queue.

chapter twenty-one

Files and Input/Output

In this chapter we look at the facilities in VHDL-AMS for file input and output. Files serve a number of purposes, one of which is to provide long-term data storage. In this context, "long-term" means beyond the lifetime of one simulation run. Files can be used to store data to be loaded into a model when it is run, or to store the results produced by a simulation. VHDL-AMS also provides specialized versions of file operations for working with text files. We show how textual input and output can be used to extend the user interface of a simulator with model-specific operations.

21.1 **Files**

We start our discussion of files by looking at the general-purpose mechanisms provided in VHDL-AMS for file input and output. VHDL-AMS provides sequential access to files using operations, such as "open", "close", "read" and "write", that are familiar to users of conventional programming languages.

File Declarations

A VHDL-AMS file is a class of object used to store data. Hence, as with other classes of objects, we must include file-type definitions in our models. The syntax rule for defining a file type is

file_type_definition ⇐ **file of** type_mark

A file-type definition simply specifies the type of objects to be stored in files of the given type. For example, the type declaration

type integer_file **is file of** integer;

defines integer_file to be a type of file that can only contain integers. A file can only contain one type of object, but that type can be almost any VHDL-AMS type, including scalar types, records and one-dimensional arrays. The only types that cannot be stored in files are multidimensional arrays, access types, protected types and other files.

Once we have defined a file type, we can then declare file objects. We do this with a new form of object declaration, described by the syntax rule

file_declaration ⇐
    file identifier ⦃ , ⦄ : subtype_indication
        ⟦ ⟦ **open** *file_open_kind*_expression ⟧ **is** *string*_expression ⟧ ;

A file declaration creates one or more file objects of a given file type. We can include a file declaration in any declarative part in which we can create objects, such as within architecture bodies, blocks, processes, packages and subprograms.

The optional parts of a file declaration allow us to make an association between the file object and a physical file in the host file system. If we include these parts, the file is automatically opened for access during simulation. The string after the keyword **is** is a file *logical name,* which identifies the host file to access. Since different host operating systems use different formats for naming files, many simulators provide some form of mapping between the logical name strings that we include in our models and the file names used in the host file system. For example, if we declare a file as

file lookup_table_file : integer_file **is** "lookup–values";

a simulator running under the UNIX operating system may associate the file object with a physical file named "lookup-values" in the current working directory. A different simulator, running under a Windows operating system, may associate the file object differently, since file names in that operating system are case independent. So it might associate the object with a physical file called "Lookup-Values" in the current working directory.

The optional expression after the keyword **open** allows us to specify how the physical file associated with the file object should be opened. This expression must have a value of the predefined type file_open_kind, declared in the package standard. The declaration is

> **type** file_open_kind **is** (read_mode, write_mode, append_mode);

If we omit the open kind information from a file declaration but include the file logical name, the physical file is opened in read mode. In the rest of this section we discuss each of these modes and see how data is read and written using files opened in each of the modes.

Reading from Files

If a file is opened in read mode, successive elements of data are read from the file using the **read** operation. Reading starts from the first element in the file, and each time an element is read the file position advances to the next element. We can use the **endfile** operation to determine when we have read the last element in the file. Given a file type declared as follows:

> **type** file_type **is file of** element_type;

the **read** and **endfile** operations are implicitly declared as

> **procedure** read (**file** f : file_type; value : **out** element_type);
> **function** endfile (**file** f : file_type) **return** boolean;

We explain subprogram file parameters later in this section.

Example   We can use file operations to initialize the contents of a read-only memory (ROM) from a file. Figure 21-1 shows an entity declaration for a ROM that includes a generic constant to specify the name of a file from which to load the ROM contents. The architecture body for the ROM uses the file name in a file declaration, creating a file object associated with a physical file of data words. The process that implements the behavior of the ROM loads the ROM storage array by reading successive words of data from the file, using **endfile** to determine when to stop.

FIGURE 21-1

```
library ieee;  use ieee.std_logic_1164.all;
entity ROM is
    generic ( load_file_name : string );
    port ( sel : in std_logic;
            address : in std_logic_vector;
            data : inout std_logic_vector );
end entity ROM;
```

```
architecture behavioral of ROM is
begin
    behavior : process is
        subtype word is std_logic_vector(0 to data'length − 1);
        type storage_array is
            array (natural range 0 to 2**address'length − 1) of word;
        variable storage : storage_array;
        variable index : natural;
        ...        −− other declarations
        type load_file_type is file of word;
        file load_file : load_file_type open read_mode is load_file_name;
    begin
        −− load ROM contents from load_file
        index := 0;
        while not endfile(load_file) loop
            read(load_file, storage(index));
            index := index + 1;
        end loop;
        −− respond to ROM accesses
        loop
            ...
        end loop;
    end process behavior;
end architecture behavioral;
```

An entity and architecture body for a ROM that reads its data from a file.

In the above example, each element of the file is a standard-logic vector of a fixed length, determined by the ROM data port width. However, we are not restricted to fixed-length arrays as file elements. We may declare a file type with an unconstrained array type for the element type, for example:

type bit_vector_file **is file of** bit_vector;

The data in a file of this type is a sequence of bit vectors, each of which may be of a different length. For such a file, the **read** operation takes a slightly different form, to allow for the fact that we do not know the length of the next element until we read it. The operation is implicitly declared as

procedure read (**file** f : file_type;
                          value : **out** element_type; length : **out** natural);

When we call this form of **read** operation, we supply an array variable large enough to receive the value we expect to read, and another variable to receive the actual length of the value read. For example, if we make the following declarations:

file vectors : bit_vector_file **open** read_mode **is** "vectors.dat";
variable next_vector : bit_vector(63 **downto** 0);
variable actual_len : natural;

we can call the read operation as follows:

read(vectors, next_vector, actual_len);

This allows us to read a bit vector up to 64 bits long. If the next value in the file is less than or equal to 64 bits long, it is placed in the leftmost part of **next_vector**, with the remaining bits being unchanged. If the value in the file is longer than 64 bits, the first 64 bits of the value are placed in **next_vector**, and the remaining bits are discarded. In both cases, **actual_len** is set to the actual length of the value in the file, whether it be shorter or longer than the length of the second argument to **read**. This allows us to test whether information has been lost. If the expression

actual_len > next_vector'length

is true, the vector variable was not long enough to receive all of the bits.

Example   Suppose we have designed a model for a network receiver and we wish to test it. We can generate network packets to stimulate the model by reading variable-length packets from a file. The outline of a process to do this is shown in Figure 21-2.

The process declares a file object, **stimulus_file**, containing variable-length bit vectors. Each file element is read into the bit-vector variable **packet**, with the length of the bit vector read from the file being stored in **packet_length**. If the bit vector in the file is longer than the bit-vector variable, the process reports the fact and ignores that stimulus packet. Otherwise, the value in **packet_length** is used to determine how many bits from **packet** should be used as data bits to stimulate the network.

FIGURE 21-2

```
stimulate_network : process is
    type packet_file is file of bit_vector;
    file stimulus_file : packet_file open read_mode is "test packets";

    variable packet : bit_vector(1 to 2048);
    variable packet_length : natural;
begin
    while not endfile(stimulus_file) loop
        read(stimulus_file, packet, packet_length);
        if packet_length > packet'length then
            report "stimulus packet too long – ignored" severity warning;
        else
            for bit_index in 1 to packet_length loop
                wait until stimulus_clock = '1';
                stimulus_network <= not stimulus_network;
                wait until stimulus_clock = '0';
                stimulus_network <= stimulus_network xor packet(bit_index);
            end loop;
        end if;
    end loop;
    wait;  -- end of stimulation: wait forever
end process stimulate_network;
```

A process that reads network test packets from a file.

Writing to Files

If a file is opened in write mode, a new empty file is created in the host computer's file system, and successive data elements are added using the **write** operation. For each file type declared, the **write** operation is implicitly declared as

procedure write (**file** f : file_type; value : **in** element_type);

One common use of output files is to save information gathered by instrumentation code. When the simulation is complete, or upon some other trigger condition, the instrumentation code can use write operations to write the data to a file for subsequent analysis.

Example   When we are designing a new CPU instruction set, it is useful to know how frequently each instruction is used in different programs. We measure this by simulating the CPU running a program and having the CPU keep count of how often it executes each instruction. When it completes the program (for example, by reaching a halt instruction), it writes the accumulated counts to a file.

The architecture body for a CPU shown in Figure 21-3 illustrates this approach. It contains a file, instruction_counts, opened in write mode. There is also

FIGURE 21-3

```
architecture instrumented of CPU is
    type count_file is file of natural;
    file instruction_counts : count_file open write_mode is "instructions";
begin
    interpreter : process is
        variable IR : word;
        alias opcode : byte is IR(0 to 7);
        variable opcode_number : natural;
        type counter_array is array (0 to 2**opcode'length – 1) of natural;
        variable counters : counter_array := (others => 0);
        …

    begin
        …      -- initialize the instruction set interpreter
        instruction_loop : loop
            …      -- fetch the next instruction into IR

            -- decode the instruction
            opcode_number := convert_to_natural(opcode);
            counters(opcode_number) := counters(opcode_number) + 1;
            …

            -- execute the decoded instruction
            case opcode is
                …
                when halt_opcode => exit instruction_loop;
                …
            end case;
        end loop instruction_loop;

        for index in counters'range loop
            write(instruction_counts, counters(index));
        end loop;
        wait;  -- program finished, wait forever
    end process interpreter;
end architecture instrumented;
```

An architecture body for a CPU that counts instruction execution frequencies.

a process, interpreter, that fetches and interprets instructions. It contains an array of counters, indexed by opcode values. As the instruction interpreter process decodes each instruction, it increments the appropriate counter. When a halt instruction is executed, the interpreter stops execution and writes the counter values as successive elements in the instruction_counts file.

If an existing physical file in the host computer's file system is opened in append mode, successive data elements are added to the end of the file using the **write** operation. If there is no host file of the given name in the host file system, opening the file object in append mode creates a new file, so that data elements are written from the beginning. Append mode is used for a file that accumulates log information or simulation results over a number of simulation runs. Each run adds its data to the end of the previously accumulated data in the file.

Example   When we are designing a cache memory to attach to a CPU, we need to measure how different cache organizations affect the miss rate, since this influences the average access time seen by the CPU. We measure the miss rate by monitoring the traffic on the buses between the CPU and cache and between the cache and main memory. At the end of a simulation run, the process monitoring the buses appends a record to a data file, storing the parameter values that determine the cache organization and the measured miss rate and average access time.

An outline of the process is shown in Figure 21-4. The process declares a record type that represents the information to be recorded for the simulation run and opens a file of records of this type in append mode. At the end of the simulation run, it creates a record value and appends it to the end of the previously existing data in the file. The record includes the values of generic constants that control the cache organization and identify the benchmark program being run, as well as the calculated values for the miss rate and average access time.

FIGURE 21-4

```
cache_monitor : process is
    type measurement_record is
        record
            cache_size, block_size, associativity : positive;
            benchmark_name : string(1 to 10);
            miss_rate : real;
            ave_access_time : delay_length;
        end record;
    type measurement_file is file of measurement_record;
    file measurements : measurement_file
        open append_mode is "cache-measurements";
    ...
```

```
    begin
        ...
    loop
            ...
        exit when halt = '1';
            ...
    end loop;
    write ( measurements, measurement_record'(
                            -- write values of generics for this run
                            cache_size, block_size, associativity, benchmark_name,
                            -- calculate performance metrics
                            miss_rate => real(miss_count) / real(total_accesses),
                            ave_access_time => total_delay / total_accesses ) );
    wait;
end process cache_monitor;
```

A process that measures cache performance and appends a data record to a log file.

Files Declared in Subprograms

In all of the previous examples, the file object is declared in an architecture body or a process. In these cases, the file is opened at the start of the simulation and automatically closed again at the end of the simulation. The same applies to files declared in packages. We can also declare files within subprograms, but the behavior in these cases is slightly different. The file is opened when the subprogram is called and is automatically closed again when the subprogram returns. Hence the file object, and its association with a physical file in the host file system, is purely local to the subprogram activation. So, for example, if we declare a file in a subprogram:

```
procedure write_to_file is
    file data_file : data_file_type open write_mode is "datafile";
begin
    ...
end procedure write_to_file;
```

each time we call the procedure a new physical file is created, replacing the old one.

Example We can initialize the value of a constant array by calling a function that reads element values from a file. Suppose the array is of the following type, containing integer elements:

```
type integer_vector is array (integer range <>) of integer;
```

The function declaration is shown in Figure 21-5. The first parameter is the name of the file from which to read data elements, and the second parameter is the size of the array that the function should return. The function creates a file object representing a file of integer values and uses the file name parameter to open the file. It then reads values from the file into an array until it reaches the end of the file or the end of the array. It returns the array as the function result. When the function returns, the file is automatically closed. We can use this function in a constant declaration as follows:

```
constant coeffs : integer_vector := read_array("coeff–data", 16);
```

The length of the constant is determined by the result of the function.

FIGURE 21-5

```
impure function read_array ( file_name : string;  array_length : natural )
                          return integer_vector is
    type integer_file is file of integer;
    file data_file : integer_file open read_mode is file_name;
    variable result : integer_vector(1 to array_length) := (others => 0);
    variable index : integer := 1;
begin
    while not endfile(data_file) and index <= array_length loop
        read(data_file, result(index));
        index := index + 1;
    end loop;
    return result;
end function read_array;
```

A function that reads integer elements from a file and returns an array of the elements.

One important point to note about files is that we should be careful not to associate more than one VHDL-AMS file object with a single physical file in the host file system. While the language does not expressly prohibit multiple associations, it does not specify what happens when we do several reads or writes to the same physical file through different VHDL-AMS file objects. Hence the results may be unpredictable and may vary from one host to another.

This restriction may seem fairly trivial, but we may violate it inadvertently. For example, we might declare a file object in an architecture body for some entity as follows:

```
file log_info : log_file open write_mode is "logfile";
```

If our design uses multiple instances of the entity, we have multiple instances of the file object, each associated with "logfile". Possible consequences include interleaving of writes from different instances and loss of data written from all but one instance. The solution to this problem depends on the desired effect. If we intend to merge log data from all instances into one file, we should declare the file in a package. On the other hand, if we intend each instance to have its own log file, we should compute separate file logical name strings for each instance.

Explicit Open and Close Operations

The syntax rule for a file object declaration, shown on page 644, indicates that the file open mode and logical name are optional. If we include either of them, the physical file is automatically opened when the file object is created. If we omit them, the file object is created but remains unassociated with any physical file. An example of a file declaration in this form is

```
file lookup_table_file, result_file : integer_file;
```

If we declare a file object in this way, we explicitly associate it with a physical file and open the file using the **file_open** operation. Given a file type declared as follows:

```
type file_type is file of element_type;
```

file_open is implicitly declared as

```
procedure file_open ( file f : file_type;
                      external_name : in string;
                      open_kind : in file_open_kind := read_mode );
```

The external_name and open_kind parameters serve exactly the same purpose as the corresponding information in the optional part of a file object declaration. For example, the declaration

```
file lookup_table_file : integer_file open read_mode is "lookup–values";
```

is equivalent to

```
file lookup_table_file : integer_file;
...
file_open ( lookup_table_file,
            external_name => "lookup–values", open_kind => read_mode );
```

The advantage of using an explicit **file_open** operation, as opposed to having the file automatically opened when the file object is created, is that we can first perform some other computation to determine how to open it. For example, we might ask the user to type in a file name.

A problem that arises with both of the previously mentioned ways of opening a file is that the operation may fail, causing the whole simulation to come to an abrupt halt. We can make a model more robust by including some error checking, using a second form of the file_open operation, implicitly declared as

```
procedure file_open ( status : out file_open_status;
                      file f : file_type;
                      external_name : in string;
                      open_kind : in file_open_kind := read_mode );
```

The extra parameter, **status**, is used to return information about the success or failure of the operation. Its type is predefined in the package standard as

```
type file_open_status is (open_ok, status_error, name_error, mode_error);
```

If the file was successfully opened, the value **open_ok** is returned, and we can proceed with **read**, **write** and **endfile** operations, according to the mode. If there was a problem during the file_open operation, one of the remaining values is returned. The value **status_error** indicates that the file object had previously been opened and associated with a physical file. (This error is different from the case in which multiple file objects are associated with the same physical file.) The value **name_error** is returned under different circumstances, depending on the mode in which we attempt to open the file. In read mode, it is returned if the named host file does not exist. In write mode, it is returned if a file of the given name cannot be created. In append mode, it is returned if the named file does not exist and a new file of that name cannot be created. Finally, the value **mode_error** is returned from the file_open operation if the file exists but cannot be opened in the specified mode. This error may arise if we attempt to write or append to a file marked read-only in the host file system.

Complementing the file_open operation, VHDL-AMS also provides a file_close operation, which can be used to close a file explicitly. The operation disassociates the file object from the physical file. When a file type is declared, a corresponding version of file_close is implicitly declared as

```
procedure file_close ( file f : file_type );
```

We can use file_open and file_close in combination, either to associate a file object with a number of different physical files in succession, or to access a particular physical file multiple times. While applying the file_close operation to a file object that is already closed has no effect, it is good style to make sure that file_open and file_close operations are always paired. We should open a file in the desired mode, perform the reads and writes required, then close the file. This discipline helps ensure that we do not inadvertently write the wrong data to the wrong file.

Example   Suppose we wish to apply stimulus vectors from a number of different files to a model during a simulation run. We create a directory file containing a list of file names to be used as stimulus files. Our test bench model then reads the stimulus file names from this directory file and opens the stimulus files one-by-one to read the stimulus data.

An outline of a process that reads the stimulus files is shown in Figure 21-6. The process has a string variable, **file_name**, into which it reads the name of the next stimulus file to be opened. Note the test to see if the actual file name is longer than this variable. This test guards against the open failing through truncation of a file name. The second form of **file_open** is used to open the stimulus file, using the slice of the **file_name** variable containing the name read from the directory. If the open fails, the stimulus file is skipped. Otherwise, the process reads the stimulus vectors from the file, then closes it. When the end of the directory is reached, all stimulus files have been read, so the process suspends.

FIGURE 21-6

```
stimulus_generator : process is
    type directory_file is file of string;
    file directory : directory_file open read_mode is "stimulus–directory";
    variable file_name : string(1 to 50);
    variable file_name_length : natural;
    variable open_status : file_open_status;

    subtype stimulus_vector is std_logic_vector(0 to 9);
    type stimulus_file is file of stimulus_vector;
    file stimuli : stimulus_file;
    variable current_stimulus : stimulus_vector;
    …
begin
    file_loop : while not endfile(directory) loop
        read( directory, file_name, file_name_length );
        if file_name_length > file_name'length then
            report "file name too long: " & file_name & "... – file skipped"
                severity warning;
            next file_loop;
        end if;
        file_open ( open_status, stimuli,
                    file_name(1 to file_name_length), read_mode );
        if open_status /= open_ok then
            report file_open_status'image(open_status) & " while opening file "
                & file_name(1 to file_name_length) & " – file skipped"
                severity warning;
            next file_loop;
        end if;
        stimulus_loop : while not endfile(stimuli) loop
            read(stimuli, current_stimulus);
```

(continued on page 656)

(continued from page 655)

```
        ...       -- apply the stimulus
      end loop stimulus_loop;
      file_close(stimuli);
    end loop file_loop;
    wait;
  end process stimulus_generator;
```

A process that reads stimulus files, using a directory of file names.

File Parameters in Subprograms

We have seen that the file operations described above take a file object as a parameter. In general, we can include a file parameter in any subprogram we write. Files form a fourth class of parameter, along with constants, variables and signals. The syntax for a file parameter in a subprogram specification is as follows:

interface_file_declaration ⇐ **file** identifier ⦃ , ... ⦄ : subtype_indication

The file parameters in the file operations we have seen conform to this syntax rule. The subtype indication must denote a file type. When the subprogram is called, a file object of that type must be supplied as an actual parameter. This object can be a file object declared by the caller, or, if the caller is itself a subprogram, a formal file parameter of the caller. The file object is passed into the subprogram and any of the file operations can be performed on it (depending on the mode in which the file object is opened).

Example   Suppose we need to initialize a number of two-dimensional transformation arrays of real numbers using data stored in a file. We cannot directly declare the file of array objects, as VHDL-AMS only allows us to store one-dimensional arrays in a file. Instead, we declare the file to be a file of real numbers and use a procedure to read numbers from the file into an array parameter. First, here are the declarations for the arrays and the file:

```
type transform_array is array (1 to 3, 1 to 3) of real;
variable transform1, transform2 : transform_array;

type transform_file is file of real;
file initial_transforms : transform_file open read_mode is "transforms.ini";
```

Next, Figure 21-7 shows the declaration of the procedure to read values into an array. It uses the **endfile** operation to test whether there is an element to read. If not, it reports the fact and returns. Otherwise, it proceeds to use the **read** operation to fetch the next element of the array.

FIGURE 21-7

```
procedure read_transform ( file f : transform_file;
                              variable transform : out transform_array ) is
begin
    for i in transform'range(1) loop
        for j in transform'range(2) loop
            if endfile(f) then
                report "unexpected end of file in read_transform – "
                    & "some array elements not read"
                    severity error;
                return;
            end if;
            read ( f, transform(i, j) );
        end loop;
    end loop;
end procedure read_transform;
```

A procedure to read values from a file into an array.

We call this procedure to read values into the two array variables as follows:

```
read_transform ( initial_transforms, transform1 );
read_transform ( initial_transforms, transform2 );
```

The file object initial_transforms remains opened between the two calls, so the second call reads values from the file beyond those read by the first call.

Portability of Files

We finish this section on VHDL-AMS's file facilities with a few comments about the way in which file data is stored. It is important to note that files of the types we have described store the data in some binary representation. The format is dependent on the host computer system and on the simulator being used. This fact raises the issue of portability of files between different systems. All we can expect is that a file of a given type written by one model can be read as a file of the same type in a different model, provided it is run on the same host computer using the same VHDL-AMS simulator. There is no guarantee that it can be read on a different host computer, even using the same simulator retargeted for that host, nor that it can be read on any host using a different simulator.

While this might seem to limit the use of files for storing data, in reality it does not present much of an obstacle. If we do need to transfer files between systems, we can use text files as the interchange medium. As we see in the next section, VHDL-AMS provides an extensive set of facilities for dealing with the textual representation of data. Furthermore, tools for transferring text files between different computer systems are commonplace. The other potential problem arises if we wish to use non-VHDL-AMS software tools to process files written by VHDL-AMS models. For example, we may wish to write a program in some conventional programming language to perform data analysis on a data file produced by an instrumented VHDL-AMS model. Again, we can use text files to write data in a form readable by other tools. Alternatively, we can consult the VHDL-AMS tool vendor's documentation to learn the details of the binary data representation in a file and write a program to read data in that format.

21.2 **The Package Textio**

The predefined package **textio** in the library **std** provides a number of useful types and operations for reading and writing text files, that is, files of character strings. In particular, it provides procedures for reading and writing textual representations of the various predefined data types provided in VHDL-AMS. These operations make it possible to write files that can be read by other software tools and transferred to other host computer systems. The package specification is shown in Figure 21-8.

FIGURE 21-8[1]

```
package textio is
    type line is access string;
    type text is file of string;
    type side is (right, left);
    subtype width is natural;
    file input : text open read_mode is "std_input";
    file output : text open write_mode is "std_output";
    procedure readline(file f: text; l: out line);
    procedure read ( L : inout line;  value: out bit;  good : out boolean );
    procedure read ( L : inout line;  value: out bit );
    procedure read ( L : inout line;  value: out bit_vector;  good : out boolean );
    procedure read ( L : inout line;  value: out bit_vector );
    procedure read ( L : inout line;  value: out boolean;  good : out boolean );
    procedure read ( L : inout line;  value: out boolean );
    procedure read ( L : inout line;  value: out character;  good : out boolean );
    procedure read ( L : inout line;  value: out character );
    procedure read ( L : inout line;  value: out integer;  good : out boolean );
    procedure read ( L : inout line;  value: out integer );
```

```
        procedure read ( L : inout line;  value: out real;  good : out boolean );
        procedure read ( L : inout line;  value: out real );

        procedure read ( L : inout line;  value: out string;  good : out boolean );
        procedure read ( L : inout line;  value: out string );

        procedure read ( L : inout line;  value: out time;  good : out boolean );
        procedure read ( L : inout line;  value: out time );

        procedure writeline ( file f : text;  L : inout line );

        procedure write ( L : inout line;  value : in bit;
                    justified: in side := right;  field: in width := 0 );

        procedure write ( L : inout line;  value : in bit_vector;
                    justified: in side := right;  field: in width := 0 );

        procedure write ( L : inout line;  value : in boolean;
                    justified: in side := right;  field: in width := 0 );

        procedure write ( L : inout line;  value : in character;
                    justified: in side := right;  field: in width := 0 );

        procedure write ( L : inout line;  value : in integer;
                    justified: in side := right;  field: in width := 0 );

        procedure write ( L : inout line;  value : in real;
                    justified: in side := right;  field: in width := 0;
                    digits: in natural := 0 );

        procedure write ( L : inout line;  value : in string;
                    justified: in side := right;  field: in width := 0 );

        procedure write ( L : inout line;  value : in time;
                    justified: in side := right;  field: in width := 0;
                    unit: in time := ns );

end package textio;
```

The textio *package.*

Input and output operations using **textio** are based on dynamic strings, accessed using pointers of the type **line**, declared in the package. We use the **readline** operation to read a complete line of text from an input file. It creates a string object in the host computer's memory and returns a pointer to the string. We then use various versions of the **read** operation to extract values of different types from the string. When we need to write text, we first use various versions of the **write** operation to form a string object in memory, then pass the string to the **writeline** operation via its pointer. The operation writes the complete line of text to the output file and resets the pointer to point to an empty string. If the pointer passed to **writeline** is **null**, the operation writes a blank line to the output file.

The reason that VHDL-AMS takes this approach to input and output is to allow multiple processes to read or write to a single file without interfering with each other. Recall that multiple processes that are resumed in the same simulation cycle execute concurrently. If processes were to write directly to the file, partial lines from different processes might be intermixed, making the output unintelligible. By having each process form a line locally, we can write each line as one atomic action. The result is an output file consisting of interleaved lines from the different processes. A similar argument applies to input. If read operations were to read directly from the file, no process would be able to read an entire line without the possibility of interference from another process also reading input. The solution is for a process to read an entire line as one atomic action and then to extract the data from the line locally.

The package **textio** declares the file type **text**, representing files of strings. The operations provided by the package act on files of this type. The package also declares the file objects **input** and **output**, respectively associated with physical files using the logical names **std_input** and **std_output**. The intention is that the host simulator associate these file objects with the standard devices used for input and output. For example, the file **input** might be associated with the workstation keyboard and the file **output** with the workstation display. A model then uses the files to interact with the user. Prompts and informational messages are displayed by writing them to **output**, and commands and data typed by the user are read from **input**.

Textio Read Operations

Let us now look at the read operations in detail. Each version of **read** has at least two parameters: a pointer to the line of text from which to read and a variable in which to store the value. The operations extract characters from the beginning of the line, looking for characters that form a textual representation of a value of the expected type. The line is modified to contain only the remaining characters, and the value represented by the extracted characters is returned.

The character version of **read** simply extracts the first character in the line and returns it. It does not look for quotation marks around the character. For example, if the line pointed to by **L** contains

```
a'bcd
```

two successive character **read** operations would return the characters 'a' and '''.

The string version extracts enough characters to fill the actual string argument. This version of **read** does not look for double quotation marks around the string. For example, if **s** is a string variable of length five, and **L** points to the line

```
fred "cat"
```

a read into **s** returns the string "fred ". A second read into **s** returns the string ""cat"". If the line does not contain enough characters to fill the string variable, the read operation fails. If this possibility could cause problems, we can resort to direct string manipulation of the line. So, for example, we can test the length of the line and extract fewer characters than the length of the string variable as follows:

```
if L'length < s'length then
    read(L, s(1 to L'length));
```

```
    else
        read(L, s);
    end if;
```

Since L is an access variable to a string, the 'length attribute applied to L returns the length of the string pointed to by L, provided that L is not **null**.

The versions of **read** for all other types of data skip over any whitespace characters in the line before the textual representation of the data. A whitespace character is a space, a non-breaking space or a horizontal tab character. These operations then extract as many characters from the line as can be used to form a valid literal of the expected type. Characters are extracted up to the first character that is not valid for a literal of that type or to the end of the line. For example, if L points to the line

```
    12          -4.27!
```

an integer read extracts the first two characters and returns the value 12. A subsequent read into a real variable skips the spaces, then extracts the characters up to but not including the '!' and returns the value –4.27.

For bit-vector values, the literal in the line should be a binary string without quotation marks or a base specifier (that is, just a string of '0' or '1' characters). For time values, the literal should be a number followed by a time unit, with at least one whitespace character between them.

The versions of the **read** operations in **textio** that include the third parameter, **good**, allow for graceful recovery if the next value on the input line is not a valid textual representation of a value of the expected type. In that case, they return with **good** set to false, the line unmodified and the **value** parameter undefined. For example, an integer read from a line containing

```
    $%@!!&
```

fails in this way. On the other hand, if the line does contain valid text, **good** is set to true, and the value is extracted as described above. The versions of **read** without the **good** parameter cause an error if the line contains invalid text.

Example   Suppose we have designed a model for a thermostat system and need to test it. The thermostat has inputs connected to a quantity **temperature**, a signal **setting** of type **real** and signals **enable** and **heater_fail** of type **bit**. We can use a text editor to write a file that specifies input stimuli to test the thermostat. Each line of the file is formatted as follows

```
    time    string    value
```

where *time* is the simulation time at which the stimulus is applied, *string* is a four-character string identifying one of the inputs and *value* is the value to be applied to the input. The allowed *string* values are "temp", "set ", "on " and "fail". We assume that the stimuli are sorted in increasing order of application time.   A sample file in this format is

```
0 ms       on     0.0
2 ms       fail   0.0
15 ms      temp   56.0
100 ms     set    70.0
1.5 sec    on     1.0
```

We write a process to interpret such a stimulus control file as shown in Figure 21-9.   The process declares a file object, **control**, associated with the stimulus control file, and an access variable, **command**, to point to a command line read from the file.   It also declares a number of variables to store values read from a line.   The process body repeatedly reads lines from the file and extracts the fields from it using read operations.   We use the forms of **read** with **good** parameters to do error checking.   In this way, we make the model less sensitive to formatting errors in the control file and report useful error information when an error is detected.   When the end of the command file is reached, the process suspends for the rest of the simulation.

FIGURE 21-9

```vhdl
stimulus_interpreter : process is
    use std.textio.all;
    file control : text open read_mode is "control";
    variable command : line;
    variable read_ok : boolean;
    variable next_time : time;
    variable whitespace : character;
    variable signal_id : string(1 to 4);
    variable temp_value, set_value : real;
    variable on_value, fail_value : bit;
begin
    command_loop : while not endfile(control) loop
        readline ( control, command );
        -- read next stimulus time, and suspend until then
        read ( command, next_time, read_ok );
        if not read_ok then
            report "error reading time from line: " & command.all
                severity warning;
            next command_loop;
        end if;
        wait for next_time - now;
```

```
                    -- skip whitespace
                    while command'length > 0
                        and ( command(command'left) = ' '   -- ordinary space
                                or command(command'left) = ' '   -- non-breaking space
                                or command(command'left) = HT ) loop
                        read ( command, whitespace );
                    end loop;
                    -- read signal identifier string
                    read ( command, signal_id, read_ok );
                    if not read_ok then
                        report "error reading signal id from line: " & command.all
                            severity warning;
                        next command_loop;
                    end if;
                    -- dispatch based on signal id
                    case signal_id is

                        when "temp" =>
                            read ( command, temp_value, read_ok );
                            if not read_ok then
                                report "error reading temperature value from line: "
                                        & command.all severity warning;
                                next command_loop;
                            end if;
                            temp_sig <= temp_value;

                        when "set " =>
                            ...      -- similar to "temp"

                        when "on  " =>
                            read ( command, on_value, read_ok );
                            if not read_ok then
                                report "error reading on value from line: "
                                        & command.all
                                    severity warning;
                                next command_loop;
                            end if;
                            enable <= on_value;

                        when "fail" =>
                            ...      -- similar to "on  "

                        when others =>
                            report "invalid signal id in line: " & signal_id
                                severity warning;
                            next command_loop;

                    end case;
                end loop command_loop;
```

(continued on page 664)

(continued from page 663)

    wait;

end process stimulus_interpreter;

A process that reads a stimulus text file to test a thermostat.

For each command line, the process first extracts the time value and suspends until simulation advances to that time. It then skips over whitespace characters in the line up to the first non-whitespace character, which should represent the signal identifier string. The process skips whitespace characters by repeatedly inspecting the first character in what remains of the command line and, if it is a whitespace character, removing it with a character read operation. Skipping whitespace in this way allows the user some flexibility in formatting the command file. The process next dispatches to different branches of a case statement depending on the signal identifier string. For each string value, the process reads a stimulus value of the appropriate type from the command line and applies it to the corresponding signal. The **temperature** quantity can then be updated by using a simple simultaneous statement as follows:

    temperature == temp_sig'ramp;

We use the 'ramp attribute to automatically handle any discontinuities in the analog inputs.

Textio Write Operations

We now turn to write operations, which form a line of text ready for output. Each version of **write** has two parameters, specifying the pointer to the line being formed and the value whose textual representation is to be added to the line. Subsequent parameters beyond these two are used to control the formatting of the textual representation. The **field** parameter specifies how many characters are used to represent the value. If the field is wider than necessary, space characters are used as padding. The characters representing the value are either left-justified or right-justified within the field, depending on the **justified** parameter. For example, if we write the integer 42 left-justified in a field of five characters, the string "42   " is added to the line. If we write the same value right-justified in a field of five characters, the string "   42" is added. If we specify a field width that is smaller than the minimum required to represent the value, that minimal representation is used with no space padding. Thus, writing the integer 123 with a specified field width of two characters or less results in the three-character string "123" being added to the line. Note that the default values for **justified** and **field** conveniently result in the minimal representation being used.

    The write operations for character, string and bit-vector values write representations that do not include quotation marks or a base specifier. Bit-vector values are written in binary. For example, if we perform the following write operations to a line, L, that is initially empty:

```
write ( L, string'( "fred" ) );
write ( L, ' ' );
write ( L, bit_vector'( X"3A" ) );
```

the resulting line is

```
fred 00111010
```

The write operation for real values has an additional parameter, **digits**, that specifies how many digits to the right of the decimal point are to be included in the textual representation of the value. For example, writing the value 3.14159 with **digits** set to 2 results in the string "3.14" being added to the line. If **digits** is set to 0 (the default value), the value is represented in exponential notation. For example, writing 123.4567 in this way results in the string "1.234567e+02" (or something similar) being added to the line.

The write operation for time values has a parameter, **unit**, that specifies the time unit to use to express the value. The output is expressed as a multiple of this unit. For example, writing the value 40 ns with **unit** set to **ps** results in the string "40000 ps" being added to the line. If the value to be written is not an integral multiple of the specified unit, a real literal is used in the textual representation. For example, writing the value 23 µs with **unit** set to **ms** results in the string "0.023 ms" being added to the line.

Example   We can write a bus monitor process for a computer system model that creates a log file of bus activity, similar to that displayed by a bus-state analyzer monitoring real hardware. Suppose the model includes the following signals connecting the CPU with memory and I/O controllers:

```
signal address : bit_vector(15 downto 0);
signal data : resolve_bytes byte;
signal rd, wr, io : bit;     -- read, write, io/mem select
signal ready : resolve_bits bit;
```

Our monitor process is written as shown in Figure 21-10. It declares an output file **log**, of type **text**, and an access variable **trace_line**, of type **line**, for accumulating each line of output. The process is resumed when the memory or I/O controller responds to a bus read or write request. It generates a formatted line using write operations. It also keeps count of how many lines are written to the log file and includes a header line after every 60 lines of trace data. A sample log file showing how the data is formatted is

```
Time    R/W I/M  Address           Data

0.4 us   R   M   0000000000000000  10011110
```

```
0.9 us    R   M    0000000000000001 00010010
  2 us    R   M    0000000000010100 11100111
2.7 us    W   I    0000000000000111 00000000
```

FIGURE 21-10

```
bus_monitor : process is
    constant header : string(1 to 44)
        := FF & "    Time  R/W I/M  Address        Data";
    use std.textio.all;

    file log : text open write_mode is "buslog";
    variable trace_line : line;
    variable line_count : natural := 0;
begin
    if line_count mod 60 = 0 then
        write ( trace_line, header );
        writeline ( log, trace_line );
        writeline ( log, trace_line );   -- empty line
    end if;
    wait until (rd = '1' or wr = '1') and ready = '1';
    write ( trace_line, now, justified => right, field => 10, unit => us );
    write ( trace_line, string'("    ") );
    if rd = '1' then
        write ( trace_line, 'R' );
    else
        write ( trace_line, 'W' );
    end if;
    write ( trace_line, string'("   ") );
    if io = '1' then
        write ( trace_line, 'I' );
    else
        write ( trace_line, 'M' );
    end if;
    write ( trace_line, string'("   ") );
    write ( trace_line, address );
    write ( trace_line, ' ');
    write ( trace_line, data );
    writeline ( log, trace_line );
    line_count := line_count + 1;
end process bus_monitor;
```

A process that monitors a computer system bus and creates a log file of bus activity.

Reading and Writing User-Defined Types

We have seen that **textio** provides read and write operations for the predefined types. If we need to read or write values of types we declare, such as new enumeration or physical types, we use the 'image and 'value attributes to convert between the values and their textual representations. For example, if we declare an enumeration type and variable as

    type speed_category is (stopped, slow, fast, maniacal);
    variable speed : speed_category;

we can write a value of the type using the 'image attribute to create a string to supply to the string version of **write**:

    write (L, speed_category'image(speed));

Reading a value of a new type we define presents more problems if we want our model to be robust in the face of invalid input. In this case, we must write VHDL-AMS code that analyzes the line of text to ensure that it contains a valid representation of a value of the expected type. If we are not so concerned with robustness, we can simply use the 'value attribute to convert the input line to a value of the expected type. For example, the statements

    readline(input, L);
    speed := speed_category'value(L.all);

convert an entire line of input to a value of type **speed_category**.

One final point to note about the read and write operations provided by **textio** is that they may deallocate storage used by lines of text passed to them as arguments. For example, when a read operation extracts characters from the beginning of a line, the storage for the extracted characters may be deallocated. Alternatively, the whole line may be deallocated and a new line formed from the remaining characters. The trap to be aware of is that if we copy the pointer to a line, using assignment of one value of type **line** to another, we may end up with dangling pointers after doing read or write operations. The best way to avoid problems is to avoid modifying variables of type **line** other than with read and write operations.

Exercises

1. [**❶** 21.1] Write declarations to define a file of real values associated with the host file "samples.dat" and opened for reading. Write a statement to read a value from the file into a variable **x**.

2. [**❶** 21.1] Write declarations to define a file of bit-vector values associated with the host file "/tmp/trace.tmp" and opened for writing. Write a statement to write the concatenation of the values of two signals, **addr** and **d_bus**, to the file.

3. [❶ 21.1] Write statements that attempt to open a file of real values called "wave-form" for reading and report any error that results from the attempt.

4. [❶ 21.2] Suppose the next line in a text file contains the characters

    ```
    123 4.5 6789
    ```

    What is the result returned by the following **read** calls?

    ```
    readline(in_file, L);
    read(L, bit_value);     -- read a value of type bit
    read(L, int_value);     -- read a value of type integer
    read(L, real_value);    -- read a value of type real
    read(L, str_value);     -- read a value of type string(1 to 3)
    ```

5. [❶ 21.2] Write declarations and statements for a process to prompt the user to enter a number and to accept the number from the user.

6. [❶ 21.2] What string is written to the output file by the following statements:

    ```
    write(L, 3.5 us, justified => right, field => 10, unit => ns);
    write(L, ' ');
    write(L, bit_vector'(X"3C"));
    write(L, ' ');
    write(L, string'("ok"), justified => left, field => 5);
    writeline(output, L);
    ```

7. [❷ 21.1] Write a function that may be called to initialize an array of bit-vector words. The words are of the subtype

    ```
    subtype word is std_logic_vector(0 to 15);
    ```

    The function should have two parameters, the first being the name of a file from which the words of data are read, and the second being the size of the array to return. If the file contains fewer words than required, the extra words in the array are initialized with all bits set to 'U'.

8. [❷ 21.1] Develop a procedure that writes the contents of a memory array to a file. The memory array is of the type **mem_array**, declared as

    ```
    subtype byte is bit_vector(7 downto 0);
    type mem_array is array (natural range <>) of byte;
    ```

    The procedure should have two parameters, one being the array whose value is to be written and the other being a file of **byte** elements into which the data is written. The procedure should assume the file has already been opened for writing.

9. [❷ 21.2] Develop a procedure that has a file name and an integer signal as parameters. The file name refers to a text file that contains a delay value and an integer on each line. The procedure should read successive lines, wait for the time specified by the delay value, then assign the integer value to the signal. When the last line has been processed, the procedure should return. Invoke the procedure using a concurrent procedure call in a test bench.

10. [❷ 21.2] Develop a procedure that logs the history of values on a real-vector signal to a file. The procedure has two parameters, the name of a text file and a real-vector signal. The procedure logs the initial value and the new values when events occur on the signal. Each log entry in the file should consist of the simulation time and the signal value at that time.

11. [❷ 21.2] Develop a procedure similar to that described in Exercise 10, but which logs values of a signal of type motor_control, declared as

```
type motor_state is (idle, forward, reverse);
type motor_control is record
       state : motor_state;
       speed : natural;
   end record motor_control;
```

The motor_control values should be written in the format of a record aggregate using positional association.

12. [❸ 21.1] Experiment with your simulator to determine the format it uses for binary files. Write a model that creates files of various data types, and use operating system utilities (for example, hexadecimal dump utilities) to see how the data is stored. Try to develop programs in a conventional programming language to write files that can be read by VHDL-AMS models run by your simulator.

13. [❸ 21.2] Develop a package that provides textual read and write operations for real-vector values.

chapter twenty-two

Attributes and Groups

VHDL-AMS provides comprehensive facilities for expressing the behavior and structure of a design. VHDL-AMS also provides the attribute *mechanism for annotating a model with additional information. In this chapter, we review the predefined attributes and show how to define new attributes. We also look at the group mechanism, which allows us to describe additional relationships between various items in a model.*

22.1 **Predefined Attributes**

Throughout this book we have seen predefined attributes that are used to retrieve information about types, objects and other items within a model. In this section we summarize the previously introduced attributes and fully describe the remaining predefined attributes.

Attributes of Scalar Types

The first group of predefined attributes gives information about the values in a scalar type. These were introduced in Chapter 2 and are summarized in Figure 22-1.

FIGURE 22-1

Attribute	Type of T	Result type	Result
T'left	any scalar type or subtype	same as T	leftmost value in T
T'right	"	"	rightmost value in T
T'low	"	"	least value in T
T'high	"	"	greatest value in T
T'ascending	"	boolean	true if T is an ascending range, false otherwise
T'image(x)	"	string	a textual representation of the value x of type T
T'value(s)	"	base type of T	value in T represented by the string s
T'pos(s)	any discrete or physical type or subtype	universal integer	position number of x in T
T'val(x)	"	base type of T	value at position x in T
T'succ(x)	"	"	value at position one greater than x in T
T'pred(x)	"	"	value at position one less than x in T
T'leftof(x)	"	"	value at position one to the left of x in T
T'rightof(x)	"	"	value at position one to the right of x in T
T'base	any type or subtype		base type of T, for use only as prefix of another attribute

The predefined attributes giving information about values in a type.

Attributes of Scalar Natures

The second group of predefined attributes gives information about the values of a scalar nature or subnature. These were also introduced in Chapter 2 and are summarized in Figure 22-2.

FIGURE 22-2

Attribute	Nature of N	Result
N'across	any nature or subnature	across type of N
N'through	any nature or subnature	through type of N

The predefined attributes giving information about values of a nature.

Attributes of Array Types and Objects

The third group of predefined attributes gives information about the index values of an array object, type or nature. These were introduced in Chapter 4 and are summarized in Figure 22-3. The prefix A in the table refers either to a constrained array type or subtype, to a constrained array nature or subnature, to an array object or to a slice of an array. If A is a variable of an access type pointing to an array object, the attribute refers to the array object, not the pointer value. Each of the attributes optionally takes an argument that selects one of the index dimensions of the array. The default is the first dimension. Note that if the prefix A is an alias for an array object, the attributes return information about the index values declared for the alias, not those declared for the original object.

FIGURE 22-3

Attribute	Result
A'left(n)	leftmost value in index range of dimension n
A'right(n)	rightmost value in index range of dimension n
A'low(n)	least value in index range of dimension n
A'high(n)	greatest value in index range of dimension n
A'range(n)	index range of dimension n
A'reverse_range(n)	index range of dimension n reversed in direction and bounds
A'length(n)	length of index range of dimension n
A'ascending(n)	true if index range of dimension n is ascending, false otherwise

The predefined attributes giving information about the index range of an array.

Attributes of Signals

The fourth group of predefined attributes gives information about signals or defines new implicit signals derived from explicitly declared signals. These attributes were introduced in Chapters 5, 6 and 15 and are summarized in Figure 22-4. The prefix **S** in the table refers to any statically named signal. Three of the attributes optionally

FIGURE 22-4

Attribute	Result type	Result
S'delayed(t)	base type of S	implicit signal, with the same value as S, but delayed by t time units (t ≥ 0 ns)
S'stable(t)	boolean	implicit signal, **true** when no event has occurred on S for t time units, **false** otherwise (t ≥ 0 ns)
S'quiet(t)	boolean	implicit signal, **true** when no transaction has occurred on S for t time units, **false** otherwise (t ≥ 0 ns)
S'transaction	bit	implicit signal, changes value in simulation cycles in which a transaction occurs on S
S'event	boolean	true if an event has occurred on S in the current simulation cycle, **false** otherwise
S'active	boolean	true if a transaction has occurred on S in the current simulation cycle, **false** otherwise
S'last_event	time	time since last event occurred on S, or time'high if no event has yet occurred
S'last_active	time	time since last transaction occurred on S, or **time'high** if no transaction has yet occurred
S'last_value	base type of S	value of S before last event occurred on it
S'driving	boolean	true if the containing process is driving S (or every element of a composite signal S), or **false** if the containing process has disconnected its driver for S (or any element of S) with a null transaction
S'driving_value	base type of S	value contributed by driver for S in the containing process
S'ramp (trise, tfall)	base type of S	quantity where each scalar subelement follows the corresponding subelement of S with a linear change of value in **trise** time units (if given) for rising values and in **tfall** time units (if given) for falling values
S'slew (rslope, fslope)	base type of S	quantity where each scalar subelement follows the corresponding subelement of S with a linear change of value governed by a maximum rising slope of **rslope** (if given) and a maximum falling slope of **fslope** (if given)

The predefined attributes giving information about signals and values of signals.

take a non-negative argument t of type **time**. The default is 0 fs. The 'ramp attribute optionally takes a rise-time argument of type **time** and an optional additional fall-time argument of type **time**. The 'slew attribute optionally takes a rising-slope argument, which is a static expression of type **real**, as well as an optional additional falling-slope argument, also a static expression of type **real**.

Attributes of Terminals

The fifth group of predefined attributes gives information about terminals. These attributes were introduced in Chapter 6 and are summarized in Figure 22-5. The prefix T in the table refers to any terminal.

FIGURE 22-5

Attribute	Result type	Result
T'reference	across type of nature of T	reference quantity of T
T'contribution	through type of nature of T	contribution quantity of T
T'tolerance	string	tolerance group of T

The predefined attributes giving information about terminals.

Attributes of Quantities

The sixth group of predefined attributes gives information about quantities. These attributes were introduced in Chapters 6 and 13 and are summarized in Figure 22-6. The prefix Q in the table refers to any quantity. Three of the attributes optionally take a non-negative argument t of type **time**. The default is 0 fs.

FIGURE 22-6

Attribute	Result type	Result
Q'tolerance	string	tolerance group of Q
Q'dot	same type as Q	derivative with respect to time of Q
Q'integ	same type as Q	time integral of Q from time 0
Q'delayed(t)	same type as Q	a quantity equal to Q but delayed by t
Q'above(E)	boolean	a signal that is true if Q > E, false otherwise
Q'zoh(t, delay)	base type of Q	a quantity whose value is that of Q sampled initially at time **delay** and every interval t thereafter

(continued on page 676)

(continued from page 675)

Attribute	Result type	Result
Q'ltf(num, den)	base type of Q	the Laplace transfer function of each scalar subelement of Q with num as the numerator and **den** as the denominator polynomial coefficients
Q'ztf(num,den, t, delay)	type of Q	the z-domain transfer function of each scalar subelement of Q with **num** as the numerator and **den** as the denominator polynomial coefficients, t as the sampling period, and **delay** as the time of the first sampling
Q'slew (rslope, fslope)	base type of Q	a quantity where each scalar subelement follows the corresponding scalar subelement of **Q**, but with its derivative with respect to time limited by the specified slopes

The predefined attributes giving information about quantities.

Attributes of Named Items

The remaining predefined attributes are applied to any declared item and return a string representation of the name of the item. These attributes are summarized in Figure 22-7. The prefix X in the table refers to any declared item. If the item is an alias, the attribute returns the name of the alias itself, not the aliased item.

The 'simple_name attribute returns a string representation of the name of an item. For example, if a package utility_definitions in a library utilities declares a constant named word_size, the attribute

    utilities.utility_definitions.word_size'simple_name

FIGURE 22-7

Attribute	Result
X'simple_name	a string representing the identifier, character or operator symbol defined in the declaration of the item X
X'path_name	a string describing the path through the elaborated design hierarchy, from the top-level entity or package to the item X
X'instance_name	a string similar to that produced by X'path_name, but including the names of the entity and architecture bound to each component instance in the path

The predefined attributes that provide names of declared items.

returns the string "**word_size**". We might ask why VHDL-AMS provides this attribute, since we need to write the simple name of the item in order to apply the attribute. It would be simpler to write the string literal directly. If nothing else, we can use the attribute to gain consistency of style in reporting item names in messages, since the 'simple_name attribute always returns a lowercase version of the name.

The 'path_name and 'instance_name attributes both return string representations of the path through the design hierarchy to an item. They are especially useful in assertion or report statements to pinpoint exactly which instance of a library unit is the source of a message. VHDL-AMS only requires that the message reported to the user by these statements indicate the name of the library unit (entity, architecture body or package) containing the statement. We can use the 'path_name or 'instance_name attribute to determine which particular instance of a process in the design hierarchy is the source of a message.

Example Suppose we have a design that includes numerous instances of a flipflop component bound to an entity **flipflop** and using an architecture **behavior**. Within this architecture we wish to include timing checks and report an error message if the constraints are violated. An outline of the architecture body incorporating these checks is shown in Figure 22-8. When a flipflop instance in the design detects a timing violation, it will issue an assertion violation message indicating that the problem arose in the architecture **behavior** of flipflop. We use the 'path_name attribute in the message string to identify which component instance bound to the flipflop entity is the one responsible for issuing the message.

FIGURE 22-8

```
architecture behavior of flipflop is
begin

    timing_check : process (clk) is
    begin
        if clk = '1' then
            assert d'last_event >= Tsetup
                report "set up violation detected in " & timing_check'path_name
                severity error;
        end if;
    end process timing_check;

    ...    -- functionality

end architecture behavior;
```

An architecture body including a process that checks for a timing constraint violation.

Unfortunately, the specification in the VHDL-AMS standard of the values to be returned by the 'path_name and 'instance_name attributes is ill-defined. It contains some ambiguities and contradictory examples. These problems were present in the VHDL-93 standard, on which VHDL-AMS is based, and were corrected in the VHDL-2001 standard. Our description here is based on the VHDL-2001 specification, as we expect future versions of VHDL-AMS will conform to that specification.

The format of the string produced by the 'path_name and 'instance_name attributes for a library, a package, or an item declared in a package is described by the EBNF rule

> package_based_path ⇐
> : *library*_logical_name : ⟦ *package*_simple_name : ⟧
> ⟨ *subprogram*_simple_name : ⟩
> ⟦ simple_name ⟦ character_literal ⟦ operator_symbol ⟧

The colon characters serve as punctuation, separating elements within the path string. If the item to which the attribute is applied is a library, the path string includes only the library name. If the item is a package, the path string includes the library name and the package name. If the item is declared in a package, the path string includes the library name, the package name and the name of the item. If the item is nested within a subprogram in the package, the string also includes the names of the containing subprogram or subprograms.

Example   Suppose we have a package **mem_pkg** stored in the library **project**. The package declaration is shown at the top of Figure 22-9. The 'path_name attribute applied to these items gives the following results:

```
mem_pkg'path_name = ":project:mem_pkg:"
word'path_name = ":project:mem_pkg:word"
word_array'path_name = ":project:mem_pkg:word_array"
load_array'path_name = ":project:mem_pkg:load_array"
```

FIGURE 22-9

```
package mem_pkg is
    subtype word is bit_vector(0 to 31);
    type word_array is array (natural range <>) of word;
    procedure load_array ( words : out word_array;  file_name : string );
end package mem_pkg;
```

```
package body mem_pkg is
    procedure load_array ( words : out word_array;  file_name : string ) is
        -- words'path_name = ":project:mem_pkg:load_array:words"
        use std.textio.all;
        file load_file : text open read_mode is file_name;
        -- load_file'path_name = ":project:mem_pkg:load_array:load_file"
```

```
        procedure read_line is
      -- read_line'path_name = ":project:mem_pkg:load_array:read_line:"
            variable current_line : line;
            -- current_line'path_name =
            --   ":project:mem_pkg:load_array:read_line:current_line"
        begin
            ...
        end procedure read_line;
    begin  -- load_array
        ...
    end procedure load_array;
end package body mem_pkg;
```

A package declaration and body, illustrating the path name attribute.

The 'instance_name attribute returns the same strings for these items. An outline of the package body is also shown in Figure 22-9. The comments indicate the values of the 'path_name attribute applied to various names within the package body. Again, the 'instance_name attribute returns the same strings as the 'path_name attribute.

If an item is declared within an entity or architecture body, the 'path_name and 'instance_name attributes return different strings depending on the structure of the elaborated design and the location of the declared item within the design hierarchy. We first look at the string returned by the 'path_name attribute, as it is the simpler of the two. The format of the string is described by the EBNF rules

instance_based_path ⇐
    : ⦃ path_instance_element : ⦄
        ⟦ simple_name ⦶ character_literal ⦶ operator_symbol ⟧

path_instance_element ⇐
    *entity*_simple_name
    ⦶ *component_instantiation*_label
    ⦶ *block*_label
    ⦶ *generate*_label ⟦ (literal) ⟧
    ⦶ ⟦ *process*_label ⟧
    ⦶ *procedural*_label
    ⦶ *subprogram*_simple_name

The string starts with the name of the topmost entity in the design and continues with the labels of any blocks, generate statements, processes, procedurals and subprograms between the top and the item. If the design hierarchy includes a component instance bound to an entity and architecture body containing the item, the attribute string includes the label of the component instantiation statement. If the item is contained within an iterative generate statement, the string includes the value of the generate parameter for the particular iteration containing the item. The value is included in parentheses after the generate statement label. If the item is included in a process that has no label, the string includes an empty element in place of a process label.

The format of the string returned by the 'instance_name attribute is described by the EBNF rules

full_instance_based_path ⇐
   : 〖 full_path_instance_element : 〗
     〖 simple_name ▯ character_literal ▯ operator_symbol 〗

full_path_instance_element ⇐
   *entity*_simple_name (architecture_simple_name)
   ▯ *component_instantiation*_label
     @ *entity*_simple_name (*architecture*_simple_name)
   ▯ *block*_label
   ▯ *generate*_label 〖 (literal) 〗
   ▯ 〖 *process*_label 〗
   ▯ *procedural*_label
   ▯ *subprogram*_simple_name signature

It is the same as that returned by 'path_name, except that the names of the entity and architecture bound to a component instance are included after the label of the component instantiation statement. Furthermore, the architecture name for the top-level design entity is also included.

Example   We illustrate the results returned by the 'path_name and 'instance_name attributes by looking at a sample design hierarchy. The top level of the hierarchy is formed by the entity **top** and its corresponding architecture **top_arch**, declared as shown in Figure 22-10. The numbered comments in this model mark points at which various declared items are visible. The values of the 'path_name and 'instance_name attributes of these items at the marked points are shown in Figure 22-11. At point 4, the string returned varies between repetitions created by the generator. Where the table shows *index* in the attribute value, the value of the generate parameter for that repetition is substituted. For example, in the repetition with the generate parameter set to 4, the result of other_sig'path_name is ":top:rep_gen(4):other_gen:other_sig".

FIGURE 22-10

```
entity top is
end entity top;
```

```
architecture top_arch of top is
    signal top_sig : ...;                            -- 1
begin
    stimulus : process is
        variable var : ...;                          -- 2
    begin
        ...
    end process stimulus;
    rep_gen : for index in 0 to 7 generate
    begin
        end_gen : if index = 7 generate
            signal end_sig : ...;                    -- 3
        begin
            ...
        end generate end_gen;
        other_gen : if index /= 7 generate
            signal other_sig : ...;                  -- 4
        begin
            other_comp : entity work.bottom(bottom_arch)
                port map ( ... );
        end generate other_gen;
    end generate rep_gen;
end architecture top_arch;
```

The top-level entity and architecture body of a design hierarchy.

FIGURE 22-11

Point	Item	Item'path_name *and item*'instance_name	
1	top	:top:	:top(top_arch):
1	top_sig	:top:top_sig	:top(top_arch):top_sig
2	stimulus	:top:stimulus:	:top(top_arch):stimulus:
2	var	:top:stimulus:var	:top(top_arch):stimulus:var
3	end_sig	:top:rep_gen(7):end_gen:end_sig	
		:top(top_arch):rep_gen(7):end_gen:end_sig	
4	other_sig	:top:rep_gen(index):other_gen:other_sig	
		:top(top_arch):rep_gen(index):other_gen:other_sig	

The results of applying the path and instance name attributes to the top-level design entity.

The entity declaration and architecture body for the bottom level of the design hierarchy, instantiated in the preceding architecture body, are shown in Figure 22-12. The values of the 'path_name and 'instance_name attributes of items within this architecture at the marked points are shown in Figure 22-13. The values shown are for the instance of the architecture corresponding to the component instantiation statement in the repetition of **rep_gen** with index set to 4. Point 8 is within a process that has no label, so the strings returned for the item **v** include an empty element (two consecutive colon characters) where the process label would otherwise be.

FIGURE 22-12

```
entity bottom is
    port ( ... );
end entity bottom;
```

```
architecture bottom_arch of bottom is
    signal bot_sig : ...;                          -- 5
    procedure proc ( ... ) is
        variable v : ...;                          -- 6
    begin
        ...
    end procedure proc;
begin
    delays : block is
        constant d : integer := 1;                 -- 7
    begin
        ...
    end block delays;
    func : block is
    begin
        process is
            variable v : ...;                      -- 8
        begin
            ...
        end process;
    end block func;
end architecture bottom_arch;
```

The bottom-level entity and architecture body of a design hierarchy.

FIGURE 22-13

Point	Item	*Item*'path_name *and item*'instance_name
5	bot_sig	:top:rep_gen(4):other_gen:other_comp:bot_sig
		:top(top_arch):rep_gen(4):other_gen:other_comp@bottom(bottom_arch):bot_sig
6	v	:top:rep_gen(4):other_gen:other_comp:proc:v
		:top(top_arch):rep_gen(4):other_gen:other_comp@bottom(bottom_arch):proc:v
7	d	:top:rep_gen(4):other_gen:other_comp:delays:d
		:top(top_arch):rep_gen(4):other_gen:other_comp@bottom(bottom_arch):delays:d
8	v	:top:rep_gen(4):other_gen:other_comp:func::v
		:top(top_arch):rep_gen(4):other_gen:other_comp@bottom(bottom_arch):func::v

The results of applying the path and instance name attributes to the bottom-level design entity.

22.2 User-Defined Attributes

The predefined attributes provide information about types, objects or other items in a VHDL-AMS model. VHDL-AMS also provides us with a way of adding additional information of our own choosing to items in our models, namely, through user-defined attributes. We can use them to add physical design information such as standard cell allocation and placements, layout constraints such as maximum wire delay and inter-wire skew or information for synthesis such as encodings for enumeration types and hints about resource allocation. In general, information of a non-structural and non-behavioral nature can be added using attributes and processed using software tools operating on the design database.

Attribute Declarations

The first step in defining an attribute is to declare the name and type of an attribute, using an *attribute declaration*. The syntax rule describing this is

attribute_declaration ⇐ **attribute** identifier : type_mark ;

An attribute declaration simply defines the identifier as representing a user-defined attribute that can take on values from the specified type. The type can be any VHDL-AMS type except an access, file or protected type or a composite type with a subelement that is an access, file or protected type. Some examples of attribute declarations are

attribute cell_name : string;
attribute pin_number : positive;

```
attribute max_wire_delay : delay_length;
attribute encoding : bit_vector;
```

The attribute type need not be a simple scalar. For example, we might define an attribute to represent cell placement as follows:

```
type length is range 0 to integer'high
    units nm;
        um = 1000 nm;
        mm = 1000 um;
        mil = 25400 nm;
    end units length;

type coordinate is record
        x, y : length;
    end record coordinate;

attribute cell_position : coordinate;
```

Attribute Specifications

Once we have defined an attribute name and type, we then use it to *decorate* items within a design. We write *attribute specifications,* nominating items that take on the attribute with particular values. The syntax rules for an attribute specification are

```
attribute_specification ⟸
    attribute identifier of entity_name_list : entity_class is expression ;

entity_name_list ⟸
    ⟨ ⟨ ⟨ identifier ⎮ character_literal ⎮ operator_symbol ⟩ ⟦ signature ⟧ ⟩ ⟨ , ... ⟩
    ⎮ others
    ⎮ all
```

```
entity_class ⟸
    entity          ⎮ architecture   ⎮ configuration  ⎮ package
    ⎮ procedure     ⎮ function        ⎮ type           ⎮ subtype
    ⎮ constant      ⎮ signal          ⎮ variable       ⎮ file
    ⎮ component     ⎮ label           ⎮ literal        ⎮ units
    ⎮ group         ⎮ nature          ⎮ subnature      ⎮ quantity
    ⎮ terminal
```

The first identifier in an attribute specification is the name of a previously declared attribute. The items to be decorated with this attribute are listed in the entity name list. Note that we use the term "entity" here to refer to any item in the design, not to be confused with an entity interface defined in an entity declaration. We adopt this terminology to remain consistent with the VHDL-AMS *Language Reference Manual,* since you may need to refer to it occasionally. However, we use the term as little as possible, preferring instead to refer to "items" in the design, to avoid confusion. The items to be decorated with the attribute are those named items of the particular kind specified by the "entity" class. The list of classes shown covers every kind of item we can name in a VHDL-AMS description, so we can decorate any part of a design with an attribute. Finally, the actual value for the attribute of the decorated items is the result of the expression included in the attribute specification. Here are some examples of attribute specifications using the attributes defined earlier:

```
attribute cell_name of std_cell : architecture is "DFF_SR_QQNN";
attribute pin_number of enable : signal is 14;
attribute max_wire_delay of clk : signal is 50 ps;
attribute encoding of idle_state : literal is b"0000";
attribute cell_position of the_fpu : label is ( 540 um, 1200 um );
```

We now look at how attribute values may be specified for each of the classes of items shown in the syntax rule. For most classes of items, an attribute specification must appear in the same group of declarations as the declaration for the item being decorated. However, the first four classes shown in the syntax rule are design units that are placed in a design library as library units when analyzed. They are not declared within any enclosing declarative part. Instead, we can consider them as being declared in the context of the design library. However, this presents a problem if we wish to decorate an item of one of these classes with an attribute. For entities, architectures, configurations and packages, we solve this problem by placing the attribute specification in the declarative part of the design unit itself. For example, we decorate an architecture std_cell with the cell_name attribute as follows:

```
architecture std_cell of flipflop is

    attribute cell_name of std_cell : architecture is "DFF_SR_QQNN";

    ...      -- other declarations

begin

    ...

end architecture std_cell;
```

In the case of packages, the attribute specification must be included in the package declaration, not the package body. For example, we can decorate a package model_utilities with the optimize attribute as follows:

```
package model_utilities is

    attribute optimize : string;
    attribute optimize of model_utilities : package is "level_4";

    ...

end package model_utilities;
```

When we decorate subprograms we may need to distinguish between several overloaded versions. The syntax rule on page 684 shows that we can include a signature to identify one version uniquely by specifying the types of its parameters and return value. Signatures were introduced in Chapter 11.

Example If we have two overloaded versions of the procedure add_with_overflow declared in a process as shown in Figure 22-14, we can decorate them using signatures in the attribute specification.

FIGURE 22-14

```
process is
    procedure add_with_overflow ( a, b : in integer;
                                sum : out integer;  overflow : out boolean ) is ...
    procedure add_with_overflow ( a, b : in bit_vector;
                                sum : out bit_vector;  overflow : out boolean ) is ...
    attribute built_in : string;
    attribute built_in of
        add_with_overflow [ integer, integer, integer, boolean ] : procedure is
        "int_add_overflow";
    attribute built_in of
        add_with_overflow [ bit_vector, bit_vector,
                            bit_vector, boolean ] : procedure is
        "bit_vector_add_overflow";
begin
    ...
end process;
```

A process using signatures in the attribute specifications for two overloaded procedures.

The syntax rule also shows that we can identify an overloaded operator by writing the operator symbol as the function name. For example, if we declare a function to concatenate two lists of stimulus vectors:

```
function "&" ( a, b : stimulus_list ) return stimulus_list;
```

we can decorate it with an attribute as follows:

```
attribute debug : string;
attribute debug of
    "&" [ stimulus_list, stimulus_list return stimulus_list ] : function is
    "source_statement_step";
```

The syntax rules for attribute specifications show the signature to be optional, and indeed, we can omit it when decorating subprograms. In this case, the attribute specification applies to all subprograms with the given name declared in the same declarative part as the attribute specification.

We can decorate a type, subtype or data objects (a constant, variable, signal or files) by including an attribute specification after the declaration of the item. The attribute specification must appear within the same declarative part as the declaration of the item. For example, if we declare a resolved subtype **resolved_mvl**:

```
type mvl is ('X', '0', '1', 'Z');
type mvl_vector is array ( integer range <>) of mvl;
function resolve_mvl ( drivers : mvl_vector ) return mvl;
subtype resolved_mvl is resolve_mvl mvl;
```

we can decorate it as follows:

```
type builtin_types is (builtin_bit, builtin_mvl, builtin_integer);
attribute builtin : builtin_types;
attribute builtin of resolved_mvl : subtype is builtin_mvl;
```

Generics and ports in the interface of a block or entity are data objects and can be decorated with attributes. Generics are objects of constant class, and ports are objects of signal class. The interface list is included in the declarative part of the block or entity. Hence, we write attribute specifications for generics and ports in the declarative part of the block or entity. Subprogram parameters are also data objects that can be decorated with attributes. The class of each parameter is specified in the interface list of the subprogram. We write the attribute specifications for subprogram parameters in the declarative part of the subprogram.

Example   Suppose the package **physical_attributes** declared the following attributes:

```
attribute layout_ignore : boolean;
attribute pin_number : positive;
```

We can declare an entity with decorated generics and ports as shown in Figure 22-15.

FIGURE 22-15

```
library ieee;  use ieee.std_logic_1164.all;
use work.physical_attributes.all;
entity \74x138\ is
    generic ( Tpd : time );
```

(continued on page 688)

(continued from page 687)

```
      port ( en1, en2a_n, en2b_n : in std_logic;
             s0, s1, s2 : in std_logic;
             y0, y1, y2, y3, y4, y5, y6, y7 : out std_logic );

      attribute layout_ignore of Tpd : constant is true;

      attribute pin_number of s0 : signal is 1;
      attribute pin_number of s1 : signal is 2;
      attribute pin_number of s2 : signal is 3;
      attribute pin_number of en2a_n : signal is 4;

      ...

  end entity \74x138\;
```

An entity declaration for a 74x138 decoder, with decorated ports.

Example   Figure 22-16 shows a procedure with three parameters of different classes. Attribute specifications for the parameters are included in the declarative part of the procedure.

FIGURE 22-16

```
procedure mem_read ( address : in natural;
                       result : out byte_vector;
                       signal memory_bus : inout ram_bus ) is
      attribute trace of address : constant is "integer/hex";
      attribute trace of result : variable is "byte/multiple/hex";
      attribute trace of memory_bus : signal is
          "custom/command=rambus.cmd";
      ...
begin
      ...
end procedure mem_read;
```

A procedure with decorated parameters.

We can decorate a component in a model by including an attribute specification along with the component declaration. An important point to realize is that the attribute decorates the template defined by the component declaration. It does not decorate component instances that use that template.

Example   Figure 22-17 shows a package specification that includes a component declaration for an and gate. The package imports two attributes, **graphic_symbol** and **graphic_style**, from the package **graphics_pkg** in the library **graphics**. It decorates the component template with each of these attributes.

FIGURE 22-17

```
library ieee;  use ieee.std_logic_1164.all;
library graphics;

package gate_components is

    use graphics.graphics_pkg.graphic_symbol,
        graphics.graphics_pkg.graphic_style;

    component and2 is
        generic ( prop_delay : delay_length );
        port ( a, b : in std_logic;  y : out std_logic );
    end component and2;

    attribute graphic_symbol of and2 : component is "and2";
    attribute graphic_style of and2 : component is "color:default, weight:bold";


    ...

end package gate_components;
```

A package that declares a component and decorates it with attributes.

===

If we wish to decorate a component instance or any other concurrent statement with an attribute, we do so by decorating the label of the statement. The label is implicitly declared in the declarative part of the architecture or block containing the concurrent statement. Hence, we place the attribute specification in that declarative part.

Example   We might decorate a component instance in an architecture body with an attribute describing cell placement as shown in Figure 22-18.

FIGURE 22-18

```
architecture cell_based of CPU is
    component fpu is
        port ( ... );
    end component;
    use work.cell_attributes.all;
```

(continued on page 690)

(continued from page 689)

```
        attribute cell_position of the_fpu : label is ( 540 um, 1200 um );

        ...

begin
    the_fpu : component fpu
        port map ( ... );

    ...

end architecture cell_based;
```

An architecture body containing a component instance whose label is decorated with an attribute.

We can decorate sequential statements within a process or a subprogram in a similar way. The syntax rules for sequential statements show that each kind of sequential statement may be labeled. We decorate a sequential statement by specifying an attribute for the label. We place the attribute specification in the declarative part of the process or subprogram containing the sequential statement.

Example If we wish to decorate a loop statement in a process with the attribute synthesis_hint, we proceed as shown in Figure 22-19.

FIGURE 22-19

```
controller : process is
    attribute synthesis_hint of control_loop : label is
        "implementation:FSM(clk)";

    ...

begin
    ...        -- initialization
    control_loop : loop
        wait until clk = '1';

        ...

    end loop;
end process controller;
```

A process containing a sequential statement whose label is decorated with an attribute.

When we introduced aliases and signatures in Chapter 11, we mentioned that enumeration literals can be thought of as functions with no parameters that return values of their enumeration types. We can take the same approach when decorating enumeration literals with attributes, in order to distinguish between literals of the same name from different enumeration types.

Example   If we have two enumeration types declared as

> **type** controller_state **is** (idle, active, fail_safe);
> **type** load_level **is** (idle, busy, overloaded);

we can decorate the literals of type controller_state as follows:

> **attribute** encoding **of** idle [**return** controller_state] : **literal is** b"00";
> **attribute** encoding **of** active [**return** controller_state] : **literal is** b"01";
> **attribute** encoding **of** fail_safe [**return** controller_state] : **literal is** b"10";

The signature associated with the literal idle indicates that it is of type controller_state, not load_level. As with attribute specifications for subprograms, if a signature is not included for a literal, all literals of the given name declared in the same declarative part as the attribute specification are decorated with the attribute.

When we declare a physical type we introduce a primary unit name and possibly a number of secondary unit names. Each of the unit names is a declared item and so may be decorated with attributes.

Example   Figure 22-20 shows a package interface that defines a physical type voltage. It also declares an attribute, resolution, and decorates each of the units of voltage with this attribute.

FIGURE 22-20

```
package voltage_defs is
    type voltage is range −2e9 to +2e9
        units
            nV;
            uV = 1000 nV;
            mV = 1000 uV;
            V = 1000 mV;
        end units voltage;
    attribute resolution : real;
    attribute resolution of nV : units is 1.0;
```

(continued on page 692)

(continued from page 691)

```
     attribute resolution of uV : units is 0.01;
     attribute resolution of mV : units is 0.01;
     attribute resolution of V : units is 0.001;
 end package voltage_defs;
```

A package that declares a physical type and decorates units of the type with attributes.

The one remaining class of items that can be decorated with attributes is groups. We introduce groups in the next section and show examples of decorated groups.

If we return to the syntax rules for attribute specifications, shown on page 684, we see that we can write the keyword **others** in place of the list of names of items to be decorated. If we do so, the attribute specification applies to all items of the given class in the declarative part that are not otherwise decorated with the attribute. Such an attribute specification must be the last one in the declarative part that refers to the given attribute name and item class.

Example   Figure 22-21 shows an architecture body in which signals are decorated with attributes specifying the maximum allowable delays due to the physical layout. The two signals recovered_clk1 and recovered_clk2 are explicitly decorated with the attribute value 100 ps. The remaining signals are decorated with the value 200 ps.

FIGURE 22-21

```
library ieee;  use ieee.std_logic_1164.all;
use work.timing_attributes.all;

architecture structural of sequencer is
     signal recovered_clk1, recovered_clk2 : std_logic;
     signal test_enable : std_logic;
     signal test_data : std_logic_vector(0 to 15);

     attribute max_wire_delay of
          recovered_clk1, recovered_clk2 : signal is 100 ps;

     attribute max_wire_delay of others : signal is 200 ps;

     ...

begin
     ...
end architecture structural;
```

An outline of an architecture body in which attributes are used to specify layout-based delays for signals.

The syntax rules also show that we can use the keyword **all** in place of a list of item names. In this case, all items of the given class defined in the declarative part containing the attribute specification are decorated. Such an attribute specification must be the only one in the declarative part to refer to the given attribute name and item class.

Although we can only decorate an item with one value for a given attribute name, we can decorate it with several different attributes. We simply write one attribute specification for each of the attributes decorating the item. For example, a component instance labeled **mult** might be decorated with several attributes as follows:

attribute cell_allocation **of** mult : **label is** "wallace_tree_multiplier";
attribute cell_position **of** mult : **label is** (1200 um, 4500 um);
attribute cell_orientation **of** mult : **label is** down;

If an item in a design is decorated with a user-defined attribute, we can refer to the attribute value using the same notation that we use for predefined attributes. The syntax rule for an attribute name referring to a user-defined attribute is

attribute_name ⇐ name ⟦ signature ⟧ ' identifier

If the name of the item is unambiguous, we can simply write an apostrophe and the attribute name after the item name. For example:

std_cell'cell_name
enable'pin_number
clk'max_wire_delay
v4 := idle_state'encoding
the_fpu'cell_position

In the case of attributes decorating subprograms or enumeration literals, it may be necessary to use a signature to distinguish between a number of alternative names. For example, we might refer to attribute values of different versions of an increment function as

increment [bit_vector **return** bit_vector] 'built_in
increment [std_logic_vector **return** std_logic_vector] 'built_in

Similarly, we might refer to attribute values of enumeration literals as

high [**return** speed_range] 'representation
high [**return** coolant_level] 'representation

While it is legal VHDL-AMS to refer to attribute values such as these in expressions, it is not good design practice to use attribute values to affect the structure or behavior of the model. It is better to describe structure and behavior using the language facilities intended for that purpose and use attributes to annotate the design with other kinds of information for use by other software tools. For this reason, we do not further discuss the use of attribute values in models. Software tools that use attributes should include documentation describing the required attribute types and their usage.

In Chapter 11, we introduced aliases as a way of defining alternate names for items in a design. In most cases, referring to an item using an alias is exactly the same as referring to it using its original name. The same interpretation holds when decorating items with attributes. When we use an alias of an item in an attribute specification, it is the original object denoted by the alias that is decorated, not the alias. This is the interpretation we saw for the predefined attributes discussed in the previous section. The exceptions are the predefined attributes that return the path name of an item and those that return information about the index ranges of arrays. One restriction on decorating data objects using aliases is that we may only do so using aliases that denote whole objects, not elements or slices of records or arrays. This restriction corresponds to the restriction that an attribute must decorate a whole object. The syntax rule for an attribute specification does not provide for naming parts of objects, since we can only write a simple identifier as an object name.

One final point to mention about user-defined attributes relates to component instantiation statements and to subprogram calls. In a component instantiation statement, actual signals are associated with formal ports of an entity. If the actual signal is decorated with an attribute, the attribute information is only visible in the context of the actual signal, namely, in the architecture body in which the signal is declared. It is not carried through to the instantiated entity. For example, if we have a signal **s** decorated with an attribute **attr**, we might use it as an actual signal in a component instantiation statement:

```
c1 : entity work.e(arch)
        port map ( p => s );
```

Within the architecture body **arch**, we cannot refer the attribute of the signal using the notation p'attr. This notation instead refers to the attribute **attr** of the port **p**, which can only be defined in the entity declaration.

In a subprogram call an actual parameter (such as a constant, variable, signal or file) is associated with a formal parameter of the subprogram. If the actual parameter is decorated with an attribute, that attribute information is likewise not carried through to the subprogram. The decoration is purely local to the region in which the actual object is declared.

The Attribute Foreign

While VHDL-AMS provides comprehensive features for modeling the structure and behavior of hardware designs, there remain some tasks for which we need to step outside of the VHDL-AMS domain. For these cases, VHDL-AMS defines the following attribute in the package **std.standard**:

```
attribute foreign : string;
```

We can use the 'foreign attribute to decorate architectures and subprograms. When we do so, the contents of the architecture body or subprogram body are given special treatment by the simulator, using information supplied in the attribute value. VHDL-AMS does not specify what special treatment is applied, leaving that to individual vendors of VHDL-AMS tools. The language simply provides the mechanism for vendors to use to interface to non-VHDL-AMS libraries and tools. We need to consult the documentation provided with each individual VHDL-AMS tool set to find out how the 'foreign attribute is treated. Note that an implementation may restrict the class, mode and type of ports and parameters of entities and subprograms decorated with the 'foreign attribute. Such restrictions may be required to limit the data types and communications mechanisms in an interface to those that are common to the VHDL-AMS tool and the non-VHDL-AMS tools. A vendor's documentation should also describe any such restrictions.

Example   One possible use of the 'foreign attribute is to specify some vendor-specific implementation for an architecture body, for example, an optimized implementation based on acceleration hardware. A vendor might require the architecture to be decorated with the 'foreign attribute as follows:

```
architecture accelerated of and2 is
    attribute foreign of accelerated : architecture is
        "accelerate/function:and_2in/nocheck";
begin
end architecture accelerated;
```

When a design using this architecture is elaborated, the VHDL-AMS simulator notes that the architecture is decorated with the 'foreign attribute and invokes special processing to use the accelerator, rather than elaborating the architecture in the normal way.

Example   The 'foreign attribute might be used to specify that a subprogram is implemented in some language other than VHDL-AMS. Figure 22-22 shows a VHDL-AMS package declaring the procedure **create_window**. The package also decorates the procedure with the 'foreign attribute, specifying that the procedure is implemented in the Ada programming language. Additional information in the attribute string specifies the Ada procedure to use and describes the mapping from the VHDL-AMS procedure parameters to the Ada procedure parameters.

FIGURE 22-22

```
package display_interface is

    ...
```

(continued on page 696)

(continued from page 695)

> **procedure** create_window (size_x, size_y : natural;
>   status : **out** status_type);
>
> **attribute** foreign **of** create_window : **procedure is**
>   "language Ada; with window_operations;" &
>   "bind to window_operations.create_window;" &
>   "parameter size_x maps to size_x : in natural;" &
>   "parameter size_y maps to size_y : in natural;" &
>   "parameter status maps to status : out window_operations.status_type;" &
>   "others map to default";
>
>   ...
>
> **end package** display_interface;

A package that declares a procedure and decorates with the 'foreign attribute.

22.3 **Groups**

The user-defined attribute facility discussed in the previous section allows us to anno-tate individual items in a design with non-structural and non-behavioral information. However, much of the additional information we may need to include can best be expressed as relationships between collections of items, rather than pertaining to in-dividual items. For this reason VHDL-AMS provides a grouping mechanism to identify a collection of items over which some relationship holds. The information about the relationship is expressed as an attribute of the group. In this section we see how to define kinds of groups, to identify particular groups of related items and to specify attributes for particular groups.

The first stage in grouping items is to define a template for the classes of items that can be included in the group. We do this with a *group template declaration,* for which the syntax rule is

> group_template_declaration ⇐
>   **group** identifier **is** (⟨ entity_class ⟦ <> ⟧ ⟩ ⟨ , ₀₀₀ ⟩) ;

A group template declaration lists one or more classes of items, in order, that may constitute a group. Note that the syntax rule uses the term "entity" here in the same way as the rules for attribute specifications, namely, to refer to any kind of item in a design. We discuss the meaning of the "<>" notation shortly. An example of a group template declaration is

> **group** signal_pair **is** (**signal, signal**);

This defines a template for groups consisting of two signals. We can use this template to define a number of groups using *group declarations*. The syntax rule for a group declaration is

> group_declaration ⇐
>   **group** identifier : *group_template*_name
>   (〖 name 〗 character_literal 〗 〖 , ₀₀₀ 〗) ;

A group declaration names a template to use for the group and lists the items that are to be members of the group. Each item in the list must be of the class specified in the corresponding position in the template. For example, if we have two clock signals in a design, clk_phase1 and clk_phase2, we can group them together using the signal_pair template defined above by writing

> **group** clock_pair : signal_pair (clk_phase1, clk_phase2);

As we mentioned earlier, the main use of groups is as a mechanism for defining relationships between items by decorating a group of items with an attribute. We decorate a group by naming it in an attribute specification, identifying it as an item of class **group**. For example, if we have an attribute declared as

> **attribute** max_skew : time;

we can decorate the clock_pair group with this attribute as follows:

> **attribute** max_skew **of** clock_pair : **group is** 200 ps;

The decoration can be interpreted as an annotation to the design, indicating to a layout tool that the maximum permissible skew between the two signals in the group is 200 ps.

The syntax rule for a group template shows that we may write the box symbol ("<>") after an item class. In fact, we may only include such a class specification once in any template, and it must be in the last position in the list of item classes. It indicates that a group based on that template may have an indefinite number of elements of the given class (including none).

Example We can define a group template for a group representing component instances to be allocated to the same physical package. The members of such a group are the labels of the component instances. The group template declaration is

> **group** component_instances **is** (**label** <>);

We can use the template to create groups of instances:

> **group** U1 : component_instances (nand1, nand2, nand3);
> **group** U2 : component_instances (inv1, inv2);

We can specify what kind of integrated circuit should be used for each group by defining an attribute and using it to decorate the group:

> **attribute** IC_allocation : string;
>
> **attribute** IC_allocation **of** U1 : **group is** "74LS00";
> **attribute** IC_allocation **of** U2 : **group is** "74LS04";

An individual item in a design can belong to more than one group. We simply include its name in the declaration of each group of which it is a member.

Example   We can use groups of signals as the basis for annotating a design entity with port-to-port timing constraints. Suppose we declare a group template port_pair and an attribute max_prop_delay in a package **constraints**:

> **group** port_pair **is** (**signal**, **signal**);
> **attribute** max_prop_delay : time;

We can then use the template to group pairs of ports of an entity and annotate them with constraint attributes, as shown in Figure 22-23. In this entity declaration, the item clock_in is a member of each of the three groups clock_to_out1, clock_to_out2 and clock_to_out3.

FIGURE 22-23

```
library ieee;  use ieee.std_logic_1164.all;
use work.constraints.port_pair, work.constraints.max_prop_delay;
entity clock_buffer is
    port ( clock_in : in std_logic;
            clock_out1, clock_out2, clock_out3 : out std_logic );
    group clock_to_out1 : port_pair ( clock_in, clock_out1 );
    group clock_to_out2 : port_pair ( clock_in, clock_out2 );
    group clock_to_out3 : port_pair ( clock_in, clock_out3 );
    attribute max_prop_delay of clock_to_out1 : group is 2 ns;
    attribute max_prop_delay of clock_to_out2 : group is 2 ns;
    attribute max_prop_delay of clock_to_out3 : group is 2 ns;
end entity clock_buffer;
```

An entity declaration in which group attributes are used to represent timing constraints.

Exercises

1. [● 22.1] Suppose we instantiate the counter entity, described in the example on page 172, in a test bench as follows:

   ```
   dut : entity work.counter(registered)
       port map ( ... );
   ```

   The test bench entity name is **test_bench**, and the architecture body name is **counter_test**. What are the values of the following attributes:

   - val0_reg'path_name in the architecture **registered** of **counter**,

   - bit0'path_name in the instance val1_reg of the **struct** architecture body of **reg4** and

   - clr'path_name in the instance **bit2** of the **behavioral** architecture body of edge_triggered_Dff, in the instance val1_reg?

   What are the values of the 'instance_name attributes of the same items?

2. [● 22.2] Given a physical type capacitance, declared as

   ```
   type capacitance is range 0 to integer'high
       units pF;
       end units capacitance;
   ```

   write an attribute declaration that represents a capacitive load and an attribute specification that decorates a signal d_in with a load of 3 pF.

3. [● 22.2] Write a physical type declaration for areas, with a primary unit of μm^2. Write an appropriate attribute declaration and specification to decorate an architecture body **library_cell** of an entity **and3** with an area of 15 μm^2.

4. [● 22.2] Given an attribute declared as

   ```
   attribute optimization : string;
   ```

   decorate the following procedure with the attribute value "inline". Assume that another overloaded version of the procedure, which must not be decorated, is visible.

   ```
   procedure test_empty ( variable list : in list_ptr; is_empty : out boolean ) is ...
   ```

5. [● 22.2] Augment the following architecture body to decorate it with the 'foreign attribute, having the value "control_unit.o control_utilities.o".

   ```
   architecture c_implementation of control_unit is
   begin
   end architecture c_implementation;
   ```

6. [● 22.3] Define a group template that allows two or more statement labels as members. Next, declare a group that includes the labels of the following two statements:

step_1 : a := b * c + k;
step_2 : n := a + 4 * j;

Then, write an attribute specification that decorates the group with the attribute resource_allocation having the value max_sharing.

7. [❷ 22.1] Since the definition in the VHDL *Language Reference Manual* of the 'path_name and 'instance_name attributes of items declared within packages is ambiguous, different simulators may produce different results. Construct some small examples, such as those shown in Section 22.1, and experiment with your simulator to see how it constructs values for these attributes.

8. [❷ 22.1] Develop an edge-triggered register model that includes generics for setup and hold times in its entity interface and that reports an assertion violation if the timing constraints are not met. The message reported should include the full instance name of the entity instance in which the violation occurs.

9. [❷ 22.2] Write an entity interface that describes a 74x138 three-to-eight decoder. Include an attribute declaration and attribute specifications to decorate the ports with pin-number information for the package shown in Figure 22-24.

10. [❷ 22.3] Write an entity interface for an and-or-invert gate that implements the following function:

$$z = \overline{a_1 \cdot a_2 \cdot a_3 + b_1 \cdot b_2 \cdot b_3}$$

Since the "and" function is commutative and associative, a layout tool should be able to permute the connections within each of the groups a_1, a_2, a_3 and b_1, b_2, b_3 without affecting the function performed by the circuit. Include in the entity interface of the and-or-invert gate a group template declaration and group declarations that encompass ports among which connections may be permuted.

FIGURE 22-24

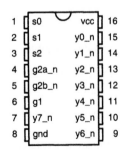

A package for a 74x138 decoder.

11. [❸ 22.2] Check the documentation for your simulator to see if it makes use of the 'foreign attribute on subprograms or architecture bodies. If it does, experiment to verify that you can use the facilities it provides. For example, if the simulator uses the 'foreign attribute as a means of specifying an implementation in a non-VHDL-AMS programming language, try writing a small procedure or function in the programming language to interact with a simulation model.

12. [❹ 22.2] If your simulator allows you to call functions written in the programming language C, develop a register model that uses the graphical display libraries of your host computer system to create a pop-up window to display the register contents. Instantiate the register model in a test bench, and step through the simulation to verify that the model creates and updates the display.

chapter twenty-three

Case Study 4: Communication System

With a contribution by Tom Egel,
Mentor Graphics Corporation

The purpose of the communication block is to transmit the encoded rudder and throttle commands to the airplane using frequency modulation (FM) techniques. This block constitutes both the ground-based transmitter and the in-flight receiver communication electronics. The key component in any communication system is the detector. In this case study, we consider two common detector architectures.

23.1 **Communication System Overview**

The RF communication system for the RC airplane is outlined by the dashed box in the system diagram in Figure 23-1. The main purpose of this block is to manipulate the digital bitstream so that it can be transmitted and received across the desired radio frequency channel. The RF block produces an output bitstream identical to the input bitstream under normal operation. The output bitstream is asynchronous with respect to the otherwise synchronous receiver electronics.

Figure 23-2, from [34], shows a basic model for a complete communication system. In a typical communication system, the source and destination are non-electrical. In the RC airplane, for example, the source is the joystick control and the destination is the rudder movement. As we saw in the first case study in Chapter 8, two transducers convert the source information (namely, joystick movements) into electrical signals. These signals are then encoded and multiplexed into a single digital bitstream. The bitstream is modulated onto a high-frequency carrier so that it can be transmitted across the RF link forming the communication channel. Once received,

FIGURE 23-1

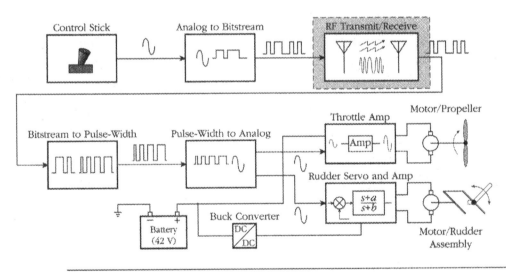

RC airplane system diagram with RF communication block highlighted.

FIGURE 23-2

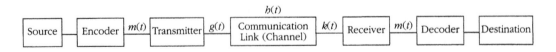

Basic communication system model.

the carrier is demodulated to reproduce the bitstream, then demultiplexed and decoded to derive electrical signals to control throttle and rudder movement. In this case study we concentrate on the modulator in the transmitter and the detector in the receiver.

The transmitted signal in an RF communication system is typically a high-frequency carrier signal modulated by the baseband signal containing the information. Modulation is the process of varying an otherwise purely sinusoidal RF carrier frequency in some way to transmit information. The common methods for doing this are amplitude modulation (AM) and frequency modulation (FM). As their names suggest, the baseband signal is superimposed on the carrier signal by varying its amplitude or frequency, respectively.

In traditional AM and FM radio broadcasting techniques the baseband signal is analog. This is sufficient when the broadcasting stations are physically far apart and is thus suitable for radio broadcasting. For more recent wireless applications, signals are transmitted over short distances and bandwidth is shared among many users using a variety of multiplexing techniques. Digital modulation techniques are widely used for these applications and offer many advantages over analog modulation. For a more complete study on communication system theory and design, see Razavi [33], Best [5] and Read [34].

23.2 **Frequency Shift Keying**

The input to the communication block in this case study is the digital bitstream of 6000 to 7000 bits/s from the encoder block described in Chapter 8. The digital nature of this baseband signal allows us to use a modulation technique called *keying*. Specifically, we use *binary frequency shift keying* (BFSK, or alternatively just FSK). BFSK modulation is the digital counterpart to FM. The binary baseband signal varies the frequency of the carrier signal by switching between two different carrier frequencies corresponding to the binary values 0 and 1. This composite high-frequency signal can then be transmitted as a radio wave and demodulated by the receiver, where the original information can be recovered.

A simple VHDL-AMS model that implements the BFSK technique is shown in Figure 23-3. The generics fc and delta_f specify the carrier frequency and the frequency change as the digital input changes between 0 and 1. In the architecture body, the constants wc and delta_w represent the frequencies in radians per second. The simultaneous if statement switches the derivative of the output phase between the two frequencies. Thus, the phase increases monotonically at a rate determined by the selected frequency. The simultaneous statement at the end of the architecture body converts the increasing phase into a sinusoidal voltage.

Figure 23-4 shows the simulation results for fc and delta_f both having the value 25 kHz. The FSK output is a signal that switches between two frequencies. When the bitstream input is '0', the output frequency is 25 kHz, and when the bitstream is '1', the output frequency jumps up to 50 kHz.

We chose these relatively low frequencies so that operation could be easily visualized in a time domain simulation. More typically, the carrier frequencies are much

FIGURE 23-3

```
library ieee, ieee_proposed;
use ieee_proposed.electrical_systems.all;
use ieee.std_logic_1164.all;
use ieee.math_real.all;

entity bfsk is
    generic ( fc : real := 1.0e6;          -- mean carrier frequency
              delta_f : real := 5.0e3;     -- difference between low and high
                                           --  carrier frequencies

              amp : voltage := 1.0;        -- amplitude of modulated signal
              offset : voltage := 0.0 );   -- output offset voltage
    port ( signal d_in : in std_logic;     -- digital input
           terminal a_out : electrical );  -- output terminal
end entity bfsk;
```

```
architecture behavioral of bfsk is
    quantity vout across iout through a_out;   -- output branch
    quantity phi : real;                       -- free quantity angle in radians
    constant wc : real := math_2_pi * fc;      -- convert fc to rad/s
    constant delta_w : real := math_2_pi * delta_f;   -- convert delta_f to rad/s
begin
    if To_X01(d_in) = '0' use
        phi'dot == wc;                     -- set to carrier frequency
    elsif To_X01(d_in) = '1' use
        phi'dot == wc + delta_w;           -- set to carrier frequency + delta
    else
        phi'dot == 0.0;
    end use;

    break on d_in;

    vout == offset + amp * sin(phi);       -- create sinusoidal output using phi
end architecture behavioral;
```

Model of a BFSK modulator.

higher and the difference between them relatively small, making the frequency change undetectable by inspection of the time domain response waveform. For these high frequencies, we can write a test-bench model to measure the frequency of the FSK output and report it as a numerical result. An example of such a model is shown in Figure 23-5. The key to this model is the **detect** process, which uses the **'above** attribute to detect when an analog signal crosses a specified threshold and trigger a digital event. The process measures the time interval between successive threshold crossings and outputs the reciprocal of the interval as the measured frequency.

FIGURE 23-4

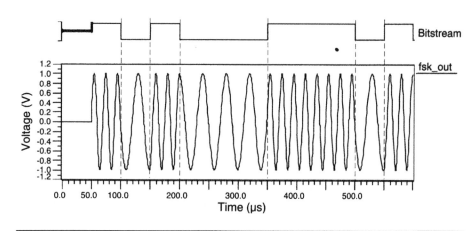

Simulation results of BFSK modulator with a bitstream input.

FIGURE 23-5

```
library ieee_proposed;  use ieee_proposed.electrical_systems.all;
entity MeasFreq is
    generic ( thres : real := 0.0 );
    port ( terminal input : electrical;
            signal f_out : out real := 0.0 );
end entity MeasFreq;
```

```
architecture ThresDetect of MeasFreq is
    quantity vin across input;
begin
    detect : process ( vin'above(thres) ) is
        variable t_old : real := real'low;
    begin
        if vin'above(thres) then
            f_out <= 1.0 / (now – t_old);
            t_old := now;
        end if;
    end process detect;
end ThresDetect;
```

Model to measure the frequency of an electrical voltage.

The simulation results for the FSK modulator with the measurement model added are shown in Figure 23-6. For this simulation, we set the carrier frequency to 455 kHz and the delta frequency to 5 kHz. These values are reflected in the output of the frequency measurement model. The rationale for this choice of frequencies will become apparent in the following sections.

23.3 FSK Detection

The carrier frequency used to transmit the information in an RC airplane system is typically around 72 MHz with a delta frequency of 5 kHz. At these high frequencies, it is difficult to design circuitry to produce a clean amplified signal at the receiver. Hence we usually down convert this frequency to an intermediate frequency (IF) of 455 kHz, maintaining the same 5 kHz delta frequency. (Real RC systems actually perform two-stage down conversion with the first IF at 10.7 MHz.) To keep the time domain simulation times reasonably short, we will forgo simulation at 72 MHz and instead program the FSK model to output at the 455 kHz IF frequency, as shown in Figure 23-6.

The next task is to design a detection mechanism to recover the original bitstream from the BFSK output signal. The frequencies at which the system operates, along with the bandwidth requirements, play a role in deciding which architecture is the best. Here we will explore two possible architectures: a non-coherent detector and a phase-locked loop detector. We will develop models at a high level of abstraction using the behavioral modeling features of VHDL-AMS. Then, in the next section, we

FIGURE 23-6

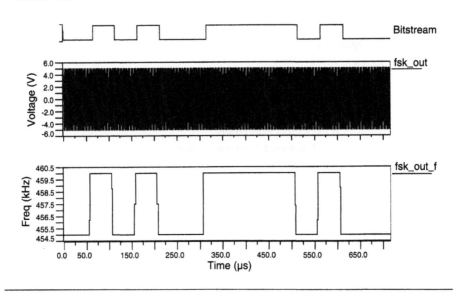

Simulation results for the FSK detector with frequency measurement.

will compare the two architectures to decide which to refine to a more detailed design. This "top-down" approach allows us to begin analysis early in the design flow and to explore alternatives with minimal effort. The key to the approach is to include just the relevant information in our abstract behavioral models to allow us to perform the required analysis. Once we have selected an architecture, we can then add detail to the behavioral model or develop a structural model corresponding to a circuit.

Non-Coherent Detection

One common method for detecting, or demodulating, an FSK signal is non-coherent detection. Unlike coherent detection, which requires phase synchronization between the carrier and the oscillator in the receiver, non-coherent detection can be achieved by much simpler means, although with some sacrifice in the bit-error rate. A block diagram of a non-coherent detector is shown in Figure 23-7. We can think of the FSK signal as two on-off keyed (OOK) signals, each with a different carrier frequency. Each OOK signal is selected using a band-pass filter centered on the carrier frequencies (455 kHz or 460 kHz). The filter outputs are connected to envelope detectors, and the resulting signals subtracted to recover the original baseband data.

Figure 23-8 shows a behavioral model of the band-pass filter implemented using the 'ltf attribute. The transfer function is

$$\frac{v_{out}}{v_{in}} = K \times \frac{\omega_0 s}{s^2 + \dfrac{\omega_0}{Q}s + \omega_0^2}$$

FIGURE 23-7

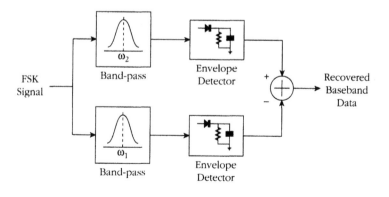

Block diagram of a non-coherent FSK detector.

FIGURE 23-8

```
library ieee;  use ieee.math_real.all;
library ieee_proposed;  use ieee_proposed.electrical_systems.all;
entity v_BPF is
        generic ( k : real := 1.0;        -- filter gain
                  fo : real := 100.0e3;   -- center frequency [Hz]
                  q : real := 0.707 );    -- quality factor
        port ( terminal input: electrical;
               terminal output : electrical );
end entity v_BPF;
--------------------------------------------------------------

architecture behavioral of v_BPF is
        quantity vin across input;
        quantity vout across iout through output;
        constant wo : real := math_2_pi * fo;      -- frequency in radians
        constant num : real_vector := (0.0, wo);   -- numerator array
        constant den : real_vector := (wo * wo, wo / q, 1.0);   -- denominator array
begin
        vout == k * vin'ltf(num, den);   -- Laplace transform of output
end architecture behavioral;
```

Band-pass filter model implemented using the 'lft attribute.

The summing junction is also implemented as a behavioral model, as shown in Figure 23-9. We combine these models with a structural implementation of the envelope detector, consisting of instances of a diode, capacitor and resistor, to form a complete FSK detector.

FIGURE 23-9

```
library IEEE_proposed;  use IEEE_proposed.electrical_systems.all;
entity v_Sum is
        generic ( k1 : real := 1.0;
                  k2 : real := -1.0 );
        port ( terminal in1, in2 : electrical;
               terminal output : electrical );
end entity v_Sum;
--------------------------------------------------------------

architecture behavioral of v_Sum is
```

```
    quantity vin1 across in1 to electrical_ref;
    quantity vin2 across in2 to electrical_ref;
    quantity vout across iout through output to electrical_ref;
begin
    vout == k1 * vin1 + k2 * vin2;
end architecture behavioral;
```

Implementation of the summing junction.

The simulation results in Figure 23-10 show the original bitstream, the FSK frequency measurement, the filter output and the successfully recovered baseband data. Because of the small frequency change (5 kHz) relative to the carrier (455 kHz), the output of the detector must be amplified and filtered in order to recover the original signal data (filter_out). Exercise 8 at the end of this chapter involves design of a behavioral threshold detector using the 'above attribute to generate a digital output.

Phase-Locked Loop Detection

Phase-locked loops (PLLs) have many applications in the communications world. The main purpose of a PLL circuit is to synchronize an output oscillator signal with a reference signal. When the phase difference between the two signals is zero, the system is "locked." A PLL is a closed-loop system with a control mechanism to reduce any phase error that may occur. Figure 23-11 shows a block diagram of a PLL.

FIGURE 23-10

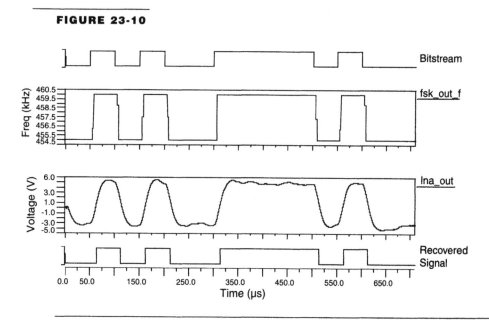

Simulation results of non-coherent FSK detector.

FIGURE 23-11

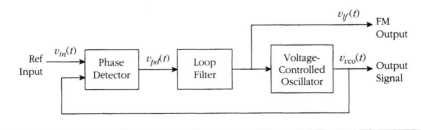

Block diagram of a PLL.

We can readily model a PLL at this level in VHDL-AMS. We implement the phase detector as an analog multiplier, the loop filter as a lag block and the VCO as a gain block whose output frequency is determined by the following relationship:

$$f_{vco}(t) = f_c + K_v v_{lf}(t) \tag{23-1}$$

where f_c is the center frequency of the VCO output signal, $v_{lf}(t)$ is the output of the loop filter and K_v is the VCO gain in units of Hz/V.

A VHDL-AMS model of a PLL is shown in Figure 23-12. Here the individual functions for each block within the PLL are combined into a single high-level behavioral model. The phase detector multiplies the reference input and the VCO output, the loop filter is implemented using the 'ltf attribute, and the VCO generates a sinusoidal output whose frequency is determined according to Equation 23-1. A high-level model such as this is useful for performing quick simulations and confirming theory, but is limited in detail. Exercise 12 involves refinement of the PLL design by modeling each of the blocks in Figure 23-11 separately.

FIGURE 23-12

```
library ieee_proposed;  use ieee_proposed.electrical_systems.all;
library ieee;  use ieee.math_real.all;

entity PLL is
        generic ( Fp : real := 20.0e3;      -- loop filter pole freq [Hz]
                  Fz : real := 1.0e6;       -- loop filter zero freq [Hz]
                  Kv : real := 100.0e3;     -- VCO gain [Hz/V]
                  Fc : real := 1.0e6 );     -- VCO center freq [Hz]
        port ( terminal input, lf_out, vco_out : electrical );
end entity PLL;
```

```
architecture behavioral of PLL is
```

```
quantity v_in across input to electrical_ref;
quantity v_lf across i_lf through lf_out to electrical_ref;
quantity v_vco across i_vco through vco_out to electrical_ref;

-- internal quantities and constants
-- multiplier
quantity mult : real;

-- loop filter (Lag)
constant wp : real  := math_2_pi * fp;              -- pole freq in rad/s
constant wz : real  := math_2_pi * fz;              -- zero freq in rad/s
constant num : real_vector := (1.0, 1.0 / wz);      -- numerator array
constant den : real_vector := (1.0, 1.0 / wp);      -- denominator array

-- VCO
quantity phi : real;                                -- used in VCO equation
constant Kv_w: real := math_2_pi * Kv;              -- change gain to (rad/s)/V
constant wc : real := math_2_pi * Fc;              -- change freq to rad/s

begin
    if domain = quiescent_domain use
        phi == 0.0;                                 -- initialize phi
    else
        phi'dot == wc + Kv_w * (v_lf);              -- calculate VCO frequency
    end use;

    mult == v_in * v_vco;                           -- multiplier output

    v_lf == mult'ltf(num, den);                     -- loop filter output

    v_vco == cos(phi);                              -- VCO output

end architecture behavioral;
```

VHDL-AMS model of a PLL.

Before integrating the PLL model with the rest of the system, we create a test bench to ensure the PLL performs as expected. One way to test it is to sweep the input over a range of frequencies and see how well the output tracks the input. For this we need a swept sine wave voltage source (see Exercise 13) and the frequency measurement model from Figure 23-5. The simulation results of such a test bench are shown in Figure 23-13. The reference input is a sinusoid whose frequency starts at 900 kHz and is swept to 1.1 MHz. The waveforms demonstrate that the PLL is able to lock onto and track the frequency of the reference input.

We now turn to the use of a PLL as a frequency detector. In our communication system, we connect the BFSK output from the model in Figure 23-3 to the PLL reference input. When the frequency of this reference signal is equal to the VCO output, the DC component of the resulting error signal (phase detector output) is zero. When the BFSK signal deviates above or below the VCO center frequency (455 kHz), the DC term of the error signal increases or decreases, respectively. The loop filter removes the unwanted high-frequency components of the error signals. The output of the loop

FIGURE 23-13

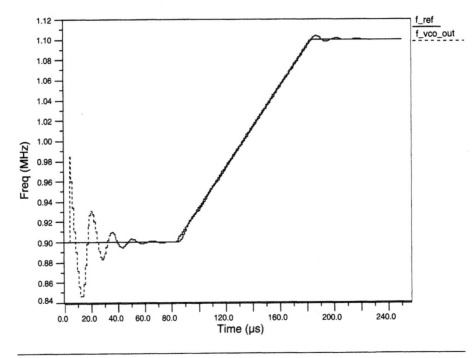

PLL simulation results.

filter ($v_{lf}(t)$ in Figure 23-11) is used to control the output frequency of the VCO and serves as the demodulated output of the PLL FM detector.

The simulation results in Figure 23-14 illustrate the operation of this detector. The waveforms include the original bitstream along with the frequency of the BFSK output (bfsk_out_f). We see that the VCO output frequency (vco_out_f) output does indeed track the BFSK signal, and that the loop filter output (lf_out) contains information related to the original bitstream. Passing the filter output through a gain block and second low-pass filter stage (lpf_out) allows us to recover the signal using threshold detection.

23.4 **Trade-Off Study**

In the previous section we examined two architectures that, at a high level, appear to be suitable for detecting the original digital bitstream used to modulate the command signals. The next step in the top-down design process is to determine which architecture is the best for our application and to examine any design trade-offs. We use VHDL-AMS in the top-down design methodology to help us make architectural design decisions prior to committing to hardware.

FIGURE 23-14

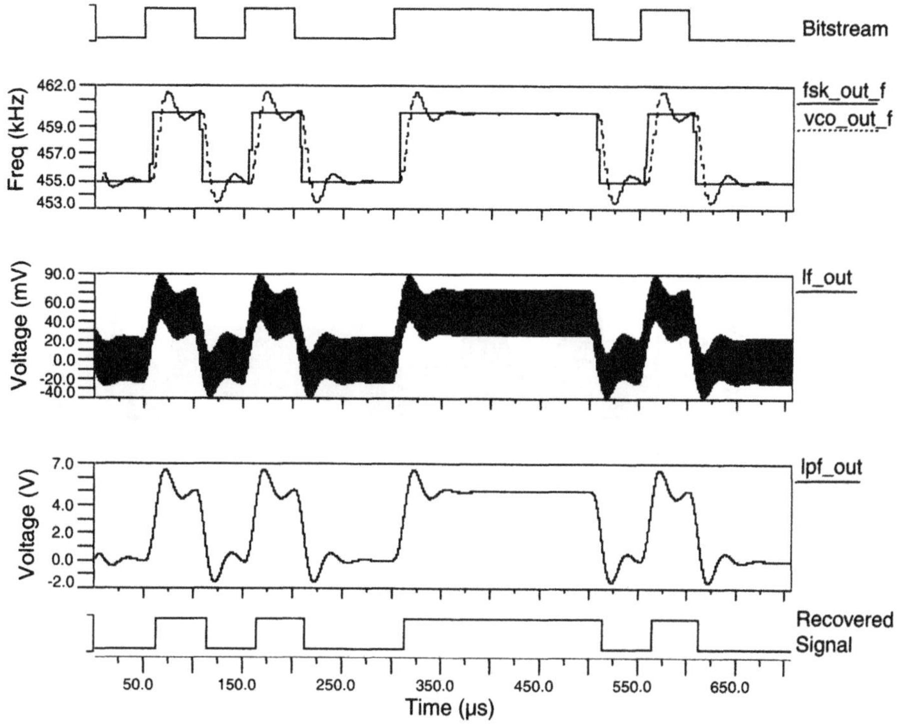

Simulation results with PLL as a frequency detector.

If we examine the simulation results for the non-coherent detector more closely, we see that the signal at the output of the summing junction of Figure 23-7 is quite small. The output signal is **sum_out**, shown in Figure 23-15. Consequently, we require a high-gain block and a high-Q filter to successfully recover the signal. The reason for the low signal level is the small delta frequency (5 kHz) compared to the carrier (455 kHz). We could improve the design in several ways. We could use higher Q band-pass filters to improve the rejection of the unwanted frequencies. Alternatively (or in addition), we could down-convert the incoming signal to a lower frequency to relax the overall filter requirements.

The FM output of the PLL, on the other hand, is a much "cleaner" signal and is less susceptible to noise. (See the signal **pll_lf_out** in Figure 23-15.) It still needs some amplification and filtering, but the requirements are much less stringent than for the non-coherent detector. Since the PLL detector is a closed-loop system, it also requires some settling time, both initially as well as when switching between frequencies. Using the high-level VHDL-AMS model, we can adjust the internal loop filter and VCO gain to obtain the desired response.

The communication system described here is far from complete, but does serve to illustrate the design process. Once we have determined the appropriate detector architecture, the next step would be to proceed with the detailed design. The intent

FIGURE 23-15

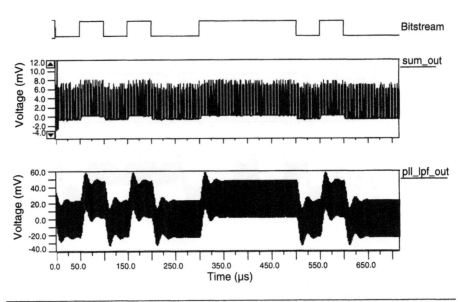

Comparison of the non-coherent and PLL detector outputs.

here, however, was to show how we can quickly create behavioral models and use them to make high-level design decisions. Our models for the BFSK modulator, filters, summing block and a PLL are simple but effective for a comparison of the two detector topologies.

Exercises

1. [**❶** 23.1] What is modulation and how is it used in communication systems?

2. [**❶** 23.1] What is the difference between analog and digital modulation?

3. [**❶** 23.2] Briefly describe FSK modulation.

4. [**❶** 23.3] Briefly describe how a phase-locked loop circuit can be used as a frequency detector.

5. [**❶** 23.3] Give two advantages for using a behavioral (equation-based) model for the PLL instead of a circuit-level implementation.

6. [**❷** 23.2] Modify the BFSK model in Figure 23-3 so that the output frequency is fc ± delta_f.

7. [**❷** 23.3] Create a low-pass filter block with the transfer function

$$\frac{v_{out}}{v_{in}} = K \times \frac{\omega_p^2}{s^2 + \frac{\omega_p}{Q}s + \omega_p^2}$$

that amplifies and filters the output of the non-coherent detector shown in Figure 23-7. Set the gain to 10,000 and f_p to 20 kHz.

8. [❷ 23.3] Create a threshold detector that uses the 'above attribute to convert the analog outputs of the two detector topologies to a digital bitstream.

9. [❸ 23.2] Develop a behavioral model for a QPSK (quadrature phase shift keying) modulator that uses the equation

$$x(t) = b_m \cos\omega_c t - b_{m+1}\sin\omega_c t$$

where ω_c is the carrier frequency, and b_m and b_{m+1} are the values of consecutive digital bits. Design the modulator so that the modulated signal has four distinct phase states generated from two consecutive bits of a digital input bitstream. Use the following Grey code mapping scheme:

'00' → −135°, '01' → +135°, '11' → +45°, '10' → −45°

10. [❸ 23.2] Develop models for a serial-to-parallel converter, a multiplier and a difference block to create the quadrature-modulation circuit design in Figure 23-16.

11. [❸ 23.3] Develop a VHDL-AMS model to generate the I (in-phase) and Q (quadrature) components of an RF signal as shown in Figure 23-17.

12. [❸ 23.3] Create models for the individual blocks within the PLL model in Figure 23-12 (the phase detector, loop filter and VCO).

FIGURE 23·16

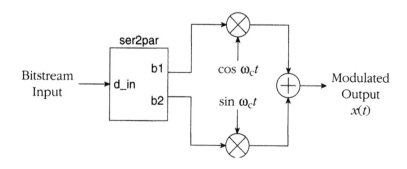

Quadrature modulation.

FIGURE 23-17

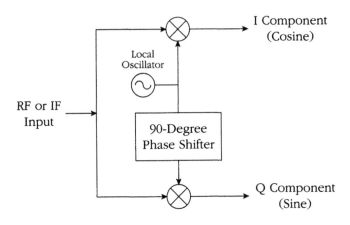

I/Q signal generator.

13. [❸ 23.3] Create a model for a sinusoidal voltage source with generics to sweep the frequency over a specified range at a specified sweep rate and use this to test the PLL model in Exercise 12.

14. [❹ 23.2] Expand the original binary FSK modulator described in this case study to be a multilevel (*M*-ary) FSK system with orthogonal signaling. As described by Bateman [3], to make the signals orthogonal, they should be of the form

$$x(t) = \cos\left(2\pi f_c t + \frac{2\pi m t}{2T_s}\right)$$

where *m* = 1, 2, ..., *M*. For *M*-ary signaling, the number of symbol states (*M*) is determined by the number of bits (*n*) as follows: $M = 2^n$.

15. [❹ 23.4] Develop a model that utilizes amplitude shift keying (ASK) modulation of a baseband signal. Develop a detector model with two architectures, coherent and non-coherent. Use simulation to show how the coherent detector provides superior noise immunity.

chapter twenty-four

Miscellaneous Topics

In the preceding chapters we have introduced most of the facilities provided by VHDL-AMS and shown how they may be used to model a variety of hardware systems at various levels of detail. However, there remain a few VHDL-AMS facilities that we have not yet discussed. In this chapter, we tie off these loose ends.

24.1 **Buffer and Linkage Ports**

When we introduced ports in Chapter 5, we identified three modes, **in**, **out** and **inout**, that control how data is passed to and from a design entity. VHDL-AMS provides two further modes, **buffer** and **linkage**. These modes may only be specified for ports of entities, blocks and components, not for generic constants or subprogram parameters.

A **buffer** mode port behaves in a similar way to an **inout** mode port, in that the port can be both read and assigned in the entity or block. The source of a **buffer** port determines the driving value of the port in the normal way. However, when the port is read, the value read is the driving value. This behavior differs from **inout** ports in that the value read for an **inout** port may be different from the driving value if the actual signal associated with the port is resolved. The behavior of a **buffer** port allows us to model a design that has a buffered output connection and internally uses the value driving the buffer. In this case we do not explicitly represent the buffer as a component, nor its input as a signal.

Example   We can implement a counter as a string of flipflops, with each stage feeding the next. This form of counter is usually called a "ripple" counter. An entity declaration for a simple 2-bit counter is shown in Figure 24-1. The corresponding architecture body drives the output ports q0 and q1 with the q outputs of the flipflops bit0 and bit1. Ports q0 and q1 are also used as the inputs to the inverters inv0 and inv1. If q0 and q1 were declared as ports of mode **out**, we could not make these internal connections. Since we really want q0 and q1 to be outputs, we declare them to be mode **buffer**, allowing us to read the ports internally as well as treating them as outputs.

FIGURE 24-1

```
entity count2 is
    port ( clk : in bit;  q0, q1 : buffer bit );
end entity count2;
```

```
architecture buffered_outputs of count2 is
    component D_flipflop is
        port ( clk, d : in bit;  q : buffer bit );
    end component D_flipflop;

    component inverter is
        port ( a : in bit;  y : out bit );
    end component inverter;

    signal q0_n, q1_n : bit;
begin
    bit0 : component D_flipflop
        port map ( clk => clk, d => q0_n, q => q0 );
```

```
    inv0 : component inverter
        port map ( a => q0, y => q0_n );
    bit1 : component D_flipflop
        port map ( clk => q0_n, d => q1_n, q => q1 );
    inv1 : component inverter
        port map ( a => q1, y => q1_n );
end architecture buffered_outputs;
```

An entity and architecture body for a 2-bit ripple counter.

At first sight, buffer ports seem to be very useful. However, VHDL-AMS imposes a number of restrictions on how buffer ports may be interconnected with other ports. First, if the actual object associated with a buffer port of a component instance is a port of the enclosing entity, it must also be a buffer port. Second, if we associate a buffer port as an actual object with some formal port of a component instance, the formal port must be of mode **in**, **buffer** or **linkage**. It may not be a port of mode **out**. Thus, the D_flipflop component in Figure 24-1 has a buffer output port. Any flipflop entity bound to the flipflop instances in the counter must also have a buffer output port. Third, a buffer port can only have one source. Hence we cannot resolve a number of sources to determine the value of a buffer port. Finally, while we can associate an actual signal with a buffer port of a component instance, that port must be the only source of the signal. Thus, we cannot use a buffer port of a component as one of a number of contributors to a resolved signal. These restrictions severely limit the uses of buffer ports, so they are not commonly used in practice. VHDL-2001 removes these restrictions, making buffer ports much more useful. Future versions of VHDL-AMS are likely to follow VHDL-2001 in removing the restrictions.

Linkage ports are provided as a means of connecting signals to foreign design entities. If the implementation of an entity is expressed in some language other than VHDL-AMS, the way in which values are generated and read within the entity may not conform to the same transaction semantics as those of VHDL-AMS. A **linkage** mode port provides the point of contact between the non-VHDL-AMS and the VHDL-AMS domains. Unless a simulator provides some additional semantics for generating and reading linkage ports, a model containing linkage ports anywhere in the hierarchy cannot be simulated.

Since the internal operation of a linkage port is not bound by the rules of VHDL-AMS, VHDL-AMS takes the safe approach and considers a linkage port connected to a signal to be both a reader and a source for the signal. Thus, if the linkage port is connected to an actual signal that is a port of an enclosing entity, the actual port cannot be of mode **in** or **out**. It must be a port of mode **inout**, **buffer** or **linkage**. One further restriction is that linkage ports may not have default expressions in their declarations.

One final point to note about linkage ports is that they are deprecated in the current version of the *VHDL Language Reference Manual* and may be removed from the language in subsequent versions. Hence, they may also be removed from the *VHDL-AMS Language Reference Manual*. Thus we should avoid using them in new designs.

24.2 Conversion Functions in Association Lists

In the preceding chapters, we have seen uses of association lists in generic maps, port maps and subprogram calls. An association list associates actual values and objects with formal objects. Let us now look at the full capabilities provided in association lists, shown by the following full syntax rules:

association_list ⟸ ⟨ ⟦ formal_part => ⟧ actual_part ⟩ ⟨ , ⋯ ⟩

formal_part ⟸
    *generic*_name
    ❘ *port*_name
    ❘ *parameter*_name
    ❘ *function*_name (⟨ *generic*_name ❘ *port*_name ❘ *parameter*_name ⟩)
    ❘ type_mark (⟨ *generic*_name ❘ *port*_name ❘ *parameter*_name ⟩)

actual_part ⟸
    expression
    ❘ *signal*_name
    ❘ *variable*_name
    ❘ *quantity*_name
    ❘ *terminal*_name
    ❘ **open**
    ❘ *function*_name (⟨ *signal*_name ❘ *variable*_name ⟩)
    ❘ type_mark (⟨ *signal*_name ❘ *variable*_name ⟩)

The simple rules for association lists we used previously allowed us to write associations of the form "formal => actual". These new rules allow us to write associations such as

```
f1 ( formal ) => actual
formal => f2 ( actual )
f1 ( formal ) => f2 ( actual )
```

These associations include *conversion functions* or *type conversions*. We discussed type conversions in Chapter 2. They allow us to convert a value from one type to another closely related type. A conversion function, on the other hand, is an explicitly or implicitly declared subprogram or operation. It can be any function with one parameter and can compute its result in any way we choose.

A conversion in the actual part of an association is invoked whenever a value is passed from the actual object to the formal object. For a variable-class subprogram parameter, conversion occurs when the subprogram is called. For a signal associated with a port, conversion occurs whenever an updated signal value is passed to the port.

For a quantity associated with a port, conversion occurs whenever an updated quantity value is passed to the port. For constant-class subprogram parameters and for generic constants, the actual values are expressions, which may directly take the form of function calls or type conversions. In these cases, the conversion is not considered to be part of the association list; instead, it is part of the expression. Conversions are not allowed in the remaining cases, namely, signal-class and file-class actual subprogram parameters and terminals associated with terminal ports.

Example   We wish to implement a limit checker, which checks whether a signed integer is out of specified bounds. The integer and bounds are represented as standard-logic vectors of the subtype **word**, declared in the package project_util as

> **subtype** word **is** std_logic_vector(31 **downto** 0);

We can use a comparison function that compares integers represented as bit vectors. The function is declared in project_util as

> **function** "<" (bv1, bv2 : bit_vector) **return** boolean;

The entity declaration and architecure body for the limit checker are shown in Figure 24-2. The process performs the comparisons by converting the word values to bit vectors, using the conversion function word_to_bitvector. Note that we cannot use the function **To_bitvector** itself in the actual part of the association list, as it has two parameters, not one. Note also that the result type of the conversion function in this example must be a constrained array type in order to specify the array index range for the actual value passed to the comparison function.

FIGURE 24-2

```
library ieee;  use ieee.std_logic_1164.all;
use work.project_util.all;

entity limit_checker is
    port ( input, lower_bound, upper_bound : in word;
           out_of_bounds : out std_logic );
end entity limit_checker;
```

```
architecture behavioral of limit_checker is
    subtype bv_word is bit_vector(31 downto 0);
    function word_to_bitvector ( w : in word ) return bv_word is
    begin
        return To_bitvector ( w, xmap => '0' );
    end function word_to_bitvector;
```

(continued on page 724)

(continued from page 723)

```
begin
    algorithm : process (input, lower_bound, upper_bound) is
    begin
        if "<" ( bv1 => word_to_bitvector(input),
                bv2 => word_to_bitvector(lower_bound) )
            or "<" ( bv1 => word_to_bitvector(upper_bound),
                    bv2 => word_to_bitvector(input) ) then
            out_of_bounds <= '1';
        else
            out_of_bounds <= '0';
        end if;
    end process algorithm;
end architecture behavioral;
```

An entity and architecture body for a flipflop.

A conversion can only be included in the actual part of an association if the interface object is of mode **in**, **inout** or **linkage**. If the conversion takes the form of a type conversion, it must name a subtype that has the same base type as the formal object and is closely related to the type of the actual object. If the conversion takes the form of a conversion function, the function must have only one parameter of the same type as the actual object and must return a result of the same type as the formal object. If the interface object is of an unconstrained array type, the type mark of the type conversion or the result type of the conversion function must be constrained. The index range of the type mark or function result is used as the index range of the interface object.

A conversion in the formal part of an association is invoked whenever a value is passed from the formal object to the actual object. For a variable-class procedure parameter, conversion occurs when the procedure returns. For a signal associated with a port, conversion occurs whenever the port drives a new value. Conversions are not allowed for signal-class and file-class formal subprogram parameters or for terminal ports.

Example   Suppose a library contains the following entity, which generates a random number at regular intervals:

```
entity random_source is
    generic ( min, max : natural;
              seed : natural;
              interval : delay_length );
    port ( number : out natural );
end entity random_source;
```

If we have a test bench including signals of type **bit**, we can use the entity to generate random stimuli. We use a conversion function to convert the numbers to bit-vector values. An outline of the test bench is shown in Figure 24-3. The function **natural_to_bv11** has a parameter that is a natural number and returns a bit-vector result. The architecture instantiates the **random_source** component, using the conversion function in the formal part of the association between the port and the signal. Each time the component instance generates a new random number, the function is invoked to convert it to a bit vector for assignment to stimulus_vector.

FIGURE 24-3

```
architecture random_test of test_bench is
    subtype bv11 is bit_vector(10 downto 0);
    function natural_to_bv11 ( n : natural ) return bv11 is
        variable result : bv11 := (others => '0');
        variable remaining_digits : natural := n;
    begin
        for index in result'reverse_range loop
            result(index) := bit'val(remaining_digits mod 2);
            remaining_digits := remaining_digits / 2;
            exit when remaining_digits = 0;
        end loop;
        return result;
    end function natural_to_bv11;

    signal stimulus_vector : bv11;
    ...
begin
    stimulus_generator : entity work.random_source
        generic map ( min => 0, max => 2**10 - 1, seed => 0,
                      interval => 100 ns )
        port map ( natural_to_bv11(number) => stimulus_vector );

    ...
end architecture random_test;
```

An outline of a test-bench architecture body, including a random stimulus generator.

The type requirements for conversions included in the formal parts of associations mirror those of conversions in actual parts. A conversion can only be included in a formal part if the interface object is of mode **out**, **inout**, **buffer** or **linkage**. If the conversion takes the form of a type conversion, it must name a subtype that has the same base type as the actual object and is closely related to the type of the formal object.

If the conversion takes the form of a conversion function, the function must have only one parameter of the same type as the formal object and must return a result of the same type as the actual object. If the interface object is of an unconstrained array type, the type mark of the type conversion or the parameter type of the conversion function must be constrained. The index range of the type mark or function parameter is used as the index range of the interface object.

Note that we can include a conversion in both the formal part and the actual part of an association if the interface object is of mode **inout** or **linkage**. The conversion on the actual side is invoked whenever a value is passed from the actual to the formal, and the conversion on the formal side is invoked whenever a value is passed from the formal to the actual.

One important use of type conversions in association lists arises when we mix arrays of unresolved and resolved elements in a model. For example, the standard-logic package declares the two types:

type std_ulogic_vector **is array** (natural **range** <>) **of** std_ulogic;

type std_logic_vector **is array** (natural **range** <>) **of** std_logic;

These are two distinct types, even though the element type of **std_logic_vector** is a subtype of the element type of **std_ulogic_vector**. Thus, we cannot directly associate a **std_ulogic_vector** signal with a **std_logic_vector** port, nor a **std_logic_vector** signal with a **std_ulogic_vector** port. However, we can use type conversions or conversion functions to deal with the type mismatch.

Example   Suppose we are developing a register-transfer-level model of a computer system. The architecture body for the processor is shown in Figure 24-4. We declare a latch component and a ROM component, both with unresolved ports. We also declare a constrained array subtype **std_logic_word** with resolved elements and a number of signals of this subtype representing the internal buses of the processor.

We instantiate the latch component and associate the **destination** bus with the d port and the **source1** bus with the q port. Since the signals and the ports are of different but closely related types, we use type conversions in the association list. Although the types **std_ulogic_vector** and **std_logic_vector** are unconstrained array types, we can name them in the type conversion in this instance, since the component ports are constrained.

FIGURE 24-4

```
architecture rtl of processor is
    component latch is
        generic ( width : positive );
        port ( d : in std_ulogic_vector(0 to width − 1);
               q : out std_ulogic_vector(0 to width − 1);
               ... );
    end component latch;
```

```
    component ROM is
        port ( d_out : out std_ulogic_vector; ... );
    end component ROM;

    subtype std_logic_word is std_logic_vector(0 to 31);

    signal source1, source2, destination : std_logic_word;
        ...

begin

    temp_register : component latch
        generic map ( width => 32 )
        port map ( d => std_ulogic_vector(destination),
                    std_logic_vector(q) => source1, ... );

    constant_ROM : component ROM
        port map ( std_logic_word(d_out) => source2, ... );

        ...

end architecture rtl;
```

An outline of a computer system model using type conversions to associate array signals with array ports.

We also instantiate the ROM component and associate the **source2** bus with the **d_out** port. Here also we use a type conversion in the association list. However, the port **d_out** is of an unconstrained type. Hence we may not use the name std_logic_vector in the type conversion, since it, too, is unconstrained. Instead, we use the constrained subtype name **std_logic_word**. The index range of this subtype is used as the index range of the port **d_out** in the component instance.

24.3 **Postponed Processes**

VHDL-AMS provides a facility, *postponed processes,* that is useful in delta-delay models. A process is made postponed by including the keyword **postponed**, as shown by the full syntax rule for a process:

process_statement ⇐
    ⟦ *process*_label : ⟧
    ⟦ **postponed** ⟧ **process** ⟦ (*signal*_name ⟨ , ⚬⚬⚬ ⟩) ⟧ ⟦ **is** ⟧
        ⟨ process_declarative_item ⟩
    begin
        ⟨ sequential_statement ⟩
    end ⟦ **postponed** ⟧ **process** ⟦ *process*_label ⟧ ;

The difference between a postponed process and a normal process lies in the way in which they are resumed during simulation. In our discussion of the simulation cycle in Chapter 5, we said that a normal process is triggered during a simulation cycle in which one of the signals to which it is sensitive changes value. The process then executes during that same simulation cycle. A postponed process is triggered in the same way, but may not execute in the same cycle. Instead, it waits until the last delta cycle at the current simulation time and executes after all non-postponed processes have suspended. It must wait until the non-postponed processes have suspended in order to ensure that there are no further delta cycles at the current simulation time. In addition, during initialization, a postponed process is started after all normal processes have been started and have suspended.

When we are writing models that use delta delays, we can use postponed processes to describe "steady state" behavior at each simulation time. The normal processes are executed over a series of delta delays, during which signal values are determined incrementally. Then, when all of the signals have settled to their final state at the current simulation time, the postponed processes execute, using these signal values as their input.

Example We can write an entity interface for a set-reset flipflop as shown in Figure 24-5. The entity declaration includes a process that verifies the outputs of the flipflop. Every implementation of the interface is required to produce complementary outputs. (The condition "now = 0 fs" is included to avoid an assertion violation during initialization.)

Figure 24-5 also shows a dataflow architecture of the flipflop. The concurrent signal assignment statements **gate_1** and **gate_2** model an implementation composed of cross-coupled gates. Assume that the flipflop is initally in the reset state. When s_n changes from '1' to '0', **gate_1** is resumed and schedules a change on q from '0' to '1' after a delta delay. In the next simulation cycle, the change on q causes **gate_2** to resume. It schedules a change on q_n from '1' to '0' after a delta delay. During the first delta cycle, q has the new value '1', but q_n still has its initial value of '1'. If we had made the verification process in the entity declaration a non-postponed process, it would be resumed in the first delta cycle and report an assertion violation. Since it is a postponed process, it is not resumed until the second delta cycle (the last delta cycle after the change on s_n), by which time q and q_n have stabilized.

FIGURE 24-5

```
entity SR_flipflop is
    port ( s_n, r_n : in bit;  q, q_n : inout bit );
begin
    postponed process (q, q_n) is
    begin
        assert now = 0 fs or q = not q_n
            report "implementation error: q /= not q_n";
    end postponed process;
end entity SR_flipflop;
```

```
architecture dataflow of SR_flipflop is
begin
    gate_1 : q <= s_n nand q_n;
    gate_2 : q_n <= r_n nand q;
end architecture dataflow;
```

An entity declaration and architecture body for a set-reset flipflop.

It is important to note that the condition that triggers a postponed process may not obtain when the process is finally executed. For example, suppose a signal **s** is updated to the value '1', causing the following postponed process to be triggered:

```
p : postponed process is
    ...
begin
    ...
    wait until s = '1';
    ...        -- s may not be '1'!!
end postponed process p;
```

Because the process is postponed, it is not executed immediately. Instead, some other process may execute, assigning '0' to **s** with delta delay. This assignment causes a delta cycle during which **s** is updated to '0'. When **p** is eventually executed, it proceeds with the statements immediately after the wait statement. However, despite the appearance of the condition in the wait statement, **s** does not have the value '1' at that point.

Since each postponed process waits until the last delta cycle at a given simulation time before executing, there may be several postponed processes triggered by different conditions in different delta cycles, all waiting to execute. Since the cycle in which the postponed processes execute must be the last delta cycle at the current simulation time, the postponed processes must not schedule transactions on signals with delta delay. If they did, they would cause another delta cycle at the current simulation time, meaning that the postponed processes should not have executed. The restriction is required to avoid this paradox.

In previous chapters, we described a number of concurrent statements that are equivalent to similar sequential statements encapsulated in processes. We can write postponed versions of each of these by including the keyword **postponed** at the beginning of the statement, as shown by the following syntax rules:

concurrent_procedure_call_statement ⇐
    ⟦ label : ⟧
    ⟦ **postponed** ⟧ *procedure*_name ⟦ (*parameter*_association_list) ⟧ ;

concurrent_assertion_statement ⇐
   ⟦ label : ⟧
   ⟦ **postponed** ⟧ **assert** *boolean*_expression
                ⟦ **report** expression ⟧ ⟦ **severity** expression ⟧ ;

concurrent_signal_assignment_statement ⇐
   ⟦ label : ⟧ ⟦ **postponed** ⟧ conditional_signal_assignment
   ❘ ⟦ label : ⟧ ⟦ **postponed** ⟧ selected_signal_assignment

Inclusion of the keyword **postponed** simply makes the encapsulating process a postponed process. Thus, we can rewrite the postponed process in the example on page 728 as

postponed assert now = 0 fs **or** q = **not** q_n
   report "implementation error: q /= not q_n";

24.4 Shared Variables

When we introduced variables in Chapter 2, we noted that they can only be declared in processes; hence only one process can access each variable. We have also seen variables declared in subprograms, in which case they are local to the invocation of the subprogram. The reason for these restrictions is to prevent indeterminate results arising from a number of processes accessing a variable in an indeterminate order during a simulation cycle. In some circumstances, however, it is desirable to allow a number of processes to share access to a variable. Either the fact of non-determinacy may be irrelevant, or the use of shared variables may allow a more concise and understandable model. VHDL-AMS provides a mechanism for sharing variables, shown by the full syntax rule for a variable declaration:

variable_declaration ⇐
   ⟦ **shared** ⟧ **variable** identifier ⟨ , ... ⟩ : subtype_indication ⟦ := expression ⟧ ;

If we include the keyword **shared** in a variable declaration, the variables defined are called shared variables and can be accessed by more than one process. We can only declare shared variables in the places in a model where we cannot declare normal variables, namely, in entity declarations and architecture bodies, in block and generate statements and in packages. For example, we might include a shared variable declaration in an architecture body as follows:

architecture instrumented **of** controller **is**

   shared variable operation_count : natural := 0;

   ...

begin

   ...

end architecture instrumented;

The value of a shared variable can be used in an expression in the same way as that of a normal variable. It can be updated using variable assignment statements and can be associated as an actual variable with variable-class subprogram parameters.

The inclusion of shared variables in VHDL-93 was a contentious issue in the development of the language. The initial language specification for shared variables did not define the behavior of concurrent reads and writes to shared variables in the same simulation cycle. For example, difficulties could arise if reads and writes were not performed as atomic operations. It would be possible for one process to write a variable (even a scalar variable) in two separate stages, and for these stages to overlap with a read performed by some other process. Hence the read would not return a predictable value, or even a legal value for the type of the variable. Similarly, concurrent writes by two processes could result in an indeterminate or illegal value being assigned to the variable. For these reasons, the VHDL-93 language specification deemed a model to be in error if it depended on the values of shared variables accessed by more than one process during any simulation cycle. Since VHDL-AMS is based on VHDL-93, the same rule applies in VHDL-AMS.

Provided we restrict access to a shared variable to one process per simulation cycle, modeling using shared variables is safe and deterministic and is similar to using signals to communicate between processes. Access to a shared variable is serialized in simulation time by the simulation algorithm, as simulation cycles occur in a strict non-overlapping order. One such use of shared variables is in instrumenting a model. A shared variable can be used by a number of processes to accumulate information about their collective behavior. While the same effect can be achieved using a signal to hold the data, it may be better to use a variable. Conceptually, a signal represents part of the structure of a design and serves to interconnect modules in the design. Instrumentation, on the other hand, is purely an artifact of the simulation, used to observe the behavior of the system under design. The use of shared variables makes this distinction clearer.

Where the logic of a design does not lead naturally to serialized access to shared variables, we need to enforce serialization explicitly. Our goal is to enforce mutual exclusion between accesses to shared variables from different processes. Mutual exclusion means that each access is allowed to complete without interference from other processes. When one process accesses a shared variable, it excludes accesses from other processes until the first access is complete. While it is possible to encode mutual exclusion algorithms in the current version of VHDL-AMS, we do not investigate this possibility. Instead, we await revision of the VHDL-AMS standard to include the mutual exclusion features provided in the 2001 revision of VHDL. The interested reader should refer to *The Designer's Guide to VHDL* for further information about these features.

Exercises

1. [❶ 24.2] Suppose we wish to associate an **out** mode port of type **std_logic** with a signal of type **bit**. Why can we not use the function **To_bit** as a conversion function in the association?

2. [❶ 24.2] Suppose we have a gate component declared as

    component nand2 **is**
        port (a, b : **in** std_logic; y_n : **out** std_logic);
    end component nand2;

    Write a component instantiation statement that instantiates the gate, with inputs connected to signals **s1** and **s2** and output connected to the signal **s3**. All of the signals are of type **bit**. Use conversion functions where required.

3. [❶ 24.4] Suppose we have a shared variable declared as follows in a package instrumentation:

    shared variable multiply_counter : natural := 0;

    We have two instances, **m1** and **m2**, of a behavioral multiplier model that includes the statement

    instrumentation.multiply_counter := instrumentation.multiply_counter + 1;

    Show how the variable may be updated incorrectly if we allow the two instances to access the variable in the same simulation cycle.

4. [❷ 24.1] Develop a structural model of an SR-flipflop constructed from nor gates as shown in Figure 24-6. Use **buffer** mode ports for q and q_n.

5. [❸ 24.2] Develop a behavioral model of a counter that counts from 0 to 255 with an output port of type **natural**. In a test bench, define and instantiate an 8-bit counter component. Write a configuration declaration for the test bench, binding the behavioral counter entity to the counter component instance. Use conversion functions in the binding indication as required. You may wish to use the conversion functions from the **bv_arithmetic** package described in Chapter 10. Note that a configuration declaration can use items, such as conversion functions, declared in separate packages.

6. [❸ 24.3] Exercise 17 in Chapter 15 describes a distributed priority arbiter for a shared-bus multiprocessor system. Each requester computes the minimum of all priorities. Develop a model of the minimization circuit that operates using delta delays. Include a number of instances of the minimizer in a test bench. Also in-

---

FIGURE 24-6

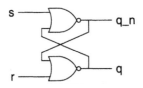

An SR-flipflop constructed from not gates.

clude a process that verifies that the result priority is the minimum of all of the request priorities when the computation is complete.

chapter twenty-five

Integrated System Modeling

The design and verification of analog, mixed-signal and mixed-technology systems can be difficult and complex. The process of top-down design for these types of systems is less straightforward than for digital systems. In this chapter we discuss how to use subsystem models with different abstraction levels to answer system-level questions, make system-level trade-offs, verify system performance and discover problematic interactions. We focus on the design process and the role played by VHDL-AMS models.

25.1 **Top-down Design**

Top-down design methodologies have had a profound impact on digital system design. They allow us to quickly and efficiently specify, design, synthesize and verify designs ready for fabrication. The key to these methodologies is synthesis, which relies on a mapping between the logical functions we use in a design and the physical circuits that realize the functions. Synthesis technology allows us to work at higher levels of abstraction and to delegate physical implementation details to automatic tools.

The number of digital building blocks required for synthesis is relatively small. Most digital designs can be implemented with a handful of basic logical gates (for example, and, or, not, nand, nor and xor gates) and storage devices (for example, registers, flipflops and latches). The same cannot be said for analog, mixed-signal and mixed-technology designs. The building blocks for these design domains are far more numerous and sophisticated. Furthermore, their behavior cannot be captured as readily as that of digital building blocks. Nonetheless, a methodical top-down design approach is appealing.

Unfortunately, analog synthesis technology is very much in its infancy. We do not have comprehensive synthesis tools for every analog, mixed-signal or mixed-technology design domain; however, we do have some tools for specific applications, such as filter design. Such tools are similar to digital synthesis tools in that they start with a function specification of a system, they rely on fixed circuit topologies and building blocks for implementation, they are retargetable to different technologies and the results are verifiable through low-level simulation.

In the absence of general synthesis tools, we must resort to manual design refinement. In this case, a well-ordered top-down design flow is even more important to manage complexity. Figure 25-1 compares a digital design flow based on top-down design and bottom-up verification with a possible flow for analog, mixed-signal and mixed-technology design. (This diagram is derived from work by Pratt [32]. It was originally developed with a focus on mixed-signal IC design, but is extended to cover the design of larger and more diverse systems.) There are many parallels and several significant differences between the two flows. In this chapter, we explore the similarities and differences, discuss the role of VHDL-AMS in each, and illustrate the steps with examples from our RC airplane case studies.

While VHDL-AMS facilitates top-down design, use of the language is not in itself sufficient to guarantee success. Top-down design also depends on proper staffing and work methodologies. The design process described here has many similarities to software development processes. The use of VHDL-AMS is not unlike the use of UML (Universal Modeling Language [15]) for software design and analysis. The suite of test benches for the system model are similar to a set of *use cases* for software analysis. Modern software development *best practices* dictate that certain methodologies increase the likelihood of success. The use of VHDL-AMS can also benefit from these practices.

Modern best practices include such concepts as *configuration management,* where an individual or group manages and controls changes to the design or code. This ensures a stable and predictable environment in which to develop new work, without confusion caused by simultaneous changes made by other developers.

FIGURE 25·1

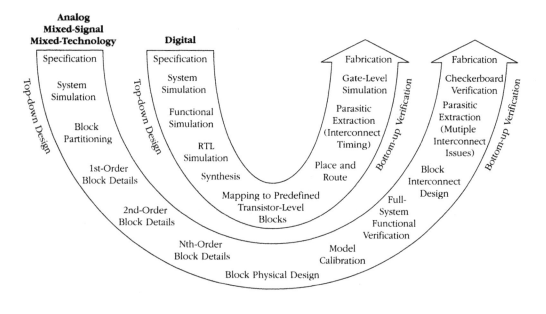

Top-down design for digital versus analog/mixed-signal/mixed-technology.

Configuration management also includes the concept of *revision control,* allowing a historical sequence of design changes to be captured, managed and, if necessary, re-called. Finally, configuration management includes the notion of orderly integration and merging of changes into a carefully controlled main flow of work destined to become the delivered product. Typically, integration is done by a *change control board,* which is a small group of individuals responsible for the final work products.

In software development projects it is common for there to be an individual (or small group) responsible for the overall management of the system architecture. It is their job to be able to answer the top-level system design and implementation questions. For top-down design using VHDL-AMS, it is also helpful to have an individual responsible for the overall architecture and its representation and simulation in VHDL-AMS. The system architect facilitates and coordinates the efforts of all of the developers and can significantly improve everyone's effectiveness.

Software development efforts often employ individuals with specialized skills, such as software builders and quality-assurance engineers. These individuals work with the software developers to integrate components into the system and verify that the system requirements are met. Specialists are also useful in top-down design projects using VHDL-AMS. They can help to integrate the VHDL-AMS models of sub-systems into an overall system model and verify performance using test benches.

25.2 System Specification

The first step of successful product development is a clear definition of the system requirements and a system architecture that implements them. Many projects use informal specification documents. Maintaining such documents as a project evolves can be difficult, particularly in large or complex projects with changing requirements. Furthermore, informal documents are not effective for communicating changes to specifications or for validating designs.

An alternative approach is to use a *system architecture model* as the starting point for a top-down design methodology. The model captures the proposed system structure and functionality and acts as an executable specification. It defines the decomposition of the system into functional blocks and specifies how the blocks are intended to work together. Each block may be hierarchically decomposed down to an appropriate level of detail. VHDL-AMS models can be associated with blocks at any level of the hierarchy, providing a mechanism to explore the system functionality through simulation. Characteristic measurements from the simulation waveforms form quantitative specifications for system performance.

The VHDL-AMS models used at this early stage of development may not have a direct correspondence to physical hardware; capturing the design intent is the highest priority. It is also important for the models to execute as fast as possible, as they may be used for repeated exploration of different topologies, algorithms and design ideas. Therefore, this phase of design may include extensive use of behavioral and transfer function models. More detailed models may be used, of course, if they are available and their performance is adequate.

As the system architecture model stabilizes, a partitioning of the system into blocks that can be physically implemented emerges. The system architecture model evolves into a *system design model*. We discuss partitioning more in Section 25.3. As the design process continues, the individual system blocks are refined, as discussed in Section 25.4. The system design model continues to be the framework upon which the design is refined and validated.

Since the system design model embodies the system requirements, it can be used in the later parts of the design flow for system verification. As detailed designs for blocks are completed, they can be integrated into the system design model. Simulation can then be used to verify that requirements are met using the detailed designs.

An important part of system verification is testing manufactured hardware when it is delivered. While test development may be expensive and time-consuming, it can be a critical factor in determining the success of the product, especially when time-to-market is important [14]. The availability of a system design model provides the test development team valuable insight into the design to be tested and validated. If models of the test equipment are also available, it is possible to create test programs and have them ready to run when the manufactured hardware is available, saving valuable time in getting the product to market.

The case studies in this book describe a mixed-signal, mixed-technology system that must meet a variety of requirements. The top-level description of this system and its requirements are reviewed in Chapter 26. In this book, for the purpose of progressively illustrating language concepts, we have developed each block of the RC airplane design assuming that the requirements for each block are well defined. In reality, the block requirements were determined from the system architecture model and the analyses performed on it.

Figure 25-2 shows the airplane system architecture diagram, which, together with the top-level behavioral models for each block, constitutes the system architecture model. The model allows us to analyze the overall functionality of the system.

25.3 **Partitioning the System**

Once we have developed the system architecture model, we can divide the system into partitions that can be assigned to individuals or design teams for further refinement. Partitioning the design has many benefits. It provides a methodical process for conducting development in parallel, which is particularly important for large projects. It also helps identify opportunities to reuse existing designs and to create reusable designs for the future.

If the blocks of a system are to be designed in parallel, it is very important that the interfaces between the blocks be well defined; otherwise integration of the blocks will be difficult. Interface definition is aided by an evolving system design model, based on the system architecture model with design detail added as it becomes available. The system design model and the simulation test cases that exercise it provide the context that enables independent development of blocks. Each team can plug their design work into the model and receive feedback without the delay or potential oversights that come with "paper" design reviews.

VHDL-AMS provides strongly typed interface constructs that ensure clarity in the interface specifications. The test benches that accompany the system model make

FIGURE 25-2

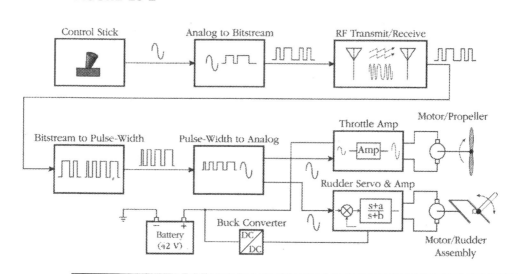

Schematic diagram for the RC airplane system architecture model.

interface "misunderstandings" evident during simulations. Sometimes detailed design work leads to discovery of problems that require changes to the interfaces or even to the architecture of the system. The VHDL-AMS system design model provides the framework for negotiating, communicating and implementing such changes.

Partitioning decisions often reflect the composition of the design organization. Different parts of the organization may specialize in different disciplines, such as analog, RF, digital or mechanical design. Partitioning may also reflect geographic distribution in the organization or the use of subcontractors. In all of these cases, a system design model helps the different teams communicate and develop a better understanding of how the system works, the role of their particular component and the opportunities for improving overall system performance and reducing costs.

VHDL-AMS, with its distinct entity declarations and library mechanisms, facilitates encapsulation of portions of a design for reuse in other designs. The language also provides clean mechanisms for replacing portions of a system with new technology when it becomes available.

In the RC airplane case studies, we divided the system into four partitions, one per case study chapter:

- mixed-signal data path,
- electromechanical control and control-surface positioning,
- power conversion and
- RF communications channel.

We chose these partitions to allow detailed analysis in each of the design disciplines. While the disciplines are separate, the blocks themselves have significant interactions. The system design model continues to be the means to allow the block designers to communicate the implications of their design decisions, even if the designers are not aware of the implications. The final case study in Chapter 26 deals with the system model that pulls the partitions together into an integrated system.

25.4 Refining the Design

Once the basic blocks of the system are defined, they can be explored and designed in detail, resulting in the information needed for the physical implementation of the blocks. Interconnect between the blocks may still be considered ideal at this point, unless knowledge of key interconnect issues already exists. Work on individual blocks can be validated using the system design model.

Refining the design of a block involves the addition of models that provide progressively more information about the block. This is the stage where design trade-offs are typically made. Concrete decisions are made that ultimately allow the design to be manufactured. Design decisions are tested, first in the narrow context of the block alone and then in the larger context of the system model. Decisions can take many forms. A schematic might be edited to make circuit design changes, component substitutions or component value changes. Equations in an analog model or logic in a digital model might be edited to change an algorithm. An entirely new model might be created, representing adoption of a new approach to implementation of the block. All of these changes are manifest in revisions to models, whether automatically generated by tools or by manual editing of model text. The changes may also result in additions to the test bench suite, allowing subsequent changes to be tested, evaluated and verified. Such tests that apply to individual block models are similar to *unit tests* described in software development processes.

The changes resulting from design decisions, as they are approved, are added to the system model. New VHDL-AMS architectures are added beside the existing architectures for entities already in the model. New entities and architectures are also added to the model hierarchy. The system architect can use the new models throughout the development process to track progress of the design. The architect can also create and document representative configurations of the system design model to facilitate communication of design information. Individual design teams should be able to select and use the configurations at a high level, without having to understand the details of each block design.

The process of successive refinement, with frequent integration and validation, continues until the bottom-level model is reached. A physical implementation can be generated from this model. In an analog IC design, the bottom-level model may be a transistor-level circuit schematic, from which the IC layout proceeds. For digital IC design, the process is more automated, with synthesis tools processing register-transfer-level models to assemble the physical design from prevalidated physical layout blocks. For a PCB design, the system schematic, with connectivity and a bill of materials (BOM), is sufficient to begin the process of board layout. Similarly, for an automotive fuel injection system, a BOM and the system connectivity (including electronic and plumbing connectivity) are sufficient to proceed to physical layout of the system.

In each of these scenarios, the physical design of a block is represented by a model, either created by the designer or automatically generated. Physical models are the lowest, most detailed models added to the hierarchy of the system design model. Lower-level models may exist, but only to generate or calibrate the physical model. Since the physical model is the closest to the final implementation, it is the natural place to represent manufacturing process variations.

The RC airplane case studies demonstrate refinement of the design partitions described in Section 25.3 and addition to the system model. The first partition is the mixed-signal data path, in which multiple channels of analog information are transformed in several ways between the joystick controls and the actuators on the airplane. The information is converted to digital signals, serialized, transmitted over an RF channel, reinterpreted as separate channels, converted to pulse-width modulated waveforms and finally provided as inputs to servo loops. In Chapter 8 we performed a detailed design of components to handle the transformations and verified the integrity of the data path. We assumed an ideal RF channel and artificially provided clock synchronization between the transmitter and receiver. Our trade-off study in that chapter compared different resolutions for the analog-to-digital and digital-to-analog converters. New models and test benches were added to the system model as design decisions were made.

We refined the rudder system partition in Chapter 14, starting with a model represented entirely as s-domain transfer functions. Next, we modified the block to include the rudder and associated components implemented as a mixed-technology system with conservation-based electromechanical models, leaving the servo modeled in the s-domain. Finally, we replaced the s-domain servo with its z-domain equivalent, illustrating how system control loop functions can be relegated to software or firmware implementations. As part of the refinement process, we performed high-level analyses of response error and system stability. We analyzed the control horns and translational linkage assemblies at the electromechanical level using the conservation-based models. Finally, we tested the feasibility of implementing the servo system in software or firmware using the z-domain capabilities of VHDL-AMS. Again, new models and test benches were added as design decisions were made.

The power conversion block is represented in the system architecture model as a simple voltage-level shifter. In Chapter 18 we described the detailed design of the block, starting with the main converter stage and then adding feedback control to regulate the output. We introduced a state-space-averaged model to perform frequency domain analysis and to verify the stability of the feedback loop. Finally, our trade-off studies involved component sizing and selection of switching frequency to optimize the design. The new models developed in this case study were added to the system model. The state-space-averaged models were particularly useful during the model calibration and system verification steps.

The final partition in the design is the RF communications channel. In the system architecture model, the RF channel is abstracted to a direct connection between the transmitter and receiver. We described the detailed design of the RF communication block in Chapter 23, including the design of non-coherent and phase-locked-loop detection schemes. As with the other refinements, the new models and test benches were added to the system model as design additions were made.

One difficulty with modeling an RF channel is the difference between the frequencies involved. The baseband signals (the serialization digitized data) are measured in kilohertz, whereas the passband signals (the carrier signals that are modulated by the baseband signals) are measured in megahertz. Techniques for efficiently managing these differences exist. For example, the passband signals can be modeled by considering only the IQ ("in-phase" and "quadrature") components instead of the time domain analog signal at the passband frequencies. (See [8] for further information.) This effectively removes the static carrier frequency from the simulations, while retaining useful modulation nonlinearities in the system model. These models are not presented in this book. IQ models are particularly useful during model calibration and system verification steps. There are also algorithms, such as modulated steady-state analysis, for efficiently simulating RF systems. (See [25], for example.) Such algorithms can be applied to a system described in VHDL-AMS.

25.5 **Model Calibration**

Top-down design of digital circuits, using synthesis to generate the physical design, produces calibrated gate-level models that are useful for bottom-up verification of the design. Top-down design in the absence of synthesis also requires models for use in bottom-up verification. In many cases, the physical models resulting from design refinement are too detailed for efficient simulations of the entire system. Hence, it is useful to identify higher-level models that include sufficient detail for system validation, but are more efficient. These models can be calibrated to match the more detailed models. The calibrated models can also be used in the next generation of the top-down design process, ensuring that physical effects are represented early in the design process.

The task of calibrating models is not trivial. Some organizations already have teams in place to characterize manufacturing processes and to create corresponding models for use in design and verification tasks. Their efforts can be extended to include calibration of higher-level behavioral models. Some organizations are also beginning to require calibrated models from their suppliers, to facilitate the use of model-based design and verification. Furthermore, tools are becoming available to help with the creation and calibration of specific types of design blocks. Where possible, simulation results should be combined with actual measured results to completely calibrate models.

Model calibration can take many forms, for example:

- A behavioral opamp model can be calibrated with parameters obtained from a transistor-level opamp model. Parameters can include gain, offset voltage, poles, zeros, power supply effects and temperature effects.

- A behavioral electromechanical motor model can be calibrated using databook information or measured data.

- A solenoid model can be calibrated using physical design information and measured force-versus-current data. Alternatively, field-solver data can be generated from the detailed 3D physical design and used to generate a calibrated behavioral model.

- Printed circuit board (PCB) traces can be modeled as transmission lines, with their characteristic impedances and coupling determined from field-solver analysis of the physical layer stackup. Similarly, interconnect anomalies such as plated-through vias can be modeled by field-solver analysis of the via structure. The resulting data can be used to calibrate behavioral models of via structures. I/O buffers for ICs mounted on PCBs can be modeled using information available in I/O Buffer Information Specification (IBIS) files (see [20]).

- A microgyroscope device manufactured with microelectromechanical system (MEMS) technology can be modeled with mixed-technology behavioral models calibrated with data from field-solvers for mixed-energy domains (see [39]).

We illustrate a simple form of model calibration in the motor models in Chapter 14. We use parameters from a motor vendor's data sheets in our calculations for the *s*-domain model and its refinements. We reuse the models with different parameters for the propeller motor in Chapter 26.

25.6 System Verification

The purpose of system verification is to ensure that the manufactured design will meet the established specifications and requirements. Verification is best performed as early in the design process as possible, since the cost of discovering and correcting problems increases dramatically in later phases of the process. We discuss three forms of verification here.

Functional verification determines that the design will work as intended, assuming perfect interconnection of components. Functional verification is most accurate when performed using the most accurate models available, typically the physical implementation models. However, as we mentioned earlier, simulating using those models is time-consuming, so it is more efficient to use calibrated higher-level models. Faster simulation allows more time to verify more aspects of the system.

Functional verification of the digital part of the design may be accomplished by comparing the gate-level models derived from synthesis with register-transfer-level models. The system model test-bench suite can be used to drive both sets of models and the results compared. A similar process can be used for analog, mixed-signal and mixed-technology system models. Detailed models or calibrated models can be compared with system design models using the system model test benches.

Interconnect verification takes into account the non-ideal nature of the interconnections between components and can uncover errors missed by functional verification. The relative placement of blocks and their interconnection can significantly affect overall system performance. Interconnect performance is especially important for high-speed integrated circuit design and for circuits implemented on printed circuit boards. It can also be important for non-electrical systems. For example, in a fuel-injection system the piping between the high-pressure fuel reservoir and the injectors is an integral part of the design. In general, the design of component interconnect must consider component placement, loading effects, interconnect and load matching and interconnect sizing effects. It is often necessary to model the interconnect mechanisms and include them in the system model.

For digital IC designs, interconnect modeling involves analysis of the drive strength of devices and the timing that is acceptable for the design. Sometimes the only way to fix the timing problems is to change the locations of blocks involved in critical timing paths.

For high-speed PCB designs, correct placement of high-speed chips on a circuit board can be very difficult. Signals must travel distances measured in tens of centimeters and have rise times measured in picoseconds. This means that an interconnect between the device must be considered as a transmission line, requiring impedance matching between drivers, transmission line and receivers. Reflections from imperfections and cross-talk coupling between traces can compromise the quality of digital waveforms. Even without these signal integrity problems, the different paths that signals take across a circuit board can cause timing skew problems. These various effects can be modeled using VHDL-AMS. The book by Hall et al. [20] offers more information on high-speed digital PCB design issues.

Interconnect verification is just as important for analog IC and PCB system design. Many of the same issues are present. However, the problems are even more critical, since analog circuits do not enjoy the same noise margins as digital systems. Likewise, interconnect verification is important for mixed-technology systems. Adverse effects can include flexing of mechanical linkages and shafts, pressure drops and loading effects in hydraulic lines, flux linkage between magnetic components and so on. Again, VHDL-AMS provides useful facilities for modeling these effects.

Checkerboard verification is a hybrid of various forms of verification, facilitated in VHDL-AMS by the use of multiple architectures for a given entity and by configurations. Checkerboard verification uses combinations of calibrated models at different levels of abstraction, possibly including interconnect models, to verify the design. It involves selection of detailed models for specific portions of the design in combination with abstract models for the remainder of the design. The detailed models allow focused analysis on the specific portion of the design, while the abstract models allow fast overall simulation.

In the RC airplane case studies we demonstrate functional verification of the most detailed design models, both for individual blocks and for the entire system. For example, in Chapter 26 we verify system functionality in the presence of component interactions, such as the dependence of servo functionality on the power supply voltage and the effect of the motor/propeller loading on the supply voltage. We demonstrate interconnect verification through the modeling of the mechanical linkage between the servos and the rudder. We also demonstrate checkerboard verification throughout the case studies as we use different architectures to achieve different analysis goals.

25.7 **Synthesis and Reuse**

As we have mentioned earlier, synthesis is a key element in top-down digital design processes. While synthesis technology is not yet available for analog, mixed-signal or mixed-technology design in general, it is available in specialized areas such as filter design. Synthesis for other specialized areas is likely to receive attention as VHDL-AMS becomes more widely accepted.

Although we cannot currently rely on synthesis of analog designs, we can reuse models to accelerate the design process. Indeed, tool-based reuse and calibration of models can be seen as a first step toward automatic synthesis. As designers go through the process of developing behavioral models, refining the designs to include more detailed effects, building the hardware and calibrating the results back to the behavioral models, the quality of the behavioral models and the confidence in their accuracy will increase. Figure 25-3, adapted from [32], shows the concept of successive improvement and reuse of behavioral models, including calibration from physical models or hardware measurements.

Many of the building blocks developed for the RC airplane are good candidates for reuse in other related systems. Examples include the RF communications channel, the multichannel serial link, the power supply, the servo control systems and the motor control. These blocks have been designed so that they can be reassembled into new systems, customized by setting generic values and configured to use the various entity/architecture pairs.

FIGURE 25-3

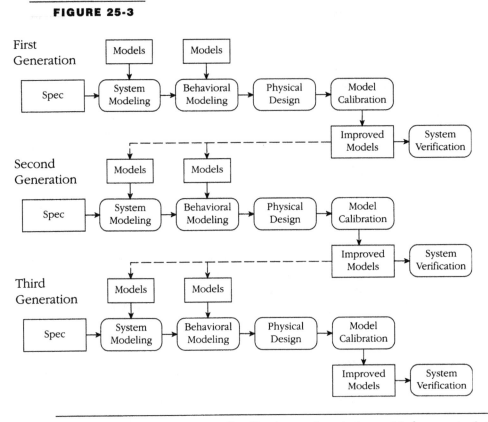

Each generation of verification produces better models for reuse in design.

25.8 Design Trade-Offs and Optimization

One of the main benefits of modeling a system is to allow us to quickly modify the design and see the consequences of the change. A model is an environment in which we can perform experiments much more readily than with real hardware. It provides opportunities for us to discover and exploit design trade-offs, allowing us to more closely match the product characteristics with the requirements of a target market. A given basic product design may have application in very different markets. By making the appropriate trade-offs, we can adapt the design to the needs of the different markets.

VHDL-AMS has three fundamental mechanisms to facilitate design trade-off analysis: structural modeling, multiple architectures per entity and generic constants. These mechanisms allow us to optimize a design through fundamental architectural changes or simple parametric adjustments. The trade-off analyses in each of the RC airplane case studies illustrate these mechanisms.

Architectural Trade-Offs

The most important decisions in a design are often the choices that are made about the structure and functional decomposition of the system. These decisions can determine whether or not the system requirements can even be met. They can also affect the future extensibility of the system, determining the adaptability of the design to future requirements and trade-offs. Finally, architectural decisions can have a significant effect on the cost structure of the system.

The architecture of the system is best determined early in the design, through the use of the system architecture model. Architectural experiments can be performed and analyzed quickly using high-level models. The trade-offs can be documented in reports using graphs from the simulation analyses. There is value in documenting those architectural attempts that are not selected, since they may be useful in the future when circumstances and requirements change. They can also help avoid repeated exploration of dead-end paths.

VHDL-AMS provides mechanisms to help make architectural exploration easier. The use of structural models (net-lists of more basic building blocks) allows for flexible assembly of higher-level models from basic building blocks. The use of multiple architectures for a given entity also makes it easier to build, configure, use and document the system architecture model with varying functionality.

Parametric Analysis

One of the most common experiments designers perform is changing the value of a design parameter to see its effect on operation of the system. The effect can often be seen in measurements taken from simulation waveforms—measurements such as rise time, fall time, overshoot, frequency, period and delay. It is useful to see these measured values plotted as a function of a design parameter as the parameter value is swept over a range. Such "design curves" are one of the most direct ways to communicate design trade-offs. Figure 25-4 is an example, showing design curves derived from multiple simulations of the switching power supply in Chapter 18. The curves directly relate competing design requirements (voltage droop and settling time) with an important design parameter (switching frequency).

VHDL-AMS facilitates parametric analysis by providing the mechanism of generic constants. The generic constants defined for an entity are the "parameters" of the entity. Sweeping the values of an entity's generics allows design curves to be generated. It is also possible to write models that include instrumentation to make measurements of quantities, producing the desired waveform characteristic as VHDL-AMS signals or quantities during a simulation.

Optimization

Optimization techniques have been in use for many years. These techniques involve automatically modifying the values of system parameters, simulating the system and measuring the response. The measurements are compared with a goal to determine

FIGURE 25-4

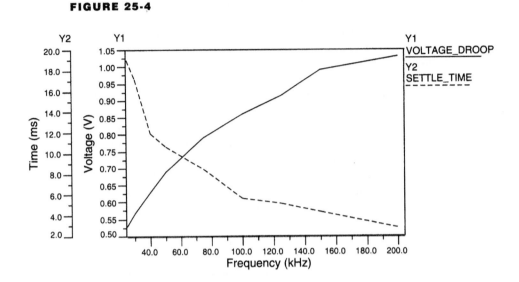

Output voltage droop and settling-time measurements as a function of switching frequency.

new values for the system parameters, and the process is repeated. Successive simulations are performed until the goal is achieved or it is determined that success is not possible.

Some optimization algorithms use gradient-based methods, where the sensitivity of waveform characteristics, as a function of a parameter value, is used to determine the direction of change for the next iteration of the parameter value. Other algorithms use so-called "simulated annealing" or "genetic" algorithms that have desirable convergence characteristics.

VHDL-AMS does not directly support optimization techniques. However, the use of generic constants to represent parameters, along with instrumentation models written specifically to measure quantities during simulation, can form the modeling basis for optimization tools.

Response Surface Models

Response surface modeling is a powerful approach for analyzing systems and identifying potential trade-offs. It is related to the *design of experiments* (DOE) concept [26] and makes use of carefully planned parametric "experiments." It is a very effective technique for mapping both the functional behavior of a system relative to parameter values and the variability of the behavior.

The DOE part of response surface modeling methodically defines the set of parameter values that will be used to map out the system response. Some of the parameters are under the control of the designer, although they may have some variability due to manufacturing tolerances. It is also helpful to include parameters that are not under the designer's control, using any known probability distributions to characterize their variability. Next, experiments are performed, varying the independent parameters and measuring the effect on quantities that have limits imposed by the system specifications or that affect system performance significantly. Finally, a statistical analysis is performed to determine the *response surface,* which consists of a set of equations that relate the means and standard deviations of the measured quantities to the independent parameters.

Producing a response surface may involve a significant amount of analysis and be resource intensive. Once it is available, however, it serves several useful functions. Design trade-offs, for example, can be performed very quickly simply by evaluating a set of algebraic equations. The effects of parameter tolerance can quickly be evaluated. It is even possible to discover ways to reduce overall system variability, *without* tightening the tolerance of system parameters, by finding areas in the design space where the design is more tolerant to variation. This can lead to significant reduction in system cost while simultaneously improving the robustness of the design.

A response surface model can be combined with optimization techniques to significantly improve the performance of system optimization. The response surface model is very efficient and focuses on the distilled performance of the system rather than on the raw data produced by detailed simulations. By modifying the desired specifications, optimization with a response surface model can be used to retarget the design to a related, but slightly different, set of requirements. This provides a mechanism to quickly evaluate the viability of creating a variant of a design for a new market.

DOE techniques have been known for many years. The work of quality experts such as Demming and Taguchi (associated with Japanese manufacturing quality improvements) are based on DOE theory. However, the use of these techniques has not been as widespread as one might think, due to the time and cost involved in conducting the required experiments. Fortunately, simulation tools offer the potential to reduce the cost, time delays and errors associated with conducting experiments using real hardware. As with other design exploration techniques, DOE techniques are facilitated by VHDL-AMS models that use generic constants to represent design parameters. Furthermore, the equations that embody a response surface model can be implemented directly in VHDL-AMS.

Exercises

1. [❶ 25.2] What is the difference between a "system architecture model" and a "system design model"?

2. [❷ 25.5] Identify blocks from the airplane design that would be good candidates for creating model calibration algorithms. (Hint: Look for entities with multiple architectures, including both detailed and high-level model abstractions.)

3. [❷ 25.8] Develop empirical equations that relate the RC airplane DC/DC converter's voltage droop and settling time to the switching frequency using the data from Figure 25-4.

4. [❸ 25.5] Create a model calibration algorithm for matching a switching power supply model with its corresponding state-space-averaged model.

5. [❹ 25.4] Create a physical design for one of the components of the system: controller/transmitter; receiver; servos; battery, power converter, motor; airframe with control surfaces.

6. [❹ 25.4] Develop "in-phase" and "quadrature" models for the modulation/demodulation blocks in the RF communications channel of the RC airplane.

7. [❹] Create a more sophisticated airplane system model by adding channels for ailerons and an elevator to the system.

8. [❹] Build an operational RC airplane and verify that the subsystems all work as modeled.

chapter twenty-six

Case Study 5: RC Airplane System

With a contribution by Scott Cooper, Mentor Graphics Corporation

The RC airplane example illustrates the diverse capabilities of the VHDL-AMS modeling language. This system is implemented with a combination of analog, digital, mechanical and s-domain models. This final case study integrates the subsystems from Case Studies 1 to 4 into a complete airplane system. The following topics are highlighted: interfacing the command and control and rudder systems; analyzing system power supply effects; designing the propeller system; and implementing the human controller into the overall system.

26.1 **RC System Overview**

Figure 26-1 shows the complete system diagram for the RC airplane system. In previous case studies, we presented the specifications for the various subsystems. We summarize them in Figure 26-2 for reference. There are many ways in which to meet the specifications. For these case studies, we have chosen design avenues that lend themselves to reader education, occasionally in opposition to the most straightforward approach available. For example, a typical RC airplane system would probably use the 1–2 ms pulse outputs from the command and control blocks as the control signals for switching amplifiers that drive the rudder and propeller, rather than including extra data conversions as we have done.

26.2 **Interfacing Command and Control to the Rudder System**

Now that we have designed the airplane's command and control and rudder systems individually, we can connect them together and analyze their combined system performance. The first check is to see how the rudder angle behaves when driven by the command and control block. The combined system is illustrated in Figure 26-3. The output of the command and control block, which is generated by a digital-to-analog converter, is connected to the input of the rudder servo block. Thus, the rudder angle is now controlled by the rudder control stick.

The rudder response to a sine wave command is shown in Figure 26-4. The waveform shows that there is some signal degradation when the two systems are

FIGURE 26-1

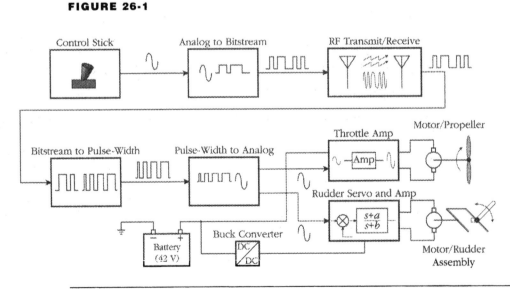

The complete RC airplane system diagram.

FIGURE 26-2

Command and Control System

Analog voltage input/output range	0–4.8 V	Channel size	16 bits
Digitization accuracy	10 bits	Frame update rate	~20 ms
Total number of channels	8	Output to servo, voltage pulse	1–2 ms
Active channels	2		

RF System

Carrier frequency	72 MHz	Delta frequency	5 kHz

Rudder System

Torque at gearbox	0.7 Nm	Servo phase margin	≥35°
Rudder speed, full scale (0 to 60°) @0.2 Nm static load	≤300 ms	Servo steady-state error to ramp input	≤1%

Propeller System

Flying time from 42 V battery	5–10 min

Power Supply Regulator

V_{in}	42 V DC	$V_{out(ripple)}$	<100 mV p-p
$F_{switching}$	25 kHz	I_{out}	15 mA to 2 A
V_{out}	4.8 V DC	$I_{out(ripple)}$	<30 mA p-p

Summary of specifications for the RC airplane.

combined. There appears to be some ripple in the rudder waveform. In order to better understand and quantify this degradation, we look once again at the servo error.

We used servo error as the performance metric for the rudder system accuracy in Case Study 2. There, we specified that the steady-state ramp error should not exceed 1%. The error measurement is taken after the position-loop summing junction inside the rudder servo block. The error results are illustrated in Figure 26-5. As shown in the bottom waveform, not only is there nearly 200 mV of ripple from the servo input, but the average steady-state ramp level is about 500 mV at 4 V input, which yields a steady-state error of 12.5% (0.5 V/4 V). This clearly does not meet the 1% error criterion. The measured ripple frequency is 50 Hz, which corresponds to the frame-update rate of the command and control system. (Recall that the command and control system updates its output every 20 ms.) Clearly, we need to filter out this unwanted ripple.

To overcome the unacceptable error level, we insert a low-pass filter between the command and controller output and the rudder system input, as indicated by the dashed box in Figure 26-6. Since our working system bandwidth needs to be around

FIGURE 26-3

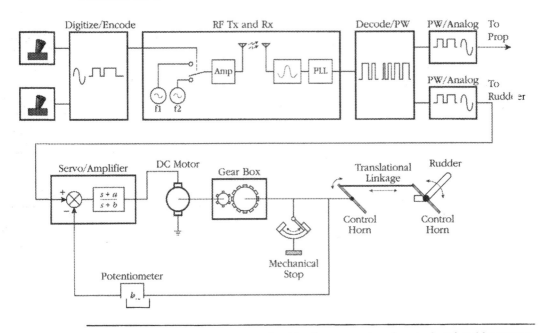

Combined command and control and rudder systems.

1 Hz and the ripple frequency is 50 Hz, we use a two-pole filter with both poles set at 10 Hz. This allows frequencies up to 1 Hz to pass through relatively cleanly, but reduces the effects of the 50 Hz ripple at the frame-update rate.

After adding the filter, the servo error signal is reduced as shown in Figure 26-7. Not only is the ripple drastically reduced by the filter, but the servo once again has an acceptable error level of 0.85% (33.9 mV/4 V). The penalty for introducing the filter, however, is that the filtered signal lags the unfiltered signal slightly, which increases the delay from the operator command to rudder actuation. The effect of the filter on the rudder's response to a sinusoidal input is illustrated in Figure 26-8. The rudder output appears much smoother than without filtering, but the signal is delayed as a result of the filtering. We will return to this delay later in the case study.

26.3 System Power Supply Effects

As we discussed in Case Study 3, the RC airplane is powered by a 42 V battery. This high voltage level is required to drive the propeller of the plane. We designed a buck converter to produce 4.8 V from the 42 V supply to drive the rest of the airplane systems.

In this section we analyze some of the effects of the power supply on the performance of the rudder system from Case Study 2. For this discussion, we assume that the digital-to-analog converter and servo electronics use small independent low-pow-

FIGURE 26-4

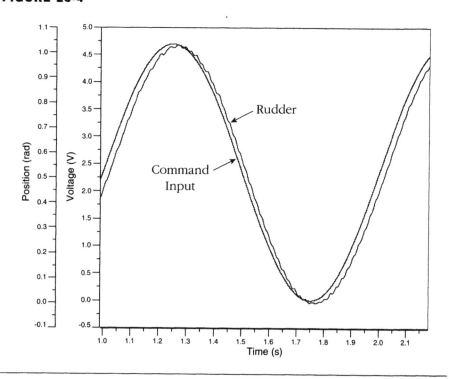

Command and control input and rudder response.

er voltage regulators that buffer the circuits from power supply fluctuations. These regulators should help the airplane components act with high precision even when the power supply voltage fluctuates. The rudder motor, however, is a high-power device that cannot be protected in this manner. The motor can draw up to 2 A of current, which is well beyond the ability of a small on-board regulator to supply. This means that the motor may be the most supply-dependent component in the airplane; hence it is the subject of our study of system power supply effects.

In previous discussions, we assumed an ideal power supply for the rudder motor. The motor is actually driven by some form of power amplifier in the complete system. Here, we investigate two aspects of the power supply and amplifier on the system. We first examine the effect of reducing the power supply voltage level on the servo error. Next, we verify that the power supply can deliver enough current to the amplifier to handle a 1 Hz sine wave command.

Supply Level and Servo Error

For this investigation, we once again take advantage of the ability of VHDL-AMS to model multiple levels of abstraction, in order to model our motor amplifier as a limiter block. Unlike a standard limiter with fixed limits (like that used in Case Study 2), the limits of the motor-amplifier limiter are determined by possibly non-static power

FIGURE 26-5

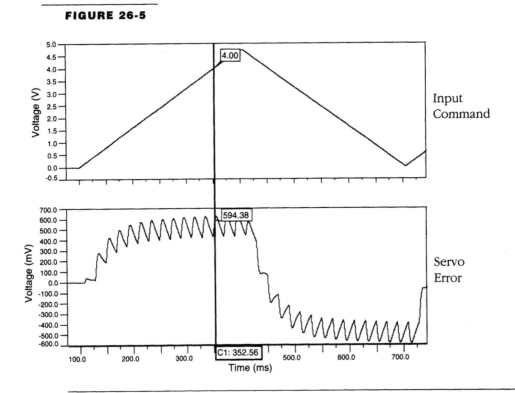

Servo error without filtering.

supply voltage levels. The model has unity gain in the non-limited region, but clips the input signal if it exceeds the power supply level.

We modify our standard rudder system to include the limiting amplifier model, outlined by the dashed box in Figure 26-9. The power amplifier is inserted between the servo/compensator block and the DC motor. The power pin of the amplifier is driven by a piecewise linear voltage source, which allows the supply voltage level to be manipulated as desired.

The supply-limited amplifier model is shown in Figure 26-10. The model uses a simultaneous if statement to pass the input voltage to the output with unity gain, or to clip the output to the power supply input level. Note that there are no loading effects built into the model. We will return to this limitation in the next section.

With the limiting amplifier in place, we can determine the effects of stepping down the power supply voltage from 4.8 V to 3.2 V in 0.4 V increments. Measurements of the steady-state ramp error at each supply voltage level are illustrated in Figure 26-11. As shown in the figure, the supply voltage does not adversely affect the steady-state system error until the voltage drops to 3.2 V, at which point the error specification is violated. Closer inspection of the error signal also reveals that the main transient error pulse grows larger as a function of reduced supply voltage, and also takes longer to settle out. For example, with a 4.4 V power level, the transient error pulse is about 60 ms; for a 4.0 V power level, it is about 75 ms; for a 3.6 V power

FIGURE 26-6

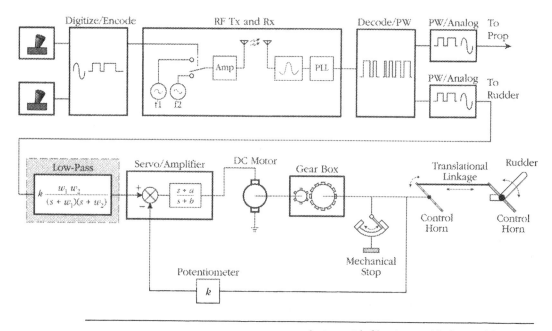

System with filter inserted before rudder servo.

level, it is about 90 ms. In general, there is more transient error for longer periods of time as a function of reduced supply levels.

Rudder Servo with Buck Converter

Now that we have performed a preliminary investigation on servo error as a function of supply voltage levels, we turn our attention to supply current. The circuit topology of Figure 26-9 works well for voltage levels; however, the amplifier model has no means to limit the current it supplies to the motor. In order to see the actual current drawn from the buck converter by the motor, we use the new topology illustrated in Figure 26-12. This figure shows the familiar rudder system, but with a power amplifier inserted between the servo controller and the motor. In addition, the power amplifier is driven by the buck converter discussed in Case Study 3.

The power amplifier circuit is illustrated in Figure 26-13. In order to deliver power to the motor directly from the buck converter, we use an H-bridge circuit driven by a pulse width modulator (PWM). The H-bridge works by simultaneously closing switches Q1 and Q4 (with Q2 and Q3 open) for clockwise motor shaft rotation, and closing Q2 and Q3 (with Q1 and Q4 open) for counterclockwise motor shaft rotation.

The PWM converts the input servo error into pulses proportional to the error amplitude. The pulses then drive the switch controls to achieve the desired current flow through the motor. The switching frequency for the PWM is 2.5 kHz, chosen to be 10 times the measured small-signal bandwidth, 250 Hz, of the rudder system.

FIGURE 26-7

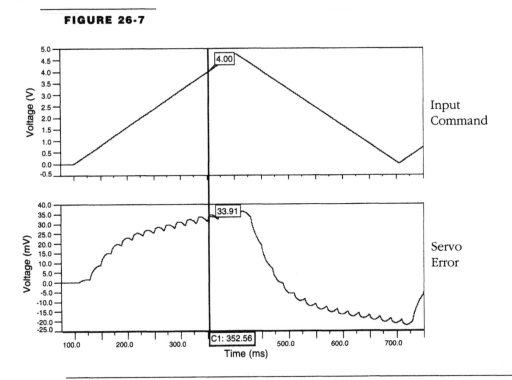

Servo error with filter.

One advantage of the H-bridge configuration is that it allows the full supply voltage to be delivered to the motor in either direction (±4.8 V). This means that the motor can be driven in either the clockwise or counterclockwise direction at maximum torque. Another advantage of this configuration is that it allows us to connect the motor to the buck converter through the switches to see how they interact. The buck converter is illustrated in Figure 26-14. If we simulate the combined system with a 1 Hz sine wave command, we see whether the converter specifications were chosen correctly. The results of this analysis are shown in Figure 26-15. As we would expect, the rudder angle waveform appears smooth and closely follows the command input.

Using this topology, we can now look at the current drawn from the buck converter. This was a key specification for the converter, which was designed to deliver up to 2 A of current. A snapshot of the current delivered through the converter's filter inductor is illustrated in Figure 26-16. This figure illustrates the current fluctuations from the buck converter as a function of PWM control voltage. The measured switching frequency is 2.5 kHz (0.4 ms), which we can see superimposed on the current waveform. The current waveform itself is well within the 2 A specification, demonstrating that the converter can handle this command scenario.

The motor current waveform also reveals an unexpected interaction between the buck converter and the motor, an interaction that is not present when the buck converter is replaced with an ideal voltage source. The symptom of the interaction is a 80 Hz to 200 Hz oscillation, upon which the PWM frequency rides. Investigation re-

FIGURE 26-8

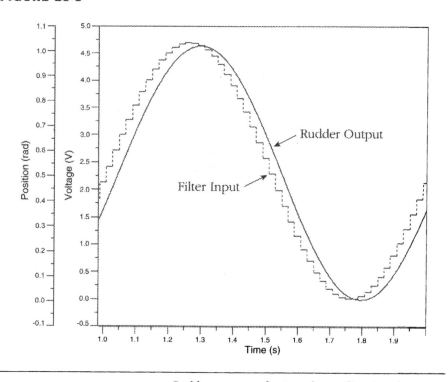

Rudder response after introducing filter into the system.

FIGURE 26-9

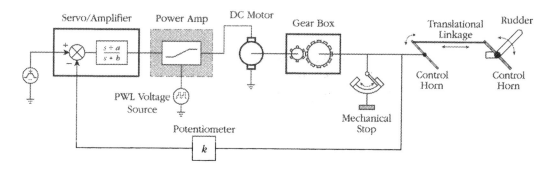

Rudder system with power amplifier driving motor.

veals that the oscillation is due to interactions between the buck converter's filter inductance and the rudder motor's parameters. As the rudder output performance appears acceptable even with this oscillation, we do not investigate it further here. However, we should ultimately perform an analysis of the complete system to fully

FIGURE 26-10

```
library ieee_proposed;  use ieee_proposed.electrical_systems.all;
entity amp_lim is
    port ( terminal ps : electrical;   -- positive supply terminal
           terminal input, output : electrical );
end entity amp_lim;
```

```
architecture simple of amp_lim is
    quantity v_pwr across i_pwr through ps to electrical_ref;
    quantity vin across iin through input to electrical_ref;
    quantity vout across iout through output to electrical_ref;
    quantity v_amplified : voltage ;
    constant gain : real := 1.0;
begin
    v_amplified == gain * vin;
    if v_amplified'above(v_pwr) use
        vout == v_pwr;
    else
        vout == v_amplified;
    end use;
    break on v_amplified'above(v_pwr);
    -- ignore loading effects
    i_pwr == 0.0;
    iin == 0.0;
end architecture simple;
```

Rudder motor amplifier model.

understand this interaction. We should measure the servo error once again and analyze system response to various motor load profiles.

In this section we have presented only a cursory examination of the interaction between the buck converter and rudder system. There are numerous further analyses that we should perform on the system. For example, we could analyze how the current from the converter is affected by changing rudder load torque. Thus far, we have used a constant rudder torque of 0.2 N, but this could change depending on wind and other flight conditions. Other examples include analyzing the effect of rudder motor stalls on the converter, and determining how well the rudder can recover from a converter voltage dropout. We should also further investigate the motor current oscillatory behavior discussed above. Using system models like those we have developed here, these and several other system-level questions can be answered.

FIGURE 26-11

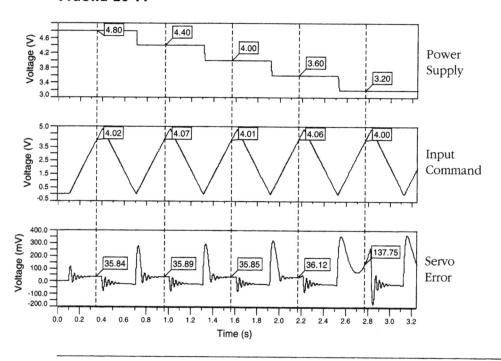

Servo error resulting from power supply voltage reduction.

FIGURE 26-12

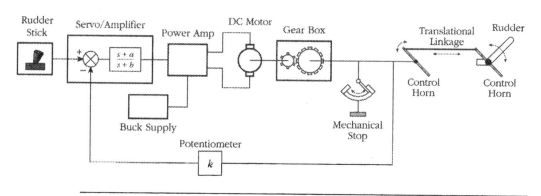

Full buck converter/amplifier topology.

FIGURE 26-13

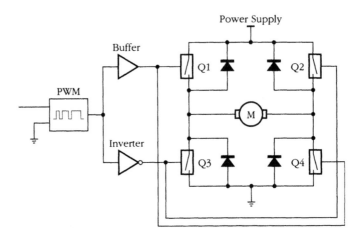

H-bridge driven by PWM.

FIGURE 26-14

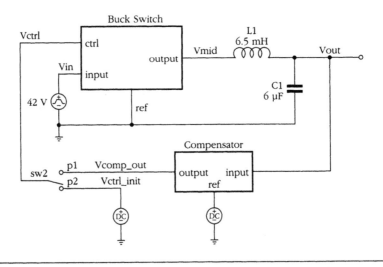

Buck converter from Case Study 3.

26.4 Propeller System

In this section, we add the propeller system to the overall RC airplane system. For simplicity in this case study, we revert to the non-switching power amplifier for the rudder system. The addition of the propeller system is indicated by the dashed box in Figure 26-17.

FIGURE 26-15

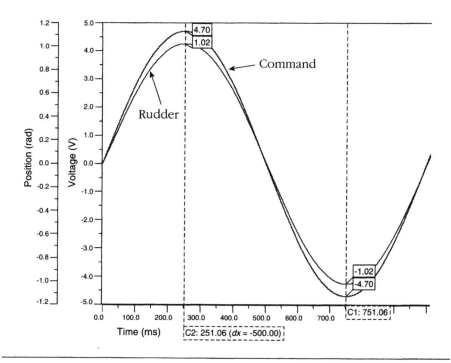

Rudder response to sine wave with buck supply and power amplifier.

The propeller system is composed of four main components: a low-pass filter to smooth out the frame-update noise; a speed controller for the propeller motor; the propeller motor; and the propeller blade. The low-pass filter is the same model that we used for the rudder, with both poles also set to 10 Hz.

The power amplifier for the propeller is configured as a basic speed controller and is illustrated in Figure 26-18. The speed controller is configured as a digitally controlled analog switch, driven by a pulse-width modulated (PWM) signal. The PWM signal is generated from the throttle command produced by the command and control system discussed in Case Study 1. A fly-back diode is included to provide the continuous current flow required by the motor's winding inductance when the switch is open.

Unlike the power amplifier used for the rudder system, this design uses only a single switch and relies on propeller drag to slow down the propeller when the switch is open. This is possible because the propeller spins in only one direction (unlike the rudder, which must respond to bidirectional control).

The PWM output ranges in duty cycle from 0% to 100% for command values of 0 V to 4.8 V. For model airplane propellers, the switching rate of the PWM is typically between 2000 Hz and 3000 Hz. This is because higher frequencies can cause interference with the radio control, due to the correspondingly fast rise and fall times of the power switch. Lower frequencies tend to make the plane inefficient when flown

FIGURE 26-16

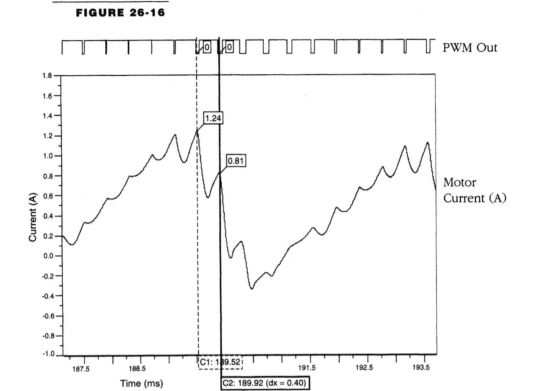

Current versus PWM pulses for complete rudder system.

at constant partial power levels [6]. For our system, we use a switching rate of 2500 Hz.

The VHDL-AMS propeller motor model is the same as that used for the rudder, but with the following parameters:

R = 0.16 Ω   armature winding resistance

L = 40 μH   armature winding inductance

J = 315 × 10^{-6} kg/m^2 shaft inertia

k_T = 30.1 mNm/A   torque (motor) constant

k_E = 30.1 mV/rad/s   voltage (back-EMF) constant

B = 5.63 × 10^{-12} Nm/rad/s   damping factor

The propeller blade is what produces actual thrust for the airplane. It is connected directly to the motor shaft rather than through a gearbox. For our airplane design, we use a 13 inch × 8 inch propeller. This means that the diameter of the blade is 13

FIGURE 26-17

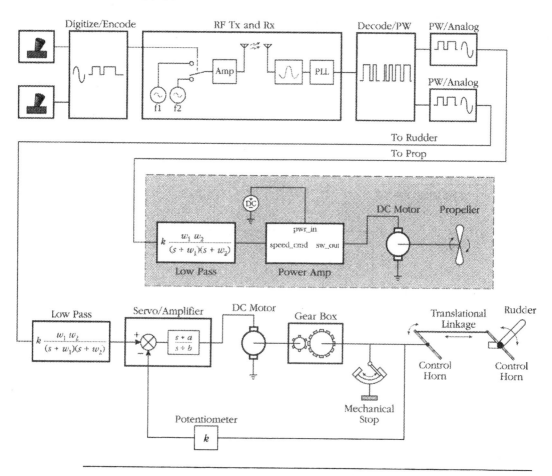

RC airplane system with propeller subsystem.

FIGURE 26-18

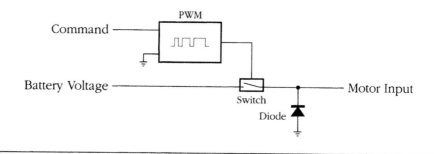

Propeller motor speed controller.

inches, and the pitch (or angle) is 8 inches. The graph in Figure 26-19 shows the relationship between torque and speed, based on measurements given in [6].

We use this data for our model of the propeller. The implementation is divided into two parts: the behavioral model, called **prop_pwl**, and a lookup function, **pwl_dim1_extrap**. Both are illustrated in Figure 26-20. The **prop_pwl** model works as follows. The measured velocity/torque data are represented using the two generic constants. The single port of the model is declared as a terminal with nature **rotational_v**, with angular velocity as the across quantity and torque as the through quantity. The simultaneous statement uses the angular velocity and the velocity/torque constants as actual parameters for the **pwl_dim1_extrap** function. The function result is the torque corresponding to the angular velocity of the propeller.

FIGURE 26·19

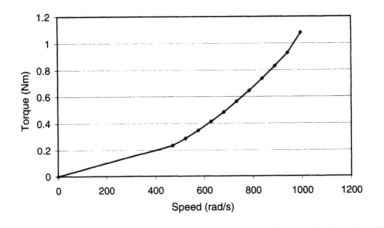

Propeller torque versus speed curve from measured data.

FIGURE 26·20

```
library ieee_proposed;  use ieee_proposed.mechanical_systems.all;
entity prop_pwl is
        generic ( ydata : real_vector;        -- torque data points
                  xdata : real_vector );      -- velocity data points
        port ( terminal shaft1 : rotational_v );
        end entity prop_pwl;
```

```
architecture ideal of prop_pwl is
        use work.pwl_functions.all;
        quantity w across torq through shaft1 to rotational_v_ref;
begin
```

```
        torq == pwl_dim1_extrap(w, xdata, ydata);
end architecture ideal;

————————————————————————————————————————————————

    function pwl_dim1_extrap ( x : in real;  xdata, ydata : in real_vector )
                             return real is
        variable xvalue, yvalue, m : real;
        variable start, fin, mid: integer;
    begin
        if x <= xdata(0) then
            yvalue := extrapolate ( x, ydata(1), ydata(0), xdata(1), xdata(0) );
            return yvalue;
        end if;

        if x >= xdata(xdata'right) then
            yvalue := extrapolate( x, ydata(ydata'right), ydata(ydata'right – 1),
                                   xdata(xdata'right), xdata(xdata'right – 1) );
            return yvalue;
        end if;

        start := 0;
        fin := xdata'right;
        while start <= fin loop
            mid := (start + fin) / 2;
            if xdata(mid) < x then
                start := mid + 1;
            else
                fin := mid – 1;
            end if;
        end loop;
        if xdata(mid) > x then
            mid := mid – 1;
        end if;
        yvalue := interpolate( x, ydata(mid + 1), ydata(mid),
                               xdata(mid + 1), xdata(mid) );
        return yvalue;
    end function pwl_dim1_extrap;
```

VHDL-AMS listing of piecewise linear lookup model.

The **pwl_dim1_extrap** function is defined in a separate package. It performs interpolation and extrapolation from the constant lookup data to determine the torque value corresponding to a velocity value. The function parameters are the current propeller velocity, **x**, and the real vectors containing the lookup data, **xdata** and **ydata**. If **x** is less than the value of the leftmost data entry in the lookup vectors, the resulting torque is determined using linear extrapolation from the leftmost two data entries. Similarly, if **x** is greater than the value of the rightmost data entry in the lookup vectors, the resulting torque is determined using linear extrapolation from the rightmost two data entries. The remaining case is where **x** lies within the range of data entries. In that case, the function performs a binary search algorithm to find the index value of the entry just less than **x**. The function then uses linear interpolation between the entries on either side of **x** to determine the resulting torque. The extrapolation and interpolation operations are both implemented using further functions defined in the package containing **pwl_dim1_extrap**.

A lack of a good closed-form characteristic equation for a model is not uncommon. In such circumstances, empirical data can serve equally well. The propeller model discussed above demonstrates how we can readily incorporate such data into a VHDL-AMS model.

Propeller System Performance

The propeller system was simulated with a 1 Hz sine wave input command. The resulting speed and torque waveforms are shown in Figure 26-21. These waveforms illustrate that the propeller rotates at a maximum velocity of about 1000 rad/s in response to a full 4.8 V input command. They also illustrate that the propeller takes quite a bit longer to spin down, due to the single switch controller relying on the propeller drag to slow down rotation.

FIGURE 26-21

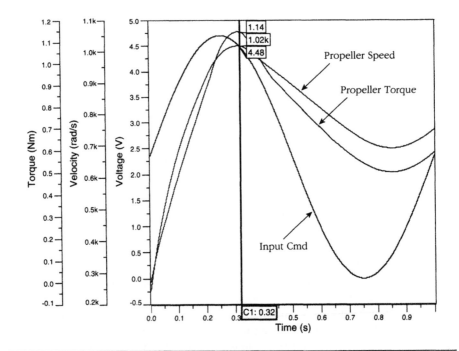

Propeller speed versus torque curves for sine wave input command.

PWM versus motor current waveforms are illustrated in Figure 26-22. As shown in the figure, the PWM switches at 2.5 kHz, resulting in the large current ripple. At this point in the simulation, the average current is about 20 A, which is the expected level when the motor is running at maximum efficiency.

The purpose of the propeller is to transform motor torque into thrust. For the combination of motor and propeller running from a 42 V battery, we expect the following performance:

- Propeller speed: 10 krpm (~1000 rad/s)

- Current at maximum motor efficiency: 20 A

- Motor efficiency: 85%

- Pitch speed: 77 mph (124 km/h)

- Thrust at pitch speed: 132 oz (36.7 N)

As we commented at the end of the previous section, we can now perform numerous further analyses on the propeller system. We can optimize the propeller system design by performing efficiency tests, evaluating alternative switches and analyzing many other design trade-offs.

FIGURE 26-22

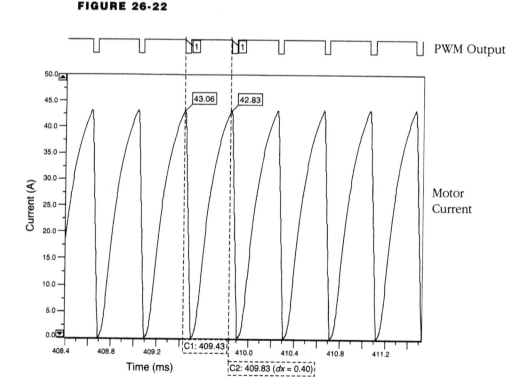

PWM control and motor current response for propeller system.

26.5 Human Controller

Thus far in our case studies, we have concentrated on the performance of the RC airplane design from a system standpoint. We have looked at the performance of individual subsystems, and then analyzed how some of these subsystems will interact with one another in the overall system. What we have not considered to this point is the human being controlling the airplane. What effects does the "human in the loop" have on overall airplane performance? In this section, we explore this aspect by introducing the airplane operator into our analysis.

Modeling the Human

Humans have differing responses to various stimuli. By taking into account such factors as cognitive processing, neural transmission to brain and muscle, sensory receptor response and muscle latency, a human response range of 113 ms to 528 ms has been measured [2]. From measurements such as these, transfer functions can be implemented to model the response time of the human brain and the human nervous system [36]. For the human brain, the transfer function is

$$G_B(s) = 1 + \frac{0.1}{s} \tag{26-1}$$

which includes position error as well as its integral. The transfer function for the human nervous system is

$$G_N(s) = \frac{(1/T)}{s + (1/T)} = \frac{4}{s + 4} \tag{26-2}$$

which represents a 250 ms time-constant delay. Representing the brain and nervous system transfer functions as control blocks leads to the configuration illustrated in Figure 26-23. This represents the overall transfer function of the human brain and nervous system.

When we add these blocks to the overall system design, the result is a system with a human in the loop. This is illustrated in Figure 26-24, in which the human control system blocks constitute a new servo loop around the rudder channel. The human brain and nervous system time delays constitute the human control loop (HCL), which consists of the control blocks shown in Figure 26-23. The airplane consists of a summing junction that outputs the difference between the commanded crosswind profile and the rudder angle. This difference represents the plane's actual position. The overall loop works as follows. The HCL "sees" the airplane's heading. If it is on track with the commanded heading, the operator issues no new control command. However, if a crosswind changes the heading, the operator sees this change and issues a compensating command through the HCL.

FIGURE 26-23

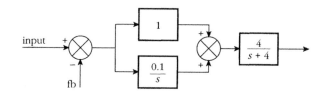

Human brain and nervous system control blocks.

FIGURE 26-24

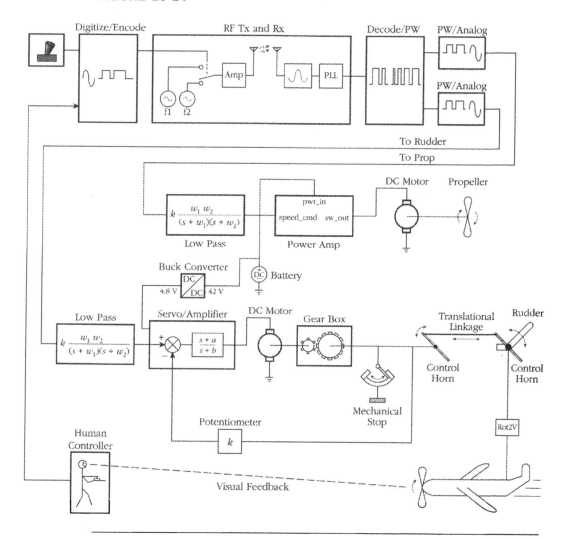

RC airplane system with human control loop.

We analyze this system as follows. First, we command a target heading through the HCL. Next, we generate a crosswind profile and drive it into the airplane. Finally, we superimpose the compensating rudder angle onto this wind profile. This gives us a representation of how well the plane operator is capable of correcting for crosswind-induced heading deviations.

The crosswind profile and compensating rudder angle are illustrated in Figure 26-25. The top waveforms illustrate the wind profile and how well it is compensated by the rudder angle. As shown, the rudder angle closely follows the wind profile, although delayed as expected by the HCL and frame filter. The bottom waveform shows the normalized difference between the wind profile and the rudder angle. This represents the plane's deviation from its commanded heading. The wind profile represents wind velocity that is translated into a value proportional to the plane's signal range (0–4.8 V). At the start of the flight, the deviation is 0. As each change in the wind is encountered, the plane deviates from its course. The operator sees this and responds with a rudder angle correction through the HCL, which drives the deviation back to near 0.

FIGURE 26-25

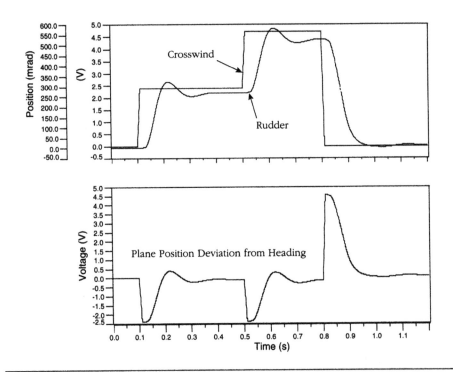

Rudder response and flight deviation to wind profile.

System Accuracy

Our last analysis of the RC airplane system involves system accuracy. The design is specified to 10 bits of accuracy for the A/D and D/A conversions. With the models we now have in place, we can measure the effects of changing the number of bits in the design.

The results of three analyses with different numbers of bits are given in Figure 26-26. The top waveforms show a linearly increasing crosswind profile and the operator's attempt to compensate for it, through the HCL, with a 10-bit system. The middle waveforms show the same scenario, but with a 6-bit system. The bottom waveforms again illustrate the same scenario, but this time with a 2-bit system. Clearly, the operator's ability to accurately compensate for wind disturbances is proportional to the number of bits representing the system signals.

26.6 Summary

In this final case study, we have integrated the previous case study systems into the overall RC airplane system. We have looked at some of the interactions that such systems can have when connected together, such as problems that can arise from

FIGURE 26-26

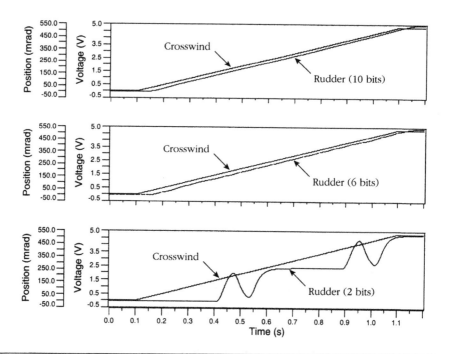

Airplane response to flight plan (with human in the loop).

insufficient specifications for system interfaces. This was the case for the command and control output signals and the effect they had on the rudder system, since no signal conditioning requirement was specified. Having the ability to integrate these two systems allowed us to determine that this requirement had been overlooked, and that the servo error specification could be violated as a result. We also added the propeller design into the overall system, introducing more mixed-signal and mixed-technology components, once again illustrating the breadth of VHDL-AMS modeling capabilities. We not only analyzed the propeller system performance, but also showed how VHDL-AMS supported the ability to incorporate measured data directly into the propeller model.

While the use of hierarchical design is evident in all of the case studies, we heavily relied upon it for the development of the command and control system in Case Study 1. The RC airplane command and control system is large and complex. The transformation of analog control stick information into digital words, to serial words, to a time-division multiplexed serial bitstream, to a variable pulse width, and back into analog signals takes quite a few subsystems. To view this as a flat design without hierarchy is both inconvenient and impractical. The ability to organize the system into hierarchical functional blocks and sub-blocks was immensely helpful.

We also illustrated the power of having the ability to represent multiple levels of abstraction in the power system of Case Study 3. Here we showed that by using an averaged model in conjunction with a switching model, both time and frequency domain analyses could be conveniently handled.

Throughout these case studies, we have shown how VHDL-AMS can be effectively used for the top-down design methodology. This approach was most clearly illustrated in the rudder system design of Case Study 2. Here we designed the system at a high level in the *s*-domain to check overall servo error and stability. We then implemented the system as a mixed-technology design to account for the true conservation-based behaviors of electromechanical systems. Finally, we illustrated the use of *z*-domain modeling to reimplement the compensator in software. Although not specifically emphasized in the case studies, a bottom-up design methodology is also supported by VHDL-AMS. In this case, low-level detailed circuits and systems can be characterized, and measured parameters can be passed into the higher-level models, resulting in systems that are both accurate and quick to simulate.

Exercises

1. [❶ 26.3] What is the advantage of an H-bridge power amplifier over a push-pull amplifier?

2. [❶ 26.4] What benefit is there of using functions for the data lookup, extrapolation and interpolation algorithms?

3. [❶ 26.4] In Figure 26-20, the prop_pwl model uses the following lookup table function call to get the value of torque that corresponds to the velocity, w:

    torq == pwl_dim1_extrap(w, xdata, ydata);

How would this be rewritten to get the torque value as a function of time rather than a function of velocity (assuming the **xdata** lookup table elements were also time values)?

4. [❶ 26.5] Why should we bother to model the human in the development of an RC airplane system?

5. [❷ 26.3] The rudder system could be controlled bidirectionally with the H-bridge configuration illustrated in Figure 26-13. What modifications would need to be made elsewhere in the overall system to support bidirectional control?

6. [❷ 26.3] Sketch out a simple pulse-width modulator (PWM) circuit that can be implemented structurally in VHDL-AMS.

7. [❷ 26.4] Create a behavioral speed controller model from the sketch in Figure 26-18 using a block statement for each component.

8. [❷ 26.5] Develop a behavioral model for the brain and nervous system functions as illustrated in Figure 26-23.

9. [❸ 26.3] Implement the PWM model you sketched out in Exercise 6 in two ways: (1) as a structural VHDL-AMS model that instantiates individual components, and (2) as a single behavioral model using separate block statements for each component.

10. [❸ 26.3] Implement the PWM model from Exercise 9 as a behavioral model, without using block statements.

11. [❸ 26.4] Using the discussion of the piecewise linear propeller model as a guide, create a piecewise linear voltage source.

12. [❸ 26.4] Write functions to perform the extrapolation and interpolation operations.

13. [❸ 26.4] Modify the lookup table model and functions from Figure 26-20 so that, rather than extrapolating the end value of the lookup data, the end values themselves are used beyond the range of data. For example, if the leftmost **xdata** value corresponds to a **yvalue** of –5, return –5 for any simulation point evaluated to the left of the leftmost **xdata** value. Similarly, if the rightmost **xdata** value corresponds to a **yvalue** of 20, return 20 for any simulation point evaluated to the right of the rightmost **xdata** value.

14. [❸ 26.5] In the RC airplane system depicted in Figure 26-24, the crosswind that influences the plane's heading is modeled as a voltage source internal to the airplane symbol shown in the figure. Create a crosswind model, with proper units (not voltage), that can be made to change the plane's heading.

15. [❹ 26.5] Create a behavioral model for the entire RC airplane system illustrated in Figure 26-24. This model should be analyzable in both the time and frequency domains.

appendix A

Using SPICE Models
in VHDL-AMS

As illustrated throughout this book, the VHDL-AMS modeling language is extremely powerful and flexible for developing simulation models. Many tool vendors extend the power of VHDL-AMS even further by supporting the incorporation of SPICE models into the simulation environment.

In this appendix, the approaches taken by several tool vendors to incorporate SPICE models into their VHDL-AMS simulation environments are presented. Examples of these approaches are also illustrated.

A.1 SystemVision/ADMS (Mentor Graphics Corporation)

www.mentor.com

The SystemVision/ADMS simulation tools by Mentor Graphics allow SPICE circuits and models to be integrated into the VHDL-AMS environment in two ways. First, a VHDL-AMS model can include SPICE sub-circuits as components; second, a SPICE net-list can include VHDL-AMS design entities as components.

VHDL-AMS Model with SPICE Component

As an example, we will demonstrate the method for using a SPICE model of a 5-pin opamp as the core of a VHDL-AMS opamp. The SPICE opamp is a LMC6482A, and the VHDL-AMS entity is called **opamp5**. The **opamp5** "VHDL-AMS on top" model is illustrated in Figure A-1.

As shown in the figure, the SPICE model is incorporated by using three propriety attributes: **Eldo_device_kind**, **Eldo_subckt_name** and **Eldo_file_name**. These attributes are declared in the **MGC_AMS** library, **Eldo** package.

FIGURE A-1

library MGC_AMS; **use** MGC_AMS.eldo.**all**;
...   *-- other lib declarations*
entity opamp5 **is**
     port (**terminal** in_neg, in_pos, output, vcc, vee : electrical);
end opamp5;
-- architecture that calls PSPICE model
architecture LMC6482A **of** opamp5 **is**
     component PSPICE_OpAmp **is**
          port (**terminal** INP, INM, VCC, VEE, VOUT : electrical);
     end component PSPICE_OpAmp;

     attribute Eldo_device **of** PSPICE_OpAmp : **component**
          is Eldo_subckt;
     attribute Eldo_subckt_name **of** PSPICE_OpAmp : **component**
          is "LMC6482A";
     attribute Eldo_file_name **of** PSPICE_OpAmp : **component**
          is "<Model Path>SPICE_models\LMC6482A.cir";
begin
     LMC6482A_1 : PSPICE_OpAmp
          port map (
               INM   => in_neg,
               INP   => in_pos,
               VOUT   => output,
               VCC   => vcc,
               VEE   => vee);
-- | |
-- | *must match names in VHDL-AMS entity declaration*
--   *must match names in PSPICE_OpAmp component port declaration*
end;

```
------------------------------------------------------

*////////////////////////////////////////////////////////
*LMC6482A CMOS Dual OP-AMP MACRO-MODEL
*////////////////////////////////////////////////////////
*
* connections:      non-inverting input
*                   |  inverting input
*                   |  |  positive power supply
*                   |  |  |  negative power supply
*                   |  |  |  |  output
*                   |  |  |  |  |
*                   |  |  |  |  |
.SUBCKT LMC6482A    1  2  99 50 40
```

```
* CAUTION:  SET .OPTIONS GMIN=1E-16
* TO CORRECTLY MODEL INPUT BIAS CURRENT.
...
```

Example of "VHDL-AMS on top" model implementation.

SPICE Model with VHDL-AMS Component

In addition to allowing a SPICE circuit to be referenced from a VHDL-AMS model, a VHDL-AMS model may also be referenced from a SPICE circuit. An example of this "SPICE on top" implementation is illustrated in Figure A-2.

FIGURE A-2

```
.model opamp5(behavioral) macro lang=vhdlams lib=work
yopamp5 opamp5(behavioral)
+ generic:
+ a0 = "1.0e5"
+ f1 = "1.0e6"
+ vos = "0.0"
+ port: in_neg in_pos output vcc vee
```

```
library MGC_AMS;
use MGC_AMS.eldo.all;
...   -- other lib declarations;
entity opamp5 is
    generic ( a0  : real := 1.0e5;    -- open loop gain
              f1  : real := 1.0e6;    -- unit gain bandwidth
              vos : real := 0.0 );    -- offset voltage
    port ( terminal in_neg, in_pos, output, vcc, vee : electrical );
end opamp5;

-- behavioral architecture
architecture behavioral of opamp5 is
    ...
begin
    ...
end architecture behavioral;
```

Example of "SPICE on top" model implementation.

A.2   **VeriasHDL (Synopsys, Inc.)**

www.synopsys.com

Synopsys's VeriasHDL simulator is a multilingual single-kernel mixed-signal simulator that supports, among other languages, VHDL-AMS and HSPICE,[1] Synopsys's version of SPICE. The simulator consists of separate analyzer front ends for VHDL-AMS and HSPICE and shared, but language-aware, analyzer back end, elaborator and simulation engines.

While the VHDL-AMS analyzer complies with IEEE Standard 1076.1-1999, the HSPICE analyzer has been designed to work with the library management scheme defined by VHDL-AMS. In particular, both analyzers understand the concepts of working libraries and resource libraries, and they place the analyzed library units into library WORK. For the HSPICE analyzer, the library units are sub-circuits defined by

```
.SUBCKT
...
.ENDS
```

or

```
.MACRO
...
.ENDM
```

The HSPICE Library

The models supported by the HSPICE simulator are provided with the VeriasHDL simulator in a resource library with the logical name HSPICE. These are TrueHspice models; that is, they use the same source code as the models that are built into the HSPICE simulator. The number of models in the HSPICE library is larger than the number of elements defined by the HSPICE manual because many HSPICE elements have several mutually exclusive sets of parameters that define and control the behavior of the element. Each such behavior is represented by a separate model with the corresponding parameters.

The HSPICE library also contains a package that provides the support needed to instantiate HSPICE models with a VHDL-AMS component instantiation statement. As shown in the next section, HSPICE .MODEL cards are represented by VHDL-AMS constants of a record type. The package includes appropriate record type declarations, a constructor function for each record type and component declarations for most models in the library.

As an example, consider a simplified diode model with just two parameters, the saturation current is0 and the emission coefficient n. The corresponding VHDL-AMS record type declaration is

---

1. VeriasHDL, HSPICE and TrueHspice are trademarks of Synopsys, Inc.

```
type DiodeModel is record
    is0: real;
    n: real;
end record;
```

The constructor function for this type creates a value of the record type from the values of its elements. It also defines the default value of each member:

```
function DiodeModelValue ( is0 : real := 1.0e–14;
                           n : real := 1.0 ) return DiodeModel is
begin
    return DiodeModel'(is0, n);
end function DiodeModelValue;
```

Finally, the component declaration for the corresponding diode is

```
component Diode is
    generic ( model : DiodeModel ;
    port ( terminal anode, cathode : electrical );
end component Diode;
```

The next section shows an example of how these building blocks can be used in a VHDL-AMS design entity.

VHDL-AMS Hierarchies

The VHDL-AMS analyzer in the VeriasHDL simulator can bind design entities to component instances without having to know what language the design entity has been written in. In particular, a VHDL-AMS component instantiation statement can instantiate an HSPICE model or sub-circuit simply by making the corresponding design entity visible using a VHDL-AMS library clause and possibly a use clause. This transparent approach is made possible by placing the HSPICE predefined models and HSPICE sub-circuit definitions in design libraries. There is one restriction: HSPICE models that cannot be written using the VHDL-AMS language cannot be instantiated with a VHDL-AMS component instantiation statement. The HSPICE K element specifying a mutual coupling between two inductors is one of these models.

As an example, an HSPICE .MODEL card can be represented in VHDL-AMS using the building blocks shown in the previous section by a constant of a record type whose initial value is defined by a call to the constructor function. For a saturation current of 10^{-15} A, and using the default for the emission coefficient:

```
constant dv : DiodeModel := DiodeModelValue(is0 => 1.0e–15);
```

This constant can now be used as the actual in the generic map of a component instantiation statement defining an instance of the diode:

```
d1: Diode
    generic map (model => dv)
    port map (anode => ..., cathode => ...);
```

HSPICE Net-Lists

The HSPICE analyzer in the VeriasHDL simulator maps an HSPICE element card to a component instantiation statement for one of the models in the HSPICE library, based on the actual parameters of the element. A sub-circuit element card, which has the syntax

```
Xyyyy n1 [n2 ...] subnam [parnam=val ...]
```

where portions in brackets are optional and an ellipsis indicates that the preceding part can be repeated, is treated slightly differently. If subnam is of the form

```
design_entity@library
```

then the design entity bound to this component instance is found in the library with the specified logical name. Otherwise, it is found in library **work**. The design_entity portion can itself have the form

```
entity(architecture)
```

to specify both entity name and architecture name. This extended syntax makes it possible to instantiate VHDL-AMS design entities from any design library in an HSPICE net-list. There is also one restriction: all ports of such design entities must be terminal ports of nature **electrical**. VHDL-AMS design entities that have ports that are not terminal ports of nature **electrical** cannot be instantiated in an HSPICE net-list.

A.3   Auriga (FTL Systems, Inc.)

www.ftlsys.com

SPICE-like design components may be readily integrated into VHDL-AMS and Verilog-AMS designs using FTL System's Auriga family of compiled-code, mixed-signal simulators. A dialect-dependent parser analyzes SPICE design decks into one or more VHDL-AMS entity-architecture pairs and a TCL command stream. Auriga compilers and runtime environments include SPICE-compatible commands. Auriga export menus provide for exporting the SPICE deck into VHDL-AMS or Verilog-AMS source.

Each top-level SPICE deck or SPICE sub-circuit translates into a VHDL-AMS entity and architecture pair. Within each architecture, most SPICE device instances are readily represented as a VHDL-AMS component instantiation. Generic parameter values come from dialect-specific default values, the SPICE device instance or a corresponding model parameter statement.

Whereas SPICE simulators build component implementations directly into the simulator, Auriga allows implementations using VHDL-AMS, Verilog-AMS, C++ code (through the VHDL-AMS programming-language interface) and on-the-fly component generators. Comparatively simple SPICE components, such as resistors, diodes and JFETs, may be readily translated into VHDL-AMS source code. Such models are loaded on demand via Auriga's file-intermediate representation. Predefined components include

- resistors (discrete and semiconductor)

- capacitors (discrete and semiconductor)

- inductors (discrete and coupled/mutual inductors)

- switches

- voltage and current sources

- transmission lines (lossless and lossy)

- diodes

- bipolar junction transistors (NPN/PNP)

- junction field effect transistors (JFET)

- MOS field effect transistors (MOSFET)

More complex models, such as the BSIM series and proprietary models, may be compiled and linked through FTL Systems' extension of the VHDL-AMS programming language interface. Several SPICE devices, such as mutual inductors, cannot readily be mapped into statically defined library components. Instead, library components are generated on demand during analysis of the SPICE deck.

Translated SPICE decks use data types and natures defined by proposed IEEE standard packages, such as **electrical_systems**. This translation facilitates tight integration of legacy SPICE decks with new HDL-based mixed-signal designs.

In order to preserve upward compatibility with SPICE decks, Auriga family tools translate common SPICE commands into TCL and then implement the commands in VHDL-AMS form. Supported commands include

- operating point analysis

- DC-sweep analysis

- AC analysis

- sensitivity analysis

- transfer function analysis

- transient analysis

- distortion analysis
- Fourier analysis
- noise analysis
- power analysis
- pole/zero analysis
- global
- gridsize
- initial conditions
- model
- nodeset
- options
- param
- table
- temp
- vector
- vrange
- width
- probe/print/plot

Analysis tools built into Auriga help to correlate the behavior of SPICE designs with their HDL-based equivalent. These tools help to increase the user's confidence in adopting the translated HDL design as the primary analog model.

appendix B

The Predefined Package Standard

The predefined types, subtypes and functions of VHDL-AMS are defined in a package called **standard**[1], stored in the library **std**. Each design unit in a design is automatically preceded by the following context clause:

library std, work; **use** std.standard.**all**;

so the predefined items are directly visible in the design. The package **standard** is listed here. The comments indicate which operators are implicitly defined for each explicitly defined type. These operators are also automatically made visible in design units. The types *universal_integer* and *universal_real* are anonymous types. They cannot be referred to explicitly.

package standard **is**
    type boolean **is** (false, true);
        -- implicitly declared for boolean operands:
        -- "and", "or", "nand", "nor", "xor", "xnor", "not" return boolean
        -- "=", "/=", "<", "<=", ">", ">=" return boolean
    type bit **is** ('0', '1');
        -- implicitly declared for bit operands:
        -- "and", "or", "nand", "nor", "xor", "xnor", "not" return bit
        -- "=", "/=", "<", "<=", ">", ">=" return boolean
    type character **is** (

nul,	soh,	stx,	etx,	eot,	enq,	ack,	bel,
bs,	ht,	lf,	vt,	ff,	cr,	so,	si,
dle,	dc1,	dc2,	dc3,	dc4,	nak,	syn,	etb,
can,	em,	sub,	esc,	fsp,	gsp,	rsp,	usp,
' ',	'!',	'"',	'#',	'$',	'%',	'&',	''',

---

1. From IEEE Standard 1076-2001. Copyright 2001 IEEE. All rights reserved.

```
'(',      ')',      '*',      '+',      ',',      '-',      '.',      '/',
'0',      '1',      '2',      '3',      '4',      '5',      '6',      '7',
'8',      '9',      ':',      ';',      '<',      '=',      '>',      '?',
'@',      'A',      'B',      'C',      'D',      'E',      'F',      'G',
'H',      'I',      'J',      'K',      'L',      'M',      'N',      'O',
'P',      'Q',      'R',      'S',      'T',      'U',      'V',      'W',
'X',      'Y',      'Z',      '[',      '\',      ']',      '^',      '_',
'`',      'a',      'b',      'c',      'd',      'e',      'f',      'g',
'h',      'i',      'j',      'k',      'l',      'm',      'n',      'o',
'p',      'q',      'r',      's',      't',      'u',      'v',      'w',
'x',      'y',      'z',      '{',      '|',      '}',      '~',      del,
c128,     c129,     c130,     c131,     c132,     c133,     c134,     c135,
c136,     c137,     c138,     c139,     c140,     c141,     c142,     c143,
c144,     c145,     c146,     c147,     c148,     c149,     c150,     c151,
c152,     c153,     c154,     c155,     c156,     c157,     c158,     c159,
' ',      '¡',      '¢',      '£',      '¤',      '¥',      '¦',      '§',
'¨',      '©',      'ª',      '«',      '¬',      '',      '®',      '¯',
'°',      '±',      '²',      '³',      '´',      'µ',      '¶',      '·',
'¸',      '¹',      'º',      '»',      '¼',      '½',      '¾',      '¿',
'À',      'Á',      'Â',      'Ã',      'Ä',      'Å',      'Æ',      'Ç',
'È',      'É',      'Ê',      'Ë',      'Ì',      'Í',      'Î',      'Ï',
'Ð',      'Ñ',      'Ò',      'Ó',      'Ô',      'Õ',      'Ö',      '×',
'Ø',      'Ù',      'Ú',      'Û',      'Ü',      'Ý',      'Þ',      'ß',
'à',      'á',      'â',      'ã',      'ä',      'å',      'æ',      'ç',
'è',      'é',      'ê',      'ë',      'ì',      'í',      'î',      'ï',
'ð',      'ñ',      'ò',      'ó',      'ô',      'õ',      'ö',      '÷',
'ø',      'ù',      'ú',      'û',      'ü',      'ý',      'þ',      'ÿ');
```

    -- implicitly declared for character operands:
    -- "=", "/=", "<", "<=", ">", ">=" return boolean

type severity_level **is** (note, warning, error, failure);

    -- implicitly declared for severity_level operands:
    -- "=", "/=", "<", "<=", ">", ">=" return boolean

type *universal_integer* **is range** *implementation_defined*;

    -- implicitly declared for universal_integer operands:
    -- "=", "/=", "<", "<=", ">", ">=" return boolean
    -- "*", "/", "+", "-", "abs", "rem", "mod" return universal_integer

type *universal_real* **is range** *implementation_defined*;

    -- implicitly declared for universal_real operands:
    -- "=", "/=", "<", "<=", ">", ">=" return boolean
    -- "*", "/", "+", "-", "abs" return universal_real

type integer **is range** *implementation_defined*;

    -- implicitly declared for integer operands:
    -- "=", "/=", "<", "<=", ">", ">=" return boolean
    -- "**", "*", "/", "+", "-", "abs", "rem", "mod" return integer

```
subtype natural is integer range 0 to integer'high;
subtype positive is integer range 1 to integer'high;

type real is range implementation_defined;

    -- implicitly declared for real operands:
    -- "=", "/=", "<", "<=", ">", ">=" return boolean
    -- "**", "*", "/", "+", "-", "abs" return real

type time is range implementation_defined
    units fs;
        ps  = 1000 fs;
        ns  = 1000 ps;
        us  = 1000 ns;
        ms  = 1000 us;
        sec = 1000 ms;
        min = 60 sec;
        hr  = 60 min;
    end units;

    -- implicitly declared for time operands:
    -- "=", "/=", "<", "<=", ">", ">=" return boolean
    -- "*", "+", "-", "abs" return time
    -- "/" return time or universal_integer

type domain_type is (quiescent_domain, time_domain, frequency_domain);

    -- implicitly declared for domain_type operands:
    -- "=", "/=", "<", "<=", ">", ">=" return boolean

signal domain : domain_type := quiescent_domain;

subtype delay_length is time range 0 fs to time'high;

impure function now return delay_length;

impure function now return real;

function frequency return real;

type real_vector is array (natural range <>) of real;

    -- implicitly declared for real_vector operands:
    -- "=", "/=", "<", "<=", ">", ">=" return boolean
    -- "&" return real_vector

type string is array (positive range <>) of character;

    -- implicitly declared for string operands:
    -- "=", "/=", "<", "<=", ">", ">=" return boolean
    -- "&" return string

type bit_vector is array (natural range <>) of bit;

    -- implicitly declared for bit_vector operands:
    -- "and", "or", "nand", "nor", "xor", "xnor", "not" return bit_vector
    -- "sll", "srl", "sla", "sra", "rol", "ror" return bit_vector
    -- "=", "/=", "<", "<=", ">", ">=" return boolean
    -- "&" return bit_vector
```

type file_open_kind **is** (read_mode, write_mode, append_mode);

—— implicitly declared for file_open_kind operands:
—— "=", "/=", "<", "<=", ">", ">=" return boolean

type file_open_status **is** (open_ok, status_error, name_error, mode_error);

—— implicitly declared for file_open_status operands:
—— "=", "/=", "<", "<=", ">", ">=" return boolean

attribute foreign : string;

end package standard;

appendix C

IEEE Standard Packages

The package declarations for the IEEE standard multivalue logic and mathematical packages are listed in this appendix. The IEEE standards also include package bodies defining the detailed meaning of each of the operators and functions provided by the packages. However, simulator vendors are allowed to substitute accelerated implementations of the packages rather than compiling the package bodies into simulations. The IEEE standards require the packages to be in a resource library named **ieee**.

C.1 Std_Logic_1164 Multivalue Logic System[1]

package std_logic_1164 **is**

```
----------------------------------------------------------
-- logic state system (unresolved)
----------------------------------------------------------
type std_ulogic is ( 'U',     -- Uninitialized
                     'X',     -- Forcing Unknown
                     '0',     -- Forcing 0
                     '1',     -- Forcing 1
                     'Z',     -- High Impedance
                     'W',     -- Weak Unknown
                     'L',     -- Weak 0
                     'H',     -- Weak 1
                     '-'      -- Don't care
                   );
----------------------------------------------------------
-- unconstrained array of std_ulogic for use with the resolution function
----------------------------------------------------------
type std_ulogic_vector is array ( natural range <> ) of std_ulogic;
```

---

1. From IEEE Standard 1164-1993. Copyright 1993 IEEE. All rights reserved.

```
--------------------------------------------------------
-- resolution function
--------------------------------------------------------

function resolved ( s : std_ulogic_vector ) return std_ulogic;


--------------------------------------------------------
-- *** industry standard logic type ***
--------------------------------------------------------

subtype std_logic is resolved std_ulogic;


-- unconstrained array of std_logic for use in declaring signal arrays
--------------------------------------------------------

type std_logic_vector is array ( natural range <>) of std_logic;


-- common subtypes
--------------------------------------------------------

subtype X01    is resolved std_ulogic range 'X' to '1';    -- ('X','0','1')
subtype X01Z   is resolved std_ulogic range 'X' to 'Z';    -- ('X','0','1','Z')
subtype UX01   is resolved std_ulogic range 'U' to '1';    -- ('U','X','0','1')
subtype UX01Z  is resolved std_ulogic range 'U' to 'Z';    -- ('U','X','0','1','Z')


-- overloaded logical operators
--------------------------------------------------------

function "and"   ( l : std_ulogic; r : std_ulogic ) return UX01;
function "nand"  ( l : std_ulogic; r : std_ulogic ) return UX01;
function "or"    ( l : std_ulogic; r : std_ulogic ) return UX01;
function "nor"   ( l : std_ulogic; r : std_ulogic ) return UX01;
function "xor"   ( l : std_ulogic; r : std_ulogic ) return UX01;
function "xnor"  ( l : std_ulogic; r : std_ulogic ) return UX01;
function "not"   ( l : std_ulogic ) return UX01;


-- vectorized overloaded logical operators
--------------------------------------------------------

function "and"   ( l, r : std_logic_vector ) return std_logic_vector;
function "and"   ( l, r : std_ulogic_vector ) return std_ulogic_vector;
function "nand"  ( l, r : std_logic_vector ) return std_logic_vector;
function "nand"  ( l, r : std_ulogic_vector ) return std_ulogic_vector;
function "or"    ( l, r : std_logic_vector ) return std_logic_vector;
function "or"    ( l, r : std_ulogic_vector ) return std_ulogic_vector;
function "nor"   ( l, r : std_logic_vector ) return std_logic_vector;
function "nor"   ( l, r : std_ulogic_vector ) return std_ulogic_vector;
function "xor"   ( l, r : std_logic_vector ) return std_logic_vector;
function "xor"   ( l, r : std_ulogic_vector ) return std_ulogic_vector;
function "xnor"  ( l, r : std_logic_vector ) return std_logic_vector;
function "xnor"  ( l, r : std_ulogic_vector ) return std_ulogic_vector;
function "not"   ( l : std_logic_vector ) return std_logic_vector;
function "not"   ( l : std_ulogic_vector ) return std_ulogic_vector;
```

```
------------------------------------------------------------
-- conversion functions
------------------------------------------------------------
function To_bit ( s : std_ulogic;  xmap : bit := '0' ) return bit;
function To_bitvector ( s : std_logic_vector;  xmap : bit := '0' ) return bit_vector;
function To_bitvector ( s : std_ulogic_vector;  xmap : bit := '0' ) return bit_vector;
function To_StdULogic ( b : bit ) return std_ulogic;
function To_StdLogicVector ( b : bit_vector ) return std_logic_vector;
function To_StdLogicVector ( s : std_ulogic_vector ) return std_logic_vector;
function To_StdULogicVector ( b : bit_vector ) return std_ulogic_vector;
function To_StdULogicVector ( s : std_logic_vector ) return std_ulogic_vector;

------------------------------------------------------------
-- strength strippers and type convertors
------------------------------------------------------------
function To_X01 ( s : std_logic_vector ) return std_logic_vector;
function To_X01 ( s : std_ulogic_vector ) return std_ulogic_vector;
function To_X01 ( s : std_ulogic ) return X01;
function To_X01 ( b : bit_vector ) return std_logic_vector;
function To_X01 ( b : bit_vector ) return std_ulogic_vector;
function To_X01 ( b : bit ) return X01;
function To_X01Z ( s : std_logic_vector ) return std_logic_vector;
function To_X01Z ( s : std_ulogic_vector ) return std_ulogic_vector;
function To_X01Z ( s : std_ulogic ) return X01Z;
function To_X01Z ( b : bit_vector ) return std_logic_vector;
function To_X01Z ( b : bit_vector ) return std_ulogic_vector;
function To_X01Z ( b : bit ) return X01Z;
function To_UX01 ( s : std_logic_vector ) return std_logic_vector;
function To_UX01 ( s : std_ulogic_vector ) return std_ulogic_vector;
function To_UX01 ( s : std_ulogic ) return UX01;
function To_UX01 ( b : bit_vector ) return std_logic_vector;
function To_UX01 ( b : bit_vector ) return std_ulogic_vector;
function To_UX01 ( b : bit ) return UX01;

------------------------------------------------------------
-- edge detection
------------------------------------------------------------
function rising_edge ( signal s : std_ulogic ) return boolean;
function falling_edge ( signal s : std_ulogic ) return boolean;

------------------------------------------------------------
-- object contains an unknown
------------------------------------------------------------
function Is_X ( s : std_ulogic_vector ) return boolean;
function Is_X ( s : std_logic_vector ) return boolean;
function Is_X ( s : std_ulogic ) return boolean;
end std_logic_1164;
```

C.2 **Standard 1076.2 VHDL Mathematical Packages**[2]

Real Mathematical Operations

package math_real **is**

    constant copyrightnotice: string := "Copyright 1996 IEEE. All rights reserved.";

    -- Constant Definitions

    ----

    constant math_e : real := 2.71828_18284_59045_23536;
    constant math_1_over_e : real := 0.36787_94411_71442_32160;
    constant math_pi : real := 3.14159_26535_89793_23846;
    constant math_2_pi : real := 6.28318_53071_79586_47693;
    constant math_1_over_pi : real := 0.31830_98861_83790_67154;
    constant math_pi_over_2 : real := 1.57079_63267_94896_61923;
    constant math_pi_over_3 : real := 1.04719_75511_96597_74615;
    constant math_pi_over_4 : real := 0.78539_81633_97448_30962;
    constant math_3_pi_over_2 : real := 4.71238_89803_84689_85769;
    constant math_log_of_2 : real := 0.69314_71805_59945_30942;
    constant math_log_of_10 : real := 2.30258_50929_94045_68402;
    constant math_log2_of_e : real := 1.44269_50408_88963_4074;
    constant math_log10_of_e: real := 0.43429_44819_03251_82765;
    constant math_sqrt_2: real := 1.41421_35623_73095_04880;
    constant math_1_over_sqrt_2: real := 0.70710_67811_86547_52440;
    constant math_sqrt_pi: real := 1.77245_38509_05516_02730;
    constant math_deg_to_rad: real := 0.01745_32925_19943_29577;
    constant math_rad_to_deg: real := 57.29577_95130_82320_87680;

    -- Function Declarations

    ----

    function sign (x : **in** real) **return** real;
    function ceil (x : **in** real) **return** real;
    function floor (x : **in** real) **return** real;
    function round (x : **in** real) **return** real;
    function trunc (x : **in** real) **return** real;

    function "mod" (x, y : **in** real) **return** real;

    function realmax (x, y : **in** real) **return** real;
    function realmin (x, y : **in** real) **return** real;

    procedure uniform (**variable** seed1,seed2 : **inout** positive; **variable** x : **out** real);

    function sqrt (x : **in** real) **return** real;
    function cbrt (x : **in** real) **return** real;

---

2. From IEEE Standard 1076.2-1996. Copyright 1997 IEEE. All rights reserved.

```
function "**" ( x : in integer;  y : in real ) return real;
function "**" ( x : in real;  y : in real ) return real;

function exp ( x : in real ) return real;
function log ( x : in real ) return real;
function log2 ( x : in real ) return real;
function log10 ( x : in real ) return real;
function log ( x : in real; base: in real ) return real;

function  sin ( x : in real ) return real;
function  cos ( x : in real ) return real;
function  tan ( x : in real ) return real;

function  arcsin ( x : in real ) return real;
function  arccos ( x : in real ) return real;
function  arctan ( y : in real ) return real;
function  arctan ( y : in real;  x : in real ) return real;

function sinh ( x : in real ) return real;
function cosh ( x : in real ) return real;
function tanh ( x : in real ) return real;

function arcsinh ( x : in real ) return real;
function arccosh ( x : in real ) return real;
function arctanh ( x : in real ) return real;
end math_real;
```

Complex Mathematical Operations

```
use work.math_real.all;

package math_complex is

    constant copyrightnotice: string := "Copyright 1996 IEEE. All rights reserved.";

    ----------------------------------------------------------
    -- Type Definitions
    ----------------------------------------------------------
    type complex is
        record
            re : real;    -- real part
            im : real;    -- imaginary part
        end record;
    subtype positive_real is real range 0.0 to real'high;
    subtype principal_value is real range -math_pi to math_pi;
    type complex_polar is
        record
            mag : positive_real; -- magnitude
            arg : principal_value;  -- angle in radians; -math_pi is illegal
        end record;
```

-- Constant Definitions
---

constant math_cbase_1 : complex := complex'(1.0, 0.0);
constant math_cbase_j : complex := complex'(0.0, 1.0);
constant math_czero : complex := complex'(0.0, 0.0);

-- Overloaded equality and inequality operators for complex_polar
-- (equality and inequality operators for complex are predefined)
---

function "=" (l : **in** complex_polar; r : **in** complex_polar) **return** boolean;
function "/=" (l : **in** complex_polar; r : **in** complex_polar) **return** boolean;

-- Function Declarations
---

function cmplx (x : **in** real; y: **in** real:= 0.0) **return** complex;

function get_principal_value (x : **in** real) **return** principal_value;

function complex_to_polar (z : **in** complex) **return** complex_polar;
function polar_to_complex (z : **in** complex_polar) **return** complex;

function "abs" (z: **in** complex) **return** positive_real;
function "abs" (z: **in** complex_polar) **return** positive_real;
function arg (z: **in** complex) **return** principal_value;
function arg (z: **in** complex_polar) **return** principal_value;

function "−" (z: **in** complex) **return** complex;
function "−" (z: **in** complex_polar) **return** complex_polar;

function conj (z: **in** complex) **return** complex;
function conj (z: **in** complex_polar) **return** complex_polar;

function sqrt (z: **in** complex) **return** complex;
function sqrt (z: **in** complex_polar) **return** complex_polar;

function exp (z: **in** complex) **return** complex;
function exp (z: **in** complex_polar) **return** complex_polar;

function log (z: **in** complex) **return** complex;
function log2 (z: **in** complex) **return** complex;
function log10 (z: **in** complex) **return** complex;
function log (z: **in** complex_polar) **return** complex_polar;
function log2 (z: **in** complex_polar) **return** complex_polar;
function log10 (z: **in** complex_polar) **return** complex_polar;
function log (z: **in** complex; base: **in** real) **return** complex;
function log (z: **in** complex_polar; base: **in** real) **return** complex_polar;

function sin (z : **in** complex) **return** complex;
function sin (z : **in** complex_polar) **return** complex_polar;
function cos (z : **in** complex) **return** complex;
function cos (z : **in** complex_polar) **return** complex_polar;

```
function sinh ( z : in complex ) return complex;
function sinh ( z : in complex_polar ) return complex_polar;
function cosh ( z : in complex ) return complex;
function cosh ( z : in complex_polar ) return complex_polar;
```

-- Arithmetic Operators

```
function "+" ( l: in complex;  r: in complex ) return complex;
function "+" ( l: in real;  r: in complex ) return complex;
function "+" ( l: in complex;  r: in real ) return complex;
function "+" ( l: in complex_polar;  r : in complex_polar ) return complex_polar;
function "+" ( l: in real;  r: in complex_polar ) return complex_polar;
function "+" ( l: in complex_polar;  r: in real ) return complex_polar;

function "−" ( l: in complex;  r: in complex ) return complex;
function "−" ( l: in real;   r: in complex ) return complex;
function "−" ( l: in complex;  r: in real ) return complex;
function "−" ( l: in complex_polar;  r : in complex_polar ) return complex_polar;
function "−" ( l: in real;  r: in complex_polar ) return complex_polar;
function "−" ( l: in complex_polar;  r: in real ) return complex_polar;

function "*" ( l: in complex;  r: in complex ) return complex;
function "*" ( l: in real;  r: in complex ) return complex;
function "*" ( l: in complex;  r: in real ) return complex;
function "*" ( l: in complex_polar;  r : in complex_polar ) return complex_polar;
function "*" ( l: in real;  r: in complex_polar ) return complex_polar;
function "*" ( l: in complex_polar;  r: in real ) return complex_polar;

function "/" ( l: in complex;  r: in complex ) return complex;
function "/" ( l: in real;  r: in complex ) return complex;
function "/" ( l: in complex;  r: in real ) return complex;
function "/" ( l: in complex_polar;  r : in complex_polar ) return complex_polar;
function "/" ( l: in real;  r: in complex_polar ) return complex_polar;
function "/" ( l: in complex_polar;  r: in real ) return complex_polar;
end math_complex;
```

appendix D

Related Standards

VHDL-AMS, as a hardware description language, is a fundamental tool for designing electronic circuits and systems. However, it does not stand alone. It must be part of a collection of methodologies, tools and utilities that form a complete electronic design automation (EDA) environment. The IEEE Design Automation Standards Committee (DASC) and other groups are actively developing standards that specify these other components of the EDA suite. In this appendix, we briefly introduce those standards related to VHDL-AMS that have been completed or are in progress and discuss future evolution of existing standards.

The IEEE practice is to designate authorized standards development projects that are in progress with the letter 'P' followed by the standard number. Several of the projects are in this state at the time of writing. When their development work is complete and the standard is passed, the 'P' will be dropped to form the official standard number.

The reader should bear in mind that the information here is a snapshot of standards at the time of writing. In the field of EDA, things move quickly. A good starting point for up-to-date information is the EDA Industry Working Groups Web page at *www.eda.org*. For each of the standards described in this appendix, we list the Web address of the group responsible for maintaining the standard.

D.1 IEEE VHDL Standards

IEEE Standard 1076 VHDL

www.eda.org/vasg/

VHDL is officially defined in IEEE Standard 1076-2001, *IEEE Standard VHDL Language Reference Manual*. This document is maintained by a subcommittee of the DASC called the VHDL Analysis and Standardization Group (VASG). At the time of writing, the VASG is preparing for the next revision of the language, scheduled for completion around 2006. The initial stages of preparation involve collecting requirements for changes and enhancements from VHDL users and other stakeholders. The group's Web pages currently include a "Bugs and Enhancements" form for users to provide input to this process.

The interested reader should see *The Designer's Guide to VHDL* for information about the differences between the 1993 version of VHDL (on which VHDL-AMS is based) and the 2001 version.

VHDL Programming Language Interface

www.eda.org/vhdlpli/

The DASC VHDL PLI Task Force is developing a specification for a programming language interface to VHDL design databases and simulators. The PLI defines a collection of C functions for accessing static information about an elaborated VHDL model, for controlling activity in a VHDL simulator, for accessing and modifying the values of VHDL objects during simulation, and for interfacing non-VHDL models with a VHDL simulation. These functions can be used for design processing tools, such as translators, delay calculators, debuggers, code profilers and coverage analyzers, and specialized behavioral models. At the time of writing, it is unclear whether the PLI will be published as an annex to the VHDL standard document, or as a separate standard document.

IEEE Standard 1076.1 VHDL-AMS

www.eda.org/vhdl-ams/

VHDL-AMS is defined in IEEE Standard 1076.1-1999, *IEEE Standard VHDL Analog and Mixed-Signal Extensions*. This standard is an extension of the 1993 version of the VHDL standard. At the time of writing, the working group responsible for the VHDL-AMS standard plans to revise the standard to track changes in the 2001 version of VHDL. However, the schedule for the revision is not yet set.

VHDL-AMS Programming Language Interface

www.lynguent.com/VHPI-AMS/

The VHDL-AMS Working Group established a subcommittee late in 2001 to develop an extension of the VHDL PLI (described above) for VHDL-AMS. At the time of writing, work was in the very preliminary stages. Interested readers can monitor progress on the subcommittee's Web site.

IEEE Standard 1076.2 Mathematical Packages

www.eda.org/math/

In Chapter 10 we described the packages math_real and math_complex. These packages are defined in IEEE Standard 1076.2-1996, *IEEE Standard VHDL Mathematical Packages*. At the time of writing, the IEEE 1076.2 Working Group has not been active. However, the standard needs to be reviewed soon, so there is an opportunity for considering enhancements when the working group reconvenes.

IEEE Standard 1076.3 Synthesis Packages

www.eda.org/vhdlsynth/

In Chapter 10 we also mentioned the packages numeric_bit and numeric_std. These packages are defined in IEEE Standard 1076.3-1997, *IEEE Standard VHDL Synthesis Packages*. The standard also specifies the interpretation by synthesis tools of the standard logic types defined in std_logic_1164. At the time of writing, the IEEE 1076.3 Working Group also has not been active. However, the 1076.3 standard also needs to be reviewed soon, providing an opportunity for considering enhancements.

IEEE Standard 1076.4 VITAL

www.eda.org/vital/

One of the most difficult aspects of designing a system is the timing. This is one reason why features to deal with timing are such a major part of VHDL and VHDL-AMS. However, these languages just provide basic mechanisms. They do not provide a complete methodology for specifying or testing the detailed timing behavior of a circuit. In response to this lack, a consortium of interested parties, including ASIC vendors and designers, formed an organization called the VHDL Initiative Towards ASIC Libraries (VITAL). They developed a standard practice for including detailed timing information in VHDL models of ASIC cells and a standard interface for back-annotation of timing data from layout tools. They also developed a library of primitive components (gates, flipflops, registers, etc.) that conform to the methodology. The goal was to allow a designer to perform "sign-off" simulation of a design, namely, a sufficiently detailed simulation to satisfy both designer and ASIC foundry that the fabricated ASIC will function as simulated. The VITAL Committee subsequently transferred the specifications to an IEEE working group, resulting in development of the IEEE standard published in 1995.

The VITAL standard specifies a package, vital_timing in library ieee, containing types for specifying detailed pin-to-pin propagation delays and timing constraints, including maximum, minimum and nominal values. The package also provides procedures for performing timing checks. The VITAL standard methodology involves the designer including generic constants for timing data in entity declarations. The names and types for the generic constants are specified by the standard, as is the way in which they should be used within architecture bodies to implement correct timing behavior and to verify timing constraints. Instead of using configuration declarations to include actual back-annotated timing data, the standard allows simulators to read the data from files in Standard Delay Format (SDF). The reasons for this approach are that SDF is widely used already and that reading the data in this format is faster than analyzing a VHDL version and reconfiguring the model. The VITAL standard also specifies a package, vital_primitives, that provides subprograms to assist in expressing the behavior of ASIC cell models. The subprograms include operations to model basic logic primitives, such as gates, multiplexers and decoders, as well as operations to model combinatorial truth tables and sequential state tables.

Since publication of the 1995 version, the VITAL Working Group has revised the standard. The current revision is IEEE Standard 1076.4-2000, *IEEE Standard VITAL ASIC (Application-Specific Integrated Circuit) Modeling Specification*. The revision addresses several usability issues that were raised with the 1995 standard. However, the most significant enhancement is inclusion of a new package, vital_memory, that defines data types and subprograms to support development of memory models.

IEEE P1076.5 VHDL Utility Library

www.eda.org/libutil/

Most organizations that use VHDL find it necessary or desirable to develop a library of packages of generally useful operations. This follows the good software engineering practice of code reuse. Since VHDL's widespread adoption, many organizations have made their utility packages freely available. However, designers often find the urge to "do it better" irresistible.

The P1076.5 Working Group was formed to develop a utility library to add to the collection of IEEE standard packages. However, very little interest was shown in the work, and the project has since lapsed. We mention it here so that the curious reader will know why the number 1076.5 is missing from the sequence of 1076 "dot" standards.

IEEE 1076.6 VHDL Synthesis Interoperability

www.eda.org/siwg/

IEEE Standard 1076.6-1999, *IEEE Standard for VHDL Register Transfer Level (RTL) Synthesis*, defines a subset of VHDL for use with digital hardware synthesis tools. The interested reader should see *The Designer's Guide to VHDL* for an overview of the standard and guidelines on writing synthesizable VHDL models. The subset of VHDL described in the standard is referred to by the IEEE 1076.6 Working Group as the Level 1 subset. It is deliberately very restrictive, in order to allow models to be accepted by as many synthesis tools as possible. At the time of writing, the working group is specifying a Level 2 subset, in which many of the restrictions are relaxed.

IEEE Standard 1164 Multivalue Logic System

www.eda.org/vhdl-std-logic/

In this book we have made extensive use of the package std_logic_1164. The package is defined in IEEE Standard 1164-1993, *IEEE Standard Multivalue Logic System for VHDL Model Interoperability (Std_logic_1164)*. At the time of writing, the working group responsible for the standard is preparing a revision to be published in 2002.

IEEE Standard 1029.1 WAVES

www.eda.org/waves/

IEEE Standard 1029.1-1998, *IEEE Standard for VHDL Waveform and Vector Exchange to Support Design and Test Verification (WAVES) Language Reference Manual,* speci-fies use of VHDL to exchange stimulus/response test vector information between sim-ulation and test environments. Because it relies purely on VHDL, it is a non-proprietary format.

A WAVES *test set* is a collection of VHDL packages, including a *waveform gener-ator procedure* that produces a stream of stimulus or expected response values (a *waveform*) for a unit under test. The procedure draws upon the resources of a num-ber of predefined WAVES packages to specify the values in the waveform and the tim-ing relationships between waveform elements. The VHDL packages in a WAVES data set may be augmented with external files containing data in a non-VHDL format. The waveform generator procedure may read data from these files to construct the wave-form.

One of the difficulties with WAVES is that it simply defines a format for describing a waveform generator. It does not indicate how a generator is to be incorporated into a VHDL test bench to test operation of a simulation model. To address this prob-lem, a group at Rome Laboratories of the United States Air Force has developed a WAVES-VHDL Tool Set. It includes a tool to generate a WAVES test set and a VHDL test bench from a VHDL entity declaration and a tool to generate automatic test equip-ment (ATE) files from a WAVES test set. The tool set is available from the WAVES Working Group Web page.

D.2 Other Design Automation Standards

While VHDL-AMS is a major tool for design of digital and mixed-signal systems, there are other standardized tools that complement it to form a complete EDA environment. Some of these are standardized by the IEEE, whereas others are specified by other organizations. In this section, we list several major EDA standards and projects that are not specifically VHDL-based.

IEEE Standard 1364 Verilog

www.ovi.org/ieee-1364/Welcome.html

Verilog is "the other" hardware description language. While it is widely used in North America and Asia, it is much less popular in Europe. It originated as a proprietary simulation language and was subsequently handed over to the IEEE and published as an IEEE standard. The working group responsible for maintaining the standard operates under the auspices of Open Verilog International (OVI), now part of the Accellera organization. It has recently completed a revision of the standard, published as IEEE Standard 1364-2001, *IEEE Standard for Verilog Hardware Description Language.*

Verilog addresses many of the same requirements of a hardware description language as VHDL. However, it lacks the emphasis on strong software-engineering discipline and support. In particular, it does not have the rich type system of VHDL. Instead, data is represented and manipulated at the bit and bit-vector level. Furthermore, Verilog does not provide support for managing complex structural design hierarchy. However, the language does offer better support than VHDL for modeling at low levels of abstraction, in particular, gate level and switch level. For these reasons, many designers choose VHDL for their models at the behavioral and register-transfer levels and use synthesis tools to generate Verilog models at the gate level. They then rely on Verilog simulation tools to perform final timing verification of the design.

The Verilog-2001 revision of the standard addresses some of the shortcomings of Verilog for behavioral-level modeling and for design configuration. For further information, see the Working Group's Web page.

IEEE P1364.1 Verilog Synthesis Interoperability

www.eda.org/vlog-synth/

The IEEE P1364.1 Working Group is developing a specification of a synthesizable subset of Verilog, analogous to the subset of VHDL defined in IEEE Standard 1076.6.

OVI Verilog-AMS

www.eda.org/verilog-ams/

The Verilog-AMS Technical Subcommittee of OVI is developing extensions to Verilog for modeling analog and mixed-signal systems. Verilog-AMS uses much of the same underlying theory for describing analog behavior as VHDL-AMS. It allows description in terms of differential and algebraic equations relating values of potential and flow quantities at nodes in the analog circuit and provides transition generators and threshold-crossing detectors for interfacing between analog and digital parts of a model. Information about the extensions and example models can be found in the Verilog-AMS Subcommittee's Web pages.

IEEE Standard 1499 OMF

www.eda.org/omf/

In this book we have described the use of VHDL-AMS for expressing models of hardware designs. We have also mentioned Verilog as an alternative hardware description language. However, in some cases, model vendors choose to express models using a programming language, such as C or C++. There are various reasons for doing so. One is that the code generated by programming language compilers is generally much more efficient, and hence higher in performance, than that generated by a VHDL or Verilog compiler. Another is the protection of intellectual property (IP) afforded by supplying compiled programming language object files instead of VHDL or Verilog source code. Furthermore, use of programming languages allows interfacing with hardware modelers and emulators to accelerate simulation.

For models written using programming languages to be portable across host platforms and different simulators, there needs to be a specification for the interface between models and simulators. Such a specification was developed by the Open Model Forum (OMF), a consortium of simulator and model vendors. The specification was subsequently standardized as IEEE Standard 1499-1998, *IEEE Standard Interface for Hardware Description Models of Electronics Components*. It specifies a set of functions to be implemented by a simulator and a model that allow the model to drive values on signals and to respond to events generated by the simulator.

Rosetta

www.sldl.org

www.eda.org/slds-rosetta/

The System Level Design Language (SLDL) Initiative was formed under the auspices of the EDA Industry Council and subsequently migrated to VHDL International, now part of the Accellera organization. Its charter was to develop languages to support high-level specification and design of microelectronic systems. This also encompasses specification and design of the environment in which the systems operate, including software, mixed-signal, optical and micro electronic/mechanical characteristics. An Accellera working group is now defining the Rosetta system-level description language, in which system-level specifications and constraints will be expressed. The group envisages that Rosetta will be used early in the design flow to capture abstract specification and constraint information and will interface with tools using languages such as VHDL-AMS for design refinement.

IEEE P1497 Standard Delay Format

www.eda.org/sdf/

Standard Delay Format (SDF) is a file format for expressing detailed timing information about a design. The data in an SDF file is a tool-independent representation of path delays, timing constraint values, interconnect delays and high-level technology parameters. The SDF specification was originally developed as a proprietary format and subsequently standardized by OVI. It has gained widespread acceptance by EDA tool vendors. Recently, the specification was handed over to an IEEE working group. At the time of writing, the draft standard has been approved and should be published in 2002.

IEEE P1603 Advanced Library Format

www.eda.org/alf/

The Advanced Library Format (ALF) Working Group has developed a specification for a format to describe ASIC library cells for use by synthesis tools, timing and power analysis tools, and other physical design tools. The description of a library cell includes specification of its function; its timing and electrical characteristics; and other data needed for synthesis, layout and test. The format also allows for specification of library information, such as interconnect models and technology physical data.

IEEE Standard 1481 Delay and Power Calculation

www.eda.org/dpc/ and *www.si2.org/ieee1481/*

The Delay and Power Calculation System (DPCS) and Delay Calculation Language (DCL) were originally developed under the auspices of the Silicon Integration Initiative (SI^2) and OVI. The specifications were subsequently standardized as IEEE Standard 1481-1999, *IEEE Standard for Delay and Power Calculation*. DCL is a language for use by an ASIC cell provider to specify how delays should be calculated for cells in a given technology library. A DCL description is compiled into a Delay Calculation Module (DCM) that is incorporated into the library. The standard specifies a procedural interface for use by EDA tools to invoke the delay calculation rules in the DCM. The DPCS also makes use of information represented in two subsidiary formats: the Physical Data Exchange Format (PDEF), for floor plan information, and the Standard Parasitic Extended File (SPEF) format, for interconnect parasitic information resulting from the detailed layout of the ASIC design. Among other applications, the DPCS can be used in timing analysis tools that generate SDF timing information for detailed timing simulation of a design.

EIA-682 Electronic Design Interchange Format (EDIF)

www.edif.org/

EDIF is a standard for exchanging electronic design information between EDA tools and for transferring the information to manufacturers. The standard originated with the Electronic Industries Alliance (EIA) and has subsequently been adopted as an international standard by the International Electrotechnical Commission (IEC). EDIF Version 3 0 0 is IEC Standard 61690-1, and EDIF Version 4 0 0 is IEC Standard 61690-2. Version 3 0 0 provides for description of schematics connectivity, design hierarchy, libraries and configuration, while Version 4 0 0 adds support for describing printed circuit boards and multichip modules.

EIA-567-A Component Modeling and Interface

No Web pages available at time of writing.

The EIA has developed the *VHDL Hardware Component Modeling and Interface Standard* to provide guidelines for component models. The standard addresses issues similar to those addressed by P1076.4, but with an emphasis on modeling existing hardware components rather than ASICs under development. The EIA-567-A standard specifies the form and content of an *electronic data sheet* for a hardware component, analogous to the paper data sheets provided by component manufacturers. The electronic data sheet includes an *electrical view*, a *timing view* and a *physical view*, all of which are written as VHDL packages. The data sheet also includes a VHDL simulation model that implements the component behavior, a test bench and stimulus/response test vectors, VHDL configuration declarations required to build a simulation and documentation for the model user. The electrical view specifies the signal voltage and current characteristics for each electrical connection of the component. The physical view specifies all of the pins of the physical package of the component, including power supply and electrically unconnected pins. The timing view specifies the values of timing parameters, such as setup and hold times, pulse widths and propagation delays for minimum, nominal and maximum operating points. The standard also describes the generic constants to be included in an entity interface to specify wire delays at inputs and load delays at outputs.

EIA/IS-103-A Library of Parameterized Modules

www.edif.org/lpmweb/

The Library of Parameterized Modules (LPM) standard allows mapping of digital designs into different implementation technologies such as programmable logic devices, gate arrays and standard cells. The standard specifies a collection of generic technology-independent logic functions that can be used by designers or synthesis tools to implement a design. Each function has a number of parameters that are used to specialize the module for a particular application. For example, the counter module has parameters that specify the width, whether the counter counts up or down, whether it loads synchronously or asynchronously, and so on. Each technology vendor supplies their own implementation of the library modules for use with their place and route tools. Versions of the LPM descriptions exist in EDIF, VHDL and Verilog formats.

appendix E

VHDL-AMS Syntax

In this appendix we present the full set of syntax rules for VHDL-AMS using the EBNF notation introduced in Chapter 1. The form of EBNF used in this book differs from that of the VHDL-AMS standard in order to make the syntax rules more intelligible to the VHDL user. The standard includes a separate syntax rule for each minor syntactic category. In this book, we condense the grammar into a smaller number of rules, each of which defines a larger part of the grammar. We introduce the EBNF symbols "〔", "〕" and "₀₀₀" as part of this simplification. Our aim is to avoid the large amount of searching required when using the standard rules to resolve a question of grammar.

Index to Syntax Rules

access_type_definition   813
across_aspect   812
actual_part   819
aggregate   820
alias_declaration   812
architecture_body   809
array_nature_definition   814
array_type_definition   813
assertion_statement   817
association_list   819
attribute_declaration   812
attribute_name   820
attribute_specification   812

based_integer   820
based_literal   820
binding_indication   812
bit_string_literal   820
block_configuration   810
block_declarative_item   815
block_statement   814
break_element   818
break_statement   818

case_statement   818
character_literal   820
choices   820
component_declaration   812
component_instantiation_statement   816
component_specification   812
concurrent_assertion_statement   815
concurrent_break_statement   816
concurrent_procedure_call_statement   815
concurrent_signal_assignment_statement   815
concurrent_statement   814
conditional_signal_assignment   816
configuration_declaration   810
configuration_specification   812
constant_declaration   811

decimal_literal   820
delay_mechanism   818
design_file   809
design_unit   809
disconnection_specification   813
discrete_range   814

entity_class   812
entity_declaration   809
entity_declarative_item   809
entity_name_list   812
enumeration_type_definition   813
exit_statement   818
expression   819

factor   820
file_declaration   812
file_type_definition   813
floating_type_definition   813
formal_part   819
function_call   820

generate_statement   816
group_declaration   813
group_template_declaration   813

identifier   820
if_statement   818
integer   820
integer_type_definition   813
interface_list   819

label   820
library_clause   809
library_unit   809
literal   820
loop_statement   818

mode   819

name   820
nature_declaration   811
nature_definition   811
nature_mark   814
next_statement   818
null_statement   818

operator_symbol   820

package_body   810
package_body_declarative_item   810
package_declaration   810
package_declarative_item   810
physical_literal   820
physical_type_definition   813
primary   820
procedural_declarative_item   817
procedure_call_statement   818
process_declarative_item   815
process_statement   815

qualified_expression   820
quantity_declaration   811

record_nature_definition   814
record_type_definition   813
relation   819
report_statement   817
return_statement   818

scalar_nature_definition   813
selected_name   820
selected_signal_assignment   816
sequential_statement   817
shift_expression   819
signal_assignment_statement   818
signal_declaration   811
signature   820
simple_expression   819
simple_simultaneous_statement   816
simultaneous_case_statement   817
simultaneous_if_statement   816
simultaneous_null_statement   817
simultaneous_procedural_statement   817
simultaneous_statement   816
source_aspect   812
step_limit_specification   813
string_literal   820
subnature_declaration   814
subnature_indication   814
subprogram_body   811
subprogram_declaration   811
subprogram_declarative_item   811
subprogram_specification   811
subtype_declaration   814
subtype_indication   814

term   819
terminal_aspect   812
terminal_declaration   811
through_aspect   812
type_declaration   811
type_definition   811
type_mark   814

use_clause   813

variable_assignment_statement   818
variable_declaration   811

wait_statement   817
waveform   818

E.1 **Design File**

design_file ⇐ design_unit ⦃ ... ⦄

design_unit ⇐
    ⦃ library_clause ▯ use_clause ⦄
    library_unit

library_unit ⇐
    entity_declaration   ▯ architecture_body
    ▯ package_declaration   ▯ package_body
    ▯ configuration_declaration

library_clause ⇐ **library** identifier ⦃ , ... ⦄ ;

E.2 **Library Unit Declarations**

entity_declaration ⇐
    entity identifier **is**
        ⟦ **generic** (*generic*_interface_list) ; ⟧
        ⟦ **port** (*port*_interface_list) ; ⟧
        ⦃ entity_declarative_item ⦄
    ⟦ **begin**
        ⦃ concurrent_assertion_statement
            ▯ *passive*_concurrent_procedure_call_statement
            ▯ *passive*_process_statement ⦄ ⟧
    end ⟦ **entity** ⟧ ⟦ identifier ⟧ ;

entity_declarative_item ⇐
    subprogram_declaration   ▯ subprogram_body
    ▯ type_declaration   ▯ subtype_declaration
    ▯ constant_declaration   ▯ signal_declaration
    ▯ *shared*_variable_declaration   ▯ file_declaration
    ▯ alias_declaration
    ▯ attribute_declaration   ▯ attribute_specification
    ▯ disconnection_specification   ▯ use_clause
    ▯ group_template_declaration   ▯ group_declaration
    ▯ step_limit_specification
    ▯ nature_declaration   ▯ subnature_declaration
    ▯ quantity_declaration   ▯ terminal_declaration

architecture_body ⇐
    architecture identifier **of** *entity*_name **is**
        ⦃ block_declarative_item ⦄
    begin
        ⦃ concurrent_statement ▯ simultaneous_statement ⦄
    end ⟦ **architecture** ⟧ ⟦ identifier ⟧ ;

configuration_declaration ⇐
    configuration identifier **of** *entity*_name **is**
        《 use_clause ▯ attribute_specification ▯ group_declaration 》
        block_configuration
    end 〚 **configuration** 〛 〚 identifier 〛 ;

block_configuration ⇐
    for 《 *architecture*_name
        ▯ *block_statement*_label
        ▯ *generate_statement*_label 〚 (《 discrete_range ▯ *static*_expression 》) 〛 》
        《 use_clause 》
        《 block_configuration
          ▯ **for** component_specification
            〚 binding_indication ; 〛
            〚 block_configuration 〛
         end for ; 》
    end for ;

package_declaration ⇐
    package identifier **is**
        《 package_declarative_item 》
    end 〚 **package** 〛 〚 identifier 〛 ;

package_declarative_item ⇐
    subprogram_declaration

▯ type_declaration	▯ subtype_declaration
▯ constant_declaration	▯ signal_declaration
▯ *shared*_variable_declaration	▯ file_declaration
▯ alias_declaration	▯ component_declaration
▯ attribute_declaration	▯ attribute_specification
▯ disconnection_specification	▯ use_clause
▯ group_template_declaration	▯ group_declaration
▯ nature_declaration	▯ subnature_declaration
▯ terminal_declaration	

package_body ⇐
    package body identifier **is**
        《 package_body_declarative_item 》
    end 〚 **package body** 〛 〚 identifier 〛 ;

package_body_declarative_item ⇐

subprogram_declaration	▯ subprogram_body
▯ type_declaration	▯ subtype_declaration
▯ constant_declaration	▯ *shared*_variable_declaration
▯ file_declaration	▯ alias_declaration
▯ use_clause	
▯ group_template_declaration	▯ group_declaration

E.3 **Declarations and Specifications**

subprogram_specification ⇐
    procedure ⟨ identifier ⫿ operator_symbol ⟩ ⟦ (*parameter*_interface_list) ⟧
    ⫿ ⟦ **pure** ⫿ **impure** ⟧
      function ⟨ identifier ⫿ operator_symbol ⟩
          ⟦ (*parameter*_interface_list) ⟧ **return** type_mark

subprogram_declaration ⇐ subprogram_specification ;

subprogram_body ⇐
    subprogram_specification **is**
      ⦃ subprogram_declarative_item ⦄
    begin
      ⦃ sequential_statement ⦄
    end ⟦ **procedure** ⫿ **function** ⟧ ⟦ identifier ⫿ operator_symbol ⟧ ;

subprogram_declarative_item ⇐
    subprogram_declaration   ⫿ subprogram_body
    ⫿ type_declaration   ⫿ subtype_declaration
    ⫿ constant_declaration   ⫿ variable_declaration
    ⫿ file_declaration   ⫿ alias_declaration
    ⫿ attribute_declaration   ⫿ attribute_specification
    ⫿ use_clause
    ⫿ group_template_declaration   ⫿ group_declaration

type_declaration ⇐
    type identifier **is** type_definition ;
    ⫿ **type** identifier ;

type_definition ⇐
    enumeration_type_definition   ⫿ integer_type_definition
    ⫿ floating_type_definition   ⫿ physical_type_definition
    ⫿ array_type_definition   ⫿ record_type_definition
    ⫿ access_type_definition   ⫿ file_type_definition⫿
protected_type_declaration⫿ protected_type_body

nature_declaration ⇐
    nature identifier **is** nature_definition ;

nature_definition ⇐
    scalar_nature_definition ⫿ array_nature_definition ⫿ record_nature_definition

constant_declaration ⇐
    constant identifier ⦃ , … ⦄ : subtype_indication ⟦ := expression ⟧ ;

signal_declaration ⇐
    signal identifier ⦃ , … ⦄ : subtype_indication ⟦ **register** ⫿ **bus** ⟧ ⟦ := expression ⟧ ;

variable_declaration ⇐
    ⟦ **shared** ⟧ **variable** identifier ⦃ , … ⦄ : subtype_indication ⟦ := expression ⟧ ;

terminal_declaration ⇐
    terminal identifier ⦃ , … ⦄ : subnature_indication ;

quantity_declaration ⇐
    quantity identifier ⦃ , ⣂ ⦄ : subtype_indication ⟦ := expression ⟧ ;
    ❘ **quantity** ⟦ across_aspect ⟧ ⟦ through_aspect ⟧ terminal_aspect ;
    ❘ **quantity** identifier ⦃ , ⣂ ⦄ : subtype_indication source_aspect ;

across_aspect ⇐
    identifier ⦃ , ⣂ ⦄ ⟦ **tolerance** *string*_expression ⟧ ⟦ := expression ⟧ **across**

through_aspect ⇐
    identifier ⦃ , ⣂ ⦄ ⟦ **tolerance** *string*_expression ⟧ ⟦ := expression ⟧ **through**

terminal_aspect ⇐
    *plus_terminal*_name ⟦ **to** *minus_terminal*_name ⟧

source_aspect ⇐
    spectrum *magnitude*_simple_expression , *phase*_simple_expression
    ❘ **noise** *power*_simple_expression

file_declaration ⇐
    file identifier ⦃ , ⣂ ⦄ : subtype_indication .
        ⟦ ⟦ **open** *file_open_kind*_expression ⟧ **is** *string*_expression ⟧ ;

alias_declaration ⇐
    alias ⦇ identifier ❘ character_literal ❘ operator_symbol ⦈
        ⟦ : ⦇ subtype_indication ❘ subnature_indication ⦈ ⟧ **is** name ⟦ signature ⟧ ;

component_declaration ⇐
    component identifier ⟦ **is** ⟧
        ⟦ **generic** (*generic*_interface_list) ; ⟧
        ⟦ **port** (*port*_interface_list) ; ⟧
    end component ⟦ identifier ⟧ ;

attribute_declaration ⇐ **attribute** identifier : type_mark ;

attribute_specification ⇐
    attribute identifier **of** entity_name_list : entity_class **is** expression ;

entity_name_list ⇐
    ⦇ ⦇ identifier ❘ character_literal ❘ operator_symbol ⦈ ⟦ signature ⟧ ⦈ ⦃ , ⣂ ⦄
    ❘ **others**
    ❘ **all**

entity_class ⇐

entity	❘ **architecture**	❘ **configuration**	❘ **package**	
❘ **procedure**	❘ **function**	❘ **type**	❘ **subtype**	
❘ **constant**	❘ **signal**	❘ **variable**	❘ **file**	
❘ **component**	❘ **label**	❘ **literal**	❘ **units**	❘ **group**
❘ **nature**	❘ **subnature**	❘ **quantity**	❘ **terminal**	

configuration_specification ⇐
    for component_specification binding_indication ;

component_specification ⇐
    ⦇ *instantiation*_label ⦃ , ⣂ ⦄ ❘ **others** ❘ **all** ⦈ : *component*_name

binding_indication ⇐
    〚 **use** 〘 **entity** *entity*_name 〚 (*architecture*_identifier) 〛
        〘 **configuration** *configuration*_name
        〘 **open** 〙 〛
    〚 **generic map** (*generic*_association_list) 〛
    〚 **port map** (*port*_association_list) 〛
disconnection_specification ⇐
    disconnect 〘 *signal*_name 〘 , ... 〙 〘 **others** 〘 **all** 〙 : type_mark
        after *time*_expression ;
step_limit_specification ⇐
    limit 〘 *quantity*_name 〘 , ... 〙 〘 **others** 〘 **all** 〙 : type_mark **with** *real*_expression ;
group_template_declaration ⇐
    group identifier **is** (〘 entity_class 〚 <> 〛 〙 〘 , ... 〙) ;
group_declaration ⇐
    group identifier : *group_template*_name (〘 name 〘 character_literal 〙 〘 , ... 〙) ;
use_clause ⇐ **use** selected_name 〘 , ... 〙 ;

E.4 Type Definitions

enumeration_type_definition ⇐ (〘 identifier 〘 character_literal 〙 〘 , ... 〙)
integer_type_definition ⇐
    range 〘 *range*_attribute_name
        〘 simple_expression 〘 **to** 〘 **downto** 〙 simple_expression 〙
floating_type_definition ⇐
    range 〘 *range*_attribute_name
        〘 simple_expression 〘 **to** 〘 **downto** 〙 simple_expression 〙
physical_type_definition ⇐
    range 〘 *range*_attribute_name
        〘 simple_expression 〘 **to** 〘 **downto** 〙 simple_expression 〙
      units
        identifier ;
        〘 identifier = physical_literal ; 〙
      end units 〚 identifier 〛
array_type_definition ⇐
    array (〘 type_mark **range** <> 〙 〘 , ... 〙) **of** *element*_subtype_indication
    〘 **array** (discrete_range 〘 , ... 〙) **of** *element*_subtype_indication
record_type_definition ⇐
    record
        〘 identifier 〘 , ... 〙 : subtype_indication ; 〙
        〘 ... 〙
    end record 〚 identifier 〛
access_type_definition ⇐ **access** subtype_indication

file_type_definition ⇐ **file of** type_mark

scalar_nature_definition ⇐
    type_mark **across** type_mark **through** identifier **reference**

array_nature_definition ⇐
    array (〔 type_mark **range** <> 〕 〔 , ⚬⚬⚬ 〕) **of** subnature_indication
    〖 **array** (discrete_range 〔 , ⚬⚬⚬ 〕) **of** subnature_indication

record_nature_definition ⇐
    record
        〔 identifier 〔 , ⚬⚬⚬ 〕 : subnature_indication ; 〕
        〔 ⚬⚬⚬ 〕
    end record 〔 identifier 〕

subtype_declaration ⇐ **subtype** identifier **is** subtype_indication ;

subtype_indication ⇐
    〔 *resolution_function*_name 〕
    type_mark 〔 **range** 〔 *range*_attribute_name
                      〖 simple_expression 〔 **to** 〖 **downto** 〕 simple_expression 〕
             〖 (discrete_range 〔 , ⚬⚬⚬ 〕) 〕
             〔 **tolerance** *string*_expression 〕

discrete_range ⇐
    *discrete*_subtype_indication
    〖 *range*_attribute_name
    〖 simple_expression 〔 **to** 〖 **downto** 〕 simple_expression

type_mark ⇐ *type*_name 〖 *subtype*_name

subnature_declaration ⇐ **subnature** identifier **is** subnature_indication ;

subnature_indication ⇐
    nature_mark
        〔 (discrete_range 〔 , ⚬⚬⚬ 〕) 〕
        〔 **tolerance** *string*_expression **across** *string*_expression **through** 〕

nature_mark ⇐ *nature*_name 〖 *subnature*_name

E.5   **Concurrent Statements**

concurrent_statement ⇐
    block_statement
    〖 process_statement
    〖 concurrent_procedure_call_statement
    〖 concurrent_assertion_statement
    〖 concurrent_signal_assignment_statement
    〖 component_instantiation_statement
    〖 generate_statement
    〖 concurrent_break_statement

block_statement ⇐
    *block*_label :
    block ⟦ (*guard*_expression) ⟧ ⟦ **is** ⟧
        ⟦ **generic** (*generic*_interface_list) ;
        ⟦ **generic map** (*generic*_association_list) ; ⟧ ⟧
        ⟦ **port** (*port*_interface_list) ;
        ⟦ **port map** (*port*_association_list) ; ⟧ ⟧
        ❴ block_declarative_item ❵
    begin
        ❴ concurrent_statement ⏐ simultaneous_statement ❵
    end block ⟦ *block*_label ⟧ ;
block_declarative_item ⇐
    subprogram_declaration   ⏐ subprogram_body
    ⏐ type_declaration   ⏐ subtype_declaration
    ⏐ constant_declaration   ⏐ signal_declaration
    ⏐ *shared*_variable_declaration   ⏐ file_declaration
    ⏐ alias_declaration   ⏐ component_declaration
    ⏐ attribute_declaration   ⏐ attribute_specification
    ⏐ configuration_specification   ⏐ disconnection_specification
    ⏐ use_clause
    ⏐ group_template_declaration   ⏐ group_declaration
    ⏐ step_limit_specification
    ⏐ nature_declaration   ⏐ subnature_declaration
    ⏐ quantity_declaration   ⏐ terminal_declaration
process_statement ⇐
    ⟦ *process*_label : ⟧
    ⟦ **postponed** ⟧ **process** ⟦ (*signal*_name ❴ , … ❵) ⟧ ⟦ **is** ⟧
        ❴ process_declarative_item ❵
    begin
        ❴ sequential_statement ❵
    end ⟦ **postponed** ⟧ **process** ⟦ *process*_label ⟧ ;
process_declarative_item ⇐
    subprogram_declaration   ⏐ subprogram_body
    ⏐ type_declaration   ⏐ subtype_declaration
    ⏐ constant_declaration   ⏐ variable_declaration
    ⏐ file_declaration   ⏐ alias_declaration
    ⏐ attribute_declaration   ⏐ attribute_specification
    ⏐ use_clause
    ⏐ group_template_declaration   ⏐ group_declaration
concurrent_procedure_call_statement ⇐
    ⟦ label : ⟧
    ⟦ **postponed** ⟧ *procedure*_name ⟦ (*parameter*_association_list) ⟧ ;
concurrent_assertion_statement ⇐
    ⟦ label : ⟧
    ⟦ **postponed** ⟧ **assert** *boolean*_expression
                ⟦ **report** expression ⟧ ⟦ **severity** expression ⟧ ;

concurrent_signal_assignment_statement ⇐
   ⟦ label : ⟧ ⟦ **postponed** ⟧ conditional_signal_assignment
   ⟨ ⟦ label : ⟧ ⟦ **postponed** ⟧ selected_signal_assignment

conditional_signal_assignment ⇐
   ⟨ name ⟨ aggregate ⟩ <= ⟦ **guarded** ⟧ ⟦ delay_mechanism ⟧
      ⟨ waveform **when** *boolean*_expression **else** ⟩
      waveform ⟦ **when** *boolean*_expression ⟧ ;

selected_signal_assignment ⇐
   with expression **select**
      ⟨ name ⟨ aggregate ⟩ <= ⟦ **guarded** ⟧ ⟦ delay_mechanism ⟧
         ⟨ waveform **when** choices , ⟩
         waveform **when** choices ;

component_instantiation_statement ⇐
   *instantiation*_label :
      ⟨ ⟦ **component** ⟧ *component*_name
         ⟨ **entity** *entity*_name ⟦ (*architecture*_identifier) ⟧
         ⟨ **configuration** *configuration*_name ⟩
      ⟦ **generic map** (*generic*_association_list) ⟧
      ⟦ **port map** (*port*_association_list) ⟧ ;

generate_statement ⇐
   *generate*_label :
   ⟨ **for** identifier **in** discrete_range ⟨ **if** *boolean*_expression ⟩ **generate**
      ⟦ ⟨ block_declarative_item ⟩
   begin ⟧
      ⟨ concurrent_statement ⟨ simultaneous_statement ⟩
   end generate ⟦ *generate*_label ⟧ ;

concurrent_break_statement ⇐
   ⟦ label : ⟧
   break ⟦ break_element ⟨ , ... ⟩ ⟧
      ⟦ **on** signal_name ⟨ , ... ⟩ ⟧
      ⟦ **when** *boolean*_expression ⟧ ;

E.6 **Simultaneous Statements**

simultaneous_statement ⇐
   simple_simultaneous_statement
   ⟨ simultaneous_if_statement   ⟨ simultaneous_case_statement
   ⟨ simultaneous_procedural_statement   ⟨ simultaneous_null_statement

simple_simultaneous_statement ⇐
   ⟦ label : ⟧
   simple_expression == simple_expression ⟦ **tolerance** *string*_expression ⟧ ;

simultaneous_if_statement ⇐
  ⟦ *if*_label : ⟧
  if *boolean*_expression **use**
    ⟨ simultaneous_statement ⟩
  ⟨ **elsif** *boolean*_expression **use**
    ⟨ simultaneous_statement ⟩ ⟩
  ⟦ **else**
    ⟨ simultaneous_statement ⟩ ⟧
  end use ⟦ *if*_label ⟧ ;

simultaneous_case_statement ⇐
  ⟦ *case*_label : ⟧
  case expression **use**
    ⟨ **when** choices => ⟨ simultaneous_statement ⟩ ⟩
    ⟨ ... ⟩
  end case ⟦ *case*_label ⟧ ;

simultaneous_procedural_statement ⇐
  ⟦ *procedural*_label : ⟧
  procedural ⟦ **is** ⟧
    ⟨ procedural_declarative_item ⟩
  begin
    ⟨ sequential_statement ⟩
  end procedural ⟦ *procedural*_label ⟧ ;

procedural_declarative_item ⇐
  subprogram_declaration   ❘ subprogram_body
  ❘ type_declaration   ❘ subtype_declaration
  ❘ constant_declaration   ❘ variable_declaration
  ❘ alias_declaration   ❘ attribute_declaration
  ❘ attribute_specification   ❘ use_clause
  ❘ group_template_declaration   ❘ group_declaration

simultaneous_null_statement ⇐ ⟦ label : ⟧ **null** ;

E.7 Sequential Statements

sequential_statement ⇐
  wait_statement   ❘ assertion_statement
  ❘ report_statement   ❘ signal_assignment_statement
  ❘ variable_assignment_statement ❘ procedure_call_statement
  ❘ if_statement   ❘ case_statement
  ❘ loop_statement   ❘ next_statement
  ❘ exit_statement   ❘ return_statement
  ❘ null_statement   ❘ break_statement

wait_statement ⇐
  ⟦ label : ⟧ **wait** ⟦ **on** *signal*_name ⟨ , ... ⟩ ⟧
        ⟦ **until** *boolean*_expression ⟧
        ⟦ **for** *time*_expression ⟧ ;

assertion_statement ⇐
    ⟦ label : ⟧ **assert** *boolean*_expression
                ⟦ **report** expression ⟧ ⟦ **severity** expression ⟧ ;

report_statement ⇐ ⟦ label : ⟧ **report** expression ⟦ **severity** expression ⟧ ;

signal_assignment_statement ⇐
    ⟦ label : ⟧ ⟨ name ⎮ aggregate ⟩ <= ⟦ delay_mechanism ⟧ waveform ;

delay_mechanism ⇐ **transport** ⎮ ⟦ **reject** *time*_expression ⟧ **inertial**

waveform ⇐
    ⟨ *value*_expression ⟦ **after** *time*_expression ⟧
       ⎮ **null** ⟦ **after** *time*_expression ⟧ ⟩ ⟨ , ₀₀₀ ⟩
    ⎮ **unaffected**

variable_assignment_statement ⇐
    ⟦ label : ⟧ ⟨ name ⎮ aggregate ⟩ := expression ;

procedure_call_statement ⇐
    ⟦ label : ⟧ *procedure*_name ⟦ (*parameter*_association_list) ⟧ ;

if_statement ⇐
    ⟦ *if*_label : ⟧
    if *boolean*_expression **then**
        ⟨ sequential_statement ⟩
    ⟨ **elsif** *boolean*_expression **then**
        ⟨ sequential_statement ⟩ ⟩
    ⟦ **else**
        ⟨ sequential_statement ⟩ ⟧
    end if ⟦ *if*_label : ⟧ ;

case_statement ⇐
    ⟦ *case*_label : ⟧
    case expression **is**
        ⟨ **when** choices => ⟨ sequential_statement ⟩ ⟩
        ⟨ ₀₀₀ ⟩
    end case ⟦ *case*_label : ⟧ ;

loop_statement ⇐
    ⟦ *loop*_label ⟧
    ⟦ **while** *boolean*_expression ⎮ **for** identifier **in** discrete_range ⟧ **loop**
        ⟨ sequential_statement ⟩
    end loop ⟦ *loop*_label ⟧ ;

next_statement ⇐ ⟦ label : ⟧ **next** ⟦ *loop*_label ⟧ ⟦ **when** *boolean*_expression ⟧ ;

exit_statement ⇐ ⟦ label : ⟧ **exit** ⟦ *loop*_label ⟧ ⟦ **when** *boolean*_expression ⟧ ;

return_statement ⇐ ⟦ label : ⟧ **return** ⟦ expression ⟧ ;

null_statement ⇐ ⟦ label : ⟧ **null** ;

break_statement ⇐
    ⟦ label : ⟧ **break** ⟦ break_element ⟨ , ₀₀₀ ⟩ ⟧ ⟦ **when** *boolean*_expression ⟧ ;

break_element ⇐ ⟦ **for** *quantity*_name **use** ⟧ *quantity*_name => expression

E.8 **Interfaces and Associations**

interface_list ⇐
 (⟦ **constant** ⟧ identifier ⟨ , ... ⟩ : ⟦ **in** ⟧ subtype_indication
             ⟦ := *static*_expression ⟧
  ⫿ ⟦ **signal** ⟧ identifier ⟨ , ... ⟩ : ⟦ mode ⟧ subtype_indication ⟦ **bus** ⟧
            ⟦ := *static*_expression ⟧
  ⫿ ⟦ **variable** ⟧ identifier ⟨ , ... ⟩ : ⟦ mode ⟧ subtype_indication
            ⟦ := *static*_expression ⟧
  ⫿ **file** identifier ⟨ , ... ⟩ : subtype_indication
  ⫿ **terminal** identifier ⟨ , ... ⟩ : subnature_indication
  ⫿ **quantity** identifier ⟨ , ... ⟩ : ⟦ **in** ⫿ **out** ⟧ subtype_indication
            ⟦ := *static*_expression ⟧
) ⟨ ; ... ⟩

mode ⇐ **in** ⫿ **out** ⫿ **inout** ⫿ **buffer** ⫿ **linkage**

association_list ⇐ (⟦ formal_part => ⟧ actual_part) ⟨ , ... ⟩

formal_part ⇐
 *generic*_name
 ⫿ *port*_name
 ⫿ *parameter*_name
 ⫿ *function*_name (⟨ *generic*_name ⫿ *port*_name ⫿ *parameter*_name ⟩)
 ⫿ type_mark (⟨ *generic*_name ⫿ *port*_name ⫿ *parameter*_name ⟩)

actual_part ⇐
 expression
 ⫿ *signal*_name
 ⫿ *variable*_name
 ⫿ *terminal*_name
 ⫿ *quantity*_name
 ⫿ **open**
 ⫿ *function*_name (⟨ *signal*_name ⫿ *variable*_name ⫿ *quantity*_name ⟩)
 ⫿ type_mark (⟨ *signal*_name ⫿ *variable*_name ⫿ *quantity*_name ⟩)

E.9 **Expressions**

expression ⇐
 relation ⟨ **and** relation ⟩ ⫿ relation ⟦ **nand** relation ⟧
 ⫿ relation ⟨ **or** relation ⟩ ⫿ relation ⟦ **nor** relation ⟧
 ⫿ relation ⟨ **xor** relation ⟩ ⫿ relation ⟨ **xnor** relation ⟩

relation ⇐ shift_expression ⟦ (= ⫿ /= ⫿ < ⫿ <= ⫿ > ⫿ >=) shift_expression ⟧

shift_expression ⇐
 simple_expression ⟦ (**sll** ⫿ **srl** ⫿ **sla** ⫿ **sra** ⫿ **rol** ⫿ **ror**) simple_expression ⟧

simple_expression ⇐ ⟦ + ⫿ − ⟧ term ⟨ (+ ⫿ − ⫿ &) term ⟩

term ⇐ factor ⟨ (* ⫿ / ⫿ **mod** ⫿ **rem**) factor ⟩

factor ⇐ primary ⟦ ** primary ⟧ ⏋ **abs** primary ⏋ **not** primary

primary ⇐
    name   ⏋ literal
    ⏋ aggregate   ⏋ function_call
    ⏋ qualified_expression   ⏋ type_mark (expression)
    ⏋ **new** subtype_indication   ⏋ **new** qualified_expression
    ⏋ (expression)

function_call ⇐ *function*_name ⟦ (*parameter*_association_list) ⟧

qualified_expression ⇐ type_mark ' (expression) ⏋ type_mark ' aggregate

name ⇐
    identifier
    ⏋ operator_symbol
    ⏋ selected_name
    ⏋ ⦅ name ⏋ function_call ⦆ (expression ⦃ , ⋯ ⦄)
    ⏋ ⦅ name ⏋ function_call ⦆ (discrete_range)
    ⏋ attribute_name

selected_name ⇐
    ⦅ name ⏋ function_call ⦆ . ⦅ identifier ⏋ character_literal ⏋ operator_symbol ⏋ **all** ⦆

operator_symbol ⇐ " ⦃ graphic_character ⦄ "

attribute_name ⇐
    ⦅ name ⏋ function_call ⦆ ⟦ signature ⟧ ' identifier ⟦ (expression ⦃ , ⋯ ⦄) ⟧

signature ⇐ [⟦ type_mark ⦃ , ⋯ ⦄ ⟧ ⟦ **return** type_mark ⟧]

literal ⇐
    decimal_literal   ⏋ based_literal
    ⏋ physical_literal   ⏋ identifier
    ⏋ character_literal   ⏋ string_literal
    ⏋ bit_string_literal   ⏋ **null**

physical_literal ⇐ ⟦ decimal_literal ⏋ based_literal ⟧ *unit*_name

decimal_literal ⇐ integer ⟦ . integer ⟧ ⟦ E ⟦ + ⟧ integer ⏋ E − integer ⟧

based_literal ⇐
    integer # based_integer ⟦ . based_integer ⟧ # ⟦ E ⟦ + ⟧ integer ⏋ E − integer ⟧

integer ⇐ digit ⦃ ⟦ _ ⟧ ⋯ ⦄

based_integer ⇐ ⦅ digit ⏋ letter ⦆ ⦃ ⟦ _ ⟧ ⋯ ⦄

character_literal ⇐ ' graphic_character '

string_literal ⇐ " ⦃ graphic_character ⦄ "

bit_string_literal ⇐ ⦅ B ⏋ O ⏋ X ⦆ " ⟦ ⦅ digit ⏋ letter ⦆ ⦃ ⟦ _ ⟧ ⋯ ⦄ ⟧ "

aggregate ⇐ (⦅ ⟦ choices => ⟧ expression ⦆ ⦃ , ⋯ ⦄)

choices ⇐ ⦅ simple_expression ⏋ discrete_range ⏋ identifier ⏋ **others** ⦆ ⦃ ⏋ ⋯ ⦄

label ⇐ identifier

identifier ⇐ letter ⦃ ⟦ _ ⟧ ⦅ letter ⏋ digit ⦆ ⦄ ⏋ \ graphic_character ⦃ ⋯ ⦄ \

appendix F

Answers to Exercises

In this appendix, we provide sample answers to the quiz-style exercises marked with the symbol "❶". Readers are encouraged to test their answers to the other, more involved, exercises by running the models on a VHDL simulator.

Chapter 1

1. Entity declaration: defines the interface to a module, in terms of its ports, their data transfer direction and their types. Behavioral architecture body: defines the function of a module in terms of an algorithm. Structural architecture body: defines an implementation of a module in terms of an interconnected composition of sub-modules. Process statement: encapsulates an algorithm in a behavioral description, contains sequential actions to be performed. Signal assignment statement: specifies values to be applied to signals at some later time. Simultaneous statement: describes equations governing analog system behavior. Port map: specifies the interconnection between signals and component instance ports in a structural architecture.

2.
```
   apply_transform : process is
   begin
       d_out <= transform(d_in) after 200 ps;
       -- debug_test <= transform(d_in);
       wait on enable, d_in;
   end process apply_transform;
```

3. Basic identifiers: last_item. Reserved words: limit. Invalid: prev item, value–1 and element#5 include characters that may not occur within identifiers; _control starts with an underscore; 93_999 starts with a digit; gain_ ends with an underscore.

4. 16#1#   16#22#   16#100.0#   16#0.8#

5. 12   132   44   250000   32768   0.625

6. The literal 16#23DF# is an integer expressed in base 16, whereas the literal X"23DF" is a string of 16 bits.

7. B"111_100_111"   B"011_111_111"   B"001_011_100_101"
    B"1111_0010"   B"0000_0000_0001_0100"
    B"0000_0000_0000_0000_0000_0000_0000_0001"

Chapter 2

1. **constant** bits_per_word : integer := 32;
    constant pi : real := 3.14159;

2. **variable** counter : integer := 0;
    variable busy_status : boolean;
    variable temp_result : std_ulogic;

3. counter := counter + 1;
    busy_status := true;
    temp_result := 'W';

4. **package** misc_types **is**
        type small_int **is range** 0 **to** 255;
        type fraction **is range** −1.0 **to** +1.0;
        type current **is range** integer'low **to** integer'high
            units nA;
                uA = 1000 nA;
                mA = 1000 uA;
                A = 1000 mA;
            end units;
        type colors **is** (red, yellow, green);
    end package misc_types;

5. **package** pneumatic_systems **is**
        subtype pressure **is** real **tolerance** "default_pressure";
        subtype volumetric_flow_rate **is** real **tolerance** "default_flow";
        nature pneumatic **is**
            pressure **across**
            volumetric_flow_rate **through**
            pneumatic_ref **reference**;
    end package pneumatic_systems;

6. **subnature** detailed_pneumatic **is** pneumatic
        tolerance "detailed_pressure" **across** "detailed_flow" **through**;

7. pulse_range'left = pulse_range'low = 1 ms
    pulse_range'right = pulse_range'high = 100 ms
    pulse_range'ascending = true

    word_index'left = 31   word_index'right = 0
    word_index'low = 0   word_index'high = 31
    word_index'ascending = false

8. state'pos(standby) = 1   state'val(2) = active1
    state'succ(active2) **is** undefined   state'pred(active1) = standby
    state'leftof(off) **is** undefined   state'rightof(off) = standby

9. 2 * 3 + 6 / 4 = 7
    3 + −4 *is syntactically incorrect*
    "cat" & character'('0') = "cat0"
    true **and** x **and not** y **or** z *is syntactically incorrect*
    B"101110" **sll** 3 = B"110000"
    (B"100010" **sra** 2) & X"2C"= B"11100000101100"

Chapter 3

1.  ```
    if n mod 2 = 1 then
         odd := '1';
    else
         odd := '0';
    end if;
    ```

2.  ```
    if year mod 400 = 0 then
         days_in_February := 29;
    elsif year mod 100 = 0 then
         days_in_February := 28;
    elsif year mod 4 = 0 then
         days_in_February := 29;
    else
         days_in_February := 28;
    end if;
    ```

3.  ```
    case x is
         when '0' | 'L' => x := '0';
         when '1' | 'H' => x := '1';
         when others => x := 'X';
    end case;
    ```

4.  ```
    case ch is
         when 'A' to 'Z' | 'a' to 'z' | 'À' to 'Ö' | 'Ø' to 'ß' | 'à' to 'ö' | 'ø' to 'ÿ' =>
              character_class := 1;
         when '0' to '9' => character_class := 2;
         when nul to usp | del | c128 to c159 => character_class := 4;
         when others => character_class := 3;
    end case;
    ```

5.  ```
    loop
         wait until clk = '1';
         exit when d = '1';
    end loop;
    ```
    ```

6.      ```
        sum := 1.0;
        term := 1.0;
        n := 0;
        while abs term > abs (sum / 1.0E5) loop
            n := n + 1;
            term := term * x / real(n);
            sum := sum + term;
        end loop;
        ```

7.      ```
        sum := 1.0;
        term := 1.0;
        for n in 1 to 7 loop
            term := term * x / real(n);
            sum := sum + term;
        end loop;
        ```

8.      ```
        assert to_X01(q) = not to_X01(q_n)
            report "flipflop outputs are not complementary";
        ```

9. Insert the statement after the comment "*-- at this point, reset = '1'*":

        ```
        report "counter is reset";
        ```

Chapter 4

1.      ```
        type num_vector is array (1 to 30) of integer;
        variable numbers : num_vector;
        ...
        sum := 0;
        for i in numbers'range loop
            sum := sum + numbers(i);
        end loop;
        average := sum / numbers'length;
        ```

2.      ```
        type std_ulogic_to_bit_array is array (std_ulogic) of bit;
        constant std_ulogic_to_bit : std_ulogic_to_bit_array
            := ( 'U' => '0', 'X' => '0', '0' => '0', '1' => '1', 'Z' => '0',
                 'W' => '0', 'L' => '0', 'H' => '1', '-' => '0' );
        ...
        for index in 0 to 15 loop
            v2(index) := std_ulogic_to_bit(v1(index));
        end loop;
        ```

3.      ```
        nature electrical_array is array (1 to 4) of electrical;
        terminal n1, n2 : electrical_array;
        quantity v across i through n1 to n2;
        ```

4.      ```
        constant scale_by_2 : matrix := (2.0, 0.0, 0.0, 0.0, 2.0, 0.0, 0.0, 0.0, 2.0);
        quantity p, q : point;
        ...
        ```
        ```

```
q(1) == scale_by_2(1, 1) * p(1) * scale_by_2(1, 2) * p(2) + scale_by_2(1, 3) * p(3);
q(2) == scale_by_2(2, 1) * p(1) * scale_by_2(2, 2) * p(2) + scale_by_2(2, 3) * p(3);
q(3) == scale_by_2(3, 1) * p(1) * scale_by_2(3, 2) * p(2) + scale_by_2(3, 3) * p(3);
```

5.
```
type trailer_connections is
    ( tail_light, brake_light, left_indicator, right_indicator, reversing_light,
        aux_light, negative_return, chassis_ground );
nature trailer_electrical is array (trailer_connections) of electrical;
```

6.
```
type free_map_array is array (0 to 1, 0 to 79, 0 to 17) of bit;
variable free_map : free_map_array;
...
found := false;
search_loop : for side in 0 to 1 loop
    for track in 0 to 79 loop
        for sector in 0 to 17 loop
            if free_map(side, track, sector) = '1' then
                found := true;  free_side := side;
                free_track := track;  free_sector := sector;
                exit search_loop;
            end if;
        end loop;
    end loop;
end loop;
```

7.
```
subtype std_ulogic_byte is std_ulogic_vector(7 downto 0);
constant Z_byte : std_ulogic_byte := "ZZZZZZZZ";
```

8.
```
count := 0;
for index in v'range loop
    if v(index) = '1' then
        count := count + 1;
    end if;
end loop;
```

9.
```
subtype coordinate is real_vector(1 to 3);
quantity hand_position : coordinate := (0.0, 0.0, 0.0);
```

10. Assuming the declarations
```
variable v1 : bit_vector(7 downto 0);
variable v2 : bit_vector(31 downto 0);
...
v2(31 downto 24) := v1;
v2 := v2 sra 24;
```

11.
```
type test_record is record
        stimulus : bit_vector(0 to 2);
        delay : delay_length;
        expected_response : bit_vector(0 to 7);
    end record test_record;
```

Chapter 5

1.
```
entity lookup_ROM is
    port ( address : in lookup_index;  data : out real );
    type lookup_table is array (lookup_index) of real;
    constant lookup_data : lookup_table
                := ( real'high, 1.0, 1.0/2.0, 1.0/3.0, 1.0/4.0, ... );
end entity lookup_ROM;
```

2. Transactions are 'Z' at 0 ns, '0' at 10 ns, '1' at 30 ns, '1' at 55 ns, 'H' at 65 ns and 'Z' at 100 ns. The signal is active at all of these times. Events occur at each time except 55 ns, since the signal already has the value '1' at that time.

3. s'delayed(5 ns): 'Z' at 5 ns, '0' at 15 ns, '1' at 35 ns, 'H' at 70 ns, 'Z' at 105 ns. s'stable(5 ns): false at 0 ns, true at 5 ns, false at 10 ns, true at 15 ns, false at 30 ns, true at 35 ns, false at 65 ns, true at 70 ns, false at 100 ns, true at 105 ns. s'quiet(5 ns): false at 0 ns, true at 5 ns, false at 10 ns, true at 15 ns, false at 30 ns, true at 35 ns, false at 55 ns, true at 60 ns, false at 65 ns, true at 70 ns, false at 100 ns, true at 105 ns. s'transaction (assuming an initial value of '0'): '1' at 0 ns, '0' at 10 ns, '1' at 30 ns, '0' at 55 ns, '1' at 65 ns, '0' at 100 ns. At time 60 ns, s'last_event is 30 ns, s'last_active is 5 ns, and s'last_value is '0'.

4. **wait on** s **until** s = '1' **and** en = '1';

5. **wait until** ready = '1' **for** 5 ms;

6. The variable v1 is assigned false, since s is not updated until the next simulation cycle. The variable v2 is assigned true, since the wait statement causes the process to resume after s is updated with the value '1'.

7. At 0 ns: schedule '1' for 6 ns. At 3 ns: schedule '0' for 7 ns. At 8 ns: schedule '1' for 14 ns. At 9 ns: delete transaction scheduled for 14 ns, schedule '0' for 13 ns. The signal z takes on the values '1' at 6 ns and '0' at 7 ns. The transaction scheduled for 13 ns does not result in an event on z.

8. At 0 ns: schedule 1 for 7 ns, 23 for 9 ns, 5 for 10 ns, 23 for 12 ns and –5 for 15 ns. At 6 ns: schedule 23 for 13 ns, delete transactions scheduled for 15 ns, 10 ns and 9 ns. The signal x takes on the values 1 at 7 ns and 23 at 12 ns.

9.
```
mux_logic : process is
begin
    if enable = '1' and sel = '0' then
        z <= a and not b after 5 ns;
    elsif enable = '1' and sel = '1' then
        z <= x or y after 6 ns;
    else
        z <= '0' after 4 ns;
    end if;
    wait on a, b, enable, sel, x, y;
end process mux_logic;
```

10.   **process is**
       begin
              case bit_vector'(s, r) **is**
                     when "00" => null;
                     when "01" => q <= '0';
                     when "10" | "11" => q <= '1';
              end case;
              wait on s, r;
       end process;

11.   **assert** clk'last_event >= T_pw_clk
       report "interval between changes on clk is too small";

12.   bit_0 : **entity** work.ttl_74x74(basic)
              port map (pr_n => '1', d => q0_n, clk => clk, clr_n => reset,
                     q => q0, q_n => q0_n);
       bit_1 : **entity** work.ttl_74x74(basic)
              port map (pr_n => '1', d => q1_n, clk => q0_n, clr_n => reset,
                     q => q1, q_n => q1_n);

13.

Chapter 6

1.   **quantity** control_voltage : voltage **tolerance** "control_voltage_tolerance" := 3.5;

2.   **library** ieee_proposed;
         use ieee_proposed.mechanical_systems.**all**, ieee_proposed.thermal_systems.**all**;

         entity spring **is**
             port (**terminal** end1, end2 : translational;
                 quantity temp : **in** temperature);
         end entity spring;

3.   **terminal** node1, node2 : electrical;
         quantity v_circuit **across** i_circuit **through** node1 **to** node2;

4.   **library** ieee_proposed; **use** ieee_proposed.electrical_systems.**all**;

         entity voltage_supply **is**
             port (**terminal** vdd_positive, vdd_negative : electrical);
         end entity voltage_supply;

5.   **library** ieee_proposed; **use** ieee_proposed.mechanical_systems.**all**;

         entity spring **is**
             port (**terminal** end1, end2 : translational;);
         end entity spring;

6.   **terminal** sensor_array : thermal_vector(1 **to** 36);
         quantity sensor_temperatures **across** sensor_array;
         quantity sensor_13_to_24_flow **through** sensor_array(13 **to** 24);

7.   **terminal** pistons : translational_vector(1 **to** 6);

8.   **quantity** position **across** stroke_force **through** pistons;

9.   **nature** piston_translational_record **is**
             record
                 piston1, piston2, piston3, piston4, piston5, piston6 : translational;
             end record piston_translational_record;
         terminal pistons : piston_translational_record;

10.   **terminal** hard_stop : translational;
         ...
         hard_stop'reference == 0.2;

11.   **quantity** v_amplified : voltage **tolerance** v_in'tolerance;

12.   temp_ok <= '0' **when** sensor_temp'above(303.0) **else**
                 '1';

13.   F == m * x'dot'dot + d * x'dot + k * x;

14.   shaft_position == shaft_velocity'integ + 0.25;

15.   v_out'slew(0.6E+6, 1.2E+6)

16.   v_res == i_res * r_res **tolerance** "high_accuracy";

17.   **if** F'above(k * (Lf – Lc)) **use**
             x == Lf – Lc;
         elsif not F'above(k * (Lf – Le)) **use**

```
        x == Lf – Le;
    else
        F == k * x;
    end use;
```

18.   **break on** F'above(k * (Lf – Lc)), F'above(k * (Lf – Le));

19.   **limit** q : vflow_rate **with** 0.01;

20. 0, 19, 26, 58, 38.

21. 21 µs.

Chapter 7

1. One possible order is suggested: analyzing all entity declarations first, followed by all architecture bodies:

```
        entity analog_switch
        entity resistor
        entity capacitor
        entity opamp
        entity inverting_integrator
        entity comparator
        entity dff
        entity volume_sensor
        architecture ideal of analog_switch
        architecture ideal of resistor
        architecture leakage of capacitor
        architecture slew_limited of opamp
        architecture structural of inverting_integrator
        architecture hysteresis of comparator
        architecture behav of dff
        architecture structural of volume_sensor
```

    An alternative is

```
        entity analog_switch
        entity resistor
        entity capacitor
        entity opamp
        entity inverting_integrator
        architecture structural of inverting_integrator
        entity comparator
        entity dff
        entity volume_sensor
        architecture structural of volume_sensor
        architecture ideal of analog_switch
        architecture ideal of resistor
        architecture leakage of capacitor
```

architecture **slew_limited** of opamp
architecture **hysteresis** of comparator
architecture **behav** of dff

2.   **library** company_lib, project_lib;
     use company_lib.in_pad, company_lib.out_pad, project_lib.**all**;

3.

Chapter 8

1.   This can be done by replacing the single constant **tran_time** with two constants, t_open and t_closed, as follows:

     constant t_open : real := 10.0e–6;   *-- transition time to open position*
     constant t_closed : real := 20.0e–6;   *-- transition time to closed position*

     ...

     r1 == r_sig1'ramp(t_open, t_closed);
     r2 == r_sig2'ramp(t_open, t_closed);

2.   We first consider the idea of using the signal **s_out** in place of variable **v_sum** in the for loop. For the individual bit voltage contributions to be correctly summed, the new **delta_v** values must be added to the running total each time the loop is executed. A *variable* assignment is needed in this case as variables take on their new values as soon as they are assigned. If the *signal* **sum_out** were updated within the loop, it would only take on the newly assigned value after the process completed.

     Next we attempt to replace the *signal* **sum_out** with the *variable* **v_sum**. In this case we contend with the fact that **v_sum** is not visible outside of the process in which it is defined. Therefore, for this basic model topology, both the variable **v_sum** and the signal **sum_out** are required.

Chapter 9

1.   **constant** operand1 : **in** integer
     operand1 : integer
     constant tag : **in** bit_vector(31 **downto** 16)
     tag : bit_vector(31 **downto** 16)
     constant trace : **in** boolean := false
     trace : boolean := false

2.   **variable** average : **out** real;
    average : **out** real
    variable identifier : **inout** string
    identifier : **inout** string

3.   **signal** clk : **out** bit
    signal data_in : **in** std_ulogic_vector
    signal data_in : std_ulogic_vector

4. Some alternatives are

    stimulate (s, 5 ns, 3);
    stimulate (target => s, delay => 5 ns, cycles => 3);

    stimulate (s, 10 ns, 1);
    stimulate (s, 10 ns);
    stimulate (target => s, delay => 10 ns, cycles => **open**);
    stimulate (target => s, cycles => **open**, delay => 10 ns);
    stimulate (target => s, delay => 10 ns);

    stimulate (s, 1 ns, 15);
    stimulate (target => s, delay => **open**, cycles => 15);
    stimulate (target => s, cycles => 15);
    stimulate (s, cycles => 15);

5.   swapper : **process is**
    begin
        shuffle_bytes (ext_data, int_data, swap_control, Tpd_swap);
        wait on ext_data, swap_control;
    end process swapper;

6.   product_size := approx_log_2(multiplicand) + approx_log_2(multiplier);

7.   **assert** now <= 20 ms
        report "simulation time has exceeded 20 ms";

8.   v_cap == v_supply * (1.0 − exp(−now/(R * C)));

9.   vector_multiply : **procedural is**
        variable result : real_vector(source_position'range);
    begin
        for index **in** source_position'range **loop**
            result(index) := source_position(index) * scale_factor;
        end loop;
        scaled_position := result;
    end procedural vector_multiply;

10. The third, first, none and third, respectively.

11.
```
architecture behavioral of computer system is
    signal internal_data : bit_vector(31 downto 0);
    interpreter : process is
        variable opcode : bit_vector(5 downto 0);
        procedure do_write is
            variable aligned_address : natural;
        begin
            ...
        end procedure do_write;
    begin
        ...
    end process interpreter;
end architecture behavioral;
```

Chapter 10

1.
```
library ieee;  use ieee.math_real.all;
library ieee_proposed;  use ieee_proposed.mechanical_systems.all;

package EMS is
    terminal engine_crankshaft : rotational_v;
    constant peak_rpm : angular_velocity := 6000.0 * math_2_pi / 60.0;
    type gear is (first, second, third, fourth, reverse);
end package EMS;
```

work.EMS.engine_crankshaft
work.EMS.peak_rpm
work.EMS.gear   work.EMS.first
work.EMS.second   work.EMS.third
work.EMS.fourth   work.EMS.reverse

2. **procedure** increment (num : **inout** integer);

3. **function** odd (num : integer) **return** boolean;

4. **constant** e : real;

5. No. The package does not contain any subprogram declarations or deferred constant declarations.

6. **use** work.EMS.engine_crankshaft;

7. **library** DSP_lib;
   use DSP_lib.systolic_FFT, DSP_lib.DSP_types.**all**;

Chapter 11

1.   **alias** received_source **is** received_packet.source;
        alias received_dest **is** received_packet.dest;
        alias received_flags **is** received_packet.flags;
        alias received_payload **is** received_packet.payload;
        alias received_checksum **is** received_packet.checksum;

2.   **alias** FET_source **is** M1.source;
        alias FET_drain **is** M1.drain;
        alias FET_gate **is** M1.gate;
        alias FET_substrate **is** M1.substrate;

3.   **alias** received_AK **is** received_packet.flags(0);
        alias received_ACKNO : bit_vector(2 **downto** 0)
               is received_packet.flags(1 **to** 3);
        alias received_SEQNO : bit_vector(2 **downto** 0)
               is received_packet.flags(4 **to** 6);
        alias received_UD **is** received_packet.flags(7);

4.   **alias** cons **is** "&" [character, string **return** string];
        report cons (grade_char, "–grade");

Chapter 12

1.   **entity** flipflop **is**
        generic (Tpw_clk_h, T_pw_clk_l : delay_length := 3 ns);
        port (clk, d : **in** bit; q, q_n : **out** bit);
     end entity flipflop;

2.   **entity** resistor **is**
        generic (r_nom : resistance := 1000.0;
               temp : temperature := 298.0;
               W : real := 0.0;
               L : real := 0.0);
        port (**terminal** node1, node2 : electrical);
     end entity resistor;

3.   clk_gen : **entity** work.clock_generator
        generic map (period => 10 ns)
        port map (clk => master_clk);

4.   **entity** adder **is**
        generic (data_length : positive);
        port (a, b : **in** std_ulogic_vector(data_length – 1 **downto** 0);
             sum : **out** std_ulogic_vector(data_length – 1 **downto** 0));
     end entity adder;

5.   io_control_reg : **entity** work.reg
                generic map (width => 4)
                port map (d => data_out(3 **downto** 0),
                            q(0) => io_en, q(1) => io_int_en, q(2) => io_dir, q(3) => io_mode,
                            clk => io_write, reset => io_reset);

Chapter 13

1. The are functionally the same. The Laplace operator s can be directly replaced by 'dot.

2. It is a more economical way of expressing transfer functions than 'dot. This is particularly true for many control system functions.

3. When the function to be modeled is nonlinear, since the coefficients of the transfer function terms must be constant to use 'ltf. Also, 'dot is preferred when the function to be modeled cannot be expressed in transfer function form, or it is for some reason difficult or inconvenient to do so.

4. Make sure the sampling rate is at least twice the highest frequency that will be sampled; incorporate an anti-aliasing filter that will restrict the high-frequency content of the data to be sampled.

5. The 'zoh and 'ztf attributes allow small-signal frequency-domain analysis to be performed on the model. Once the system is truly discretized, small-signal frequency-domain analysis cannot be performed.

6. It is a VHDL-AMS primitive that samples and holds a continuous quantity, thereby transforming it into a discontinuous or discrete quantity.

7. In effect, it samples an input quantity ('zoh) and delays certain terms in the transfer function ('delayed).

8. This analysis capability allows us to test z-domain designs, and in particular, z-domain function coefficients, without the need for an actual software or firmware platform on which to test. This can be extended to allow direct testing of software algorithms prior to having the hardware built on which they will eventually be implemented.

9. As sample rate is increased, the sampled system response will approach its continuous counterpart. As sample rate is decreased, accuracy is lost and incorrect results may occur due to violation of the Nyquist criterion.

10. Discrete systems are commonly used for software and firmware implementations of systems.

11. It becomes a discrete quantity whose value is only updated with each new sample clock.

Chapter 14

1. Quantity ports only deal with real numbers, so conservation laws do not apply to them. Terminals, on the other hand, deal with both through and across variables, allowing conservation laws to be enforced.

2. The **break on** statement informs the simulator that a first derivative discontinuity exists at the points where either limit is reached in the model. This allows the simulator to reinitialize the analog solver at that point.

3. Since a through variable is not specified for the input terminal, the simulator will assume that this is an ideal input that draws zero current.

4. The motor torque is defined as a branch variable from the model pin shaft_rotv to mechanical reference, rotational_v_ref. A positive value for the quantity torq implies it drives from shaft_rotv to rotational_v_ref, which "pulls" torque from whatever is connected to port shaft_rotv. A negative value for the quantity torq implies torque flows from rotational_v_ref to shaft_rotv, which "pushes" torque into whatever is connected to shaft_rotv. By convention, a positive torque generated by the motor is pushed or added to whatever is connected to it.

5. They are different because the gear model accepts a rotational velocity at its input and, because it integrates this signal, delivers a rotational position (angle) at its output. These differences are reflected in the port declarations for the model.

6. The sequence of the variable updates is set by the statement

    z_new := 0.6163507 * input – 0.6144184 * zi_dly1 + 0.2307692 * zo_dly1;

    Each time it is executed, the equation requires three new pieces of information: the current input value, input; the previous input value, zi_dly1; and the previous output value, zo_dly1. To get both the current and previous input values in the statement, the delayed input value must be set to the current input value after the equation is calculated; otherwise the delayed input value would simply be rewritten as the current input value.

    The delayed output value, zo_dly1, is actually updated after the equation is executed as well, since it takes on the value of z_out, which is updated at the end of the process.

7. Gearbox control horn:

        port (**terminal** theta : rotational;   *-- input angular position port*
            terminal pos : translational);   *-- output translational position port*

    Rudder control horn:

        port (**terminal** pos : translational;   *-- input translational position port*
            terminal theta : rotational);   *-- output angular position port*

8. The 'ramp attribute is used to transform the discontinuous signal z_out into a continuous quantity, output.

Chapter 15

1. (a) '1'.

    (b) '0'.

    (c) Either '1' or '0'. The order of contributions within the array passed to the resolution function is not defined. This particular resolution function returns the leftmost non-'Z' value in the array, so the result depends on the order in which the simulator assembles the contributions.

2.   **subtype** wired_and_logic **is** wired_and tri_state_logic;
        signal synch_control : wired_and_logic := '0';

3. The initial value is 'X'. The default initial value of type **MVL4**, 'X', is used as the initial value of each driver of **int_req**. These contributions are passed to the resolution function, which returns the value 'X'.

4. No, since the operation represented by the table in the resolution function is commutative and associative, with 'Z' as its identity.

5. (a) "ZZZZ0011"

    (b) "XXXX0011"

    (c) "0011XX11"

6. "XXXXZZZZ00111100"

7. (a) '0'

    (b) '0'

    (c) 'W'

    (d) 'U'

    (e) 'X'

8.

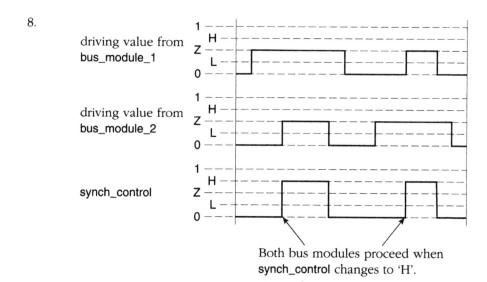

driving value from
bus_module_1

driving value from
bus_module_2

synch_control

Both bus modules proceed when
synch_control changes to 'H'.

9. The resolution function is invoked seven times: for the Mem port, the Cache port, the CPU/Mem Section port, the Serial port, the DMA port, the I/O Section port and the Data Bus signal.

10. We cannot simply invert the value read from the port, since the value may differ from that driven by the process. Instead, we use the **'driving_value** attribute:

```
synch_T <= not synch_T'driving_value;
```

Chapter 16

1. An entity declaration uses the keyword **entity** where a component declaration uses the keyword **component**. An entity declaration is a design unit that is analyzed and placed into a design library, whereas a component declaration is simply a declaration in an architecture body or a package. An entity declaration has a declarative part and a statement part, providing part of the implementation of the interface, whereas a component declaration simply declares an interface with no implementation information. An entity declaration represents the interface of a "real" electronic circuit, whereas a component declaration represents a "virtual" or "template" interface.

2.
```
component magnitude_comparator is
    generic ( width : positive; Tpd : delay_length );
    port ( a, b : in std_logic_vector(width – 1 downto 0);
        a_equals_b, a_less_than_b : out std_logic );
end component magnitude_comparator;
```

3.
```
position_comparator : component magnitude_comparator
    generic map ( width => current_position'length, Tpd => 12 ns )
    port map ( a => current_position, b => upper_limit,
        a_less_than_b => position_ok, a_equals_b => open );
```

4.
```
package small_number_pkg is
    subtype small_number is natural range 0 to 255;
    component adder is
        port ( a, b : in small_number;  s : out small_number );
    end component adder;
end package small_number_pkg;
```

5.
```
library ieee_proposed;  use ieee_proposed.electrical_systems.all;
package device_pkg is
    component resistor is
        generic ( r : resistance );
        port ( terminal p1, p2 : electrical );
    end component resistor;

    component capacitor is
        generic ( c : capacitance );
        port ( terminal p1, p2 : electrical );
    end component capacitor;

    component opamp is
        port ( terminal plus_in, minus_in, output : electrical );
    end component opamp;

end package device_pkg;
```

6.
```
library ieee_proposed;  use ieee_proposed.electrical_systems.all;
entity low_pass_filter is
    port ( terminal v_in, v_out : electrical );
end entity low_pass_filter;

architecture structural of low_pass_filter is
    use work.device_package.all;
    terminal n1, n2 : electrical;
begin
    amp : component opamp
        port map ( plus_in => n2, minus_in => v_out, output => v_out );
    r1 : component resistor
        generic map ( 10.0E+3 )
        port map ( v_in, n1 );
    r2 : component resistor
        generic map ( 10.0E+3 )
        port map ( n1, n2 );
    c1 : component capacitor
        generic map ( 15.0E-9 )
        port map ( n1, v_out );
    c2 : component capacitor
        generic map ( 15.0E-9 )
        port map ( n2, electrical_ref );
end architecture structural;
```

7.  ```
    library ieee_proposed;
    use ieee_proposed.electrical_systems.all, ieee_proposed.thermal_systems.all;
    package transistor_pkg is
        component nmos is
            port ( terminal gate, source, drain : electrical;
                   quantity temp : in temperature );
        end component nmos;

        component pmos is
            port ( terminal gate, source, drain : electrical;
                   quantity temp : in temperature );
        end component pmos;

    end package transistor_pkg;
    ```

8.  ```
    library dsp_lib;
    configuration digital_filter_rtl of digital_filter is
        for register_transfer
            for coeff_1_multiplier : multiplier
                use entity dsp_lib.fixed_point_mult(algorithmic);
            end for;
        end for;
    end configuration digital_filter_rtl;
    ```

9.  ```
    library dsp_lib;
    configuration digital_filter_std_cell of digital_filter is
        for register_transfer
            for coeff_1_multiplier : multiplier
                use configuration dsp_lib.fixed_point_mult_std_cell;
            end for;
        end for;
    end configuration digital_filter_std_cell;
    ```

10. ```
    library dsp_lib;
    architecture register_transfer of digital_filter is
        ...
    begin
        coeff_1_multiplier : configuration dsp_lib.fixed_point_mult_std_cell
            port map ( ... );
        ...
    end architecture register_transfer;
    ```

11. ```
    use entity work.multiplexer
        generic map ( Tpd => 3.5 ns );
    ```
    ```

12.

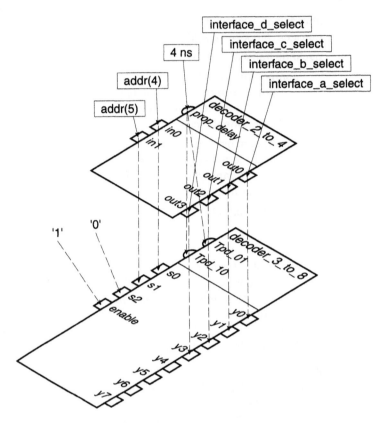

13.   **generic map** (Tpd_01 => **open**, Tpd_10 => **open**)
       port map (a => a, b => b, c => c, d => **open**, y => y)

14.   **library** ideal_lib;
       configuration ideal_low_pass_filter **of** low_pass_filter **is**
              for structural
                     for all : resistor
                            use entity ideal_lib.resistor(ideal);
                     end for;
                     for all : capacitor
                            use entity ideal_lib.capacitor(ideal);
                     end for;
                     for amp : opamp
                            use entity ideal_lib.opamp(ideal);
                     end for;
              end for;
       end configuration ideal_low_pass_filter;

15.   **library** bipolar;
       configuration bipolar_active_filter **of** active_filter **is**
              for structural
                     for opamp1 : opamp

```
                    use entity bipolar.uA741_opamp(behavioral);
                  end for;
                  …
              end for;
            end configuration bipolar_active_filter;
```

16.
```
            library bipolar;
            configuration discrete_741_active_filter of active_filter is
                for structural
                    for opamp1 : opamp
                        use configuration bipolar.discrete_uA741_opamp;
                    end for;
                    …
                end for;
            end configuration discrete_741_active_filter;
```

17.
```
            library bipolar;
           'architecture structural of active_filter is
                …
            begin
                opamp1 : configuration bipolar.discrete_uA741_opamp
                    port map ( … );
                …
            end architecture structural;
```

18.
```
        for interface_decoder : decoder_2_to_4
            use entity work.decoder_3_to_8(basic)
            generic map ( Tpd_01 => prop_delay, Tpd_10 => prop_delay )
            port map ( s0 => in0, s1 => in1, s2 => '0',
                        enable => '1',
                        y0 => out0, y1 => out1, y2 => out2, y3 => out3,
                        y4 => open, y5 => open, y6 => open, y7 => open );
```

19.
```
        configuration rebound of computer_system is
            for structure
                for interface_decoder : decoder_2_to_4
                    generic map ( Tpd_01 => 4.3 ns, Tpd_10 => 3.8 ns );
                end for;
            end for;
        end configuration rebound;
```

Chapter 17

1.

2.
```
inverter_array : for index in data_in'range generate
    inv : component inverter
        port map ( i => data_in(index), y_n => data_out_n(index) );
end generate inverter_array;
```

3.
```
direct_clock : if positive_clock generate
    internal_clock <= external_clock;
end generate direct_clock;

inverting_clock : if not positive_clock generate
    clock_inverter : component inverter
        port map ( i => external_clock, y => internal_clock );
end generate inverting_clock;
```

4.
```
for synch_delay_line(1)
    for delay_ff : d_ff
        use entity parts_lib.d_flipflop(low_input_load);
    end for;
end for;
for synch_delay_line(2 to 4)
    for delay_ff : d_ff
        use entity parts_lib.d_flipflop(standard_input_load);
    end for;
end for;
```

5. A block configuration is not required for the statement that directly connects the signals, since the statement does not include any component instances. The following block configuration for the statement that instantiates the inverter component is only used if the generic **positive_clock** is false when the design is elaborated:

```
for inverting_clock
    for clock_inverter : inverter
        use entity parts_lib.inverter;
    end for;
end for;
```

Chapter 18

1. $V_{out} = V_{in} \times D$

2. Boost converter.

3. It provides isolation between the input and output to protect against a switch failure.

4. The circuit begins to operate in discontinuous mode.

5. The transistor in a buck converter is either saturated or off. As a result, a complex transistor model is not really needed and can be replaced by a simple ideal switch model written in VHDL-AMS.

6. The averaged model simulates much faster and allows us to also examine the frequency response of the system useful for designing the compensation.

7. It provides loop stability by compensating for the poles and zeros present in the buck circuit. The 'ltf attribute allows us to create a high-level model whose pole and zero locations can be easily adjusted as the overall system requirements are defined.

8. It allows us to easily open and close the loop, depending on the desired analysis.

9. It is generated by running a frequency (AC) analysis on the buck converter in the open-loop configuration and is used to aid in compensator design.

10. It is an inverse relationship. As the switching frequency increases, the values for the inductor and capacitor decrease.

Chapter 19

1. **signal** serial_bus : wired_or_bit **bus**;
    signal d_node : unique_bit **register**;

2. When the resolution function for a standard-logic signal is passed an empty vector, it returns the value 'Z'. Thus, the values on rx_bus are 'Z', '0' after 10 ns, '1' after 20 ns, '0' after 30 ns, 'X' after 35 ns, '1' after 40 ns, '0' after 45 ns and 'Z' after 55 ns.

3. 'U', '0' after 10 ns, '1' after 20 ns, '0' after 30 ns, 'X' after 35 ns, '1' after 40 ns, '0' after 45 ns.

4.   vote <= 3 **after** 2 us, **null after** 5 us;

5. Initially false, true at 160 ns, false at 270 ns.

6. It should return the byte "1111_1111", since this is the identity value for the logical "and" operation.

7.
```
inverting_latch : block ( en = '1' or en = 'H' ) is
begin
      q_out_n <= guarded not d_in;
end block inverting_latch;
```

8.
```
disconnect source1 : wired_word after 3.5 ns;
disconnect others : wired_word after 3.2 ns;
disconnect all : wired_bit after 2.8 ns;
```

9. Initially 0, 3 at 51 ns, 5 at 81 ns, 0 at 102 ns.

10.
```
inverting_ff : block is
      signal q_internal : bit;
begin
     the_dff : component dff
           port map ( clk => sys_clk, d => d_in, q => q_internal );
     the_inverter : component inverter
           port map ( i => q_internal, y => q_out_n );
end block inverting_ff;
```

11.
```
for inverting_ff
     for the_dff : dff
          use entity work.d_flipflop(basic);
     end for;
     for the_inverter : inverter
          use entity work.inverter(basic);
     end for;
end for;
```

12.
```
library ieee_proposed;  use ieee_proposed.electrical_systems.all;

entity capacitor is
     generic ( cap : capacitance := 1.0e–6;
                 rleak : resistance := 10.0e9 ) ;
     port ( terminal p1, p2 : electrical );
end entity capacitor;

architecture leakage of capacitor is
     quantity vcap across icap, ileak through p1 to p2;
begin
     leak : block is
     begin
          ileak == vcap / rleak;
     end block leak;

     cap : block is
     begin
          icap == cap * vcap'dot;
     end block capacitor;

end architecture leakage;
```

13.
```
library ieee_proposed;  use ieee_proposed.electrical_systems.all;

entity lowpass_filter is
    generic ( c : capacitance := 1.0e–6;
                r : resistance := 15.9e3 );
    port ( terminal p1, p2 : electrical );
end entity lowpass_filter;

architecture ideal of lowpass_filter is
    quantity vr across ir through p1 to p2;
    quantity vc across ic through p2 to electrical_ref;
begin

    resistor : block is
    begin
        vr == ir * r;
    end block resistor;

    capacitor : block is
    begin
        ic == c * vc'dot;
    end block capacitor;

end architecture ideal;
```

Chapter 20

1.
```
type character_ptr is access character;
variable char : character_ptr := new character'(ETX);
...
char.all := 'A';
```

2. The statement "r := r + 1.0;" should be "r.all := r.all + 1.0;". The name r in the statement denotes the pointer, rather than the value pointed to. It is an error to perform an arithmetic operation on a pointer value.

3.

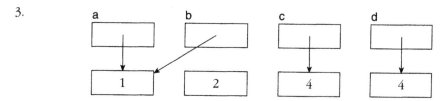

4. a = b is true, a.all = b.all is true, c = d is false, c.all = d.all is true.

5.
```
type string_ptr is access string;
variable str : string_ptr := new string'("    ");
...
str(1) := NUL;
```

6.
```
z.re := x.re * y.re – x.im * y.im;
z.im := x.re * y.im + x.im * y.re;
```

7.   **type** message_cell;
      type message_ptr **is access** message_cell;
      type message_cell **is record**
          source, destination : natural;
          data : bit_vector(0 **to** 255);
          next_cell : message_ptr;
       end record message_cell;
      variable message_list : message_ptr;
      ...
      message_list := **new** message_cell'(source => 1, destination => 5,
                          data => (**others** => '0'),
                          next_cell => message_list);

8. The first statement copies the pointer to the first cell to the access variable cell_to_be_deleted and leaves value_list also pointing to that cell. The call to **de-allocate** reclaims the storage and sets cell_to_be_deleted to the null pointer, but leaves value_list unchanged. The host computer system is free to reuse or remove the reclaimed storage, so the access using value_list in the third statement may not be valid.

9.   **use** work.bounded_buffer_adt.**all**;
      ...
    loop
        test_full(test_buffer, buffer_full);
        exit when buffer_full;
        write(test_buffer, X"00");
    end loop;

Chapter 21

1.   **type** real_file **is file of** real;
      file sample_file : real_file **open** read_mode **is** "samples.dat";
      ...
      read (sample_file, x);

2.   **type** bv_file **is file of** bit_vector;
      file trace_file : bv_file **open** write_mode **is** "/tmp/trace.tmp";
      ...
      write (trace_file, addr & d_bus);

3.   file_open (status => waveform_status, f => waveform_file,
            external_name => "waveform", open_kind => read_mode);
      assert waveform_status = open_ok
        report file_open_status'image(waveform_status)
          & " occurred opening waveform file" **severity** error;

4. The first call returns the bit value '1'. The second call returns the integer value 23. The third call returns the real value 4.5. The fourth call returns the three-character string " 67".

5.   **use** std.textio.**all**;
      variable prompt_line, input_line : line;
      variable number : integer;

      ...

      write(prompt_line, string'("Enter a number:"));
      writeline(output, prompt_line);
      readline(input, input_line);
      read(input_line, number);

6.   "   3500 ns 00111100 ok   "

Chapter 22

1.   val0_reg'path_name = ":test_bench:dut:val0_reg:"
      val0_reg'instance_name =
          ":test_bench(counter_test)"
          && ":dut@counter(registered):val0_reg@reg4(struct):"
      bit0'path_name = ":test_bench:dut:val1_reg:bit0"
      bit0'instance_name =
          ":test_bench(counter_test)"
          && ":dut@counter(registered):val1_reg@reg4(struct)"
          && ":bit0@edge_triggered_dff(behavioral):"
      clr'path_name = ":test_bench:dut:val1_reg:bit0:clr"
      clr'instance_name =
          ":test_bench(counter_test)"
          && ":dut@counter(registered):val1_reg@reg4(struct)"
          && ":bit0@edge_triggered_dff(behavioral):clr"

2.   **attribute** load : capacitance;
      attribute load **of** d_in : **signal is** 3 pF;

3.   **type** area **is range** 0 **to** integer'high
          units um_2;
          end units area;
      attribute cell_area : area;
      attribute cell_area **of** library_cell : **architecture is** 15 um_2;

4.   **attribute** optimization **of**
          test_empty [list_ptr, boolean] : **procedure is** "inline";

5.   **architecture** c_implementation **of** control_unit **is**
          attribute foreign **of**
              c_implementation : **architecture is**
              "control_unit.o control_utilities.o";
      begin
      end architecture c_implementation;

6.   **group** statement_set **is** (**label, label** <>);
          group steps_1_and_2 : statement_set (step_1, step_2);
          attribute resource_allocation **of** steps_1_and_2 : **group is** max_sharing;

Chapter 23

1. Modulation is the process of varying an otherwise purely sinusoidal signal in some fashion. In communications systems the transmittable high-frequency carrier signal is modulated by the baseband, and the resulting composite signal is then transmitted and demodulated by the receiver to recover the original baseband signal.

2. For analog modulation, the baseband signal is analog, and for digital modulation, the baseband signal is digital.

3. Frequency shift keying is a modulation technique where the value of a binary baseband signal is used to modulate a carrier signal between two different frequencies.

4. The output of the loop filter that controls the VCO also contains the original baseband information. The original signal can then be easily recovered with some additional filtering and threshold detection.

5. Simulation speed: The high-level behavioral PLL model substantially reduces simulation time, while still providing the appropriate amount of accuracy.

    Top-down design: If the system requirements change, the behavioral model parameters can be adjusted much more easily than changing the detailed circuit design. For example, if a quicker response time is needed, the VCO gain can be increased and the system resimulated to verify operation. As the system requirements are solidified, the behavioral models can be replaced by their detailed circuit implementations.

Chapter 24

1. The function **To_bit** has two parameters: the value to be converted and the parameter **xmap** that indicates how an unknown logic level should be converted. A conversion function in an association list must have only one parameter.

2. We need to define a conversion function from **std_ulogic** to **bit**:

        function cvt_to_bit (s : std_ulogic) **return** bit **is**
        begin
            return To_bit(s);
        end function cvt_to_bit;

    We can use this function and the standard-logic conversion function **To_stdulogic** in the association list:

```
gate1 : component nand2
    port map ( a => To_stdlogic(s1), b => To_stdlogic(s2),
              cvt_to_bit(y_n) => s3 );
```

3. If the host computer system has multiple processors, m1 and m2 may be resumed
    concurrently on different processors. Suppose the variable starts with the value
    0. A possible sequence of events is the following: m1 reads the variable and gets
    the value 0, m2 reads the variable and gets the value 0, m1 updates the variable
    with the value 1, m1 updates the variable with the value 1. Thus, the final value
    of the variable is 1, even though there were two increments performed.

Chapter 25

1. The system architecture model and system design model are both abstractions im-
    plemented using the VHDL-AMS language, but they differ in their usage. The ar-
    chitecture model is used for high-level specification and exploration. The design
    model is used for iteratively developing a design that can be physically imple-
    mented. In some cases, from a VHDL-AMS perspective, the architecture model
    may be just the top level of an incomplete design model. In other cases, the top
    level of the design model maps more closely to the physical design than does the
    architecture model.

Chapter 26

1. The main advantage of an H-bridge configuration for a single-supply system is
    that full power is available to drive the motor in either direction. A push-pull am-
    plifier can source the full supply voltage ($+V_{supply}$) to the load, but can only sink
    it to ground (not to $-V_{supply}$). If the supply power is split, then equal sourcing/
    sinking capability can be established, but with only half the supply voltage avail-
    able.

2. The main advantage of using functions is that they can be reused by several mod-
    els. For example, the **pwl_dim1_extrap** function can also be used in a variety of
    applications, including a piecewise linear voltage source.

3.   torq == pwl_dim1_extrap(now, xdata, ydata);

4. When operating the plane, the human operator actually becomes part of the over-
    all control system within which the plane functions. Jamming a control stick from
    rail to rail might cause a condition from which the plane control loop becomes
    unstable. Also, the bandwidth of the plane's response is affected by the human
    operator's response time (as shown in Figure 26-25.)

appendix G

CD-ROM Guide

Contents of the CD-ROM

The CD-ROM includes

- the VHDL-AMS source code for all the examples and case studies provided in this book

- an educational model library

- VHDL-AMS quick-reference guides

- links to VHDL-AMS resources

- links to an educational version of Mentor Graphics SystemVision, a simulation and modeling environment that includes a schematic entry tool, a VHDL-AMS simulator and a waveform viewing facility

The file *index.html* in the top-level directory of the CD-ROM provides access to these items.

Source Code Files

The files are located in the directory hierarchy within the *vhdl-ams-code* directory. There is a separate directory for each chapter, with the directory name based on the chapter title. In addition, the directory named *util* contains a number of utility packages and models. Within each directory there is an index file named *index-ams.txt*. It lists the files within the directory and indicates their contents.

There are three classes of files within each directory:

- Files containing code from figures within the book. The file names are based on the names of the entities, packages and configurations contained in the files. The index file identifies the corresponding figures.

- Files containing code appearing in line in the text of the book. The file names are of the form *inline_nn.vhd*. The index file identifies the corresponding section of the book.

- Files containing test-bench code. The file names are based on the name of the source file tested, with the prefix *tb_* added. The index file identifies the corresponding source file tested.

A small number of the models encounter limitations in the release of SystemVision available at the time of writing. In some of these cases, we have provided alternative "work-around" versions, identified by the suffix *_wa* in the file names, that avoid the limitations. Future releases of SystemVision should obviate these versions.

In many of the code examples in the book, segments of code are elided, indicated by ellipsis points (...). Their treatment in the source code files varies, depending on the reason for elision. If the code is elided for brevity, the code is included in full in the file. If the code is elided because it is not relevant to the example, it is also elided in the file. The file contains the ellipsis points commented out. If the elision results in syntactically incorrect code, "fix-up" code may be inserted to allow the file to be analyzed without error. In some cases, test-bench code may also be inserted.

Educational Library of Models

An "educational library," consisting of a wide range of useful VHDL-AMS model listings, is included on the CD-ROM. The models provide the reader with an array of "ready to simulate" building blocks. The files are located in the *EduLib* directory and contain code for multiple energy domains grouped into subdirectories as follows:

- *ControlSystems*
- *Digital*
- *Electrical*
- *Hydraulic*
- *Magnetic*
- *MixedSignal*
- *MixedTechnology*
- *Rotational*
- *Thermal*
- *Translational*

References

[1] P. J. Ashenden, *The Designer's Guide to VHDL,* 2nd edition, Morgan Kaufmann Publishers, San Francisco, 2002.

[2] R. W. Baily, *Human Performance Engineering: Using Human Factors/Ergonomics to Achieve Computer System Usability,* 2nd edition, Prentice-Hall, Englewood Cliffs, NJ, 1989.

[3] A. Bateman, *Digital Communications,* Addison Wesley, Reading, MA, 1999.

[4] C. G. Bell and A. Newell, *Computer Structures: Readings and Examples,* McGraw-Hill, New York, 1971.

[5] R. Best, *Phase-Locked Loops—Design, Simulation, and Applications,* McGraw-Hill, New York, 1999.

[6] R. J. Boucher, *Electric Motor Handbook,* Astro Flight, Marina Del Rey, CA, 2001.

[7] M. Brown, *Practical Switching Power Supply Design,* Academic Press, San Diego, 1990.

[8] J. Chen, J. Phillips, L. M. Silveira and K. Kundert, "Modeling RF Circuits for Systems Analysis," *Proceedings of the Cadence Technical Conference,* San Antonio, TX, May 1998.

[9] E. Christen, K. Bakalar, A. Dewey and E. Moser, "Analog and Mixed-Signal Modeling Using the VHDL-AMS Language," Tutorial presented at *36th Design Automation Conference,* New Orleans, 1999, *www.eda.org/vhdl-ams/ftp_files/documentation/tutdac99.pdf.*

[10] R. S. Cooper, *The Designer's Guide to Analog and Mixed-Signal Modeling,* Avant! Corp., Beaverton, OR, 2001.

[11] J. D'Azzo and C. H. Houpis, *Linear Control System Analysis and Design: Conventional and Modern,* 3rd edition, McGraw-Hill, New York, 1988.

[12] M. B. Feldman, *Data Structures with Ada,* Prentice-Hall, Englewood Cliffs, NJ, 1985.

[13] T. A. Fjeldly, T. Ytterdal and M. Shur, *Introduction to Device Modeling and Circuit Simulation,* Wiley Interscience, New York, 1998.

[14] C. Force, "Integrating Design and Test Using New Tools and Techniques," *Integrated System Design Magazine,* February 1999.

[15] M. Fowler and K. Scott, *UML Distilled: A Brief Guide to the Standard Object Modeling Language,* Addison-Wesley, Reading, MA, 1997.

[16] S. Franco, *Design with Operational Amplifiers and Analog Integrated Circuits,* 2nd edition, McGraw-Hill, New York, 1998.

[17] B. Friedland, *Control System Design: An Introduction to State-Space Methods,* McGraw-Hill, New York, 1986.

[18] D. D. Gajski and R. H. Kuhn, "New VLSI Tools," *IEEE Computer,* Vol. 16, no. 12 (December 1983), pp. 11–14.

[19] P. R. Gray, P. J. Hurst, S. H. Lewis and R. G. Meyer, *Analysis and Design of Analog Integrated Circuits,* 4th edition, John Wiley and Sons, New York, 2001.

[20] S. H. Hall, G. W. Hall and J. A. McCall, *High-Speed Digital System Design: A Handbook of Interconnect Theory and Design Practices,* Wiley-Interscience, New York, 2000.

[21] Institute for Electrical and Electronic Engineers, *Information Technology—Microprocessor Systems—Futurebus+—Logical Protocol Specification,* ISO/IEC 10857, ANSI/IEEE Std. 896.1, IEEE, New York, 1994.

[22] E. J. Kennedy, *Operational Amplifier Circuits: Theory and Applications,* Holt, Rinehart and Winston, New York, 1988.

[23] R. Kielkowski, *Inside SPICE,* 2nd edition, McGraw-Hill, New York, 1998.

[24] W. Liu, *MOSFET Models for SPICE Simulation Including BSIM3v3 and BSIM4,* John Wiley and Sons, New York, 2001.

[25] Mentor Graphics Corporation, *Eldo RF User's Manual,* Version 5.7_1, December 2001, pp. 1–4.

[26] D. C. Montgomery, *Design and Analysis of Experiments,* 5th edition, John Wiley and Sons, New York, 2000.

[27] H. Nyquist, "Certain Topics in Telegraph Transmission Theory," *IEE Transactions,* Vol. 47 (January 1928), pp. 617–644.

[28] K. Ogata, *Modern Control Engineering,* Prentice-Hall, Englewood Cliffs, NJ, 1970.

[29] K. Ogata, *Discrete-Time Control Systems,* Prentice-Hall, Englewood Cliffs, NJ, 1987.

[30] A. V. Oppenheim and A. S. Willsky, with S. H. Nawab, *Signals and Systems,* 2nd edition, Prentice-Hall, Englewood Cliffs, NJ, 1997.

[31] L. T. Pillage, R. A. Rohrer and C. Visweswariah, *Electronic Circuit and System Simulation Methods,* McGraw-Hill, New York, 1995.

[32] G. Pratt, "Automated Top-Down Design Rapidly Becoming Essential for Mixed-Signal Circuitry," *Electronic Design Magazine,* March 5, 2001.

[33] B. Razavi, *RF Microelectronics,* Prentice-Hall, Englewood Cliffs, NJ, 1998.

[34] R. Read, *The Essence of Communications Theory,* Prentice-Hall, Englewood Cliffs, NJ, 1998.

[35] S. P. Smith and R. D. Acosta, "Value System for Switch-Level Modeling," *IEEE Design & Test of Computers,* Vol. 7, No. 3 (June 1990), pp. 33–41.

[36] R. T. Stefani, B. Shahian, C. J. Savant and G. H. Hostetter, *Design of Feedback Control Systems,* Oxford University Press, Oxford, England, 2001.

[37] I. E. Sutherland, C. E. Molnar, R. F. Sproull and J. C. Mudge, "The TRIMOSBUS," *Proceedings of the Caltech Conference on VLSI,* January 1979.

[38] A. S. Tanenbaum, *Structured Computer Organization,* 3rd edition, Prentice-Hall, Englewood Cliffs, NJ, 1990.

[39] D. Teegarden, G. Lorenz and R. Neul, "How to Model and Simulate Microgyroscope Systems," *IEEE Spectrum,* Vol. 35, No. 7 (July 1998), pp. 66–75.

[40] Texas Instruments, *Understanding Buck Power Stages in Switchmode Power Supplies,* Application Report SLVA057, March 1999.

[41] S. A. Ward and R. H. Halstead Jr., *Computation Structures,* MIT Press, Cambridge, MA, and McGraw-Hill, New York, 1990.

[42] N. Weste and K. Eshraghian, *Principles of CMOS VLSI Design: A Systems Perspective,* Addison-Wesley, Reading, MA, 1985.

Index

*Page numbers in bold face denote whole sections
and subsections that address a topic.*

A

above
    predefined attribute, 78, 202, **203**, 205, 249,
            278, 675
        case selector expression, 226
        in concurrent break statement, 242
        initialization, 277
        in simultaneous if statement, 222
absolute value operator (**abs**), 71, 370
    See also arithmetic operator
abstract data type (ADT), 355, **626**
    container, **631**
abstraction, 5, 151
AC analysis, **402**
acceleration
    standard subtype, 373
acceleration due to gravity, 372
accelerometer
    exercise, 259
access type, **613**
    allocator, **614**, 620, 623
    array, **618**
    array attribute, 673
    attribute declaration, 683
    constant, 614
    dangling pointer, 626, 667
    deallocation, **625**
    declaration, **614**
    equality, **617**
    file element, 644
    garbage, 618, 625
    line deallocation, 667
    linked data structure, **620**, **631**
        circular list example, 636
        deletion, 625

        search, 623
        traversal, 623
    null, 614, 618, 622, 623, 625
    parameter, 627
    quantity, 614
    record, **618**
    signal, 614
    terminal, 614
    variable assignment, 615, **617**
accuracy, **295**, 431, 451, **773**
across
    predefined attribute, 69, 246, 673
across quantity, 18, 62, **193**, 272
across type, 62, 64, 65, 69, 192, 194
    array, 110
    record, 131
active, 142
active
    predefined attribute, 144, 674
actuator
    exercise, 257, 258
ADC. *See* analog-to-digital converter
adder
    behavioral example, 139, 147
    entity example, 136
    exercise, 181, 183, 185, 399, 521, 525, 551,
            552, 610
    functional example, 166
    procedure example, 312
addition
    function example, 382
addition operator (+), 71, 370
    See also arithmetic operator
address alignment
    exercise, 347
address decoder
    exercise, 182
    functional example, 351
ADT. *See* abstract data type
Advanced Library Format (ALF), **804**

aggregate
    array, **113**, 120, 166, 616, 620
        target of assignment, 116, 167
    multidimensional array, 115
    record, **131**, 616
ALF. *See* Advanced Library Format
alias, **377**
    array, 381
    array attribute, 673
    attribute specification, 694
    data object, **378**
    non-data item, **383**
    path name attribute, 676
    reference terminal, 379
    slice, 381
    subnature indication, 381
    subtype indication, 381
    unconstrained array parameter, 382
alias declaration, 378, 383
aliasing, 431
all
    access reference, 615, 618
    attribute specification, 693
    configuration declaration, 499
    disconnection specification, 600
    step limit specification, 246
    use clause, 361
allocator. *See* access type, allocator
alternative
    case statement, 80
ALU. *See* arithmetic/logic unit
amplifier, **455**, 756, 757
    behavioral example, 18
    exercise, 36, 133, 612
amplitude modulation, 705
amplitude shift keying (ASK)
    exercise, 718
analog output interface
    structural example, 353
analog package, **371**
analog solution point, 25, 218, 233, 244, 278, 329, 335
analog solver, 25, 26, 194, 200, 218, 223, 227, 232, 235, 242, 244, 250, 254, 271, 275, 278, 329, 330, 335
analog switch, **285**
    behavioral example, 241
analog-to-digital converter, 2, 203, **248**, **287**, **295**
    behavioral example, 12, 16, 248, 249
    configuration example, 507
    entity example, 15, 506
    exercise, 36, 259, 300, 435
    functional example, 602
    instantiation example, 231, 506
    structural example, 18
analysis, 24, **262**, 500

order, 262, 360
anchor, 373, 379
and gate
    behavioral example, 122, 159
    foreign example, 695
    functional example, 390
    instantiation example, 176, 178, 391
and operator, 72
    See also logical operator
and-or-invert gate
    entity example, 137
    exercise, 133, 700
    instantiation example, 177
    structural example, 140
angle
    standard subtype, 373
angular_accel
    standard subtype, 374
angular momentum, 243
angular_velocity
    standard subtype, 374
anti-aliasing filter, 432
antilock brake
    exercise, 435
arbiter
    exercise, 184, 490
arccos
    math_real function, 368
arccosh
    math_real function, 368
architectural trade-off, **747**
architecture body, 16, **138**, 262, 514, 730, 746
    attribute specification, 685
    component instantiation statement, 172
    declarative part, 139, 305, 514
    most recently analyzed, 172, 499
arcsin
    math_real function, 368
arcsinh
    math_real function, 368
arctan
    math_real function, 368
arctanh
    math_real function, 368
arithmetic/logic unit (ALU)
    behavioral example, 305, 311
    exercise, 73, 103
    functional example, 79
    test bench example, 368
arithmetic operation
    procedure example, 305, 311
arithmetic operator, 45, 47, 49, 70
    package example, 359
armature, 444
array, **106**
    access type, **618**

across type, 110
aggregate, **113**, 120, 166, 616, 620
    target of assignment, 116, 167
alias, 381
alias for element, 380, 694
assigment, 127
attribute, **117**, 320, 378, **673**, 694
branch quantity, 110
element indexing, 106, 108, 112, 175
file element, 644
guarded signal, 589
index range, 106, 111, 117, 119, 723
    allocator, 620
    parameter, 319
index type, 107, 118, 119
initialization from file, 651
    exercise, 668
multidimensional, **111**
    aggregate, 115
nature definition, 106
object declaration, 108
operator, **123**
port, 175, 212, 394
quantity, 212
resolved
    package example, 474
resolved element, 477, 726
signal, 173
slice, **125**, 175, 381, 694
    null, 125
terminal, 110, 197, 199
through type, 110
type conversion, **126**
type definition, 106
unconstrained, **118**, 470, 619, 724, 726
    file element, 646
    resolved elements, 477
unconstrained constant, 119
unconstrained parameter, **319**, 382
unconstrained port, **122**, 176, 178
ascending
    predefined attribute, 66, 117, 672, 673
ascending range, 44, 59, 69
ASCII character set, 52
ASK. *See* amplitude shift keying
assertion statement, **96**, 677
    concurrent, **167**, 169, 729
assertion violation, 97, 168
assignment statement
    signal. *See* signal assignment statement
    variable. *See* variable assignment statement
association list, 171, **722**
asynchronous clear, 145
attribute, 70
    array, **117**, 320, 378, **673**, 694
    path name, **676**, 694

predefined, **672**
quantity, **202**, 277
scalar nature, **66**
scalar type, **66**
signal, **144**, **213**, 277, **674**
terminal, **202**
type, **672**, **673**
user defined. *See* attribute declaration; at-
    tribute name; attribute specification
attribute declaration, **683**
attribute name
    enumeration literal, 693
    subprogram, 693
    user-defined, 693
attribute specification, **684**
    alias, 694
    design unit, 685
    group, 692, 697
    subprogram, 685
augmentation set, 25
average
    procedure example, 304
averaged model, **569**, 580
    exercise, 584
averager
    example, 248
    exercise, 103

B

back annotation, 507, 518
back-EMF, 444, 456, 764
Backus-Naur Form (BNF), 32
ball
    behavioral example, 237
band-pass filter
    behavioral example, 709
bandwidth, 574, 708, 753
barrel shifter
    exercise, 611
base
    predefined attribute, 69, 672
baseband, 705, 709
based literal, 30
base specifier, 31
base type, 57, 69, 94
basic identifier, 27
battery, 559, 754
    behavioral example, 275
    exercise, 280, 584
beam
    exercise, 526
behavioral modeling, 5, 10, **16**, **141**, **217**, **390**,
    533, 614, 626
    mixed structural/behavioral, **21**
best practice, 736

BFSK. *See* frequency shift keying
bilinear transform, 423, 463
binary base specifier, 31
binary frequency shift keying (BFSK). *See* frequency shift keying
binary search tree
    exercise, 642
binding indication, **498**, 498, 501, 505, 510, 514
    default, 499, 511, 519
    deferred, **512**
    incremental, **515**
bit
    predefined type, 55
bit reverser
    exercise, 387
bit string literal, 31, **121**
bit_vector
    predefined type, **121**
bit vector arithmetic
    package example, 359
bit vector I/O
    exercise, 669
block configuration. *See* configuration declaration, block configuration
block statement, **595**, **601**, 730
    declarative part, 514, 602
    generic constant, **604**
    port, **604**
BNF. *See* Backus-Naur Form
Bode plot, 573
Boltzmann constant, 372
boolean
    predefined type, 54, 55
boolean equation, 340, 384
boolean expression. *See* condition
boost converter, 558
bottom-up verification, 736
bouncing ball
    behavioral example, 237
brake system
    exercise, 524
    structural example, 497
branch quantity, 16, 18, 62, 188, **193**, 228, 246, 271
    array, 110
    composite, 196, 198
    parallel, 195
break element, 236, 238, 240
break quantity, 236, 238
break statement, 223, **232**, 251, 335, 443
    concurrent, 232, **239**
    in process, 235
buck converter, **558**, 754, **757**
buffer
    calibration, 743
    functional example, 596

buffer mode. *See* port, buffer mode
burglar alarm
    exercise, 185
bus monitor
    behavioral example, 665
bus port, 591
bus signal, 586
byte shuffler
    exercise, 345
byte swapper
    behavioral example, 126

C

cache memory
    behavioral example, 342
cache performance monitor
    behavioral example, 650
calibration, **742**
    exercise, 749, 750
capacitance
    standard subtype, 373
capacitive strength
    exercise, 491
capacitor, 558, 562, **565**
    charging example, 233, 236, 239
    exercise, 259, 346, 399, 521, 583, 609
    instantiation example, 228, 263
    leakage example, 195
car park counter
    exercise, 186
carrier, 704, 705, 709
carry chain
    configuration example, 548
    structural example, 537
case statement, **79**, 84, 165, 224
    simultaneous. *See* simultaneous case statement
cbrt
    math_real function, 367
ceil
    math_real function, 367
change control, 737
character
    predefined type, 52
characteristic expression, 24, 269, 271, 275, 278, 279, 403, 405
character literal, 31, 51, 383, 385
charge
    standard subtype, 373
checkerboard verification, 745
choice
    array aggregate, 114
    case statement, 80, 118, 225
    record aggregate, 131

circular buffer
  ADT example, 628
circular list
  ADT example, 636
clamp transistor
  example, 233
class, 40
  entity (item), 685, 696
  parameter. *See* parameter, class
clock buffer
  entity example, 698
clock distribution tree
  structural example, 541
clock generator
  behavioral example, 143, 148, 149
  exercise, 74
  procedure example, 324
clock signal
  package example, 353
closed loop, **571**, 576, 711
closely related type, 61, 126
command and control, **282**, **752**
comment, 27, 35
communication, **704**
comparator, 568, 569
  behavioral example, 18, 204, 249
  exercise, 133, 521, 584
  instantiation example, 264
  pulse-width modulation, 290
compensator, 449, 451, **451**, **462**, 565, 571, **572**, 580
  exercise, 468, 583, 584
complex number, 369
component, **493**
  attribute specification, 688
component declaration, **494**, 514
  package, **496**
component instance, 18, 138, **170**, **228**, 269, 271, 275, **495**, 510, 604, 679
  attribute specification, 689
  configuration, **498**
  direct, 122, 170, 498, **504**
  generic map, 391
  unbound, 499, **512**
component modeling, **805**
composite quantity, 207, 208, 212, 219, 220
composite signal, 215, 216
composite terminal, 193
composite type, **105**
computer system
  behavioral example, 128, 151, 598
  configuration example, 541, 544
  exercise, 184
  instrumented example, 539, 544
  register-transfer example, 726
  structural example, 475, 484, 508, 512, 587

concatenation operator (&), 31, 71, 125
concurrent assertion statement. *See* assertion statement, concurrent
concurrent break statement. *See* break statement, concurrent
concurrent procedure call statement. *See* procedure call statement, concurrent
concurrent statement, 21, **139**, 160, 217, 269, 530, 604
  attribute specification, 689
  postponed, 729
condition, 76, 87, 90, 91, 97, 161, 221
  break statement, 237
  concurrent assertion statement, 167
  generate statement, 537
  guard. *See* expression, guard
  wait statement, 148
conditional signal assignment statement. *See* signal assignment statement, conditional
condition clause
  wait statement, 146, 148, 149
configuration declaration, **498**
  attribute specification, 685
  binding. *See* binding indication
  block configuration, 503, 544, **605**
  direct instantiation, **504**
  generate statement, **543**
  generic map, **505**
  hierarchical, **501**
  nested, 503
  port map, **505**
configuration management, 736
configuration specification, **514**, 515
conformance, 358
conservation, 13, 15, 188, 193, 272, 441, 455
constant, **40**, 94, 108, 117, 218
  access type, 614
  alias, 378
  mathematical, 366, 369
  natural, 372
  unconstrained array, 119
constant class parameter. *See* parameter, class
constant declaration, **40**, 137, 139, 304, 334, 350, 530, 602
  deferred, **356**, 358, 359
constraint. *See* range constraint
context clause, 363
continuous mode, 559, 569
contradictory, 277
contribution
  predefined attribute, 202, 272, 675
contribution expression, 272
contribution quantity, 272
control character, 52
control horn, 438, **458**
  exercise, 612

control section, 8
    structural example, 516
control sequencer
    behavioral example, 308
control stick, **283**
    example, 85
control structure, 75
control system
    exercise, 259, 435
    signal flow example, 190
convergence, 214, 223, 330
conversion
    type. *See* type conversion
conversion function
    association list, **722**
    bit vector to number example, 326
    standard logic, 365, 480
coordinate transformation
    behavioral example, 112
cos
    math_real function, 368
cosh
    math_real function, 368
cosine
    behavioral example, 92, 95
cosine function
    exercise, 348
counter
    behavioral example, 86, 88
    exercise, 73, 103, 181, 183, 186, 399, 550, 552, 732
    pulse-width modulation, 290
    structural example, 172, 720
CPU
    behavioral example, 128, 151, 306, 309, 357, 362, 380
    entity example, 475
    functional example, 596
    instrumented example, 648
    package example, 350, 356
    register transfer example, 8, 308, 588
    structural example, 175, 516, 518
crossover frequency, 574
crosswind, 770, 773
    exercise, 775
ctok
    standard constant, 372
cycle pure, 329, 331

D

damper
    exercise, 257, 526, 610
damping, 444, 456, 764
damping
    standard subtype, 373

dashpot
    behavioral example, 209
    exercise, 259
data acquisition system
    exercise, 259
data logger
    behavioral example, 593
data path, 8
DC-DC converter, **558**
    exercise, 584
DCL. *See* Delay Calculation Language
DC operating point, 52, 403
    See also quiescent point
deallocate
    implicit procedure, 625
deallocation, **625**
debugging, 392, 539
declarative part, 341, 361, 644
    architecture body, 139, 305, 514
    block statement, 514, 602
    entity, 137, **168**
    function, 325
    generate statement, 530
    procedural, 334
    procedure, 304
    process statement, 41, 160
decoder, **290**, 705
    configuration example, 508
    entity example, 508
    exercise, 133, 182, 183, 553, 610, 700
    functional example, 351
    instantiation example, 508
decoration. *See* attribute specification
default binding, 499, 511, 519
default initial value, 46, 47, 50, 52, 189, 615
    signal, 277, 472
default value
    generic constant, 392
    parameter, **317**, 321, 339
    port, 137, 177, 230
deferred binding, **512**
deferred constant. *See* constant declaration, deferred
delay
    signal asignment statement, 141
Delay and Power Calculation System (DCPS), **804**
Delay Calculation Language (DCL), **804**
delayed
    predefined attribute, 144, 202, **206**, 424, 674, 675
    initialization, 277
delay element
    behavioral example, 155
    exercise, 182, 258, 549
    functional example, 164

delay_length
  predefined subtype, 60
delay line
  exercise, 550
delay mechanism, 141, **153**, 164, 165, 590
delta cycle, 235
delta delay, 145, **150**, 727
demodulation, 705, **708**
  exercise, 750
demultiplexer, 705
density
  standard subtype, 374
dependency
  between library units, 262
derivative, 202, 207, 208, 236, 237, 239, 705
descending range, 44, 59, 69
design library. *See* library
design of experiments, 748
design unit, 24, 262, 350, 360, 363, 500
  attribute specification, 685
detector, **708**
difference equations, 462, **464**
differencer, 442
  exercise, 717
differentiation, 417
digital-to-analog converter, 2, **250**, **292**, **295**, 752
  behavioral example, 214, 216, 251
  exercise, 552
digitizer. *See* analog-to-digital converter
dimension, 256
diode, 558
  exercise, 347, 434, 583
  fly-back, 763
  linearization example, 403
  mixed-technology example, 254
diode array
  exercise, 550
direct instantiation
  configuration, **504**
  entity, 122, 170, 498
direction, 59, 82
directly visible. *See* visibility, directly visible
disconnection. *See* signal, disconnection
disconnection specification, **600**
  delay, 600
discontinuity, 214, 223, **232**, 251, 443
  function, 330
discontinuous mode, 559
discrete event simulation, 142
discrete range, 81, 93, 106, 119, 530, 544, 547
discrete transfer function, **423**
discrete type, 57, 80, 82, 93
  attribute, 67
displacement
  standard subtype, 373
display

configuration example, 546
structural example, 530
display package
  foreign example, 695
division operator (/), 71, 370
  See also arithmetic operator
DMA controller
  package example, 385
domain
  predefined signal, 52, 278, 404
domain_type
  predefined type, 52, 278, 404
"don't care" value, 56, 480
dot
  predefined attribute, 202, **206**, 416, 675
    break statement, 237, 239
    initialization, 277
DPCS. *See* Delay and Power Calculation System
driver. *See* signal, driver
driving
  predefined attribute, **591**, 674
driving value, 178, 481, 484, 720
driving_value
  predefined attribute, **485**, 674
duty cycle, 559, 561, 568
dynamic storage, 586

E

EBNF. *See* Extended Backus-Naur Form
edge checker
  exercise, 347
edge triggered, 100, 145
EDIF. *See* Electronic Design Interchange Format
effective value, 178, 484
elaboration, 24, **269**, 500, 543
electrical
  standard nature, 64, 373
electrical nature, 62, 64, 192
electrical_ref, 62, 194, 373
electrical_systems
  standard package, 373
electron charge, 372
Electronic Design Interchange Format (EDIF),
  805
encoder, 283, 704
  exercise, 133
endfile
  implicit function, 645
energy, 64
energy
  standard subtype, 371
energy domains, 12
energy_systems
  standard package, 371

engine management system
    exercise, 375
entity, 15
    attribute specification, 685
    declarative part, 137, **168**
    instantiation. *See* component instance, direct
entity (item)
    attribute specification, 684
    group template declaration, 696
entity declaration, 15, **136**, 262, 363, 390, 494,
    730, 740
enumeration literal, 51, 352, 383, 384
    attribute name, 693
    attribute specification, 691
    overloading, 51
enumeration type, **51**, 57, 383, 474
envelope detector, 709
eps0
    standard constant, 372
eps_si
    standard constant, 372
eps_sio2
    standard constant, 372
equality operator (=), 72, 370
    See also relational operator
equivalent series resistance, 566, 573
    exercise, 583
error, 448, 462, 464, 568, 713, 753, **755**
error detection, 284
error detector and corrector
    exercise, 185
error rate, 709
error severity level, 98
e_si
    standard constant, 372
e_sio2
    standard constant, 372
event, 25, 142, 278
event
    predefined attribute, 144, 674
exclusive nor operator. *See* **xnor** operator
exclusive or operator. *See* **xor** operator
execution, **277**
    See also simulation
execution time, 403
exit statement, **87**, 91, 95
exp
    math_real function, 367
explicit set, 25, 275
exponential function
    exercise, 102, 103
exponential notation, 30
exponentiation operator (**), 71, 367
    See also arithmetic operator
expression, **70**, 165, 218
    actual generic constant, 391

actual parameter, 312
association with port, 171, 177, 178, 230
boolean. *See* condition
case statement selector, 80, 224
characteristic. *See* characteristic expression
function call, 325
generate configuration, 544, 547
guard, 595, 602
initialization, 40, 41, 120
parameter default value, **317**, 321, 339
primary, 70, 615
qualified, **60**, 70, 80, 167, 352, 616
return statement, 325
variable assignment statement, 42
Extended Backus Naur Form (EBNF), 32
extended identifier, 28
extension
    exercise, 133
extrapolation, 767
    exercise, 775

F

failure severity level, 98
falling_edge
    standard logic function, 365
fcapacitance
    standard subtype, 374
feedback, **571**
FIFO buffer
    ADT example, 627
FIFO queue
    exercise, 550, 553
file, 614, **643**
    alias, 378
    appending, 650
    attribute declaration, 683
    closing, 651, **653**
    end of file test, 645
    logical name, 644, 653
    multiple association, 652
    opening, 644, 651, **653**
        status, 654
    parameter. *See* parameter, file class
    portability, **657**
    reading, **645**
    unconstrained array, 646
    writing, **648**
file_close
    implicit procedure, 654
file declaration, **644**
    subprogram, **651**
file_open
    implicit procedure, 653, 654
file_open_kind
    predefined type, 52, 645

file_open_status
    predefined type, 52, 654
filter, 445, 713, 715, 753, 759, 763
    behavioral example, 415, 428, 709
    configuration example, 501, 503
    device-level model, 11
    exercise, 259, 434, 435, 521, 523, 524, 609,
        610, 716, 717
    instantiation example, 505
    Laplace transfer function example, 417, 428
    structural example, 413, 428, 501
    z-domain transfer function example, 426, 428,
        431
    zero order hold example, 423, 428
finite-state machine (FSM), 284
    behavioral example, 115
    encoder, **289**
    transition matrix, 115
first bit set
    procedure example, 319
flicker noise, 410
flipflop
    behavioral example, 18, 98, 145, 264, 677
    component example, 494
    dataflow example, 728
    entity example, 169
    exercise, 103, 181, 184, 732
    functional example, 167
    instantiation example, 172, 394
    timing example, 331
floating point comparison, 205
floating point type, **46**, 57, 59, 62, 69, 188
floor
    math_real function, 367
fluidic
    standard nature, 64, 374
fluidic nature, 64
fluidic_ref, 374
fluidic_systems
    standard package, 374
fluid sensor
    structural example, 263
flux
    standard subtype, 373
fly-back diode, 763
force
    standard subtype, 373
forcing strength, 56, 480
foreign, 466
foreign
    predefined attribute, **694**
for generate. *See* generate statement, iterative
for loop, **93**, 118
Fourier series, 402
Fourier transform, 403, 405
free quantity, 16, **188**, 228, 246, 275, 276

free sector map
    exercise, 132
frequency
    predefined function, 407
frequency analysis, 573
frequency dependent noise, 410
frequency detector, 706, 713
    behavioral example, 332
frequency domain, 25, 52, 188, 203, **402**, 405,
        431, 569
frequency_domain
    predefined enumeration value, 279
frequency domain augmentation set, 405
frequency modulation, 705
frequency response, 412
frequency shift keying (FSK), **705**
    exercise, 716, 718
fresistance
    standard subtype, 374
FSK. *See* frequency shift keying
FSM. *See* finite-state machine
function, **325**, 383
    call, 325, 338
        simultaneous statement, **329**
    declarative part, 325
    impure, **327**
    nested, 342
    overloading, **338**
    parameter list, 325
    procedural equivalent, 335
    pure, **327**, 329, 479
    resolution. *See* resolution function
    result type, 325, 355, 384
    See also subprogram
functional modeling, 161, **327**, 340
functional verification, 744
function declaration, 325
fundamental frequency, 402

G

gain, 441, 444, 446, **446**, 451, 574, 715
    behavioral example, 440, 441
garbage. *See* access type, garbage
gate
    behavioral example, 122, 156, 159
    configuration example, 519, 520
    entity example, 137, 514
    exercise, 133, 523, 524, 700
    foreign example, 695
    functional example, 390
    instantiation example, 176, 177, 178, 391, 514,
        518, 520
    structural example, 140
gearbox, 438, **446**, **457**
    exercise, 258, 468

generate parameter, 383, 530, 537
generate statement, **529**, 604, 730
    conditional, **536**, 544
    configuration, **543**
    declarative part, 530
    iterative, **530**, 546
    nested, 534, 547
    recursive, **541**
generic constant, **389**, 506, 530, 537, 539, 746
    actual, 391, 495, 510, 722
    attribute specification, 687
    block statement, **604**
    default value, 392
    formal, 390, 510, 514
    local, 510, 514
    unassociated, 516
    visibility, 391
generic interface list, 390
generic map, 391, 495, 504, 510, 515
    block statement, **604**
    configuration declaration, **505**
genetic algorithm, 748
globally static, 177
gradient-based methods, 748
graphics transformation
    behavioral example, 533
grav
    standard constant, 372
greater than operator (>), 72
    See also relational operator
greater than or equal operator (>=), 72
    See also relational operator
ground, 373, 379
group, **696**
    attribute specification, 692, 697
group declaration, 697
group template declaration, 696
guard
    implicit signal. *See* signal, **guard**
guarded port, **591**
guarded signal, **586**, 589, 596
guarded signal assignment, **595**
    disconnection specification, **600**
guarded signal parameter, **593**
guard expression, 595, 602

H

Hamming code generator
    exercise, 185
hard stop. *See* stop
H-bridge, 757
heat_flow
    standard subtype, 374
hexadecimal base specifier, 31
hiding. *See* visibility, hiding

high
    predefined attribute, 66, 117, 672, 673
high impedance, 470, 480, 586
hold time, 331
Hooke's law, 219
human
    exercise, 775
human controller, **770**
hypercube
    exercise, 555

I

identifier, 27, 70
    basic, 27
    enumeration literal, 51
    extended, 28
identifier table
    exercise, 376
identity operator (+), 71
    See also arithmetic operator
ieee
    standard library, 352, 364
ieee_proposed
    standard library, 65, 362, 371
IF. *See* intermediate frequency
if generate. *See* generate statement, conditional
if statement, **76**, 80, 161, 221
    simultaneous. *See* simultaneous if statement
illuminance
    standard subtype, 374
image
    predefined attribute, 66, 672
        textual output, 667
impedance, 417
implicit equation, 13, 217
impure function, **327**
incomplete type declaration, 621
incremental binding. *See* binding indication, incremental
incrementer
    procedure example, 318
indefinite wait, 150, 323
index range. *See* array, index range
index type, 107, 118, 119
inductance, 759
inductance
    standard subtype, 373
inductor, 558, 562
    behavioral example, 207, 209
    exercise, 583
inelastic, 457
inequality operator (/=), 72, 370
    See also relational operator
inertance
    standard subtype, 374

inertia, 444, 456, 764
inertial delay, **153**, 210, 590
infinite loop, 86
information hiding, 355, 356
initialization, 566
initialization expression, 40, 41, 120
initialization phase, 25, 277
initial value, 188, 189, 200, 201
    default initial value, 46, 47, 50, 52, 277, 472, 615
    signal, 140, 277, 472
        ramp and **slew** attributes, **217**
in-phase component
    exercise, 717
input
    textio file object, 660
input/output, **643**
    user-defined type, **667**
input/output controller
    structural example, 353
instability, 566
instance_name
    predefined attribute, 378, 676
instantiation. *See* component instance
instruction fetch
    procedure example, 306
instruction set
    example, 128
instruction set interpreter
    behavioral example, 306, 309, 357, 362
instrumentation, 539
integ
    predefined attribute, 202, **208**, 675
        break statement, 237, 239
        initialization, 277
integer
    universal, 68
integer
    predefined type, 44
integer literal, 29
integer type, **44**, 57
integral, 202, 208
integration, 417
integrator, 446, **447**, 457
    exercise, 73, 468
    structural example, 228, 263
interconnect verification, 744
interface, 739
intermediate frequency, 708
interpolation, 767
    exercise, 775
inverter, 569
    behavioral example, 156
    exercise, 549
ISO character set, 52

is_X
    standard logic function, 366

K

k
    standard constant, 372
keying, 705
keypad controller
    exercise, 491
Kirchoff's law, 13, 194, 272, 274

L

label, 383
    assertion statement, 97
    attribute specification, 689, 690
    block statement, 595, 602, 606
    break statement, 233
    case statement, 79
    component instance, 495, 499
    concurrent assertion statement, 167
    concurrent procedure call statement, 322
    concurrent signal assignment statement, 161
    exit statement, 87
    generate statement, 530, 537, 544
    if statement, 76
    loop statement, 89, 91, 95
    next statement, 90
    null statement, 85
    procedure call statement, 305
    process statement, 160
    return statement, 309, 325
    signal assignment statement, 141
    simultaneous statement, 218, 221, 225, 227, 334
    variable assignment statement, 42
    wait statement, 146
ladder network
    exercise, 550
lag, 444, **445**, 712
Language Reference Manual (LRM), **797**
Laplace transfer function, 203, 403, **412**, 426, 428
    See also s-domain transfer function
Laplace transform, 403
last_active
    predefined attribute, 144, 674
last_event
    predefined attribute, 144, 674
last_value
    predefined attribute, 144, 674
latch
    exercise, 181, 183, 398
    functional example, 597

latching multiplexer
    exercise, 609
layout constraint, 683
lead-lag compensator, 451, **451**, **462**
    exercise, 468
left
    predefined attribute, 66, 117, 320, 672, 673
leftof
    predefined attribute, 67, 672
length
    physical type example, 49
length
    predefined attribute, 117, 661, 673
less than operator (<), 72
    See also relational operator
less than or equal operator (<=), 72
    See also relational operator
lexical elements, **27**
library, 24, 262, **267**, 499, 740
    ieee, 352, 364
    ieee_proposed, 65, 362, 371
    resource, 267, 352
    std, 363, 658
    working, 171, 267, 350, 363, 500
library clause, **267**, 362, 500
    example, 267
library name, 351, 352, 361
Library of Parameterized Modules (LPM), **805**
library unit, 262, 351, 360, 500
light emitting diode (LED)
    instantiation example, 531
limiter, 441, **443**, 446, 451, 755
    behavioral example, 723
    exercise, 103
    function example, 326
line
    textio type, 659
linearized form, 403
linearly independent, 277
line regulation, **578**, 580
linkage. *See* control horn
linkage mode, **721**
linked data structure. *See* access type, linked data
        structure
linked list
    exercise, 641
literal, 70, 218
    based, 30
    bit string, 31, **121**
    character, 31, 51, 383, 385
    enumeration. *See* enumeration literal
    integer, 29
    numeric, 358
    physical, 48
    real, 29
    string, 31, **121**

load, **447**, 560, 571, 572, 576
    exercise, 584
load regulation, **576**
load resistance, 563
local declaration, 304, 325
locally static, 45, 82, 357
logarithm
    math_real function, 367
logarithm function
    exercise, 345
log file
    exercise, 669
logical name. *See* file, logical name
logical operator, 54, 55, 57, 70, 340
    array operands, 123
    exercise, 348
    standard logic, 365, 480
logic block
    functional example, 340, 474
    structural example, 514, 520
loop parameter, 93, 118, 383
loop statement, **86**
    for loop, **93**, 118
    infinite, 86
    labelled, 89, 91, 95
    nested, 89
    summary, **96**
    while loop, **91**
low
    predefined attribute, 66, 117, 672, 673
LPM. *See* Library of Parameterized Modules
LRM. *See* Language Reference Manual
ltf
    predefined attribute, 203, 412, 428, 446, 453,
        676

M

magnetic
    standard nature, 64, 373
magnetic_ref, 373
magnitude, 402, 405, 407, 573
majority
    exercise, 348, 525
Manchester carry chain
    configuration example, 548
    structural example, 537
mass
    behavioral example, 209
    exercise, 257, 259, 526, 610
mass
    standard subtype, 373
math_complex
    standard package, 369, **793**, **799**
mathematical packages, **366**

math_real
    standard package, 366, **792**, **799**
maximum
    behavioral example, 99
    exercise, 133, 347
mechanical modeling, **454**
mechanical nature, 64, 69
mechanical_systems
    standard package, 373
memory
    behavioral example, 109, 128, 151
    configuration example, 547
    entity example, 475, 477
    exercise, 186, 399, 525, 526, 610, 668
    package example, 678
    structural example, 478, 534
memory access
    procedure example, 306, 309
metastability, 263
methodology, 736
microgyroscope, 743
microprocessor. *See* CPU
minimum
    exercise, 347
mixed-signal, 2, 190, 201, 204, 232, **247**, **281**, 736
    example, 12
mixed-technology, 190, **253**, **437**, 736
mixer
    procedural example, 334
mmf
    standard subtype, 373
mmoment_i
    standard subtype, 374
mode_error
    predefined literal, 654
model, 3
modem
    behavioral example, 115
modulation, 704
    exercise, 750
modulo operator (**mod**), 71, 367
    See also arithmetic operator
momentum, 64
MOSFET, 566
motor, 438, 441, **444**, **455**, 578, 755, 757, 763
    calibration, 743
    exercise, 612
    state space example, 335
mu0
    standard constant, 372
Muller-C element
    exercise, 182
multiplexer, 704
    behavioral example, 83, 143, 147
    exercise, 36, 181, 399, 490, 522, 550, 552
    functional example, 161, 162, 595

instantiation example, 177
multiplication operator (*), 71, 370
    See also arithmetic operator
multiplier, 712
    analog example, 189
    exercise, 522, 553, 717
multivalued logic, 472, 477, 479
    package example, 472
mutual exclusion, 731

N

named association, 228
    array aggregate, 114, 120
    generic map, 392
    parameter, 321
    port map, 171
    record aggregate, 131
name_error
    predefined literal, 654
nand gate
    configuration example, 520
    entity example, 514
    exercise, 523
    instantiation example, 514, 520
nand operator, 72
    See also logical operator
natural
    predefined subtype, 60
natural constant, 372
nature, 15, 192, 254
    electrical, 62, 64, 192
    fluidic, 64
    mechanical, 64, 69
    optical. *See* nature, radiant
    radiant, 63, 192
    record, 130, 199, 219, 380
    scalar, **61**
    thermal, 63
nature declaration, **61**, 118, 602
negation
    procedure example, 314
negation operator (–), 30, 71, 370
    See also arithmetic operator
negation operator (**not**), 71
    See also logical operator
negative logic, 56
net, 269
network interface
    behavioral example, 328
network packet generator
    behavioral example, 647
network receiver
    behavioral example, 315, 628
new. *See* access type, allocator
Newton's law of cooling, 13

Newton's law of motion, 208, 209, 237
next statement, **90**, 91, 95
NMOS transistor
    behavioral example, 223, 225
noise, 25, 52, 188
noise simulation, 403
noise source quantity, **409**
non-coherent detector, 709
non-conservative, 13, 188, 190
non-contradictory, 277
nor gate
    configuration example, 519
    instantiation example, 518
nor operator, 72
    See also logical operator
note severity level, 97
now
    predefined function, 100, **330**
null access value. *See* access type, null
null range, 95
null slice, 125
null statement, **84**, 165, 227
    simultaneous. *See* simultaneous null state-
        ment
null transaction, 586, 590, 593, 596, 600
number of equations, 227, 275
numeric_bit
    standard package, **366**, **799**
numeric literal, 358
numeric_std
    standard package, **366**, **799**
nu_si
    standard constant, 372
Nyquist criterion, 431

O

octal base specifier, 31
Ohm's law, 18, 192, 218, 227, 391, 533
    exercise, 257
OMF. *See* Open Model Forum
opamp
    behavioral example, 211, 212
    calibration, 743
    configuration example, 500
    exercise, 36, 259, 399, 434, 435, 521, 523, 524,
        610
    instantiation example, 228, 263
    Laplace transfer function example, 419
    procedural example, 396
    saturating example, 221
    structural example, 495
open
    actual parameter, 318
    binding indication, 512
    file declaration, 645

port map, 177, 508
    See also unassociated
open collector, 482
    exercise, 489
open drain, 482
open loop, 571
Open Model Forum (OMF), **803**
open_ok
    predefined literal, 654
operational amplifier. *See* opamp
operator, **70**, 70
    arithmetic, 45, 47, 49, 70
    array, **123**
    concatenation (&), 31, 71, 125
    logical, 54, 55, 57, 70, 340
        array operands, 123
    overloading
        See operator symbol, overloading
    overloading. *See* operator symbol, overload-
        ing
    precedence, 70
    relational, 54, 70, 222
        array operands, 124
    shift, 70, 124
    short circuit, 54, 340, 624
operator symbol, 383
    attribute specification, 686
    overloading, **339**, 384
optical nature. *See* nature, radiant
optic_flux
    standard subtype, 374
optimization, **746**, **747**
ordered collection
    ADT example, 632
    exercise, 642
or operator, 72
    See also logical operator
oscillation, 758
oscillator, 711
others
    array aggregate, 114
    attribute specification, 692
    case statement, 81
    configuration declaration, 499
    disconnection specification, 601
    record aggregate, 131
    step limit specification, 246
output
    textio file object, 660
overloading, 344, 383, 384
    enumeration literal, 51
    operator symbol, **339**, 384
    subprogram, **338**

P

package, 43, **349**, 378, 730
    attribute specification, 685
    component declaration, **496**
    example, 385
    IEEE standard, **364**
    selected name, 351, 352, 360
    standard analog, **371**
    template, 632
package body, 350, **358**, 627
package declaration, **350**, 358, 363, 627
    subprogram, **355**
parallel branch quantity, 195
parameter, **310**, 384
    access type, 627
    actual, 311, 312, 313, 315, 316, 318, 319, 321,
        322, 338, 485, 593, 722
        attribute specification, 694
        file, 656
    array index range, 319
    attribute specification, 687
    class, 312, 313, 318, 321, 325, 327
    default value, **317**, 321, 339
    direction. *See* parameter, mode
    file class, **656**
    formal, 311, 313, 315, 316, 319, 321, 338, 358,
        593, 724
    generate, 383, 530, 537
    guarded signal, **593**
    list, 310, 321, 325, 355
    loop, 93, 118, 383
    mode, 311, 312, 313, 314, 316, 317, 321, 325,
        327
    resolved signal, **485**
    shared variable, 731
    signal class, **314**
    summary, **321**
    type, 311, 319, 321, 338
    unassociated, 318
    unconstrained array, **319**, 382
parametric analysis, **747**
parent, 328
parentheses, 70
parity checker
    exercise, 183
parity tree
    exercise, 552
partitioning, **739**
passive process, **168**
passive switch, 560
pass transistor
    exercise, 489, 610
path name
    attribute, **676**, 694
path_name

predefined attribute, 378, 676
pendulum
    behavioral example, 242
periodicity
    standard subtype, 372
permeability of vacuum, 372
permittivity of silicon, 372
permittivity of silicon dioxide, 372
permittivity of vacuum, 372
phase, 402, 405, 407, 573, 705
phase detector, 712, 713
    exercise, 717
phase error, 711
phase locked loop (PLL), **711**
    behavioral example, 712
phase margin, 449, 574
phasor, 402, 417
physical design, 741
    exercise, 750
physical literal, 48
physical type, **48**, 57, 384
    attribute, 67
    mixed dimensional arithmetic, 68
pipeline
    behavioral example, 533
pipeline interlock control
    structural example, 518
piston
    behavioral example, 208
    exercise, 257
placement, 683
PLI. *See* programming language interface
PLL. *See* phase locked loop
pointer. *See* access type
Poisson's ratio for silicon, 372
pole, 412, 417, 445, 449, 573, 580, 754
    exercise, 583
port, 15, 136, 269, 471
    actual, 510, 722
    array, 175, 212, 394
    association, 171, 477
    association with expression, 171, 177, 178,
        230
    association with resolved signal, **481**
    attribute specification, 687
    bidirectional, 137
    block statement, **604**
    buffer mode, **720**
    bus kind, 591
    composite, 174
    default value, 137, 177, 230
    direction, 136, 190, 201
    driving value, 178, 720
    effective value, 178
    formal, 510, 514, 724
    guarded, **591**

port (continued)
    inout mode, 137
    linkage mode, **721**
    local, 510, 514
    mode, 136, 190, 201, 232
    quantity, 15, **190**, 228, 230, 232, 271, 275, 277
    record, 174
    register kind, 591
    resolved, **483**, 591
    signal, 136, 190
    source, 483, 720, 721
    terminal, 15, **200**, 228, 230, 271
    type, 43, 136
    unassociated, 171, 178, 230, 274, 277, 508, 512, 516
    unconstrained array, **122**, 176, 178
    unused input, 177
port map, 18, **170**, **228**, 275, 477, 495, 504, 510, 515
    block statement, **604**
    configuration declaration, **505**
pos
    predefined attribute, 67, 672
positional association, 228
    array aggregate, 113, 120
    generic map, 392
    parameter, 321
    port map, 171
    record aggregate, 131
position number, 68
positive
    predefined subtype, 60
positive logic, 55
positive_real
    math_complex subtype, 369
postponed process, **727**
potentiometer, 439, 446
    exercise, 468
power, 64, 409
power
    standard subtype, 372
power amplifier, 757
power converter, **558**
power supply, **754**
    example, 65
power switch, 558
power terminal
    package example, 353
precedence
    EBNF, 34
    operator, 70
pred
    predefined attribute, 67, 672
pressure
    standard subtype, 374

pressure sensor
    exercise, 258
primary binding. *See* binding indication, incremental
primary expression, 70, 615
primary unit
    design unit, 262, 360, 363, 500
    physical type, 48
principal_value
    math_complex subtype, 369
priority encoder
    exercise, 133
priority minimizer
    exercise, 732
procedural, **333**
    declarative part, 334
    function equivalent, 335
    opamp example, 396
procedure, **304**
    abstraction of a process, 324
    declarative part, 304
    nested, 342
    overloading, **338**
    parameter. *See* parameter
    parameter list, 310
    return, 305, **309**
    See also subprogram
procedure call statement, 305, 308, 321, 322, 338
    concurrent, 169, **322**, 729
        example, 324
    example, 311, 313, 314
procedure declaration, 304
processor. *See* CPU
process statement, 16, 138, 139, 141, **160**, 247, 254, 269, 533
    declarative part, 41, 160
    elaboration, 271
    example, 78
    execution, 151
    passive, **168**
    postponed, **727**
    resumption, 26, 146, 278, 727
    sensitivity, 17, 26, 278, 316, 728
    sensitivity list, 78, 87, 147, 160, 249
    suspension, 17, 26, 160, 278, 316, 323, 728
    timeout, 278
producer/consumer
    exercise, 182
programming language interface (PLI), **798**
propagation delay, 142, 156, 159, 390, 392, 518, 600
    functional example, 602, 606
propellor, **762**
propulsion system
    example, 21
    test bench example, 23

protected type
    attribute declaration, 683
    file element, 644
pull-up, 586
    exercise, 489
    functional example, 482
pulse-code modulation, 283
pulse generator, 569
    exercise, 347
pulse rejection limit, 157, 600
pulse source
    exercise, 583
pulse-width check, 145
pulse-width modulation (PWM), **290**, 558, 568,
    757, 763
    accuracy, 297
    exercise, 775
pump
    exercise, 259
pure function, **327**, 329

Q

q
    standard constant, 372
QPSK. *See* quadrature phase shift keying
quadrature component
    exercise, 717
quadrature modulation
    exercise, 717
quadrature phase shift keying (QPSK)
    exercise, 717
qualified expression, **60**, 70, 80, 167, 352, 616
quantity, 108, 117, 218, 247, 254, 269
    access type, 614
    across, 18, 62, **193**, 272
    alias, 378
    array, 212
    attribute, **202**
    branch, 16, 18, 62, 188, **193**, 228, 246, 271
        array, 110
        composite, 196, 198
        parallel, 195
    break, 236, 238
    case selector expression, 226
    composite, 207, 208, 212, 219, 220
    contribution, 272
    free, 16, **188**, 228, 246, 275, 276
    port, 15, **190**, 228, 230, 232, 271, 275, 277
    procedural, 335
    reference, 271
    scalar, 203, 204
    selector, 236, 238
    source, 188, **405**, **409**, 414
    through, 18, **193**, 275
quantity declaration, 188, 244, 530, 602

quantization error, **295**
queue ADT
    exercise, 642
quiescent domain, 52, 404
quiescent_domain
    predefined enumeration value, 278
quiescent point, 25, 278, 406, 409
quiescent state augmentation set, 279
quiet
    predefined attribute, 144, 674

R

radiant
    standard nature, 65, 374
radiant nature, 63, 192
radiant_ref, 374
radiant_systems
    standard package, 374
radio
    structural example, 505
RAM. *See* memory
ramp
    predefined attribute, 144, **213**, 246, 251
        initialization, 277
        signal initialization, **217**
random number generator, 366
    test bench example, 368, 724
range, 82, 118
    direction, 44
    null range, 95
range
    predefined attribute, 117, 122, 319, 320, 673
range constraint, 44, 47, 48, 58, 59, 82, 93, 106,
    107, 118, 119
read
    implicit procedure, 645, 647
    textio procedure, 659, **660**
        invalid input, 661
readline
    textio procedure, 659
read only memory (ROM)
    behavioral example, 326, 645
    entity example, 137, 477
    exercise, 179
real
    predefined type, 47
real literal, 29
realmax
    math_real function, 367
realmin
    math_real function, 367
real number, **46**, 57
real_vector
    predefined type, **120**
receiver, 705

record, **127**
　access type, **618**
　across type, 131
　aggregate, **131**, 616
　alias for element, 380, 694
　element selection, 128
　nature, 130, 199, 219, 380
　port, 174
　selected name, 128
　terminal, 199
　through type, 131
　type definition, 127
recursive structure, **541**
reference
　predefined attribute, 202, 272, 675
reference quantity, 271
reference terminal, 62, 192, 194, 202
　alias, 379
refinement, 736, **740**
register
　behavioral example, 100, 395
　configuration example, 517
　entity example, 516
　exercise, 610, 700, 701
　instantiation example, 172, 175, 395, 516
　structural example, 172
register file
　exercise, 133
register signal, 586
register transfer language, 8
register transfer modeling, 8
regulator, 558
rejection. *See* pulse rejection limit
relational operation
　procedure example, 320
relational operator, 54, 70, 222
　array operands, 124
　function example, 364
remainder operator (**rem**), 71
　See also arithmetic operator
report clause
　assertion statement, 97
　concurrent assertion statement, 167
report statement, **96**, 101, 392, 677
reserved word, 28, 339
reset generator
　functional example, 163
resistance
　physical type example, 48
resistance
　standard subtype, 373
resistor, 218
　behavioral example, 18, 227, 391
　exercise, 434, 521, 583
　instantiation example, 228, 263, 531
　temperature dependent, 197, 199, 532

　behavioral example, 191
resistor package
　behavioral example, 197, 199, 532
resolution, 294, 298, 431, 773
resolution function, 470, 471, 484, 586, 587
　example, 592
　summary, **478**
resolution limit, 50, 317
resolved
　signal, 721
resolved
　standard logic resolution function, 479
resolved port, **483**, 591
resolved signal. *See* signal, resolved
resolved signal parameter, **485**
resolved subtype. *See* subtype, resolved
response surface modeling, **748**
response time, 573
resumption. *See* process statement, resumption
return
　procedure, 305
return statement, 335
　function, 325
　procedure, **309**
reuse, 740, **745**
reverser
　exercise, 387
reverse_range
　predefined attribute, 117, 673
revision control, 737
RF communication system, **704**
right
　predefined attribute, 66, 117, 672, 673
rightof
　predefined attribute, 67, 672
ripple, 562, 573, 753, 769
rising_edge
　standard logic function, 365
ROM. *See* read only memory
root locus techniques, 449
root terminal, 272, 274
Rosetta, **803**
rotate left operator (**rol**), 72
　See also shift operator
rotate right operator (**ror**), 72
　See also shift operator
rotational
　standard nature, 64, 373
rotational_ref, 373
rotational_v
　standard nature, 64, 373
rotational_v_ref, 373
round
　math_real function, 367
rudder, **460**, **752**

S

safety switch
    example, 379
sample, 203, 287
    example, 248
sample frequency, 431
sample-hold, 423
    exercise, 434
sampling, **423**, **431**, 462
    exercise, 435
saturated, 567
scalar nature, **61**
    attribute, **66**
scalar quantity, 203, 204
scalar terminal, 193
scalar type, **43**, 57
    attribute, **66**
scheduler
    functional example, 164
SDF. *See* Standard Delay Format
s-domain transfer function, **440**, **454**
    See also Laplace transfer function
secondary unit
    design unit, 262, 360, 363
    physical type, 48, 49
selected name, 269, 344, 358, 385
    package item, 351, 352, 360
    predefined item, 363
    record element, 128
selected signal assignment statement. *See* signal
        assignment statement, selected
selector expression
    case statement, 80
selector quantity, 236, 238
self-timed logic
    exercise, 492
semantics, 24, 26, 262
    EBNF, 35
sensitivity, 17, 26, 278, 316, 728
    concurrent assertion statement, 167
    concurrent break statement, 240
    concurrent procedure call statement, 323
    conditional signal assignment statement, 161
    selected signal assignment statement, 165
sensitivity clause, 146, 149, 164, 240
sensitivity list, 78, 87, 147, 160, 249
sensor
    analog modeling example, 10
    elaboration example, 269
    exercise, 256
    mixed-signal example, 12
    structural example, 263, 506
sensor grid
    example, 112
sequence number generator

function example, 328
sequencer
    structural example, 353
sequential break statement. *See* break statement
sequential statement, 16, **75**, 139, 160, 278, 304,
        321, 325, 334
    attribute specification, 690
serial-to-parallel converter
    exercise, 717
servo, 290, 438, **441**, **455**, 462, 752, **755**, **757**,
        770
    exercise, 468, 612
settling time, 580
setup time, 145, 323
seven-segment decoder
    exercise, 183
seven segment LED
    instantiation example, 230
severity clause
    assertion statement, 97
    concurrent assertion statement, 167
severity_level
    predefined type, 52, 97
shared variable. *See* variable, shared
shift left arithmetic operator (**sla**), 72
    See also shift operator
shift left logical operator (**sll**), 72
    See also shift operator
shift operator, 70, 124
shift register
    exercise, 524
shift right arithmetic operator (**sra**), 72
    See also shift operator
shift right logical operator (**srl**), 72
    See also shift operator
short circuit operator, 54, 340, 624
sign
    math_real function, 367
signal, 108, 117, 138, 218, 247, 250, 254, 269
    access type, 614
    active, 142
    alias, 378
    array, 173
    array of resolved elements, 477
    association with port, 171
    attribute, **144**, **213**, **674**
    attribute specification, 694
    bus kind, 586
    composite, 215, 216
    default initial value, 277, 472
    disconnection, **586**, 596
    driver, 144, 154, 158, 271, 277, 471, 481, 485,
        586, 587, 590, 593, 596
        actual parameter, 316
    driving value, 481, 484
    effective value, 484

signal (continued)
 event, 25, 142, 278
 global, 352
 guard, 595, 596, **598**
 guarded, **586**, 596
  array, 589
 guarded parameter. *See* parameter, guarded
   signal
 initial value, 140, 277, 472
  ramp and **slew** attributes, **217**
 kind, 586, 593
 net, 269
 null transaction, 586, 590, 593, 596, 600
 parameter, **314**
 port, 136, 190
 register kind, 586
 resolved, 144, **469**, 586, 720, 721
  array of resolved elements, 477
  associated with port, **481**
  composite, **474**
  declaration, 470
  parameter. *See* parameter, resolved signal
  summary, **478**
 resolved array
  package example, 474
 source, 144, 471, 595
 transaction, 24, 142, 154, 156, 158, 278, 316,
  471, 587, 729
 type, 140
 update, 151, 278
signal assignment statement, 16, 17, 116, 141,
  141, 150, 154, 156, 158, 162, 169, 271, 335,
  485
 concurrent, **161**, 327, 596, 729
 conditional, 161, 596
 guarded, **595**
  disconnection specification, **600**
 in a procedure, 316, 317
 selected, 161, 165, 596
signal class parameter. *See* parameter, signal class
signal declaration, 18, 137, 139, **140**, 350, 530,
  586, 602
 package, 352
 resolved, 470
signal flow modeling, 188
signal generator
 behavioral example, 316
signal processing
 behavioral example, 92
signature
 alias, 384
 attribute name, 693
 attribute specification, 685, 690
signed magnitude number
 exercise, 375

sign extension
 exercise, 133
simple_name
 predefined attribute, 378, 676
simple simultaneous statement, **218**
simulated annealing, 748
simulation, 24, 97, 261, **277**, 479, 500, 512, 539
simulation cycle, 25, 142, 151, 235, 250, 254, 277,
  727
simulation time, 142, 154, 277, 330
simultaneous case statement, **224**, 276
simultaneous if statement, **221**, 276
simultaneous null statement, **227**, 276
simultaneous procedural statement. *See* procedural
simultaneous statement, 16, **217**, 247, 250, 254,
  269, 275, 277, 333, 530, 595, 604
 function call, **329**
sin
 math_real function, 331, 368
sinh
 math_real function, 368
slew
 predefined attribute, 144, 203, **210**, **215**, 247,
  251, 674, 676
  initialization, 277
  signal initialization, **217**
slice, **125**, 175, 694
 alias, 381
 null, 125
small signal, 403, 405, 409, 569
solenoid
 calibration, 743
solvability, **275**, 353, 403
source
 port, 483, 720, 721
 signal, 144, 471, 595
source quantity, 188, **405**, **409**, 414
special symbols, 28
specification, **738**
spectral component, 402
spectral source quantity, **405**, 414
speed controller, 763
 exercise, 775
spring, 219, 447, 460
 behavioral example, 209
 exercise, 256, 257, 259, 399, 526, 610
sqrt
 math_real function, 367
stability, 451, 462, 464, 565, 569, 571
stable
 predefined attribute, 144, 674
stack ADT
 exercise, 641
standard
 predefined package, **363**, 694, **785**

standard analog package, **371**
Standard Delay Format (SDF), **804**
standard logic, 56, **121**, 159, **801**
state, 64
state averaged model, **569**, 580
state machine. *See* finite-state machine
static, 45, 204
   See also globally static
status_error
   predefined literal, 654
std
   predefined library, 363, 658
std_input
   textio logical name, 660
std_logic
   standard logic subtype, 365, 479
std_logic_1164
   standard logic package, 56, 121, 340, 352,
    364, **479**, **789**, **801**
std_logic_vector
   standard logic type, 365, 479, 726
std_output
   textio logical name, 660
std_ulogic
   standard logic type, 56, 340, 365, 479
std_ulogic_vector
   standard logic type, 121, 340, 365, 479, 726
step limit specification, **244**, 278
stiffness, 457
stiffness
   standard subtype, 373
stimulus
   exercise, 641
stimulus/response test
   exercise, 133
stimulus file reader
   behavioral example, 654
   exercise, 668
stimulus generator
   example, 150, 368
   exercise, 348
stimulus list
   example, 620, 625, 634
stop, 443, 446, 457
   exercise, 257
stop-watch
   exercise, 526
strength weakener
   exercise, 347
string
   assertion statement, 97
   literal, 31, **121**
   textio, 659
string
   predefined type, **120**

structural modeling, **18**, **170**, **228**, **394**, **493**, 506,
   530, **536**, **601**, 746
   mixed structural/behavioral, **21**
structural set, 25, 269, 271, 275, 277
subelement association, 174, 230
subnature, **65**
subnature declaration, 65, 118, 119, 602
subnature indication, 106
   alias, 381
subnature indications, 65
subprogram, **303**, 350
   alias, 384
   attribute name, 693
   attribute specification, 685
   file declaration, **651**
   overloading, **338**
   package declaration, **355**
   See also function; procedure
subprogram declaration, 358, 530, 602
subtraction operator (–), 71, 370
   See also arithmetic operator
subtype, **57**, 121
   resolved, 471
    composite, **474**
    summary, **478**
   resolved array
    package example, 474
subtype declaration, 58, 118, 119, 304, 334, 350,
   530, 602
subtype indication, 58, 82, 106, 119, 471, 586, 614
   alias, 381
   allocator, 615
succ
   predefined attribute, 67, 672
successive approximation, 287
   exercise, 300
summer, 441, **442**, 444, 770
   behavioral example, 197, 710
sum of squares procedure
   exercise, 347
superposition, 402
suspension. *See* process statement, suspension
switch, **285**, **566**
   behavioral example, 241
   exercise, 299, 584
   instantiation example, 263
switching frequency, 562, 574, **579**
switching power converter, **558**
switch-mode power supply, 558
switch strength
   exercise, 492
symbol
   standard attribute, 372
synchronization, 284
   behavioral example, 482
   exercise, 300, 492

synchronization (continued)
    procedure example, 486
syntax, 24, 26, **32**, 262
synthesis, 4, 56, 97, 177, 261, 479, 539, 683, 736,
    745, 800, 802
synthesis packages, **366, 799**
system architecture, 737
system architecture model, 738
system design model, 738
system specification, **738**
systolic array
    exercise, 555

T

tan
    math_real function, 368
tanh
    math_real function, 368
temperature
    standard subtype, 374
terminal, 61, 117, 228, 247, 254, 269
    access type, 614
    alias, 378
    array, 110, 197, 199
    attribute, **202**
    composite, 193
    global, 352
    port, 15, **200**, 228, 230, 271
    record, 199
    reference, 62, 192, 194, 202, 379
    root, 272, 274
    scalar, 193
terminal declaration, 18, **192**, 530, 602
    package, 352
terminator
    functional example, 482
test bench, **21**, 736
testing, 3, 738
text
    textio file type, 660
textio
    predefined package, **658**
        deallocation, 667
thermal
    standard nature, 64, 374
thermal nature, 63
thermal noise, 410
thermal_ref, 374
thermal_systems
    standard package, 374
thermostat
    behavioral example, 78
    test bench example, 661
threshold detector
    exercise, 717

through
    predefined attribute, 69, 246, 673
through quantity, 18, **193**, 275
through type, 62, 64, 65, 69, 192, 194
    array, 110
    record, 131
time
    floating point, 51, 149, 206, 330
time
    predefined type, 50
time constant, 415, 418, 444
time division multiplexer, 283
time domain, 25, 52, 405, 406, 409, 431, 566, 569
time_domain
    predefined enumeration value, 279
time of day
    exercise, 375
timeout
    process statement, 278
timeout clause
    wait statement, 146, 149
timer
    behavioral example, 233, 236, 239, 393
time step, 223, 236, **244**, 278
timing constraint, 100, 145, 167, 330, 506
    attribute example, 698
    example, 331
    exercise, 347, 348
    procedure example, 323
to_bit
    standard logic function, 365
to_bitvector
    standard logic function, 365, 723
tolerance
    predefined attribute, 69, 202, **203**, 675
tolerance group, 59, 62, 65, 69, 106, 188, 200, 202,
    203, 209, 218, 220
top-down design, **736**
torque, 444, 456
torque
    standard subtype, 373
torque constant, 764
to_StdLogicVector
    standard logic function, 365
to_StdULogic
    standard logic function, 365
to_StdULogicVector
    standard logic function, 365
to_X01
    standard logic function, 102, 365
to_X01Z
    standard logic function, 365
trace write, 101
    exercise, 103
tracing, 539

transaction
   signal. *See* signal, transaction
transaction
   predefined attribute, 144, 674
transceiver
   exercise, 489, 490, 524
transfer function, 203, 403, 428, 572, 580, 709
   behavioral example, 574
   human, 770
transformation array initialization
   procedure example, 656
transformer, 559
   exercise, 584
transient error pulse, 756
transistor, 566
   behavioral example, 223, 225
   exercise, 259, 435, 522
   instantiation example, 495, 537
   noise example, 410
translational
   standard nature, 64, 373
translational_ref, 373
translational_v
   standard nature, 64, 373
translational_v_ref, 373
transmission
   exercise, 258
transmission line
   behavioral example, 110, 154, 206
   calibration, 743
   exercise, 551
transmitter, 705
transport delay, **153**
tree structure, 541
TRIMOSBUS
   exercise, 492
tristate, 470, 472
tristate buffer
   behavioral example, 473
   exercise, 74, 490, 609, 610
tristate register
   behavioral example, 592
trunc
   math_real function, 367
truth table
   functional example, 166
type
   across, 62, 64, 65, 69, 192, 194
      array, 110
      record, 131
   alias, 383
   attribute, **672**, **673**
   classification, **57**
   composite, **105**
   declaration, 304, 334
   parameter, 311, 319, 321, 338

   port, 43, 136
   scalar, **43**, 57
   signal, 140
   through, 62, 64, 65, 69, 192, 194
      array, 110
      record, 131
type conversion, **60**, 70, 212
   array, **126**
   association list, 477, **722**
type declaration, **43**, 118, 137, 350, 530, 602
   incomplete, 621
type qualification. *See* qualified expression

U

unaffected waveform, 164, 165
unassociated
   generic constant, 516
   parameter, 318
   port, 171, 178, 230, 274, 277, 508, 512, 516
unbound. *See* binding indication, deferred
unconnected. *See* port, unassociated
uniform
   math_real procedure, 366
uninitialized value, 56, 480
unit
   design. *See* design unit
   library. *See* library unit
   multiplier, 372
   physical type, 48, 49, 384
      attribute specification, 691
unit test, 741
universal integer, 68
unknown value, 56, 472, 480
use case, 736
use clause, 44, 268, **360**, 500
UX01
   standard logic subtype, 365, 480
UX01Z
   standard logic subtype, 365, 480

V

val
   predefined attribute, 67, 672
value
   predefined attribute, 66, 672
      textual input, 667
valve
   entity example, 497
   exercise, 524
   package example, 497
variable, 17, **40**, 108, 117, 160, 247, 250, 254, 271
   access type, 614, 617
   actual parameter, 313

variable (continued)
    alias, 378
    shared, 41, **730**
variable assignment statement, **42**, 116, 313
    access type, 615, **617**, 622
    shared variable, 731
variable class parameter. *See* parameter, class
variable declaration, **40**, 304, 334
    shared, 730
VCO. *See* voltage controlled oscillator
vector multiply
    exercise, 346
    function example, 329
velocity
    standard subtype, 373
verification, 3, 97, 167, **744**
    example, 728
Verilog, **802**
vflow_rate
    standard subtype, 374
via
    calibration, 743
viscosity
    standard subtype, 374
visibility, 141, **341**, 391, 511, 595, 602, 604
    directly visible, 268, 343, 352, 360, 363, 378,
        500
    hiding, 94, 344
    visible by selection, 344
VITAL, **799**
voltage
    standard subtype, 373
voltage controlled oscillator (VCO), 712
    exercise, 717
voltage mode control, **568**
voltage reference, 571
voltage regulator, 755
voltage source, 713, 756
    behavioral example, 331
    behavioral model, 275
    exercise, 258, 347, 583, 718, 775
    spectral example, 406, 408
volume
    standard subtype, 374

W

wait statement, 17, 26, 86, **146**, 160, 204, 249,
        278, 335
    in concurrent break statement, 240
    indefinite, 150, 323
    in a procedure, 315
warning severity level, 98
waveform, 141, 161, 165, 587
    unaffected, 164, 165
waveform element, 141, 158

waveform generator
    behavioral example, 245
WAVES, **801**
weak strength, 56, 480
when clause
    case statement, 80
    exit statement, 87
    next statement, 90
while loop, **91**
white noise, 410
winding inductance, 456, 763, 764
winding resistance, 456, 764
wired-and
    behavioral example, 482
write
    implicit procedure, 648
    textio procedure, 659, **664**
writeline
    textio procedure, 659

X

X01
    standard logic subtype, 365, 480
X01Z
    standard logic subtype, 365, 480
xnor operator, 72
    See also logical operator
xor operator, 72
    See also logical operator

Y

Young's modulus, 372

Z

z-domain transfer function, 203, 403, 423, **426**,
        428, **431**, 462
    exercise, 435
zero, 412, 451, 566, 573, 580
    exercise, 583
zero order hold, 203, **423**, 428
zoh
    predefined attribute, 203, **423**, 428, 675
ztf
    predefined attribute, 203, **426**, 428, 462, 676

A Radio-Controlled, Electric-Powered Airplane System
Case Studies

In *The Systems Designer's Guide to VHDL-AMS*, five case studies focus on different aspects of the design of a radio-controlled, electric-powered airplane system. Each case study illustrates the VHDL-AMS language features presented in the preceding chapters. The numbers in the diagram below identify the case study focusing on that aspect of the design.

Case Study 1: Mixed-Signal Focus

Focuses on the encoding, transmission and decoding of the analog throttle and rudder command signals as they make their way through the system, highlighting analog-to-digital and digital-to-analog conversions to show mixed-signal modeling with VHDL-AMS. Illustrates concepts presented in Chapters 1–7.

Case Study 2: Mixed-Technology Focus

Focuses on the mixed-technology (mixed-domain) capabilities of VHDL-AMS, discussing the s-domain servo control blocks and the electrical and mechanical system. Illustrates concepts presented in Chapters 9–13.

Case Study 3: DC-DC Power Converter

Demonstrates how to model power systems with VHDL-AMS, modeling a Buck converter with two useful levels of abstraction and simulating the effects of power fluctuations on the system. Illustrates concepts presented in Chapters 15–17.

Case Study 4: Communications System

Compares phase-locked loop and discrimination methods for signal recovery in the RF receiver. Illustrates concepts presented in Chapters 19–22.

Case Study 5: RC Airplane System

Analyzes the RC airplane as an entire system, highlighting how different modeling abstraction levels may be used efficiently for large-system simulations and exploring the value of early requirements capture, frequent subsystem integration and validation, and bottom-up design verification. Illustrates concepts presented in Chapters 24–25.

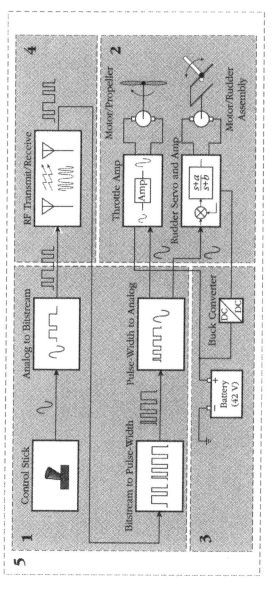

A radio-controlled, electric-powered airplane system

The ground-based operator gives analog throttle (propeller) and rudder commands using the control joysticks as shown in the upper left-hand corner of the diagram. The command signals are digitized, encoded into a serial format and transmitted over an FM radio link. The signals are picked up by receiver electronics on the airplane, decoded and converted to pulse-width modulated signals that are proportional to the original analog control settings. These varying pulse-width signals are converted back to analog signals and sent to the amplifiers and servos controlling the propeller speed and the rudder position.